A TESTAMENT TO FREEDOM

A TESTAMENT TO FREEDOM

FREEDOM

The Essential Writings of Dietrich Bonhoeffer

Edited by

Geffrey B. Kelly

and

F. Burton Nelson

HarperSanFrancisco

A Division of HarperCollins*Publishers*

A TESTAMENT TO FREEDOM: *The Essential Writings of Dietrich Bonhoeffer.* Introduction and explanatory notes copyright © 1990 by Geffrey B. Kelly and F. Burton Nelson. All rights reserved. Printed in the United States of America. No part of this book may be used or reproduced in any manner whatsoever without written permission except in the case of brief quotations embodied in critical articles and reviews. For information address HarperCollins Publishers, 10 East 53rd Street, New York, NY 10022.

Credits appear on pages xvii–xviii, which is a continuation of the copyright page.

FIRST EDITION

Library of Congress Cataloging-in-Publication Data

Bonhoeffer, Dietrich, 1906–1945
    A testament to freedom: the essential writings of Dietrich
Bonhoeffer / edited by Geffrey B. Kelly and F. Burton Nelson.
      p.   cm.
    Includes bibliographical references.
    ISBN 0-06-060813-7
    1. Theology. I. Kelly, Geffrey B. II. Nelson, F. Burton.
III. Title.
BR50.B63   1990   89-45514
230'.044—dc20   CIP

90 91 92 93 94 RINAM 10 9 8 7 6 5 4 3 2 1

This edition is printed on acid-free paper that meets the American National Standards Institute Z39.48 Standard.

Contents

Part 3   Bonhoeffer's Confession of Faith
Introduction: The Church Struggle and
Nazi Racial Policies   131

Part 4   Bonhoeffer the Pastor
Introduction: The Word of God in
Sermon and Spiritual Ministry   181

Sermons, 1928–1932   194

Part 6   Bonhoeffer's Ethics
Introduction: Freedom and Responsibility   359

Part 7   Bonhoeffer's Correspondence
Introduction: Who *Is* Jesus Christ for Us Today?   393

Poems

Foreword

Many questions will undoubtedly be raised with the publication of this new collection of the essential writings of Dietrich Bonhoeffer. Will *A Testament to Freedom* actually serve as the guide to the Bonhoeffer legacy, seen as a whole? Does this reader with its own special method of selection capture the full richness of that phenomenon: the German Lutheran theologian, pastor, and ecumenist; that fighter on behalf of the First Commandment against the idolatrous syncretisms of his time and of our time as well; the composer of devout prayers and inspiring sermons; the fascinating author of spiritual literature; the exciting writer of the letters from prison; the sophisticated analyst of the Christian situation in the post-Enlightenment era; the witness to faith in Jesus Christ both now and in the future?

After some forty years of entangled and often confusing use of selected formulations from Bonhoeffer's theology, we can confidently answer: "Yes, it does!" This book genuinely does achieve these aims. Perhaps we have needed these forty years of bold popularizations of Bonhoeffer and shortcutting theories of interpreting his theology to whet our appetite for such a book. We still observe a growing interest in certain of Bonhoeffer's catchphrases as well as in the self-sacrifice and prophetic vision of this young pastor-theologian. Such is certainly part of the background for this text, which offers an important cross section of all of the periods and all of the literary genre of the religious genius that was Dietrich Bonhoeffer. Professors Kelly and Nelson bring to this timely and useful volume their own experiences in analyzing these past forty years of study. They know well that their work is the fruit of even longer periods of exploration and participation in the theological controversies that have surrounded research into the religious thought of Bonhoeffer.

Kelly and Nelson have likewise brought to this book an intention that is complex even in its simplicity. They wish to present the whole of Bonhoeffer's life and theology in the context of his particular place in German and Christian history. They wish to open their readers' eyes to the different ways Bonhoeffer expressed his ongoing reaction to that history. Such a task is, as they acknowledge in their preface, extremely complex. Translators of Bonhoeffer's writings in the first two decades after 1945 were accustomed to being asked to work on only one of the books, for example, *The Cost of Discipleship*. Another person would be contacted by a different publisher to translate an additional book, perhaps without any deep knowledge of the former volume or even of the later stage of Bonhoeffer's language and terminology in the changing circumstances of his life. The resulting discrepancy often irritated the more discerning reader and helped to create the unjustified impression that Bonhoeffer's thinking and writings were filled with inconsistencies. Kelly and Nelson have attempted to counteract this impression through their own ordering of Bonhoeffer's literary legacy under the consistent theme of his known advocacy of freedom for the people oppressed by the Hitler regime and of freedom within the churches to obey the call of Jesus Christ. They have done this remarkably well.

Second, Kelly and Nelson are also aware of the major problems created in mixing various approaches to the interpretation of Bonhoeffer. There is, for example, the clash of American and German theological terminology. There are the special issues and needs confronting churches in their diverse settings. Kelly and Nelson have seen what can happen when the content and form of the specific issues faced by Bonhoeffer become forced into alien contexts and contorted in unfamiliar traditions. The isolated, unconvincing perspectives of some interpreters and the short-circuited conclusions of others stand as a reminder to observe caution in any attempt to decipher Bonhoeffer or to transpose his thought onto issues facing churches and people today.

Finally, *A Testament to Freedom* has been assembled and edited by experienced teachers. Professors Kelly and Nelson have been engaged for many years in conveying Bonhoeffer's message in all its nuances and emphasis to classes of students, to religious congregations, at scholarly conferences, and to many readers of their publications who have simply expressed interest in Bonhoeffer's life and theology. They are conscious of the risk involved in offering a more comprehensive collection of the writings of Bonhoeffer set in their proper place and time. They understand the enormous task of commentary and interpretation. This selection of the essential writings includes extensive and careful introductions into particular sources and into the circumstances in which individual texts came to be. Thanks to these perceptive, comprehensive introductions, in which the editors become authors in their own rights, the local historical setting of Bonhoeffer's writings comes alive. Readers will be helped to understand the distance and the nearness of Bonhoeffer's voice in our present time in all of its softness and loudness, its attractiveness, its inspiration, and its call to action.

We can thus appreciate this book as the fruit of a long period of exciting and intense cooperation. It is an excellent aid for teaching Bonhoeffer. It vitalizes the very special contribution of this witness to Jesus Christ who prepares us for our journey into the twenty-first century of our Christian existence.

Eberhard Bethge
Bonn
Federal Republic of Germany

Preface

Over the course of many years, we have met countless persons who have expressed a need for a Dietrich Bonhoeffer reader. Teachers, pastors, leaders of adult education courses, students, and others have looked for a text that offers a cross section of the entire Bonhoeffer literary legacy while setting the writings themselves in an appropriate biographical-historical context. Their interest has been both gratifying and encouraging to us during these years. It is this need and interest that influenced our decision to undertake this project.

Selecting which materials to incorporate has been difficult. Part of this problem stemmed from the sheer multitude of inspirational passages at every turn of Bonhoeffer's career as university teacher, pastor, seminary director, ecumenist, Confessing Church leader, conspirator, and finally prisoner. Choosing what to include took longer than we had anticipated. We were also aware of the demands that space limitations would make on decisions of what to include.

In excerpting from Bonhoeffer's writings—books, conference lectures, sermons, letters—we searched for those passages that would best capture the primary point that Bonhoeffer wished to make within an individual work. We wished, moreover, to retain those passages of either special literary beauty or unusual inspiration. As the project was undergoing its initial labor pains, we realized that, even at the risk of annoying those persons who might look in vain for a favorite passage, we had to keep the commentaries and the selections to a manageable size.

In this process we were guided by our goal of acquainting readers with more than the usual works encountered in courses on Bonhoeffer: *Life Together, The Cost of Discipleship, Ethics,* and *Letters and Papers from Prison.* Often even these are read by the public without the benefit of any adequate introduction that might provide insight into the personal life and history that make these readings so exciting to the person who "knows" Bonhoeffer. For those who may be aware only that Bonhoeffer wrote the prison letters and the more "devotional" *The Cost of Discipleship,* this book, we believe, will alert them to the diversity and richness of the theological, biblical, pastoral, ecumenical literature that comprises an equally impressive part of this legacy to Christianity in the late twentieth century.

Further, we detected in our readings of Bonhoeffer, themes that would come to dominate Bonhoeffer's life and writings during the years of the church struggle, the resistance, and his imprisonment, namely his growing solidarity with the oppressed in their quest for freedom together with his incessant demand that the churches themselves be free to follow the call to discipleship of Jesus Christ. We took as cue for this perception both the phrase from his poignant essay "After Ten Years" and the whole thrust of his poem "Stations on the Road to Freedom." In the essay Bonhoeffer points out to his fellow conspirators that for once they have "learned to see the great events of world history from below, from the perspective of the outcast, the suspects, the maltreated, the powerless, the oppressed, the reviled—in short, from the perspective of those who suffer." We were not surprised to observe Bonhoeffer making common cause with those who lived under economic and political oppression from the earliest days of his Barcelona pastorate. It is this recurring theme, animated, of course, by Bonhoeffer's desire, in discovering the concrete presence of Jesus Christ in the world and in being a disciple of Jesus Christ, to set these people free, that led us to entitle our book *A Testament to Freedom*. The "oppressed" whom he gave his life to liberate seem to represent for Bonhoeffer the principal answer to his question from Tegel prison in 1944: "Who really is Jesus Christ for us today?" This concern would turn Bonhoeffer's attention to peace and the protection of civil, ecclesial, and fundamental human rights during the crisis years of the 1930s and the catastrophe that was World War II.

This book is not the first Bonhoeffer reader. One of Bonhoeffer's Finkenwalde students, Otto Dudzus, collected the sermons, conference lectures, and meditations into single volumes published in Germany in 1984 and 1985. He has likewise published a compact reader *Dietrich Bonhoeffer: Lesebuch* (Munich: Kaiser Verlag, 1985). This book is quite different. We are including a rather comprehensive text, containing the widest possible selection of Bonhoeffer's writings arranged according to both chronology and genre. Hence, there are separate sections incorporating the early writings, lectures, conferences, sermons, books, and correspondence.

In this volume we have made a conscious decision to use gender-inclusive language whenever possible and appropriate. In so doing, we desire to signify the universal appreciation of Dietrich Bonhoeffer's theological and spiritual reflections.

Despite the comprehensive scope of this total venture, we do not intend it to serve as a substitute for reading the entire book, conference lecture, or sermon excerpted here. It is, on the contrary, our hope that this reader will encourage persons to encounter the entire corpus of Bonhoeffer literature, especially the individual volumes of the *Bonhoeffer Werke* project, the new editions of Bonhoeffer's collected writings, now underway in both Germany and the United States. We anticipate that some of the translations appearing here for the first time will be incorporated into this substantial publication.

That Bonhoeffer's writings have ever reached the stage of a "definitive edition" of his entire literary legacy is due in no small measure to the energetic dedication of Eberhard and Renate Bethge of Bonn, Germany. Just as it was once said of the church that all paths led to Rome, so it must be said of Bonhoeffer research that all paths eventually lead to the Bethges. We recognize that many of these "paths" began with Eberhard, Bonhoeffer's biographer and confidant, and editor of the posthumous writings. In recent years, scholars have come to recognize increasingly the contribution of Renate Bethge, Bonhoeffer's niece, to the task of editing and preserving Bonhoeffer's collected writings, and as a principal source, along with Eberhard, of the living history that has breathed so much life into the literature. Without the Bethges, it is unlikely that this project could have been fulfilled. We are indebted to them for not only making available the literature that is the heart of this book, but also for evoking within us the appreciation of Bonhoeffer's life and inspiration that made this project so appealing to us, and, we hope, to the readers of this volume. In so many ways, we sense that we have discovered in the Bethges some of the influence behind Bonhoeffer's courageous stand during the crisis years of the rise and fall of Hitler's Third Reich.

This project has been nourished by the encouragement of the International Bonhoeffer Society. Within this circle of colleagues, a pastoral concern and conviviality that seems very natural exists when the society regularly convenes to discuss Bonhoeffer's thought and the implications of that thought for problems besetting the modern world. The society has evolved into a brotherhood and sisterhood as well. As one international scholar recently remarked, the members genuinely seem to like one another.

We acknowledge, too, the contributions that have been made toward the completion of this project. First, to our respective schools—North Park Theological Seminary and La Salle University—and the academic colleagues of the institutions, Provost Robert Johnston and Dean Klyne Snodgrass of North Park, Provost Emery Mollenhauer, Dean James Muldoon, and Chairman David Efroymson of the Religion Department of La Salle. The periodic released time from teaching duties has been deeply appreciated.

Daniel Bloesch has been a special friend to this project. His linguistic expertise has notably augmented translations, enhancing both accuracy and word flow.

The preparation of the manuscript has been guided chiefly by Carol J. McHugh, Thomas Walker, Elizabeth Kim, and Susan Zimmerman. Others who have given substantial assistance have been Emily Nelson, Sonia Nelson, Ingrid Nelson, Martha Nelson, Betty Coyne, Terry

Mattson, and Mary Train. We are grateful, too, for the advice and encouragement in preparation of the text given us by, first, Roy M. Carlisle while he was editor in charge of our project at HarperSanFrancisco, and, then, by Christine M. Anderson, who shepherded this project through to its completion. To Arla Ertz and Terri Goff we offer special thanks for their help during the many phases of the production process.

Finally, we owe our heartfelt gratitude to the two persons who have provided us continual inspiration, encouragement, nurture, and, at times, heroic patience—our wives, Joan Wingert Kelly and Grace Johnson Nelson. We dedicate this book to them with the deepest affection.

Geffrey B. Kelly
La Salle University
Philadelphia, Pennsylvania

F. Burton Nelson
North Park Theological Seminary
Chicago, Illinois

Acknowledgments

The authors and publisher acknowledge with appreciation the permissions granted for the use of the following copyrighted materials:

Christian Kaiser Verlag

Excerpts from the following:

Dietrich Bonhoeffer, *Gesammelten Schriften*, vols. 1–6. Edited by Eberhard Bethge, 1958–1974.

Dietrich Bonhoeffer, *Widerstand und Ergebung*. Edited by Eberhard Bethge, 1977.

Ein Briefwechsel zwischen Dietrich Bonhoeffer und Karl Barth, 1985.

Dietrich Bonhoeffer, *Schöpfung und Fall*, 1937.

Fortress Press

Excerpts from Dietrich Bonhoeffer, *Spiritual Care*. Edited by Jay Rochelle, 1985.

Excerpts from John Godsey, *Preface to Bonhoeffer: The Man and Two of His Shorter Writings*, 1965.

Photos from *Dietrich Bonhoeffer: A Life in Pictures*. Edited by Eberhard Bethge, Renate Bethge, and Christian Gremmels, 1986:

"Dietrich Bonhoeffer as a student"

"Bonhoeffer after a service in Trinity Church, talking with Hanns Lilje"

"With Jean Lasserre at the Fanø Conference, August 1934"

"Participants in the Fanø Conference, August 1934"

"Dietrich Bonhoeffer, August 1935"

"3 March 1986, arrival in Stockholm"

"Gross-Schlönwitz, summer 1938, Eberhard Bethge and Dietrich Bonhoeffer, the collective pastorate of Gross-Schlönwitz"

"Dietrich Bonhoeffer in the courtyard of the military interrogation prison at Tegel (summer 1944)"

Harper & Row

Excerpts from the following:

Dietrich Bonhoeffer, *Act and Being*. Translated by Bernard Noble, 1962.

Dietrich Bonhoeffer, *Christ the Center*. Revised translation by Edwin H. Robertson, 1978.

Dietrich Bonhoeffer, *The Communion of Saints*. Translated by Ronald Gregor Smith et al., 1963.

Dietrich Bonhoeffer, *Life Together*. Translated by John Doberstein, 1954.

Dietrich Bonhoeffer, *No Rusty Swords: Letters, Lectures and Notes, 1928–1936*. Translated by Edwin H. Robertson and John Bowden, 1965.

Dietrich Bonhoeffer, *True Patriotism: Letters, Lectures and Notes, 1939–1945*. Translated by Edwin H. Robertson and John Bowden, 1973.
Dietrich Bonhoeffer, *The Way to Freedom: Letters, Lectures and Notes, 1935–1939*. Translated by Edwin H. Robertson and John Bowden, 1966.

Macmillan Publishing Company

Excerpts from the following:
Dietrich Bonhoeffer, *The Cost of Discipleship*. Translated by R. H. Fuller, revised by Irmgard Booth, 1963.
Dietrich Bonhoeffer, *Ethics*. Translated by Neville Horton Smith, 1965.
Dietrich Bonhoeffer, *Letters and Papers from Prison*. Enlarged edition. Translated by R. H. Fuller, et al., 1972.

Keystone Pressedienst

Photo, "Bischop Ludwig Müller on the steps of the Rathaus at Wittenberg, 1933."

Translations

The authors acknowledge with appreciation the following translations from
German into English, many of them appearing in translated form for the first
time:

Daniel W. Bloesch:

Sermon on "Death Sunday," November 26, 1933 (*GS*, IV, pp. 160–65)
Sermon for the First Sunday in Advent, December 3, 1933 (*GS*, IV,
  pp. 166–70)
Sermon for the Sixth Sunday after Trinity, July 8, 1934 (*GS*, V, pp. 521–27)
Sermon, the end of September 1934 (*GS*, V, pp. 527–33)
Sermon for the Twentieth Sunday after Trinity Sunday (*GS*, V, pp. 534–42)
Sermon for the Thirty-first Sunday after Trinity Sunday (*GS*, V, pp. 542–49)
Sermon for Reformation Sunday, November 4, 1934 (*GS*, V, pp. 555–60)
Sermon on Vengeance and Deliverance, July 11, 1937 (*GS*, IV, pp. 413–22)

John Godsey:

Letter of May 17, 1942 from Dietrich Bonhoeffer to Karl Barth (*Ein Briefwechsel
  Zwischen Dietrich Bonhoeffer und Karl Barth*)

Geffrey B. Kelly:

Christ and Peace (*GS*, V, pp. 359–62)
Jesus Christ and the Essence of Christianity (*GS*, V, pp. 134–36, 149–50,
  152–54)
Sermon at the Religious Service marking the End of the Semester, Ninth Sunday
  after Trinity Sunday, July 24, 1932 (*GS*, IV, pp. 79, 86–87)
Letter to Rüdiger Schleicher (*GS*, I, pp. 37–47)
Letter to Grandmother (*GS*, II, pp. 77–79)
Letter to Martin Niemöller (*GS*, II, pp. 149–52)
Letter to Grandmother (*GS*, II, pp. 180–82)
Letter to the Old Prussian Council of the Brethren (*GS*, II, pp. 308–15)
Letter to Karl Friedrich (*GS*, III, pp. 24–25)
Letter to Rüdiger Schleicher (*GS*, III, pp. 26–29)
Selections from *Creation and Fall* (*Schöpfung und Fall*)

Martha Corcoran Luemers:

Exaudi Sermon on Psalm 42, June 1935 (*GS*, IV, pp. 391–99)
Sermon on Forgiveness, November 17, 1935 (*GS*, IV, pp. 399–406)
Sermon on Memorial Day, November 24, 1935 (*GS*, IV, pp. 568–76)

Funeral Sermon for Julie Bonhoeffer, January 15, 1936 (*GS*, IV, pp. 456–60)
Marriage Sermon for H. and A. Schönherr, April 15, 1936 (*GS*, IV,
   pp. 460–63)
Sermon on Third Sunday after Epiphany, January 23, 1938 (*GS*, IV,
   pp. 427–34)
Sermon on Romans 5, March 1938 (*GS*, IV, pp. 434–41)
Confirmation Sermon, April 9, 1938 (*GS*, IV, pp. 441–47)
Communion Address on Memorial Day, November 26, 1939 (*GS*, IV,
   pp. 453–55)

Nancy Lukens:

Poem: The Death of Moses (*GS*, IV, pp. 613–20)
Poem: Christians and Pagans (*Widerstand und Ergebung*, p. 382)
Poem: Stations on the Way to Freedom (*Widerstand und Ergebung*, pp. 403–4)

David Manrodt:

Sermon for the First Sunday in Advent, November 29, 1931 (*GS*, IV,
   pp. 26–33)
Evening Sermon for Day of National Mourning, February 21, 1932 (*GS*, IV,
   pp. 38–40)
Sermon for the First Sunday after Trinity, May 29, 1932 (*GS*, IV, pp. 52–53)
Sermon for Repentance Sunday, November 19, 1933 (*GS*, IV, pp. 154–59)
Outline for a Reformation Festival, 1936 (*GS*, IV, pp. 193–96)

In addition to the new translations included in this volume, the authors gratefully acknowledge the work of the translators of previously published Bonhoeffer texts, which are listed in the bibliography, pp. 569–70. Some of these texts have been edited and emended for the purpose of providing gender inclusive language where possible and, in some instances, to offer a translation that is closer to the original German.

Abbreviations

BOOKS BY DIETRICH BONHOEFFER

AB   *Act and Being*. Translated by Bernard Noble. New York: Harper & Row, 1962. Reprint (same pagination); New York: Octagon Books, 1983.

CC   *Christ the Center*. Revised translation by Edwin H. Robertson. New York: Harper & Row, 1978.

CD   *The Cost of Discipleship*. Translated by R. H. Fuller, revised by Irmgard Booth. New York: Macmillan, 1963. Hardcover reissue (same pagination); Gloucester, MA: Peter Smith, 1983.

CS   *The Communion of Saints*. Translated by Ronald Gregor Smith et al. New York: Harper & Row, 1963.

DBW   *Dietrich Bonhoeffer Werke*. Sixteen volumes when completed. Munich: Kaiser Verlag, 1986–1993.

E   *Ethics*. Translated by Neville Horton Smith. Rearranged edition. New York: Macmillan, 1965.

GS   *Gesammelte Schriften*, I to VI. Munich: Kaiser Verlag, 1958–1974.

LPP   *Letters and Papers from Prison*. The Enlarged Edition. Edited by Eberhard Bethge. Translated by R. H. Fuller, John Bowden, et al. New York: Macmillan, 1972.

LT   *Life Together*. Translated by John W. Doberstein. New York: Harper & Row, 1954. Paperback edition (same pagination), 1976.

NRS   *No Rusty Swords: Letters, Lectures and Notes, 1939–1945*. Edited by Edwin H. Robertson. Translation revised by John Bowden and Eberhard Bethge. London: Collins, 1970. Cleveland, OH: Collins-World, 1977.

SC   *Spiritual Care*. Translated and with an introduction by Jay C. Rochelle, Philadelphia: Fortress Press, 1985.

TP   *True Patriotism: Letters, Lectures and Notes, 1949–1945*. Edited by Edwin H. Robertson. Translated by Edwin H. Robertson and John Bowden. New York: Harper & Row, 1973. Paperback edition (same pagination); Cleveland, OH: Collins-World, 1977.

WF   *The Way to Freedom: Letters, Lectures and Notes, 1935–1939*. Edited by Edwin H. Robertson. Translated by Edwin H. Robertson and John Bowden. New York: Harper & Row, 1966. Paperback edition (same pagination); London: Collins, 1972; Cleveland, OH: Collins-World, 1977.

DOCUMENTS BY DIETRICH BONHOEFFER

MW   *Die Mündige Welt: Dokumente*
      zur Bonhoeffer-Forschung,
      1928–1949. Munich: Kaiser
      Verlag, 1969.

SECONDARY LITERATURE

BEM   Eberhard Bethge. *Bonhoeffer:*
      Exile and Martyr. Edited and
      with an essay by John W. de
      Gruchy. New York: Seabury
      Press, 1975.

DB   Eberhard Bethge, *Dietrich*
      Bonhoeffer: Man of Vision, Man
      of Courage. Edited by Edwin
      H. Robertson. Translated by
      Eric Mosbacher, et al. New
      York: Harper & Row, 1970.

      Paperback edition (same pa-
      gination), 1977.

IKDB *I Knew Dietrich Bonhoeffer.* Ed-
      ited by Wolf-Dieter Zimmer-
      mann and Ronald Gregor
      Smith. Translated by Käthe
      Gregor Smith. New York and
      Evanston: Harper & Row,
      1966. Paperback edition
      (same pagination); London:
      Collins, 1973.

Editors' Introduction

SOLIDARITY WITH THE OPPRESSED: BONHOEFFER THE MAN

Dietrich Bonhoeffer, August 1935.
From: Eberhard Bethge, Renate Bethge, Christian Gremmels, *Dietrich Bonhoeffer: A Life in Pictures* (Philadelphia: Fortress Press, 1986) p. 141.

Editors' Introduction

In one of his most autobiographical poems from prison, Dietrich Bonhoeffer ponders who he *really* is. His verses betray a distrust of the admiration and praise cast his way by warders and fellow prisoners alike. Bonhoeffer seems aware of his having achieved almost heroic status in their eyes. But at that other level, where he knows all too well of his own inner turmoil, he detects not heroism but contradiction. "Who am I?" he wonders, the one able to "bear the days of misfortune equably, smilingly, proudly, like one accustomed to win." Or is he that other only he could be aware of, "restless and longing and sick, like a bird in a cage, struggling for breath, as though hands were compressing my throat . . . trembling with anger at despotisms and petty humiliation . . . powerlessly trembling for friends at an infinite distance, weary and empty at praying, at thinking, at doing, faint, and ready to say farewell to it all?"[1]

When we read that poem, after having followed Bonhoeffer's career and perhaps even having traveled a similar route in coping with the call to Christian discipleship, we realize that the "stuff" of which heroes like Bonhoeffer are made is still very mortal. He was, in his own personal musings, weaker than most people might have perceived. One could answer Bonhoeffer's question "Who am I?" with a long list both of his accomplishments and of the various turning points in his life's inevitable journey to a Nazi scaffold. He was the brilliant student at the University of Berlin, awarded the doctorate in theology at the age of twenty-one. He was the promising young teacher at the university. He was also the catechist in a Berlin slum. He was the pastor, the ecumenist, the pacifist, the director of an illegal seminary, the conspirator, the prisoner, and, finally, the martyr.

For sheer drama, it is Bonhoeffer's martyrdom that excites the literary and historical imagination for the problems described in his poem. Who was he? People are fascinated by the questions and issues raised in his being executed for a cause that was at once deeply Christian and highly political, the peace of Christ and a treasonous conspiracy to end the evils of a world war and the Nazi Holocaust. In all the confusion of the directions his life took, Bonhoeffer knew the ground on which he stood to be as firm as his abiding faith in God. "In Jesus, God has said Yes and Amen to it all," he wrote from prison, "and that Yes and Amen is the firm ground on which we stand."[2] This is why he concludes his poem by insisting that all the lonely questions about his true identity only mocked him. His life was a unity in that mysterious oneness where all contradictions are resolved in the experience of God's abiding love and forgiveness. "Whoever I am, thou knowest, O God, I am thine."

Bonhoeffer's execution took place on April 9, 1945, only four weeks before the defeat of Nazi Germany. His actions to bring the war to an end were accomplished at a time when few Germans dared publicly question Hitler's rhetoric of blood and battle or failed to snap at the bait of "patriotism" and national pride by joining the Nazi war effort. History tells us that patriotism has often lured people to enlist blindly in causes about which they know little more than the propagandist slogans with which political-military leaders fire up morale. Nazism's brutal conquest of Europe and the reign of terror in both Germany and occupied territories were no exception. The extermination of Jews, Slavs, gypsies, and political dissenters was construed by Heinrich Himmler and the officers of the S.S. as the "patriotic deed," distasteful to be sure, but part of their "master plan" to deliver on the promise of a Nazi millennium.

Yet in this morally inverted world of the Third Reich, the "treason" of the conspirators became *true* patriotism for Bonhoeffer and what was normally viewed as nazism's "patriotic" actions were viewed by him as, in fact, a treacherous undermining of Germany's spiritual heritage. The "survival tactics" of the churches, which, for the most part, gave loyal acquiescence in political decisions and prayerful support of the troops, he rejected as a hypocritical evasion of responsibility for the violence and bloodshed of both war and death camps. In contrast to church leaders who avowed that meddling in matters of state, especially in the fate of Jews, was not part of any explicit gospel mandate, Bonhoeffer argued before his fellow conspirators that the ultimate question was not how to extricate themselves with "clean hands" from moral dilemmas, such as those presented by military oaths and the separation of one's "sacred" life from the profane, but the responsibility of individual Christians and of Christian churches to "shape history" for the sake of the coming generation. The war was, he insisted, a time for decisions of conscience and even of martyrdom. Death in the cause of bringing about peace would not, however, be like the "glorious martyrdom" portrayed in more euphoric literature about early Christianity. Rather, as Bonhoeffer declared in a strangely prophetic sermon, they were living in a macabre age in which martyrs' blood "will not be so innocent."[3] Theirs, he admitted, was to be a sacrifice tainted by the "great guilt" of betraying their nation.

What moved Bonhoeffer, a dedicated pacifist in the 1930s and an agitator on behalf of world peace at ecumenical gatherings, into the role of double agent for German military intelligence—a center of the resistance movement within Germany—and conspirator against the Nazi regime, can best be seen as a growing solidarity with those who represented for him the compassion of Jesus regardless of their religious affiliation. This meant, above all, entering into solidarity with the victims of the national heartlessness then sweeping Germany. Bonhoeffer's resistance group had, he remarked in a New Year's essay-gift to his fellow conspirators, "for once learned to see the great events of world history from below, from the perspective of the outcast, the suspects, the maltreated, the powerless, the oppressed, the reviled—in short, from the perspective of those who suffer."[4]

FAMILY ROOTS

Indeed, solidarity with the innocent victims of racial hatred and with the multitudes of suffering strewn in the mass graves and rubble of a world war became a passion with Bonhoeffer. Yet the sparks of that passion are barely detectable in Bonhoeffer's earliest years spent in an atmosphere of relative affluence. He came from a family that enjoyed abundance, even privilege. More important, however, Dietrich's family provided a context for developing maturity of judgment and an esteem for freedom that was uncommon in the years of tight Nazi control over the lives and speech of German citizenry. Dietrich's father, Karl Bonhoeffer, the noted neurologist, professor of psychiatry at the University of Berlin, and director of the psychiatric and neurological clinic at the Charité Hospital Complex in Berlin, encouraged his children to be disciplined and independent in their thinking. In his prison letters Dietrich acknowledges this strong formative influence on his personality. From his mother, Paula von Hase, came an equally significant influence and the source of his early religious upbringing, though Dietrich's interest in religion seemed to have been strongest only in the way he used it in daring to be different from his more skeptical, only nominally religious, father and older brothers. His mother's side of the family could boast of a distinguished church historian, Dietrich's great-grandfather, Karl-August von Hase. Dietrich's grandfather, Karl-Alfred von Hase, was preacher to the court of Kaiser Wilhelm II; he fell "out of grace" with the kaiser for his bold contradiction of the emperor who had referred to the common people as "rabble." Dietrich's vocation would take him even further out of step with a German leader's attitude, even to making common cause with the Third Reich's "rabble," the Jewish community.

IN PURSUIT OF ACADEMIC EXCELLENCE

If it is true that Dietrich's home life nurtured the mature independence and savoring of freedom that are the spine of any resistance movement against state policies, these qualities acquired more specific shape during his theological schooling and in the pastoral-academic career that later become so troublesome to him. What we note in the early years of his academic training is the interlocking of concrete personal experience with both passing and permanent theological insight that have made his religious writings appear so true to life. Even in the more abstruse Berlin dissertations, one is able to trace with Bonhoeffer the beginnings of a lifelong search to discover the concrete locus of both God's revelation and Christian faith.

Bonhoeffer had matriculated at the University of Berlin in 1924, after having spent his first university year at the University of Tübingen. His time at Tübingen introduced him to the critical philosophy of Immanuel Kant and to the exegesis of Adolf Schlatter. Before returning to Berlin he visited Rome and came away conscious, as never before, of the universality of the church. Eberhard Bethge, in his definitive biography, traces Bonhoeffer's fascination with the "larger" church to his experience of Catholic Rome. Bonhoeffer began to see for the first time how nationalistic, narrow-minded, and sectarian was the outlook of his own church. In his diary one reads: "I believe I am beginning to understand the concept of the church."[5]

Bonhoeffer's career at Berlin expanded his initial understanding of church, an understanding he achieved in the more theatrical setting of the Catholic epicenter. Closer to home he profited not only from the liberal theology then in vogue but also from the presence of the great teachers with whom he associated, albeit in an increasingly critical way. These included men like Adolf von Harnack, the noted church historian; Lutheran scholar Karl Holl; and Reinhold Seeberg, the prime dogmatician at the University of Berlin. In the meantime, too, he discovered the writings of Karl Barth, who had fired up both theological imaginations and liberal opposition with his *Epistle to the Romans,* his early essays on the Word of God, and the "crisis theology" that indicted liberal theology for compromising Christianity and making national hatreds and war possible. From Barth, Bonhoeffer now seemed to receive the greatest intellectual stimulation. His enthusiasm for Barth was, however, a source of regret to Adolf von Harnack, who proceeded to caution Bonhoeffer against the threat posed by Barth's "contempt for scientific theology."[6] Von Harnack's feud with Barth in the *Christliche Welt* was well known at the time. Bethge recalls that Bonhoeffer became a propagandist of sorts for Barth's collected lectures, *Das Wort Gottes und die Theologie* (The Word of God and the Word of Man). He pored over the handwritten notes of Barth's lectures on the Christian religion, then being circulated among interested students of other universities. These notes were later incorporated into the first volume of his *Church Dogmatics.* The young Bonhoeffer had, indeed, been won over to Barth's dialectical theology, but not without critical reservations and that flair for maintaining his independence from any system regardless of the insights he might absorb from Barth or any other source of inspiration.

Bonhoeffer was not beyond criticizing Barth, but he did so "as an ally."[7] Barth had given Bonhoeffer the student a direction and the joy of finding an integrative key to the many facets of his calling to be a theologian, pastor, preacher, but, above all else, a Christian. With Barth, Bonhoeffer began to anchor his theology in the Word of God and with attention to God's judgment on human pretentiousness. Curiously enough, with all his admiration for Barth, Bonhoeffer continued to harbor and to express his misgivings over several aspects of Barth's theology that conflicted with the more deeply ingrained convictions animating his own understanding of how theology was related to both faith and experience. Barth's emphasis on God's majesty, for example, seemed to Bonhoeffer to downplay, even volatilize, the concreteness, the earthliness, of the human condition as the ground of faith and revelation. God's freedom is not, as Barth claimed, to be free *from* us, Bonhoeffer would declare in his second dissertation, but to be free *for* us. Bonhoeffer leaned more toward the Lutheran insistence on God's existing "for us," making it possible for finite, limited creatures to become bearers of the infinite (*finitum capax infiniti*), whereas Barth remained much more closely tied to the Calvinist emphasis on God's glory and his judgment against all finite claims to have "grasped" the infinite (*finitum incapax infiniti*). But at this stage Barth had become a trusted guide in Bonhoeffer's own attempts to discern the manner in which he was seeking to understand and integrate his theological-pastoral mission in the church. Later he would be linked closely with Barth in the church struggle against Nazi policies.

Bonhoeffer's doctoral dissertation, completed in 1927, was, in fact, praised by Barth as a "theological miracle." He was twenty-one years old at the time. In this dissertation Bonhoeffer describes the church as a reality in which "Christ exists as community." If the church is a "communion of saints," that communion can exist nowhere else but in the congregation of sinners who experience God's graciousness in word, sacrament, and the special gift of being enabled to live for each other. God becomes more tangible because Christ exists in this community in word, in sacrament, and in the mutual love of the members. The Christian community, in turn, becomes most real, as Bonhoeffer states in this dissertation, when the human, graced by God, is enhanced in promise, demand, love, and service. Here he attempted to harness social philosophy to the chariot of ecclesiology in an effort to project his own ideals of what a congregation of believers should be against the reality of what the church had hardly ever been: the credible presence of Christ in the world. From affirming the social nature of the human person, Bonhoeffer moved toward an assessment of how that sociality, though sundered by sin, can nonetheless be shaped by Christ's command into a communion of loving people who enjoy serving each other. This, for Bonhoeffer, is God's reign at that Archimedean point of justification where Christ's incarnate presence and true believers encounter each other.

PASTORAL MINISTRY IN BARCELONA

Between completion of this study at the University of Berlin and writing a second dissertation needed to secure a coveted academic appointment to the university faculty, Bonhoeffer accepted his first church position in 1928, that of assistant pastor to the German congregation in Barcelona. Compared to the theological excitement in Berlin, this was a dull year, spent catering to the "spiritual needs" of a couple of hundred German businesspeople, in a community already rocked with the destructive waves of the Depression, bankruptcy, and unemployment. Though Bonhoeffer had only hints of the more pathetic plight of the poor beyond his own congregation, he helped organize the charity his parish extended to its own unemployed. What he began to perceive more clearly, however, was the impact of the international economic crisis as it generated nearly total confusion about "educational, ethical, and religious questions."[8] "All at once and without warning," he wrote, "the ground from under our feet, or rather the bourgeois rug from under our feet, has been pulled away and now it is a question of seeking the solid ground on which we stand."[9]

Although his family's social and economic status had insulated him from the distressing touch of poverty, Bonhoeffer seemed to experience for the first time the trauma of seeing traditional values in decline. This moved him to seek, as he put it, the firmer ground on which he and his fellow Germans could take a stand. This stand was not to be on the more abstract churchiness that some interpreters of his ecclesiology tried to read into his Berlin dissertations, and that he openly abhorred. Rather, he urged that it was in looking to God alone that the believing community could find the "solid strength" to stand firm. Such strength could only be where the community's center was God's own humanity in Christ.[10]

In the Barcelona phase of his theology and separated from the support of family, it is not surprising that Bonhoeffer should describe the plight of individuals left in isolation to undertake their lonely search for meaning. We discover in his papers of this period the hints of his later bitter indictment of the church for its having buried Jesus in a repelling heap of religiosity. It is God who brings meaning out of that chaos suffered by those whom society has rejected, the "little people," the "neglected, the insignificant people, the weak, the unknown, the inferior, the oppressed, the despised."[11] It seemed to Bonhoeffer that his parish and, indeed, the entire church were anywhere but where Christ commanded his community of followers to be in responding to human need, by sharing with the needy the love of Christ in some tangible form. "God wanders among us in human form," Bonhoeffer proclaimed in a Barcelona sermon, "speaking to us in those who cross our paths, be they stranger, beggar, sick, or even in those nearest to us in everyday life, becoming Christ's demand on our faith in him."[12]

ACT AND BEING: CREDENTIALS FOR TEACHING

Bonhoeffer returned to Germany from Barcelona in February 1929, still determined to integrate his ambitions for an academic career with his desire to be a pastor. The German people had begun to see by this time that the Weimar Republic seemed to mirror their own declining sense of self-worth. They were beset by the conflicting emotions of resentment, despair, and the confusion generated by an apparently inept government and Hitler's demagogic intrigues. Bonhoeffer's second dissertation was his credential into a more attractive world of university life and what promised to be a base of effecting some change in national outlook. *Act and Being,* for all its encyclopedic typology of philosophies and theologies offering either an "act" or a "being" version of revelation, is at a deeper level an effort on Bonhoeffer's part to cope with the crises of faith then sweeping across him as an individual as well as across nation and church as loci of that individuality. What appears to be a disingenuous attempt to understand revelation from within its concreteness in sociality and freedom is also a strong effort to relate God's liberating Word to the way an individual can be freed from a narcissistic turning in on oneself. Clearly we see exposed here some of Bonhoeffer's deepest fears about himself, namely his own personal struggle between the lure of academe's comfortable, heady existence and the powerful call of Christ to accept more courageously the gospel's challenge to genuine faith within a truly believing community.

Such a challenge was hardly accepted in the wimpish accommodation to society's values and whims that animated most supposedly Christian congregations. Bonhoeffer's concern in this second dissertation was soteriological; in this case, to offer serious reflection on the way individuals and communities can become locked into self-deceiving, idolatrous substitutes for God's own gift of himself. Revelation was not to be reduced to those "heavenly doubles" of the living God even if these paraded under the guise of inerrant Bible or infallible, sacred institution. Bonhoeffer considered it theologically offensive to claim that one was capable of bestowing truth on oneself and of yoking God to human reflection and individualistic religiosity. Only in community, or in God's relationship to us from "without," can one encounter God in Christ. The Christian church, Bonhoeffer charged, in its power-hungry appropriation of revelation through doctrine, psychic experience, or institution, had tried to reduce God to itself. His revulsion at what he considered a flirtation with idolatry would later stir Bonhoeffer to criticize and then openly oppose nazism's claims to be "positive Christianity in action."[13]

FIRST AMERICAN VISIT: BUDDING PACIFISM

With his academic appointment safely in tow, Bonhoeffer's main decision in 1929 was to accept a Sloane Fellowship to Union Theological

Seminary in New York for studies to begin in the autumn of 1930. At the time he felt himself drawn more to the pastor's pulpit than to the academic podium. Further, he was convinced beforehand that America had nothing to offer him theologically, an opinion he reiterated in his on-scene, somewhat arrogant assessment of American theology. Union Theological Seminary represented for him the worst and the best of America's liberal humanism and the church's social gospel. The seminary, he wrote, "had evidently forgotten what Christian theology by its very nature stands for."[14] Whatever his prejudgement and motivations for being at Union might be, theology at Union was obviously not cut from the same cloth as that of the more closely and heavily textured Germanic-European approach to theology. There was a seriousness about doing theology at the University of Berlin that Bonhoeffer would miss. His zest for travel and broadening of his experience that travel offered could, nonetheless, make even a year in what promised to be a theological desert worthwhile.

What his year in America did give him appears to have been much more than he could then admit. In its own way, his American experience was foundational for some of the later developments in Bonhoeffer's growing solidarity with the oppressed and his espousal of the cause of world peace. For Bonhoeffer, social activism was not coterminous with Christianity, and the weekly sermons he heard were more akin to self-congratulatory pap than to the gospel's biting scorn of society's typical pretentiousness. Yet for all his critique of the mundaneness of American church sermons and seminary theology, it is not mere speculation to suggest that Union Theological Seminary had a lasting impact on Bonhoeffer. Reinhold Niebuhr's seminar, for example, introduced him to a political-economic insight into the makeup of American society, a vision laced with Niebuhr's "social" interpretation of the gospel. Though Bonhoeffer would never place Niebuhr's main concern at the center of his own theology and did, in fact, lament that even in Niebuhr one detected a lack of foundational strength in Christology, Bonhoeffer had to concede in so many ways that one could hardly be a responsible Christian without such a sensitivity to social problems.[15]

In Professor Eugene W. Lyman, Bonhoeffer met a trusted guide to the world of American pragmatism and realism. Here he encountered the strongest critique yet of his tendency to separate the world of systematic theology from the realm of decision, the world of ideas from the world of reality. Lyman, as well as Niebuhr, urged Bonhoeffer to bridge the apparent gaps between theory, God's grace, and concrete reality. Niebuhr commented on one of Bonhoeffer's papers that he had over-emphasized grace in respect to ethical action: "In making grace as transcendent as you do, I don't see how you can ascribe any ethical significance to it. Obedience to God's will may be a religious experience but it is not an ethical one until it issues in actions which can be socially valued. . . . So any other interpretation of 'ethical' than one which measures an action in terms of consequences and judges actions purely in terms of motive empties the ethical life of content and makes it purely formal."[16]

Bonhoeffer may have resisted these professional inroads into his Berlin theology for a time, but the circumstances in Nazi Germany demanded from him precisely the pragmatism and emphasis on responsible action that would later animate his anti-Hitler activities and portions of *Ethics*. What was more obvious to those who noticed the changes on his return home was the impact his friendships at Union had made on his thinking. Through a black student friend from Alabama, the Rev. Frank Fisher, Bonhoeffer was able to spend nearly every Sunday and several evenings preaching and teaching the catechism at the Abyssinian Baptist Church in Harlem. He marveled at the warmth and happiness of their life-affirming liturgies. Later he took recordings of the spirituals back to Germany and taught them to his students at the University of Berlin as well as to his seminarians in the anti-Nazi Confessing Church. But he also experienced firsthand the squalor and sense of disenfranchisement of young blacks. He was aware of the blistering unrest that threatened to scar America, all the while church sermons counseled patience in enduring injustices. Racial injustices disturbed him profoundly because they were hardly alleviated by the seeming ineptness of the churches in bringing about an integration of the races or at least in making black Americans feel a part of mainstream America. He stated categorically that if the blacks ever became godless, he would hold white America responsible.[17] He correctly predicted, following his second trip to America, that racism would become "one of the most critical future problems for the white church."[18] In 1931 he believed that there was nothing analogous to America's racial situation in Germany; by 1933, on the other hand, it was clear to him that Germany's Jews were even worse off than America's blacks.

Bonhoeffer's passion for social justice can be traced at least in part to the influence of a fellow student, Paul Lehmann, who became Bonhoeffer's closest American friend. Bonhoeffer visited Paul and Marion Lehmann nearly every evening and was a frequent dinner guest at their apartment. Together they discussed the urgent theological issues then fermenting both locally and internationally. Lehmann, in these daily conversations as well as in his preaching and entire attitude, showed Bonhoeffer that the theological made sense only when it intersected ethically with one's social and political concerns. Lehmann helped Bonhoeffer deepen his appreciation of the plight of America's blacks and his recognition of church failure and the obvious need for the church to become involved in civil rights and the cause of economic justice. Though Lehmann disclaims such an influence, it is evident that his own attempt to harmonize the gospel with social activism reverberated in Bonhoeffer's later teaching and career as his theology became more and more politically oriented and ethically focused. Bonhoeffer began, as he would later write, to see things from the point of view of the oppressed.[19]

Part of that "oppression" he came more and more to associate with the evils of war. Perhaps the most significant shift in Bonhoeffer's attitude toward war and peace in the decade of the 1930s came as a result of his friendship with the pacifist Jean Lasserre, founder of the "Movement for Reconciliation" in his native France. Given the gospel's insistence on universal brotherhood and sisterhood in Jesus Christ, Bonhoeffer began to see for the first time the absurdity of Christians killing people for the sake of national pride or territorial ambitions. Lasserre tells us that he was drawn to Bonhoeffer and to a third foreign student, the Swiss seminarian Erwin Sutz, because they were Sloane fellows from abroad, but also because they represented for him the serious European approach to theology. Lasserre suspected that his convictions on social Christianity and pacifism may have shocked Bonhoeffer because Bonhoeffer was, like most Germans, resentful of the harsh conditions imposed on Germany by the Treaty of Versailles following the Great War. In an interview just before his death, Lasserre described an important aspect of his initial interest in Bonhoeffer: "It was clear we interested him in our quality as human beings and as Christians. In short, he took us seriously. He never crushed us with his theological superiority. He never let us feel that he disapproved of something in us or our behavior. He totally respected our freedom, that of living as well as thinking."[20]

Under the impact of this friendship, Bonhoeffer the German began to see the need to transcend the national setting of his faith and loyalty. It was a struggle with his own attachment to Germany, but eventually the struggle wrung from him a deeper commitment to the principles of the Sermon on the Mount and a devotion to the cause of world peace. Paradoxically, this commitment led to a truer loyalty to Germany in the higher integrity of service to country he and his fellow conspirators displayed. Lasserre pinpointed the turning point in Bonhoeffer's own pacifism to a Saturday afternoon when together they viewed the film *All Quiet on the Western Front*. They were aghast and deeply saddened to the point of tears at the lighthearted reaction of the children in the theater to the killing portrayed on screen. Lasserre said that it was a shocking, even tragic, experience for both of them: "I think it was there both of us discovered that the communion, the community of the church is much more important than the national community." Lasserre adds in his recollection of the event: "I think this has been very important in his path toward pacifism because he has discovered that war is not the most important thing from the church's viewpoint. The important, the only really important thing, is that the church *be* the church, and that it *remain* the church and that it would keep in fellowship all Christians. And what is absolutely awful and unacceptable in war is that Christians are compelled to forget their Christian faith and Christian belonging to the church, to the universal, to the real church."[21] Bonhoeffer the student would soon become the promoter of world peace at ecumenical gatherings. His experiences in America became part of what he described in a letter to a friend as "a great liberation."[22]

UNIVERSITY LECTURER AND PASTOR

Back in Germany, Bonhoeffer hastened to fulfill an ambition that had lingered with him since his student days, to meet Karl Barth at Bonn. The visit, for the final three weeks of the summer term beginning July 10, 1931, had been arranged through Erwin Sutz. Once having met Barth, Bonhoeffer wrote that he had never "regretted anything that I have failed to do in my theological past as much as the fact that I did not come here earlier."[23] One of Bonhoeffer's later students and seminarians, Winfried Maechler, often cited the story that Bonhoeffer caught Barth's attention during one of his seminars by quoting Luther to the effect that "the curses of the godless sometimes sound better in God's ear than the hallelujahs of the pious." Barth's delight at this intervention was the beginning of their acquaintance.[24] There is no doubt that Bonhoeffer enjoyed his personal encounters with Barth. The seminars, meetings with students, open evenings, and a luncheon together that lasted a couple of hours, moved him to remark that he had "been impressed even more by discussions with him than by his writings and his lectures."[25] Bonhoeffer had already praised Barth at Union Theological Seminary as belonging to the great tradition of the apostle Paul, Martin Luther, and Søren Kierkegaard, each exemplifying "genuine Christian thinking."[26] Later their respective roles in the church struggle strengthened their mutual esteem. Now the two men had become friends and colleagues. For Barth, Bonhoeffer was a young theologian of promise.

That "promise" began to be fulfilled on Bonhoeffer's return to Berlin and the beginning of his career at the university in 1931. Bonhoeffer's energies were quickly directed to the ecclesiastical and political crises provoked by Hitler's rise to power. He had arrived at a crossroads. Ordained on November 15, 1931, Bonhoeffer had already been functioning at the university as a lecturer. These classes and his seminars continued to attract those students who did not gravitate, as did a majority of theological students at the time, to nazism. Bethge explains Bonhoeffer's initial popularity with this kind of student in terms of his critical independence and integrity, adding that "a teacher who maintained his independence in the face of the approaching storm necessarily attracted students who did not react strongly to the new magnetic forces." During his two years' work at the University of Berlin, Bonhoeffer gradually acquired a substantial audience and a dedicated following in his seminars. The very young lecturer became a minor sensation to those who took his courses and was widely talked about.

His regular followers were attracted to the intellectual and personal standards he required. There were none of the "German Christians" among them, except perhaps some who believed for a time that a political alliance with the Nazi party would not adversely affect their theology.[27] Bonhoeffer's students would become part of the core opposition to Nazi policies in 1933 and 1934. He had also become popular among those students who attended his talks to the Christian Student Movement in Berlin. From student notes, already in 1931 and 1932 we see emerging the emphasis on peace and discipleship for which Bonhoeffer became known in the late 1930s, especially in his *The Cost of Discipleship*.

As an ordained minister, Bonhoeffer was appointed chaplain to the Technical University at Charlottenburg in 1931. His work in this capacity seemed to suffer, however, from the pinch of the growing attraction of nazism for students and the lack of interest in his ministry on the part of a faculty succumbing gradually to the lure of advancement and the pressures of a totalitarian regime. The post served in the longer run only to fulfill the preliminary condition for obtaining the pulpit Bonhoeffer coveted. In the meantime he took over a confirmation class in the Zion parish of the poverty-ridden section of Prenzlauer Berg, Berlin. His devotion to the "refractory" lads in the class was remarkable; Bonhoeffer even went to the point of moving out of his comfortable surroundings to share more closely in their poverty, visiting their families and taking them on weekend trips to youth hostels and a rented cottage in the country area of Biesenthal, in sum, teaching them something about the nature of Christian community. As he remarked in a letter to Erwin Sutz, his method of relating to his students was a free departure from the catechism then in vogue and something unknown in most German parishes. "I have developed all my instructions on the idea of community," he wrote, "and these young men, who are always listening to party political speeches, know quite well what I'm getting at. . . . And again and again we have found our way from faith in the communion of saints to the forgiveness of sins, and I believe that they have now grasped something of it."[28] One of the students who survived the war remembered that Bonhoeffer had made the catechism come alive in a way he had never experienced before.[29]

Bonhoeffer also ran a short-lived youth club. But these activities were all part of his drive to secure a parish appointment. Eventually, an opening did occur in Friedrichshain, in the eastern section of Berlin, but he was defeated for the post. The reasons given included: "too young, his preaching too severe, and the demands he made on his congregation too strange. His rival was too popular."[30] His next setback was a more bitter experience. Both he and his young minister friend of Jewish descent, Franz Hildebrandt, were in line for an appointment to the Lazarus Church in Berlin. However, this prospect ran into the Aryan Clause, which excluded Jews from civil service. Inasmuch as ministers were considered civil servants, Hildebrandt's appointment became unlikely. In the backlash of this new example of the church's caving in to state policy, Bonhoeffer wrote to Karl Barth, "I could not accept the ministry I had wanted unless I were willing to give up my attitude of unconditional opposition to *this* church, unless I were willing to make my ministry unconvincing in advance, and were willing to drop my solidarity with the Jewish-Christian ministers—my closest friend is one of them and is now faced with a void."[31] His move away from the university and from the Berlin pulpits seemed inevitable. These had become mere focal points in the rising accommodation of both teachers and church leaders to nazism's insidious denial of civil rights.

What was happening in German churches at this time served to confirm the suspicions Bonhoeffer had voiced in a radio address delivered only two days after Hitler had become chancellor. In his talk he warned against the possibility of Germany slipping into an idolatrous cult of the *Führer* (leader), who could very well turn out to be a *Verführer* (misleader) and one who mocks God himself. He was cut off the air at that juncture, in what may have been the first governmental action against free speech. Bonhoeffer was so fearful that the talk might be distorted into an endorsement of the *Führer* that he privately circulated the entire script and presented a lecture incorporating the element missing from the radio broadcast.[32]

EARLY ENCOUNTER WITH NAZI ANTI-SEMITISM

While there was much about nazism that disturbed Bonhoeffer and his family, the nub of Bonhoeffer's disquiet seemed to center on the bullying and virulent anti-Semitism that rapidly became official government policy. On April 7, 1933, the passage of the Aryan Clause excluded Jews from civil service. Six days previously, the boycott of Jewish stores prompted Dietrich and his brother Klaus to discuss with Paul Lehmann, Dietrich's friend from Union Theological Seminary days, how they might alert the proper circles in America to the plight of the Jews. Bonhoeffer's essay "The Church and the Jewish Question," delivered that same month to a group of pastors who met regularly to discuss matters of theological interest, was his first public response to both the legislation and the question of church responsibility for the Jews. Bonhoeffer had revised the original manuscript after the boycott and anti-Jewish legislation in order to incorporate a section to deal with possible church action on behalf of nonbaptized as well as baptized Jews.

This new section so stirred his colleagues that some left the audience. What particularly upset them was the seeming sedition in Bonhoeffer's insistence that the so-called Jewish Question was in reality a critical question for Christianity and church-state relations. The church had the right, he argued, to question and even admonish the state. Further, the church had a responsibility to the victims of state injustice, regardless of their religious affiliation. Finally, taking a long stride away from traditional interpretations of Martin Luther's two kingdoms theory, Bonhoeffer urged jamming the spoke of the wheel of state (*dem Rad selbst in die Speichen zu fallen*) if the injustices continued. He added that such action would be incumbent on a church were the state to fail in its functions by unrestrainedly bringing "about too much or too little law and order."[33] Nazism's anti-Jewish legislation had, in Bonhoeffer's opinion, been an unmerited, ill-conceived intervention in church affairs and had exposed the Jewish community to the worst disorder, aggression in the name of the law. It was a crisis begging the church "to protect the state *qua* state from itself and to preserve it."[34]

Bonhoeffer seemed to be alone in these critical remarks of 1933. Nevertheless, the lingering Jewish stereotypes reflected in Bonhoeffer's words showed that even he had a long way to go in purging his theology of the deep-clutching roots of Christian anti-Semitism.[35] The struggle over nazism's attempts to Aryanize the churches and co-opt pastors to Hitler's policies with the bait of a purified and united *Volkskirche* (a "folk church" along national lines), helped to galvanize Bonhoeffer's perception of the real issue for Christianity. As he wrote in a letter to his grandmother in August 1933: "The conflict is really Germanism or Christianity and the sooner the conflict comes out in the open, the better."[36]

Seared into Bonhoeffer's thoughts at the time of that letter and as he worked on the Bethel Confession (a theological declaration of faith motivated by a sense of urgency over the threat of Nazi policies) was the rejection of his earlier efforts to arouse church opposition to what he now recognized to be heresy seeping into the Evangelical Church of Germany. He and his group of Young Reformers had not only urged convocation of a general council to attack the heresy but also proclamation by clergy and bishops of a "spiritual interdict." It seemed to many in one audience Bonhoeffer addressed on this issue that he was "routing out ancient halberds from dusty armories."[37] Bethge remarks that Bonhoeffer "displayed a faith in the concreteness of the church that astounded his audience."[38]

Whatever his obvious sincerity and convictions about the issue of nazism in the churches, it was equally obvious that many church members were threatened by Bonhoeffer's seeming intransigence. Few pastors recognized the potential of a spiritual interdict on all religious services as a force against the racist dictatorship. The suggestion that a council root out the new heresy struck some as an infringement on the liberalism and tolerance that were a boast of twentieth-century Protestantism. Yet the idea of a council was to be realized to some degree a year later in the Barmen and Dahlem Synods, though what was accomplished at these gatherings was but a shadow of the radical steps and uncompromising declarations Bonhoeffer dreamed of provoking. One can only surmise the effect a spiritual interdict would have had on Nazi policies.

Later in the war the very tactic Bonhoeffer had proposed was, in fact, adopted by the Norwegian church in the aftermath of actions against Provost Fjelibu and Bishop Berggrav. There followed a pastors' strike and wholesale church resignations. Berlin was moved to intervene on the bishop's behalf. Ironically, it was Bonhoeffer and Count von Moltke, two members of the German resistance, who were sent by the *Abwehr* (German Military Intelligence) to examine the Norwegian church struggle and its "danger" to the morale of German troops. Bonhoeffer used the occasion to encourage the Norwegians to resist even to the point of martyrdom. From his own experience in having his suggestion that the church invoke an interdict against Nazi Germany rejected in 1933, he warned the pastors in Norway not to give way to state persuasion or control in the matter of church government.[39] That personal experience was bitter. Indeed, Bonhoeffer's move to London in 1933 to accept the pastorate of two German-speaking parishes was, in part at least, an escape from the frustration of seeing the resistance to nazism checkmated by timidity and, consequently, watching the erosion of Christianity within Germany.

Part of that erosion was the victory of the "German Christians" (Protestants in support of Hitler) in the national church election of July 23, 1933, enabling them to occupy key positions in the church. Bonhoeffer called for a new confession of faith in his sermon of that day: "For the times, which are times of collapse to the human understanding, may well be for it a great time of building. . . . Church, remain a church! . . . confess, confess, confess."[40]

THE BETHEL CONFESSION

As the German Christians assumed more power in the church, the opposing pastors united more closely in the struggle for what they hoped would supersede that power, namely, truth and justice. It was a time begging for the confession of faith Bonhoeffer had urged in his sermon of July 23, 1933. Many confessions were, in fact, being formulated by ministers concerned about what was happening within their churches. But these were too scattered to be effective in arousing individual and community consciences. Bonhoeffer and Professor Hermann Sasse of Erlangen were deputized by the Council of Young Reformers, therefore, to retreat to the community of Bethel, a Christian settlement grown out of a treatment center for epileptics, to produce a confession of faith that would challenge the German Christians. The aim was to compel the German Christians to declare their beliefs openly. They also wished to create a new creed to combat distortions in the church struggle. What they finally wrote was a solid, uncompromising, statement of the theological basis of the church struggle. It contained, moreover, a spirited defense of the Jews. Bonhoeffer and Sasse reiterated God's choice of Israel in wholly theological terms and insisted that God had not retracted that choice. "The 'holy remnant,'" the document affirms, "can neither be absorbed into another nation by emancipation and assimilation . . . nor be exterminated by Pharaoh-like measures. This 'holy remnant' bears the indelible stamp of the chosen people. . . . No nation can ever be commissioned to avenge on the Jews the murder at Golgotha. We oppose the attempt to deprive the Evangelical Church of Germany of its promise by the attempt to change it into a national church of Christians of Aryan descent."[41] The Bethel Confession, despite its obvious shortcomings in properly assessing Judaism, is a clear repudiation of Aryanism and the Nazi attempt to rid nation and church of any Jewish presence. The confession was then circulated to some twenty theologians, who proceeded to whittle away at its call to uncompromising commitment in the struggle. Attempts were made to dilute criticism of the state in the document. For Bonhoeffer, the suggested corrections were an emasculation of the challenge he had incorporated as one of the central purposes of the confession. Disappointed, he refused to sign the final toothless copy that Martin Niemöller circulated.

THE PASTORS' EMERGENCY LEAGUE

By that time, however, Bonhoeffer, Niemöller, and Franz Hildebrandt had already met at the house of the young pastor Gerhard Jacobi to organize the *Pfarrernotbund* (Pastors' Emergency League), whose pledge was to fight for a confession of faith within the church. Their four resolutions were the first organized statements of resistance to the events of the Brown Synod of September 4, 1933, so-called because so many of the ministers appeared in brown shirts, sporting the swastika, as a declaration of loyalty to Adolf Hitler. It had been heralded as the "the party day of the faith." In effect, it had succeeded in deposing the general superintendents of the church and replacing them with ten German Christian bishops sympathetic to the Hitler regime. It also rammed through passage of the Aryan Clause as official church policy for ministers. It was a bitter moment for those who gathered at Jacobi's house. To resist this strongest move to Aryanize the church, they declared the following: (1) the Aryan Clause was an unlawful intrusion into the teaching office of the church, bound only to its authorized calling; (2) ordained ministers have the right to proclaim the Word and administer the sacraments based on the Confessions of the Reformation; (3) Because the action taken at the synod was a breach of those confessions and a separation from the church's true communion, the law must be repealed; (4) help must be given to those affected by the new unjust laws. For Bonhoeffer, these resolutions declared that the church of the Brown Synod had separated itself from the church of Jesus Christ.[42]

Over 2,000 signatures had been added to the protest by the time of the National Synod at Wittenberg in late September 1933. Bonhoeffer and Hildebrandt nailed their protest leaflets to the trees when it appeared that the pro-Nazi bishop Ludwig Müller would ignore their demands to comment on the church law passed during the infamous Brown Synod. The synod at Wittenberg was another disappointment; the bishops again remained silent. On an impulse, Bonhoeffer and Hildebrandt visited the "Old Lutherans" in Berlin-Wilmersdorf to inquire about the possibility of joining the Lutheran Free Church. There they learned that they would have to bring their congregations with them. Leaving the church on that condition did not seem feasible; Bonhoeffer, therefore, abandoned the plan.[43] But his pastor friend Gerhard Jacobi, who would eventually preside over the Confessing Church in Berlin, later recalled the deep impression Bonhoeffer was able to make at subsequent meetings of pastors, though he spoke only briefly. "Twice he quoted to them nothing but the words: 'One man asks: What is to come? The other: What is right? And that is the difference between the free man and the slave.' He said nothing more, but those few words spoken in calmness and certainty, and out of personal freedom, found their mark."[44]

Inwardly, however, Bonhoeffer felt himself more and more isolated in his radical suggestions. The dilution of his Bethel Confession to palliate pastors who were less than enthusiastic about pushing for a more forceful stand on behalf of the Jews bothered him. Even before his work on the confession, he had been haunted by personal doubts about what was the best course of action against the German Christians now so boldly entrenched in roles of leadership within the church. In the midst of that turmoil and prior to his mission at Bethel, Bonhoeffer accepted the pastorate of two German-speaking parishes in the Sydenham section of London. As he put it in a letter to Karl Barth, he wanted "to go into the wilderness for a spell" to get his bearings. He arrived at his London vicarage on October 17, 1933, and was joined by Hildebrandt a month later.

PASTORAL MINISTRY IN LONDON

London was hardly a "wilderness," but the overseas assignment did provide Bonhoeffer the distance he needed to renew the church struggle from a different perspective, that of bringing pressure from outside to weigh on the German Christians. Barth responded to Bonhoeffer's letter stating his reasons for the retreat with a sharp rebuke of Bonhoeffer for depriving the German church of his "splendid theological armory" and "upright German figure" at the time he was most needed. Barth pointed out to Bonhoeffer "that the house of your church is on fire, that you know enough and can say what you know well enough to be able to help." He suggested Bonhoeffer return to Berlin "by the next ship" or "the ship after next."[45] Bonhoeffer's return was to be several ships later. His stay in London was not, as Barth's letter implied, an abandonment of the struggle. In his foreign post he continued his involvement with the church in Berlin, running up a staggeringly high telephone bill to stay in touch with Niemöller through his mother. And in gatherings of overseas pastors as well as in ecumenical discussions, he rallied people to an awareness of and an opposition to the German Christians' heretical attempt to amalgamate Nazi racism with the Christian gospel. Bishop Heckel, charged with the Ecclesiastical Foreign Ministry, traveled to London determined to deal with the overseas threat to church polity by asking Bonhoeffer to sign an agreement to abstain from any ecumenical activities not directly authorized by Berlin. Bonhoeffer refused.[46]

It was, in fact, these ecumenical activities that led to his lasting friendship with George K. A. Bell, bishop of Chichester and, in 1933–1934, president of the Universal Christian Council for Life and Work. Bell's church position gave Bonhoeffer the benefit of having in that office an advocate who could effectively pressure the churches for decisions favorable to the Confessing Church. Indeed, it was Bell who succeeded in having Bonhoeffer and Präses Koch, head of the Confessing Synod, chosen to become members of the Ecumenical Council. It was Bell to whom Bonhoeffer would address his last words prior to his execution at the Flossenbürg Concentration Camp in April 1945. When the English edition of *The Cost of Discipleship* appeared after the war years, it was Bell who wrote the foreword, offering one of the most sterling tributes to Bonhoeffer's life and witness: "I knew him in London in the early days of the evil regime, and from him, more than from any other German, I learned the true character of the conflict, in an intimate friendship. I have no doubt that he did fine work with his German congregation; but he taught many besides his fellow countrymen while a pastor in England. He was crystal clear in his convictions; and young as he was, and humble-minded as he was, he saw the truth, and spoke it with a complete absence of fear." At Bonhoeffer's behest, Bell undertook to compose an alert to the churches in the Universal Christian Council for Life and Work telling them of "the dangers to which the spiritual life of the Evangelical Church is exposed." There were, he observed, "other problems which the Evangelical Church of Germany is facing, which are the common concern of the whole of Christendom. These are such fundamental questions as those respecting the nature of the Church, its witness, its freedom and its relation to the secular power."[47] That message, known as Bell's "Ascensiontide Message," appeared just three weeks before the famous Synod of Barmen in Wuppertal.

THE BARMEN CONFESSION

It was in the "Barmen Confession" and not in the Bethel Confession, as Bonhoeffer had hoped, that the Confessing Church took its strongest stand against Hitler. This was the first organized Confessing Synod, held on May 29–31, 1934, with representatives from nineteen provincial churches. They were unanimous in stating their opposition to the Nazi posturing of the Reich Church under the pro-Hitler bishop Ludwig Müller. The Confessing Church's claim to be the true Protestant church of Germany was based on the confession of faith drawn up substantially by Karl Barth. Especially significant is the lucid theological premise of the association of the German churches that opens the declaration: "The impregnable foundation of the German Evangelical Church is the Gospel of Jesus Christ, as it was revealed in Holy Scripture and came again to the light in the creeds of the Reformation." One important clause later became the battle cry of the church struggle and made many signers of the declaration marked men with the secret police. "We repudiate the false teaching that there are areas of our life in which we belong not to Jesus Christ but to other lords, areas in which we do not need justification and sanctification through him."[48] This was the matter of principle: the church demanded the right and the freedom to be the church of Jesus Christ.

Bonhoeffer himself, though not present at Barmen, would look back on that moment as an affirmation that church order was bound solely to Jesus Christ. This affirmation, for him, was a clear rejection of the heresy that a church could be allowed to suit its convictions to the dictates of politics or public opinion. The church was, to put it simply, the body of Christ.[49] Bishop Bell hailed the document as "a thunderbolt in the very middle of the National Socialist campaign to unify the Church by means of force, corruption and insincere practices."[50] If this was the strength of the Barmen Confession, its weakness lay in its seeming insensitivity to the plight of the Jews. Some who revel in the memory of Barmen are still not aware of this. Karl Barth would later regret the omission. The church did not take, as Bethge puts it, "the road which might have led to an unprecedented new encounter with the Jews."[51]

ECUMENICAL ACTIVIST

Bonhoeffer became an outspoken advocate for the Barmen Confession as a rallying point for the anti-Nazi stand of the churches. In his ecumenical activities especially, he directed his energies toward having the Confessing Church recognized officially as the only valid representative of the Evangelical Church of Germany. Prior to the ecumenical meeting at Fanø, Denmark, in late August 1934, Bonhoeffer caucused with Präses Karl Koch and Martin Niemöller in Berlin. They agreed that unless one of their number were invited and, therefore, the Confessing Church officially represented at Fanø, they would not collaborate in the conference. They pressured the World Alliance for Promoting International Friendship through the Churches on this. From Henry L. Henriod in Geneva, secretary of the World Alliance, however, they received only sympathy and the suggestion that the Confessing Synod take the step of declaring itself a church alongside the Reich Church as prelude to a formal invitation.

For Bonhoeffer, this step meant abandoning their claim to be the *only* Evangelical Church of Germany. This much seemed clear to him from the Barmen Synod. Bonhoeffer then turned to Bishop Bell for help. When Bell had secured the backing of Bishop Ammundsen, chairman of the World Alliance, Bell wrote Koch "to invite you to attend the Meeting of the Council and to bring a colleague with you; or if you are for any reason unable to attend yourself, to send two representatives. . . . I invite you and your colleague or representatives as guests and as authoritative spokesmen in a very difficult situation, from whose information and advice the Universal Christian Council would be certain to derive much benefit."[52] This was not the invitation giving some substance to their church claims, as Bonhoeffer had desired. Nonetheless, his decision to attend the Fanø Conference became important for two reasons: first, because of the political situation in Berlin, neither Koch nor his colleague Fritz von Bodelschwingh, the former national bishop and outspoken critic of the German Christians, was able to attend; thus, Bonhoeffer became the sole "official" representative of the Confessing Church at Fanø. Second, Bonhoeffer's contributions to the council would be hailed as among the most significant for the future of the ecumenical movement.

If Bonhoeffer was alone as "official" representative of the Confessing Church at the Fanø gathering, he was not alone in the deliberations of the Ecumenical Youth Commission in which he functioned as secretary. Many of those present were former students of Bonhoeffer from Berlin, and, like their teacher, they were disenchanted with the nationalism then sweeping Germany. Most of these would also be at his side as members of his Finkenwalde Seminary during the coming years of the church struggle. In their history of the ecumenical movement, Ruth Rouse and Stephen Neill make special mention of how Bonhoeffer's Ecumenical Youth Commission was the most radical of all the groups at Fanø.[53] Indeed, their resolutions were certainly a courageous departure from the usual diplomatic couching of church statements at ecumenical meetings. One striking resolution insisted that the church's essential task was "to proclaim the Word of God." Because of this, its proclamation had to be "independent of purely nationalistic aims. In particular, the church may under no circumstances lend its spiritual support to a war. In the face of the increasing claims of the state, the church must abandon its passive attitude and proclaim the will of God come what may." The conference bluntly urged the churches to refuse even to recognize as Christian any church that denied its universal character in favor of being a mere adjunct of state policy unable to challenge the people with God's Word.[54] The German Christians were not mentioned by name in this implied accusation, but most delegates knew the intent behind the words.

Bonhoeffer's main contribution at Fanø, however, went beyond these tough words against the Reich Church heresy. As the recognized leader of the German youth delegation, he denounced the distortion of the gospel of Christ that would permit war between Christians. His most memorable words on behalf of world peace have been preserved in his sermon "The Church and the Peoples of the World," delivered at one of the morning services. "From the first moment the assembly was breathless with tension," Otto Dudzus wrote of that event. "Many may have felt that they would never forget what they had just heard. . . . Bonhoeffer had charged so far ahead that the conference could not follow him. Did that surprise anybody? But on the other hand: Could anybody have good conscience about it?"[55] Bonhoeffer's words were a challenge to those who were attempting to maintain a good conscience, all the while avoiding the real issue of whether one could be a Christian at all without committing oneself to the gospel of peace. "Peace on earth is not a problem," he said, "but a commandment given at Christ's coming." He attacked those attempts to soften that command by interjections in favor of national security and legitimate defense needs. God, he retorted, did not say anything about that, but he did clearly enjoin peace among all peoples. The church, he declared, must be in the vanguard of this struggle for peace. "There shall be peace because Christ is in the world, that is to say, there shall be peace because there is a church of Christ for whose sake alone the whole world still exists. And this church of Christ exists at one and the same time in all peoples, yet beyond all boundaries, whether national, political, social, or racial."[56] The real issue, he argued in that sermon, was whether the churches could justify their existence if they did not take steps to halt the march toward war. The churches must not mistake peace for security. "Peace means to give oneself altogether to the law of God, wanting no security, but in faith and obedience laying the destiny of the nations in the hand of Almighty God, not trying to direct it for selfish purposes. Battles are won, not with weapons, but with God. They are won where the way leads to the cross." He asked the ecumenical council finally to begin to act like the holy church of Christ by speaking out "so that the world, though it gnash its teeth, will have to hear, so that the peoples will rejoice because the church of Christ in the name of Christ has taken the weapons from the hands of their sons, forbidden war, proclaimed the peace of Christ against the raging world."[57] The effect of his words on the delegates was electrifying. Could they, as Otto Dudzus asked, have a good conscience about not following Bonhoeffer's lead in taking concrete steps to promote peace and stop war? Unfortunately, many churches and church leaders seemed to have adjusted their consciences for the coming turbulence in Europe.

Some of Bonhoeffer's words from that sermon at Fanø are reminiscent of the philosophy and pacifist tactics of Mahatma Gandhi. "Which of us can say he knows what it might mean for the world," Bonhoeffer speculated, "if one nation should meet the aggressor, not with weapons in hand, but praying, defenseless, and for that very reason protected by 'a bulwark never failing'?"[58] Several letters written prior to the Fanø gathering do indeed reveal Bonhoeffer's growing interest in visiting India and learning firsthand Gandhi's way of life and the successful tactics of Gandhi's nonviolent resistance.

To this end, Bonhoeffer spent part of 1934 preparing for such a journey, not only procuring letters of introduction for his encounter with Gandhi but also seeking out British disciples of Gandhi to discover more about life in the East and about a method of resistance to structured evil seemingly closer to Christ than the Westernized versions of Christianity Bonhoeffer so openly abhorred. "Must we be put to shame by heathens in the East?" he asked at Fanø.[59] He had already alluded to this "shameful" discrepancy in a letter to his grandmother informing her of his plans for travel to India. "Sometimes it even seems to me that there's more Christianity in their 'paganism' than in the whole of our Reich Church. Of course Christianity did come from the East originally, but it has been so Westernized and so permeated by civilized thought that, as we can now see, it is almost lost to us. Unfortunately I have little confidence left in the church opposition. I don't at all like the way they're going about things, and really dread the time when they assume responsibility and we may be compelled yet again to witness the discrediting of Christianity."[60] He had also written Reinhold Niebuhr of his intentions. Niebuhr was less than enthusiastic, pointing out in his own incisive, pragmatic manner that the move was unwise for two reasons. Gandhi's philosophy was a world removed from Bonhoeffer's upbringing and his own German Lutheran worldview. Secondly, Gandhi's tactics would ultimately be ineffective in Nazi Germany. Hitler's S.S. and Gestapo would have none of the compunction of conscience of the British in squelching a Gandhi-like resistance.[61] Bonhoeffer remained unconvinced by Niebuhr's arguments and pushed ahead with his travel plans. The invitation finally arrived. Bonhoeffer was invited to share in Gandhi's community life, living at his ashram, and to accompany him on journeys throughout India.

THE SEMINARY AT FINKENWALDE

The encounter with Gandhi was, however, a dream that was never realized. More important considerations made it necessary for Bonhoeffer to return to Germany. The Confessing Church had been further squeezed by the national bishop and leaders of the German Christians. The Old Prussian Preachers' Seminaries had been shut down in March 1934. Theological students had been forbidden to take the special examinations leading to ordination unless they could provide full proof of their pure Aryan blood. This additional nazification of church policy moved Confessing Church leaders at the Dahlem Synod of October

1934 to take the radical step of organizing their own training of candidates, a venture to be supported by freewill donations. It was a new undertaking, demanding in turn a rare combination of scholarship, a passion for the principles of the Reformation, and a certain fearlessness in those who would direct these seminaries. Gerhard Jacobi, not unexpectedly, proposed Bonhoeffer to the church leadership for what would eventually be directorship of the seminary for Prussia in Pomerania. Bonhoeffer, having been approached earlier about his availability, had let it be known that he would be willing to accept such a mission. Despite some objections that he might be neither discreet nor pliable enough from those who remembered his bold intransigence in the church struggle of 1933, he was named and approved for the post.

His eventual acceptance was not without its inner cost, however, as he revealed in a letter to Erwin Sutz, his friend of Union Theological Seminary days. "I am struggling," he wrote, "over the decision on whether I should go back to Germany as director of the New Preachers' Seminary still to be established or whether I should remain here or go to India. I no longer believe in the University, and never really have believed in it—a fact that used to rile you. The entire training of young theologians belongs today in church, monastic-like schools in which the pure doctrine, the Sermon on the Mount, and worship can be taken seriously which is really not the case with all three things at the university and, in present-day circumstances, is impossible."[62]

Indeed, his desire to incorporate "pure doctrine, the Sermon on the Mount, and worship" into the training of his seminarians prompted Bonhoeffer to request additional preparation time and to postpone opening the seminary until the spring of 1935. This additional time allowed him to visit several Anglican seminaries and religious communities to experience firsthand their manner of living the common life and to assess their methods of training for the ministry. He thus drew from several spiritual wells confirmation of his conviction that the "formation" of seminarians demanded a lively sense of what Christ was demanding of his followers in the Sermon on the Mount. For Bonhoeffer, this could only be done in a community shaped by Christian service and sustained by regular spiritual exercises and worship. If the venture appeared to some as "too Catholic," for Bonhoeffer life in the seminary was to be based in part on a healthy blend of some of the better elements of the Catholic-Christian tradition with a rigorous adherence to the demands and principles of the Reformation. Given his stated purpose, to make of the seminary a vortex from which "Christianity can be a vital force for our people," and thereby "also make a definite stand for peace by conscientious objection,"[63] there would be included in his seminary something of Gandhi's ashram.

Those seminarians who gathered, first, at the lovely seaside setting of Zingst and later in the more "permanent" quarters of an abandoned, rambling estate converted into a private school at Finkenwalde noticed their director's strong commitment to peace. The first realization of this came early in May 1935 when Hitler proclaimed Germany's rebirth as a military power muscular enough to reverse the shame of the Treaty of Versailles. As a result, the ordinands were excited about the prospect of donning uniform and disproving the accusation that the Confessing Church was a disloyal religious fifth column within Nazi Germany. But Bonhoeffer himself dampened the euphoria with a reminder of the other and more compelling options enjoined on Christians by the gospel: pacifism and conscientious objection to military service. Such a viewpoint was unexpected not just to the seminarians but within mainstream Lutheranism and its innocuous fallback on Luther's doctrine of the two kingdoms to solve that possible dilemma. It was then they discovered that their director was a pacifist. Yet Bonhoeffer's commitment to pacifism and his strong difference of opinion on what was the better option for a Christian did not destroy the seminarians' admiration for him. He was not overbearing in the way he defended conscientious objection to military service, arguing not for fanaticism in the cause of peace but rather in favor of a more sympathetic attitude on their part for those who adopted a pacifist stand in their own following of Christ. Many of the seminarians would later die at the front.

The regimen at Finkenwalde was built around a monasticlike schedule. The seminarians began and ended the day with a half hour of common prayer drawn from the Psalms read antiphonally, a hymn for the day, then readings from the Hebrew and Christian Scriptures, extempore prayer, recitation of the Our Father, and a closing hymn. On Sundays there was a full liturgical service with the usual sermon. In the mornings this was followed by a half-hour meditation. The rest of the day was taken up with course lectures, readings, meals together, fraternal service, and imaginative recreation. In all the day's order and routine, however, Bonhoeffer insisted that the Bible was the seminary's guiding spirit, just as the ecclesial-political situation was its concrete context. We read this in his October "Greeting" from the seminary to the Confessing Church pastors and benefactors. "The special character of a seminary of the Confessing Church derives from the difficult situation in which we have been placed by the church struggle. The Bible forms the focal point of our work. It has once again become for us the starting point and the center of our theological work and of all our Christian action. We have learned here to read the Bible once again prayerfully."[64] Each day was lightened by leisure in which Bonhoeffer's and others' skills at the piano were appreciated. Bonhoeffer taught them the black spirituals he had learned in America and had made part of his record collection. They liked to sing together, often substituting a hymn for the table grace. In short, the mood was both festive and serious.

The highlight of many days was, of course, Bonhoeffer's lectures on discipleship. This was what Bethge would call the "nerve center" of the seminary, which distinguished his seminary from all others. The seminarians felt "they were witnessing a theological event which would stimulate every area of their professional life."[65] As a teacher, Bonhoeffer was without equal. His style was intense, drawing students into thinking deeply about and even openly disputing the point in question. He had developed the knack of communicating well, a trait enhanced by his ability to maintain eye contact and to listen attentively and to debate an issue with energy but also with respect. He was, as his assistant, Wilhelm Rott, remembered, one "who always had time for his brethren."[66]

This availability carried over into the daily life of the seminarians, but it was of a piece with the Christian service and love of God's Word galvanized in one's daily meditation. Bonhoeffer often had to defend the practice of daily meditation. Not many, even among the seminarians, understood what it was about in the beginning. Left to themselves at the outset of their training by one of Bonhoeffer's forced absences, they realized their own trials and "errors" with the practice, some sleeping, some working on sermons during the time, some reading commentaries, some not knowing what to do and so daydreaming the time away. From outside the seminary came complaints of Bonhoeffer's catholicizing the seminary. Even Barth remarked in a letter to Bonhoeffer that he was uneasy over what appeared "an almost indefinable odor of monastic eros and pathos."[67]

Bonhoeffer was willing to discuss any difficulty and objection; however, he considered the practice of meditation essential to the training of ordinands. It was not something to be put to a majority vote for approval. Even at the height of the war years, he urged his former seminarians to keep up the practice of meditation. "The daily, silent meditation upon the Word of God," he wrote, "with which I am concerned—even if it is only for a few minutes—must be for me the crystallization of everything that brings order into my life, both inwardly and outwardly. In these days when our old rules of life have had to be discarded, and there is great danger of finding our inner order endangered by the rush of events . . . meditation gives our life a kind of stability, maintaining a link with our earlier life, from baptism to confirmation and ordination, preserving us in the saving fellowship of our community, our brothers, and our spiritual home."[68]

Barth's remark was typical of those who suspected that the seminarians were being cloistered to the point of losing touch with the real world of Nazi Germany and church politics. Far from walling themselves off from the world, however, the "Finkenwaldians" were constantly confronted by Bonhoeffer with a down-to-earth theology that emphasized the gospel challenge, the care of souls, and their mission to bring God's Word to decisions affecting service to both church and state. Other seminaries did not include prayer in their curricula. With Bonhoeffer, prayer was taught as much by his personal example as in formal classes. Bonhoeffer was clearly the leader in the largely extemporized prayers of thanksgiving, forgiveness, and intercession. Bethge recalled that "into these prayers he would put his will, his understanding and his heart."[69]

Much of the intent behind the regular life of prayer, lecture, service, and meditation on God's Word is revealed most forcefully in Bonhoeffer's proposal to establish a "House of Brethren" at the seminary to provide a needed continuity as some finished their training and began parish work. The "brethren" would be, therefore, a spiritual leaven for new candidates. He put the need squarely in the context of that attachment to God's Word and dedication to Christian service which for him were the only raison d'être of a seminary. "They must be ready to be where their service is needed whatever the external circumstances, even renouncing all the privileges of clergy, financial or otherwise. They will find their home and all the fellowship they need for their service in the community from which they come and to which they return continually. The aim is not the seclusion of a monastery, but a place of the deepest inward concentration for service outside."[70] The official proposal for such a community, to be called the "Evangelical House of Brethren," was submitted on September 6, 1935. What Bonhoeffer desired was a genuine experiment in communal living for ministers beyond their all-too-rapid six months of training. They would thus be sustained by a more intense mode of Christian life in their preaching and service. Finkenwalde would be for them a continual haven for renewal. Their life together would be simple, without clerical privilege, "a communal life in daily and strict obedience to the will of Christ Jesus, in the exercise of the humblest and highest service one Christian brother can perform for another. . . . " In this he hoped they would "learn to recognize the strength and liberation to be founded in brotherly service and communal life in a Christian community."[71]

Six of the Finkenwaldians, including Eberhard Bethge, who had become Bonhoeffer's friend, confidant, confessor, and, in many ways, spiritual guide, received permission to stay on. They shared their financial resources, with Bonhoeffer contributing the most money for the venture, and became, as Bonhoeffer intended, the brotherhood that preserved "the inner continuity" of the Finkenwalde seminary. This experiment in Christianity and ministry was not destined to last. The Gestapo closed the seminary in October 1937. Bonhoeffer's efforts to continue the training of ordinands by conducting a "seminary on the run" proved only moderately successful. Finkenwalde survives today in the books *The Cost of Discipleship* and *Life Together* but especially in Finkenwaldians such as Eberhard Bethge, Winfried Maechler, Werner Koch, Albrecht Schönherr, Wolf-Dieter Zimmermann, Otto Dudzus, Joachim Kanitz, and others who have kept alive the Bonhoeffer legacy of dedication to God's Word in the modern world.

THE CHURCH STRUGGLE

Even before the Gestapo moved against the seminary, the church struggle had taken several unpleasant twists for Bonhoeffer and his ordinands. The Confessing Church seemed gradually to be losing its will to speak clearly on behalf of a more active resistance to nazism. The promise of the Barmen Confession was in the process of being blunted by compromise and the seductive siren of patriotism. Barth had been dismissed from his post in Bonn without an outcry from the Confessing Church; his opposition to the civil service oath, the immediate reason for his dismissal, was considered "too political." Bonhoeffer refused to make such a distinction and warned that failure to support Barth "would give the impression of a deviation from the Confessing Church's original and true course."[72] Barth would leave Germany but not before expressing his consternation that the Confessing Church still had not shown any "sympathy for the millions who are suffering injustice. It has not once spoken out on the most simple matters of public integrity. And if and when it does speak, it is always on its own behalf."[73] These accusations were true of all the churches and would be echoed in Bonhoeffer's own denunciation of the churches from prison.

Barth's "farewell letter" was circulated by Bonhoeffer's ordinands, who still had hopes of provoking a more spirited church resistance to the latest infringements on personal and ecclesial rights within the nation. These hopes were again to be disappointed when in June 1935 the Third National Synod of the Confessing Church's meeting in Augsburg ignored the more urgent issues, namely that the church insist on freedom for its pastors to refuse the requirement of a civil oath to Hitler. More sadly for Bonhoeffer, nothing was said about the increasingly systematic persecution of the Jewish people. Similar frustrations were experienced at the synod held in Berlin-Steglitz on September 23–26, 1935. Bonhoeffer subscribed to what his friend Superintendent Martin Albertz wished to convey to the Steglitz Synod in the aftermath of the silence of Confessing Church delegates at Augsburg. He himself was unable to speak because he was not a member of the Steglitz Synod. Albertz voiced the concerns of Bonhoeffer, who demanded more than a focus on Jewish baptism and the mission to the Jews. Someone needed to ask the question, as Albertz did: "Where is Abel your brother? In our case too, in the case of the Confessing Church, there can be no other answer than that given by Cain. . . . And if the church, afraid for its own destruction, can in many instances do nothing, why is it not at least conscious of its guilt? Why does it not pray for those who are afflicted by this undeserved suffering and persecution? Why are there no services of intercession as there were for the imprisoned pastors?"[74] These became the questions of conscience for the assembly. But the focus of Steglitz was mainly on how to secure state recognition and how to achieve financial autonomy. In face of this, how could the Confessing Church "dare assume that they are entitled, even called, to preach to Jews, whose present sufferings are our crime . . . ?"[75] For Bonhoeffer, the failure of Steglitz was the failure of the church to be a voice for those who have no voice, in this case the disenfranchised Jew.

The entire church, it seemed, was being split into camps supporting, on the one side, conformity with state laws for the sake of recognition and financial support, and, on the other, resistance for what they perceived to be the call of God's Word and the demand of faith. In a talk for the clergy assembled at Stettin-Bredow on January 10, 1936, for a meeting preliminary to the important synod scheduled for Bad Oeynhausen in February, Bonhoeffer accused the church of muddling the real issues and stalling the spirit of the Barmen and Dahlem synods. The church had, in short, become susceptible to skilled subversion by state propaganda. In standing still, he said, they "destroy the church." He urged them to move forward, pinning their hopes on decisive action to be taken at the Bad Oeynhausen Synod. "A third synod must now provide protection against the subversion of the church by the world which, in the shape of the National Socialist State, is intervening through its finance departments, legislative authority, and committees, and is now splitting into groups the church of those who uphold the 'Confession.' Here we cannot and must not yield for one moment."[76]

But this determination, too, would be frustrated as the resolutions of Oeynhausen only thrust the young ministers into the greater dilemma of having to make the personal choice of dissent themselves, unsupported by any corporate decision on the question of submission or resistance. The new restrictive, laws seemed to isolate the Confessing Church into a position of further open defiance of the state. Now the newly established church committees offered opposition pastors a third option, namely the possibility of exercising a legitimate ministry within an officially recognized church without having to subscribe to the Reich Church ideology.

Bonhoeffer had hoped the Bad Oeynhausen Synod would rule out this neutral position—for him, one did not compromise with the forces of the AntiChrist—or any compromise with nazism. Instead, the synod shifted its own responsibility onto the consciences of individual pastors. This prompted Bonhoeffer and his seminarians to complain: "How shall we younger brethren make up our minds about them [the resolutions]? Are we to choose between accepting the resolutions or losing our office as ministers? What separates us from those who accept these resolutions, a matter of wide choice or the Word of God? We expect guidance on these matters from the Provisional Committee."[77] The tactic of making a corporate peace with Hitler's church committees without upholding individual dissenting pastors seemed to Bonhoeffer merely a reckless skirting of responsibility by overanxious church leaders. The synod had produced, not the uncompromising declaration of faith Bonhoeffer desired, but an abdication of leadership that could lead, as it did, to dissension and further splitting of the church.

Bonhoeffer's strongest word against the "neutral path" offered by the church committees came in his controversial essay *Zur Frage nach der Kirchengemeinschaft* (On the Question of the Church Community). Here Bonhoeffer stated somewhat categorically that "whoever knowingly cuts himself off from the Confessing Church in Germany cuts himself off from salvation."[78] Earlier in the paper he extended this stricture to "anyone who takes part in the governmental functions of the committees," claiming that they had separated themselves "from the church of Jesus."[79] Although those shocked by his radical attitude toward church affiliation and confessions of faith accused him of legalism, Bonhoeffer insisted that he did not intend his statements in their no-compromise form to be taken legalistically.

The issue, as he saw it, was how seriously one was to take the confession of faith and the decisions of Barmen and Dahlem. The church of Christ was not constituted by its members but by God's Word, which confronts and shapes the church, and by the sacraments that become gathering points in faith for each congregation. In the spirit of Barmen and Dahlem, the Confessing Church and its synods had no business abandoning its dissenting pastors to the obscurity of its own indecision. Criticizing the Oeynhausen Synod for its equivocation, Bonhoeffer declared that their "obscurity is pernicious."[80] It is the duty of the Confessing Church, he argued, to take "its confident way between the Scylla of orthodoxy and the Charybdis of confessionlessness. It bears the responsibility of being the true church of Jesus."[81] The harsh starkness of Bonhoeffer's paper roused many church people to revile its author. Within a month all the copies of the journal were sold-out. This surprised Bonhoeffer because his whole argument seemed so axiomatic. To him either one followed the gospel integrally or one did not. The issue to which Bonhoeffer constantly returned was the incompatibility between the Christian gospel and the national church's self-acquiescence to state domination, to the extent of absorbing the racist policies of that state into its confession.

Even the strong words of this paper were incapable of stiffening the resolve of church synods. The failure of Oeynhausen was compounded by the timid resolutions of the Sixth Confessing Church Synod at Nikolasse in June 1938. This time the danger to dissenting pastors seemed more ominous. Dr. Friedrich Werner, state commissar for the Prussian Church, had threatened to remove from office any pastor refusing to take a civil oath of loyalty to be presented by the churches as a "birthday offering" to Adolf Hitler. On the pretext that the oath in question was more a "state requirement," the synod hesitated to take a corporate stance in the name of church freedom and the gospel. Instead, it left all responsibility for such decisions to individual pastors, though it was fully aware of the vulnerability its official stance cast upon these pastors.

Bonhoeffer's ensuing letter to the Berlin Council of Brethren was strewn with the bitterness of his disappointment. "It is a heavy decision for a confessing pastor," he began, "to have to contradict a confessing synod." Again Bonhoeffer pleaded for the church to accept fully its call to be the Church of Jesus Christ and to stand with the weak and defenseless, in this case the dissenting pastors of the Confessing Church, who were now forced to withstand more political pressures alone. He contended that a majority vote toward neutrality on the synod's part was hardly a mandate and so the decision could and should be reversed. He closed his argument with a series of questions aimed at disturbing the "peace" of the Council and the synodal members: "Will the Confessing Church be willing openly to confess its guilt and disunity? Will it have room for prayer for forgiveness and a new beginning . . . ? Will Confessing Synods learn that it is important to counsel and to decide in defiance of all dangers and difficulties . . . ? Will they ever learn that majority decision in matters of conscience kills the spirit?"[82]

Bonhoeffer was rapidly becoming a man without a government he could live with and without a church that could live with his ideals. The church leaders seemed content, as he observed in the above letter, with killing the spirit of God's Word. On the ecumenical front, where he had impressed so many as both a person of peace and a young agitator against the Reich Church, he continued to function as youth secretary. He and Bethge participated in the ecumenical conference for "Life and Work" at Chamby in August 1936. As it turned out, this was to be the only conference attended by official representatives of the Confessing Church. The Reich Church delegates were led by Dr. Wilhelm Zoellner, a man soon to be replaced because of his own anxiety about antigospel policies of so many within the Reich Church leadership. The conference served only to confirm Bonhoeffer in his opinion that the Confessing Church should refuse to participate in any future ecumenical conferences in which the heretical Reich Church would be seated. He was intransigent on this point, demanding that "the ecumenical movement should be asked whether it intended to recognize the Confessing Church as the only lawful church. This was the best service that could be rendered to 'Life and Work' for it would protect the latter against the danger of non-committal theologizing."[83]

Beyond the stalemate achieved at Chamby lay Bonhoeffer's efforts to fend off any suggestion that the diverse church factions could equally represent the Protestant churches of Germany. Dr. Henry L. Henriod, secretary for the Ecumenical Council in Geneva, attempted to mediate the dispute, urging equal representation of all the churches, however heretical or fanatical one viewed the other.[84] It is evident from his letters to Bonhoeffer, however, that he missed the importance of the stand Bonhoeffer wished the Ecumenical Council to take. The minutes of the Youth Commission meeting in London to prepare for the London conference note that "Dr. Bonhoeffer declared the differences between the churches to be so great that he would be unwilling to secure a German youth delegation in which the Reich Church would be represented."[85] At the same meeting, Bonhoeffer resigned as youth secretary.

INNER EXILE

Within his own church Bonhoeffer was becoming isolated, drifting into what Bethge has described as an "inner exile."[86] Alienated from the majority of pastors who took the oath to Hitler and thus legalized themselves before the government, Bonhoeffer's efforts to drum up resistance to the oath met with little success. As late as September 1938, he received a draft of a new ordinance to regulate appointments to church administration. What he read there, however, was a strong desire to reestablish unity within the church by harnessing all the widely divergent sides together in a "pacification" grounded in compromise. This would bring together the Church of the Old Prussian Union, the Evangelical Church of Germany, confessing pastors drawing inspiration from Dahlem, and so-called neutrals. Bonhoeffer announced at the outset of his reply that he rejected the proposal because it was a betrayal of the Barmen and Dahlem synods. He alluded in the letter to the great disappointment of Nikolasse. "After this defeat we had indeed expected a different, far more spiritual word from our church leadership. But now what is proposed to us is the surrender of the Confessing Church. Here we will no longer follow."[87] It was obvious that Bonhoeffer preferred solidarity with the shrinking remnant of dissenting pastors left unsupported by church leadership.

On November 9, 1938, storm troopers mobilized hordes of willing citizens to terrorize the Jewish population, breaking windows of houses and stores and burning the synagogues. Though they knew that this was a well-orchestrated escalation of making life miserable for Jews, not even the atrocities of *Kristallnacht* (Crystal Night) kept church leaders from retreating into a pious silence. When Bonhoeffer reached Berlin, part of his angry reaction was to argue how reprehensible it was for Christians to make the connection, as many did, between the destruction of Jewish property and the so-called curse on Jews because of their alleged participation in the death of Christ. His seminarians recalled his remark at one of their ensuing discussions that, "if the synagogues are set afire today, tomorrow the churches will burn." In the Bible he used for prayer and meditation, these words from Psalm 74:8 are marked with the date, November 9, 1938: "they say to themselves: Let us plunder them! *They burn all the houses of God in the land*" (these last words are underlined in his Bible).[88] Within his own church, only a few pastors spoke out against this latest violence against the Jews and their places of worship.

This dishonorable silence was one reason Bonhoeffer at the time was seriously considering the possibility of again emigrating to the United

States. The restrictions against dissenting pastors of the Confessing Church were continuing with renewed intensity. Soon the substance of his own dissent would have to take on an important decision with regard to military service. Those who knew him as a pacifist and a firebrand of opposition to the Nazi government were aware that he would undoubtedly refuse to be drafted into the military when his age group was called to arms. Around this same period, a perceptible change began to emerge in Bonhoeffer's attitude toward the open, public defiance and denunciation of Nazi policies by church leaders. Under the influence of his brother-in-law Hans von Dohnanyi, former personal assistant to Franz Gürtner, minister of justice, Bonhoeffer began to see the wisdom of amassing enough power to topple the regime.

Though von Dohnanyi had been dismissed from his position in the Ministry of Justice in 1938, he had managed to become a member of the Supreme Court in Leipzig in that same year. While working in the Ministry of Justice, von Dohnanyi kept a secret record of those Nazi crimes and atrocities that were brought to his attention. At the outbreak of war, he had himself assigned to the *Abwehr*, an arrangement he had made earlier with Admiral Wilhelm Canaris and Colonel Hans Oster, who from 1938 on had been plotting against Nazi rule. For their planned coup to be successful, they needed to convince the military to take the necessary steps to dethrone Hitler and remove his entire entourage. For this, too, they needed a trusted group, much circumspection and secrecy, and delicate timing. Bonhoeffer's own outspoken criticism of the government was not a useful tool for conspiracy.[89]

SECOND AMERICAN VISIT

It is difficult in any event to untangle the arguments that brought Bonhoeffer to leave Germany again for a foreign refuge. He wished to avoid the draft for reasons of conscience and feared the consequences of such an action for his closest brethren, the dissenting pastors. Bonhoeffer, therefore, sent out feelers to Paul Lehmann to explore the possibility of a lecture tour in the United States. Lehmann enlisted the aid of Reinhold Niebuhr, from whom came the official invitation to lecture at Union Theological Seminary in the summer of 1939. This permitted Bonhoeffer to ask the ecumenical delegate of the Lutheran Union, Hans Böhm, to provide him with "official" commissions abroad.

There were many questions he hoped a respite in the United States might answer. For one, it would give him more time to consider the repercussions of his refusing the draft, a move frowned on by most Christians and their churches at that time. In a letter to Bishop Bell, Bonhoeffer states that this was his main concern.

It seems to me conscientiously impossible to join in a war under the present circumstances. . . . I should cause a tremendous damage to my brethren if I would make a stand on this point which would be regarded by the regime as typical of the hostility of our church towards the state. Perhaps the worst thing of all is the military oath which I should have to swear. So I am rather puzzled in this situation, and perhaps even more because, I feel, it is really only on Christian grounds that I find it difficult to do military service under the present conditions, and yet there are only very few friends who would approve of my attitude.[90]

There was also the futility of his attempts to stir up the consciences of his own church leaders in the question of the oath. This frustration had worn his sense of loyalty to the Confessing Church thin except for those brethren who maintained their integrity. Finally there was the question of his association with those who already were active in the nascent conspiracy. Would his stand against nazism bring suspicion on them and disrupt their plans?

In the midst of these incertitudes, Bonhoeffer obtained the needed leave of absence from the Council of Brethren and quickly conveyed that news to Reinhold Niebuhr, noting that the church leaders seemed happy to have him out of the way. In a separate letter to Dr. Henry Leiper, general secretary of the Federal Council of Churches and one of his American sponsors, he emphasized more the desirability of his being "an ecumenic link between our isolated church in Germany and our friends over here [the United States]. My personal question and difficulty with regard to military service etc. came in only as a second consideration. Of course, my colleagues were glad, that I would be able to postpone my decision for at least one year."[91] This letter was written in America when Bonhoeffer was close to a decision to return.

Bonhoeffer left for England on March 10, 1939, and there made arrangements to meet with Dr. Willem Visser 't Hooft, newly appointed general secretary of the provisional World Council of Churches headquartered in Geneva. Immediately after the war Visser 't Hooft wrote of their discussion on the German church situation: "He spoke in a way that was remarkably free from illusions, and sometimes almost clairvoyant, about the coming war, which would start soon . . . and which would cause the Confessing Church to be forced into even greater distress. . . . Had not the time now come to refuse to serve a government that was heading straight for war and breaking all the Commandments?"[92] Their meeting restored Bonhoeffer's confidence that the Confessing Church's interests would be represented in some way in the World Council in Geneva.

Bonhoeffer's return to Germany from London on April 18, 1939, coincided with Hitler's birthday parade, an event signaled as one of "exultant joy" by Dr. Friedrich Werner, the lawyer-head of the church committee and official engineer and enforcer of the pastors' oath of loyalty to Hitler. His rhapsodical report added: "In him God has given the German people a real miracle worker. . . . Let our thanks be the resolute and inflexible will not to disappoint . . . our *Führer* and the great historic hour."[93] For the Bonhoeffer family, it was an "hour" of sadness.

A month and a half later, Bonhoeffer left for London and then for America. He was leaving behind a church being even further squeezed by Werner's intensified pressure on the dissenting pastors. He cut off their stipends in parishes not acting in accordance with his own views on the collections. Werner had likewise pressed for church leaders to endorse the Godesberg Declaration containing the odious phrase that all members were enjoined "to join fully and devotedly in the *Führer's* national political constructive work. . . . In the national sphere of life there must be serious and responsible racial policy of maintaining the purity of our nation."[94] The thought of his brethren facing persecutions from unfeeling civil servants like Werner profoundly disturbed the peace of Bonhoeffer's journey. In his diary we read of the inner torment. He wanted to return to Germany eventually, but was not sure when. The plan for him to teach a summer course at Union Theological Seminary appealed to him. The more important proposal from his American friends who wanted to rescue him from possible imprisonment in Germany was that of his being a pastor caring for refugees. This was on behalf of the American Committee for Christian German Refugees. That post, if accepted, would mean abandoning the possibility of any immediate return to Germany. His inward conflict over the prospect is noted in the entry in his diary for June 13, 1939: "My starting point for everything is that I intend to go back in one year at the latest. Surprise. But I am quite clear that I must go back." While staying at Dr. Henry Sloane Coffin's house in Lakeville, Connecticut, he wrote: "I do not know why I am here, whether it is wise, whether the result will be worthwhile."[95] The decision to return to Germany came after an aimless walk about Times Square. On June 21, 1939, he declined Leiper's invitation, mentioning in his diary that the scriptural reading for the day shows how God "certainly sees how personal a matter today's decision is, and how full of anxiety, however brave it may appear. The reasons that one gives to others and to oneself for an action are certainly inadequate. We can, in fact, justify anything; but in the last resort we are acting from a plane that is hidden from us; and so we can only ask God to judge and forgive us."[96] Even these entries give us only a vague idea of the anxiety provoked by his decision. His farewell letter to Reinhold Niebuhr and his American brethren states the outcome of his resolution as succinctly and as memorably as one could hope for.

> I have made a mistake in coming to America. I must live through this difficult period of our national history with the Christian people of Germany. I will have no right to participate in the reconstruction of Christian life in Germany after the war if I do not share the trials of this time with my people. . . . Christians in Germany will face the terrible alternative of either willing the defeat of their nation in order that Christian civilization may survive, or willing the victory of their nation and thereby destroying our civilization. I know

which of these alternatives I must choose; but I cannot make that choice in security.[97]

His boat departed on July 8, 1939. Seeing him off was his closest American friend, Paul Lehmann, who had come to New York "with great heaviness of spirit," too late to persuade him to change his mind.

The outbreak of World War II was less than two months away when Bonhoeffer returned to Berlin, determined in some way to bring about the defeat of his nation so that "Christian civilization" might survive. Soon he would be commenting in a circular letter to his Finkenwaldians on the first of the seminarians to be killed in action.

A DOUBLE AGENT

In the meantime Bonhoeffer had learned of the work of a small resistance group through one of the leading men in the movement, his own brother-in-law, Hans von Dohnanyi. He had also been present at Dohnanyi's house for a discussion by a group of *Abwehr* members led by Colonel Hans Oster. They were attempting to turn into a memorandum a report from Josef Müller, who, as a secret agent, had contacted British authorities through the Vatican seeking terms of an armistice should a coup d'état against Hitler succeed. Müller's negotiations were called the "X-report."[98] Dohnanyi was able to incorporate some of his own documentation on the atrocities of the S.S., the gradual erosion of the army's independence, and moral counterarguments to the fears of breaking military oaths and treason itself in a possible military putsch. Unfortunately, this memorandum came too late. The army leaders, including Major General Franz Halder and Field Marshall von Brauchitsch, were already in the process of planning the invasion of Scandinavia and the West. The *Blitzkrieg* was on. Halder himself risked arrest in delivering the memorandum.[99] Those sympathetic to the aims of the plotters and able to make the necessary military moves against Nazi leaders were caught up in the uncanny successes of Hitler himself. Again, Oster and Dohnanyi were checked by the speed of Hitler's moves and triumphs. They could only hope that their contacts would realize that Germany had that other side of decency ready for future course of action on behalf of peace and justice.[100] Bonhoeffer would soon be a vital part of the moral force they were attempting to muster to further convince the generals of the necessity of overthrowing Hitler.

Not long after this meeting, Bonhoeffer learned through Dohnanyi of Oster's attempt to block Hitler's war successes by alerting Holland to the coming German attack. This was an action he admired, a "true patriotism" in the face of moral paralysis in those who might have more effectively stymied the Nazi lust for blood and battle. Oster was risking his name and a traitor's fate. For Bonhoeffer, this sort of "treason" was, in the topsy-turvy morality of the Nazi era, a true love of one's country.[101] But here, too, Hitler's quick military successes confounded the conspiracy leaders, who expected Germany to suffer a World War I–like bleeding in the trenches, thus causing the citizenry to waver in their support of the government's euphoric promises. Now the conspirators could not count on the people's disaffection. New tactics and more deception were needed.

By July 1940 Bonhoeffer was again under suspicion in Berlin. He had violated an ordinance prohibiting his giving courses to theological students. At the time, he had been acting, along with Eberhard Bethge, as a roving visitor of Confessing Church parishes in East Prussia. Two months later, on September 9, 1940, he was forbidden to speak in public and ordered to report regularly to the police. Bonhoeffer's protest of these strictures, which even included a cynical "Heil Hitler" at the end, went unanswered.[102] The freedom to continue his work came, not unexpectedly, through Oster and Dohnanyi, who brought Bonhoeffer into their scheming and arranged to have him declared indispensable to their *Abwehr* work, thus preventing not only his being drafted into the army but also his possible arrest by an increasingly more suspicious Gestapo. He was assigned to their Munich office to distance him as much as possible from Gestapo surveillance in the Berlin epicenter of nazism.

Now his journeys as "church visitor" were to be considered a "front" for information gathering. The requirement that he report regularly to the police was suspended. Bonhoeffer was now officially a "confidential," though unpaid, agent for the *Abwehr*. Josef Müller, introduced him to the abbot of Ettal Monastery, where he would find refuge for his theological work—sections of *Ethics* were written there—and place of residence when he was not directly involved in missions for the *Abwehr*. This arrangement also allowed him to continue contacts with his Finkenwalde students and to become a vital part in the moral inspiration needed by the conspirators to keep up their own courage and to convince the generals. To his students at the front he wrote: "The great difference between your existence, my dear brothers in the field, and ours, who still have freedom for our ministry, is that we can put ourselves in a place which in a certain sense we have chosen for ourselves, freely, through our profession, whereas you now share the life of millions of people who have never been free in this sense because of the conditions governing their life and work."[103] The "difference" could have been more accurately described in the ways they were doing their "patriotic" duty.

For Bonhoeffer, this already had come to mean his continuing the deception required to aid the work of the conspiracy. The conspirators' motivation came from many sources, not the least of which was the moral outrage of learning about new atrocities at the front and the beginnings of the deportation of the Jews. At the end of 1942, Bonhoeffer gave the following message as part of a "Christmas gift" to the main conspirators: "We have for once learned to see the great events of world history from below, from the perspective of the outcast, the suspects, the maltreated, the powerless, the oppressed, the reviled—in short, from the perspective of those who suffer."[104]

This sense of solidarity with those being oppressed under Nazi rule led Bonhoeffer and the *Abwehr* leaders to become involved in "Operation 7." This was a daring initiative to smuggle a small group of Jews out of Germany on the pretext that they were *Abwehr* agents. The "U 7" designation was in reference to the first seven people whom Admiral Canaris and Oster wanted to save from the deportations. It took an extraordinary amount of time and subterfuge, but the ploy was successful in its initial phase. Eventually, however, it would lead to the intense suspicions that later became grounds for the arrest of all the leading figures, including Bonhoeffer.

Among his trips for the conspirators, few were as significant as Bonhoeffer's journey to Sigtuna, Sweden, in May 1942. Bonhoeffer himself had been on assignment to Switzerland when he learned that Bishop Bell was to be in Sweden for three weeks beginning May 11, ostensibly to renew ecumenical contacts. Bonhoeffer, therefore, put to his *Abwehr* friends in Berlin the proposal for a quick meeting to seek further support from Great Britain through the bishop's intervention, should the plot succeed. Specifically, they wanted time to form a new government after the assassination of Hitler. Bonhoeffer would convey through Bell the information that the intentions of the conspirators were peaceful and friendly toward Britain. That view would have to be maintained despite some appearances to the contrary aimed at bringing the German nation in line with the aims of a peaceful settlement. The conspirators feared a military move by Britain immediately after the execution of their plans and before an effective takeover of power. Hans Schönfeld, secretary of research for the Ecumenical Council, was also in Sweden to represent a resistance group in the Foreign Ministry. Neither knew of the other's coming or mission. For Bonhoeffer, it was the occasion for a warm reunion with his old friend, Bishop Bell. He was able to confirm what Schönfeld had already reported and to add specific information on the names of those principals who could be counted on within Nazi Germany to engineer a coup d'état. It was an impressive show not only of the serious intent of the conspirators but also of the quality of people who represented that other, more decent, Germany.

Bell's report of their conversation shows, however, a fundamental difference in the approach of Schönfeld and Bonhoeffer. Schönfeld, it seems, tried to convey the impression that he represented a group speaking from a position of strength. He reminded Bell that the German army still occupied 1,000 miles of Russian territory. He wanted more comfortable terms of surrender. According to Bell, at this juncture, "Bonhoeffer broke in. His Christian conscience, he said, was not quite at ease with Schönfeld's ideas. There must be punishment by God. We should not be worthy of such a solution. Our action must be such that the world will understand it as an act of repentance. Christians do not wish to escape repentance, or chaos, if it is God's will to bring it upon us. We must take this judgment as Christians."[105] Bell brought the information back to England and presented it to the foreign secretary, asking on behalf of the conspirators for terms that could encourage the planned coup d'état. The British government had, unfortunately, already hardened its attitude into what became an allied battle cry, "Unconditional Surrender." That this evoked images of harsh reprisals and a Nazi-like reign of terror among the German population and stiffened their resolve to fight to the end is now history. On Bell's part, he never ceased his agitation for a more statesmanlike approach toward expediting the war's end and planning the reconstruction of Europe. It did not help his case that the resistance movement was so well hidden within the top echelons of the military, including the *Abwehr* to which Bonhoeffer belonged.

ARREST AND IMPRISONMENT

By now, a suspicious Gestapo had Bonhoeffer and Dohnanyi under surveillance; their telephones were tapped. The assassination attempts of March 13 and 21, 1943 failed because of strange quirks, a fuse not igniting the bomb on the first try, and a miscalculation of time preventing an agent's getting close enough to detonate both Hitler and himself. Two weeks later, Bonhoeffer, Dohnanyi, and Josef Müller were arrested. The Gestapo had been in the process of investigating the *Abwehr* for two years and, having arrested Bonhoeffer's two immediate superiors in Munich, they began to shift focus to the Berlin *Abwehr* office. There thus began a period in which the leading figures in that resistance movement covered many of their illegal tracks, leaving faked documents where the Gestapo were surely to find them and composing letters justifying Bonhoeffer's employment despite his known opposition to nazism as a Confessing Church pastor. They had to convince the Security Office of the legitimacy for the Nazi cause of Operation 7. In short, everything done to counteract the Hitler government had to appear geared to promote the war effort. All this served only to stall the inevitable once the arrests began. At Dohnanyi's detention, Oster himself was placed under house arrest. Admiral Canaris would be caught in the Gestapo's web after the failure of the plot of July 20, 1944.

For Bonhoeffer, the harsh shock of the first days of his imprisonment and the thought that he might, under torture, break down and drag others to their death with him led him to consider suicide. Among the stray notes he had jotted down on a leaf from a writing pad his father had to use in the guardroom to list the exact contents of a food parcel, we are able to read of his intense preoccupation with the time on his hands and the incertitude it had brought. "Waiting—but, e.g., quite composed for death. . . . Flight before the experience of time in dreams, terror on awakening here in the dream past = future, timeless. . . . Emptiness of time despite all that fills it. . . . Suicide, not because of consciousness of guilt but because basically I am already dead."[106] Later he would write about those "grim experiences" that often pursued him "into the night."[107]

Those depressing first days in Tegel prison were alleviated by the support of his family and by Frau von Wedemeyer's finally having made public his engagement to her young daughter, Maria. Dietrich had fallen in love with Maria between his journies to Sweden and Italy during the winter prior to his imprisonment. He had been charmed by her personal beauty, verve, and unique sense of independence. She was, likewise, the inspiration for his hope in the future. Her response to his love was full of admiring joy. For her part, she was attracted by his self-control in the midst of the progressive chaos of the war and the strength of his convictions in the resistance movement. She also enjoyed his company, not only because of his ability as a raconteur but especially for that "*hilaritas*" that he himself praised in Karl Barth, Martin Luther, and others. They could laugh for long moments together, she recalled. He had that serenity and confidence in his own work, boldness, even "defiance of the world and of popular opinion," and a "steadfast certainty" in his own work.[108] At first, her family objected to their engagement because of her age—she was only seventeen and he a mature thirty-seven—and the danger of his political involvement. However, they became engaged on January 17, 1943, having promised not to make any immediate public announcement.

All that changed with Bonhoeffer's arrest. Maria's family made the engagement public in a show of support that was an unexpected comfort to him. Through Maria, he would come to appreciate "what the warmth that radiates from the love of a wife and family can mean in the cold air of imprisonment." Later he would write to Maria that their love "can only be a sign of God's grace and kindness, which calls us to faith. We would be blind if we did not see it. . . . This is where faith belongs. May God give it to us daily. And I do not mean faith which flees the world, but the one that endures the world and which loves and remains true to the world in spite of all the suffering which it contains for us. Our marriage shall be a yes to God's earth; it shall strengthen our courage to act and accomplish something on the earth."[109]

This letter was composed on August 12, 1943. Eight months later, Bonhoeffer would be raising questions in his prison correspondence that shattered complacencies in the postwar theological world. These letters, smuggled out by a friendly guard, reveal much of the poignancy of his imprisonment and of the bitterness against the churches for their not having checked in any significant way the evils perpetrated by nazism. Surprisingly, however, there is none of the self-pity one might expect in these circumstances. The letters seem, rather, a tonic of mental release from the strain of worrying about his own fate and the future of Christianity in Germany. The greater number of these, addressed to Eberhard Bethge, are among the most inspiring of the Bonhoeffer theological legacy.

For Bonhoeffer, the letters became a way of renewing the spiritual strength and growth in personal conviction he seemed to derive from his closest friend and confidant. Readers recognize in this correspondence the creative mind anxious to probe the meaning of Christianity, which was then open to the most radical critique because of the moral catastrophe of the war and the systematic massacres of the death camps. "What is bothering me incessantly," Bonhoeffer wrote to Bethge,

> is the question what Christianity really is, or indeed who Christ really is, for us today. The time when people could be told everything by means of words, whether theological or pious, is over, and so is the time of inwardness and conscience—and that means the time of religion in general. We are moving towards a completely religionless time; people as they are now simply cannot be religious any more. Even those who honestly describe themselves as "religious" do not in the least act up to it, and so they presumably mean something quite different by "religious."[110]

The letters that followed elaborated on the meaning of that startling passage from the letter of April 30, 1944.

THEOLOGY FROM A PRISON CELL

For Bonhoeffer, in his prison cell, the right questions had to be asked if Christianity were ever to have a future in a world apparently able to exist rather well without the hypothesis of God. The world appeared to have come of age. It had reached adulthood and no longer needed the tutelage of religion for problems formerly unsolved except by recourse to religion. The world was entering a time of nonreligious Christianity that would call for the nonreligious interpretation of biblical concepts. Even before this correspondence, Bonhoeffer had come to see in religion a form of culture, turned in on itself, conscious of clerical privilege, and bent on its own survival in the destruction of war.

In prison Bonhoeffer accused religion of offering only an escapist flight from the real world. It was, therefore, only like a garment of faith. Religion, he continued, had pushed God to the boundaries of life, available only on call to answer prayers of deliverance or of favor. "The 'religious act,'" he argued, "is always something partial; 'faith' is something whole, involving the whole of one's life. Jesus calls a person not to a new religion, but to life."[111] In the process, religion had produced a distorted view of God, enshrining him in world of metaphysical abstraction to be spoken of only at the edges of life: sin, guilt, and death. And the clergy used this view to blackmail their people with the threat of hellish consequences for those sins the clergy were adept at sniffing out, all the while ignoring the real evil beyond their cathedrals and churches. "I should like to speak of God," he wrote, "not on the boundaries but at the center, not in weaknesses but in strength; and therefore not in death and guilt but in man's life and goodness. . . . God is beyond in the midst of our life. The church stands, not at the boundaries where human powers give out, but in the middle of the village."[112]

Because his church was not standing in the middle of that "village" where people were being destroyed in the name of an evil ideology and under cover of German Christianity, Bonhoeffer's most bitter words were reserved for the churches. The churches, he said, were interested in fighting only a rearguard action for survival and preservation of their privileges and perquisites. Instead of reflecting the compassion and courage of Christ to the world, they had cowered behind their Bibles and buildings, offering only self-serving piffle to the masses and failing to speak the prophetic word or to do the responsible deed for fear of losing what they most had to give, their lives in imitation of Jesus Christ. In *Ethics*, Bonhoeffer declared that the church was "guilty of the deaths of the weakest and most defenseless brothers of Jesus Christ."[113] For him, this meant the killing of his Jewish "brothers and sisters" as well as the countless innocents perishing in Nazi death camps. In prison this confession of guilt took the form of a bitter complaint to the family against his own Confessing Church, still proud of its stand at Barmen. The Confessing Church, he said, was good at standing up only "for the church's 'cause'"; it had "little personal faith in Christ."[114] He urged the churches, therefore, to come out of their "stagnation" and "move out again into the open air of intellectual discussion with the world, and risk saying controversial things, if we are to get down to the serious problems of life."[115] He began a book that would call for a complete renewal of the Christian church with the intent of "planning to lay the conceptual explosives within the walls of the ecclesiastical establishment, and 'in this way to perform a service for the future of the church.'"[116] The outline for this book, which is all that has survived, is very clear in its insistence that "the church is the church only when it exists for others."

The model here, as in Bonhoeffer's earlier ecclesiology, is Jesus Christ. If Jesus is "the man for others," then the church is only the church when it exists to be of service to people and not of service to clerical self-esteem. "To make a start," he wrote, "it should give away all its property to those in need. The clergy must live solely on the free-will offerings of their congregations, or possibly engage in some secular calling. The church must share in the secular problems of ordinary human life, not dominating, but helping and serving. It must tell people of every calling what it means to live in Christ, to exist for others."[117]

The biblical passage that seemed best to encapsulate the Christic attitude he wished for the churches was Mark 15:34: "My God, my God, why hast thou forsaken me?" This was for him the climax of Christ's life of faith that had such a strong this-worldly dimension. Christ's cry of near despair from the cross meant to Bonhoeffer that Christ chose not to avoid the human consequences of sacrificing himself for the sake of others. He did not, like a *deus ex machina*, remain supremely aloof from the human condition, able to intervene with opportune miracles, then to depart virtually unscathed by the inexorability of the death that is a prophet's fate. Nor did he, like the church bearing his name, play it safe during a time calling for stark confrontation with the powers of evil. Bonhoeffer insisted that the church, like the Christian, had to "drink the earthly cup to the dregs"[118] and "share in the sufferings of God at the hands of a godless world," if it was to be the true church of Jesus Christ.[119]

FINAL DAYS

Bonhoeffer's final sufferings at the hands of that godless world came soon enough after the failure of the attempted assassination of Hitler on July 20, 1944. Hitler had escaped death by a seemingly diabolical quirk. By the end of the day, Colonel Klaus von Stauffenberg, who had planted the bomb, and several in his resistance circle, had been executed. More executions and arrests were to follow. In September the Gestapo discovered Canaris's secret file in Zossen. It contained indisputable evidence against Dohnanyi, Bonhoeffer, and those members of the *Abwehr* involved in the conspiracy. Soon Bonhoeffer's brother Klaus and brother-in-law Rüdiger Schleicher were arrested. Eberhard Bethge was recalled from active duty and imprisoned with them. The imprisonment of his brother would become a factor in Dietrich's eventual death, though he had no way of knowing this at the time. With the arrests of Hans John, a legal assistant to Rüdiger Schleicher, in possession of damning evidence against the conspiracy, and of Hans von Dohnanyi, as well as the discovery of the incriminating papers at Zossen, Bonhoeffer had seriously considered escaping. Indeed, a plan for his escape had already been organized. His trusted guard and friend Corporal Knobloch had agreed to "disappear" with Dietrich while he was on duty. The family succeeded in obtaining and handing over to Knobloch a mechanic's uniform, money, and food coupons, with more provisions waiting at a "safe place." All was set for their flight from prison in the early days of October. They needed only false passports and contacts with the chaplain at the Swedish embassy. But Klaus's arrest in October moved Dietrich to inform the family that he wanted to abandon the plan in order not to make matters more difficult for his brother and further endanger the family. Rüdiger Schleicher was arrested on October 4, 1944. The next day Dietrich wrote his poem on Jonah containing the lines:

> Thus they besought. And Jonah said, "Behold, I
> sinned before the Lord of hosts. My life is
> forfeit.
>
> Cast me away! My guilt must bear the wrath of God;
> the righteous shall not perish with the sinner!"[121]

Four days later, on October 8, Bonhoeffer was transferred to the cellar of the Gestapo prison in the Prinz Albrecht Strasse in Berlin. Interrogations took a more serious bend as the Gestapo began furiously to search out the long roots of resistance within Nazi Germany. The prisoners' only hope seemed to lie in further delays, as they played for time, and in the possibility of an imminent Allied victory.

Three days after his thirty-ninth birthday, on February 7, 1945, Bonhoeffer and several other "important" prisoners were taken by van to the concentration camp at Buchenwald. There Bonhoeffer was introduced to the English captain Payne Best, an officer of the British Secret Service, kidnapped by the Gestapo in 1939. Best is the source for much of what we know about Bonhoeffer's last days. In later describing his fellow prisoners, Best wrote of Bonhoeffer that he "always seemed to diffuse an atmosphere of happiness, of joy in every smallest event in life, and a deep gratitude for the mere fact that he was alive. . . . He was one of the very few men I have ever met to whom his God was real and ever close to him." In a letter to the family he added that "Bonhoeffer was different (from the other prisoners); just quite calm and normal, seemingly perfectly at his ease . . . his soul really shone in the dark desperation of our prison."[122] Best and Bonhoeffer were among those "special prisoners" herded into a van and moved south from Buchenwald, with an ostensible destination of the death camp at Flossenbürg. The van broke down outside Regensburg and the prisoners were transferred to a bus that would take them to the Bavarian village of Schönberg. There they were locked up in the first floor of the school building. A British air force officer, Hugh Falconer, would later mention to Bonhoeffer's twin sister, Sabine, that Bonhoeffer "did a great deal to keep some of the weaker brethren from depression and anxiety."[123]

Behind the scenes, however, the fate of Dohnanyi, Bonhoeffer, and the other conspirators was now being decided in Berlin. Ernst Kaltenbrunner of the Reich Security Headquarters and Hitler himself issued their death sentences, execution pending the formality of a court marital. Von Dohnanyi was to be executed at Sachsenhausen; court proceedings were set up for the other condemned men at Flossenbürg. Because Bonhoeffer, by some mistake, was not there, Gestapo officers were sent to Schönberg. It was Low Sunday, April 8, 1945. Bonhoeffer had just conducted a prayer service on the Bible verses of the day. First he meditated on Isaiah's words, "With his wounds we are healed." Then he commented and prayed on the opening portion of 1 Peter: "Blessed be the God and Father of our Lord Jesus Christ! By his great mercy we have been born anew to a living hope through the resurrection of Jesus Christ from the dead." Best recorded in his book that Bonhoeffer "reached the hearts of all, finding just the right words to express the spirit of our imprisonment, and the thoughts and resolutions which it had brought."[124] The quiet that immediately followed the service was quickly interrupted as the door was flung open and "two evil-looking men in civilian clothes" entered. They called out Bonhoeffer's name with instructions to follow them; this had come to mean only one thing for the prisoners, the death penalty. Bonhoeffer was able to bid a farewell to each one in the room. To Payne Best he spoke his final recorded words, a message to his old friend Bishop Bell of Chichester, "This is the end—for me, the beginning of life. Tell him (Bell) . . . with him I believe in the principle of our universal Christian brotherhood which rises above all national interests, and that our victory is certain—tell him, too, that I have never forgotten his words at our last meeting."[125] Early the next morning, Bonhoeffer, Canaris, Oster, and coconspirators Sack, Strunck, and Gehre were hanged on the Flossenbürg gallows.

The only account of Bonhoeffer's death was given by the prison doctor, who wrote that, after the sentences had been read out to the condemned men, he saw "Pastor Bonhoeffer, before taking off his prison garb, kneeling on the floor praying fervently to his God. I was most deeply moved by the way this lovable man prayed, so devout and so certain that God heard his prayer." He added: "At the place of execution he again said a short prayer and then climbed the steps to the gallows, brave and composed. . . . In the almost 50 years that I worked as a doctor, I have hardly ever seen a man die so entirely submissive to the will of God."[126] The commemorative plaque in the church at Flossenbürg reads simply: "To Dietrich Bonhoeffer, 1906–1945, A Witness to Jesus Christ among his brethren." Indeed, his death seemed to be a final act of solidarity not only with the cross of Jesus Christ but also with the countless victims of Nazi evil, as he himself became one of the last to die for having dared to resist that evil.

Part 1

CHRIST AS COMMUNITY

Dietrich Bonhoeffer as a student. 1923 photograph.
From Eberhard Bethge, Renate Bethge, Christian Gremmels, *Dietrich Bonhoeffer: A Life in Pictures* (Philadelphia: Fortress Press, 1986), p. 49

Introduction: A Lecture in Barcelona, Dissertations in Berlin

Though we have limited part 1 to three of Bonhoeffer's most important early writings, an address he gave as assistant pastor in Barcelona, his doctoral dissertation, and his *Habilitationsschrift* at the University of Berlin, these works are not the sum total of his literary activity during that period. Four volumes of the *Dietrich Bonhoeffer Werke*, the new edition of the collected writings of Bonhoeffer now underway in both Germany and the United States, are devoted to his writings from 1918 to 1931.[1] What we have excerpted here, although restricted, is highly significant in tracing Bonhoeffer's earliest attempts to grapple with the centrality of Jesus Christ for one's faith commitment within the Christian community.

Bonhoeffer began his pastoral ministry in Barcelona. It was a completely new experience for him, thrusting him into an entirely different environment and among a people with whom he had little in common. These were the German businessmen and their families living abroad, petit bourgeois types with little interest in Bonhoeffer's academic world or even his refined cultural taste for theatre and music. Gone were the informed conversations at meals and the gratifying discussions in seminars. In their place, Bonhoeffer did his "pastoral" duties, attending committee meetings and helping to organize social activities for the German enclave in addition to the usual preparation of services and parish visitations. It was, as he stated in a letter to Helmut Rössler, "a very singular experience when one sees work and life really converging," something he had not found in his student days.

But the work had its frustrating side. The pastor, the Reverend Fritz Olbricht, made few demands on his congregation, allowing them a kind of "cheap grace," which Bonhoeffer tried gently to challenge. Bethge reports that Pastor Olbricht was somewhat disquieted by Bonhoeffer's energetic approach to his ministry.[2]

Beyond the social activities that were part of the German community's identity and to which he contributed with his skills at tennis, chess, and music, Bonhoeffer's pastoral skills were most evident in his visits to parishioners both old and young. In these encounters he saw the underside of the picture of prosperity that was the surface impression of the community. He encountered his first suicide, and several cases of extreme poverty and unemployment. He also became involved in the social work of the German Welfare Society. Some of his reaction to the encounter with poverty and his early involvement with the poor comes across in the address excerpted here. The lectures Bonhoeffer gave in Barcelona (his lecture on Christian ethics is excerpted in part 6) were, in a way, the offspring of his failed attempt to arrange regular religion lessons at the secondary school level. It was evident that Pastor Olbricht was uninterested in becoming involved in a project that might fall to him on Bonhoeffer's return to Germany. Bonhoeffer's popularity among the young children attests to the success of his work among the German youth of Barcelona. In fact, he was formally invited by the presbytery to remain in the Barcelona ministry, but he declined. The lure of an academic appointment was too overpowering.

In a way, Bonhoeffer's pastoral ministry in Barcelona was a hiatus between the two phases of his academic career in Berlin. Though we have included selections only from his two dissertations, Bonhoeffer's student writings are, in fact, voluminous. This is not to say that they are of high quality or even of interest to any but researchers into Bonhoeffer's first theological steps. These writings include term papers, student reports, seminar research, student notes, children's worship services, catechism outlines, and early sermons, all of uneven character, many only roughed out with little care to producing a polished text. They seem of value more as documentation of Bonhoeffer's academic development in tandem with the earliest unfolding of his career as theologian and pastor.

His two dissertations, on the other hand, are remarkable not only in that they are Bonhoeffer's first published books, but also in that they provide interpretative directions to the theological foundations of his later religious thought. No less a theologian than Karl Barth praised Bonhoeffer's doctoral dissertation, *The Communion of Saints*, with its "broad and deep vision" as a "theological miracle."[3] Unfortunately, the book's prose is, to cite one commentator, "dense and involuted," with a clumsiness that "results from the intricate weaving of sundry threads to support one central thought."[4] The book, for all its neo-Hegelianism, is nonetheless part of the vital groundwork for Bonhoeffer's understanding of church as the locus for a knowledge of God in the context of human sociality and historical concreteness. Bonhoeffer's starting point during that phase of his theological career was an idealized concept of church structured by Christ's presence and an advancing insight into the interwoven realities of person, community, and God. Neither the neoorthodox theologian nor the empirical sociologist was pleased with Bonhoeffer's achievement. Yet Bonhoeffer's dissertation laid the foundation for his theology of sociality, which in turn affected much of his later reflections on the Christian community and ethical responsibility. It is valuable not only as a study of the sociality of Christian faith but as an illustration of Bonhoeffer's earliest interests in doing theology and his budding skills as a theologian.

Like *The Communion of Saints, Act and Being* was written in a ponderous, dissertation style, pleasing to his mentors but more suitable to academic debate than to the interests of the gereral public. Neither book was a best-seller. Bonhoeffer was accused of oversimplification, one-sidedness in his interpretations, and distortion in use of his sources by some of the reviewers. For all that, *Act and Being* is one of Bonhoeffer's most important works, not because it yielded the needed credential for an academic appointment to the University of Berlin, nor even because it enabled Bonhoeffer to probe more deeply into the writings of those philosophers and theologians who represented the polarities of act and being in a theology of revelation. Rather, this second dissertation reveals the inner tensions haunting Bonhoeffer's own faith equilibrium and provides, therefore, an autobiographical clue to the way his theology paralleled his life's journey and his desire not merely to become a skilled teacher and pastor but a committed Christian as well. The key to this reading of *Act and Being* is, as the theologian Clifford Green has shown so conclusively, the theological anthropology that Bonhoeffer develops in the book.[5]

In *Act and Being,* we see expressed most clearly Bonhoeffer's personal struggle with the tensions of pursuing one's personal ambitions, heart all "turned in on oneself," or giving oneself wholeheartedly to Christ through service in and through the community. His accusation that "thought is as little able as good works to deliver the *cor curvum in se* ('heart turned in on itself') from itself," reflects one of his main concerns in the book, the soteriological. How does God in Christ deliver the human person from that isolated individualism that alienates one from God, from others, and even from oneself? Bonhoeffer decries "the idea that one need only arrive at himself to be in God." Such a person, he chillingly observes, "is doomed to hideous disillusion in experiencing the utter introversion, the treadmill confinement to the self, of the very loneliest solitude, with its tormenting desolation and sterility." If such an assertion seems overly bleak, we must remember that in the context of his life, it is also a revealing statement of Bonhoeffer's deepest anxiety about his own faith. At the time he wrote *Act and Being,* Bonhoeffer was still working through a power struggle between the allure of his more self-serving academic ambitiousness and the attraction of the powerful personality of Jesus Christ. He wondered if one could ever resist for long the temptation to reduce God's transcendence to one's own inner subjectivity. He acknowledged, accordingly, the need for a transcendental approach, if only to counteract being dominated by one's hubris as a thinking-knowing subject. How Bonhoeffer countered that "hubris" has been discussed in the editors' introduction and can be further explored in subsequent selections here that reflect his growing involvement in the church struggle, in the "Jewish Question," and in the conspiracy against Hitler. *Act and Being* is a difficult book to excerpt because of its tightly knit structure. The selections that follow are placed in the context not only of the book's developed theme but also of the underlying anthropological-autobiographical concerns.

Jesus Christ and the
Essence of Christianity

(Jesus Christ und vom Wesen des Christentums)

December 11, 1928

This address, presented in Barcelona on December 11, 1928, shows how Bonhoeffer's pastoral concerns blended in with the strong academic training he had received at the University of Berlin. We see, too, some of the theological issues that he confronted throughout his life. Here he states his understanding of the "essence of Christianity" at a very early phase of his career. Christianity for him was not a religion, but a person, Christ, who made difficult demands on people. We find in this essay some of the themes that were later to electrify readers of the prison letters: Bonhoeffer's criticism of reducing Christ and God to a small compartment of our lives; his criticism of religion and churchiness; and his placing the cross of Jesus Christ at the very center of the essence of Christianity.

We note, too, Bonhoeffer's sense of God's having sided with the poor and oppressed. The light of God's love, he insists, shines down on the weak, struggling masses. Bonhoeffer encountered his first experience of poverty in Barcelona, so his declaration of solidarity with the lowly and oppressed is not included by accident in this address. The faces of "Christ existing as community" are those of the grubby poor, and the cross is a more immediate symbol of the essence of that community.

Here as in the prison letters Bonhoeffer invokes the cross of Christ in order to home in on the meaning of Christianity and to come to grips with the experience of deprivation, death, and the seeming desertion of the Christian by Jesus' Father God. The paradoxical cry of Mark 15:34 does not mean that God has abandoned his people but that, in the death of his son, God has given proof of his undying love, a love stronger than death. In the cross, Bonhoeffer points out, one learns that God's greatest gift is not religion but the love and mercy he has shown in Christ.

Whether in our time Christ can still occupy a place where we make decisions on the deepest matters known to us, over our own life and over the life of our people, that is the question which we will consider today. Whether or not the Spirit of Christ has anything final, definitive, and decisive to say to us, that is what we want to speak about. We all know that Christ has, in effect, been eliminated from our lives. Of course, we build him a temple, but we live in our own houses. Christ has become a matter of the church or, rather, of the churchiness of a group, not a matter of life. Religion plays for the psyche of the nineteenth and twentieth centuries the role of the so-called Sunday room into which one gladly withdraws for a couple of hours but only to get back to one's place of work immediately afterwards. However, one thing is clear: we understand Christ only if we commit ourselves to him in a stark "Either-Or." He did not go to the cross to ornament and embellish our life. If we wish to have him, then he demands the right to say something decisive about our entire life. We do not understand him if we arrange for him only a small compartment in our spiritual life. Rather, we understand our spiritual life only if we then orientate it to him alone or give him a flat "No." However, there are persons who would not even bother to take Christ seriously in the demand he makes on us by his question: will you follow me wholeheartedly or not at all? Such persons had better not mix their own cause with the Christian one. That separation would only help the Christian cause since they no longer have anything in common with Christ. The religion of Christ is not a tidbit after one's bread; on the contrary, it is bread or it is nothing. People should at least understand and concede this if they call themselves Christian.

Many attempts have been made to eliminate Christ from the present life of the spirit. Indeed, what is so seductive about these attempts is that it appears as if Christ would be promoted, for the first time, to his proper place, that is, a place worthy of him. One admires Christ according to aesthetic categories as an aesthetic genius, calls him the greatest ethicist; one admires his going to his death as a heroic sacrifice for his ideas. Only one thing one doesn't do: one doesn't take him seriously. That is, one doesn't bring the center of his or her own life into contact with the claim of Christ to speak the revelation of God and to be that revelation. One maintains a distance between himself or herself and the word of Christ, and allows no serious encounter to take place. I can doubtless live with or without Jesus as a religious genius, as an ethicist, as a gentleman—just as, after all, I can also live without Plato and Kant—all that has only relative meaning. Should, however, there be something in Christ that claims my life entirely with the full seriousness that here God himself speaks and if the word of God once became present only in Christ, then Christ has not only relative but absolute, urgent significance for me. To be sure, I still have the free choice of "yes" or "no," but in the end I am indifferent to such a choice, Understanding Christ means taking Christ seriously. Understanding this claim means taking seriously his absolute claim on our commitment.

And it is now of importance for us to clarify the seriousness of this matter and to extricate Christ from the secularization process in which he has been incorporated since the Enlightenment, and finally, to show that even in our days the question to which Christ gives an answer is so completely crucial that here is where the Spirit of Christ justly makes his claim. Thus is raised our first and main question about the essence of the Christian message, the essence of Christianity. . . .

There is pronounced, therefore, a fundamental criticism against the most grandiose of all human attempts to approach the divine—against the church. Christianity contains a seed of animosity to the church since we wish to base a demand on God on our devotion to Christ and church. Thereby, we again fully misunderstand the Christian idea and fail in our efforts. Yet Christianity needs the church. That is the paradox. . . . And here lies the enormous responsibility the church has to bear.

Ethics and religion lie in the direction of humans toward God. Christ, however, speaks alone, entirely alone, of the direction of God to people; not of the human way to God but of the way of God to humans. Therefore, it is likewise completely perverse to seek a new morality in Christianity. Factually speaking, Christ has given scarcely any ethical prescriptions that were not to be found already with the contemporary Jewish rabbis or in pagan literature. The essence of Christianity lies in the message of the sovereign God to whom alone belongs glory over all the world. It is the message of the eternally other, the one who is far above the world, yet who from the depth of his being has mercy on the person who gives glory to him alone. He is the one who goes on the way to people in order to seek vessels of his glory where the human person is no longer anything, where he becomes silent, where he gives way to God alone.

Here the light of eternity shines down on those who are ever neglected, insignificant, weak, ignoble, unknown, inferior, oppressed, despised; here it radiates over the houses of prostitutes and tax collectors. . . . Here the light of eternity has been cast on the toiling, struggling, and sinning masses. The word of grace spreads across the stale sultriness of the big cities, but it halts before the houses of the satisfied, the knowledgeable, and the "haves" of this world in a spiritual sense. It speaks over the death of individuals and peoples its everlasting word: I have loved you from eternity; remain with me; thus will you live. Christianity preaches the unending worth of the apparently worthless and the unending worthlessness of what is apparently so valuable. The weak shall be made strong through God and the dying shall live. . . .

Has Christianity only pointed to another religion, a new idea of culture? Has it shown only a human way to God that had not yet been used? No; the Christian idea is the way of God to people and has as the visible objectification of this, the cross. Here lies the point at which we are accustomed to turn away shaking our heads about the Christian cause. The cross was probably first set at the center of the Christian message by Paul. Jesus has said nothing about this. And yet the correct meaning of the cross of Christ is nothing else than radical development of the concept of God held by Jesus himself. It is, so to speak, the historically visible form which this concept of God has assumed. God comes to people who have nothing but room for God—and this hollow space, this emptiness in people is called in Christian speech, faith. This means that in Jesus of Nazareth, his revealer, God inclines to the sinner; Jesus seeks the companionship of the sinner, goes after him or her in boundless love. He wants to be where a human person is no longer anything. The meaning of the life of Jesus is the demonstration of this divine will for sinners, for those who are unworthy. Where Jesus is, there is the love of God. However, the demonstration becomes complete, not when Jesus or God's love exists where the human person lives in sin and misery, but only when Jesus also takes upon himself the fate that hangs over every life, namely death. That is when Jesus who is God's love really dies. Only then can a person be certain that God's love accompanies and leads him or her through death. The death of Jesus on the cross of criminals, however, shows that the divine love even finds its way to the death of the criminal. And when Jesus dies on the cross with the cry, "My God why have you abandoned me" (Mark 15:34), does this mean that God's eternal will to love does not abandon people even when in the experience of being abandoned by God, they are plunged into despair? Jesus dies really despairing of his work, of God, but that of all things just signifies the culmination of his message that God so loves people that he takes death upon himself for their sake as proof of his own will to love. And, only because in the humiliation on the cross Jesus demonstrates his own and God's love for the world, resurrection follows after death. Death cannot restrain love. "Love is stronger than death" (Song of Songs 8:6).

That is the meaning of Good Friday and Easter Sunday: the way of God to people leads back to God. In this way Jesus' own concept of God is joined together with Paul's interpretation of the cross. Thus the cross becomes the central and paradoxical symbol of the Christian message. A king who goes to the cross must be the king of a wonderful kingdom. Only the one who understands the deep paradox of the idea of the cross can understand the entire meaning of the word of Jesus: my kingdom is not of this world. Jesus had to reject the king's crown that was offered him, had to deny the idea of the Roman imperium which would have been a temptation for him at every turn, if he were to remain true to his idea of God which led him to the cross.

The answer to another pressing question follows from this interpretation of the cross of Christ: what are we to think of other religions? Are they as nothing compared to Christianity? We answer that the Christian religion as religion is not of God. It is rather another example of a human way to God, like the Buddhist and others, too, though of course these are of a different nature. Christ is not the bringer of a new religion, but rather the one who brings God. Therefore, as an impossible way from the human to God, the Christian religion stands with other religions. The Christian can never pride himself on his Christianity, for it remains human, all too human. He lives, however, by the grace of God, which comes to people and comes to every person who opens his or her heart to it and learns to understand it in the cross of Christ. And, therefore, the gift of Christ is not the Christian religion, but the grace and love of God which culminate in the cross. [GS, V, pp.134–54]

The Communion of Saints

(Sanctorum Communio)

1930

Bonhoeffer's doctoral dissertation, *The Communion of Saints,* was written under the supervision of Professor Reinhold Seeberg and presented to the Faculty of Theology in the University of Berlin in 1927. An extensively edited version was first published in 1930 by the firm of Trowitzsch in 1930 with the proviso that Bonhoeffer pay the printing costs. The publishing house later complained of Bonhoeffer's lack of interest in publicizing the book. The English edition, translated by Ronald Gregor Smith, was published by William B. Collins, London; the American edition by Harper & Row, New York, in 1963. A new critical edition has been published as volume 1 in the *Dietrich Bonhoeffer Werke* series.[6] The selections here are taken from the English language edition of 1963 based on the third German edition of 1960. The text has been corrected where necessary.

This dissertation stands out as an academic beginning of Bonhoeffer's lifelong interest in exploring the nature and vocation of the church within the wider context of human sociality and historical concreteness. This lengthy study is not the dogmatically structured ecclesiology set in sociological and sociophilosophical categories that its dense use of sources once made it appear for many critics. Nor is it an imperialistic, theological co-opting of sociology, as Peter Berger once suggested.[7] It is rather a researched effort on Bonhoeffer's part to understand the very basis of God's relationship with peoples and communities in terms of human sociality. Throughout the multilayered approach to the social conceptuality that inspirits much of his understanding of both human life and church there is evidence that Bonhoeffer intended to interpret all of theology and anthropology in terms of the "social."[8] We see traces here, too, of Bonhoeffer's earliest stated appreciation of Christ's central relationship to people within the specifically Christian congregation as well as within the wider world of humanity itself. Structured by Christ, the "communion of saints" is declared to be the locus of that solidarity with people Bonhoeffer would later see as the life of a church and the strength and test of faith.

To this end, Bonhoeffer's dissertation roams widely around the basic Christian concepts structuring church and society: Christ, revelation, creation, sin, person,

and community. One's existence, Bonhoeffer argues, can only be understood socially. Individual life is so interwoven into those relationships with others and with
social communities that any interpretation of how God makes himself known in the
world must take into account revelation's grounding in human sociality. God's revelation in Christ reaches people only in their corporeal and communal concreteness. In Christ, God has not only entered human history but has in a striking way
shaped that history in ways more extensive than even the Bible or Christian imagination could acclaim. In effect, because of creation, God's life has become inescapably bound up into human life. Christ's role in this history lies in the formation
of one's personal and social existence by his standing as our representative at the
point where human community has been disrupted and healed. He is the Lord
through whom God's love, the basis and bond of all community, overcomes sin
and brings about the reconciliation of individuals with themselves and of people
with each other.

If, as Bonhoeffer insists, Christ's presence does indeed transform communities
into spiritual centers for God's healing power in the world, then, through Christ,
God's Word for that world assumes not mere visibility but incarnate specificity
within his church. This, in turn, invests the theological concepts of God's transcendence and freedom with more personal meaning for Bonhoeffer. God's otherness is not, he contends, that of an eternal being aloof in his heaven. Rather, God
has become in Jesus a God for people in the context of our social existence. The
Christian community is destined to reflect the everlasting God's relationship to his
people in the course of history. Christian communities become, in turn, the stories
of how God has entered into a solidarity with his creatures. God's otherness thus
becomes real in the form of individuals and communities whose relationship structure a person's very life. Moreover, it is in the context of one's personal identity
with God and with human community that Bonhoeffer's idea of the "collective
person" or his description of church, "Christ existing as community," have any
meaningful content.

In *The Communion of Saints* we see, too, a statement of the ideal ground of
those actions on behalf of the oppressed that would become the pulse of Bonhoeffer's own resistance to nazism and of his role in the conspiracy. Bonhoeffer writes
glowingly of Christ's vicarious action as the basis of that communion of people
whose oneness would be structured by "agapeic" love, their living and acting for
others rather than for themselves. It is self-sacrificing love, not necessarily aimed at
receiving love or acknowledgement in return, that shapes the community into concrete resemblance to Jesus Christ. The Christic attitude of service he idealizes here
can never be restricted to one's own circle of believers. Bonhoeffer sees the
Christian community as more the vortex of that new existence in which sociality
would be delivered from the evil of those human introversions that destroy community.

Throughout *The Communion of Saints*, Bonhoeffer takes issue with those ideologies that tend toward exclusivity and divisiveness precisely because such ideologies
negate community in favor of a self-assured but triumphalist identity. His negative
reaction to any *cor curvum in se* (heart turned in on itself) extended to the self-
serving egocentrism that reduces God to a "heavenly double" of corporate ideol-

ogy and personal ambitiousness. Though this dissertation does not offer a developed Christology but rather focuses on the church itself as collective person or "Christ existing as community" and the concrete sociality of the community, Bonhoeffer insists that Christ, not the self-seeking individual and not the ecclesiastical establishment, is the center of Christian community. The excerpts that follow begin with Bonhoeffer's statement of the relationship of Christ to the church derived from a New Testament perspective.

. . . The local church is the concrete form of the whole church of God (1 Cor. 1.2). But it is also itself the church of God. It is "the form in which the whole church appears in one place." The whole church is real only in the local church. By ecclesia, therefore, Paul always thinks of what God has established on earth, even when he speaks of the local church. The church exists by the work of Christ and the work of the Holy Spirit, which have to be distinguished. The church has been chosen by Christ from eternity (Eph. 1:4ff.; 2 Thess. 2:13; John 15:16 in the *Diatessaron*). The new mankind lives in him; it has been created by his death (Eph. 2:15). It is the second, the new Adam (1 Cor. 15:45). Thus mankind is really redeemed in him, for he gave himself for the church (Eph. 5:25), and the building up of the church means exclusively the actualizing of what has been accomplished in Christ . . . . Christ's relation to the church is twofold: he is the creator of its whole life, which rests on him, the master builder of the church, and he is also really present at all times in his church, for the church is his body; he rules over it as the head does over the body. The body, again, is ruled throughout by the Holy Spirit (1 Cor. 12:13; Eph. 2:18, 4:4), and here again we have to distinguish between the Spirit of Christ and the Holy Spirit, which are not identical in their power. What Christ is for the whole church, the Holy Spirit is for the individual. The Holy Spirit impels the individual to Christ, he brings Christ to them (Rom. 8:14; Eph. 2:22), he gives them community (2 Cor. 13:3; Phil. 2:1), that is, his power extends to man's social life, and makes use of man's social bonds and social will, whereas the Spirit of Christ is directed toward the historical nature of human life together.

If we now look at the church not in terms of how it is built up, but as a unified reality, then the image of the body of Christ must dominate. What does this really mean? In the church Christ is at work as with an instrument. He is present in it; as the Holy Spirit is with the individual, so Christ makes himself present in the congregation of the saints. If we take the thought of the body seriously, then it means that this "image" identifies Christ and the church, as Paul himself clearly does (1 Cor. 12:12, 6:5); for where my body is, there too am I. Thus when the church is split, Paul can ask, "Is Christ divided?" (1 Cor. 1:13). From this conviction that Christ himself is the church there arises the idea of an organic life in the church, in accordance with the will of Christ, from this image of a living organism. It is clear that both ideas conflict with the reality of sinfulness, and that there is need of systematic work at this point. Thus Christ is really present only in the church. The church is in him and he is in the church (1 Cor. 1:30, 3:16; 2 Cor. 6:16, 13:5; Col. 3:9, 2:17), and "to be in Christ" is the same as "to be in the church." ... [*CS*, pp. 98–100]

The problem becomes more complicated when we add, as we must, the idea of *pneuma*. For clearly the Holy Spirit is personally at work in the creation of the church. He gives community (see above) and is also the principle of unity (1 Cor. 12:4ff., especially vv. 11–13; Eph. 4:4, though this is not very clear in Paul: for the body as such is also unity). The church is the body of Christ, but only under the gathering and uniting influence of the Holy Spirit. So once more the identification of Christ and the church is made difficult, and yet it has to be made, and it is made.

The social significance of Christ is decisive. He is only present in the church, that is, where the Christian community is united by preaching and the Lord's Supper for brotherly love. The real presence of Christ is also decisive. The relation of this presence to the problem of the Word and of preaching is only indicated by Paul. The sole content of the church is in any case the revelation of God in Christ. He is present to the church in his Word, by which the community is constituted ever anew. The church is the presence of Christ, as Christ is the presence of God. ... [*CS*, pp. 99–100]

The relation of Christ to the church can now be stated as follows: essentially Jesus Christ was no more a founder of the Christian religious community than he was the founder of a religion. The credit for both these things belongs to the primitive church, that is, to the apostles. That is why the question whether Christ founded a church is so ambiguous. He brought, established and proclaimed the reality of the new mankind. The circle of disciples about him was not a church; but they simply sketched out the church's inner dialectic. This was not a new religion seeking adherents, which is a picture drawn by a later time. But God established the reality of the church, of mankind pardoned in Jesus Christ. Not religion, but revelation, not a religious community, but the church: that is what the reality of Jesus Christ means. And yet there is a necessary connection between revelation and religion, as there is between religious community and the church. Nowadays that connection is often overlooked, and yet it is only because it exists that Paul can call Jesus the foundation, the cornerstone of the building of the church. As a pioneer and model Jesus is also the founder of a religious community, though not of the Christian church (for this only came into existence after Pentecost—Matt. 16:18 and the Lord's Supper give expression to this fact). And then after the resurrection Christ restores the shattered fellowship, in the case of Peter by appearing to him, as presumably the first to whom this happened (1 Cor. 15:5), and perhaps expressly entrusting him with this new office (John 21:15f.), and then in the case of the Twelve by appearing in their midst (1 Cor. 15:5; John 20:19). Thus Christ is the sole foundation upon which the edifice of the church rests, the reality from which the historical "collective life" arose. Thus the relation of Jesus Christ to the Christian church is to be understood in a dual sense. (1) *The church is consummated in him and time is annulled.* (2) *Within time the church is to be built up on him as the foundation. He is the church's historical principle.* The vertical direction, time, belongs, as it were, to him. These statements correspond to a truth long since known from the New Testament concerning the presence and the coming of the kingdom of God, but they are not identical with it, for the church is not identical with the kingdom of God, any more than the *iustus peccator* is actually perfected, although he is essentially perfected. The kingdom of God is a purely eschatological concept, which from the point of view of God is present every moment in the church, but for us remains an object of hope, whereas the church is an object of faith here and now. The church is identical with the kingdom of Christ, but the kingdom of Christ is the kingdom of God which has been realized in history since the coming of Christ. . . . [*CS,* pp. 111–12]

CORPORATE PRAYER

If we now consider intercession from God's standpoint, it is seen to be the individual's organization of himself to realize God's will for the other man, so that he may serve the realization of God's rule in the church. Here is where the meaning and strength of the corporate prayer of the church resides, as Luther speaks of it in the sermon on good works. In this corporate prayer God possesses his strongest means for organizing the whole church toward his purpose. The church recognizes itself in prayer as an instrument of his will and organizes itself accordingly in active obedience. This provides the church with its chief impulse; the devil fears a roof of thatch beneath which the church is at prayer more than he does a splendid church in which many masses are celebrated. Thus it is of decisive significance for the church that it should give to corporate prayer its proper, central place. The church that leads to one life must also have and practice one prayer. In this prayer it takes upon itself the burden of the many individuals who already or still belong to it, and bears it to God. In the church each man bears the other's burden, and it is knowing that intercession is a means supplied by God for the realization of his aim that we can recognize and practice it with meaning. In intercession, too, we confirm the nature of Christian love as making us act "with," "for" and finally "in place of" our neighbor, thereby drawing him deeper and deeper into the church. Thus when a man is interceding for another in Jesus' name the whole church is praying with him, but praying as "Christ existing as the church." We thus modify Hegel's conception. [*CS,* p. 134]

THE PRINCIPLE OF PROGRESS IN THE CHURCH

Similarly the Christian evaluation of history gives rise to the principle of progress in the church. The church must be a church of the present day, it must take and prove all the forces that accrue to it from present-day life. Past history is in principle no more right than the present. As a modern Christian I have both the right and duty to criticize history and give form to the gospel for the present. And every local congregation has this duty vis-à-vis the whole church. On the Protestant view this makes for a balance between the retarding and the progressive element. The sociological expression of the progressive element in the church is the idea of organism. The entire life of the community comes from the cooperation of the members. Any concrete case of the rejection of something new, or the throwing off of a dead tradition, must be decided by the conscience of the church authorities. Their finest task is to make every possible power of renewal and vitality fruitful for the work of the church. To this task belongs the handing over of certain offices in the church to charismatically gifted personalities, whether in the exposition of Scripture or works of love or powers of organization. Further, there should be a constant watchfulness over the interests of the young generation, and a prudent use of the situation where similar thoughts are stirring, and attentiveness to what is being said outside the church. Fundamentally it is in this lively attitude that the law of life for every community is fulfilled: a fighting movement all the time (such as the Roman Catholic church does not have—the institution and the people as a mass). Only when every door is open to this movement, and when on the other hand the retarding element is powerful enough to reject the useless and to deal critically with the fruitful, will there be a quickening mingling of proper progress in the church.

Although both powers are at work in every national church and every gathered church, since they arise from the Protestant view of history and from historical life as a whole, although, further, there are national churches with a great will to progress, and gathered churches, certainly, which are crassly conservative, in general one can say that the national type of church tends more to the historical past and the gathered type of church more to the new and progressive. In view of all we have said, especially of the necessity of the national church from a dogmatic standpoint, we can now affirm that the national church and the gathered church belong together, and that it is all too obvious today that a national church, which is not continually pressing forward to be a confessing church, is in the greatest inner peril. There is a moment when the church dare not continue to be a national church, and this moment has come when the national church can no longer see how it can win through to being a gathered church (see above, on baptism and confirmation), but on the contrary is moving into complete petrifaction and emptiness in the use of its forms, with evil effects on the living members as well. We have today reached the point where such questions must be decided. We are more than ever grateful for the grace of the national church, but we are also more than ever keeping our eyes open for the danger of its complete degeneration. . . . [CS, pp. 188–90]

CHURCH AND PROLETARIAT

"What is the state of . . . the question concerning the significance of Christianity for the solution of the modern social problem? That is the problem of capitalist economics and the industrial proletariat created by it; the problem of gigantic bureaucratic and military states, and of immense increase in population leading to world politics and colonial policies; the problem of mechanized activity producing huge amounts of material, and mobilizing and combining everything in world traffic, but also mechanizing men and labor. We only need to formulate the question in this way to recognize that the most important answer is that this is a problem which is entirely new and unprecedented for Christian social work" (Troeltsch).

We can no longer make the last of Troeltsch's assertions in his form, and yet we must recognize that for the church of today everything depends on its once more approaching the masses which have turned away from it, and moreover in such a way that the church brings the gospel into real contact with the present situation of the proletariat, in full attentiveness to how these masses look upon the gospel.

The objective spirit of the church in its present historical conditions has not yet shown much awareness of this problem. Christian social work has had some admirable achievements. But where is there to be found any objective discussion of the gospel, the church, and the proletariat? On my view it cannot be gainsaid that the future and the hope for our "bourgeois" church lies in a renewal of its lifeblood, which is only possible if the church succeeds in winning the proletariat. If the church does not see this, then it will spurn a moment of the most serious decision. Nor is it hard to see that the churchliness of the modern bourgeoisie is threadbare, and that its living power in the church is at an end. On the other hand it seems to me as if, despite outward opposition in the proletariat, there is no modern power that is basically more open to the Christian gospel than the proletariat. The living proletariat knows only one affliction, isolation, and cries out for one thing, community. These ideas are of course entangled and confined in class consciousness. Nevertheless they are seeking something more intensively than the bourgeoisie ever did. The church dare not let the proletariat proclaim "human peace" without speaking its own word in this situation. It must not let the socialist youth movements speak of community without calling into their midst the word of the *sanctorum communio*. It must not shrug off the interest in sport shown by modern youth (not just the proletarians), but it must recognize that this, too, is a cry for community in discipline and struggle, and that here, too, the word of the *sanctorum communio* could find attentive response. Certainly it will not be heard, and cannot be heard, in the way it often speaks today. For above all the gospel must deal with the present—and that means at this moment the proletarian mass—in a concrete way, "serving the Lord" (Rom. 12:11). But let there be no apotheosis of the proletariat! It is neither the bourgeois nor the proletarian which is right, but the gospel alone. Here there is neither Jew nor Greek. Nevertheless the gospel must be concretely proclaimed in history, and that is why it brings us today face to face with the problem of the proletariat. It is not very easy to offer a proof for something which is more instinctive than conceptual, in this case to prove that our modern church is "bourgeois." The best proof is that the proletariat has turned away from the church, whereas the bourgeois (the petty official, the artisan and the merchant) have remained. So the sermon is aimed at relatively secure people, living adequately in orderly family circumstances, relatively "educated" and morally relatively solid. So the sermon meets the need for having something fine and educated and moral for the free hours of Sunday. Hence that all-too-familiar type of sermon which is called an "address," in which proof is offered of the preacher's literary culture and the corresponding interest of the "public." The danger of the church's becoming a mere association is obvious. (In this context we also find the mischievous habit of individual artistic efforts, such as solos by a professional singer, in the framework of the service.) If I consider the pictures hanging in church halls and meeting places, or the architectural styles of churches of recent decades, or the church music provided by Mendelssohn and others, I cannot help thinking that in none of these things is there the slightest understanding of the church's essential social nature. It would be an interesting task for a sociology of the church to make a historical examination of its artistic products; I believe one could perhaps get a better insight in this way than by any examination of the charitable works done by the church. [*CS,* pp. 190–92]

God's judgment and grace cover persons, that is, all the individual persons in the church; the multiplicity of spirit as we have described it earlier, as well as the marriages and friendships that have entered into the *sanctorum communio,* and finally what unites them all, the collective person of the church, spiritual unity. Ultimately, however, these are persons solely in the fellowship they have with each other—this is something we must in conclusion emphasize once more—that is to say, in community of spirit. Community of spirit, however, demands whole persons in a corporeality which must be thought of as the full expression of the new spirituality. This precludes any mystical ideas of a final absorption in God as the person who is one and all, of fusion of our divine being with his. The Creator and the creature remain distinct as persons. But the creatures too are distinct from one another, and yet taken all together form the mighty unity of the congregation of God. They are now "entirely justified and sanctified," one in Christ and yet all individuals. Their community of spirit is based upon and is kindled at their mutual love. They surrender themselves to each other and to God, and thereby form a community both with man and with God. And this community, which in history is never more than incipiently realized and is constantly breaking up, is real and eternal here. Whereas in the church too the I and the Thou confronted each other as strangers, in an estrangement overcome only in the eschatological signs of sanctification, here the revelation of one heart to the other is consummated in divine love. We behold the community of love in the mutual revelation of hearts which are filled by the Spirit. "I seeks I. They find one another and flow together ... reality and truth become the same. ... " The meaning of love is consummated where one's own person is no longer seen, and so reaches its "self" in the most intimate communion with the other, a communion which may be called blessed. It remains a community of will of free persons, and its blessedness has nothing to do with a mystic fusion. It is the highest potentialization of personal life, just as losing this communion means death. The mystic has no understanding of the power and the glory of love. From man's dual destiny of being under God's lordship and in God's kingdom arises his dual function of seeing the eternal truth—as formerly he believed it—and practicing the love that is now perfect, the perfect service of the Spirit. The movement upward cannot be separated from the movement toward our neighbor. Both belong indissolubly together. Ritschl's distinction breaks down. Standing under God's lordship means living in communion with him and with the members of the church. God wills to be the King and Father of his subjects and children, he wills to reign over spirits whose will is free, to have communion with them, but not, as the primal ground of all being, to be the death of all true being. He is the God of living persons. [CS, pp. 202–3]

CHRIST EXISTING AS THE CHURCH

Now the objective spirit of the church has really become the Holy Spirit; the experience of the "religious" community is now really the experience of the church and the collective person of the church really "Christ existing as the church." How they all become one and yet each man remains himself, how they are all in God and yet each is separate from him, how they are all in each other, and yet each man will be alone, how each has God entirely and alone in the merciful dual loneliness of seeing and serving truth and love, and is yet never lonely but always really lives only in the church—these are things it is not given us to conceive. We walk in faith. But we shall see not God alone but his church too; we shall no longer only believe in its love and faith, but see it. We shall know that God's purpose to rule is constantly over us, and we shall put it into action in the kingdom of the church. Here the kingdom of Christ has become the kingdom of God; here the *ministerium* of Christ the Holy Spirit and the Word is at an end. Christ himself gives his church into his Father's keeping (1 Cor. 15:24), that God may be all in all. [*CS*, p. 203]

3

Act and Being

(Akt und Sein)

1931

Act and Being, Bonhoeffer's *Habilitationsschrift* (a second dissertation required of young scholars in order to obtain an appointment as lecturer in theology at the University of Berlin), was completed in 1929 and published in 1931. It had been approved by the theological faculty in July 1930 and became the basis for Bonhoeffer's inaugural lecture at the university, "The Question of Man in Contemporary Philosophy and Theology," delivered July 31, 1930. The English edition was translated by Bernard Noble and published by Collins, London, and Harper & Row, New York, in 1961. The selections here are from that English language edition, with changes in the text where necessary.

The dialectic of act and being that Bonhoeffer attempts to set in motion here is "recognizable in theological terms as the dialectic of faith and the community of Christ; neither to be imagined without the other. . . . " This is Bonhoeffer's stated aim. It can, however, be misleading. *Act and Being,* because of its subjective matter, ranges into all the principal concepts dealt with in systematic theology under the approach of either "act" categories of thought or "being" categories, hence the epistemological problem with its dialectic swinging either to transcendental or ontological understanding of human existence, the revelation problem with its solution in church, and the anthropological problem with its solution as a "being in Christ" and not "being in Adam." For all of its heaviness and lumbering pace, the book is a tour de force, attempting to integrate a quasi-encyclopedic list of vying and inadequate theories into a more convincing, faith-inspirited way of doing theology, understanding church, and coping with what it means to "be in Christ." Throughout *Act and Being,* Bonhoeffer picks apart the philosophical presuppositions behind the way people have coped with the reality of revelation. He criticizes these efforts as merely feeding one's egocentric pretentiousness and maskir҈ the individualistic attitude that places human autonomy rather than God at the center of Christian maturity. God is thus harnessed to human consciousness in another glorification of reason and proclamation of justification by works, here the lofty work of intellection.

In this context the question of how one truly attains freedom arises. Freedom, for Bonhoeffer, had to be more than giving in to the near infinite vagaries of mind in the quest for truth. One needed to correct this attitude with a proper understanding of how God liberates people from themselves and of how this frees people to be in relationship with God. The act of faith, Bonhoeffer tells us, is an act of *direct* relationship with God in Christ; as such, it evades being drawn into the orbit of one's domineering ego. It is Christ alone who can create the social sensitivity by which the individual can respect God's priority and command, uncontrolled by human reflection and human categorizations. God's freedom is not freedom *from* his creatures but the freedom to be *for* his people; in a way to be "'haveable,' graspable in his Word within the church." But in this, too, God is free from all human efforts to manipulate his words and domesticate his dynamic presence within the books, podiums, pulpits, and tabernacles of a clericalized, churchy existence.

For Bonhoeffer, God's revelation of himself is necessarily a social event. The quest for truth is pursued within the context of what sociality demands of Christians—that Christians engage in self-sacrificing service of others. God's word becomes his revelation for us only in community. This is the model for the authentic freedom in which genuine, loving believers are related to God and to others in Christ. In *Act and Being*, Bonhoeffer concludes that revelation cannot fit into any categorical system. The church community, he argues, not some philosophical or theological system of thought, "is God's final revelation of himself as Christ existing as community."

Moreover, the encounter with God in Christ takes place in the community at that level where others are affirmed in their freedom and strengthened in both their personal and social relationships without danger of being reduced to reflections of one's own self-image. A community is neither a collection of isolated egos nor a conglomeration of preconceived ideals. If God's truth is to be Christ and the Christian community, then social apathy and the denial of one's sociality are the greatest untruths. From this we can appreciate Bonhoeffer's attempt in *Act and Being* to see in the presence and even in the demands placed upon us by others in the community the mode and locus of Christ's own liberating presence. We live either "in Adam" without love and with no time for people and, therefore, without Christ, or we live in Christ, in the truth that we must break out of the solitude of self to live on behalf of people, especially those in need. Faith is, then, epitomized in the person of Jesus Christ creating Christian community and becoming thereby "the free Lord of my existence."

Bonhoeffer relates this faith to "new existence" in Christ. It is Christ who in community has shattered the walls of solitary concentration on self in order to inspire a true knowledge of self in an other-centered outlook on life. This is the death of the narcissistic "I" experienced in living in and for Christ. Awareness of this transformation is never attained by any intellectual dissection of the act of justification and faith. It is achieved only in direct relationship with and contemplation of Jesus Christ. This is a deliberate, grace-initiated turning toward Christ, whose person and word move an individual and the community to acknowledge their solidarity with others in Christ. Bonhoeffer refuses to hand faith's creative energies over either to the domination of the thinking, reflecting "I" or to manipulation by an ecclesiastical establishment turned in on itself.

Beclouding the ideal in faith of fully accepting Christ in self-sacrificing response to his word in both individual and community, there still exists the problem of the egocentric tendency to turn in on oneself and to control the uncontrollable Word of God. In short, theological and ecclesial reflection tend, in Bonhoeffer's opinion, to appropriate God's revelation as doctrine, law, and institution, even in bureaucratic structures, thus reducing the unknown and warding off fears of the risks of what God may demand in the future. In this way, the anxious, manipulative self may become an obstacle to Christ's life in the community by an introverted dulling of one's sensitivity to God's call to be the courageous, responsible church not only of the present but also of the future. It is up against this seeming dead end of ecclesialized, biblicized, and juridicized reduction of revelation to a nonthreatening minimum of worship and service that Bonhoeffer proposes the model of the child forever turned toward the future, open to wonder and refreshingly eager to become the person God has destined him or her to be. Bonhoeffer's *Act and Being* ends on this note. So do the selections that follow.

Hegel wrote a philosophy of angels, but not of human existence. It simply is not true that a concrete human being (including even the philosopher) is in full possession of the mind. Whoever countenances the idea that he need only arrive at himself to be in God is doomed to hideous disillusion in experiencing the utter introversion, the treadmill confinement to the self, of the very loneliest solitude, with its tormenting desolation and sterility. [*AB*, p. 27–28]

The gospel of mind finding itself in God and God in itself was preached too seductively by idealism for theology to resist its blandishments, and all too readily it reasoned thus: if being is essentially consciousness, God must "be" in religious experiences, and the reborn I must find God in reflection on itself. Where else could God be found but in my consciousness? Even if I can never pass beyond it, it must be what constitutes being in general. God, then, is the God of my consciousness. He "is" only in my religious consciousness. But this was jumping to conclusions. [*AB*, pp. 38–39]

ACT AND BEING

This is where Seeberg's theory of the religious a priori comes into play; humankind, he says, is "charged with the capacity" for "becoming directly conscious of pure mind." According to this theory, man is able to receive God into himself, that is, to experience his immediate contact in feeling and intuition, and on these premises it is a thoroughly justified transcendental inference to attribute a being to God insofar as a being-conceived corresponds to him. But at the same time it is also genuinely transcendental to refrain from an absolute negative judgment as to being; in the present case that restraint is exercised. Be that as it may, we are told of a direct becoming-aware, of God directly touching the human. The religious a priori is said to be fundamentally open to the divine will; there is said to be a form in the human wherein the divine content of revelation may pour. In other words, revelation must become religion, and that is its nature. Revelation is religion. But this represents a trend from pure transcendentalism to idealism, in the absolute, to use Seeberg's terms, enters here again into "direct" contact, union, with the I, my will is subjected to the primal will and now God's will is active in me. The difficulty lies in the idea of the religious a priori, in spite of the latitude Seeberg accords the concept. If we are to suppose that the urgent capacity to receive revelation is given with this a priori, that is, in implication, the capacity of faith, that is already going too far. Natural man has a *cor curvum in se.* Even natural religion remains flesh, and strives after the flesh. If revelation is to come to man, he must be wholly transformed. Faith itself must be created in him. In this case there is no ability to "hear" before the "hearing." These are thoughts which Seeberg himself expresses, and refers to in Luther. But faith stands as the work of God, in a sense inapplicable to natural religiosity, for which the religious a priori noted by Seeberg certainly holds good. According to Luther, revelation and faith are bound to the concrete message, and the Word is the mediator of the contact between God and man, admitting no other "directness." But then the idea of the a priori can only be understood to imply that certain mental forms are preposited for the formal understanding of the Word, in which case, it must be admitted, a specifically religious a priori loses meaning. All that pertains to personal appropriation of the fact of Christ is not a prioristic, but is owed to the contingent action of God on man. What Seeberg calls feeling [*Empfindung*] and intuition come under the same criticism, for the purely formal understanding of the Word requires no other noetic forms than are supplied by the a priori of thought itself. . . . [*AB*, pp. 46–47]

Per se, a philosophy cannot spare room for revelation; let it then recognize revelation and confess itself Christian philosophy, knowing that the place it wished to usurp *is already* occupied by another—Christ. . . .

What offends Christian thought in any autonomous self-understanding is that it considers man capable of bestowing truth on himself, of transporting himself into the truth by his own resources, since it is reasonable to suppose that the "basis" of existence must somehow be within truth (likeness to God). Here, however, "truth" comprises only that reference to God which Christian theology does not hold possible save in the *Word* spoken, of man and to man, in the law and the gospel. It is in this sense that formal validity may be conceded to the proposition, common to transcendentalism and idealism, that knowledge about oneself or about God is no "disconnected possession," but places the knower in a direct "possessive" relation to the known; employing a terminology which must be further explained below, this means that knowledge in truth about oneself, or about God, is already "being in . . . "—whether in "Adam" or in "Christ."

"Never being able to give oneself truth" represents the unattainability of a systematic metaphysics; for such knowledge as that would imply would signify a self-placing into the truth. But neither is such knowledge a possibility for any "critical philosophy"; a philosophy with such great expectations of itself would be highly uncritical. Thought is as little able as good works to deliver the *cor curvum in se* from itself. Is it merely by chance that the most profound German philosophy finishes in the I-confinement of the All? No, the knowledge it represents is likewise a self-placing into truth—for the world of the I untouched by grace is confined to the I—though not the truth of God's word, because it simply "is" not in this truth; if it were, it would be unable to celebrate here the triumph of the I, but would have to recognize, in its eternal loneliness, the curse of lost communion with God. Only thought which, bound to the obedience of Christ, "is" *from* the truth—can be placed into the truth. Thus our way is pointed onward to revelation itself, yet we cannot understand this step merely as a final possible step, but as one which must already have been taken, or us to be able to take it. . . . [*AB*, pp. 70–72]

THE CONTINGENCY OF REVELATION

God reveals himself only in acts freely initiated by himself. "Man is touched with grace when, and from the fact that, the Word of God comes to him, no sooner, no later, and not otherwise. So far as is known, the heavenly manna in the wilderness could not be put into storage." God's Word has no being in independence of his self-revelation to man and its being heard and belived by man. This, however, is where we may recognize the transcendental thesis. Because God himself creates the hearing and belief, and is indeed himself hearing and believing, in man, "God's Word is only in the act of belief, never in that abstraction from the strictly occasional event, at God's sole discretion, which we call grace." God's being is solely act, is consequently in man only as act, and that in such a way that any reflection on the accomplished act has *ipso facto* lost contact with the act itself, with the result the act can never be grasped in conceptual form and cannot therefore be enlisted into systematic thought. It follows that although Barth has no hesitation in making use of temporal categories (moment, here and now, before, after, etc.) his concept of the act must not be regarded as temporal. The freedom of God and the act of belief are essentially supratemporal; if Barth nevertheless stresses the act which, recurrently "beginning at the beginning," is at all times free, so that there can be no inference from one act to the next, we must understand that he is endeavoring to translate the transcendental concept of the act into terms of the *geschichtlich* [historic]. However, this attempt is bound to come to grief against the fact that (according to Barth) no "historical" moment is *capax infiniti* [capable of the infinite], so that the empirical action of man—"belief," "obedience"—becomes at most a pointer to God's activity and can never, *in* its historicality, be faith and obedience themselves.

Thus the problem of transcendental philosophy, which we discovered at the beginning, presents itself afresh. God recedes into the nonobjective, the nonavailable. That is a necessary consequence of the formal conception of his freedom, which might be traced without difficulty to the combination of nominalism and the idea of contingency in the closing stages of medievalism.

God remains always the master, always the subject, so that if any man should think he has God as an object, it is no longer *God* whom he "has"; God is always the "coming," not the "existing" deity (Barth).

It was inevitable that this formal understanding of God's contingent activity should lead Barth to develop his idea of the "dialectical." "God's Word is not bound, and never will be bound. Theological dialectic is genuine dialectic to the extent that it is open to this idea, to the extent—in fact—that it will subserve this idea, subserve the freedom of the Word of God. The freedom of God's Word cannot be pinned down by unequivocal theological statements. It snaps their pronouncement in twain: thus there are only theological statements under "critical reservation." All Barth's theological propositions are rooted in the necessity of saying *not-God* when I speak of God (because *I* speak of *him*), and *not-I* when I speak of the believing I; thus due regard is paid to the idea that genuinely theological concepts do not fit into fixed ontological abstractions, and the concept of contingency would be excluded: the "coming" changed to the "existing" God. Revelation would have sunk to rest in the theological system. This is countered by the critical reservation. But it is not as if the "systematic" formula for a theology of revelation had at last been found in a dialectical theology; no, "for theology too, there is a justification only by faith." The reservation made by dialectical theology is not a logical one, such as might be suspended in the antithesis, but one real and recurrent view of predestination; however, as such no theological idea can ever seize God: it remains, "strictly speaking, a testimony from the Devil" (Barth). God remains free, nonobjective, pure act, but he can, if he choose to do so, make use of a theology in order to attest himself therein. That does not lie within the power of the theology but, again, within the freedom of God. Thought is a cohesive whole, incapable of radical self-disturbance; of this Barth is conscious—that even dialectical theology is no way to catch God. How could it be otherwise, since before all thought stands unfathomable predestination?

This attempt at unsystematic thinking, corresponding to God's freedom as formally understood, finds its parallel in a new trend of philosophy, which itself takes part with lively interest in the development of modern theology. E. Grisebach has tried in various works to clarify the idea of—or rather, point the way to—reality: every system, in one way or another, conflates reality, truth and the I; purports to understand reality and have it at its disposal. In his "satanity," man is tempted to draw reality, the absolute, his fellowman, into himself, but in this way he remains alone with himself in his system, and fails to arrive at reality. Theory is unable to form a concept of reality. Reality is "experienced" in the contingent fact of the claim of "others." Only what comes from "outside" can show man the way to his reality, his existence. In "sustaining" the "claim of my neighbor" I exist in reality, I act ethically; that is the sense of an ethics not of timeless truths but of the "present." Man can never have the absolute at his disposal, that is, bear it within him, and for that reason he never arrives at the system.

Friedrich Gogarten and H. Knittermeyer have developed this thesis for theology in such a way that the place of man's encounter with the absolute, with God, is taken by his encounter with the Thou of his neighbor, his restriction by the other as working itself out in history—if not actually constituting history. Faced with this Thou, all "humanistic-systematic" thought, tending to ontological concepts must confess its impotence. For we are dealing with history: that is, the meeting of I and Thou. The meaning of the gospel is that the claim of one's neighbor was met once and for all in Christ.

Undeniably, the objection to be raised against this thesis is that in the attempt to avoid any postulation of an absolute, the Thou is in effect made absolute. If the I's claim to be absolute is to be transferred merely to the Thou, not to him who is above both and above the absolute, we appear to be heading for a wholly ethicalized version of the gospel; worse, even the concepts of history and theology are growing obscure, which means that revelation is being lost to sight.... [*AB*, pp. 82–87]

That follows from the formal understanding of God's freedom. In this way theological thought seems condemned to remain in principle profane; it can only, in the event, stand "under the sign of God" (thus Barth). But the following objection has to be made: what can it mean to say that theology requires a justification by faith (see above), when it can only be a question of justifying the theologian who thinks the theology? Indeed it is open to doubt whether the existence of the theologian, placed in truth, serves to distinguish his systematic thought from profane thought, whether there is any such possibility at all (if so, on what basis?). Seen from the viewpoint of a formalistic understanding of God's freedom, the theory of revelation as pure act can only serve to deny the possibility of a distinction between profane and theological or—if we may anticipate—ecclesiastical thought.

The whole situation impels one to ask whether a formalistic understanding of God's freedom in contingent revelation, conceived wholly in terms of of the act, is really the proper groundwork for theology. In revelation it is a question less of God's freedom on the far side from us, that is, his eternal isolation and aseity, than of his forth-proceeding, his *given* Word, his bond in which he has bound himself, of his freedom as it is most strongly attested in his having freely bound himself to historical man, having placed himself at man's disposal. God is not free *of* man but *for* man. Christ is the Word of his freedom. God *is there*, which is to say: not in eternal nonobjectivity but (looking ahead for the moment) "haveable," graspable in his Word within the Church. Here an understanding of God's freedom based on its essential meaning supplants the more formal approach. If it should prove itself, it will suggest a redirection of our attention from revelation seen in terms of the act towards ontological ideas. But we may be sure that from the new standpoint, with its reappraisal of revelation, the problem of the theological system will assume quite a different aspect and resolve itself in quite a different way. It would remain to be seen to what extent one would still be justified in using concepts of the act to explain revelation. . . . [*AB*, pp. 90–91]

KNOWLEDGE OF REVELATION

If in this way God is apprehended as the subject of cognition, it is equally pressing, on one side, to understand the human *I* as subject of the knowledge of God (since otherwise the act of belief would have no contact with human existence) and, on the other side, to avoid identifying the human with the divine *I*. Thus one asks what mediation there is between the divine and the human acts of belief, what relation, in other words, subsists between grace and religion, revelation and history, with reference to the problem of knowledge.

This is the point where the profound difference between genuine transcendentalism and idealism stands clearly exposed. If in the latter (as has been shown, above) revelation was essentially religion through the identification of *I* and being, the original transcendental thesis marks a sharp contrast between the two. God "is" only in belief, but the subject of the believing is God himself. Hence faith is something essentially different from religion. But (even in Barth) no light is shed on how we can envisage the human religious act in conjunction with the divine act of belief, unless we sever them to allot them essentially different spheres, or suppress the "subjectivity" of God if not, alternatively, the existential impact of revelation. Religious acts of every kind may be stimulated by man, but only God himself can bestow faith, as full readiness to hear the Word; only he indeed can hear. The act of belief as reflected on cannot be distinguished from the religious act; belief, because effected by God, is only in the act, never something left for the finding. But from that it follows that the *I* of belief, supposedly mine and God's together, can never be anything already present, but only something acting in the act of belief. Whether *I* do or do not believe is therefore something *I* cannot learn from any reflection on my religious acts, but it is equally impossible, while *I* am in the process of believing, to center my attention on my belief. Belief is never directed to itself, but only on Christ, on something extrinsic. And so it is only in the believing in Christ that *I* know that *I* believe, which is to say that here and now *I* do not know it, and in reflection on this believing *I* know nothing. From the nonobjectivity of God there follows necessarily the nonobjectivity of the subject in knowing God—but that implies the nonobjectivity of faith. . . . [*AB*, pp. 94–95]

REVELATION'S MODE OF BEING WITHIN THE CHURCH

Revelation should be envisaged only with reference to the Church, where the Church is regarded as constituted by the present proclamation, within the community*, for the community, of Christ's death and resurrection. "Present," because it is only in this proclamation that the event of revelation is realized in and for the community and because, secondly, this is the only way in which its contingent (that is, extrinsic) character makes itself known—for contingency is only in presence, viz. the present. What is past, as "having" happened, is "background," unless the proclamation "coming to" us in the future should raise it to "presence." In the concept of contingency as happening which is "coming to" us from outside, the present is determined by the future; in the system, inasmuch as the (in principle) "beforeness" of the rational background obtains, the present is determined by the past. At all events the present is determined by one or the other or both; it is never *per se*. But the decision lies with us. Of the Christian revelation it may be said that the proclamation of cross and resurrection, determined by eschatology and predestination, together with the event effective within it, serves even to raise the past to the present and, paradoxically, to something future yet "to come." It follows, therefore, that we may not interpret the Christian revelation as "having happened," that for the human living in the church, in the present, this unique occurrence is qualified as future. Conversely, for the very reason that the Christian revelation, in its special qualification of the unique event of the cross and resurrection, is always "yet to come," it must happen in the present: that is to say, it must be considered within the church, for the church is the Christ of the present, "Christ existing as community." In the proclamation within the community for the community, Christ is the "subject" common to the proclamation (Word and sacrament) and community alike. The proclamation and the community are so interdependent that each, regarded

*Throughout this section Bonhoeffer uses the word *Gemeinde*, and we have translated this as "community"; however, the sense of this term in Bonhoeffer's usage is the "local community or congregation".

for itself alone, loses its meaning altogether. Christ is the corporate person of the Christian community. The Church is the body of Christ: 1 Cor. 12:12ff.; Rom. 12:4ff.; Eph. 1:23, 4:15f.; Col. 1:18. Christ is in the community as the community is in Christ: 1 Cor. 1:30, 3:16; 2 Cor. 6:16, 13:5; Col. 2:17, 3:11. The community is a corporate person whose name is also Christ: Gal. 3:28; Col. 3:10f.; cf. Eph. 1:23. Note also the expression "put on the new man," which sometimes takes the form, "put on the Lord Jesus": Col. 3:10; Eph. 4:24; Rom. 13:14; Gal. 3:27.

This is why the evangelical idea of the church is conceived in personal terms, *scil* [namely]. God reveals himself as a person in the church. The Christian community is God's final revelation: God as "Christ existing as community," ordained for the rest of time until the end of the world and the return of Christ. It is here that Christ has come the very nearest to humanity, here given himself to his new humanity, so that his person enfolds in itself all whom he has won, binding itself in duty to them, and them reciprocally in duty to him. The "church" therefore has not the meaning of a human community to which Christ is or is not self-superadded, nor of a union among such as individually seek or think to have Christ and wish to cultivate this common "possession"; no, it is a community created by Christ and founded upon him, one in which Christ reveals himself as the *deuteros anthropos,* the new man—or rather, the new humanity itself.

This is where the question of explaining revelation in terms of act or being assumes an entirely new aspect. God gives himself in Christ to his community, and to each individual as a member of that community. This he does in such a way that the active subject in the community, of both the proclamation and the believing of the Word, is Christ. It is in the personal community, and only there, that the gospel can truly be declared and believed. There, it follows, revelation is in some way secured or possessed. God's freedom has bound itself, woven itself into the personal community, and it is precisely that which proves it God's freedom—that he should bind himself to people. The community genuinely has at its disposal the Word of forgiveness; in the community it may not only be said, existentially, "I have been forgiven," but also—by the Christian Church as such, in preaching and sacrament—"thou art forgiven"; furthermore, every member of the Church may and should "become a Christ" to every other in so proclaiming the gospel. [*AB,* pp. 119–22]

REVELATION HAPPENS WITHIN THE COMMUNITY

Revelation, then, happens within the community; it demands primarily a Christian sociology of its own. The distinction between thinking of revelation individualistically and thinking of it in relation to community is fundamental. All the problematics we have examined so far have had an individualist orientation. Both the transcendental essay at act-subjectivism and the ontological attempt to establish the continuity of the *I* envisaged consistently the individual man, and he was the rock on which they both foundered. They overlooked, in searching for "reality," that a person in reality is never *only* the single unit, not even the *one* "claimed by the Thou," but invariably finds himself in some community, whether in "Adam" or in "Christ." The Word of God is given to mankind, the gospel to the community of Christ. When the sociological category is thus introduced, the problem of act and being—and also the problem of knowledge—is presented in a wholly fresh light.

The being of revelation does not lie in a unique occurrence of the past, in an entity which in principle is at my disposal and has no direct connection with my old or my new existence, neither can the being of revelation be conceived solely as the ever-free, pure and non-objective act which at certain times impinges on the existence of individuals. No, the being of revelation "is" the being of the community of persons, constituted and embraced by the person of Christ, wherein the individual finds himself to be already in his new existence.... [*AB*, pp. 122–23]

But the existence of the individual man, hearing the Word on concrete occasions, is vitally affected by this community, inasmuch as, drawn into it, he finds himself already there and as one placed into the truth of his old and new existence. This fact derives from the personal quality of the Christian community, in that its subject is Christ. For only through persons, and only through the person of Christ, can the existence of man be affected, placed into truth and transplanted into a new manner of existing. Since moreover the person of Christ has revealed itself in the community, the human existence can only be so affected through the community. It is only from the person of Christ that other persons acquire for us the character of personhood. In this way they even become Christ for us in what they both demand and promise, in their existential impositions upon us from without. At the same time they become, as such, the pledge of revelation's continuity. If the existence of man were unaffected by revelation within the community, all we have said about the being of revelation in the community would be pointless. Continuity which does not also impinge on existence is not the continuity of the Christian revelation, not present being but bygone entity. In other words, the community guarantees the continuity of revelation only by the fact that I know and believe myself to be in this community. Here the problem of act and being receives its final clarification by taking the shape of the dialectic of faith and church. But more on that later.

If the being of revelation is fixed in entity, it remains past, existentially impotent; if it is volatilized into the nonobjective, its continuity is lost. And so the being of revelation must enjoy a mode of being which satisfies both claims, embodying both the continuity proper to being and the existential significance of the act. It is as such a mode of being that we understand the person and the community. Here the possibility of existential impact is bound up with genuine objectivity in the sense of a concrete standing-over-against: this lets itself be drawn into the power of the *I* because it itself imposes a constraint on existence, because it is *the* extrinsicality.

The community in question is concretely visible, is the Christian Church which hears and believes the preaching of the Word. The Word of this community is preaching and sacrament, its conduct is believing and loving. It is in this concretion that one must think of the being of revelation in "Christ existing as community." [*AB*, pp. 124–25]

Being in Christ, being-directed to Christ, makes existence free; man exists for and through Christ; he believes because he looks on Christ. In defining this faith in terms of pure intentionality one must avoid on the one hand the desire to pinpoint the temporality of faith . . . and on the other hand the desire to locate in the act of belief itself the reflection which discovers faith only in the reflected form of wishful belief. That is the danger in Barth. Faith and "wishful belief" lie together in the same act. Every act of belief is "wishful" in so far as it is a happening embedded in the psychic and there accessible to reflection. But faith properly so called lies in the act's intention toward Christ, which is found in being in the community of Christ. A faith which grows doubtful of itself because it considers itself unworthy is a faith which stands in temptation. Faith *itself* knows that it is not faith *qua opus* (as work) which justifies, but Christ alone, and this it does not need to be told by a reflection which in addition says something quite different, inasmuch as it questions faith and brings it into temptation. Though Barth has theological right on his side when he chides Schleiermacher for his "great confusion" of religion and grace, he undermines his position by introducing reflection into the act of faith itself, therefore indirectly on Christ. This is the penalty paid for inadequately distinguishing between knowing in faith and theological cognition. Furthermore, there is a danger here of inadvertently allowing that more wishful belief truly grasps Christ, whereupon all such ominous words as enthusiasm, the lively sense or religious "experience," piety, feeling, conversion of the will must perforce return to currency. It must be plainly said that within the community of Christ faith takes shape in religion, that therefore religion is here called faith, that, as I look on Christ, I may and must say for my consolation "I believe"—only to add, of course, as I turn to look on myself, "Help Thou my unbelief." All praying, all searching for God in his Word, all clinging to his promise, all entreaty for his grace, all hoping in sight of the cross, all this for reflection is "religion," "wishful belief"; but in the communion of Christ, while it is still a human work, it is God-given faith, faith willed by God, wherein by God's mercy he may really be found. If faith wished to question its own sufficiency it would already have lapsed from intentionality into temptation. Say rather, then, that it assures itself of its content, inasmuch as it holds fast to it, draws it to itself, dwelling thus with undivided attention in the contemplation of Christ, which is destroyed only by reflection on the self. Being in Christ is being turned to Christ, and this is possible only through "being already" (as we have described above) in the community of Christ. And so the transcendental and ontological theses are reunited. . . . [AB, pp. 175–77]

In faith the future is present; but inasmuch as faith suspends itself before the future (knowing itself as the future's mode of being, but not as productive of it), the human "is" in the future of Christ, i.e. never in actless being, never in beingless act.

Willingness to be determined by the future is the eschatological possibility of the child. The child sees itself, in all fear and wonderment, gripped by the onrush of things to come; therefore it can live only for the present, but the grown person, willing to be determined by the present, lapses into the past, into himself, into death and guilt. It is only out of the future that the present can be lived. . . . [AB, p. 182]

The echoless crying out from solitude into the solitude of self, the protest against all kinds of duress, has unexpectedly received an answer: gradually it is resolved into the still and prayerful converse of the child with the Father in the Word of Jesus Christ. In contemplation of Christ, the tormented knowledge of the I's laceration finds the "joyful conscience," confidence, and courage. The slave is unbound. He who has grown to the man in exile and wretchedness grows to be the child as he finds his home. Home is the communion of Christ, which is always "future," the present "in faith," because we are children of the future; always act, because of being; always being, because act.

Here in faith becoming a reality, there in vision perfected, this is the new creation of the new man of the future, who no longer looks back on himself but only away from himself to the revelation of God, to Christ; the man who is born out of the narrowness of the world into the breadth of Heaven, who becomes what he was or, it may be, never was: a creature of God—a child. [AB, pp. 183–84]

Part 2

BONHOEFFER THE TEACHER
AND LECTURER

With his confirmation class, 1932.
From Eberhard Bethge, *Dietrich Bonhoeffer* (New York: Harper & Row, 1970).

Introduction: Christ, the Church, and Peace

Eberhard Bethge reports in his biography that Bonhoeffer began his teaching career as an unsalaried, nonexamining lecturer. As such, he was permitted by university authorities to give as many lectures as he liked on topics of his own concern. He was likewise a nonregistered assistant in the seminar on systematic theology, and not long into his first term he was allowed to take over the actual running of the seminar. Remuneration for this work was slender at best, depending, in the case of his elective lectures, solely on fees from those attracted enough to register for his lectures.[1]

What was Bonhoeffer like as a teacher? Even before his star had begun to rise at the University of Berlin and around the time of his ordination, he took over a confirmation class in the impoverished Zion parish of Prenzlauer Berg, Berlin. The young lads of that class were hardly conditioned by their economic backgrounds and youthful pursuits of chaos for an eager acceptance of catechism lessons. They had driven Bonhoeffer's predecessor to near despair and, according to Bonhoeffer, to an early grave. Bonhoeffer brought quiet and order into the lives of the boys through his own unflappable calm and through the interesting stories of personal experiences and of the black community of Harlem with which he regaled them. After the war, one of these students, Richard Rother, was to describe Bonhoeffer as a "gifted man." Rother considered his companions "fortunate to have such a man as its teacher." He added, "What do boys of that age normally care about the greatness of a man? But we may have felt something of it even then. He was so composed that it was easy for him to guide us; he made us familiar with the catechism in quite a new way, making it alive for us by telling us of many personal experiences. Our class was hardly ever restless, because all of us were keen to have enough time to hear what he had to say to us."[2] Bonhoeffer further endeared himself to these young boys by renting a room in their slumlike neighborhood and instructing his landlady to give them free access to his room during his absences. He also used his more steady income from the university seminar to rent a piece of land in the rural, peaceful countryside of Biesenthal, and he had a hut constructed there to provide the boys weekends away from their drab surroundings.[3]

Accessibility, concern for his students' personal problems, and a giftedness for translating the gospel into practical everyday experience—these were the attributes of Bonhoeffer the catechist for the young confirmands, and they were the same qualities noted by the much older students at the university. We know there soon developed in his classes a firm, loyal following of the young lecturer, many of whom were drawn toward him by the novelty of both his substance and style. His former students have mentioned that part of Bonhoeffer's charm lay in his talent for turning theology into a search for personal meaning. His lectures on the nature of the church, for instance, provoked one student to write that he was fascinated from the very beginning by "the way he saw things; he 'turned them round,' away from where they were stored for everyday use, to the place God had ordained for them. And in the process the values which had been so familiar and natural to us were transformed as if by themselves. To tell the genuine from the unreal question was of the greatest importance for theology. I should have liked to write the whole lecture down, word for word. Every sentence went home; here was a concern for what troubled me, and indeed all of us young people, what we asked and wanted to know."[4] An effort was made in the seminars "to find straight ways of thinking and to learn not to slink off into side issues or to be satisfied with premature cheap answers."[5] Another student praised Bonhoeffer for what he surmised to be a "Kierkegaardian depth" and an "Harnack-like ability for analysis."[6] This was, the student observed, tempered by a pastoral concern for the students and their needs both spiritual and intellectual. Bonhoeffer was, in short, noticed as a rising young sensation in the university world.

But Bonhoeffer was also remembered as "an outsider, not only for the students, but also for the professors."[7] Very quickly he became part of the core of young theologians in opposition to the "Aryanization" of the churches. For this and for what they perceived to be an utter integrity in his presentation of theology, Bonhoeffer's circle of students became in a short span of time his closest colleagues in the church struggle; some would become members of the Confessing Church seminary at Finkenwalde. Reich Church members among professors and students, however, saw in Bonhoeffer only the enigma of a man out of step with the rising political-ecclesial future of Germany. One of Bonhoeffer's former students, Albrecht Schönherr, who later became director of a Preachers' Seminary in Brandenberg-Havel and a bishop in East Germany, once wrote about what it was in Bonhoeffer that fascinated him and other young people. "Nothing in particular," he noted. "His appearance was imposing but not elegant; his voice high, but not rich; his formulations were laborious, not brilliant. Perhaps it was that here we met a quite single-hearted, or in the words of Matthew 6:22, a 'sound' man. Never did I discover in him anything low, undisciplined, mean. He could be relaxed, but he never let himself go. It is for such a life of one piece, such an example that a young person longs. Bonhoeffer detested binding men to himself; perhaps for that very reason so many were drawn to him."[8] Schönherr added that Bonhoeffer represented the "sound life" to which they all aspired. "He willed what he thought. And he thought sharply, logically."[9]

Much of that strength of will and sharpness of mind comes across in the ecumenical conferences and lectures that marked Bonhoeffer as a perceptive interpreter of contemporary events for the churches. Bonhoeffer's interventions in the ecumenical movement of the 1930s were to have far-reaching consequences. Willem Visser 't Hooft, former secretary general of the World Council of Churches, has made it clear that Bonhoeffer's agitating role on behalf of world peace caused the meeting at Fanø, Denmark, to become "a turning point in ecumenical history."[10] According to Otto

Dudzus, it was Bonhoeffer who played the decisive role in the direction the Fanø conference took, seeing "to it that it did not become a non-committal academic event." Dudzus also remembered Visser 't Hooft's comment that "Dietrich Bonhoeffer threw heavy lumps at our feet and said: 'Pick them up.'"[11] One detects in Bonhoeffer's conferences during this phase in his life an eagerness to mobilize support for the Confessing Church through his contacts with the primary movers of the ecumenical movement. But he was even more hopeful that the ecumenical movement might become, in fact, the one church of Jesus Christ, leaving behind the misplaced patriotism and treacherous nationalism that so often became the overriding motivation of individual churches. There is in his conferences a passion for the truth the church is called to be and for Christ's legacy of peace that the church is supposed to foster by its word and witness.

Bethge remarks that Bonhoeffer mobilized his drive to invigorate the ecumenical movement on three fronts. He was, first of all, critical of the movement's leadership for failing to develop a theological foundation sufficiently strong to withstand counterpressures from the watchdogs of national pride. Secondly, he decried the nationalism that would reduce churches to moralizing adjuncts of public policy. Thirdly, he blasted the escapist tactics of the churches to issue face-saving but ineffective resolutions that only covered up the idle talk, timidity, and lack of consciousness of their mission to be church. The only attitude he could countenance was that the ecumenical movement cease its dependence on politics and answer the challenge to be church by effectively delivering the gospel call for peace.[12] He had the knack, as Otto Dudzus has remarked of his sermon at Fanø, for charging "so far ahead that the Conference could not follow him."[13] Few would join Bonhoeffer in his unpopular stands against the easy diplomatic routes the churches preferred to take in the face of rising militarism and the cruel suppression of human rights so characteristic of the Nazi era. His vindication would come only after the war, when the demands and concerns of Bonhoeffer were incorporated into the declared theological foundations and ecumenical agenda of the World Council of Churches.

The selections included in part 2 are divided into three sections. The first of these include his lectures and conferences of 1931–1932: his lectures at Berlin on the nature of the church, his address, "Thy Kingdom Come: The Prayer of the Church for the Kingdom of God," for the "week of repentance," in Potsdam-Hermannswerder, his talk on "Christ and Peace" for the German Student Christian Movement, an ecumenical conference in Czechoslovakia on the theological basis of the ecumenical movement, and the unsettling lecture at the international youth conference in Switzerland, entitled "The Church Is Dead." The second set of excerpts are from his lectures on "Creation and Fall," delivered during the winter semester, 1932–1933 in Berlin. This is followed by selections from the lectures on Christ during the summer semester, 1933. Although they are not the sum total of Bonhoeffer's teaching career, it is hoped that these selections illustrate both the style and the substance of Bonhoeffer as a teacher revered by his students both as a person and for what he had to say.

4

The Nature of the Church

(Das Wesen der Kirche)

Summer 1932

Bonhoeffer's lectures "The Nature of the Church" were delivered in a political-ecclesial tension that had led people cynically to question whether there was any need at all for a church. Bonhoeffer addressed this question in these lectures to his students and attempted, at least in part, to answer it. Gone are the ponderous analyses of the Berlin dissertations. Bonhoeffer's ecclesiology had in the meantime been tempered by his experiences among both bourgeois businessmen and the newly impoverished in Barcelona, by his associations with the socially active church of North America, and by influential friends, such as Paul Lehmann and Jean Lasserre, whose thought turned so readily to social responsibility and the call to be an international brotherhood and sisterhood in Christ. It was this newly acquired sensitivity to the wider responsibility of Christians that would excite his students most. While most of the theology students at the University of Berlin were pro-Nazi, those who sat for Bonhoeffer's lectures were soon recognized for their opposition to the Nazi regime. Later, they would form the core group who met with Bonhoeffer evenings and weekends to discuss politics, church, and a gospel service to the poor. Many of these students would likewise become part of Bonhoeffer's "Youth Delegation" to international ecumenical conferences and comprise the first classes at the illegal seminary at Finkenwalde that Bonhoeffer directed in the mid-1930s.

What is noteworthy about these lectures, reproduced here in chapter 4, is the manner in which Bonhoeffer depicted the church's location and mission within the everyday reality of secular life. The church, he insisted, is not called to be a tiny, sacred haven from the world but, like Jesus, a presence in the very midst of the world. The world of the present time itself, not some heavenly cloud, is the only locus of church life, though this way of understanding its mission might lead the church into difficult and controversial areas of struggle with evil where it would be impossible to maintain an untainted ecclesial purity. This church is to be neither a church of privilege nor a church totally absorbed into the secularisms of the day. It is to be, rather, the community of Jesus Christ within the world, yet free enough from the world to deny secular idolatries, to confess faith in the one Lord Jesus, and to do the courageous deed of service to others. Such service was to be not only the church's primary mode of obeying God's commanding Word in any age but also the church's primary confession of faith before the world. We see here the initial references by Bonhoeffer to a "Discipline of the Secret" (*Arkanum*), a phrase that became an important aspect of his concepts of religion and worldliness in the later prison letters. In one of his most memorable sentences, Bonhoeffer declared that "the primary confession of the Christian before the world is the deed which interprets itself."

The selections from these lectures that follow appear in English translation for the first time. They are based on a text that derives from the synthesis of the student notes of Hanns Rüppell and Wolf-Dieter Zimmermann, edited by Eberhard Bethge in collaboration with Otto Dudzus for *Gesammelte Schriften*, III. The text, such as it is, emphasizes Bonhoeffer's attempt to give a balanced assessment of the church as worldly and of the church as embodying the service of people that character- ized Christ's own mission and his present mandate to Christian communities' prom- ise of fulfilling their citizens' dreams of freedom through a law and order that enhance and protect human life. Such law and order are themselves under the judgment of Christ's cross, Bonhoeffer is quick to point out, and therefore limited by, the meaning of that cross for the hopes of all people. Here again Christ be- comes in Bonhoeffer's lectures the center for any judgment on what is meaningful or demeaning human life and what is responsible and free in human action. Christ is, as the selections (taken from a corrected translation published by William Col- lins Sons & Co., London, 1978) that follow show, the Word of meaning and re- sponsibility both in the Christian communities and in the history to be shaped by him. These lectures marked the end of Bonhoeffer's university career, prompting Professor Arthur Titius, who held the other chair of systematic theology at the uni- versity, to lament: "It is a great pity that our best hope in the faculty is being wasted on the church struggle."[14] Historians of the ecumenical movement and of the church struggle have argued that, far from squandering his energies in moving away from the university, Bonhoeffer's decision to enter the "real world" of the church conflict with nazism would have momentous consequences for the future.

The new situation is marked on the one hand by our church's lack of a place. It wants to be everywhere and is, therefore, nowhere. It cannot be grasped and, therefore, cannot be attacked. It exists only in disguise. It would turn into the world without the world's becoming church. Being without a place is the "being of Cain," the fugitive. On the run from itself, the church has fallen today into a deep contempt. People have taken sects more seriously than church, since they at least stand for something definite. A thing can be depicted only within a particular place. In this way the nature and claims of a specific reality achieve some sort of clarity. While the specific place is occupied no other reality can lay claim to it. Like the church itself, so the church's concept of God is without concrete demand and place, everywhere and nowhere. The church no longer had heart for solitude in its specific place in the world.

On the other hand, the church in forfeiting its own place can now be found only in the privileged places of the world. It feels itself more at home in one place than in another. The decision in favor of a specific place demonstrates degrees of difference in its capacity for adaptation. It has lost the measure for determining its *true* place. Now the church is hated for having occupied the privileged places. Such are those where its strong identification with commitments of an outmoded time is still cherished: among the bourgeois and that spurious conservatism which clings to the old ways of doing things. In contrast with this, there is also a conservatism linked with a specific commitment but which knows something about the relativity of every succeeding social organization and structure. Our church, however, has settled into only the former kind of conservatism. Its religious services meet the needs only of the petit bourgeois. The needs of the business leaders, of intellectuals, of the enemies of the churches, of revolutionaries, are ignored. It has settled down in a swirl of worldly ceremonies and has itself become radically secularized.

According to Otto Dibelius, for the first time since 1918, the church is fully independent. But in no way is this independence that of its having achieved its own place. Rather, it exists only in the place dictated to it as a "gracious gift" by the autonomous culture. Autonomous only in its own imagination, it has been harmoniously absorbed into culture as a whole! One cultural form next to another, in bondage to the culture as a whole! One superficial view of this also makes it clear that it is not a question here of a proper *place* but of a *privileged* place.

What is the proper place of the church? It is certainly not concretely declared beforehand. It is the place of Christ present in the world. God's will chooses this or that locus for it. Therefore it is neither demonstrable nor receivable by people beforehand. God qualifies it through his gracious presence. One must confess that this place belongs to him. The order to make some historical place into God's place has not been confided to the church. Neither the state church nor some petit bourgeois center, for no human person, but God alone determines this place. The church which is aware of this waits for the word that transforms it into God's place in the world. Waiting on God's choice, it avoids becoming established in some privileged place. Such a church has the promise of God. Only in this way has it escaped the vagaries of human placelessness. Where no human place can any longer be the ground of the church, God will be there with his community, even in the midst of culture. Hence the same "yes!" and the same "no!" is pronounced on every "human" place of the church. All of these are in need in a similar way of God's coming, where God speaks with his community. This community is the absolute center of every human place, even though at this precise point it may appear to be superfluous in certain human situations. However, whether it is loved or hated, no longer is it about its proper calling for the sake of the gospel, since it has settled down in places of privilege. It is called to be the critical center from which everything will be judged. God himself is the judgment, not the pastor and not the church. Nobody knows beforehand where this center may be. If we follow historical criteria it may be entirely on the periphery, just as Galilee in the Roman world or Wittenberg in the sixteenth century. But God will make this place visible and each one must take notice of it. The church can only witness from the midst of the world that God alone creates. It must try to make space for God's action in the world.

THE PLACE OF THE CHURCH IN CHRISTIANITY

The church and Christianity are not identical. What is the basis of hatred against the church since such hatred is apparently not directed against Christians? Would such hatred be fired up by the fact that the church exists only on the periphery of life, where the life of an individual experiences high or turning points of church activity? There the church is especially to be found. Nature and celebration go together, we believe. The church serves as link between them. Thus church celebrations of nature are bestowed upon us. The church becomes the exception to what happens daily; it becomes feast. It is sought out and is in demand in order to break up the humdrum of daily existence. Commonplace thoughts ought to be covered over in church festivity. The church has to divert, deepen, and ennoble. Religious services are oriented toward church feasts under the law and dictate of everyday existence. What the common person under the stress of raising his standard of living expects from the church, that it also does. It feels itself to be indispensable in this matter. But because of this the churches only become more empty. The cinema meets the need to celebrate better than the church. Here at least one remains tragic or comic or even criminal but in the secular realm. The extent of this is revealed when one goes to the cinema and not to the church for the holiday celebration. The present-day church is Christianity celebrating only from afar. It thereby stands at the periphery and not at the center of life. It would like, however, to stand at the center and speak from the periphery about the central questions of life in a censuring and condemning way. It thus makes itself contemptuous and hated.

What is the proper place of the church in Christianity? The entire daily reality of the world and not any one single aspect, even if it be the ethical or religious. . . . [GS, V, pp. 231–33]

FORM OF THE CHURCH: THE CONFESSION OF FAITH

Gathering together and the office of preaching belong to the community. However, in this regard, it must acknowledge that it lives by God's Word alone. It does this in confessing its faith. By preaching it thereby confesses this and where this is confessed, there new preaching arises. No religious service should be without confession of faith. This differentiates the community from the general public. The community must either confess its faith or disavow it. It cannot, like the general public, remain undecided. Aesthetic hesitations do not count for much here. Confession of faith is the only genuine attitude with which the community entrusts itself. It orders its life both inwardly and outwardly through the confession of faith. Through this confession the community distinguishes itself from the world.

The confession of faith must be a wholly sincere response to God's Word of truth. Confession of faith is a matter of immediate presence. It doesn't pertain to aesthetic judgments; nor is it prayed for; it can only be confessed: "I acknowledge and confess your truth, O God." The apostolic confession doesn't suffice. Here the questions raised by Harnack and liberal theology are far from being settled. Confession of faith is a matter of our true, present stance before God. Here no definitive role has been granted to mere tradition. The spoken word itself, and not just what is meant, must be genuine in our confession of faith. For the sake of our love of the community our word ought to be clear and unequivocal. The community has a right to this since such serves its well-being. Often the confession of faith is a deterrent in our religious services.

Likewise, with respect to nonbelievers our word ought to be clear and unequivocal so that we don't drive them away from the church. The perspective of mutuality with all of Christendom that is ever again alleged against any change or setting aside of the "apostolic" tradition doesn't work here. The Bible, the Our Father, and baptism are held in common, but they are not the confession of faith. . . .

Confession of faith is not to be confused with professing a religion. Such profession uses the confession as propaganda and ammunition against the Godless. The confession of faith belongs rather to the "Discipline of the Secret" (Arkanum) in the Christian gathering of those who believe. Nowhere else is it tenable. It is, for example, untenable in the new "Confession sessions" now coming into vogue in which one dialogues with those antagonistic to faith. The primary confession of the Christian before the world is the deed which interprets itself. If this deed is to have become a force, then the world itself will long to confess the Word. This is not the same as loudly shrieking out propaganda. This Word must be preserved as the most sacred possession of the community. This is a matter between God and the community, not between the community and the world. It is the Word of recognition between friends, not a word to use against enemies. This attitude was first learned at baptism. The deed alone is our confession of faith before the world. [GS, V, pp. 258–59]

WORLDINESS AND CHRISTIANITY OF THE CHURCH (1932)

All this time we have been speaking about our concrete church. It is the real church. We don't wait for it to become a reality, but rather it is already there. We live with a view to church, not in a kind of Advent but in the fulfillment that has dawned. Christ is present in his church today. This church is no ideal church, but a reality in the world, a bit of the world reality. The secularity of the church follows from the incarnation of Christ. The church, like Christ, has become world. It is a denial of the real humanity of Jesus and also heretical to take the concrete church as only a phantom church or an illusion. It is entirely world. This means that it is subjected to all the weakness and suffering of the world. The church can at times, like Christ himself, be without a roof over its head. This must be so. For the sake of real people, the church must be thoroughly worldly. It is a worldly reality for our sakes. Real secularity consists in the church's being able to renounce all privileges and all its property but never Christ's Word and the forgiveness of sins. With Christ and the forgiveness of sins to fall back on, the church is free to give up everything else.

While the church is in the world and is even a bit of the world, it cannot hope to represent itself as a visible communion of saints. Secularity means renunciation of the ideal of purity. This has nothing to do with secularization. The church has been in process of becoming world, not some "pure" entity, since its origins. Not even primitive Christianity was "pure." Otherwise, one confuses church with a religious community and the gospel with the ideal of an experience. Perfectionistic sectarianism from Greek mysticism to Tolstoy has attempted to usurp the Kingdom of God for itself (Matt. 11:12). They pretend to have revealed this kingdom. They pretend to have made it clearly visible in the holiness of people. However, the church, having become the worldly form of revelation, ought not to succumb to this temptation. It ought not to seek to justify itself before itself and before the world. Its justification comes from God alone. It cannot anticipate the last judgment. "You shall not judge!" also applies here. God has reserved to himself the separation of the wheat from the chaff.

The church likewise remains the church of the baptized and, therefore, a communion of sinners. Every baptized person belongs to it, no matter what his works may seem to be. Renunciation of its claims to "purity" leads the church back to its solidarity with the sinful world. Through courageous acknowledgment of its being world, the church is perfectly free from the world to become Christian. It has no more respect for the "shrines" of the world. Face to face with outcasts, it is as free as the nobility. It has as its place not only with the poor but also with the rich; not only with the pious, but also with the Godless. All are world. It faces both groups with the same impartiality. There is no sphere from which it distances itself out of anxiety over going astray. Faith has completely conquered the world both for the outcast and for the rich. Only this kind of church is wholly free, the church that confesses its secularity and thereby claims to be an *ecclesia perfecta*, or perfect church. [*GS*, V, pp. 270–71]

5

Thy Kingdom Come:
The Prayer of the Church for
the Kingdom of God on Earth

(Dein Reich Komme)

November 19, 1932

The lectures on the nature of the church and Bonhoeffer's address of November 19, 1932, "Thy Kingdom Come," indicate that the strong Christian secularity emphasized in the prison letters is a processive echo to the worldliness of church he was affirming in 1932. This worldliness, he would argue, was the God-given setting of Christian faith. Awareness of its own sociohistorical grounding in the human should have forced Christianity to purge itself of all traces of the mythical, otherworldly debris that had hidden the true calling of the church to be the church of Christ. Christianity was neither an archaic replica of the heavenly world nor a cluster of sacred shrines and hallowed sanctuaries, magic escape routes from earthly turmoil. Rather, the Christian is to live faith as much in the marketplace and factory as at church altars. Faith is thus to be embedded in the way each Christian becomes strong in his or her service of earth and its people.

Bonhoeffer had been asked as lecturer at the university to speak at this conference by Johannes Kuhne, then director of studies of the Hoffbauer School in Potsdam-Hermannswerder, as part of a series of lectures to be presented during the last week of the church year, the "Week of Repentance." As his subtitle indicates, he is offering his own commentary on the petition of the church's prayer that begs for God's kingdom to come upon this earth. But he quickly turns the commentary into an exhortation for the church to divest itself of its escapist otherworldliness and to recognize its responsibility to shape this world in the image of Christ by truly becoming strong in God's Word and Christ's compassion for the oppressed.

This attitude has enormous implications for the relationship between church and state. Here, as in the ecumenical conferences of the same period, Bonhoeffer argues that the "orders" that define the responsibilities of the individual Christian and the church toward the world and, likewise, the responsibilities of states toward their people are not "orders of creation" but "orders of preservation." He feared that in the hands of opportunists the idea, "order of creation," could be twisted to mean that the state had a right, God given from the very fact of creation, to declare its actions, decisions, and laws fully in accord with some divine plan. In this way blatant evils like war, class struggle, racism, and the economic exploitation of the poor could be justified as bound up in the creation itself.

The selection that follows is from John D. Godsey's translation, *Preface to Bonhoeffer: The Man and Two of His Shorter Writings*. Godsey's translation is based on the edition by Eberhard Bethge, *Dein Reich Komme* (Hamburg: Furche Verlag, 1957). It first appeared, together with a similar address by Johannes Schneider, a colleague of Bonhoeffer at the University of Berlin who had spoken on "The Biblical Message of the Kingdom of God," as Number 78 in the series published by Furche Verlag and called *Stimmen aus der deutschen christlichen Studentenbewegung* (Voices from the Christian Student Movement in Germany).

We are otherworldly—ever since we hit upon the devious trick of being religious, yes even "Christian," at the expense of the earth. Otherworldliness affords a splendid environment in which to live. Whenever life begins to become oppressive and troublesome a person just leaps into the air with a bold kick and soars relieved and unencumbered into so-called eternal fields. He leaps over the present. He disdains the earth; he is better than it. After all, besides the temporal defeats he still has his eternal victories, and they are so easily achieved. Otherworldliness also makes it easy to preach and to speak words of comfort. An otherworldly church can be certain that it will in no time win over all the weaklings, all who are only too glad to be deceived and deluded, all utopianists, all disloyal sons of the earth. When an explosion seems imminent, who would not be so human as to quickly mount the chariot that comes down from the skies with the promise of taking him to a better world beyond? What church would be so merciless, so inhuman, as not to deal compassionately with this weakness of suffering men— thereby save souls for the kingdom of heaven? Man is weak; he cannot bear having the earth so near, the earth that bears him. He cannot stand it, because the earth is stronger than he and because he wants to be better than the evil earth. So he extricates himself from it; he refuses to take it seriously. Who could blame him for that—who but the have-nots in their envy? Man is weak, that's just the way he is; and this weakling man is open to the religion of otherworldliness. "Should it be denied him? Should the weakling remain without help? Would that be in the spirit of Jesus Christ? No, the weak man should receive help. He does in fact receive help, from Christ. However, Christ does not will or intend this weakness; instead, he makes man strong. He does not lead man in a religious flight from this world to other worlds beyond; rather, he gives him back to the earth as its loyal son.

Be not otherworldly, but be strong!

Or we are children of the world. Whoever feels that what has been said thus far does not apply to him at all had better watch out that what is now about to be said does not strike painfully home. We have fallen into secularism, and by secularism I mean pious, Christian secularism. Not the godlessness of atheism or cultural bolshevism, but the Christian renunciation of God as the Lord of the earth. In this renunciation it becomes evident that we are indeed bound to the earth. We have to struggle with the earth to come to terms with it. There is no other way. Power stands against power. World stands against church, worldliness against religion. How could it be otherwise than that religion and church are forced into this controversy, into this struggle? Moreover, faith is compelled to harden into religious habit and into morality, and the church must become an organ for effecting religious and moral reconstruction. So faith spruces up its weapons because the powers of the earth compel it to do so. After all, we are supposed to represent God's cause. We have to build for ourselves a strong fortress in which we dwell safe and secure with God. We will build the kingdom.

This joyous secularism also affords a splendid environment in which to live. Man—even religious man—likes a good fight; he likes to put his strength to the test. Who would begrudge him this gift of nature—who but the have-nots in their envy? This pious secularism also makes it possible to preach and to say nice things. The church may be certain, if only it makes a somewhat more spirited effort in this direction, that it soon will have on its side in this happy war all the brave, the resolute, the well-intentioned, all the overly loyal sons of the earth. What upright man would not gladly represent the cause of God in this wicked world and do as the ancient Egyptians are said to have done? They carried the images of their gods against the enemy—in order to hide behind them! Only now man wants to hide not just from the enemy, the world, but from God himself, from that God who destroys whoever would front for him on earth. It is not God's will that any man, on the sheer strength of his own superabundant power, should take over for God on earth, like the strong take care of the helpless. On the contrary, God manages his own cause; and out of his own free grace he accepts man, or does not accept him. God himself intends to be Lord on earth, and he regards all man's exuberant zeal on his behalf as a real disservice. Herein lies our Christian secularism, that in our very desire to see that God gets everything that is his due in the world we actually evade God himself, and so love the earth for its own sake, for the sake of this struggle. But we do not thereby really elude God. He always brings us back under his own lordship.

Become weak in the world and let God be the Lord? . . . [*Thy Kingdom Come*, pp. 28–31]

The kingdom of God exists in our world exclusively in the duality of church and state. Each is necessarily related to the other; neither exists for itself. Every attempt of one to take control of the other disregards this relationship of the kingdom of God on earth. Every prayer for the coming of the kingdom to us that does not have in mind both church and state is either otherworldliness or secularism. It is, in any case, disbelief in the kingdom of God.

The kingdom of God assumes form in the church insofar as the church bears witness to the miracle of God. The function of the church is to witness to the resurrection of Christ from the dead, to the end of the law of death of this world that stands under the curse, and to the power of God in the new creation. The kingdom of God assumes form in the state insofar as the state acknowledges and maintains the order of the preservation of life, and insofar as it holds itself responsible for protecting this world from flying to pieces and for exercising its authority here in preventing the destruction of life. Its function is not to create new life, but to preserve the life that is given.

Therefore, the power of death, of which we spoke, is destroyed in the church by the authoritative witness to the miracle of the resurrection, whereas in the state it is restrained by the order of the preservation of life. With its complete authority, with which it knows itself solely responsible for the order of life, the state points to the church's witness to the breaking up of the law of death in the world of the resurrection; and with its witness to the resurrection, the church points to the preserving, ordering action of the state in the preserved world of the curse. Thus they both witness to the kingdom of God, which is entirely God's kingdom and wholly a kingdom for us.

The kingdom of God assumes form in the church insofar as here the loneliness of man is overcome through the miracle of confession and forgiveness. This is because in the church, which is the communion of saints created by the resurrection, one person can and should bear the guilt of another, and for this reason the last shackle of loneliness, hatred of others, is removed, and community is established and created anew. It is through the miracle of confession, which is beyond all our understanding, that all hitherto existing community is shown to have been an illusion and is abolished, destroyed, and broken asunder, and that here and now the new congregation of the resurrection world is created.

The kingdom of God assumes form in the state insofar as here the orders of existing communities are maintained with authority and responsibility. Lest mankind fall apart through the desires of individuals who want simply to go their own way, the state takes the responsibility in a world under the curse for the preservation of the orders of communities, such as marriage, family, and nation. Not the creation of new communities, but the preservation of communities is given in the function of the state.

In the church the power of loneliness is destroyed in the confession-occurrence; in the state it is restrained through the preservation of community order. And, again, in its limited action the state points to the final miracle of God in the resurrection, just as in its authoritative witness to God's breaking through to the world, the church points to the maintenance of order in the world under the curse.... [*Thy Kingdom Come* pp. 40–42]

In the church the power of desire is overcome and transfigured, whereas in the state it is regulated and held in check. Here also the limited action of the state points to the authoritative testimony of the church, just as the church points to the order of the state, which in this world under the curse carries out its function.

The church limits the state, just as the state limits the church, and each must remain conscious of this mutual limitation. Furthermore, each must bear the tension of coexistence, which in this world must never be a coalescence. Only thus do both together, and never one alone, point to the kingdom of God, which here is attested in such a wonderful twofold form.... [*Thy Kingdom Come* pp. 42–43]

The kingdom of Christ is God's kingdom, but God's kingdom in the form appointed for us. It does not appear as one, visible, powerful empire, nor yet as the "new" kingdom of the world; on the contrary, it manifests itself as the kingdom of the other world that has entered completely into the discord and contradiction of this world. It appears as the powerless, defenseless gospel of the resurrection, of the miracle; and, at the very same time, as the state that possesses authority and power and maintains order. The kingdom of Christ becomes a reality only when these two are genuinely related to each other and yet mutually limit one another.

What has been said so far may sound sober, and it is supposed to; only in this way are we called to obedience, namely, when it is understood as obedience to God in the church and in the state. The kingdom of God is not to be found in some other world beyond, but in the midst of this world. Our obedience is demanded in terms of its contradictory appearance, and, then, through our obedience, the miracle, like lightning, is allowed to flash up again and again from the perfect, blessed new world of the final promise. God wants us to honor him on earth; he wants us to honor him in our fellow man and woman—and nowhere else. He sinks his kingdom down into the cursed ground. Let us open our eyes, become sober, and obey him here. "Come, O blessed of my Father, inherit the kingdom!" This the Lord will say to no other than the one to whom he says, "I was hungry and you gave me food, I was thirsty and you gave me drink.... As you did it to one of the least of my brethren, you did it to me" (Matt. 25:34, 35, 40). [*Thy Kingdom Come*, pp. 44–45]

6

Christ and Peace

(Christus und der Friede)

Fall, 1932

Bonhoeffer delivered this as an introductory talk to a discussion of the German Student Christian Movement in Berlin sometime in late summer or the fall of 1932. The address shows the concrete direction he would take his proposal that Christian students of Germany become strong advocates of peace through solidarity with peoples in their common humanity and in their common faith in Jesus. His point of departure, according to the surviving notes, was the recent failure of the Geneva conference on disarmament, a failure attributed to Papen's announcement that Germany would no longer take part in the negotiations. This talk was the highlight of an "ecumenical evening" sponsored by the German Student Christian Movement and became a catalyst for the discussions of that evening. Using Matthew 28:37–38 as his foundation, Bonhoeffer jolted his audience with a sharp, uncompromising insistence on uniting a professed faith in Christ with the peace issue. From the notes that we have translated here in their entirety for the first time, we can see that even before the anti-Jewish legislation of 1933, the initial phase of the church struggle, and his disturbing indictment of "cheap grace" in *The Cost of Discipleship*, Bonhoeffer was already attempting to challenge his church to take seriously the demands that the church itself become the means of achieving Christ's legacy of peace to the world. The text here is taken from the notes by Jürgen Winterhager in *Gesammette Schriften,* V.

You shall love the Lord, your God, with all your heart, with all your soul, and with all your strength. This is the first and greatest commandment. The other is like unto this. You shall love your neighbor as yourself. (Matt. 22:37–39)

Once again we observe human authorities who, having attempted to set up peace on a political basis, have now come to grief. And it would be good to ponder this and not find it too astonishing since, for all they do, *worldly courts of justice* are still set up by humans. They lack, therefore, any absolute authority. There is only one authority, the one who has spoken in a binding way on this question, and that is Jesus Christ.

Christ has, indeed, not given us precise instructions for every possibility in the political, economic, or other aspects of the life of people confronting complicated and unique situations. That doesn't mean, however, that the message of Jesus Christ has nothing clear to say to the problems set before us. For the simple reader, the Sermon on the Mount says things that are entirely unmistakable.

We wish to proceed here from this central issue of the New Testament. Hence we will consider these questions from the point of view of the highest and most important commandment, and in this perspective we will examine what the Lord has preached on this. We do not want to remove a single word about worldly authority from the entire context of the New Testament, for such would deny that Christ proclaimed the kingdom of God against which the whole world, including ruling powers, lives in enmity.

First of all, let us take up those individual points that readily give rise to misunderstandings.

1. For Christ it is not a question of changing the conditions of this world for the sake of our security and quiet. Still less ought we to think we are able to do away with the horror of war through political agreements that serve only to give expression to our sins. So long as the world is without God, there will be wars. For Christ, rather, it is a matter of our loving God and standing in discipleship to Jesus in whom we are called with the promise of blessedness to become witnesses for peace.

This *discipleship of Christ* comes from and depends entirely on simple *faith.* On the other hand this faith is genuine only in discipleship. Thus believers are addressed and the world is judged by Christ's witness for peace. This faith must, however, be simple. Otherwise it produces mere reflection on itself, not obedience. It might also learn only the wrong slant on things; doing what is "correct" but not really engaged in discipleship that knows nothing of the fine distinction between good and evil. Only from the viewpoint of such discipleship do we likewise have the right attitude toward those who give their lives in war.

There are, therefore, no human possibilities of assuring or organizing peace. Indeed, this human effort, using political means to achieve peace, can lead directly to the sins of domineering over an independent people. There is no assured peace. The Christian can aspire to peace only from faith. There is no direct achievement of brotherhood and sisterhood among people. There is access to one's enemy only through prayer to the Lord of all peoples and nations.

2. On the other hand, the relationship between law and gospel is often misunderstood. The gospel is then interpreted as the message of that forgiveness of sins which does not in any special way affect civil life and,

indeed, the entire earthly existence of people. There people are emphatically informed they are sinners but they are, however, not called away from either their sins or their evil situation. How are we to go on believing in God with pure hearts if we refuse to follow the path of obedience by our sinning in expectation of the grace of forgiveness and our not taking seriously that grace and especially our prayer to God? We thus make grace cheap and with the justification of the sinner through the cross of Christ, we thereby forget the cry of the Lord who never justifies sin. The command, "you shall not kill," and the Word, "love your enemy," are given to us simply to obey. Every form of war service, unless it be Good Samaritan service, and every preparation for war, is forbidden for the Christian. Faith that sees freedom from the law as a mere arbitrary disposal of the law is only human faith in defiance of God. Simple obedience knows nothing of the fine distinction between good and evil. It lives in the discipleship of Christ and does the good work as something self-evident.

3. We Christians are above all addressed by the command of love to the point that we ourselves must live in peace with every person, just like Christ when he preached peace to the community, exemplified in peace with one's brother and sister, with one's neighbor, with the Samaritan. Unless we have this peace, we cannot preach peace to people. Most who are annoyed at the word of peace among peoples, moreover, are already calling in question the love of enemies over against the personal enemy. When we wish to speak about the conditions for peace, therefore, we would do well always to keep before our eyes the fact that relationships between two nations bear close analogy to relationships between two individuals. The conditions that are opposed to peace are in the one as in the other relationship: lust for power, pride, inordinate desire for glory and honor, arrogance, feelings of inferiority, and strife over more living space and over one's "bread" or life. What is sin for an individual is never virtue for an entire people or nation. What is proclaimed as the gospel to the church, the congregation, and, thereby, the individual Christian, is spoken to the world as a judgment. When a people refuses to hear this command, then Christians are called forth from that people to give witness to peace. Let us take care, however, that we miserable sinners proclaim peace from a spirit of love and not from any zeal for security or from any mere political aim.

4. Peace with whom? True peace lies only in God and from God. This peace is given us with Christ; that is to say, this peace is inseparably bound up with the gospel. Peace cannot, therefore, consist in harmonizing the gospel with religious worldviews. Jesus delcares this: "I am not called to send peace but a sword" (Matt. 10:34). Forgiveness of sins is extended to the repentant sinner and to the sinner who has gone astray. We ought to love him, not pass judgment on him. But there is no reconciliation either with sin or with false teaching. In the struggle of the gospel with these earthly forces, the Christian is separated from father

and mother. The struggle of the Christian is thus a struggle for the "cause" of the gospel. The weapons in this conflict with the enemy of the gospel are faith and love, which is purified by suffering. How much greater this than the conflict for mere earthly goods. [*GS*, pp. 359–62]

7

On the Theological Basis of the Work of the World Alliance

(Zur theologischen Begründung der Weltbundarbeit)

July 26, 1932

Bonhoeffer's passionate outspokenness on the issue of peace was never so much in evidence as at the Youth Peace Conference at Cernohorske-Kupele, Czechoslovakia. The announced title of the lecture Bonhoeffer presented there, listed above, is deceptive. Indeed, in the company of talks entitled "Present-day Youth and Its Attitude to Spiritual Ideals" and "Public Opinion and World Peace," Bonhoeffer's lecture title seemed to promise in advance only tediousness. In retrospect, the others were the tedious lectures and part of the reason Bonhoeffer complained afterward that the conference itself was "mediocre." His own contribution is now considered a vital step toward the later, postwar commitment of the World Council of Churches to world peace. What he said on that occasion would have enormous implications for the ecumenical movement's self-understanding, even though he realized then that the assembled delegates were not ready for what he was proposing. His views were hardly popular in the rampant nationalism of the 1930s.

Yet, as his address so clearly indicates, unless the World Alliance for Promoting International Friendship through the Churches could move in the direction he suggested, it was doomed to remain a vapid, clublike gathering of isolated churches wasting "their time in idle talk," and issuing pious, ineffective resolutions. In other words, the World Alliance, forerunner of the World Council of Churches, was being urged by Bonhoeffer to accept the mission, then seen as impossible, to become the one church of Jesus Christ. This would mean leaving behind the easy busywork of compiling statistics of membership and buildings, the comfortable teas and polite chatter, and undertaking to confess the one faith in Jesus and to test their professed unity with enough courage to tackle the problem of peace in a divided world.

In this lecture, Bonhoeffer reiterated his attack on the concept of "orders of creation" and the criticism of the reasoning of its principal advocate, Professor Wilhelm

Stahlin of Münster, that he had made at a Berlin Youth Conference of 1932. In that conference, he had stated that "it was impossible to single out some features of the world above others as orders of creation and base a course of Christian moral action upon them." Advocates of these "orders" had made it easy for the churches to overlook the evidence of individual and corporate evil in government policies; indeed, to claim that such evil may have God's own blessing. Bonhoeffer proposed, instead, that in the mutuality of church and state, each affirms the "orders of preservation."[15]

In elaborating on the significance in this change of terminology, Bonhoeffer argued that, if God's revelation in Christ can turn the church inside out toward the world to preserve the world in Christ's truth, the state, in turn, exists to preserve life and to prevent the destruction of life. All actions of the state are, therefore, subjected to God's revelation in Christ. It is for his sake that an order is to be preserved. It is because an "order" of the state can be so anti-Christ that the church in the name of Christ can oppose it. It is not difficult to see in that section of the conference Bonhoeffer's rejection of the absolutist claims of the state to use people for its own destructive ends. Both church and state must witness to God's kingdom in a world under "the power of God in the new creation." The church reminds the state that God is to be honored in one's fellow man and woman. Both church and state must live in solidarity with even the "least" of their people.

We see coming together in this talk nearly all of the main concerns of Bonhoeffer in the 1930s. He demands that the church come to grips with its claim to be Christ for the world, to become the "one community of the Lord Jesus" and to proclaim that the whole world belongs to Christ, that the church be brave enough to speak the concrete word and not cower behind the cover of pious generalities, and, in particular, that the church not fudge the most obvious test of its courage in confessing faith in Jesus, and in commitment in word and deeds to the forgiveness of sins and the peace issue. This is, he claims, the ultimate ground on which the ecumenical work of the church stands or falls.

Qualified silence might perhaps be more appropriate for the church today than talk which is very unqualified. That means protest against any form of the church which does not honor the question of truth above all things. And the next thing is the demand that this question now be put again in all seriousness. The concern of youth deeply involved in ecumenical work is this: How does our ecumenical work, or the work of the World Alliance, look in the mirror of the truth of the gospel? And we feel that we cannot approach such questions in any other way than by new, strict theological work on the biblical and Reformation basis of our ecumenical understanding of the church, in complete seriousness and without regard for its consequences or its success. We ask for a responsible theology of the ecumenical movement for the sake of the truth and the certainty of our cause.

What follows is intended as an attempt to show the outlines of some of the basic theological questions which particularly concern our work in the World Alliance and to demonstrate their theological significance. We are unreservedly concerned with the questions which are put from within, not from outside, from the place of an onlooker. But to those who nevertheless consider these questions to be questions "from the outside," let it be said that it is just these questions which *today* are being put from within.

Our work in the World Alliance is based—consciously or unconsciously—on a quite definite view of the church. The church as the one community of the Lord Jesus Christ, who is Lord of the world, has the commission to say his Word to the whole world. The territory of the one church of Christ is the whole world. Each individual church has geographical limits drawn to its own preaching, but the *one* church has no limits. And the churches of the World Alliance have associated themselves together the better to be able to express this their claim to the whole world, or rather this claim of their Lord's to the whole world. They understand it as the task of the church to make the claim of Jesus Christ clear to the whole world. And this includes the repudiation of the idea that there are divinely willed, special spheres of life which are removed from the lordship of Jesus Christ, which need not hear this word. It is not a holy sacred part of the world which belongs to Christ, but the whole world. . . .

Because of the *Christus praesens*, the word of the church here and now must be a valid, binding word. Someone can only speak to me with authority if a word from the deepest knowledge of my humanity encounters me here and now in all my reality. Any other word is impotent. The word of the church to the world must therefore encounter the world in all its present reality from the deepest knowledge of the world, if it is to be authoritative. The church must be able to say the Word of God, the word of authority, here and now, in the most concrete way possible, from knowledge of the situation. The church may not therefore preach timeless principles however true, but only commandments which are true today. God is "always" *God* to us "*today.*"

How can the gospel and how can the commandment of the church be preached with authority, i.e., in quite concrete form? Here lies a problem of the utmost difficulty and magnitude. Can the church preach the commandment of God with the same certainty with which it preaches the gospel? Can the church say, "We need a socialist ordering of economics," or "Do not engage in war" with the same certainty as it can say, "Thy sins be forgiven"? Evidently both gospel and commandment will only be preached with authority where they are spoken in a quite concrete way. Otherwise things remain in the sphere of what is generally known, human, impotent, false. Where does this principle of concreteness lie in the case of the gospel? Where does it lie in the case of commandment? This is where the question must be decided. *The gospel becomes concrete in the hearers, the commandment becomes concrete in those who preach it.* The phrase "Thy sins be forgiven thee" is, as the word spoken to the community in proclamation in the sermon, in the Eucharist, framed in such a way that it encounters the hearer in concrete form. In contrast to this, the commandment needs to be given concrete content by the person who preaches it; the commandment "Thou shalt love thy neighbor as thyself" is in itself so general that it needs to be made as concrete as possible if I am to hear what it means for me here and now. And only as a concrete saying is it the Word of God to me. The preacher must therefore be concerned so to incorporate the contemporary situation in his shaping of the commandment that the commandment is itself relevant to the real situation. In the event of taking up a stand about war the church cannot just say, "There should really be no war, but there are necessary wars" and leave the application of this principle to each individual; it should be able to say quite definitely: "Engage in this war" or "Do not engage in this war." Or in social questions: the last word of the church should not be to say, "It is wrong for one man to have too much while another goes hungry, but personal property is God-willed and may not be appropriated," and once again leave the application to the individual. But, if the church really has a commandment of God, it must proclaim it in the most definite form possible, from the fullest knowledge of the matter, and it must utter a summons to obedience. A commandment must be definite, otherwise it is not a commandment. God's commandment now requires something quite definite from us. And the church should proclaim this to the community. . . .

Whence does the church know God's commandment for the moment? For it is evidently by no means obvious. "We know not what to do" (2 Chron. 20:12), "O hide not thy commandments from me" (Ps. 119:19). The recognition of God's command is an act of God's revelation. Where does the church receive this revelation? The *first answer* could be *"The Biblical Law, the Sermon on the Mount."* We have simply to take the Sermon on the Mount seriously, and to realize it. That is our obedience toward God's commandment. To this we must say: even the Sermon on the Mount may not become the letter of the law to us. In its commandments it is the demonstration of what God's commandment can be, not what it is, today, for us. No one can hear that except ourselves, and God must say it to us today. The commandment is not there once and for all, but it is given afresh, again and again. Only in this way are we free from the law, which interposes itself between us and God; only in this way do we hear God.

The *second answer* would find God's commandment in the *orders of creation.* Because certain orders are evident in creation, one should not rebel against them, but simply accept them. One can then argue: Because the nations have been created different, each one is obliged to preserve and develop its characteristics. That is obedience toward the Creator. And if this obedience leads one to struggles and to war, these too must be regarded as belonging to the order of creation. Here too, the commandment of God is thought of as something which has been given once and for all, in definite ordinances which permit of discovery. Now there is a special danger in this argument, and because it is the one most used at the moment it must be given special attention. The danger of the argument lies in the fact that just about everything can be defended by it. One need only hold out something to be God-willed and God-created for it to be vindicated forever, the division of man into nations, national struggles, war, class struggle, the exploitation of the weak by the strong, the cutthroat competition of economics. Nothing is simpler than to describe all this—because it is there—as God-willed and therefore to sanction it. But the mistake lies in the fact that in the solution of this apparently so simple equation the great unknown factor is overlooked, the factor which makes this solution impossible. It is not realized in all seriousness that the world is fallen and that now sin prevails and the creation and sin are so bound up together that no human eye can any longer separate the one from the other, that each human order is an order of the fallen world and not an order of creation. There is no longer any possibility of regarding any features *per se* as orders of creation and of perceiving the will of God *directly* in them. The so-called orders of creation are no longer *per se* revelations of the divine commandment, they are concealed and invisible. Thus the concept of orders of creation must be rejected as a basis for the knowledge of the commandment of God. Hence, neither the biblical law as such nor the so-called orders of creation as such are for us the divine commandment which we perceive today.

The commandment cannot stem from anywhere but the origin of promise and fulfillment, from Christ. From Christ alone must we know what we should do. But not from him as the preaching prophet of the Sermon on the Mount, but from him as the one who gives us life and forgiveness, as the one who has fulfilled the commandment of God in our place, as the one who brings and promises the new world. We can only perceive the commandment where the law is fulfilled, where the new world of the new order of God is established. Thus we are completely directed toward Christ. Now with this we also understand the whole world order of fallen creation as directed solely toward Christ, toward the new creation. What has hitherto been dark and obscure from our sight comes into a new light. It is not as though we now knew all at once from Jesus Christ what features we should regard as orders of creation and what not, but that we know that all the orders of the world only exist in that they are directed toward Christ; they all stand under the preservation of God as long as they are still open for Christ, they are *orders of preservation,* not orders of creation. They obtain their value wholly from outside themselves, from Christ, from the new creation. Their value does not rest in themselves, in other words they are not to be regarded as orders of creation which *per se* are "very good," but they are God's orders of preservation, which only exist as long as they are open for the revelation in Christ. Preservation is God's act with the fallen world, through which he guarantees the possibility of the new creation. Orders of preservation are forms of working against sin in the direction of the gospel *Any order*—however ancient and sacred it may be—*can be dissolved,* and must be dissolved when it closes itself up in itself, grows rigid, and no longer permits the proclamation of revelation. From this standpoint the church of Christ has to pass its verdict on the orders of the world. And it is from this standpoint that the commandment of God must be heard. In the historical change of the orders of the world it has to keep in mind only one thing: which orders can best restrain this radical falling of the world into death and sin and hold the way open for the gospel? The church hears the commandment only from Christ, not from any fixed law or from any eternal order, and it hears it in the orders of preservation. The commandment of Christ is therefore quite simply the critical and radical commandment, which is limited by nothing else, by no so-called "orders of creation." It can demand the most radical destruction simply for the sake of the one who builds up. For the church to venture a decision for or against an order of preservation would be an impossibility if it did not happen in faith in the God who in Christ forgives even the church its sins. But in this faith the decision must be ventured. . . .

There can only be a community of peace when it does not rest on lies and on *injustice.* Where a community of peace endangers or chokes truth and justice, the community of peace must be broken and battle joined. If the battle is then on both sides really waged for truth and for justice, the community of peace, though outwardly destroyed, is made all the deeper and stronger in the battle over this same cause. But should it become clear that one of the combatants is only fighting for his own selfish ends, should even this form of the community of peace be broken, there is revealed that reality which is the ultimate and only tolerable ground of any community of peace, the forgiveness of sins. There is a community of peace for Christians only because one will forgive the other his sins. The forgiveness of sins still remains the sole ground of all peace, even where the order of external peace remains preserved in truth and justice. It is therefore also the ultimate ground on which all ecumenical work rests, precisely where the cleavage appears hopeless. [NRS, pp. 160–69]

8

The Church Is Dead

(Die Kirche ist Tot)

August 29, 1932

Bonhoeffer presented this lecture to the International Youth Conference of the Universal Christian Council on Life and Work and the World Alliance for Promoting International Friendship through the Churches in Gland, Switzerland on August 29, 1932. Bonhoeffer's talk seemed a slight reversal of his previous positive affirmation of the church's inherent secularity in the preceding conference. Here he calls this world "sinful" and "out of joint." This conference of the World Alliance and the Universal Christian Council caused Bonhoeffer to have several misgivings, not the least of which was his fear that the program would focus too much on the economic and international crises and not enough on the need to be decisive in the faith of both the individual Christian and the church. He was also apprehensive of the British tendency to push toward statements and resolutions to buoy up people's spirits and effect change, as if Christianity was more its captivating statements rather than the deeds that were, for Bonhoeffer, the church's primary confession of faith before the world. Here, as later, he preferred a "qualified silence" to official proposals and well-worded, pious resolutions.

Bonhoeffer's talk at Gland, which became, in effect, a summing-up message, was to have been delivered by Bishop Ammundsen. But when Ammundsen was unable to do this, the task fell to Bonhoeffer. His talk moved even the British to admire him and to correct their initial view that he represented too pessimistic an attitude toward the world situation and church effectiveness in rectifying things.

Bonhoeffer was, however, pessimistic in his inspiring examination of the church's call to help Europe and the world "be conquered a second time by Christ." His opening words were that the church was "dead." Bonhoeffer did, in fact, dwell on the delegates' common anxiety that "everything which we undertake here as church action could be too late, superfluous, even trivial." But this gathering was also, he contended, the church in which Christ has proclaimed "life to the dying." Because "death and life come into contact in the cross of Christ," the Christian cannot sink into pessimism or get overly buoyed up in optimism. Bonhoeffer saw the possibility of the church becoming entrapped by a naive trust in the world that

threatens the very life of the church. The church, near death because of its compromising alliance with the world, should rather live "in the midst of death only
because God calls it from death to life, because he does the impossible toward us
and through us." What should the church do to proclaim Christ in such a world is
the heart of the selection that follows, summed up in Bonhoeffer's passionate plea
to "let Christ be Christ."

The unbelieving world says: the church is dead; let us celebrate its funeral with speeches and conferences and resolutions, which all do it
honor. The unbelieving world, full of pious illusion, says: the church is
not dead; it is only weak, and we will serve it with all our might and
put it on its feet again. Only goodwill can do that; let us make a new
morality.

The believer says: the church lives in the midst of death, only because
God calls it from death to life, because he does the impossible toward
us and through us—so would we all say. . . .

In all that we say and do we are concerned with nothing but Christ
and his honor among people. Let no one think that we are concerned
with our own cause, with a particular view of the world, a definite theology or even with the honor of the church. We are concerned with
Christ and nothing else. Let Christ be Christ.

We come together to hear Christ. Have we heard him? I can only put
the question; each person must answer for himself. But I will say at least
this: Is it not precisely the significance of these conferences that where
someone approaches us appearing so utterly strange and incomprehensible in his concerns and yet demands a hearing of us, we perceive in
the voice of our brother or sister the voice of Christ himself, and do not
evade this voice, but take it quite seriously and listen and love the other
precisely in his strangeness? That brother encounters brother in all
openness and truthfulness and need, and claims the attention of others
is the sole way in which Christ encounters us at such a conference. We
are here and we are joined together not as the community of those who
know, but of those who all look for the Word of their Lord and seek
everywhere if they cannot hear it, not as those who know, but as those
who seek, those who are hungry, those who wait, those who are in need,
those who hope. Christ encounters us in our brother and sister, in the
English, the French, the German. . . .

The World Alliance is the community of those who would hearken to
the Lord as they cry fearfully to their lord in the world and in the night,
and as they mean not to escape from the world, but to hear in it the call
of Christ in faith and obedience, and as they know themselves responsible to the world through this call. It is not the organ of church action,
grown weary of meditating upon the Word of God, but it is the church
which knows of the sinfulness of the world and of Christianity, which

expects all good things from God, and which would be obedient to this God in the world.

Why does the community of brothers as it is shown forth in the World Alliance have fear in the church of Christ? Because it knows of the command for peace and yet with the open eyes which are given to the church sees reality dominated by hate, enmity, and power. It is as though all the powers of the world had conspired together against peace; money, business, the lust for power, indeed even love for the fatherland have been pressed into the service of hate. Hate of nations, hate of people against their own countrymen. It is already flaring up here and there—what are the events in the Far East and in South America but a proof that all human ties are dissolving to nothing, that there is no fear of anything where the passion of hate is nourished and breaks out? Events are coming to a head more terribly than ever before—*millions hungry,* people with cruelly deferred and unfulfilled wishes, desperate men who have nothing to lose but their lives and will lose nothing in losing them—humiliated and degraded nations who cannot get over their shame—*political extreme against political extreme, fanatic against fanatic,* idol against idol, and behind it all a world which bristles with weapons as never before, a world which feverishly arms to guarantee peace through arming, a world whose idol has become the word *security*—a world without sacrifice, full of mistrust and suspicion, because past fears are still with it—a humanity which trembles at itself, a humanity which is not sure of itself and is ready at any time to lay violent hands on itself—how can one close one's eyes at the fact that the demons themselves have taken over the rule of the world, that it is the powers of darkness who have here made an awful conspiracy and could break out at any moment?—How could one think that these demons could be driven out, these powers annihilated with a bit of education in international understanding, with a bit of goodwill? . . .

Christ must become present to us in preaching and in the sacraments just as in being the crucified one he has made peace with God and with humanity. The crucified Christ is our peace. He alone exorcizes the idols and the demons. The world trembles only before the cross, not before us.

And now the cross enters this world out of joint. Christ is not far from the world, not in a distant region, of our existence. He went into the lowest depths of our world, his cross is in the midst of the world. And this cross of Christ now calls wrath and judgment over the world of hate and proclaims peace. Today there must be no more war—the cross will not have it. People must realize that nothing happens without strife in the world fallen from God, but there must be no war. War in its present form annihilates the creation of God and obscures the sight of revelation. War as a means of struggle can as little be justified from the necessity of struggle as torture as a legal means can be justified from the need for law. The church renounces obedience should she sanction war.

The church of Christ stands against war for peace among people, between nations, classes, and races.

But the church also knows that there is no peace unless righteousness and truth are preserved. A peace which does damage to righteousness and truth is no peace, and the church of Christ must protest against such peace. There can be a peace which is *worse than struggle*. But it must be a struggle out of love for the other, a struggle *of the spirit, and not of the flesh*. [NRS, pp. 184–86]

9

Creation and Fall:
The Image of God on Earth

(Schöpfung und Fall)

1932–1933

In the winter semester 1932–1933, Bonhoeffer ventured to give his first lectures on a specifically biblical topic, "a theological exposition of Genesis 1–3," as he subtitled the published version. What we read in the book *Creation and Fall,* published originally in 1937, is neither an exegesis nor a full biblical theology. Instead, we see the scriptural text absorbed into Bonhoeffer's own systematic coping with the theology of created life, freedom, sin, and grace. The God-given, "revealed" meaning of all these dimensions of being human is strained by Bonhoeffer through his Christocentrism. He asserts, for example, that we find in Christ's resurrection the ultimate manifestation of God's own personal freedom. In the word of resurrection God witnesses to his being the creator of life that is good and to the freedom that is at once his "mercy, grace, forgiveness, and comfort." Bonhoeffer attempts to draw from Christ's resurrection the conclusion that God is under no compulsion to create, but that because of resurrection we can affirm the world as the most meaningful realm of God's freedom and graced presence in human life.

What is curious about these lectures is Bonhoeffer's portrayal of sin as a power struggle between the forces of darkness and humans who must choose either to accept the created form of Jesus Christ or "to follow the serpent" and reject that form in senseless rebellion. Cain's murder of Abel is but a violent denial of life akin to the rejection of Christ's form of life symbolized in the original fall. Jesus himself is the victim of a Cainlike aggression against God's rule over life and death on earth. The rebellion-sin that darkens the light of God's creating in the image of his son is cast by Bonhoeffer into a socio-Christological context. To be created in God's image is not merely an individualistic attribute of being God's child. Rather, it implies that one is in a special relationship with God and is, thereby, placed as individual in binding social relationships with other people. According to Bonhoeffer, it is in personal and social wholeness alone that one images God.

With such a reading of the biblical text, Bonhoeffer rejects a classical theological tradition that would proclaim only the rational individual in the full strength of his intellectual prowess to be God's image on earth. Here Bonhoeffer tries a new linguistic approach to understanding God in the way God gives himself to his people, coining the expression *Analogia relationis* (analogy of relationship), and insisting that, not by "analogy of being," but by an analogy of God's gift of a relationship with him can we speak about the manifestation of God's presence in the human heart. Freedom, in this perspective, is always a being *free for* the other, just as God is free, not for himself but for his people. God's love is, therefore, manifest in the way his faithful people, from the power of their relationship with God, are enabled to live, like God in Christ, to serve others. The newly translated section from these lectures that follow form the heart of Bonhoeffer's moving the biblical account in the sociotheological direction of an affirmation of the special impact God's gift of himself has had on our freedom to be in a specifically "Christic" relationship with others.

Then God said, "Let us make human beings in our image, after our likeness." Human beings are to proceed from God as the ultimate, the new, and as the image of God in his works. There is no transition here from somewhere or other; here there is new creation. This has nothing at all to do with Darwinism. Quite independently of this, the human person remains the new, free, and unconstricted work of God. We certainly have no wish to deny our connection with the animal world: rather it is just the opposite. But we are very anxious not to lose the unique relationship of humans and God in the process. In our concern with the origin and nature of human beings, it would be a hopeless effort for us to attempt to make a gigantic leap back into the world of the lost beginning. It is hopeless for us to want to know for ourselves what the original human being was like, to identify one's own ideal of the human with the creational reality of God. Such attempts fail to understand that we can know about the original human beings only if we start from Christ. This hopeless, though understandable, attempt has again and again delivered the church up to unbridled speculation on this dangerous point. Only in the middle, as those who live from Christ, do we know of the beginning.

God creates his image on earth in the human. This means that humans are like the Creator in that they are free. Actually one is free only through God's creation, by means of the Word of God; one is free for the worship of the Creator. In the language of the Bible, freedom is not something persons have for themselves but something they have for others. No one enjoys freedom "in itself," that is, in a vacuum, the same way that one may be musical, intelligent, or blind as such. Freedom is not a quality of the human person. Nor is it an ability, a disposition, a kind of being that somehow deeply germinates in a person. Whoever scrutinizes the human to discover freedom will find nothing of it. Why?

Because freedom is not a quality that can be discovered. It is not a possession, a presence, or an object. Nor is it a pattern for existence. Rather, it is a relationship; otherwise, it is nothing. Indeed it is a relationship between two persons. Being free means "being free for the other," because the other has bound me to himself or herself. Only in relationship with the other am I free.

No substantial or individualistic concept of freedom has the ability to encompass freedom. Freedom is something over which I have no control as a possession. It is simply the event, the experience, that happens to me through the other. If we ask how we know this, or whether this is not just another speculation about the beginning that results from being in the middle, we can answer that it is the message of the gospel itself, that God's freedom has bound us to himself, that his free grace becomes real only in this relationship with us, and that God does not will to be free for himself but for man and woman. Because God in Christ is free for us humans, because he does not hoard his freedom for himself, we can envision freedom only as a "being free for." For us who live in the middle through Christ and know our humanity in his resurrection, that God is free means nothing more than that we are free for God. The freedom of the Creator is confirmed by the fact that he allows us to be free for him, and that means nothing other than that he creates his image on earth. The paradox of created freedom is not eliminated. Indeed, it ought even to be made the primary focal point. Here created *freedom* means—and this is what surpasses all the previous deeds of God, deeds which are unique for their excellence—that God himself enters into his creation.

Now God not only commands and his word becomes deed, but he himself enters into creation and thus creates freedom. In this, human beings differ from the other creatures in that God himself is in them, in that they are God's very image in whom the free Creator views himself. The old dogmatists meant this when they spoke of the "indwelling" of the Trinity in Adam. In the free creature the Holy Spirit worships the Creator, the uncreated freedom is praised in created freedom. The creature loves the Creator, because the Creator loves the creature. Created *freedom* is freedom in the Holy Spirit, but as *created* freedom, it is the freedom of *humans* themselves. How does the created being of the free person express itself? In what way does the freedom of the Creator differ from the freedom of the creature? How is the created one free?

Those who are created are free in that they are in relationship with other creatures; the human person is free for others. And he created them a man and a woman. The man is not alone; he exists in duality and it is in this dependence on the other that his creatureliness consists. The creatureliness of humans, no more than their freedom, is neither a quality, nor a disposition to be encountered, nor is it a mode of being. It is to be defined, rather, as absolutely nothing other than the relations of human beings with one another, over against one another, in dependence on one another. The "image . . . after God's likeness" is, consequently, not an *analogia entis* (analogy of being) by which humans, in their existence in and for themselves, would in their being live in the likeness to God's being. Indeed, there is no such analogy between God and the human. This is because God, who in his underived being (*aseität*) is the only one existing in and for himself and at the same time existing for his creatures, binding and giving his freedom to human beings, must not be thought of as only "being," since he is the God who in Christ witnesses to his "being for people." The likeness, the analogy of the human to God, is not *analogia entis* but *analogia relationis* (analogy of relationship). This means, first of all, that the relationship is not a capacity, possibility, or structure proper to the human. It is rather a relationship that is given as a gift and decreed as passive justice. *Justitia passiva!* And in this decreed relationship, freedom is established. From this it follows, secondly, that this analogy must not be understood as though humans somehow have this likeness in their possession, or at their disposal. On the contrary, the analogy, the likeness, must be understood so very strictly, that the likeness in question derives its resemblance from the original image *alone*. Thus it always refers us *only* to the original exemplar himself, and is "likeness" *only* in reference to this. *Analogia relationis* is, therefore, the relationship established by God himself and is an analogy only in this relationship decreed by God. The relationship of creature with creature is a God-given relationship because it exists in freedom and freedom originates from God.

Human beings in their duality—husband and wife—are brought into this world of the stars and of living things in their likeness to God. And just as one's freedom over/against people consisted in the fact that one was to be free *for* them, one's freedom over/against the rest of the created world is to be free *from* it. This means that they are its master; they have command over it; they rule it. And here is precisely the other side of their created likeness to God. Humans are to rule; indeed, to rule over God's creation, to rule like one who as such receives the mission and power of dominion from God. Being free from what is created is not the ideal freedom of the spirit from nature. Rather, this freedom of the one who has dominion includes one's being directly bound to the creatures who are ruled. The soil and the animals, over which I have dominion, are the world in which I live, without which I cease to be. It is my world, my earth, over which I rule. I am not free from it in the sense that my own being, my spirit, has no need of that nature, which is foreign to my spirit. On the contrary, in my entire being, in my creatureliness, I belong completely to this world. It bears me, nurtures me, and holds me. But my freedom from it consists in the fact that this world, to which I am bound like master to his servant, like the peasant to his earth, is subjected to me, and I am supposed to be *master* over the earth which is and remains my earth. Because it is *my* earth, all the more strongly do I rule over it. It is nothing other than the authority conferred by God's word on humans that so uniquely binds them to and sets them over/against other creatures.

This much has been told to us. We are those who live in the middle and who know nothing more about all this and to whom all this is pious myth or a lost world. Indeed, we also attempt to dominate, but the same thing happens here as on Walpurgis Night. We think that we are the ones doing the moving, but we are the ones being moved. We do not rule; rather, we are being ruled. The thing, the world, rules the human. Human beings are made prisoners, slaves of the world. Their rule is an illusion. Technology is the power with which the earth grips people and subdues them. And because we no longer are in command, we lose ground. The earth is, therefore, no longer *our* earth, and thus we become strangers to the earth. But we do not rule over it, since we do not know the world as God's creation and because we do not receive our dominion as God-given but seize hold of it for ourselves. Here there is no "being-free-from" without the "being-free-for." There is no dominion without serving God. With the one, people necessarily lose the other. Without God, without our brother or sister, we lose the earth. In the sentimental aversion to exercising dominion over the earth, however, one has so far always lost God and one's brother and sister. God, brother and sister, and the earth belong together. But for those who have once lost the earth, for us in the middle, there is no way back to the earth except the way to God and to one's brother and sister. From the very beginning the way of human beings to the earth has only been possible as God's way to people. Only where God and brother and sister come to us can we find our way back to the earth. Our being-free-for God and other people and our being-free-from the creature in our dominion over it is the likeness to God of the first human beings. [*Schöpfung und Fall*, pp. 40–45]

10

Christ the Center

(Christologie)

Summer, 1933

When Bonhoeffer began his Christology lectures in the University of Berlin's summer session in 1933, Hitler had been chancellor for three months. The arson of the Reichstag had been cunningly staged in February. That and the massive jailing of the Communist leaders were used by Nazi propaganda to manipulate German citizens into thinking they needed protection from the trumped up conspiracy of atheist Bolshevists and non-Aryan Jews alike. The "Enabling Law," granting absolute dictatorial powers to Hitler to deal with these "threats" to state security had been passed in March 1933. In that same month concentration camps had been set up; a month later, Goering officially instituted the Gestapo. The one-day boycott of all Jewish businesses and doctors on April 1, was only a mild phase of an anti-Jewish crescendo marked by the "Law for the Restoration of the Civil Service" passed on April 7, which forced retirement on Jewish officials, including university professors, and through its "Aryan clauses" forbade Jews to hold offices in churches—Jews being defined as those having one Jewish parent or grandparent, regardless of church affiliation.

To Bonhoeffer's dismay, this legislation was accepted with enthusiasm by many church people either eager to vent their own anti-Semitic feelings or to protect their newly guaranteed perquisites. Nazism had, in fact, pandered to a privilege-seeking clergy in Germany that saw in the misfortunes of Communists and Jews only an opportunity to reinforce the Christian churches with further status and power. The Nazi "millennium," then beginning, would be hailed as Christianity's finest hour as well, and Hitler would be hailed as the twentieth-century savior of Germany. Not surprisingly, one school catechism of the Third Reich proclaimed that "as Jesus set men free from sin and hell, so Hitler rescued the German people from destruction. . . . Jesus built for heaven; Hitler, for the German earth." It did not take this piece of crude prose to convince Bonhoeffer that, under Hitler, Germany was sinking into a hell of inhumanity and moving against a newly created group of outcasts, Jews, and political dissenters. For him, it was Germany's and

Christianity's worst hour. Given the legalized oppressiveness of it all, Bonhoeffer's frustrations over his inability to rally sufficient opposition, even within his own ecclesial community, soured somewhat his attitude toward institutions like the church and the university. The university seemed too tied into the world of the "phraseological" for it to get overly excited by evidence of injustice even within its own walls, as in the case of the Jewish professors. The churches, in turn, kept silent for the sake of their privileges and because in their spiritual obtuseness they could declare with the Reich Church that National Socialism was only "positive Christianity" in action.

In an atmosphere that stifled the freedom to be an effective critic of either state or church, Bonhoeffer delivered what were to be his last university lectures. Bethge calls them "the high point of Bonhoeffer's academic career." Bonhoeffer himself felt they were his stiffest teaching challenge, since in developing his Christology he was finally trying to bring together all the disparate threads of his new understanding of both himself and of his commitment to Jesus Christ. In these lectures his life and his theology appeared to converge. What is more, his Christology had become the interpretive key to reading the Bible and to his vinegary judgments on church and society, on contemporary ethics, and on the liberal reduction of dogmatics to what Barth correctly detected to be merely a humanistic domestication of God himself. Christ in all the robustness of the prophetic Sermon on the Mount now stood at the very center of Bonhoeffer's vocation as a minister. For the last time at the university, he would attempt to portray this conviction about Christ with systematic consistency to his students in the wider contexts of church, state, and history itself. One student jotted down that Bonhoeffer "looked like a student himself when he mounted the platform. But then what he had to say so gripped us all that we were no longer there to listen to this very young man but we were there because of what he had to say—even though it was dreadfully early in the morning. I have never heard a lecture that impressed me nearly so much."[16]

From the outset of these lectures Bonhoeffer seems to be urging his church to ask itself the haunting Christological questions: Who is Jesus in the world of 1933 and where is he to be found? Bonhoeffer eschews that abstract Christology so characteristic of church efforts to deaden the impact of Jesus' word by pushing him behind protective layers of dogmatic wordiness, clearly enunciated legalisms, and triumphalist slogans. For the better part of the year prior to these lectures, Bonhoeffer had conducted discussions with his students on how the church could take the initiative on behalf of the poor and in opposition to war and to Nazi racist policies. In these discussions he decried the church's hesitation to hear Christ's gospel in movements toward social justice. Crass opportunism coupled with cowardly passivity had rendered the church irrelevant to average workers who had as little use for a capitalist Christ impervious to their needs as for a church rallying the troops around the flag of privilege.

Here Bonhoeffer demands that Christology must begin in the prayerful silence of the ecclesial community. Christ must be allowed, as few church leaders permitted, to disturb the peace of the churches. Jesus' life and prophetic words, Bonhoeffer points out, call into question all those forms of political and ecclesial pretentiousness that, in effect, succeed in neutralizing God's Word in the world.

Bonhoeffer's Christological questions thus quickly become challenges to the church. He argues that people can encounter Christ only as a person in relationship with other people. It is, therefore, the duty of the believing community to recognize and enable people to recognize Christ's personal presence in the world. This is a primary form obedience to his word must take. Instead of trying to fit Christ into some preconceived theological schema with questions of "How was Christ possible?" and "What categories can we fit him into?" the believing community must set out to follow Christ. For the church to dally while waiting for "proofs" of the rightness of particular Christian action is, for Bonhoeffer, to fall into the deceptive trap of reducing Christ to only the clear images that guarantee safety and church purity. In reality the church would, by this deception, avoid Christ's historical incognitos and the very risk his cross betokens. In other words, the Christian church may be guilty in Bonhoeffer's day, as it was in Kierkegaard's day, of avoiding the scandal of Christ because Christ's humiliation in the various incognitos he assumes is more than a triumphalist church can take. It continues to honor Christ in tabernacle and church but not in the leper and outcast of society. And, paradoxically, it may unwittingly be inflicting a new and more terrible humiliation when, as church, it becomes hopelessly locked into worshipping a Christ replica of its own lust for privilege. In the lectures this point comes out most strongly in Bonhoeffer's indictment of the church for having become "one with the stupefied and oppressive capitalist system." The average worker could come "to depict Christ as allied with the church of the bourgeois society." The churches thus close their eyes to the possibility that Jesus could very well be acting in the socialist movement or be the humanly human "idiot" of Dostoyevsky's novel who "clumsily causes offense everywhere. He does not go around with the great ones, but with children. He is laughed at and loved. He is the fool and he is the wise man. He bears everything and he forgives everything. He is revolutionary and yet he conforms." "Who is Christ?" Bonhoeffer asks. Socialist, revolutionary, good man, idealist, brother, and master? All these and more, as "Christ goes through the ages, questioned anew, misunderstood anew, and again and again put to death." For Bonhoeffer, the incognitos of Christ should be reminders to the church to face the ambiguities of its own claims to be Christ for the world. The church, he insists, must listen in prayer and silence in order to allow God's word to shape the new social community at the specific moment in history into the image of his Christ.

The main issue of the lectures is still the way Christ's gospel penetrates the community and moves it to confess its faith in the Christ of the present who embodies that truth. "God is only God *pro me* [for me,] Christ is only Christ *pro me*," he asserted, standing "vicariously where mankind should stand. . . . " How to stand with Jesus Christ becomes Bonhoeffer's Christo-ecclesiological question in the new dark age of massive manipulation of peoples and seduction of the churches. National Socialist racism and belligerence depended, as Bonhoeffer's lectures seem to imply, on church failure to recognize the Christ of the present, his sociohumanistic structural character in word, sacrament, and community. Christ as church should have been the locus of freedom and responsibility moving Christians to stand with Christ on behalf of the "new humanity," a world community united in the affirmation of brotherhood and sisterhood in him.

THE UNFOLDING OF THE CHRISTOLOGICAL QUESTION

Teaching about Christ begins in silence. "Be still, for that is the absolute," writes Kierkegaard. That has nothing to do with the silence of the mystics, who in their dumbness chatter away secretly in their soul by themselves. The silence of the church is silence before the Word. In so far as the church proclaims the Word, it falls down silently in truth before the inexpressible; "In silence I worship the unutterable" (Cyril of Alexandria). The spoken Word is the inexpressible; this unutterable is the Word. "It must become spoken, it is the great battle" (Luther). Although it is cried out by the church in the world, it remains the inexpressible. To speak of Christ means to keep silent; to keep silent about Christ means to speak. When the church speaks rightly out of a proper silence, then Christ is proclaimed.

What we wish to concern ourselves with here is the study of this proclamation. The object of our study can only be shown to us again in the proclamation itself. Here to speak of Christ will be thus to speak in the silent places of the church. In the humble silence of the worshipping congregation we concern ourselves with Christology. To pray is to be silent and at the same time to cry out, before God and in the presence of his Word. It is for the study of Christ, that is, God's Word, that we have gathered together as a congregation. Yet, we are not in church, we are in a lecture hall. We have to work within an academic discipline. . . . [CC, p. 27]

Two questions therefore must remain forever excluded from Christological thought:

1. The question of whether the answer already given and the church's corresponding question, "Who?", can be justified or not. This question has no basis, because the human logos can have no authority to doubt the truth of the other Logos. The testimony of Jesus to himself stands by itself, self-authenticating. That is the backbone of every theology. The "truth" of the revelation of God in Christ cannot be scientifically established or disputed.

2. The question of how the "truth" of the revelation can be conceived. This question would mean going behind Christ's claim and finding an independent reason for it. In that way the human logos would be claiming to be the beginning and the father of Jesus Christ. With such an inordinate claim, the human logos strives for a trinitarian form. . . . [CC, p. 32]

For the proletariat, it is easy to depict Christ as allied with the Church of the bourgeois society. Then the worker sees no reason anymore to give Jesus a qualified place or status. The church is one with the stupefied and oppressive capitalist system. But at this very point the working class may distinguish between Jesus and his church; he is not the guilty party. Jesus, yes; Church, no! Jesus can then become the idealist, the socialist. What does it mean when the proletarian says, in his world of distrust, "Jesus was a good man"? It means that nobody needs to mistrust him. The proletarian does not say, "Jesus is God." But when he says, "Jesus is a good man," he is saying more than the bourgeois says when he repeats, "Jesus is God." God is for him something belonging to the church. But, Jesus can be present on the factory floor as the socialist; at a political meeting, as an idealist; in the worker's world, as a good man. He fights in their ranks against the enemy, capitalism. Who are you? Are you brother and master? Are they evading the question? Or are they in their own way putting it seriously?

Dostoyevsky let the figure of Christ appear in Russian literature as the idiot. He does not separate himself, but clumsily causes offense everywhere. He does not go around with the great ones, but with children. He is laughed at and loved. He is the fool and he is the wise man. He bears everything and he forgives everything. He is revolutionary and yet he conforms. He does not want to—but he does—call attention to himself just by his existence. Who are you? Idiot or Christ?

One thinks of Gerhard Hauptmann's novel *Der Narr in Christo Emanuel Quint.* Or of the presentation of Christ and the misrepresentation in the writing of Wilhelm Gross and Georg Grosz, behind which lurks the question, "Who are you really?" Christ goes through the ages, questioned anew, misunderstood anew, and again and again put to death.

It is the same temptation for the theologian who tries to encounter Christ and yet to avoid that encounter. Theologians betray him and simulate concern. Christ is still betrayed by the kiss. Wishing to be done with him means always to fall down with the mockers and say, "Greetings, Master!" There are only two ways possible of encountering Jesus: one must die or one must put Jesus to death.

The question "Who are you?" remains ambiguous. It can be the question of one who knows already that he has been encountered in his very questioning and who hears the responding question "Who then are you?." But it can also be the question which when asked means "How will I deal with you?." And that is a disguised form of the old question "How?" The question "Who?" can be put to Jesus only when the responding question has already been heard. Then it is not man who has dealt with Jesus, but Jesus who has dealt with man. Thus the question "Who?" which already contains in it the responding question and answer can only be spoken in faith. . . . [*CC*, pp. 35–36]

Only if I know who does the work can I have access to the work of Christ. Here everything depends upon knowing the person in order to recognize the work. If he was an idealistic founder of a religion, I can be elevated by his work and stimulated to follow his example. But my sin is not forgiven, God remains angry, and I am still in the power of death. Then the work of Jesus drives me to despair about myself, because I cannot follow his example. But if Jesus is the Christ, the Word of God, then I am not primarily called to do the things that he does; I am met in his work as one who cannot possibly do the work he does. It is through his work that I recognize the gracious God. My sin is forgiven, I am no longer in death, but in life. All this depends upon the person of Christ, whether *his* work perishes in the world of death or abides in a new world of life. But how can the person of Christ be comprehended other than by his work, i.e., otherwise than through history? This objection contains a most profound error. For even Christ's work is not unequivocal. It remains open to various interpretations. His work can also be interpreted to show that he is a hero, and his cross can be interpreted as the consummate act of a brave man, true to his convictions. There is no point in the life of Jesus of which one can say with unambiguous conviction that here we see the Son of God, proved to be such by one of his works. He does his work rather in the incognito of history, in the flesh. The incognito of the incarnation makes it doubly impossible to recognize the person by his works:

1. Jesus is man and the argument back from works to person is ambiguous.
2. Jesus is God and the argument back from history to God is impossible.

If this way of understanding is closed there remains just one more chance to gain access to Jesus Christ. This is the attempt to be in the place where the person of Christ reveals himself in his own being, without any compulsion. That is the place of prayer to Christ. Only by the Word freely revealing himself is the person of Christ available and with that also his work.

Thus the priority in theology of the Christological question over the soteriological has been established. When I know *who* he is, who does this, I will know *what* it is he does. However, it would be wrong to conclude from this that the person and the work can be separated. We are concerned here with the epistemological connection between Person and Work, as we know it, not as it is in reality. The separation of the question of Christology from that of soteriology is necessary only to establish a theological method. For the Christological question, by its very nature, must be addressed to the one complete Christ. This complete Christ is the historical Jesus, who can never in any way be separated from his work. He is asked and he answers as the one, who is his own work. But Christology is primarily concerned with who he is rather than what he does. To put that into an academic formula: the subject of Christology is the personal structure of being of the complete, historical Jesus Christ. . . . [*CC*, pp. 38–39]

Here we meet the first Christological problem: If Christ is present, not only as power, but in his person, how are we to think of this presence so that it does not violate this person? To be present means a particular time and place, i.e., to be there. Even as the risen one, Jesus Christ remains the man Jesus in time and space. Because Jesus Christ is man, he is present in time and space; because Jesus Christ is God, he is eternally present. The presence of Christ requires the statement "Jesus is fully man"; but it also requires the other statement "Jesus is fully God." The presence of Jesus Christ in the church, at a particular time and place, is because of the fact that there is one whole person of the God-Man. It is therefore an impossible question to ask how the man Jesus, limited by space and time, can be contemporary with us. This Jesus does not exist in isolation. Equally impossible is the other question, how God can be in time. This isolated God does not exist. The only possible and meaningful question is "Who is there, present in time and place?" The answer is "The one person of the God-Man, Jesus Christ." I do not know who the man Jesus is unless I can at the same time say, "Jesus Christ is God"; I do not know who the God Jesus Christ is, unless I can at the same time say, "Jesus Christ is man." The two factors cannot be isolated, because they are not separable. God in timeless eternity is not God; Jesus limited by time is not Jesus. Rather we may say that in the man Jesus, God is God. In this Jesus Christ, God is present. The one God-Man. In this Jesus Christ, God is present. This one God-Man is the starting point for Christology.

The space-time continuum is not only the human definition of the God-Man, but also the divine definition. This space-time presence of the God-Man is hidden "in the likeness of sinful flesh" (Rom. 8:3). The presence is a hidden presence. It is not that God is hidden in man, but rather that this God-Man as a whole is hidden in "the likeness of sinful flesh." That means that the principle of hiddenness is not man as such, not space and time, but the "likeness of sinful flesh," i.e., the world between temptation and sin.

In this way the whole problem of Christology is shifted. For here the issue is now that relationship between the already given God-Man and the "likeness of sinful flesh," not a discussion on how to relate an isolated God to an isolated man in Christ. This God-Man, Jesus Christ, is present and contemporary in the form which is in the "likeness of sinful flesh," i.e., in hidden form, in the form of a stumbling block. That is the central problem of Christology.

The presence of the already given God-Man, Jesus Christ, is hidden from us, and exists in the offensive form of preaching. The Christ who is preached is the real Christ. The proclamation is not a second incarnation. The offense of Jesus Christ is not his incarnation—that indeed is revelation—but his humiliation. The humanity of Christ and the humiliation of Christ need to be distinguished with care. Jesus Christ is man both when he is humilated and when he is exalted. Only the humiliation is an offense. The doctrine of the offense, the *scandalon*, is found not in the incarnation of God, but in the doctrine of the humiliated God-Man. It is the "likeness of sinful flesh" which belongs to the humiliation. But for us that means that Christ is present as the risen and exalted one only in preaching; and that means only by way of a new humiliation. Thus, in proclamation, the risen and exalted one is present in his humiliation. This presence has a threefold form in the church: that of the Word, that of the Sacrament, and that of the congregation.

But the basic question of the presence of Christ is not yet answered. The question "How can the Man Jesus or the God Christ be present here and now?" is quite inadmissible. The fact of his presence is not in question. The question is really about the kind of structure of his person which enables Christ to be present in the church. . . . [CC, pp. 45–47].

It is the nature of the person of Christ to be in the center both spatially and temporally. The one who is present in Word, Sacrament, and church is in the center of human existence, of history, and of nature. It belongs to the structure of his person to be in the center. When we turn the question "Where?" back into the question "Who?" we get the answer. Christ is the mediator as the one who exists *pro me*. That is his nature and his mode of existence. In three ways, he is in the center: in being there for humans, in being there for history, in being there for nature.

1. CHRIST AS THE CENTER OF HUMAN EXISTENCE

That Christ is the center of our existence does not mean that he is central in our personality, our thinking, and our feeling. Christ is also our center when he stands, in terms of our consciousness, on our periphery, also when Christian piety is displaced to the periphery of our being. The statement made about his centrality is not psychological, but has the character of an ontological and theological statement. It does not refer to our personality, but to our being a person before God. The center of the person cannot be demonstrated. The truth of the statement that Christ is our center does not allow of confirmation by proof. For it concerns the center in which we believe within the space of the person in whom we believe. In the fallen world the center is also the boundary. Man stands between law and fulfillment. He has the law, but he cannot fulfill it. Now Christ stands where man has failed before the law. Christ as the center means that he is the fulfillment of the law. So he is in turn the boundary and the judgment of man, but also the beginning of his new existence, its center. Christ as the center of human existence means that he is the judgment and justification of man.

2. CHRIST AS THE CENTER OF HISTORY

Every attempt to give a philosophical basis for the fact that Christ is the center of history must be rejected. There can be no question of proving that he is the center and consummation of religious and secular history. Here too it is not a matter of finding the center of historical space. Were Christ shown to be the high point of all religion, that would still have nothing to do with his being the center. A comparison with other relative appearances and, resulting from that, a possible proof that Christ was the center of history would at the most give us a relative, not an absolute, conclusion. All question about his absolute claim are wrongly stated. Comparisons with relative objects and conclusions to relative questions do not result in an absolute. The question about absolute claims is a liberal and rationalistic question and only serves to distort the question which is appropriate here. The question about Christ as center and boundary of history must be stated quite differently.

History lives between promise and fulfillment. It carries the promise within itself, to become full of God, the womb of the birth of God. The promise of a Messiah is everywhere alive in history. History lives in and from this expectation. That is what gives it significance, the coming of the Messiah. But history relates itself to his promise much as the individual relates to the law: it cannot fulfill it. The promise is corrupted by sin. Man has the law only in the corrupted form sin itself has caused. History has the promise only as it is corrupted in itself. It lives from the corrupted promises of "fulfilled time," from its kairos. It must always make visible its own center. In this situation it is forced to glory in its own messiahs. A Messiah at the center of history is, from the point of view of the philosophy of history, quite a respectable theory. But this promise remains unfulfilled. History is tormented by the impossibility of fulfilling corrupt messianic promises. It knows of its messianic determination and comes to grief on it.

Only at one point does the thought break through that the Messiah cannot be the visible and demonstrated center of history, but must be the hidden center appointed by God. This is the point at which there is a stream against the popular movement of corrupted messianism—it is in Israel. With its prophetic hope, it stands alone among the nations. And Israel becomes the place at which God fulfills his promise.

This fulfilled promise is not to be proved by anything, it is only to be proclaimed. This means that the Messiah, Christ, is at one and the same time the destroyer and the fulfiller of all the messianic expectations of history. He is the destroyer in so far as the visible Messiah does not appear and the fulfillment takes place in secret. He is the fulfiller insofar as God really enters history and he who is expected is really there. The meaning of history is tied up with an event which takes place in the depth and hiddenness of a man who ended on the cross. The meaning of history is found in the humiliated Christ.

With this every other claim of history is judged and settled. History is here led to its boundary with its own promises. By its nature it has come to an end. Yet, by setting this boundary, Christ has at the same time again become its center and its fulfillment. When the totality of history should stand before God, there Christ stands. He is also the *pro me* for history. He is also the mediator for history.

Because Christ, since the cross and resurrection, is present in the church, the church also must be understood as the center of history. It is the center of a history which is being made by the state. Again this is a hidden and not an evident center of the realm of the state. The church does not show itself to be the center by visibly standing at the center of the state or by letting itself be put at the center, as when it is made a state church. It is not its visible position in the realm of the state that shows its relation to the state. The meaning and the promise of the state is hidden in it, it judges and justifies the state in its nature. Its nature, i.e. the nature of the state, is to bring a people nearer to its fulfillment by law and the order it creates. With the thought of an order-creating state, that messianic claim dwells hidden within.

So, just as the church is the center of the state, it is also its boundary. It is the boundary of the state in proclaiming with the cross the breaking through of all human order. Just as it recognizes and believes in the cross, as the fulfillment of the law, so it also believes the cross to be the fulfillment of the order of the state. When it recognizes the cross and proclaims it, the church does not judge by a new law, according to which the state would have to act. But it proclaims that by God's entry into history and his death through history, the order of the state has been finally broken through and dissolved, but also finally affirmed and fulfilled.

Therefore the relationship of church and state since the cross is new. There is a state, in the proper sense, only when there is a church. The state has its proper origin since and with the cross (like the church) in so far as this cross destroys and fulfills and affirms its order.

Christ is present to us in the forms both of church and state. But he is this only for us, who receive him as Word and Sacrament and church; for us, who since the cross must see the state in the light of Christ. The state is God's "rule with his left hand" (Luther, W.A. 36, 385, 6–9; 52, 26, 20–6). So long as Christ was on earth, he was the kingdom of God. When he was crucified the kingdom broke up into one ruled by God's right hand and one ruled by his left hand. Now, it can only be recognized in a twofold form, as church and as state. But the complete Christ is present in his church. And this church is the hidden center of the state. The state need not know that the church is this center, but in fact it lives from this center and has no effective existence without it.

Christ as the center of history is the mediator between state and God in the form of the church. In the same way, he is as center of history also mediator between church and God. He is also the center of this church, only so can it be the center of history.

3. CHRIST AS THE CENTER BETWEEN GOD AND NATURE

There has been little consideration of this question in Protestant theology in the past.

Christ is *the* new creature. Thereby he shows all other creatures to be old creatures. Nature stands under the curse which God laid upon Adam's ground. It was the originally created Word of God, proclaiming it freely. As the fallen creation it is now dumb, enslaved under the guilt of man. Like history, it suffers from the loss of its meaning and its freedom. It waits expectantly for a new freedom. Nature, unlike man and history, will not be reconciled, but it will be set free for a new freedom. Its catastrophes are the dull will to set itself free, to show its power over man and by its own right to be a new creature, which it has made anew itself.

In the sacrament of the church, the old enslaved creature is set free to its new freedom. As the center of human existence and of history, Christ was the fulfillment of the unfulfilled law, i.e., their reconciliation. But nature is creation under the curse—not guilt, for it lacks freedom. Thus nature finds in Christ as its center, not reconciliation, but redemption. Once again, this redemption, which happens in Christ, is not evident, nor can it be proved, but it is proclaimed. The word of preaching is that enslaved nature is redeemed in hope. A sign of this is given in the sacraments, where elements of the old creation are become elements of the new. In the sacraments they are set free from their dumbness and proclaim directly to the believer the new creative Word of God. They no longer need the explanation of man. Enslaved nature does not speak the Word of God to us directly. But the sacraments do. In the sacrament, Christ is the mediator between nature and God and stands for all creation before God.

To sum up, we must continue to emphasize that Christ is truly the center of human existence, the center of history, and now also the center of nature. But these three aspects can only be distinguished from each other *in abstracto*. In fact, human existence is also and always history, always and also nature. The mediator as fulfiller of the law and liberator of creation is all this for the whole human existence. He is the same who is intercessor and *pro me,* and who is himself the end of the old world and the beginning of the new world of God. . . . [CC, pp. 62–65]

POSITIVE CHRISTOLOGY

1. THE INCARNATE ONE

The question may not run, "How is the incarnate one thinkable?", but "Who is he?" He is not the one adopted by God, he is not the one clothed in human characteristics. He is God who became man, as we became man. He lacks nothing belonging to man. There is no gift of this world or of man that he has not received. This protest against *enhypostasis* must remain. Jesus Christ had his own human, individual *hystasis* and his own human mode of existence. The man whom I am, Jesus has also been. Of him only is it valid to say that nothing human was alien to him. Of this man, we say: "This is God for us."

Two points of denial must be carefully made:

a) We do not mean that we knew something before about what and who God was, apart from Jesus Christ, and then applied it to Christ. No, this is a direct statement of identity; all that we are here able to say about God, we have gained by a glance at him, or better, this man compels us.

b) We do not mean that the statement "This man is God," adds any-thing to his humanity. That is the essential point. Against that it could be argued that something was added to this man Jesus, which we do not have, namely his deity. That is true, but we must be careful here. We are not to think of God and man in Christ being joined together by a concept of nature (being, *ousia*). Being God is not for Jesus an extension of his being man. It is also not a continuity of his being as man, which he goes on to achieve. Rather, it is a statement which comes upon this man from above. It takes nothing from him and it adds nothing to him, but it qualifies this whole man Jesus as God. It is the judgment and Word of God on this man. This qualification, this judgment and Word of God, which "comes from above," must not however be thought of as something added. Rather than something added, this Word coming down from God is that man Jesus Christ himself. And therefore, be-cause Jesus Christ *is* also God's judgment on himself, he points, at one and the same time, to both God and to himself.

Thereby what is avoided is the idea of two isolated given entities being united with each other. Jesus the man is believed in as God. And that, as man, not despite his humanity, nor over the top of it. In the man Jesus, faith is kindled in the Word. Jesus Christ is not God in a divine nature, *ousia*, substance, being, nor is he God in a way that can be demonstrated or described, he is God in faith. There is no such thing as this divine being. If Jesus Christ is to be described as God, we may not speak of this divine being, nor of his omnipotence, nor his omnis-cience; but we must speak of this weak man among sinners, of his man-ger and his cross. If we are to deal with the deity of Jesus, we must speak of his weakness. In Christology, one looks at the whole historical man Jesus and says of him that he is God. One does not first look at a human nature and then beyond it to a divine nature, but one has to do with the one man Jesus Christ, who is wholly God.

The accounts of the birth and the baptism of Jesus stand side by side. In the birth story, we are directed totally toward Jesus himself. In the story of the baptism, we are directed toward the Holy Spirit who comes from above. The reason why we find it difficult to take the two stories together is because of the doctrine of the two natures. The two stories are not teaching two natures. If we put this doctrine aside, we see that the one story concerns the being of the Word of God in Jesus, while the other concerns the coming of the Word of God upon Jesus. The child in the manger is wholly God: note Luther's Christology in the Christmas hymns. The call at the baptism is confirmation of the first happening, there is no adoptionism in it. The manger directs our attention to the man, who is God; the baptism directs our attention, as we look at Jesus, to the God who calls.

If we speak of Jesus Christ as God, we may not say of him that he is the representative of an idea of God, which possesses the characteristics of omniscience and omnipotence (there is no such thing as this abstract divine nature!); rather, we must speak of his weakness, his manger, his cross. This man is no abstract God.

Strictly speaking we should not talk of the incarnation, but of the incarnate one. The former interest arises out of the question "How?" The question "How?" for example, underlies the hypothesis of the virgin birth. Both historically and dogmatically it can be questioned. The biblical witness is ambiguous. If the biblical witness gave clear evidence of the fact, then the dogmatic obscurity might not have been so important. The doctrine of the virgin birth is meant to express the incarnation of God, not only the fact of the incarnate one. But does it not fail at the decisive point of the incarnation, namely that in it Jesus has not become man just like us? The question remains open, as and because it is already open in the Bible.

The incarnate one is the glorified God: "The Word was made flesh and we beheld his glory." God glorifies himself in man. That is the ultimate secret of the Trinity. The humanity is taken up into the Trinity. Not from all eternity, but "from now on even unto eternity"; the trinitarian God is seen as the incarnate one. The glorification of God in the flesh is now at the same time, the glorification of man, who shall have life through eternity with the trinitarian God. This does not mean that we should see the Incarnation of God as God's judgment on man. God remains the incarnate one even in the last Judgment. The Incarnation is the message of the glorification of God, who sees his honor in becoming man. It must be noted that the Incarnation is first and foremost true revelation, of the Creator in the creature, and not veiled revelation. Jesus Christ is the unveiled image of God. . . . [CC, pp. 102–5]

Between humiliation and exaltation lies oppressively the stark historical fact of the empty tomb. What is the meaning of the news of the empty tomb, before the news of the resurrection? Is it the deciding fact of Christology? Was it really empty? Is it the visible evidence, penetrating the incognito, of the Sonship of Jesus, open to everyone and therefore making faith superfluous? If it was not empty, is then Christ not risen and our faith futile? It looks as though our faith in the resurrection were bound up with the news of the empty tomb. Is our faith then ultimately only faith in the empty tomb?

This is and remains a final stumbling block, which the believer in Christ must learn to live with in one way or another. Empty or not empty, it remains a stumbling block. We cannot be sure of its historicity. The Bible itself shows this stumbling block, when it makes clear how hard it was to prove that the disciples had not stolen the body. Even here we cannot escape the realm of ambiguity. We cannot find a way round it. Even in the testimony of Scripture, Jesus enters in a form which is a stumbling block. Even as the risen one he does not lift his incognito. He will lift it only when he returns in glory. Then the incarnate one will no longer be the humiliated one. Then the decision over faith or unbelief is already taken. Then the humanity of God is really and now only the glorifying of God.

All that we know today only through the encounter with the humiliated one. It is with this humiliated one that the church goes its own way of humilation. It cannot strive after visible confirmation of its way while he renounces it with every step. But neither can it, as the humble church, look upon itself with futile self-complacency, as though its very lowliness were visible proof that Christ is present in it. Humiliation is no proof, or at least one cannot call upon it as proof! There is here no law or principle which the church has to follow, but simply a fact—put bluntly, it is God's way with the church. As Paul says of himself that he can be exalted or lowly, so long as it happens for the sake of Christ, so the church also can be exalted or lowly, so long as in both cases it is the way of Christ with it. This way is the enemy of pride, whether it is wrapped in the purple robe or the crown of martyrdom is set upon it. The church gazes always only at the humiliated Christ, whether it itself is exalted or made low.

It is not good when the church is anxious to praise itself too readily for its humble state. Equally, it is not good for it to boast of its power and its influence too soon. It is only good when the church humbly confesses its sins, allows itself to be forgiven, and confesses its Lord. Daily must it receive the will of God from Christ anew. It receives it because of the presence of the incarnate, the humiliated, and the exalted one. Daily, this Christ becomes a stumbling block to its own hopes and wishes. Daily, it stumbles at the words afresh, "You will all be offended because of me" (Matt. 26:31). And daily it holds anew to the promise, "Blessed is he who is not offended in me" (Matt. 11:6). [*CC*, pp. 112–13]

Part 3

BONHOEFFER'S
CONFESSION OF FAITH

Bonhoeffer after a service in
Trinity Church, talking with
Hanns Lilje.

With Jean Lasserre at the Fanø
Conference, August 1934.

National Synod at Wittenberg, 1933. From: Eberhard Bethge,
Dietrich Bonhoeffer
(New York: Harper & Row, 1970), p. 361.
Top left/right taken from: Eberhard Bethge, Renate Bethge,
Christian Gremmels, *Dietrich Bonhoeffer: A Life in Pictures*
(Philadelphia: Fortress Press, 1986), pp. 100, 117.

Introduction: The Church Struggle and Nazi Racial Policies

At the time of Hitler's accession to power on January 30, 1933, Bonhoeffer had himself been wavering between a decision to devote his life to the teaching profession or to direct his energies toward a parish ministry. The battery of laws against Jews, bearing on what to Bonhoeffer was the even larger issue of the freedom of a Christian church to be a church independent of state interference, gave his life a new sense of purpose beyond the call of either academe or of parish life. In this he would become an enigma to many of his colleagues in the church who were attempting by political quietism, indifference, and religious compromise to survive a difficult situation. His church, the Evangelical Church in Germany, comprising both Lutheran and Reformed confessions, was considered a state church. All its pastors, therefore, were ranked among the state officials, expected to enforce Nazi policies in their public life both civil and ecclesial. This had led to the adoption of the Aryan Clause at the infamous Brown Synod of September 4, 1933, denying pastors of Jewish descent their rights as ordained ministers. That this legislation could have been supported by the German Christians (those who endorsed the nazification of the churches), seemed to Bonhoeffer evidence enough that the national church had substituted racial purity for baptism and the call of Christ and had, thereby, fallen into heresy. The issue for Bonhoeffer was simply that there could be no retreat from a commitment to Jesus Christ. Caving in to nazism in the matter of church legislation and Christian praxis was the pursuit of "cheap grace." This to him was a modern-day denial of Christ in the person of the oppressed. It had to be counteracted with all the courage a church could muster if that church was to be free enough to suffer for the sake of its fidelity to Jesus' gospel.

Bonhoeffer's own freedom and sense of what was a just cause for the church led him in the period represented by the selections of this chapter to a passionate effort to arouse the churches and church people from their slumber. It is not surprising, therefore, that, when the Nazi government passed the Aryan legislation on April 7, 1933, he was the first scholar-minister to attempt an analysis of the consequences of these laws for the relationship of church to state. That analysis became his controversial address "The Church and the Jewish Question." His was the first voice raised in defense of the Jews, in what would become a lonely, bitter undertaking during the 1930s and the war years. Of more immediate concern in 1933 was the insidious Nazi takeover of the churches. This was not unrelated to the so-called "Jewish Question." Prior to the Brown Synod, and despite Bonhoeffer's plea to the church to "stay a church" and to "confess, confess, confess!," the rigged national church elections in July brought in a known Hitler sympathizer, Ludwig Müller, as Reich bishop, an ecclesiastical counterpart to the political leadership of Adolf Hitler.

Such a situation called for some kind of Christian action. In his early resistance to the policies of Hitler and the Nazi state, Bonhoeffer was an active agitator for more direct church intervention. He even suggested that his church convoke a council. This suggestion, delivered at a meeting on June 22, 1933, between the German Christians and the Young Reformers, as Bonhoeffer and his group were called, was dismissed as anachronistic, "like routing out ancient halberds from dusty ecclesial armories."[1] The plea for a council to root out the new heresy also hinted of an infringement of that liberalism and tolerance which were a boast of twentieth-century Protestantism. Yet the idea of a council was itself to be somewhat realized a year later in the Barmen and Dahlem synods, though what was accomplished at these synods and later in the ecumenical gatherings of the 1930s was but a shadow of the radical steps and uncompromising declarations that Bonhoeffer dreamed of provoking.

Bonhoeffer himself recognized that the struggle was not merely an internal church squabble but one which meant dramatic conflict with the Nazi government. In the church assemblies of July 1933, he and his friend Franz Hildebrandt, an ordained Christian minister of Jewish ancestry, threatened by the new laws, advocated the view that clergy and bishops should proclaim what would amount to a spiritual interdict on all religious services so long as state commissars controlled the affairs of the church. The reaction of the pastors was less than sanguine. Few recognized the potential of spiritual interdict as a force against the Hitler dictatorship; some saw in the proposal only the intransigence of Bonhoeffer and Hildebrandt. We can only surmise the effect such an action would have had on Nazi policies. The time known as the "church struggle" had begun.

For Bonhoeffer, this was a time of "confession of faith." He, Martin Niemöller, Franz Hildebrandt, and Gerhard Jacobi met to form the Pastors' Emergency League. Many in this group would shortly help to organize the Confessing Church of Germany. In search of a solid spiritual rationale, they commissioned Bonhoeffer and a fellow Confessing Church pastor, Hermann Sasse, to draft a Confession of Faith that would counter the Nazi incursion into the public life of the German Evangelical Church with its consequent corruption of attitudes toward the Jews. Since they composed this document at the retreat center of Bethel, it became known as the Bethel Confession. In retrospect, it is viewed as one of the most pointed condemnations yet of the Nazi ideology that had invaded and threatened to conquer the Christian churches of Germany. Yet, Bonhoeffer was himself dismayed at the watered-down version of the text eventually circulated among the pastors in November 1933.

The softening up of his own tough prose and the continuing failure of his church to mount a wholehearted resistance to nazism only served to reinforce Bonhoeffer's decision, taken the previous summer, to leave Berlin for a pastorate among two German-speaking parishes in London. There he continued the church struggle by correctly interpreting the German situation to his British friends, especially Bishop Bell of Chichester, himself a leading figure in the ecumenical movement and a strong advocate of the Confessing Church at the international meetings. With Bell on his side, Bonhoeffer was able with more confidence to pester the ecumenical leadership for recognition of the Confessing Church as the only true German Evangelical Church and to push the delegates to take notice of the causes dearest to him: church freedom, justice for the oppressed, and world peace. His eloquence on these issues reached a high point with his electrifying sermon "The Church and the Peoples of the World" (see part 4). This was the sermon that, according to Otto Dudzus, left the assembly "breathless with tension." He had troubled the consciences of the delgates at the ecumenical conference, even of those who would not follow his lead in seeking freedom for the church and peace in a world "choked with weapons."

On his return to Germany from his self-imposed "exile" in London, Bonhoeffer, now director of the Confessing Church seminary in Finkenwalde, became one of the most vehement defenders of the stand he and his colleagues had taken against the Reich Church. They rested their case on the Barmen and Dahlem confessions, to be sure, but also, and more ultimately, on the nature of the church as they interpreted it from the gospel of Jesus Christ. Papers from those years of conflict as well as Bonhoeffer's correspondence (see part 7) bear out the reasons for his unwillingness to compromise with the Reich Church, especially for the sake of appearances on the ecumenical scene. The selections from these papers included here show how Bonhoeffer attempted to infuse his theological insights as well as his pastoral energies into that struggle.

11

The Church and the Jewish Question

(Die Kirche vor der Juden Frage)

April 1933

This essay, written for a discussion group of pastors meeting at the house of Gerhard Jacobi in April 1933, was intended by Bonhoeffer to address the major questions that had come to dominate church discussions at that time, namely, the rising demand for an Aryan Clause in the church and its potential effects on baptized non-Aryans, especially those who held office in the congregations. These were facing not only discrimination but also rejection by the German Christians. Originally, Bonhoeffer had drawn up six theses that analyzed this problem. However, in the meantime, the boycott directed against Jewish merchants and the passage of the discriminatory laws of April 7, 1933 moved Bonhoeffer to write a completely new section to precede discussion of the six theses. This new section dealt solely with the question of discrimination against and victimization of the Jews without any reference to differentiating between the baptized and the nonbaptized Jew. It was this wholly new section, presented in the beginning, that created such a stir among the pastors that some left the gathering.[2]

One must, therefore, examine this paper in context. If originally Bonhoeffer's paper was to constitute an argument against the demeaning status the Reich Church would force on baptized non-Aryans, the new section was calling for church action in defense of Jews regardless of their baptismal status. Bonhoeffer advocated, first, that the church admonish the state; second, that it help the victims regardless of their religious affiliation; and, third, that the church consider jamming the spokes in the wheel of state. This third challenge is what proved too much for the more conservative, order-loving members of the church. It smacked of revolution and sedition.

This challenge is what those present took to be the essence of the paper, not the later published introductory statements with the lingering, unconscious anti-Semitism that some recent commentators have deracinated from context and seized upon to make a biased case against Bonhoeffer as merely the best of a universally bad lot of Germans.[3] In retrospect, the published essay is weakened by the anti-Semitism common among theologians at the time. It likewise remains somewhat problematic in its interpretation of Luther's doctrine of the "two realms," appearing to advocate a certain deference to the state in a moment that called for stark confrontation. Despite these deficiencies, the essay stands as an important, courageous call for the church to *act* at a time when few dared even speak out in defense of the Jews. There is little doubt that Bonhoeffer's assessment of the situation created by Nazi persecution of Jews, then in its beginning stage, was both precocious and accurate. In his opinion, to accept this "legalized" denial of civil rights of a whole group of people threatened the integrity of all Christians in Germany. Even if these initial observations on the issue lacked the later, more daring affirmation of the church's duty to intervene, he did succeed in drawing attention within his church to something most church leaders preferred to ignore: the Christian proclamation itself had been endangered by the Aryan legislation. His call to the revolutionary act of "jamming a spoke in the wheel" of state would be issued only when, according to Bonhoeffer, the state had failed in its duty either by the excess of law and order that led to tyranny or by the defect of law and order that led to anarchy. In a way, nazism had sinned in both directions in its laws denying basic human rights and in the anarchy of its criminal government. The church, he said, was approaching the point where it would "be called to protect the state *qua* state from itself and to preserve it."

It seems clear from this that Bonhoeffer had broadened Luther's doctrine of two realms to include confrontation of the sword of state with the gospel. He makes the "Jewish Question" a Christian church question. He raised what was to become the test question of Christian identity: how closely a Christian identifies with the Jewish people whether baptized or not. Admittedly, these issues represent only the beginning of a new phase in an eventual reconciliation with Judaism. Nonetheless, as German theologian Heinz Eduard Tödt has noted, it was an important beginning: "In 1933 Bonhoeffer was almost alone in his opinions; he was the only one who considered solidarity with the Jews, especially with non-Christian Jews, to be a matter of such importance as to obligate the Christian churches to risk a massive conflict with that state—a risk which could threaten their very existence."[4] In Hitler's Third Reich such a paper was a rarity.

Did Bonhoeffer ever retract the anti-Semitism that has hung over the published text from centuries of Christian anti-Jewish bias? There is ample evidence that he did. His later judgment on Confessing Church synods always seemed to depend on whether the resolutions included defense of the Jewish people, not merely the baptized among them. His biographer, Eberhard Bethge, reports that he dampened the enthusiastic reception of many a seemingly courageous synodal pronouncement with his own disappointment if the synod in question failed to speak out for the Jews. Church timidity on this issue was one of the reasons he joined the political resistance movement.[5] Some of the beginning of that resistance to Hitler is evidenced in the selection that follows.

Now here, of course, the state sees itself to be limited in two respects. Both too much law and order and too little law and order compel the church to speak. There is too little law and order where a group of people becomes lawless, though in real life it is sometimes extraordinarily difficult to distinguish real lawlessness from a formally permitted minimum of law. Even in slavery a minimum of law and order was preserved, and yet a reintroduction of slavery would mean real lawlessness. It is at any rate worth noting that Christian churches tolerated slavery for eighteen centuries and that a new law was made only at a time when the Christian substance of the church could at least be put in question, with the help of the churches, but not essentially or even solely by them. Nevertheless, a step back in this direction would be to the church the expression of a lawless state. It therefore follows that the concept of law is subject to historical change, and this in its turn once again confirms the state in its characteristic history-making law. It is not the church, but the state, which makes and changes the law.

Too little law and order stands in contrast to too much law and order. That means that the state develops its power to such an extent that it deprives Christian preaching and Christian faith (not freedom of conscience—that would be the humanitarian illusion, which is illusory because any life in a state constrains the so-called "free conscience") of their rights—a grotesque situation, as the state only receives its peculiar rights from this proclamation and from this faith, and enthrones itself by means of them. The church must reject this encroachment of the order of the state precisely because of its better knowledge of the state and of the limitations of its action. The state which endangers the Christian proclamation negates itself.

All this means that there are three possible ways in which the church can act toward the state: in the first place, as has been said, it can ask the state whether its actions are legitimate and in accordance with its character as state, i.e., it can throw the state back on its responsibilities. Second, it can aid the victims of state action. The church has an unconditional obligation to the victims of any ordering of society, even if they do not belong to the Christian community. "Do good to all people." In both these courses of action, the church serves the free state in its free way, and at times when laws are changed the church may in no way withdraw itself from these two tasks. The third possibility is not just to bandage the victims under the wheel, but to jam a spoke in the wheel itself. Such action would be direct political action, and is only possible and desirable when the church sees the state fail in its function of creating law and order, i.e., when it sees the state unrestrainedly bring about too much or too little law and order. In both these cases it must see the existence of the state, and with it its own existence, threatened. There would be too little law if any group of subjects were deprived of their rights, too much where the state intervened in the character of the church and its proclamation, e.g., in the forced exclusion of baptized Jews from our Christian congregations or in the prohibition of our mission to the Jews. Here the Christian church would find itself *in status confessionis* and here the state would be in the act of negating itself. A state which includes within itself a terrorized church has lost its most faithful servant. But even this third action of the church, which on occasion leads to conflict with the existing state, is only the paradoxical expression of its ultimate recognition of the state; indeed, the church itself knows itself to be called here to protect the state *qua* state from itself and to preserve it. In the Jewish problem the first two possibilities will be the compelling demands of the hour. The necessity of direct political action by the church is, on the other hand, to be decided at any time by an "Evangelical Council" and cannot therefore ever be casuistically decided beforehand. . . . [*NRS*, pp. 224–26]

12

The Bethel Confession

(Das Betheles Bekenntnis)

August 1933

Here we excerpt from the section on "The Church and the Jews," drafted in August 1933 by Bonhoeffer and Wilhelm Vischer as part of the Bethel Confession. This was a period in German church history that for many religious leaders called for a confession of faith. For this reason, the Bethel Confession has special significance in the history of the church struggle as that struggle pertained to one of the most important yet overlooked aspects of the turmoil: Christian solidarity with the Jewish people. The Bethel Confession is a landmark in this phase of the church struggle, not because of any success it had in sensitizing Christians to the evils of nazism but for the way it expresses new beginnings in the church's attitude toward Jews. Much of this shift stems from Bonhoeffer's interest in this issue and from his having composed, in collaboration with Wilhelm Vischer, the chapter on "The Church and the Jews," reproduced here. Vischer was a teacher in the School of Theology at Bethel, a center for the treatment of epileptics. Bonhoeffer and Hermann Sasse had been deputed by Confessing Church leaders to go into retreat at Bethel in order to compose a first draft of a "binding confession." Because the strengths of the section Bonhoeffer and Sasse wrote were diluted by heavy editing and because of other changes to make the overall text more acceptable, Bonhoeffer would eventually refuse to sign the document at its November 1933 publication by Martin Niemöller.[6]

Yet this confession remains important because it is so revealing of the theological clash between the German Christians and the group represented by Bonhoeffer and Vischer. The fact that the confession was directed against the German Christians with their announced intention to enforce the Aryan Clause in the church might mitigate somewhat the conscious and unconscious anti-Judaisms of the authors. We still find mention of the Jews being blamed for having rejected their Messiah, the Christ. We also see repeated the disinheritance theory: the Christian church has displaced the Jewish people of the "old" covenant. And, there is the inevitable affirmation of the Christian church's "mission" to convert the Jews. On this latter point, however, a qualification is needed. As William Jay Peck has noted, one must not overlook Bonhoeffer's intention to "keep the church open to the conversion of the Jews at a time when there was pressure to exclude them and thereby put racial limits on the fellowship of the church."[7] The "disinheritance theory" is likewise couched in terms that deny the "world mission" of a chosen "master race" now able to establish a national church with a purely Aryan composition. Hence the emphasis in the confession was to deny that the place of the Jewish people of the Old Testament had been "taken by another *nation*." The place was taken, so the document asserted, "by the Christian church called out of and living among all *nations*."[8] Here the intent is to counteract setting God's choice of Israel aside in favor of a new choice of Nazi Germany to bring about the supposed messianic kingdom, or so the Nazi mythology would have it.

What is particularly significant about the Bethel Confession is its reiteration of God's choice of Israel in wholly theological terms and its insistence that God has not retracted that choice. "The 'holy remnant'," the document states, "can neither be absorbed into another nation by emancipation and assimilation . . . nor be exterminated by Pharaohlike measures. This 'holy remnant' bears the indelible stamp of the chosen people. . . . No nation can ever be commissioned to avenge on the Jews the murder at Golgotha. . . . We oppose the attempt to deprive the German Evangelical Church of its promise by the attempt to change it into a national church of Christians of Aryan descent." From that unambiguous declaration, we can see that this confession, despite its obvious shortcomings in properly assessing Judaism, is a sharp repudiation of Aryanism and the Nazi aims to rid the German nation and church of any Jewish presence and influence. In its own way, it represents a major move away from some of the old slogans that have been used to slander the Jewish people and to make the persecution of them seem religiously justified. This confession criticizes the attitudes of church leaders who themselves subscribed to the nation's racist policies and, what is startling, given the long history of Christian anti-Semitism, emphasized God's continued fidelity to Israel and the indestructibility of the Jewish people themselves. These were formulations close to treason in those days of racial hatred. The selections from the Bethel Confession included here constitute Bonhoeffer's strongest written critique of the spirit and pseudotheological justification of the anti-Jewish policies adopted by both church and state in 1933. It is followed by a "Declaration" from Bonhoeffer and Martin Niemöller calling for repeal of the unjust Aryan Clauses.

The church teaches that God chose Israel from among all the nations of the earth to be his people. He chose them solely in the power of his Word and for the sake of his loving-kindness, and not because they were in any way preeminent (Exod. 19:5–6; Deut. 7:7–11). The Sanhedrin and the Jewish people rejected Christ Jesus, promised by the law and the prophets, in accordance with Scripture. They wanted a national Messiah, who would bring them political freedom and the rule of the world. Jesus Christ was not this, and did not do this. He died at their hands and for their sakes. The barrier between Jew and Gentile has been broken down by the crucifixion and resurrection of Jesus Christ

(Eph. 2). The place of the Old Testament people of the covenant was not taken by another nation, but by the Christian church, called out of and living among all nations.

God abundantly shows his faithfulness by still keeping faith with Israel after the flesh, from whom was born Christ after the flesh, despite all their unfaithfulness, even after the crucifixion. It is his will to complete the salvation of the world, which he began with the election of Israel, through these selfsame Jews (Rom. 9–11). Therefore he continues to preserve a "holy remnant" of Israel after the flesh, which can neither be absorbed into another nation by emancipation and assimilation, nor become one nation among others as a result of the efforts of Zionist and other similar movements, nor be exterminated by Pharaoh-like measures. This "holy remnant" bears the indelible stamp of the chosen people. The church has received from its Lord the commission to call the Jews to repentance and to baptize those who believe in Jesus Christ to the forgiveness of sins (Matt. 10:5f.; Acts 2:38ff., 3:19–26). A mission to the Jews which for cultural or political considerations refuses to baptize any more Jews at all is refusing to be obedient to its Lord. The crucified Christ is to the Jews a stumbling block and to the Greeks folly (1 Cor. 1:22f.). "The Crucified One" as little accords with the religious ideal of the Jewish soul as it does with the religious ideal of the soul of any other nation. Faith in him cannot be given by flesh and blood even to a Jew, but only by the Father in heaven through his spirit (Matt. 16:17).

The community of those who belong to the church is not determined by blood and therefore not by race, but by the Holy Spirit and baptism.

We reject any attempt to identify or confuse the historical mission of any nation with Israel's commission in sacred history.

No nation can ever be commissioned to avenge on the Jews the murder at Golgotha. "Vengeance is mine, says the Lord" (Deut. 32:35, Heb. 10:30). We reject any attempt to misuse the miracle of God's especial faithfulness toward Israel after the flesh as an indication of the religious significance of the Jewish people or of another people.

We oppose the assertion that the faith of Jewish Christians is, as opposed to that of Gentile Christians, affected by their descent and is Judaistic heresy.

We oppose the attempt to deprive the German Evangelical Church of its promise by the attempt to change it into a national church of Christians of Aryan descent. This would be to erect a racial barrier against entering the church and would make such a church itself a Jewish Christian community regulated by the Law. We therefore reject the forming of Jewish Christian communities, because the false presupposition for such action is the view that the special element in Jewish Christianity can be appropriately compared with, for example, the historically determined peculiarity of the communities of French refugees in Germany, and that Christians from Judaism must develop a form of

Christianity appropriate to their character. The special element in the Jewish Christian does not lie in his race or his character or his history, but in God's special faithfulness toward Israel after the flesh and in that alone. The way in which the Jewish Christian has a special position in the church which is not based on any legal ruling in itself makes him a living memorial of God's faithfulness within the church and is a sign that the barrier between Jew and Gentile has been broken down and that faith in Christ may not be perverted into a national religion or a racially determined Christianity. It is the task of the Christians who come from the Gentile world to expose themselves to persecution rather than to surrender, willingly or unwillingly, even in one single respect, their brotherhood with Jewish Christians in the church, founded on Word and Sacrament. . . . [NRS, pp. 240–42.]

13

Declaration

(Erklärung)

September 7, 1933

This declaration became incorporated into the draft of a call to form the Pastors' Emergency League and the basis of the petition to the National Synod signed by 2,000 evangelical pastors.

According to the confession of our church, the teaching office of the church is bound up with a call in accordance with the order of the church and with that call alone. The "Aryan Clauses" of the new enactment concerning offices in the church put forward a principle which contradicts this basic clause of the confession. As a result, a position which must be regarded as unjust is proclaimed as church law, and the confession is violated.

There can be no doubt that as long as the ordained ministers affected by the enactment are not dispossessed of the rights which belong to their status as ministers by formal proceedings they have under all circumstances the right to preach the Word and administer the sacraments freely in the Evangelical Church of the Old Prussian Union which rests on the confessions of the Reformation.

Anyone who gives his assent to a breach of the confession thereby excludes himself from the community of the church. We therefore demand that this law, which separates the Evangelical Church of the Old Prussian Union from the Christian church, be repealed forthwith.

Martin Niemöller
Dietrich Bonhoeffer

[*NRS*, p. 249.]

14

The Confessing Church and the Ecumenical Movement

(Die Bekennende Kirche und die Ökumene)

August 1935

This paper was written in Finkenwalde in June and July 1935 and published in August in *Evangelische Theologie*, vol. 7.

Eberhard Bethge mentions in his biography that Bonhoeffer's involvement with the seminary in Finkenwalde kept his involvement with the ecumenical movement at a minimum after the peak moments of 1934 at Fanø. He maintained, however, a steady dialogue with the senior members of the movement in 1935. More and more, Bonhoeffer had come to feel that the ecumenical leaders could no longer avoid the difficult problem of the Confessing Church's representation at all future conferences. To that end, he steadfastly declined to participate in any meetings at which equal representation was accorded to both the Reich Church and the Confessing Church. Matters came to a crisis point at the Hanover Conference of mid-May 1935, during which Bonhoeffer emphasized the impossibility of any kind of joint cooperation of the two opposing churches in preparation for the important Oxford Conference of 1937. Further, he insisted that the Confessing Church, backed up by the Barmen and Dahlem confessions, could no longer afford to be equivocal in this matter. In his opinion, the Oxford Conference needed a theology emanating from the true church, not from an heretical group outside the pale of the gospel. He accused the ecumenical officers in Geneva, who had treated the church struggle as a mere ecclesiastical rift, of a wimpish approach to the real issue, namely, the need to make a concrete decision in favor of the Confessing Church's claims. At the same time, he pressed for the recognition and establishment of an ecumenical office for the Confessing Church but without success.

After having again refused to take part on an equal level with delegates from the Reich Church in a Faith and Order Conference at Hindsgavl, Bonhoeffer wrote of his feelings on the matter to Canon Leonard Hodgson, stating that, in essence, his rejection of the invitation was not traceable to a simple difference of opinion between the churches, but the more fundamental issue of a church having fallen away from Christ. Citing the Dahlem Confession, he argued "that the Reich Church government has dissociated itself from the Church of Christ. This solemn declaration has been given in full power and in obedience to the Word of Jesus Christ; it states clearly that the Reich Church government can no longer claim to compose the church of Christ in Germany nor any part of it. . . . Being a minister of the Confessing Church I cannot attend an ecumenical conference unless it either excludes the Reich Church or ventures openly to charge both the Reich Church and the Confessing Church with responsibility."[9] This letter makes it clear that the relations between the Reich Church and the Confessing Church had deteriorated to such an extent that participation in the ecumenical movement was threatened.

Bonhoeffer was thoroughly convinced that he had to snap the ecumenical movement to an awareness of the extent of the crisis. Hence, his article, excerpted here, that puts into sharp theological perspective the relationship of the Confessing Church to the ecumenical movement. The church struggle, he noted, puts demand both on the ecumenical movement, to live up to the spirit of Fanø and so live up to its promise to be the church of Jesus Christ, and on the Confessing Church, to see the struggle as one for the very life of Christianity. If the ecumenical movement has backed the Confessing Church, so "the Confessing Church must vindicate itself before the ecumenical movement" and remain faithful to the gospel and the confession.

Preliminary observation: From the beginning, the struggle of the Confessing Church has been of deep concern to Christian churches outside Germany. This has often been noted with suspicion and condemned both by churchpeople and by politicians. It is understandable that this should have been a surprise for the politicians, and one that could give rise to false interpretations, for the evangelical ecumenical world has never been so much in evidence on the occasion of a church dispute as in the past two years, and the position of ecumenical Christianity on a matter of faith has never been so clear and unambiguous as here. The German church struggle marks the second great stage in the history of the ecumenical movement and will in a decisive way be normative for its future. It was less understandable, on the other hand, that in our church people should on the whole have been so unprepared for and so nonplussed at this turn of events that they were almost ashamed at the voices of our foreign brethren and felt them to be painful, instead of rejoicing at their fellowship and their testimony. The anxiety and confusion called forth by the outlawry of the political concept of internationalism in church circles had made them blind to something completely new which had begun to thrust itself forward, the evangelical ecumenical world. Under the onslaught of new nationalism, the fact that the church of Christ does not stop at national and racial boundaries but reaches beyond them, so powerfully attested in the New Testament and in the confessional writings, has been far too easily forgotten and denied. Even where it was found impossible to make a theoretical refutation, voices have never ceased to declare emphatically that of course a conversation with foreign Christians about so-called internal German church matters was unthinkable, and that a judgment or even an open attitude toward these things was impossible and reprehensible. Attempts have been made on a number of sides to convince the ecumenical organizations that nothing but scandal would attach itself to such goings-on. Ecumenical relationships have been largely regarded from the viewpoint of church-political tactics. In this, a sin has been committed against the seriousness of the ecumenicity of the Evangelical Church. It is just an expression of ecumenical thought that, despite all the fear, despite all the inner defences, despite all the attempts, honest and dishonest, to disinterest the ecumenical movement, the ecumenical movement has shared in the struggle and the suffering of German Protestantism, that it has raised its voice again and again: when the Bishop of Chichester, as president of the Ecumenical Council, wrote his letter to the national bishop in which he implored him to remain mindful of his position as guardian of evangelical Christianity in Germany, when he then in his Ascension message of 1934 drew the attention of all Christian churches to the seriousness of the position of the church in Germany and invited them to a council session, and when finally in the memorable conference at Fanø in August 1934, the ecumenical movement framed its clear and brotherly resolution on the German church dispute and at the same time elected the president of the Confessing Synod, Dr. Koch, to the Ecumenical Council. It was in those days that many leading churchpeople for the first time came to see the reality of the ecumenical movement.

In all this, the spokespeople of the ecumenical movement have begun from two recognitions: first, that the struggle of the Confessing Church is bound up with the whole preaching of the gospel, and second, that the struggle has been brought to a head and undergone by the Confessing Church vicariously for all Christianity, and particularly for Western Christianity. This recognition of necessity led to a twofold attitude. First, the natural inward and outward concern, which could not be prevented by any sort of objection, in this struggle is regarded as a common cause. Prayers have been offered in countless foreign churches for the pastors of the Confessing Church, numerous conventions of clergy have sent messages to the Confessing Church to assure it of their inward concern, and in theological seminaries young students have thought every day in their prayers of the Confessing Church and its struggles. Second, such concern can only consist in the churches' firm attitude of brotherly help and common attention to the gospel and the right of its being preached throughout the world without hindrance or intimidation.

Because this support was governed by a sense of the responsibility of the church and not by any arbitrariness, on the one hand all attempts to make a church-political business here by confusing and muddling the situation had of necessity to fail from the start. On the other hand, for the same reason, the spokespeople of the ecumenical movement could preserve the moderate and pastoral bounds of their task and continue their way unerringly.

The ecumenical movement and the Confessing Church have made an encounter. The ecumenical movement has stood sponsor at the coming-to-be of the Confessing Church, in prayer for her and in commitment toward her. That is a fact, even if it is an extremely remarkable fact, which is most offensive to many people. It is extremely remarkable, because an understanding of ecumenical work might *a priori* have been least expected in the circles of the Confessing Church, and an interest in the theological questioning of the Confessing Church might *a priori* have been least expected in ecumenical circles. It is offensive, because it is vexatious to the German nationalist for once to have to see his church from the outside, because no one gladly shows his wounds to a stranger. But it is not only a remarkable and an offensive fact, it is still more a tremendously promising fact, because in this encounter the ecumenical movement and the Confessing Church ask each other the reason for their existence. The ecumenical movement must vindicate itself before the Confessing Church and the Confessing Church must vindicate itself before the ecumenical movement, and just as the ecumenical movement is led to a serious inward concern and crisis by the Confessing Church, so too the Confessing Church is led to a serious inward concern and crisis by the ecumenical movement. This reciprocal questioning must now be developed. . . .

The Confessing Church represents a genuine question for the ecumenical movement insofar as it confronts the latter in all its totality with the question of the confession. The Confessing Church is the church which would be exclusively governed in all its totality by the confession. It is fundamentally impossible to enter into conversation with this church at any point without immediately raising the question of the confession. Because the Confessing Church has learnt in the church struggle that from the preaching of the gospel to the taxing of the churches the church must be governed by the confession and the confession alone, because there is no neutral ground, divorced from the confession, within her, she immediately confronts any partner in conversation with the question of the confession. There is no other approach to the Confessing Church than through the question of the confession. There is no possibility of common tactical action outside of the question of the confession. Here the Confessing Church seals herself off hermetically against any political, social, or humanitarian inroads. The confession occupies her whole sphere.

To this confession as it has been *authoritatively* expounded in the decisions of the synods of Barmen and Dahlem, there is only a Yes or a

No. Thus here too neutrality is impossible, here too an assent to this or that point outside the question of the confession remains excluded. No, the Confessing Church must insist that in any responsible church discussion it is taken seriously enough for this claim to be recognized and accepted. It must further insist that in any conversation with it the solidarity of the churches be shown by the partner in the conversations not entering into discussions with it and with the churches which it accuses of heresy at one and the same time, indeed that even for the ecumenical partner in the conversations the conversations be finally broken off where in its responsibility as a church it declares that they are broken off.

This is an unheard-of claim. But this is the only way in which the Confessing Church can enter ecumenical conversations. And this must be known if the Confessing Church is to be understood and its remarks rightly interpreted. If the Confessing Church departed from this claim, the church struggle in Germany (and with it the struggle for Christendom) would already have been decided against her. Seeing that the ecumenical movement has taken up conversations with the Confessing Church, it has consciously or unconsciously heard this claim, and the Confessing Church may gratefully start from this presupposition. At the same time, however, the ecumenical movement has by this allowed itself to be driven into a severe internal crisis, as the characteristic claim of the Confessing Church remains at the same time precisely within the sphere of the ecumenical movement. The questions of the Confessing Church, which the ecumenical movement declares that it has already heard, stand open there and can no longer be suppressed. . . .

Is the ecumenical movement, in its visible representation, a church? Or to put it the other way round: Has the real ecumenicity of the church as witnessed in the New Testament found visible and appropriate expression in the ecumenical organization? This question is generally put today with great emphasis by the younger generations of theologians who take part in ecumenical work. And the importance of the question is immediately clear. It is the question of the authority with which the ecumenical movement speaks and acts. "With what authority doest thou that?" they ask. This question of authority is decisive, and it is not without the most serious internal damage to the work that it remains unanswered. If the ecumenical movement claims to be the church of Christ, it is as imperishable as the church of Christ itself; in that case its work has ultimate importance and ultimate authority; in that case there is fulfilled in it either the old hope of evangelical Christianity for the one true church of Christ among all the nations of the earth *or* the titanic and anti-Christian attempt of humanity to make visible what God would hide from our eyes. In that case, the unity of this ecumenical church is either obedience to the promise of Jesus Christ that there should be one flock and one shepherd or it is the kingdom of false peace and false unity built on the lies of the devil in angelic form. In that case, the ecumenical movement stands in this dilemma, in which any church stands.

It is indeed understandable, if there have been long-continued attempts to avoid answering this question; it is indeed more pious to confess ignorance where one knows nothing of these matters than to say a false word. But now this question has been raised afresh by the Confessing Church and demands clarity. Now it can no longer be left open in *docta ignorantia*. Now it threatens every word and every deed of the ecumenical movement, and in this lies the first service of the Confessing Church to the ecumenical movement. . . .

Living confession does not mean the putting of one dogmatic thesis up against another, but it means a confession in which it is really a matter of life or death. A naturally formulated, clear, theologically based, true confession. But theology itself is not the fighting part here; it stands wholly at the service of the living, confessing, and struggling church.

It is clear that despite all theological analogies the ecumenical situation is fundamentally different from this. The Confessing Church faces the churches alien to a confession not as though they were deadly enemies, which sought its life, but in the encounter it helps to bear the guilt for the brokenness of Christianity, it shares in this guilt and in all the false theology it may encounter recognizes first of all its own guilt, the want of power in its own preaching. It recognizes God's incomprehensible ways with his church, it shudders before the gravity of a cleavage in the church and before the burden which it is laying upon subsequent generations, and it hears at this point the call and the admonition to responsibility and to repentance. In the face of this picture it will experience afresh the whole need of its own decision and in this situation its confession will be first a *confession of sin*. . . .

With this the page turns, and the Confessing Church no longer stands, does not stand at all, as the one who enquires and demands, but stands as the party being questioned by the ecumenical movement, as the church put in question—and now the surprising thing is this, that after hearing the questions of the Confessing Church, the ecumenical movement throws back the selfsame questions at the Confessing Church itself. The weapon used against the ecumenical movement is now turned against the Confessing Church. How can the confession "Christ alone, grace alone, Scripture alone," how can the confession of justification by faith alone be true in any other way than in that the confession of the Confessing Church is in the first place a confession of sin, a confession that this church with all its theology and cultus and order lives solely from the grace of God and Jesus Christ and is in need of justification? The confession of the Confessing Church becomes serious only *in actu,* i.e., here in the confession of sins, in repentance. Does the Confessing Church therefore know that the confession of the Fathers and the confession against the enemies of Jesus Christ is only credible and authoritative where the confession has first gone out against itself, where the *damnamus* has first been directed against its own front? Is this the presupposition on which the Confessing Church will enter the ecumenical community?

These questions are put to the Confessing Church by the ecumenical movement *first of all* by its existence. The mere fact that the Christian churches of the whole world—with the exception of the Roman church—have met to engage in conversation with one another and to make common decisions is there, whether the Confessing Church says Yes or No to it. It is a fact that a shattered Christianity is coming together in unanimous acknowledgment of its needs and in unanimous prayer for the promised unity of the church of Jesus Christ, indeed that services are being held together, sermons being heard, even Eucharists being celebrated together and that there is still, or again, a possibility of ecumenical Christianity, and that all is being done calling upon the name of Jesus Christ and asking for the support of the Holy Spirit. In view of this fact, can we simply set it up against it a pathetic "Impossible," is it really right *a priori* to call down the anathema over all such actions? Is not this witness of all Christian churches at least a fact which first of all requires a moment's pause and reflection? It must indeed be openly and clearly recognized that the actual existence of the ecumenical movement constitutes no proof of its truth or of its Christian legitimacy. But if it cannot be a proof, cannot it be at least an indication of the promise which God means to lay upon this action? Is there still honest prayer for the unity of the church where anyone *a priori* excludes himself or herself from this community? Should not it be the church, which is seriously concerned about truth, which should first of all be questioned about this truth? Should it not be a church within the confines of Germany, that finds it so difficult to cast its eyes beyond its own borders, which should take notice here? Should it not be a church that is fighting for its very existence, which is thankful and watchful for the prayers and the fellowship of all Christendom? Of course, it remains the fact that all this can never be a proof, but it is an indication of the promise of God and as such it is to be taken seriously and carefully examined. It is to be examined of course in no other way than through the question of the confession, through the test of Scripture. It would not be good if the Confessing Church were to act as though it had first to call the ecumenical movement to life, but it will befit its humility to recognize that here is something, outside it, independent of its Yes or No, which it has encountered on its way and by which it knows itself to be asked and summoned; the Confessing Church must encounter the ecumenical movement in repentance. It would indeed be a bad theology which prohibited the Confessing Church from taking these things very seriously.

But with this the last word has not been said. A place must be found in the foundations of the Confessing Church *qua* church from which ecumenical work becomes an ultimate obligation. This work must be a theological necessity, as well as a practical one.

Second: It is understandable that the ecumenical movement should lay great stress on just this question of innermost necessity. For on this depends whether the intentions of the Confessing Church toward the ecumenical movement are chance, possibly merely utilitarian, or whether they are necessary, and therefore permanent. Thus the question which the ecumenical movement returns to the Confessing Church comes to a head: Should the Confessing Church so isolate itself in its claim of a confession that its confession leaves no more room for ecumenical thought. The question should be asked with all seriousness, whether there is still a church of Christ in the Confessing Church. Where the claim of a confession sets itself up so absolutely that it declares that conversations with any church without a confession are broken off from the start, if in its blind zeal it can look upon all the other churches only as a mission field, if the mere readiness to hear is already branded as a betrayal of the gospel, if orthodoxy in unlimited self-glorification remains wholly with itself, and if, finally, only the Western belief in progress is detected in the continual protests of the ecumenical movement against unrighteousness and oppression—then the moment has come when it must seriously be asked whether the place of Jesus Christ over his church has not been taken by human dominion, that of the grace of God by human ordinances, and that of Christ by AntiChrist. And if—and thus the questions come full circle—it is precisely such a church which asks the ecumenical movement whether it is itself a church, the ecumenical movement will be right in seeing only the insane claim to rule of a self-divinizing church and will have to keep itself from giving this voice a hearing.

The question of the church has been returned to the Confessing Church. The Confessing Church must say where the limits of the claims of its confession lie.

The Confessing Church gives its answer first by taking a practical part in ecumenical work, sharing in it in prayer and worship, in theological and in practical work. It does this because it is called to it and because it takes this call seriously. It leaves to God what he will make out of the encounter, and waits for him to work.

The Confessing Church takes the call of the ecumenical movement seriously because it knows itself to be bound to its members by the sacrament of holy baptism. It knows that the sum total of the baptized is still not the church. It knows that despite the one baptism the churches are divided, and it does not forget its origin. But it recognizes in baptism the grace and the promise of the one church which is alone gathered by the Holy Spirit through his word. The Reformation churches recognized the baptism, for example, of the Roman church, not thereby to weaken the seriousness of the division in the church—the fact that the churches must still excommunicate each other despite the one baptism makes this division still more acute—but rather to raise the claim of desiring to be nothing but the purified Catholic church itself, the heritage of the church of Rome, and to advance their own claim to catholicity. With this at the same time the grace of God is put *above* church doctrine, once again not in such a way that the division of the church ceases to be serious and can be revoked by us, but so that it may thus be felt to be all the more fearful. In coming together on the basis of their common baptism, the Reformed churches of the ecumenical movement thereby consciously claim the heritage of the original Catholic Church, and only now does the question of the right and the legitimacy of this claim, i.e., of the scriptural purity of these churches, arise.

The Confessing Church is the church which lives not by its purity but in its impurity—the church of sinners, the church of repentance and grace, the church which can live only through Christ, through grace, and through faith. As such a church, which daily stands penitent, it is a church which confesses its guilt in the division of Christendom and which knows itself to be directed at every moment to the gift of the grace of God. It therefore exists only as a listening church; it is free for listening to the other, which calls it to repentance. Thus in its recognition of the gospel as the sole grace of God through Jesus Christ, brother and Lord, lies the necessity and the possibility of listening and of ecumenical encounter. Because this church receives its life not from itself, but from without, it therefore already exists in each word that it says from the ecumenical movement. That is its innermost compulsion to ecumenical work.

The Confessing Church takes the recognition of the gospel given to it by God through Holy Scripture in the confession of the Fathers and given afresh today with infinite seriousness. It has learned that this truth alone is its weapon in the struggle for life and death. It cannot depart from this truth in the slightest degree, but with this truth it knows itself to be called not to rule, but to serve and to listen, and it will exercise this its unrestricted service in the ecumenical movement.

The Confessing Church takes part in ecumenical work as *a church*. Its word is intended to be heard as a word of the church, simply because it does not mean to attest its own word, but the authoritative word of God. It means to speak as a church to churches. Therefore it compels a decision with its word.

The Confessing Church will recognize the right of the ecumenical movement to brotherly help, brotherly admonition, and brotherly remonstrance at any time, and will thereby testify that the unity of Christendom and love for Jesus Christ breaks through all bounds. *It will never be ashamed of the voice of its brothers,* but will give and will seek to secure for it a grateful hearing.

The question has been raised. The future of the ecumenical movement and of the Confessing Church depends on its being taken up. There can be no qualifications. No one knows the crises into which all this will lead the ecumenical movement and the Confessing Church. What remains as a positive "program"? Nothing, except that this question, now raised, be not allowed to rest. Because it has within it the real power of the church, we commit ourselves to it.

Whether the hopes laid on the Ecumenical Council of Evangelical Christendom will be fulfilled, whether such a council will not only bear witness to the truth and the unity of the church of Christ with authority but also be able to bear witness against the enemies of Christianity throughout the world, whether it will speak a word of judgment about war, race hatred, and social exploitation, whether through such true ecumenical unity of all evangelical Christians among all nations war itself will become impossible, whether the witness of such a council will find ears to hear—all this depends on our obedience toward the question which has been put to us and on the way in which God will use our obedience. What is set up is not an ideal, but a command and a promise—what is demanded is not our own realization of our own aims, but obedience. The question has been raised. [*NRS,* pp. 326–44.]

15

The Interpretation of the New Testament

(Vergegenwärtigung neutestamentlicher Texte)

August 23, 1935

Bonhoeffer delivered this lecture to the auxiliary preachers and curates of the Saxony province of the Confessing Church, in Hauteroda. One crucial aspect of the struggle of the Confessing Church with the Reich Church and Nazi theologians at the time was over the correct interpretation of Scripture. Representatives of the Reich Church were not beyond distorting the Bible texts in order to justify the racial policies then in place or to reinforce from a seemingly spiritual point of view the discriminatory laws against the Jews. Bonhoeffer waged that battle on several fronts: in his classes with the seminarians at Finkenwalde, in his preaching and teaching, and in his correspondence of the period. The lecture excerpted here shows how he proposed to interpret and use Scripture in a manner at once loyal to the correct sense of the text, but also with reverence for the power of the Word of God to cast the judgment of God on the attitudes, pretensions, and actions of the present age. Here Bonhoeffer takes issue with the manipulation of Scripture by the German Christians, accusing them of pursuing an ersatz relevance in order to evade the facts, thus sacrificing the truth to a pagan ideology. Their approach to Scripture, he argues, is an inversion in which they would germanize Christianity, making Christianity justify itself before the "present age," the popular wave of nazism. As he points out, it is, rather, the present age which must be asked to justify itself before the Christian message.

In principle, it is possible to explain the interpretation of the New Testament message in two ways. Either the biblical message must justify itself in the present age and must therefore show itself capable of interpretation or the present age must justify itself before the biblical message and therefore the message must become real. Where the question

of interpretation is put with that uncanny urgency that we know so well*
indeed is the central question of theology, it is always bound to serve
the first purpose. The New Testament is bound to justify itself in the
present age.

The question in this form became acute for the first time in the age
of the emancipation of the autonomous reason, i.e., in rationalism, and
it has influenced theology right up to the German Christian theology.
So far as rationalism was nothing but the emergence of the hitherto
latent claim of a person to shape his own life from the resources of the
world at his disposal, the question was one that implied the human claim
to autonomy, i.e., the autonomous person who would at the same time
profess Christianity demands the justification of the Christian message
before the forum of his autonomy. If this succeeds, he calls himself a
Christian; if it does not, he calls himself a *pagan.* It does not make the
slightest difference whether the forum before which the biblical message
has to justify itself is called, as in the eighteenth century, reason, as in
the nineteenth century, culture, or as in the twentieth century, the people, viz., the year 1933 and all that that includes; *the question is exactly
the same:* "Can Christianity make itself real to us, just as we are?" It is
exactly the same urgent need of all those who would lay claim to the
name of Christian on any grounds, be they those of reason, of culture,
or of politics, to justify Christianity in the present age; there is *exactly
the same presupposition,* namely that the Archimedean point, the firm
starting point which stands beyond all doubt, has already been found
(be it in reason, culture, or the idea of the people) and the movable,
questionable, uncertain element is the Christian message; and there is
exactly the same method, namely to go about the interpretation in such a
way that the biblical message is passed through the sieve of humanity's
own knowledge—what will not go through is scorned and tossed away.
The message is trimmed and cropped until it fits the frame which has
been decided, and the result is that the eagle (with its clipped wings)
can no longer rise and fly away to its true element but can be pointed
out as a special showpiece among the other household animals. It is like
a farmer who needs a horse for his fields; he leaves the fiery stallion on
one side and buys the tame, broken-in horse. This is just the way people
have tamed for themselves a usable Christianity, and it is only a matter
of time and honest thought before they lose interest in their creation
and get rid of it. *This interpretation* of the Christian message leads directly
to paganism. It therefore follows that the only difference between the
German Christians and the so-called neo-pagans is one of *honesty.* Second, however, there also follows the cry, doubtless in part uttered with
great passion and subjective earnestness, for the relevance of the
Christian message, which went up at the beginning of the German

---

*German Christians' reasons for the people's mission.

Christian movement. This is surely not to be taken seriously either by the church or by the theologians; it was at best the terror-stricken shout of those who saw the gulf between Christianity and the world opening up beneath them, who, conscious of their complete conformity to the world, recognized that it was all up with Christianity for themselves, but were not strong enough to say a clear "Yes" and an equally clear "No," and cravenly pulled down Christianity with themselves in their fall into the world. The clearest indication of this is the fact that no one here found the courage to ask afresh after the *fact* of the Christian message; they sought only its *relevance,* precisely—unlike liberal theology, e.g., Naumann!—*in order to evade the fact.* But where the question of relevance becomes the *theme of theology,* we can be certain that the cause has already been betrayed and sold out. We will have to be very much on our guard against letting the struggle get us entangled in false questions and false themes. The danger is always there. I need only recall theological writing of the last two years—and from our side too! (Althaus' *German Hour of the Church,* Heim, even Schlatter, *New German Characteristics in the Church*)—to make my point. This question of *relevance* all too easily acquires a false emphasis and displaces the question of *fact.* What is the sense in talking about presentation when we cannot even feel completely sure about what we are presenting?

Anyone who is thirsty will drink water from any utensil, even if it is somewhat inconvenient. And it is better to take some trouble in getting the water pure than to drink polluted water out of a glass. Anyone who is thirsty has always found living water in the Bible itself or in a sermon *in fact* based on the Bible, even if it were a little out-of-date—and it is an acknowledgment of a dangerous decadence of faith if the question of the relevance of the message, as a methodological question, becomes too loud. Anyone really concerned with the salvation of his or her soul has found that Luther's German version of Holy Scripture still best fulfills the demand for the presentation of the gospel in a German way. Here is Christianity which is both real and German.

That should be enough of the negative side of the definition for the moment; now the positive significance of this question of interpretation can be put in the right light. The intention should be not to justify Christianity in this present age, but *to justify the present age before the Christian message.* Interpretation then means that the present age is brought before the forum of the Christian message, in other words that the question is of the *fact,* the "value" (!) of the Christian message instead of being of the character of the present age, as in the false concept of relevance. True relevance lies in this question of the fact. It is felt of the *fact itself* that where it is really expressed it is in itself completely and utterly relevant; it therefore needs no other special act of interpretation, because the interpretation is achieved in the fact itself. This, however, is only so because *this* fact is the concern of the New Testament, because the fact here is Christ and his word. Where Christ is spoken of in the word of the New Testament, relevance is achieved. *The relevant* is not where the present age announces its claim before Christ, but where the present age stands before the claims of Christ, for the concept of the present age is determined not by a temporal definition but by the Word of Christ as the Word of God. The relevant has no feeling of time, no interpretation of time, no atmosphere of time, but the Holy Ghost, and the Holy Ghost alone. The relevant is and begins where God himself is in his Word. The Holy Ghost is the relevant subject, not we ourselves, so the Holy Ghost is also the subject of the interpretation. *The most essential element of the Christian message* and of textual exposition is not a human act of interpretation but is always God himself, it is the Holy Spirit. Because the "fact" of the New Testament is this, that Christ speaks to us through his Holy Spirit, and because this does not happen outside or alongside, but solely and exclusively *through the word* of Scripture, *being factual,* i.e., the adherence of preaching to the Scriptures, is itself interpretation—"being factual" both as a method (of which we shall soon be speaking) and as obedience and trust toward the fact of the Holy Spirit. For what is factual about this fact is the Holy Spirit himself, and he is the presence of both God and Christ. . . . [*NRS*, pp. 308–11]

16

The Visible Church in the New Testament

(Sichtbare Kirche im Neuen Testament)

1935–1936

This lecture, given at the Finkenwalde seminary during the winter semester, 1935–1936, and included in a circular letter from the seminary, was also presented during Bonhoeffer's visit to Sweden and Denmark with several of his students from February 29 to March 10, 1936, and shows Bonhoeffer's efforts to relate the church struggle to the larger question of just how the community of Christ came to be the church. The church, he argues, is not a mere religious fellowship but a fellowship in the Holy Spirit. Obedience to the Word of God and fidelity to the teachings of the apostles (*didache*) determined the nature and growth of the church. That obedience and fidelity should be the case, too, in the crisis years when, as Bonhoeffer points out in the beginning of the essay, the church could easily succumb to two dangers: it could become an incorporeal concept; it could become secularized. Nazism seemed to have accomplished both. Bonhoeffer's paper is a less-than-subtle call for a critical assessment of the present church situation based on a harkening to origins; in this case, the founding spirit of Jesus and fidelity to the Word of God in the Spirit of God.

The present situation in theology and in the church poses the following question: Does the church of the Word of God have a place in the world, and if so, what is the nature of this place? It is basically the question raised by the whole theological discussion with the state.

There are two dangers:

(a) A docetic eschatology, derived from idealism; the very claim that the church has a place in the world is called in question; the church is regarded as being by nature an incorporeal concept, which can lay no claim to such a place;

(b) A secular ecclesiology, derived from materialism, associated with a magical attitude to the sacrament.

Both these dangers are very acute in our case, in Protestantism. The former danger arises from the theology of Barth, understood wrongly; the latter from the theology of Dibelius, understood correctly. The problem for Protestants, in their discussion with the state concerning orders of nature, etc., is this question of place, keeping clear of both dangers. It is a question of finding the right way. We have such difficulty in answering all concrete questions because we have no clear view of the preliminary question, of the place the church has itself to claim by virtue of the Word of God. Is the place of the church merely the mathematical point of the Word of God, which flashes out here and there? Is it the *punctum mathematicum* of justification? Is everything all right so long as the church is left this place? Experience over recent years has taught us that the church reacts more acutely, over and above our theological consciousness, at certain limits of its body, limits of which it had earlier been unconscious. It has felt that a line must be drawn where beforehand the dogmatic view was that there were no limits at all. The church has felt itself to be a wider place, a wider body, than had formerly seemed to be the case. This is the explanation of the theological problems of the theological faculties, the academic world, and the parishes. The church struggle has been carried on by pastors and parishes, not by university theologians. The reason for this is that it has been the pastors and the parishes, not the faculties, who have realized the question of the place of the church. Theology and the question of the church stem from the empirical experiences of the church in her encounters. The church suffers blows and recognizes that the body of the church is pursuing its way in the world. The question is, how is the place of the church to be marked out in a recognizable way from the other spheres surrounding it? Is the relationship between church and state that they stand side by side (Rome)? Is the former set above the latter (Geneva)? Is the one in the other (the theology of Rothe)? Is the state above and the church under it (false Lutheran Orthodoxy of the eighteenth century)? This is where the New Testament comes into play. . . . The presupposition is that the church is a church of the Word. The question is that of the place occupied by this church in all these relationships. Therefore a visible church. . . .

THE NEW COMMUNITY

(a) The coming of the Spirit is a new creation, simply because it leads the community into fellowship with Christ. *Kaine ktisis* (2 Cor. 5:17; Gal. 6:15), the second creation after the old, corrupt creation, is humanity in the community, the community itself (Eph. 2:15). Part of the world is made afresh after the image of God (Col. 3:10). Thus no new religion has been founded; a part of the world has been made anew. That is the founding of the church. The event of Whitsuntide thus does not consist primarily in a new religiousness, but in the proclamation of a new creative act of God. And that means that the whole of life is requisitioned. It is not for a moment a matter of putting the religious before the profane, but of putting God's act before both religious and profane. Here is the essential difference between the church and a "religious fellowship." A "religious fellowship" is concerned to put the religious above the profane, to divide life into the religious and the profane; it is concerned with an ordering of value and status. A religious fellowship has its end in itself in the "religious" as the highest—one might go on to say "God-given"—value. The church, as a part of the world and of humankind created afresh by God's Spirit, demands total obedience to the Spirit which creates anew both the religious and the profane. Because the church is concerned with God, the Holy Spirit, and his Word, it is therefore not specially concerned with religion, but with *obedience* to the Word, with the *work* of the Father, i.e., with the completion of the new creation in the Spirit. It is not the religious question or religious concern of any form which constitutes the church—from a human point of view—but obedience to the Word of the new creation of grace. In other words, the church is constituted not by religious formulae, by dogma, but by the practical doing of what is commanded. The pure teaching of the gospel is not a religious concern, but a desire to execute the will of God for a new creation. In the church, the Holy Spirit and obedience take the place of "the religious." The second creation of God by Christ in the Holy Spirit is as little a "religious matter" as was the first creation. It is a reality of God. The total claim of the church, which is not content with the priority of the "religious," is grounded in the claim of the Holy Spirit to be creator in the church. Where the Word and the action of God are torn apart to the extent that they are in the Orthodox churches, the church must become a religious institution and there is no longer any protection against the pietistic, total dissolution of the concept of the church in which piety constitutes the church—and the action of God is identified with human, pious work.

(b) In Acts 2:42ff., 4:32ff., we can already find the first beginnings and the hints of the direction in which this new creation is to take shape. The place of preaching and the confession, the teaching of the Apostles, breaking of bread, prayer, the place of officers and of gifts, signs and wonders, the place of the Christian commandments, of discipleship and community of goods, and the limits of this place, toward the people in Acts 2:47 and toward the kingdom of God in the mission.

(c) Acts 2:42. "They remained steadfastly in the Apostles' doctrine." Each word is significant. The testimony of the Apostles following Peter's sermon is called *didache*. In contrast to any form of religious speaking, instruction, the imparting of past events, is meant here. That something has happened is testified, is taught—and also that something is to happen (Acts 2:38ff.). The content of what is to be said is therefore fixed, it needs only to be handed on. *Didache* is the work of mediation between firm facts and an audience—mediation understood in a purely formal way, and nothing else. *Didache* has of itself no "religious" character. Now it is only meaningful to impart something that is not already known. The imparting of something already known is senseless. Thus it seems to be a feature of the concept of *didache* that makes itself superfluous. *Didache* is only sought as long as its subject is unknown. But this is contradicted in a very strange way in our text by the word "steadfastly". . . . There must therefore be something in this *didache* which distinguishes it from any other, so that it does not make itself superfluous. The steadfastness is essential and necessary. Why? Is there a sense of duty, that the assembly must be kept up? Is it responsibility for the others? I.e., has this "steadfastly" an ethical basis? Or is it the feeling of being at home in some church or assembly, a mere emotional love of liturgy? I.e., has this "steadfastly" an emotional basis? All this, as we can see today, would not have the power to build a community. There is rather a practical necessity in the linking of this *didache* with steadfastness. It lies in the fact that this testimony, precisely as *didache*, is a work of God, of the Holy Spirit himself. The Holy Spirit himself speaks in this *didache*. He himself is the fact of this *didache*. And because the church is the church of the Holy Spirit, it builds itself up daily through this *didache*. The Holy Spirit exists in the *didache*. The guarantee of this lies in the third thing that is mentioned, namely that it is the teaching of the Apostles. The Apostles are the witnesses of the facts, chosen by the triune God, not as onlookers, but as those of whom God has made use in a special way, as his instruments. They are the witnesses whom the Holy Spirit has chosen and to whom he has made himself known. They are the foundation on which the church is built up, with Jesus Christ the chief cornerstone (Eph. 2:20). They are the living link of the Holy Spirit with the teaching—and each further sermon must be able to be called apostolic preaching on this foundation if it is to be the *didache* to which the community devotes itself steadfastly, i.e., *didache* which has the promise of the Holy Spirit.

The second special feature of this *didache* is that it does not leave the listener as an individual, like any other simple imparting of facts, such as a lecture. Each one does not take up his things and go home—this *didache* creates *koinonia*. The listeners do not remain a public. This is the way the close sentence construction must be understood. Even here no ethical norms, no emotional elements go to form the community—even here a practical compulsion must be sought. It will again be found in the fact that it pleased the Holy Spirit to promise himself not to the individual but to the gathering. It is the visible gathering which receives the Spirit and which is brought to *koinonia* through the Spirit. The liturgical gathering is the origin of the *koinonia* and is similarly its goal. Brotherly fellowship grows only with the hearing of the Word, and all brotherly life in turn stands in the service of proclaiming the Word. It is not without significance that *koinonia* is mentioned in between the teaching of the Apostles and the breaking of the bread. That is in fact the place of Christian brotherliness. Founded on and made possible by the preaching, fulfilled by and directed toward the breaking of the bread, in the community of the body of the Lord. Fellowship in the Lord's supper is the goal of brotherly fellowship and is its fulfillment. *Koinonia* is the waiting to share in the eternal Lord's supper that Christ will drink with us new in his Father's kingdom. Fellowship stands between Word and sacrament, between the earthly feast and the eternal feast. It is from here that it receives its orientation on eternity. From this fellowship there grows a fellowship of prayer, of thanksgiving, and of intercession. And in this prayer is contained a confession of God, who has given himself in Word, in brotherliness, and in sacrament. [*WF,* pp. 42–51]

17

The Question of the Boundaries of the Church and Church Union

(Zur Frage nach der Kirchengemeinschaft)

April 22, 1936

This lecture to the students at Finkenwalde was delivered in April and published in *Evangelische Theologie* in June 1936. Though this paper was presented in the milder atmosphere of Finkenwalde, its setting was the turmoil with which the Confessing Church had been convulsed at the time. The leadership of the church seemed willing to backtrack on the pivotal decisions of the Barmen and Dahlem synods, particularly through compromises on its standing rejection of interference in its affairs by the official national church government. Pressure was increased on it to conform to Nazi policies and thus acquire legality and political "respectability." Several dissenting pastors had been arrested. Bonhoeffer wished to set his seminarians, and, indeed, the churches themselves straight on the question of membership in the true church of Jesus Christ, now that so many were being tempted to compromise and some church leaders were, in his opinion, avoiding the real issue of what constituted the truth. The Oeynhausen Synod of February 1936, for example, had failed to clarify the issues or even offer any protection to younger pastors being pressured by the government to become "legal." On an index card prior to the Oeynhausen Synod, Bonhoeffer had written: "A third synod [Oeynhausen] must now provide protection against the subversion of the church by the world which, in the shape of the National Socialist State, is intervening through its finance departments, legislative authority, and committees, and is now splitting into groups the church of those who uphold the 'Confession.' Here we cannot and must not yield for one moment."[10]

Because the Oeynhausen Synod was a disappointment to these pastors and ordinands, Bonhoeffer published his clarification and theological justification for courageously clinging to the Barmen and Dahlem confessions and for their remaining in opposition to the Reich Church. One phrase from the paper, after it had been published in the June 1936 issue of *Evangelische Theologie,* "whoever knowingly separates himself from the Confessing Church in Germany separates himself from salvation," branded Bonhoeffer as a hopeless fanatic in the eyes of many in the German churches. One of Bonhoeffer's colleagues, Helmut Gollwitzer, later clarified Bonhoeffer's use of the expression, "outside the church there is no salvation" (*extra ecclesiam nulla salus*), indicating that Bonhoeffer meant this in the universalist concept of church. But Gollwitzer lost no time in turning the complaints of Bonhoeffer's assailants against them, accusing them of "their own particular brand of 'legalism,' 'enthusiasm' and 'Romanism.'"[11] While the essay was not intended by Bonhoeffer to be a judgment on the salvation or damnation of individuals in the Reich Church, he nonetheless insists that the obligation to belong to the Confessing Church as the only visible church is a strong one. His position here is consistent with his constant identification of the church with God's Word. The church boundaries were necessarily the boundaries of Christian revelation. When the leaders of the Reich Church accomodated the principles of nazism in the church's confession of faith, as far as Bonhoeffer was concerned, they were guilty of disrupting the revelation itself and of thus separating themselves from the grace of God.

The Reformation set free the question of the nature of the church from the question of who belongs to it. This was a decisive stage. Roman Catholicism and the pre-Reformation church had thought that the question of the nature of the church could be answered by a definition of its extent. The Reformation, and particularly the Lutheran concept, first says what the church is and leaves the question of its boundaries open. Its first concern is not the unveiling of the divine mystery of who belongs to the church and who does not, the question of election and rejection, it is not aimed first and foremost at judging and distinguishing people; the most important thing is that the manifest saving act of God, the present Christ, his Word and his sacrament, should be seen and adored. There are no theoretical statements about the saved and the lost, there is no verdict "This person belongs to the church, that person does not," but simply the joyful cry of those who have been granted a share in a great, astonishing gift, "Here is the gospel!" "Here are the pure sacraments!" "Here is the church!" "Come here!"

The bearing of this on relations with other churches, on the boundaries of the church, was a completely secondary question. The nature of the church is not determined by those who belong to it but by the Word and sacrament of Jesus Christ which, where they are effective, gather for themselves a community in accordance with the promise. It was a firm belief, grounded on the promise, that if only the Word and the sacrament were administered purely, those who belonged to the church would always be there. Who those are, the Lord, who calls and assembles, knows. That was enough.

The prime concern could never be the possibility of calling these by name and enumerating them, of distinguishing them from those who did not belong or who only seemed to belong; these have already been judged. Moreover, the Last Day will bring this to light. Why then should the believer be so eager to know already today where the boundaries are, where the distinctions lie? Does he not know enough if he is permitted to know the gracious saving act of God? Why should the believer be concerned to unmask the hypocrite and the heretic? How can he desire to uncover the fearful mystery of rejection prematurely, before the joy of eternal life with Christ helps him to overcome his terror and his grief at the last judgment of God? The believer indeed knows the sort of terror concealed in this concept of "the extent of the church," which seems so harmless. And he thanks God daily that he is still blind here, that he can still stand in intercession, that he can still keep to the church of salvation with the community of believers in all the joy of his knowledge of salvation. The believer thanks God that he has again been given his word and sacrament pure and entire, and that he knows where the church of God is. Why should he ask where it is not, if he is completely swallowed up in this joy?

So primitive Christianity and the Reformation did nothing more at this point than to cry confidently one after the other "Here is the church!," "The true Church of Jesus Christ!" This cry is one of humility and thankfulness. It is not boasting, but praise of God. If he has really heard and believed, who thinks of asking still whether the church might not perhaps also be found somewhere else? Who is concerned with such a question except those who do not want to hear and believe at this point? If we heard and believed that an inexhaustible vein of gold had been found which would yield enough for all people and all times, then we would hardly be interested in the question whether perhaps some gold might possibly be found somewhere else. Maybe so, maybe not— what does it matter in view of the fact that here there is enough and to spare? Would we not then also give this joyful message to all those who were struggling hard to discover other veins, would we not shout to them to come along, to abandon all their efforts and simply run and take from where everything was to be found in the utmost abundance? We might then have doubts about the seriousness of their search if they did not come, but insisted on saying "I'm looking for my own gold." Here obstinacy is stronger than the wish to find gold. We would have to leave them behind with great sorrow, for who knows whether in the end they might not go away empty? We would have to run to where the great offer was made.

So it is with the Reformation message of the church. Here is the true church. Might it not also be found somewhere else? But that is not the question. God has given it to us here. Will you stand aside and obstinately search to see whether God could not also give it to you somewhere else? It might be so—but then it really might also not be so.

Would we risk that? Anyone who takes the risk has in fact already lost, for he has not heard and believed that the true church is already there. Otherwise he would no longer take the risk at such moments. And if he has not heard, neither does he know what the true church is, and so he does not know what he is really looking for and will never find it. In that case the search is an end in itself and therefore no longer a genuine search.

So the church, always beginning with the recognized truth of what and where the church is, now proclaims to the world, "Come here, the church is here!" And that is the reason why it does not enter into discussions about where else the church might be. In face of the certainty that the church is here, everything else is uncertainty, nonchurch. . . . [WF, pp. 75–77]

The Confessing Synod of Barmen has repudiated the teaching of the German Christians in its decisive points as false teaching. This repudiation means that this false teaching has no place in the Church of Jesus Christ. The Confessing Synod of Dahlem took it upon itself to declare that the government of the national church has separated itself from the Christian church by teaching and by action. It did not bring about any exclusion from the church, but stated a *fait accompli*. At the same time it formed its own church government and claimed to represent the true Church of Jesus Christ in Germany. Since then the Confessing Church has recognized that it has the responsibility of being and the commission to be the one true Church of Jesus Christ in Germany. That is a fact of church history.

What does this mean? What does it express? Everything in the Confessing Church centers on this question. To make the inevitably vain and never conclusive attempt of asking about the views of those who were responsible for this decision of the synod is no sufficient answer. If we take this statement of the synod at all seriously we will recognize that God the Lord himself wills to be responsible for it. But in that case the statement must be received as it was issued and we must look for the will of God in it. So on the presupposition that here in all human weakness and differences of opinion, through all kinds of human moods, anxieties and hastinesses, the Word of the Lord became clear to the church when the synod declared that the government of the national church had cut itself off from the church of Jesus Christ, we must ask what this statement means. Anyone who does not share this presupposition does not speak of Barmen and Dahlem as Christian synods, and does not share the presuppositions of the Confessing Church. Things are really in a bad way if today in large circles of the Confessing Church there is willful and undisciplined talk, more among the clergy than among the laity. We can no longer go back behind Barmen and Dahlem not because they are historical facts of our church to which we must show due reverence, but because we can no longer go back behind the Word of God.

The question then is: What did God say about his church and its course of action when he spoke through Barmen and Dahlem? The government of the national church has cut itself off from the Christian church. The Confessing Church is the true church of Jesus Christ in Germany. What does that mean? It undoubtedly means that a definitive boundary has been recognized and confirmed between the government of the national church and the true church of Christ. The government of the national church is heretical. But does that mean that the person in office who continues to offer obedience to this repudiated church government falls under the same verdict? Has each German Christian pastor cut himself off from the church of Jesus? Furthermore, must we also regard the German Christians among members of the congregations and those parishes which accept their German Christian pastor without protest as cut off from the Christian church? Can the pastor of the Confessing Church claim the German Christian members of the congregation as members of his congregation? Is he permitted to exercise his office without distinction both to members of the Confessing Church and to German Christians? Where are the boundaries of the congregation for the pastor of the Confessing Church? Is there here a difference in principle between church government and congregation? And in addition, what is the position of the so-called neutrals? Finally, does anyone engaged in common church work or even church government with the German Christians share in their sin of destroying the church? Does the Dahlem verdict also apply to the church committees? Does it apply to all those who obey the church committees? To sum up, must that division which has grown up between the government of the national church and the Confessing Church now extend consistently to all these others just mentioned? An answer must be given. The congregation must know to whom they may listen and to whom not. The pastor must know how he is to understand his office rightly. Pastors and congregations largely do not know this today, and they cannot know it because they have not been told.

It would certainly be the easiest solution either to draw all the above-mentioned conclusions on the whole or to stand blindly by Dahlem and to draw no conclusions at all. Both these courses are equally unchurch-like according to everything that has been said hitherto. Drawing conclusions is no help at all, because the Word of God demands not conclusions, but obedience. But to draw no conclusions at all can be willful disobedience toward the Word. Thus each single question must be examined and a decision must be sought step by step. In this way it is possible to reach a certain degree of clarity, for example, in the case of those who hold German Christian office. In parishes in which there are only ministers of this kind the Confessing Church has taken care that the true preaching and the true ministry is preserved. It has instituted emergency ministries and in this way demonstrated that the German Christian minister is deprived of his office. Nothing of this sort has happened in the case of the neutrals. The attitude toward the congregations is of a completely different nature. The mere fact of the institution of emergency pastorates is an expression of the full claim of the Confessing Church on the congregation. The attitude of the Confessing Church toward the committees and toward the members of the committees who belong to the Confessing Church, and also to pastors who offer allegiance to the committees, is completely obscure. . . . This obscurity is pernicious. Before anything is said on the subject, however, we must look at the situation from yet another aspect.

Whereas on the one hand a continued process of separation is going on, on the other hand an extremely significant understanding is coming about between the churches of Lutheran and Reformed confessions. Since Barmen, Lutherans and Reformed have been speaking with one voice in synodal declarations. Schismatic differences of confession no longer make it impossible to form a Confessing Synod, though of course the synods are without intercommunion. This is to be taken into consideration as an actual fact. Of course disputes arise on the Confessing side. But the fact is there, and it is up to God to make what he will of it.

It cannot be disputed by any means of the confession that this fact, the recognition of "Confessing churches of equal rights," is already a decisive breach of the Augsburg Confession. The Confessing Synods cannot be justified by the letter of the Lutheran Confession. How then are we to understand the formation of the Confessing Synods despite continual reference to this very point? How are we to understand the participation of decidedly Lutheran theologians in them? We must begin by establishing the facts, that the Confessing Synods exist, and that in view of this only two attitudes are possible: either one repudiates these Synods *a limine* in the light of the Augsburg Confession or one accepts them in wonderment and humility and allows God to make of this what pleases him. In any case, the present situation is significant and instructive enough for the question of church union. On the other hand, the inexorably consistent application of the doctrinal concept leads to division of the churches, on the other hand there is a manifest neglect of the doctrinal concept, and a church union which disregards decisive and hitherto divisive differences in doctrine has already been pioneered. If we imagined the inexorably consistent application of the doctrinal concept as it is exercised against the German Christians directed say against the Reformed Churches, it would be theoretically conceivable that the old divisive differences in eucharistic doctrine or Christology would break out again here as well. Analogously a slackening of consistency could create a common basis with the German Christians. This, in any case, is how the situation must look to confessional orthodoxy. What is at the bottom of this absurd possibility? Is some sordid game being played here with church union?

At this point there is a further complication. The Confessing Church has found ecumenism. This meeting has up till now brought about two distinctive results. At Fanø, in 1934, in the presence of representatives of the Confessing Church the ecumenical movement declared the "principles and methods" of the German Christian church government to be "incompatible with the nature of the church of Christ." By the election of a representative of the Confessing Church to the ecumenical council it has asked for the cooperation of the Confessing Church and has been given this church's promise. The Confessing Church has not yet, however, sent official representatives to any ecumenical conference. The reason for this must be found in the presence of representatives of the government of the national church with whom conversation even on neutral ground is no longer possible for the Confessing Church. So while conversation with other, erring "churches" would be possible, such a possibility no longer exists for conversation between the national church and the Confessing Church. Doubtless it would be easy to point out the false doctrines of the German Christians in many other churches. Nevertheless the Confessing Church recognizes a qualitative difference.

All this must appear both incomprehensible and contradictory both to the orthodox and to those in principle without a confession. The orthodox person does not understand how it can be possible to treat the clauses of the confession in a different way. He does not understand the openness of the Lutherans of the Confessing Church toward the Reformed or toward the ecumenical movement. Those without a confession, among them the great number of pastors under the sway of pietism and liberal theology, do not, on the other hand, understand the obstinacy in the application of the doctrinal concept against the German Christians.

The Confessing Church takes its confident way between the Scylla of orthodoxy and the Charybdis of confessionlessness. It bears the burden of the responsibility of being the true Church of Jesus. It proclaims "Here is the church!" "Come here!" In proclaiming this it comes up against both friends and enemies. Where it recognizes enemies it confirms the barriers they have drawn consistently and without compromise. Where it recognizes friends, it finds common ground and is ready for conversation in the hope of communion. The church will recognize friend or enemy by the confession, but the confession is not an ultimate, clear-cut measure. The church must decide where the enemy is standing. Because he can stand now on eucharistic doctrine, another time on the doctrine of justification, a third time on the doctrine of the church, the church has to decide. And in deciding it makes its confession. Orthodoxy confuses confession with a theological system. The confession-less confuse the church's confession with the testimony of piety. It would be very much easier if the Confessing Church could think in a clear-cut way here. But by so doing it would be unfaithful to its commission to give the call to salvation; in that, it is at the same time both open and bounded.

If it is thus clear that decisions about the boundaries of the church can only be taken in each individual instance, it is now necessary to consider briefly the concrete questions raised earlier.

1. That the German Christian ministers have cut themselves off from the church is a recognition which needed only synodal confirmation. In Lutheran teaching it is only possible to institute an emergency pastorate if it is clearly declared that a person has forfeited office. Otherwise this would be an impermissible encroachment on someone else's ministry, a matter against which Luther could not utter enough warnings. Hand in hand with this should have gone a direction to the congregations to abstain from all ministerial acts of a false teacher for the sake of the Word of God and the salvation of their souls, and to live and die without word or sacrament rather than go to a false teacher.

2. In this matter a distinction must be made between ministers and members of the congregations, the leaders and those who are led. It is impossible to argue the exclusion of a congregation by the mere fact of the exclusion of its minister. The Lutheran confessional writings did not declare individual Catholics but the pope, i.e., the church government, to be AntiChrist. The Dahlem Synod spoke in the same way. The government of the church has become heretical. But this is in no way to give up any claim on the congregations. The congregations must be helped to find the right ministers. Of course, the congregation itself is also called to pass judgment on false teaching. If it does not do that, if despite warning and admonition it persists with the false teacher, here too after some time a limit must be set to patience and church membership must be regarded as dissolved, with all the consequences of the denying of ministerial functions, etc. This is the last act of mercy of the church to the congregation, the last call to communion, the "strange work" through which the call to salvation is given. It is, however, also an obligation of the church toward the office which would otherwise be guilty daily of the dissipation of the sacrament.

3. The Confessing Church can no longer avoid a clear decision about the church committees. The statement of the Oeynhausen Synod is not enough. It is impossible to see where the Church government of the committees differs from the government of the national church. Indubitably the church committees are more dangerous to the true church government than the government of the national church. It has been stated by the Confessing Synod that this church government cannot be recognized, but hitherto the unequivocal prohibition against taking part in it has not been given. This makes for confusion. Where the boundaries are recognized, the practical conclusions must be drawn. In the

same way as a member of the Confessing Church who joined the government of the National Church would cut himself off from the church of Jesus, so according to the fundamental insight expressed in the Oeynhausen Synod anyone who takes part in the governmental functions of the committees does the same thing. But from this there necessarily follows the prohibition of such participation. This and nothing else applies to those ministers who submit to the committees. It is not good to practice on ordinands what one is willing to drop in the case of pastors. The longer the government of the church avoids the decision laid upon it, the more it confuses the congregations, the more unmerciful it is toward the pastors and the less it can give its own call.

4. The neutrals are a particular problem. First of all it must be said that there are really no neutrals. They belong on the other side. But they themselves want to be neutral. It is therefore impossible to have an unequivocal attitude toward them as their own attitude is not unequivocal, because the boundary drawn by them against the true church is not clear. Jesus Christ spoke twice about the neutrals: "He who is not with me is against me" (Matt. 12:30) and "He that is not against us is for us" (Mark 9:40). The neutrals cannot claim just the second saying for themselves, neither can the church use just the first saying against them. But it must continually be demonstrated that the neutrals are in just this questionable situation described by the two sayings. Of course, if neutrality is elevated to the status of a principle, it is then possible to use just the first saying. For in that case a clear position has been taken up outside the church and a boundary has clearly been erected against the claim of the true church.

These brief remarks cannot have the significance of anticipating the decision of the church. But they must serve to remind the government of the church that it must take this decision. In doing it step by step, it will be doing the strange work so as to be able to pursue its true work rightly. The dissolution of fellowship is the last offer of fellowship!

Extra ecclesiam nulla salus. The question of church membership is the question of salvation. The boundaries of the church are the boundaries of salvation. Whoever knowingly cuts himself off from the Confessing Church in Germany cuts himself off from salvation. That is the recognition which has always forced itself upon the true church. That is its humble confession. Whoever separates the question of the Confessing Church from the question of his own salvation does not understand that the struggle of the Confessing Church is the struggle for his own salvation. . . . .

It must be said again and again that for the church to deny its boundaries is no work of mercy. The true church comes up against boundaries. In recognizing them it does the work of loving others by honoring the truth. *Extra ecclesiam nulla salus.* If this statement is indisputable, the other one must also be added which has its analogy in the doctrine of God. True, God is everywhere, "but it is not his will that you should look for him everywhere." There is a difference between the presence of God and the possibility of knowing him. As surely as the known God is our God and the unknown God can never be our God, so surely must this distinction be preserved precisely as an expression of faith which holds by the revealed God and in so doing celebrates the uniqueness and the wonder of the revelation. So now it can also be said of the church that it is only known where the promise of God rests, in the visible church. Not there is it our church. But the believer who has become certain of his salvation in the visible church celebrates the wonder of this salvation precisely in daring to speak of a being of the church beyond the manifest church of salvation. He can never do this to negate the sole salvation through the visible church, he can never do it even for the sake of this or that pious person who stands outside, he can never do it to judge and to discover himself where the "church beyond" is. It remains unknown, believed in by the church of salvation so as to praise all the more highly the glory of the known revelation of salvation. Woe to those who make this, the last possibility of faith of the church which lives by faith, *extra ecclesiam nulla salus,* into a presupposition for their pious speculation on the saved and the lost. This is not our task. We must rather flee from the temptation of such questions to the manifest salvation of God in the true church.

The question of the boundaries of the church can become a temptation for faith. But it should only serve to make faith more certain. It is the cause of the church to make this continually clearer and to make the congregation more certain of its salvation in any decision about its boundaries. [*WF* pp. 86–96]

18

Our Way According to the Testimony of Scripture

(Unser Weg nach dem Zeugnis der Schrift)

October 26, 1938

This address to the "Illegal Young Brothers" in Pomerania, later sent out as a circular letter, was given in the midst of the terrible state of indecision among the young pastors of the Confessing Church and the Councils of Brethren. The "illegal" pastors had been pressured to apply personally for the legalization of their status within the national church. Bonhoeffer had himself sent each pastor a letter urging them to endure the struggle in the spirit of fidelity to the gospel. Many of the provincial churches had already begun to negotiate "bargains" with the government, attempting to work out compromise language that would allow them a guilt-free conscience while placating the national consistories. Some felt that the Confessing Church had already failed in the matter of the civil oath and had all but completely surrendered. Some stated their worries about the future of the Confessing Church itself, wondering if it might be better to disband. In the midst of that confusion, the Pomeranian Council of Brethren summoned all the loyal pastors to an extraordinary assembly in October and invited Bonhoeffer to give the principal address that is excerpted here. In his remarks, we can see expressed again his strong insistence that the "way" of the Confessing Church is the only one justified by Holy Scripture and the Barmen and Dahlem confessions. Bethge reports that he roused "the consciences of those who were ready to compromise."[12] In a moving way he pled with the pastors to stand by each other in "brotherly solidarity" in the struggle for the truth of the gospel and the integrity of the church. This selection ends on that note of solidarity so characteristic of Bonhoeffer's challenge to the churches in the years of crisis.

These remarks are meant to provoke you to serious reflection and renewed joy over the way of the church of Jesus Christ. Only Holy Scrip-

ture can guide our reflections aright and give us utter joy and confidence. So we would ask you to examine with us what our church has done in the light of the testimony of Scripture and so to allow yourselves to be set upon the firm ground of the divine Word. The question we must consider again today is this: Was the teaching of the synods of Barmen and Dahlem in accordance with Scripture? The fact that this question has to be discussed afresh after four years must certainly make us think. It could indeed be that we really have been working and acting for four years without deciding this question before God, that you have allowed yourselves to be trained, tested, and ordained by the Council of Brethren without being compelled to by the Word of God. In that case, our situation now would in fact be the same as that of 1934. Were that so, at least the position would be clear, and the question whether Barmen and Dahlem were commensurate with Scripture would be a belated, but nevertheless a real, question. It could also be that at one time we allowed ourselves to be led by Scripture along the way of Barmen and Dahlem and that today we are once again compelled by Scripture alone to raise objections to our former decisions. In other words, that we have a better knowledge of Scripture to set alongside Barmen and Dahlem. In that case, we would have to recall you from a course contrary to Scripture to a course in accordance with it. You would then have moved towards the Council of Brethren not thoughtlessly, but wrongly. But this situation too would be clear, and our present question about Scripture would be a real one. But it could also be that while we were once convinced of the scriptural character of the Confessing Synods, today, in view of a number of circumstances, for example, the failure of the church government, the departure of brethren we admired, hindrance and oppression from all sides, we have been overcome by wholesale doubt and now, to avoid all further theological, ecclesiastical, and personal difficulties, we resign ourselves to take the only positive step we can, the only one that seems to offer some support, some work, some security, namely the step to a pastorate under the consistory of the national church. But in any case, we have to be quite clear today what we are really doubtful about. Have we become doubtful whether we weak human beings could carry out what has been laid upon us? Or have we become doubtful whether the Confessing Synods are in accordance with Scripture? Or have we gone so far as to doubt whether Holy Scripture can still show us God's will if we look for it? . . .
[*WF,* pp. 173–174]

Dahlem acted representatively for the whole church. It spoke "in the church's cause" and thus indicated that the whole church is not made up by adding the individual communities together, but is the church in itself. Each individual community is merely a part or member of the whole church, just as the Confessing Church is a part of the one Christian church. So Dahlem, being responsible to Scripture, did not think congregationally, i.e., in terms of the individual communities, but in terms of the whole church. The church is originally and essentially one. The members do not come before the body; they are members only as members of the one body. Paul writes to "the church of God which is in Corinth" (1 Cor. 1:1). He sums up the community to which he writes with his own, "saints together with all those who in every place call on the name of our Lord Jesus Christ" (1 Cor. 1:2). For the sake of the church's unity, Dahlem did not leave the struggle against destruction to the individual communities, but acted in responsibility for the whole church. The whole church was threatened, so action had to be taken on its behalf. Let us notice one thing: we met for the sake of the unity of the church, to prevent separation and schism. But who are the ones who are causing the schism, those who break up and destroy the teaching and order of the church or those who maintain it and restore it? Let us put an end to the perverse self-accusations that the Confessing Church has caused divisions. We are ready to be penitent where we have sinned. But that is a false call to penitence, it comes from the mouths of the German Christians. We are concerned with "one body and one spirit," but how can that be possible unless there is "one Lord, one faith" (Eph. 4:5)? The church of Jesus Christ can only be truly one where the one faith corresponds to the one Lord and at present there is only one place where this is, and has been, the case. All self-made unity, whether it is based on organization, or temperament, or expediency, was revealed as heresy. Dahlem called for the true unity of the church on the basis of the saying, "Every one who acknowledges me before the world, I also will acknowledge before my Father who is in heaven" (Matt. 10:32).

From this standpoint, Dahlem had to advance the claims of the newly appointed church government upon the whole church and in so doing to set itself against all congregationalist, free-church tendencies from the start. Since the Confessing Church meant to be the one, true church of the gospel, it could not (and cannot ever) become a sect, surrendering its claim to be the whole church and only looking for and caring for its own life. As long as the church holds to the decisions of Dahlem, it may be a persecuted, suffering church, but it can never go the way of self-sufficiency, by separating itself from the whole church. It will not be lured or forced into that. But as soon as the church abandons the decisions of Dahlem, it must become a sect; for in so doing it separates itself from the one true Catholic church. Indeed, it will be lucky if it gets away with its life. By appealing to the confessions of the church recognized in the church constitution, the church government must make its claim upon the whole church, just as the Apostolic Church once decided for the whole church.

Because the matter at stake was the true unity of the church in the sense of John 17, because a word for the whole church had been spoken here, it had to be matched by fellowship in action and in suffering. God has made the church one body, "that there may be no discord in the

body, but that the members may have the same care for one another"
(1 Cor. 12:25). Suffering together and rejoicing together corresponds
with this reciprocal action. "If one member suffers, all suffer together. . . ." It is in the nature of a body that no question, no problem, no
reflection can be raised as to whether one member should care for another or suffer with another; such a question is itself the end of membership of the body. Among members of a body, one cares entirely of
its own accord for the others, and suffers and rejoices with the others.
Being for one another and with each other is simply taken for granted.
Anyone who wants to get out of that gets out of the body. It has been
asked whether action within the church must always be in common. The
New Testament is not conscious of this question. It knows that in any
case, members can act for one another only as long as they are members.
Isolated action, action which is not for one another, cuts people off from
the church as the body of Christ. For the New Testament, to be for one
another means that the members are also one in mind and judgment
(1 Cor. 1:10). They should say the same thing, think the same thing
(2 Cor. 13:11; Rom. 15:5; Rom. 12:16). The common decision at the
Apostolic Council arose from the concern of Jewish and Gentile
Christians for one another. It is clear that this mutual responsibility can
and will have different forms. The weak act differently than the strong.
But the limits of the difference are clear. All act in obedience to the
only Lord. Disobedient action cuts people off from the fellowship of the
body. I shall discuss what constitutes disobedience later.

We should also add a word here about the often misunderstood saying
about "brotherly solidarity." The word is not important here. We speak
of active and brotherly love. It is so remarkable that we theologians keep
forgetting that our obedience to Jesus Christ also demands simple,
brotherly love to our brethren in office, to those who suffer, and to those
who are in the front line. It is almost too obvious to be worth mentioning
that we do not leave a brother in distress, that we stand by a brother
who is attacked for the sake of the gospel, even if by chance we ourselves
are not attacked, that we side with one another in danger, battle, and
suffering. Every question, even if it is put unconditionally, already makes
this situation problematical and can only lead to evasion. We are again
asking about good works instead of doing this work ourselves in such a
way that the left hand does not know what the right hand is doing. Let
us remember that splendid witness of the Old Testament about the East
Jordanian tribes, though as an example, not as a scriptural proof. The
Promised Land is being conquered. Reuben and Gad want to remain
and settle east of the Jordan. They come to Moses and ask for permission. But Moses lays conditions upon them. They must first help their
brothers to settle in *their* land, and so must go before them into battle.
Then they may occupy their own lands. We should read Numbers 32:5–
6, 32:16–23, and Joshua 22:3–4 thoroughly once more.

We ought also to remember the cry of the prisoner Paul to Timothy, to come to Rome to him, to suffering, not to be ashamed of his fetters but to suffer with him. "Suffer with"—that is in the end what 2 Timothy is all about—and it is the last appeal we have from the Apostle Paul. So much for the question of "solidarity." We spoke of the true unity and the true fellowship of the church. . . . [WF, pp. 180–83]

Part 4

BONHOEFFER THE PASTOR

Participants in the Fanø Youth Conference, August 22-29, 1934.
From: Eberhard Bethge, Renate Bethge, Christian Gremmels, *Dietrich Bonhoeffer: A Life in Pictures*
(Philadelphia: Fortress Press, 1986) p. 132.

Introduction: The Word of God in Sermon and Spiritual Ministry

Dietrich Bonhoeffer served the church of Christ in a number of settings—in Berlin, in Barcelona, in London—and knew from personal experience what was involved in pastoral ministry. Preaching was central to his understanding of the pastoral role, but he also developed a keen awareness of the multiple facets of ministry, such as leading worship, teaching the tenets of faith, providing spiritual care, counseling the troubled, visiting the sick, and comforting the bereaved. In Barcelona Bonhoeffer was moved by the poverty many of his parishioners experienced during the Depression. He was deeply touched by the economic distress and subtle oppression that seemed to be the lot of his black parishioners in Harlem during his stay at Union Theological Seminary in New York. In London he was alert to the need to comfort those who had been separated from their cultural roots in Germany, reminding them of the hope that was always theirs in God's Word and the Sacrament. To his seminarians he was not only the model of what a pastor should be, but he was also a spiritual guide to the sharing of their experience of God's care in the ministry to which they had been called. They remembered his extraordinary power to touch their hearts and to stiffen their resolve to be genuine disciples of Christ their brother.

It is significant in this aspect of Bonhoeffer's life as pastor and seminary director that in the multivolume series, *Twenty Centuries of Great Preaching,* (edited by Clyde E. Fant and William J. Pinson, Jr., Waco: Word Books, 1971) Dietrich Bonhoeffer is presented as one of the representatives of great preaching in this century. Even as a young adult he understood that the sermon could be a powerful channel for the communication of the Word of God. As early as age twenty-two, he was preaching in a German-speaking congregation in Barcelona, Spain. For the following fifteen years, until the time of his imprisonment in Tegel prison, preaching and pastoral care in the context of his call to be a follower of Christ were undertaken by Bonhoeffer with diligence, seriousness, and dedication, even to the point of his willingness to give his life in that cause.

Bonhoeffer's biographer Eberhard Bethge has called our attention, moreover, to the importance of preaching in Bonhoeffer's understanding of the Church's ministry: "Preaching was the great event in his life; the hard theologizing and all the critical love of his church were all for its sake, for in it the message of Christ, the bringer of peace, was proclaimed. To Bonhoeffer nothing in his calling competed with preaching."[1]

This attitude on his part became evident when, as a young pastor in Barcelona, Bonhoeffer labored for hours in his preparation of a single sermon. As he wrote to his parents: "Writing sermons still takes up a great deal of my time. I work on them a whole week, devoting some time to them every day."[2] Bethge suggests that these first sermons of the Barcelona pastorate "reveal the whole gamut of his theological work and outlook."[3] Here we can see too the distinction that Bonhoeffer was to develop between faith and religion and also his commitment to the concrete. Sermons were not to be, in his understanding of them, finely honed, harmless homilies; they were, rather, to be purposely relevant to the moral and human struggles of real people. Self-serving clerical bromides for the people and pompous showing off of one's rhetorical skills in the pulpit were to him part of the huckstering of cheap grace that he abhorred. This early phase of his preaching reveals his sensitivity to people in their personal daily dilemmas.

Bonhoeffer's sense of what a pastor needed to be and to do as a preacher continued to evolve during the years following Barcelona, although there was no single congregation that challenged his sermonic abilities each week. He was on occasion invited to preach in the Kaiser Wilhelm Memorial Church in Berlin and other Protestant churches in Germany.

With his acceptance of the pastoral responsibilities for two German-speaking congregations in London in 1933, Bonhoeffer entered into the most demanding and systematic preaching of his life.

Week by week he prepared sermons for the worshippers of the German Evangelical Congregation of Sydenham and of St. Paul's. The congregations themselves were small in number, about thirty to forty in Sydenham and about fifty in St. Paul's. Many of Bonhoeffer's sermons from this period have survived and remain models of exegetical preaching for the time. It was clear that Bonhoeffer conceived the sermon to be a grappling with the biblical text for the day, certainly not in a sealed vacuum, but in relationship to the context of time and place. For Bonhoeffer, this reality became a particular channel for Christ to live on as community.

The London sermons are as instructive for their incisive language and biblical content as they are revealing of Bonhoeffer's concern for his parishioners' spiritual lives. His continued insistence on the Christian call to agapeic love and to justice is set in the developing menace of nazism and human insensitivities. This is the constant challenge to the pastor and preacher—to refrain from vapid moralizing and to build bridges between the Bible and real life. Bonhoeffer's sermons during these months illustrate his dedication to making the Bible come alive. They also show his abiding commitment to the rhythm of the church year, and his growing attachment to the biblical texts prescribed by the church's lectionary. Editorial titles for most of the sermons have been added in order to provide a focus for their content. Bonhoeffer himself usually used headings suggested by the Sundays of the church year, or by special occasions.

In 1935 Bonhoeffer was called back to Germany to assume the leadership of one of the Confessing Church's seminaries, initially situated in Zingst, high up by the Baltic Sea, and then at Finkenwalde. For the next years his preaching, in the context of the pastoral care he was extending to his seminarians, continued to be both regular and intensive. Becoming a teacher of preaching served to increase his awareness of the crucial role of the sermon in Christian worship. His lectures on preaching are still, after an entire half century, worthy additions to studies of the art and craft of proclaiming God's Word.[4]

Bonhoeffer's effectiveness as a preacher of God's Word was enhanced by the obvious sincerity of his words and the concrete deeds of concern and kindness that made him known among his parishioners and students as a dedicated pastor and teacher. They remembered him as someone who was willing to listen and be a presence in their hopes and successes as well as in their troubles and sorrows. In essence, what people noticed in this young pastor was the way he lived out the observations that later became his written description of the spirit that must bind members of a Christian community together, in this case the brethren of his Finkenwalde seminary. Their ministry, he declares must involve control of the tongue, meekness, listening, helpfulness, bearing with people, and proclamation. But in advocating the kind of attitude that must be theirs in serving the people, Bonhoeffer seemed to be urging the seminarians to be as eager to help others as they knew him to be. He was one who was extremely generous with his time, never "taking the importance of his own career too solemnly." Likewise, as he reminded the seminarians, they must be open to the many moments in which their lives will "be interrupted by God." "God," he states, "will be constantly crossing our paths and canceling our plans by sending us people with claims and petitions." To ignore them would be, in Bonhoeffer's words, to "pass by the visible sign of the cross raised athwart our path to show us that, not our way, but God's way must be done."[5] That Bonhoeffer was one who seemed always to be searching for "God's way" gave added power to his words and work as pastor.

After the Gestapo closed the Finkenwalde seminary in 1937, the occasions for Bonhoeffer's preaching and direct pastoral work lessened considerably. Three years later, by 1940, he was prohibited by the government from preaching and teaching. His commitment to the importance of the spiritual ministry of a pastor, however, continued unabated. As late as 1942, he wrote: "I eagerly want to preach once again."[6]

Bonhoeffer's final religious service was given in a quasi-apocalyptic setting, as the Nazi web of death ensnared him and other "important" prisoners of the Third Reich. On Palm Sunday 1945, his fellow prisoners prevailed on him to lead them in worship. He preached to that small congregation about their experience of the mystery of suffering and on the deliverance that would be theirs through the Christian hope of resurrection. The following day he was executed at Flossenbürg.[7]

19

The Pastor and Spiritual Care

(Seelsorge)

1935–1939

It will soon be fifty years since Bonhoeffer's martyrdom. Among his legacy of writings, nothing surpasses his sermons in revealing his solidarity both with those under his pastoral care and the wider world of those enduring pain and oppression. In a word, his life reflected in a unique way what he had taught to his seminarians about the role of the pastor in fostering a Christlike spirit within the Christian community. These sermons illustrate, likewise, the spiritual care he desired to extend to his people in the form of proclaiming God's Word in the midst of the decadence and suffering he had come to associate with the criminal government then controlling Nazi Germany. The selections in part 4 begin, accordingly, with some significant passages about the way he envisioned the caring mission of the pastor, taken from the lectures on spiritual care that Bonhoeffer gave regularly to his Finkenwalde seminarians during the years 1935–1939. The sermons excerpted in the following chapters were for Bonhoeffer a privileged form of the caring encounter that the minister is called to facilitate between Christ and the Christian.

THE MISSION OF SPIRITUAL CARE

The mission of spiritual care falls under the general mission of proclamation. Caring for the soul is a special sort of proclamation. The minister should proclaim wherever possible. The minister is the pastor, that is, the shepherd of the congregation which needs daily care (2 Tim. 4:2). "Preach the word, be urgent in season and out of season, convince, rebuke, and exhort, be unfailing in patience and in teaching." Caring for souls is a proclamation to the individual which is part of the office of preaching. It is not a matter of "spiritual direction;" Asmussen's concept is misleading. In confidence that God alone cares for the soul, the preacher conducts spiritual care. "Spiritual direction" is carried out on a plane between two people, one of whom subjects himself to the other.

Spiritual care, on the other hand, comes down "from above," from God to the human being. For this reason the New Testament teaches reverence for the "Teacher" (Heb. 13:7). Spiritual direction is a task of educating the populace carried out by the "priest of the people." In spiritual care, God wants to act. In the midst of all anxiety and sorrow we are to trust God. God alone can be a help and a comfort. The goal of spiritual care should never be a change of mental condition. The mission itself is the decisive element, not the goal. All false hope and every false comfort must be eliminated. I do not provide decisive help for anyone if I turn a sad person into a cheerful one, a timid person into a courageous one. That would be a secular—and not a real—help. Beyond and within circumstances such as sadness and timidity it should be believed that God is our help and comfort. Christ and his victory over health and sickness, luck and misfortune, birth and death must be proclaimed. The help he brings is forgiveness and new life out of death.

Spiritual care is part of a special mission within *diakonia*. It is related to the office of proclamation but not identical to it. The diaconate of spiritual care arises from a specific problem of proclamation: a person is no longer able to hear the gospel. The more often a person hears it, the more he withdraws from the living Word. Repentance turns into its opposite, into impenitence and callousness. One hears and yet does not hear. One receives and yet is not helped. God's forgiveness is not accepted but the person learns how to deal with himself gracefully. Forgiveness is taken into one's own hands. A special *diakonia* is needed in order to bring people (who have become callous) back to the arena of proclamation. A love is needed which will lead people back to hearing the proclamation of the gospel. This *diakonia* itself cannot be an act of preaching. Spiritual care presumes the previous proclamation of the gospel and moves toward a future proclamation. Spiritual care as a *diakonia* is thus different from that spiritual care which takes place in and through preaching. In this process of spiritual care as *diakonia* the pastor's task is to listen and the parishioner's is to talk. The pastor's duty in this form of spiritual care may be to be silent for a long time in order to become free of all "priestly" behavior and conceited clericalism. That silence, which is the unconditional prerequisite for spiritual care, aids our preaching, for only after a long period of listening is one able to preach appropriately. . . . [*SC*, pp. 30–31]

Spiritual care as *diakonia* thus follows the pathway from counsel to commandment, from expression of need to confession of sin, from speech to hearing the promise. It is a path of familial assistance toward hearing the proclamation. The proclamation must not jump over all the preliminary stages. Should we oppose the question immediately with the commandment, we're likely to hear, "I can't." The pure commandment does not help the situation but rather hardens it. The other person must be helped along the path from recognition of sin and confession to voluntary obedience and faith. The questioner is to be led to ask for God's commandment. In this way, opposition to God turns to submission.

The path of spiritual care as *diakonia* has its presuppositions:

No pastoral conversation is possible without constant prayer. Other people must know that I stand before God as I stand before them. I depend on the guidance of the Holy Spirit. There is no immediate path to another person. The path to the Christian brother leads by way of prayer and hearing God's Word. No psychology is able to help me find the way to another person's soul. That path is grounded in the mediatorial function of Christ. Christ the mediator stands between me and God, between me and my brother. Therefore, spiritual care never seeks to exercise direct psychic influence. Direct influence remains wholly on the surface. True encounter is only facilitated through the spirit of Christ. The other person must deal with Christ if he is to be helped. Even my piety is useless. The only imprint he should and can receive is that one which is in accordance with the *imago Dei*. That way we keep the atmosphere clear between us and others. The direct path contains deliberations and suggestions, but they leave the other person to himself. What I am able to do for another person will be shown me in prayer. Prayer commends the others into the faithful hands of Christ and Christ will deal with them. In order to pray correctly, we must be able to listen to the other person. Those who cannot hear another person are also no longer able to hear God's Word . . . or to pray! Our love for another consists first of all in listening.

The pastor who will never confront the other person in a calculating or investigative manner has long experience with what is essential. The other person is a sinner whom God's mercy wants to encounter. That is the difference between spiritual care and psychotherapy, for which the method of investigation is all-important. Spiritual care puts no stock in such methods. There are no "psychologically interesting cases" for spiritual care; to approach the matter in such a way would be a disavowal of the office. What is supposed to be learned that is new beyond sin? The pastor remains fundamentally premethodical and prepsychological, in the best sense naive. Otherwise spiritual care could get to the point where magic and daimonism begin to take precedence over the purity and simplicity of familial love. The psychic connects to magical powers. The psychic seeks immediacy in the encounter of two souls. In psychoanalysis the "doctor complex" occurs after the first phase; one becomes dependent on this particular doctor. Although in a later stage of analysis one tries to reduce this complex, the solution never quite solves anything; we wind up with a different form of dependence. The pastor, on the other hand, does not bind anyone to himself at any stage, but only to the Word and Spirit of Christ. Where people try to enter into dependence on the pastor, the pastor must be firm and resistant without being unkind. The uneasy atmosphere of psychic immediacy must not be allowed to enter into spiritual care. The pastor loves the other person so much as to risk being hated by the other. Through dependency on Word, prayer, and faith the other person is freed from bondage to his own ego.

The true pastor will certainly ask investigative questions but only in order to get the person to talk. The immodest manner of interrogation is eliminated by familial love. The pastor only wants to know in order to help. Afterward he quickly forgets what he knows. Naiveté serves a better purpose than the dark magic of exercising control. Other people are to be placed before God alone and, through God, their eyes are to be opened.

Despite the immediacy of attachment, distance is still maintained between doctor and patient in psychotherapy. This happens because the patient submits to the doctor's knowledge and ability and thus feels dependent on the doctor. The doctor is comparable to a magician. The distance between pastor and parishioner is of another order. It is not based on differing gifts and personal powers but on the office God has given the pastor. Fundamentally there is no difference at all between pastor and parishioner. The pastor comes empty-handed like all others. It is a distance into which God places a seeker with a helper. It is not a question of power relationships but of a difference in commission. All questions of personal worthiness are beside the point and put us in the realm of psychotherapy. To those who come to us for spiritual care our ability has less than no authority. Only the mission binds us and calls us together. The pastor as spiritual curate is not a person of unusual experience, ability, or maturity. He should not pass himself off as such, as a "person you can trust," "a priestly person," or the like. If he does, he will only put himself in Jesus' place and arouse expectations he will of necessity disappoint. People will most likely confide in us. But they ought rather place their trust in the Word, Christ, alone. To this end we can serve and aid. The more they turn to Christ the less will we steer any attention to ourselves.

It would certainly be most misleading to remove the distance between pastor and parishioner which is established by God's commission. The pastor should not—out of a misguided idea of solidarity—speak about personal unworthiness or sin. As a rule this is not helpful for the other person. By doing this, we interpose ourselves and our own problems between the other person and Christ. It could also be an evasion of the mission of spiritual care. The relationship may proceed naturally to the point where one doesn't know who is pastor and who is parishioner. But we shouldn't make a method of that which is an ultimate possibility and a genuine grace. The office of spiritual care does not exist to declare solidarity but to listen and to proclaim the gospel. Proper distance helps establish proper closeness. . . . [SC, pp. 35–37]

The person who is puzzled about faith means to take God seriously when he doubts that God is gracious toward him. But God is not taken seriously when one's own lostness is taken more seriously than the grace of God, which is able to take away and emerge victorious over that lost condition. It is also not taking God seriously when we elevate our concept of God as divine wrath above God's essence, namely the reality of God's grace. God is gracious above and beyond all our sins. Those who want to take God seriously should look upon Christ. In Christ God's wrath is revealed as nowhere else, yet at the same time God's grace is revealed as nowhere else. If you think you are under God's wrath, then cleave to Christ! "For his anger is but for a moment, and his favor is for a lifetime" (Ps. 30:5).

Hidden and unknown temptations are the most dangerous. They are objectively present to us but subjectively we do not reckon them. Their aim is general ruin of our spiritual state. Signs of such temptations are that we can no longer pray, sense our sin, take refuge in grace and forgiveness, or have anything conclusive in which to believe. The whole Christian terminology is known and even respected; it rolls out of our mouths without a hitch, but it has no grip on our hearts. God's wrath is concealed in such circumstances. But the human heart is hardened to the point where one cannot recognize God's wrath even once. "To have no temptation is the worst temptation" (Luther). Here our spiritual care must clarify where the foundation lies for such self-induced impenitence. This is one of the most difficult problems the pastor will face. He can only rely on the Word, which is sharper than any two-edged sword, and before which the thoughts and intentions of the human heart are laid bare (Heb. 4:12).

A brief word might be said in conclusion about those who are troubled by a lack of personal experience of God. To begin with, we should inquire about their thankfulness, hope, and obedience. Where these remain parenthetical and marginal to a person's being, grace will always be cheap grace. No doubt the best information is in remembering 2 Corinthians 12 where Paul asks for the removal of the "thorn in the flesh" and receives the answer, "my grace is sufficient for you." We have no claim to experiences of God. We will not be saved by experiences but by grace, not even through an *experience of grace* but by grace alone. Grace is more than what we "experience" of it. Grace has to be *believed*. Thus we mustn't gloss over sins. We would badly distort Paul's words if we did that. Sin is never a "thorn in the flesh" with whose presence we are to become content or comfortable. Sin must come to the light of day under all circumstances.

SPIRITUAL CARE TO THE SICK

Sick visits should be regular. Bear in mind that they are for the sake of the sick person. People never expect others to show up so much as they do when sick. It is best to schedule the visit in advance so the sick person can get presentable. Announced visits are more worthwhile than surprise visits. The pastor mustn't ignore a scheduled visit. You can't imagine how much damage you'll do if you don't show up. Scheduling regular visits pledges the pastor to be prepared and the sick person to be ready. If possible, the visits should always be scheduled at the same hour and on the same day of the week.

Regular visits are also good for the pastor. He should be present with the sick often. In such a way he will learn that sickness and health go together. This is not abnormal. Sickness and pain are a law of the fallen world. A person who happens to experience fallenness in this special way is an image of the One who bore our sickness and was so afflicted that people hid their faces from him (Isa. 53). If Jesus came among the sick, that signifies that he bore the law of this world and fulfilled it. "He took our infirmities and bore our diseases" (Matt. 8:17). Jesus saves in that he bears. His salvation has nothing to do with magic, which is able to make people well from a distance. In Jesus' healings the cross is prefigured. Healing shows that Jesus receives and bears the sick in their weakness, a weakness he will bear on the cross. Only as the crucified One is he the healer.

Among the sick we learn more about the world and come closer to the pangs of Jesus' cross than we do among the well. Guilt, sin, and decay are more recognizable where everyone participates in the subjection of those who suffer without any particular discernible reason. The same curse rests upon us all. Some, however, experience it more deeply and painfully than all the rest. Such participation helps us recognize the true condition of the world. Our health is endangered in each moment. All sickness is enclosed within our health. The law of this world calls for a cross and not health. It's not good that the sick are shut up, concentrated in large hospitals to put them far out of sight of the well. At Bethel the sick and the healthy live with one another, sharing as a matter of course daily life and worship: a continual reminder to the sick of wholeness.

Love toward sick members should have a special place in the Christian congregation. Christ comes near to us in the sick. The pastor who neglects the visitation of the sick must ask whether or not he can exercise his office on the whole.

Sick people ask for healing. They cry for release from this body of death into a new and healthy body. They cry for the new world in which "God will wipe away every tear, and there will be no more suffering or crying or pain" (Rev. 21:4). Insofar as this happens, the sick inquire about Christ more than do the well. Christ fulfills this conscious or unconscious expectation through his promise, "I am the Lord, your physician" (Exod. 15:26). Nevertheless the proclamation should not be limited to this one aspect. No proper spiritual care occurs without the offer of the forgiveness of sins. The mandate to proclaim the forgiveness of sins applies here, too. Often concrete sins will come to light. Not only past sins come to light, but also those related to the sickness and those the sickness itself creates. Sickness can make one egocentric and sullen, driven to extreme resistance toward Christ, a resistance which is itself unhealthy. The sickbed then becomes burdened with great guilt. So in spiritual care compassion cannot stand alone; we must also bring the whole truth of sin and grace. [SC, pp. 53–57]

SERMONS, 1928–1932
BARCELONA, NEW YORK, BERLIN

As a young preacher in Barcelona, Bonhoeffer was very diligent in preparing his sermons. Indeed, Eberhard Bethge suggests that these first sermons of Bonhoeffer's Barcelona pastorate "reveal the whole gamut of his theological work and outlook." Here we can see the distinction that he later developed between faith and religion, and also his commitment to the "concrete." In this fledgling year as a preacher, during which he wrote and preached nineteen sermons, Bonhoeffer likewise manifests a remarkable sensitivity to his parishioners in their daily problems and personal anxieties. The pastorate in Barcelona was, as we have seen in the biographical introduction, Bonhoeffer's first encounter with poverty. Many of his congregation were experiencing the effects of the depression then afflicting Europe. Bonhoeffer speaks to them of the advent of Christ who will not leave people alone in their troubles, but who promises to bring peace of heart and to make all things new. He asks his people to draw on the reserves of their Christian trust in the Lord, seeking not the kind of peace that the world gives.

In the sermon we have included here from his year in New York, we read of God's love breaking down the barriers of race, religion, and nation. It is the Lord alone, he claims, who can satisfy the great need for peace after the traumatic experience of World War I and the divisiveness and mistrust between nations. He declares in one inspiring passage that "above all differences of race, nationality and custom there is an invisible community of the children of God. There each one prays for the others, be he or she, American or German or African; here each one loves the others without reservation. Let us in this hour gratefully consider that we all belong to this church. . . ." This sermon is an early expression of his passionate concern for peace on earth.

In his preaching, having returned to Berlin, Bonhoeffer returns to the theme of God's loving care and the solace given to people in suffering. In the sermon at the Harvest Festival he reminds people of God's goodness and mercy in the gifts of plenty and a kind of prosperity. But he asks, too, for a true, gospel understanding of this sign of God's goodness. It means that the "haves" of this world must share with the "have-nots" and become the extension of God's graciousness to them. In other sermons Bonhoeffer emphasizes the hope that overcomes even the threat of death and the power of the cross of Christ to be the light of the world in the dark pathos of a nation mourning its dead. Finally, we see Bonhoeffer's call to the people to accept the revolutionary word of the gospel. Christians, he declares, should be the most revolutionary force in society as they make real in their following of Christ the true meaning of freedom.

Though some segments of the sermons may have gone over the heads of his hearers, Bonhoeffer nevertheless developed a rapport with the various congregations that was drawn out of his genuine pastoral concern and regular contacts with the people. His sermons were timely, pointed in their emphasis on Christ and faith, and from the heart. The selections that follow illustrate these qualities.

20

The Coming of Jesus in Our Midst

(First Sunday in Advent, Barcelona)

December 2, 1928

TEXT: "Behold, I stand at the door and knock; if anyone hears my voice and opens the door, I will come in to him and eat with him, and he with me." (Rev. 3:20)

When the old Christianity spoke of the return of the Lord Jesus, they thought of a great day of judgment. Even though this thought may appear to us to be so unlike Christmas, it is original Christianity and to be taken extremely seriously. When we hear Jesus knocking, our conscience first of all pricks us: Are we rightly prepared? Is our heart capable of becoming God's dwelling place? Thus Advent becomes a time of self-examination. "Put the desires of your heart in order, O human beings!" (Valentin Thilo), as the old song sings. It is very remarkable that we face the thought that God himself is coming, so calmly, whereas previously peoples trembled at the day of God, whereas the world fell into trembling when Jesus Christ walked over the earth. That is why it is so strange when we see the marks of God in the world so often together with the marks of human suffering, with the marks of the cross on Golgotha. We have become so accustomed to the idea of divine love and of his coming at Christmas that we no longer feel the shiver of fear that God's coming should arouse in us. We are indifferent to the message, taking only the pleasant and agreeable out of it and forgetting the serious aspect, that the God of the world draws near to the people of our little earth and lays claim to us. The coming of God is truly not only glad tidings, but first of all frightening news for every one who has a conscience.

Only when we have felt the terror of the matter, can we recognize the incomparable kindness. God comes into the very midst of evil and of death, and judges the evil in us and in the world. And by judging us, he cleanses and sanctifies us, comes to us with his grace and love. He makes us happy as only children can be happy. He wants to always be with us, wherever we may be—in our sin, in our suffering and death. We are no longer alone; God is with us. We are no longer homeless; a bit of the eternal home itself has moved into us. Therefore we adults can rejoice deeply within our hearts under the Christmas tree, perhaps much more than the children are able. We know that God's goodness will once again draw near. We think of all of God's goodness that came our way last year and sense something of this marvelous home. Jesus comes in judgment and grace: "Behold I stand at the door. . . . Open wide the gates!" (Ps. 24:7).

. . . One day, at the last judgment, he will separate the sheep and the goats and will say to those on his right: "Come, you blessed, . . . I was hungry and you fed me. . . ." (Matt. 25:34ff.). To the astonished question of when and where, he answered: "What you did to the least of these, you have done to me. . . ." (Matt. 25:40). With that we are faced with the shocking reality: Jesus stands at the door and knocks, in complete reality. He asks you for help in the form of a beggar, in the form of a ruined human being in torn clothing. He confronts you in every person that you meet. Christ walks on the earth as your neighbor as long as there are people. He walks on the earth as the one through whom God calls you, speaks to you and makes his demands. That is the greatest seriousness and the greatest blessedness of the Advent message. Christ stands at the door. He lives in the form of the person in our midst. Will you keep the door locked or open it to him?

Christ is still knocking. It is not yet Christmas. But it is also not the great final Advent, the final coming of Christ. Through all the Advents of our life that we celebrate goes the longing for the final Advent, where it says: "Behold, I make all things new" (Rev. 21:5). Advent is a time of waiting. Our whole life, however, is Advent—that is, a time of waiting for the ultimate, for the time when there will be a new heaven and a new earth, when all people are brothers and sisters and one rejoices in the words of the angels: "On earth peace to men on whom his favor rests." Learn to wait, because he has promised to come. "I stand at the door. . . ." We however call him: "Yes, come soon, Lord Jesus!" Amen.
[*GS*, V, pp. 473–78]

21

On God's Message of Love to Germany and the Community of Nations

(New York)

Autumn 1930

TEXT: "God is love; and he who abides in love abides in God and God in him." (1 John 4:16b)

It is indeed a strange feeling for me just coming over here from Germany to stand now in an American pulpit and before an American Christian congregation. In this hour the worldwide extent of our faith and hope occurs anew to my mind. I am overwhelmed, considering the idea of God, the Father, who dwells beyond the stars and looks down upon his children in the whole world—in America and Germany, in India and in Africa. There is not any difference before God, as Paul says: "There is neither Jew nor Greek, there is neither bond nor free, there is neither male nor female, for ye are all one in Christ Jesus." God has erected a strange, marvelous, and wonderful sign in the world, where we all could find him—I mean the cross of Jesus Christ, the cross of the suffering love of God. Under the cross of Christ we know that we all belong to one another, that we all are brethren and sisters in the same need and in the same hope, that we are bound together by the same destiny, human beings with all our suffering and all our joys, with sorrows and with desires, with disappointments and fulfillments—and most important, human beings with our sin and guilt, with our faith and hope. Before the cross of Christ and his inconceivable suffering all our external differences disappear, we are no longer rich or poor, wise or simple, good or bad; we are no longer Americans or Germans, we are one large congregation of brethren; we recognize that nobody is good before God, as Paul says: "For all have sinned and come short of the glory of God, being justified freely by his grace."

Let us look at the love of Christ, who without guilt bore the cross—why? Because he had loved his people more than himself. And then let us consider our own feebleness and our own want of courage, our anxiety when sorrow and grief threaten, our selfish desire to live a comfortable and careless life. In profound and serious humility we Christian people must confess that we are not worthy of such great love of God. If you ask me: What is Christendom?—I answer: Christendom is the great congregation of people who humble themselves before God and who put all their hope and faith in the love and the help of God. Christendom is the community in which people stand for each other, as a brother stands for his brother. Christendom is one great people composed of persons of every country in concord in their faith and their love because there is One God, One Lord, One Spirit, One Hope. That is the marvelous mystery of the people of God. Above all differences of race, nationality, and custom there is an invisible community of the children of God. There each one prays for the others, be he or she American or German or African; here each one loves the others without reservation. Let us in this hour gratefully consider that we all belong to this church, that God has called us to be his children and made us brethren, that there cannot be any hate and enmity, but only the best will to understand each other. Otherwise we would not be worthy to bear the name of Christ, we would offend the glory of God, who is a God of love and not of hate.

Now I stand before you not only as a Christian, but also as a German, who rejoices with his people and who suffers when he sees his people suffering, who confesses gratefully that he received from his people all that he has and is. So I bring you this morning a double message: the message of Germany and the message of Christianity in Germany. I hope you will hear this message with a Christian heart, with the readiness of a Christian soul to understand and to love, wherever and whomever it might be.

November 11, 1918, brought to Germany the end of a frightful and unparalleled time, a time which we pray, if God wills, will never return. For four years German men and lads stood for their home with an unheard-of tenacity and intrepidity, with the imperturbable consciousness of their duty, with an inexorable self-discipline and with a glowing love for their fatherland, and with a belief in its future. For weeks and months these people suffered privations of every kind; they persevered in hunger and thirst, in pain and affliction, in craving after home, after mothers and wives and brothers and children. In the country the stream of tears of old and young people did not cease. Every day the message came to more than a thousand families that the husband, the father, the brother had died in a foreign country. Hardly any family was spared.

(. . . I tell you from my personal experience, two brothers of mine stood at the front. The older one, eighteen years old, was wounded, the younger one, seventeen years old, was killed. Three first cousins of mine were also killed, boys of eighteen to twenty years old. Although I was then a small boy I never can forget those most gloomy days of the war.) Death stood at the door of almost every house and called for entrance. Once the message came about the death of many thousands of seventeen- and eighteen-year-old boys killed in a few hours. Germany was made a house of mourning. The breakdown could not be delayed longer. Famine and enervation were too powerful and destructive.

I think you will release me from talking about our feeling in Germany those days. The recollection of this time is gloomy and sad. Very seldom will you hear today in Germany anybody talking about those days. We will not reopen an old and painful wound. But however we felt, the war and its dreadful killing and dying was finished. Our minds were still too confused and bewildered; we could not yet conceive and quietly consider the meaning of all the events of the last years and months. But gradually we saw more and more clearly; and Christian people in Germany, who took the course and the end of the war seriously, could not help seeing here a judgment of God upon this fallen world and especially upon our people.

Before the war we lived too far from God; we believed too much in our own power, in our almightiness and righteousness. We attempted to be a strong and good people, but we were too proud of our endeavor, we felt too much satisfaction with our scientific, economic, and social progress, and we identified this progress with the coming of the kingdom of God. We felt too happy and complacent in this world; our souls were too much at home in this world. Then the great disillusionment came. We saw the impotence and the weakness of humanity, we were suddenly awakened from our dream, we recognised our guiltiness before God and we humbled ourselves under the mighty hand of God. When I was speaking of "guiltiness," I added on purpose: "guilt before God," Let me tell you frankly that no German and no stranger who knows well the history of the origin of the war believes that Germany bears the sole guilt of the war—a sentence which we were compelled to sign in the Treaty of Versailles. (The Allied and Associated governments affirm and Germany accepts the responsibility of Germany and her allies for causing all the loss and the damage to which the Allied and Associated governments and their nations have been subjected as a consequence of the war imposed upon them by the aggression of Germany and her allies.) I personally do not believe, on the other hand, that Germany was the only guiltless country, but as a Christian I see the main guilt of Germany in quite a different light. I see it in Germany's complacency, in her belief in her almightiness, in the lack of humility and faith in God and fear of God. It seems to me that this is the meaning of the war for Germany: we had to recognize the limits of humanity and by that means we discovered anew God in his glory and almightiness, in his wrath and his grace.

The same November 11, 1918, which brought to us the end of the war, was the beginning of a new epoch of suffering and grief. The first years after the war showed to us the corruption in our public life. The general poverty caused by the hunger blockade had dreadful consequences. Germany was starved out. (. . . The consequences of the blockade were frightful. I myself was in these years a schoolboy and I can assure you that not only I had in those days to learn what hunger means. I should wish that you would have to eat this food for only one day that we had for three or four years and I think you would get a glimpse of the privations which Germany had to endure. Put yourself in the situation of the German mothers whose husbands were standing [serving] or were killed in the war and who had to provide for growing hungry children. Countless tears were shed in these last years of the war and the first years of peace by the desperate mothers and hungry children. As a matter of fact instead of a good meal there was largely sawdust in our bread and the fixed portion for every day was five or six slices of that kind of bread. You could not get any butter at all. Instead of sugar we had saccharin tablets. The substitute for meat, fish, vegetables, even for coffee, jam and toast—were turnips for breakfast, lunch, and supper. Germany really was starved out. Thousands and thousands of old and young people, of little children, died simply because there was not enough to eat. Fatal epidemics ran through the country. The flu epidemic of 1918 demanded more than a hundred thousand victims. People were physically too enervated and could not resist. When the wintertime came we had not enough coal for heating our rooms. We had no cloth for our clothes; it is no exaggeration to say that many people had to buy suits made more of paper than of real cloth. In the street you could see the undernourished and poorly dressed people, the pale and sick children. The number of suicides increased in a terrifying way. I remember very well I had on the way to my school to pass by a bridge and in the winters from 1917 to 1919 almost every morning when I came to this bridge I saw a group of people standing on the river and everybody who passed by knew what had happened. These impressions were hard for young boys.

(I will stop picturing these frightful months and years. But before I go on, I will not forget to tell you that the Quaker congregations of the States were the first who after the war in an admirable work supported the German children. Many thousand children were saved from starvation. Germany remembers in deep thankfulness this work of love of the Quaker society. . . .)

(. . . there was one wound which was much more painful than all these privations and needs, that was the Article 231 of the Treaty of Versailles. I will tell you frankly, that this is the wound which still is open and bleeds in Germany. I will try to explain to you briefly what our attitude toward this question was and is. When the war broke out the German people did not consider very much the question of guilt. We thought it to be our duty to stand for our country and we believed of course in our essential guiltlessness. You cannot expect in such a moment of excitement an objective and detached valuation of the present conditions. The war has its own psychology. The German soldiers stood in the war in the confident faith in the righteousness of their country. But already during the war you could hear in Germany some skeptical voices: Who can tell who is wrong and who is right? We all fight for our country and believe in it, Germans no less than French. Now twelve years after the war the whole question has been thoroughly searched historically. I personally see many faults in our policy before the war, I am not going to defend my country in every point. But a study of the diplomatic documents of Belgium of the years before the war for instance shows irrefutably that other countries had committed the same or greater faults than Germany. I mean especially Russia and France. In 1914 everybody in Europe expected more a war caused by Russia and France than by Germany. It can be proved historically that the Article 231 of the Treaty of Versailles is an injustice against our country and we have a right to protest. That fact is recognized by the largest parts of educated people in Europe and in America.)

Everyone who is familiar with the conditions in Germany today, twelve years after the war, knows that in spite of some changes in their external aspect, social conditions are almost as unhappy as ten or twelve years ago. The debts of the war press us not only with regard to our financial standard, but likewise in regard to our whole behavior, we see the hopelessness of our work. It is impossible for us to provide social and economic conditions for our children of the future in which we can trust for security. The Germans are a suffering people today, but they will not despair. They will work for building up a new and better home, they will work for peace in their country, they will work for peace in the world. When I came over here, I was astonished on being asked again and again, what German people think about a future war. I tell you the truth: German people do not speak at all about that; they don't even think of it. You almost never hear in Germany talk about war and much less about a future war. We know what a war means for a people.

I have been accustomed once in every year since my boyhood to wander on foot through our country, and so I happen to know many classes of German people very well. Many evenings I have sat with the families of peasants around the big stove talking about past and future, about the next generation and their chances. But always when the talk happened to touch the war, I observed how deep the wound was which the past war had caused to everyone. The German people need and want above all *peace*. (. . . They want to work peacefully in their fields, they fear any disturbance. But it is not different among other classes in Germany. In the working class for instance started the German peace movement and the interest for an international trade makes those people naturally pacifistic. It was in Germany that the thought arose that the workers in France and in Germany are closer to one another than the various classes within each country [which] separately belong to one another. You will find large worker organizations with a particularly pacifistic program; especially also the Christian organizations of workers work in this very direction. The bourgeois in Germany had to bear the hardest burden after the war, but nevertheless I can assure you that by far the most of them would abominate a war more than anything else. You might be interested in hearing something about the attitude of the youth toward war and peace. The youth movement which started immediately after the war was in its tendencies entirely pacifist. In a deep religious feeling we recognized all people as brothers, as children of God. We wanted to forget all hard and bitter feeling after the war. We had anew discovered a genuine and true love for our home country and that helped us to get a great and deep love for other people, for all mankind. You see there are many various motives working for peace, but whatever motive it might be there is one great aim and one great work; the peace movement in Germany is an enormous power.) As a Christian minister I think that just here is one of the greatest tasks for our church: to strengthen the work of peace in every country and in the whole world. It must never more happen that a Christian people fights against a Christian people, brother against brother, since both have one Father. Our churches have already begun this international work. But more important than that is, it seems to me, that every Christian man and woman, boy and girl, take seriously the great idea of the unity of Christianity, above all personal and national desires, of the one Christian people in the whole world, of the brotherhood of mankind of the love, about which Paul says: "Love is patient and kind; love is not jealous or boastful; love is not arrogant or rude. Love does not insist on its own way; it is not irritable or resentful; it does not rejoice at wrong, but rejoices in the right. Love bears all things, believes all things, hopes all things, endures all things. Love never ends." Let us consider that the judgment comes for every man and woman, boy and girl, in America and Germany, in Russia and in India; and God will judge us according to our faith and love. How can the man who hates his brother expect grace from God? That is my message as a German and as a Christian to you: let us love one another, let us build in faith and love one holy Christianity, one brotherhood, with God the Father, and Christ the Lord, and the Holy Spirit as the sanctifying power. Nobody is too little or too poor for this work; we need every will and force.

I address now especially you, boys and girls of the United States, future bearers and leaders of the culture of your country. You have brothers and sisters in our people and in every people; do not forget that. Come what may, let us never more forget that one Christian people is the people of God, that if we are in accord, no nationalism, no hate of races or classes can execute its designs, and then the world will have its peace forever and ever. (. . . This is my message for you: hear the voice of your German brothers and sisters, take their stretched out hand. We know it is not enough only to talk and to feel the necessity of peace; we must work seriously. There is so much meanness, selfishness, slander, hatred, prejudice among the nations. But we must overcome it. Today as never before nations of Europe—except Germany—are preparing for war. This makes our work very urgent. We must no longer waste time. Let us work together for an everlasting peace.) Let us remember the prayer of Christ spoken shortly before his end: "I pray for them which shall believe in me: that they all may be one; as thou, Father, art in me, and I in thee, that they also may be one in us."

And the peace of God, which passeth all understanding, shall keep your hearts and minds through Christ Jesus. Amen. (At this time there comes to my mind an evening, which I spent not a long time ago with a group of young people from our German youth movement. It was a glorious summer night. We were outdoors far away from the noise and bustle of the city on the top of a mountain, above us the sky with its millions of stars, the quietness of the evening, below us the lights of the villages, the misty fields and the black woods; not one of us spoke a word. We heard nothing but the peaceful rustling of the brooks and the trees. On that evening a great and deep love came anew in our hearts, a love for our home and for the starry sky. The boys had carried branches of trees and lit a big fire on the top of the mountain and while we were staring into the blazing fire in silence, a boy began to speak about his love for his country and for the starry sky, which at that very time was shining upon people of all nations, upon all humankind, and he said: "How wonderful it would be if people of all nations lived in peace and quiet as the stars in the heaven above, if only all nations could live together like brothers as they do in their own country." When he finished all the boys and girls raised their hands as a sign that they were willing to work for this peace for everyone in his place, for the peace in the country and the world. Then we sat down and while the fire was burning out we sang our most beautiful folk songs about the love of our country and the peace of all mankind. With the deep understanding of our great task before us we went home.)

(More than a year has passed since that time and I wish to bring this message from my German students to the students of this great country.) [NRS, pp. 76–85]

22

God's Loving Care and Human Suffering

(Harvest Festival, Berlin)

October 4, 1931

TEXT: "For thy goodness is better than life." (Ps. 63:3)

Two and a half millennia have now passed since the ancient Jewish saint, far from Jerusalem and his homeland, devoured by misery in body and soul, surrounded by mockers and enemies of his God, pondered the strange and wonderful ways God had led him. It was no easy, peaceful meditation. It was a struggle for God and his faithfulness. The pillars of life had crumbled away. Where his hand thought it had found firm support it reached into an empty nothingness. "God, where are you? God, who am I? My life falls crashing down into the bottomless abyss. God, I am afraid, where has your goodness gone? And yet, you are my God and your goodness is better than life," That is one of the words that does not let you go once you have understood it, a word that seems to shine gently, but is inwardly hard, a word of passion that is engendered where two worlds clash, that is, a word from the world of the Bible and not from our own.

The words of this text, "Thy goodness is better than life," seem to shine gently, but inwardly they are hard words. These words are full of passion conceived in the conflict of two different worlds, the world of the Bible in conflict with our own.

"Your goodness is better than life": It is the exultant cry of the wretched and abandoned, of the weary and overburdened; the cry of longing uttered by the sick and the oppressed; the song of praise among the unemployed and the hungry in the great cities; the prayer of thanksgiving prayed by tax collectors and prostitutes, by sinners known and unknown. Well is that really their shout of joy? No, it is not, not in our world, at any rate not in our age. It is the shout of joy for the peculiar world of the Bible, which frightens and angers us with its strangeness, at least as far as we still listen to its message and have not become insensitive to the reality of the Bible. Or perhaps the verse does not seem so particularly remarkable after all. Perhaps we think that it is perfectly self-evident. These things have become part of the life of a Christian. If that is how we think, we shall have to discover what the psalmist is really saying here and whether it really is so obvious.

At some point in our psalmist's life something quite decisive happened: God came into his life. From that moment his life was changed. I don't mean that suddenly he became good and pious—it may well be that he was that before God came. But now God himself had come and had drawn near to him. What made his life remarkable was simply that God was always there with him and he could no longer get away from God. It completely tore his life apart. We so often hear and say that religion makes people happy and harmonious and peaceful and content. Maybe that's true of religion; but it is not true of God and dealings with humankind. It is utterly wrong. This is what the psalmist discovered. Something had burst open inside him. He felt as if he were split in two. A struggle flared up within him, which every day became more and more heated and terrible. He experienced hour by hour how his old beliefs were being torn out of his inner being. He struggled desperately to hold on to them; but God, standing ever before him, had taken them from him and would never give them back. And the more he loses, the more firmly and eagerly he grabs at what is left; but the more firmly he holds on to what he has, the harder must God strike to break it free and the more it hurts when it is torn away. And so the breathless struggle goes on, with God the victor and the person defeated; he no longer knows where it will all lead to and he sees that he is lost; he does not know whether he hates or loves the one who has forced his way so violently into his life and destroyed his peace. He struggles for every inch and in despair yields to the weapons of God. And his position would not be quite so hopeless were it not for the fact that God's weapons are so strange and wonderful, that they cast down and lift up, that they wound and yet heal, that they kill and yet bring life; God speaks: "If you want my mercy, then let me gain the victory over you; if you want my life, then let me hate and destroy that which is evil in you; if you want my goodness, then let me take your life." And now it has come to the final struggle. Everything has been surrendered up and only one thing has been left to the person, which he is determined to hold on to: his life. Still God will not call a halt, but storms this last citadel of all. And so the battle rages on for the last thing which he has; the individual defends himself like a mad person. God cannot want this; God is not cruel; God is good and kind. And yet the answer comes back: "If you want my goodness then give me the last thing that you have, give me your life. Now choose!"

Such heights terrify us; it is as if someone led us to the limits of the world and as if we looked down into an abyss and he said: "Now jump!" We feel as if we had been torn apart. How can we choose between God's goodness and our life? What is our life? Everything that we see, touch, hear, taste, feel; everything which surrounds us, which we possess, which we are used to, which we love. What is God's goodness? In any case everything which we cannot see, cannot touch, cannot comprehend, and indeed cannot believe; something which we do not possess, something quite improbable, something outside this world, standing above and behind all events, and yet which speaks to us so directly. Who would venture to make a free choice here? God himself gains the victory, and it seems humanly impossible that we should now hear from the psalmist's lips the words: "God, you are my God. Your goodness is better than life."

Some of you will by now be indignant and you will begin to object: What sort of exaggerated and wild talk is this? You can't talk about the goodness of God in that way. That I'm in good health, that I've still got food and drink to share with my family, that I've got work and a house, that's what God's goodness means to me and that's what I should thank him for. But I neither know nor understand anything of this struggle with God's goodness.

My friends, today is harvest festival and a very proper time for us to reflect seriously about what God's goodness means to us. Unmoved by the bitter worries and unrest of our time, nature goes about her work in the world. She produces food for the peoples of the earth. When she withholds her gifts, millions die; when she bestows them lavishly humankind flourishes. No person has control over her and when he is confronted by her power, the person grows silent and is reminded of him who has the power over nature. Today we celebrate our harvest festival in particular circumstances and with specific thoughts in mind. The harvest has not brought us what we hoped for. This has already caused us great sorrow. But on top of this comes one of the worst plagues which can ever be inflicted on a people, and which is now spreading across the world, unemployment. We must be prepared for the fact that this winter seven million people in Germany will find no work, which means hunger for fifteen to twenty million people next winter. Another twelve million or more in England, twenty or more in America, while at this very moment sixteen million are starving in China and the situation is not much better in India. These are the cold statistics behind which stands a terrible reality. Should we overlook these millions of people when we celebrate our harvest festival in church? We dare not. Rather we should want to measure our Christian thinking and intentions by how well we respond to these facts.

When we sit down this evening to a full table and say grace and thank God for his goodness, we shall not be able to avoid a strange feeling of uneasiness. It will seem incomprehensible to us that we should be the ones to receive such gifts and we will be overwhelmed by such thoughts and will think that we have not in any way deserved these gifts more than our hungry brothers in our town. What if, precisely at the moment when we are thanking God for his goodness toward us, there is a ring at the door, as so often happens these days, and we find someone standing there who also would like to thank God for some small gift, but to whom such a gift has been denied and who is starving with his children and who will go to bed in bitterness? What becomes of our grace in such moments? Will we really feel like saying that God is merciful to *us* and angry with *him,* or that the fact that we still have something to eat proves that we have won a special position of favor in God's sight, that God feeds his favorite children and lets the unworthy go hungry? May the merciful God protect us from the temptation of such gratitude. May he lead us to a true understanding of his goodness. Don't we see that the gifts of his goodness become a curse for us if we have such thoughts about them and act in such a way; if we look upon ourselves as models of virtue, instead of growing humble as we look at the incomprehensibility of God and the worry and anxiety our wealth creates in us and if we thank God only for his goodness to us instead of becoming conscious of the immeasurable responsibility which is laid upon us by his goodness? If we want to understand God's goodness in his gifts, then we must think of them as a responsibility we bear for our brothers. Let no one say: God has blessed me with money and possessions, and then live as if he and his God were alone in the world. For the time will come when he realizes that he has been worshipping the idols of his good fortune and his selfishness. Possessions are not God's blessing and goodness, but the opportunities of service which he entrusts to us.

This has already brought us some distance along the way toward understanding what God's goodness is. Whoever has a task laid upon him by God sees himself set between two worlds: "If you want my goodness to stay with you, then serve your neighbor, for in him God comes to you himself"; such a person sees in his neighbor the material and spiritual need for which he is now called to account. And now the struggle is played out of which the psalmist speaks. "If you want my mercy, then give your neighbor a share of your possessions. If you want my love, then give your neighbor your soul. If you want my goodness then stake your life for your neighbor. And if you don't do all this then that which was God's goodness to you, the gifts which he showered on your body and soul, will turn into a curse on you." Which of us would care to say that he had done all this, that in his thoughts and particularly in his actions he had really understood that God's goodness leads us into a struggle, that it is not something which we receive and then simply possess, so that we live on, somewhat happier, somewhat richer, but essentially unaltered. But how miserably we enter on this struggle; with so little passion and with so much fear, weakness, trembling, and sadness; and how little does it really take hold of the roots of our being.

Yet we shall not understand this struggle at all until we understand how radical and basic it is. "Thy goodness is better than life" does not just mean better than your house, than your food, than your work, than your reputation, than your honor, than your physical, artistic, and spiritual pleasures, than your wife or husband and children, but it means more than all that; it means that it is better than the one thing you still have when you have lost everything, better than your life. Which of us has already come to know that God's goodness leads us into a conflict, which involves the physical side of our life, and not only that but also our work, our honor, and even our family? Who would allow himself to be drawn into such a conflict and who would see in such a conflict God's goodness? And above all, who sees that we have not grasped the meaning of God's goodness until the conflict goes much deeper and seizes hold of our life and reaches out beyond even that? . . .

But now comes the greatest wonder that the world has ever known. In the very place where we have fallen away from God, where we have become dead and unreceptive to him, in our guilt, God's goodness searches us out, and he reveals himself to us again as *the* eternal promise of God, in Jesus Christ, which far surpasses all guilt and all life. Only the person who, in the darkness of guilt, of unfaithfulness, of enmity toward God, has felt himself or herself touched by the love which never ceases, which forgives everything and which points beyond all misery to the world of God, only such a person really knows what God's goodness means.

But of course we are not lifted out of life. Our task still remains with us and we are continually asked by God: "What is my love worth to you?" But the more deeply we recognize what God's goodness is, the more lively our answer will be, and again we shall be led by God's goodness to assume our responsibility and will be brought to him again through our acknowledged guilt. When will the time come that, at least in the Christian community, the world of our psalmist will break in, and in happiness or in misery, in hunger or in sickness, in fear or trouble, in sadness or guilt, in good or bad harvest we can make a truly joyful thanksgiving:

> And though they take our life,
> Goods, honor, children, wife,
> yet is their profit small;
> These things shall vanish all:
> The City of God remaineth!

O God, thy goodness is better than life—Amen. [*NRS*, pp. 125–32]

23

On Being People
Waiting for the Lord

(First Sunday in Advent, Berlin)

November 29, 1931

TEXT: "Let your loins be girded and your lamps burning, and be like men who are waiting for their master to come home from the marriage feast, so that they may open to him at once when he comes and knocks. Blessed are those servants whom the master finds awake when he comes; truly, I say to you, he will gird himself and have them sit at table, and he will come and serve them. If he comes in the second watch, or in the third, and finds them so, blessed are those servants! But know this, that if the householder had known at what hour the thief was coming, he would not have left his house to be broken into. You also must be ready; for the Son of man is coming at an unexpected hour." (Luke 12:35–40)

. . . But the strange thing is: he does not speak of one man, who brought his ideals into reality by struggling, nor of the wrestling, striving man, but he sees this man already totally taken up in God's peace, free from strife, wounds, and dying. He sees him here already under the power of the kingdom in which the souls who overcame are blessed. Because Jesus so sees humankind in this way we stand there where Jesus is blessing, as the unblessed—outside, close by, distant. Therefore we know that he is not talking about us. In any case not because we are what we really are today, but that the people here are seen in an entirely different perspective, namely, as those who are never anything in themselves, as those who are already covered by the eternal peace and eternal salvation of God; as the persons over whom the approach of the new heaven and the new earth has already won power; that is, as the people in the perspective of the future of God, in which the suffering, struggling, dying God of human history reveals himself as the First and the Last, to whom the kingdom belonged from the beginning. And because Christ knows of this future out of his mysterious, eternal knowledge, for that reason he blesses them; blessed as one to whom God will someday come, and who lives today totally for this coming, this being over-powered by God. Blessed are those who wait, blessed are those who watch and wait. Be like those who wait for their Lord! Blessed are those servants whom the Lord finds watching when he comes.

. . . Humankind wishes to remain Lord of the world, the Lord of the future. . . . And now Jesus praises those servants and says to the disciples: therefore be like the servants who wait for the Lord; you also be prepared! Be waiting people. . . .

Then hope is not a melancholy fantasy which makes his torture only greater but it is life itself. . . . Without his doing anything this wonderful happening draws near, in the time of God, in the future of God, in his coming on the earth. Here the future becomes for him a living reality, here he lives today under the shadow of the coming, not some kind of threatening misfortune, a fate, but the righteousness of the coming God, of love, and of peace. Not that he goes self-assured on the path into the future of God; no, he takes the future from God. He knows that he cannot go to God but that God must go to him in his inconceivable grace, otherwise he has waited in vain and would lose his life. He can do nothing else but watch and wait, which means enthusiastically, totally taken up, deaf toward everyone who would make him confused with doubts, blind to every force that comes between him and that future of God. Only one thing is of importance to him. He wants to see God; he wants to hear God; he wants to receive God; he wants to know God; he wants to serve God. He wants inconceivably nothing else, in any case nothing like he wants God. [GS, IV, pp. 26–33]

24

The Cross of Christ and Remembrance of the Dead

(Day of National Mourning, Berlin)

February 21, 1932

TEXT: Matt. 24:6–14

... Who would not be disturbed and ask: What is the meaning of the 1914–1918 event, what is the meaning of the millions of dead German men—for me—for us today? How does God speak through this? That means still one more time to ask quite simply: How can I put into one thought the idea of God, Christ, and the event of war? Should I say: it was an action of God, or should I give up hope and say: here God's might was at an end? Here Christ was far distant?

We must undertake these questions with vigor—and what places us close to the beginning of the Lententide?—to see first of all what has happened on the cross of Golgotha. Are not the same questions posted here, only incomparably more sharply and more impressively: How can I think of cross and God at the same time? And is it not precisely here that *the* answer is given, that stands over the whole Christian message: Christ goes through the cross, and only through the cross to life, to the resurrection, to victory? The wondrous theme of the Bible that frightens so many people is that the only visible sign of God in the world is the cross. Christ is not carried away from earth to heaven in glory, but he must go to the cross. And precisely there, where the cross stands, the resurrection is near; even there, where everyone begins to doubt God, where everyone despairs of God's power, there God is whole, there Christ is active and near. Where it is on a razor's edge, whether one becomes faithless or remains loyal—there God is, and there Christ is. Where the power of darkness does violence to the light of God, there God triumphs and judges the darkness. So is it also, when Christ thinks about the day that is approaching his congregation. His disciples ask him about the signs of his return after his death. This is not a return, happening but once. The end time in the Bible is the whole time and every day between the death of Christ and the last judgment. Yes, so seriously, so decisively does the New Testament see the death of Christ.

Christ, however, knows that his way goes to the cross, that also the way for his disciples does not lead gloriously and safely directly into heaven, but that they also must go through the darkness, through the cross. Also, they must struggle, For that reason the first sign of the nearness of Christ—worthy enough of him!—is that his enemies become great, that the power of temptation, of apostasy, of unfaithfulness, becomes strong, that his congregation would be led right up to the abyss of confusion about God. The first will be that his enemies are concealed behind the name of Christ, and now under the appearance of Christlikeness would entice us away from him. That is, the name "Christ" doesn't do it; and how easy it is in times of confusion as at present, to fight in the name of Christ against the true Christ. Then, however, when the spirits are once confused, the powers of the world are revealed, and burst forth openly. The powers* that want to snatch the disciples from him, that want to show them that it is madness to go with him, that Christ has no power,* only words; that they, the powers of reality, speak the language of facts and this language is more convincing than the language of Christ. The world bands together against the spirit of Christ, the demons are enraged: it is a revolt† against Christ. And the great power of the rebellion is called—war! The others are called pestilence and expensive times. Thus, war, sickness, and hunger are the powers, who wish to take Christ's lordship, and they are all incited by the archenemy of Christ, who is the living one from death. It would thus appear as though with Christ the victory is won. Christ has conquered Death, but now howl these powers: we are here! Look at us and be terrified. We have might! Our might has not been taken from us. Christ has not won the victory, but we are winning the victory. Christ is dead. But we are living. We are called war, sickness, and hunger. Why do you let yourselves be bewitched by these false prophets who speak about peace and life, about God and his kingdom? We are here!

And they fall upon the people and tear into them. Death goes all around and holds a great harvest; he mows over millions.

And now comes the great breaking asunder of Christendom. Their kingdoms will disintegrate and be torn up. Terrible confusion and fear comes over the followers of Christ. They must recognize that all of these attacks are basically attacks against Christ and his Word. Yes,

---

*Gewalt: power, authority

†Aufruhr: uproar, mutiny.

that this word obviously has no power over them. The previous war has confused thousands, even millions, about Christ, even among those who took his Word seriously, and now see themselves so bitterly disappointed. Read war letters; read the compilation of reports from the working class about church and Christendom that was published by a Berlin pastor. All these things are written there so that anyone can read them. "The war has shown me that Christ is not right." "The war robbed me of faith in God." "Since the war, I know that belief is madness." Those are clear words about war and the church of Christ—it is very pharisaical to simply say here: "Well now, they never really had a right faith." Dear Congregation: indeed one must have had a right faith to feel so clearly that one's faith is destroyed. And who among us wishes to say that he or she has the right faith which nothing, absolutely nothing, can jeopardize. If someone thinks that he or she has such a faith may he or she ponder over it very sharply, as to whether this faith has become more one of indifference which nothing can disturb. Therefore, let there be caution with such pharisaic reproaches. Didn't those millions also have a right to Christ, who was snatched away from them? What are we going to say about this, we who were pulled into this event of 1914–1918, and thus are partially to blame for the fact their faith was taken from them?

From this perspective things look different. Would we not be a conceited, harsh Christendom if under such circumstances even the most faithful were not overcome with unspeakable fear that Christ could be snatched from us, if not even the true people of God were not deeply depressed, and if the frightened congregation of Christ did not have to cry out over the plague of the war: "My God, why have you forsaken me?" Christ himself cried out in this manner from the cross, and died with this cry, according to the report of one evangelist. Oh, it is all too understandable, that millions became unfaithful, that under so much hate their love became cold. Truly despair would surround us if the Word of Christ were not here: "When all this happens to you, look up and do not be afraid. All this must happen first." Jesus had to say so often to his disciples: "Do not be afraid, for I am with you." "Fear not, for I have called you by name . . ." so says the Old Testament. "Fear not," the angel called to the frightened shepherds. "Fear not, only believe," says Jesus. "Fear not, you small flock, since it is the Father's pleasure to give you the kingdom." "When you see such things, do not be afraid. All these things must come to pass, for the end is not yet here." We ask: Why must all this happen? Because Christ himself must go through death, because where Christ, where God himself is truly present, there the darkness itself most terribly rebels and of its own accord nails him to the cross. Therefore, we also must go through it. All this must happen so that the end can come.

God's way in the world leads to the cross and through the cross to life. Therefore, do not be afraid; fear not; be faithful! But what is meant here by being faithful is namely: to stand and to fall with the Word of Christ, with his sermon about the kingdom of peace, to know that the Words of Christ in spite of all are mightier than the powers of evil. What is meant here by being faithful as a congregation of Christ is namely: to be in this furious storm even to exhaustion, even to vexation, even to the call to martyrdom for the Word of Christ, so that there will be peace, so that there will be love, so that there will be salvation, and so that he is our peace and that God is a God of peace. And the more they storm, the more shall we call. And the more we call, the more wildly will they storm because where the Word of Christ is truly said, there the world feels that it is either a destructive madness or rather a destructive truth, which is a matter then of life and death. Where truly peace has been spoken, there the war must doubly rage, since it perceives that it is to be finished off. Christ wishes to be its death.

But the more passionately and the more faithfully will the church of Christ stand with its Lord and preach his Word of peace, even if it goes through abuse and persecution. It knows that its Lord had to go to the cross. But now it understands the promise that Jesus is for it. The war will not be the end. But it [the war] must be, so that the end comes. "The gospel of the kingdom will be preached in the whole world as a witness to all people, and then the end will come." Here our vision broadens, and will be lifted up to the Lord, who rules all, whom even the demons and devils must serve. War, sickness, and hunger must come so that the gospel of the kingdom of peace, of love and salvation may be said and heard so much more clearly and deeply. The evil powers must serve the gospel; the powers of enmity and of the nations' opposition must also serve, to bring the gospel to all nations, so that it may be heard by all; all these must serve the kingdom which shall belong to all humankind. War serves peace, hate serves love, the devil serves God, the cross serves life. And then, when that becomes manifest, then the end will come; then the Lord of the church will lay his hand of blessing and protection on them, as on his faithful servant.

The Day of National Mourning in the church! What does it mean? It means the raising up of the one great hope, from which we all live, the sermon concerning the kingdom of God. It means that we see the past, about which we think today, with all its terrors and in all its godlessness and we are still not to be afraid, but we hear the sermon on peace. It means that all this must come about, so that the end comes, so that God remains the Lord. It means that we rightly mourn over the dead of the world war, when we stand in the same faithfulness in which they stood out there, so we now deliver the message of peace and preach so much louder, the kingdom on which account death had to be. It means to look beyond the borders of our people, over the whole earth, and pray that the gospel of the kingdom that sets an end to all war, will come to all peoples, and that then the end comes and Christ draws near.

Day of National Mourning in the Church! That means that God is near us in the cross; it means looking at Christ upon the cross, who conquered through the cross. Day of National Mourning in the Church: that means knowing that Christ alone conquers. Amen. [*GS* IV, pp. 38–40]

25

The Gospel of the New Order

(First Sunday after Trinity Sunday, Berlin)

May 29, 1932

TEXT: Luke 16:19–31

Blessed are you outcasts and despised, you casualties of society, you men and women without work, you broken and ruined ones, you lonely and forsaken, you who endure violence and unjustly suffer, you who suffer in body and soul. Blessed are you since God's joy will come over you and will remain eternally with you. That is the gospel of the dawn* of the new world, the new order, that is the world of God and the order of God. The deaf hear, the blind see, the lame walk, and the gospel is preached to the poor. . . . So seriously does he take suffering that he must immediately destroy it. The power of the demons must be broken wherever Christ is—for that reason he healed and for that reason he said to his disciples: "If you have faith, you will do greater works than I." The kingdom of God is still in the dawning.† The deeds of healing are like summer lightnings, flashes out of the new world—but now the glad tidings [were] so much more powerful. Blessed are you who weep since you shall laugh, you who hunger since you will be satisfied. No cynical consolation, but it is the one great hope, the new world, the joyous tidings, the merciful God! [GS, IV, pp. 52–53]

---

*Anbrechen: dawn, the breaking in.

†Anbruch (m.): beginning, opening, the breaking in.

26

On Freedom

(Religious service marking the end of the semester,
Ninth Sunday after Trinity Sunday, Berlin)

July 24, 1932

TEXT: "The truth shall set you free." (John 8:32)

That is perhaps the most revolutionary word of the New Testament. Therefore, it is not addressed to the masses. It is, however, grasped by the few genuine revolutionaries. It is an exclusive word. . . .

"The truth shall set you free." Not our deed, not our courage or strength, not our people, not our truth, but God's truth alone. Why? Because to be *free* does not mean to be *great* in the world, to be free *against* our brethren, to be free *against* God; but it means to be free from ourselves, from our untruth, in which it seems as if I alone were there, as if I were the center of the world; to be free from the hatred with which I destroy God's creation; to be free from myself in order to be free for others. God's truth alone allows me to see others. It directs my attention, bent in on myself, to what is beyond and shows me the other person. And, as it does this, I experience the love and the grace of God. It destroys our untruth and creates truth. It destroys hatred and creates love. God's truth is God's love, and God's love frees us from ourselves to be free for others. To be free means nothing else than to be in this love, and to be in this love means nothing else than to be in God's truth.

The person who loves, because he is freed through the truth of God, is the most revolutionary person on earth. He is the one who upsets all values; he is the explosive in human society. Such a one is the most dangerous person. For he has recognized that people are untruthful in the extreme, and he is ready at any time, and just for the sake of love, to permit the light of truth to fall on them. This disturbance of peace, which comes to the world through these people, provokes the world's hatred. Therefore, the knight of truth and love is not the hero whom people worship and honor, who is free of enemies, but the one whom they cast out, whom they want to get rid of, whom they declare an outlaw, whom they kill. The way, which God's truth in the world has gone, leads to the cross.

From this we know that all truth which exists in the presence of God must lead to the cross. The community that follows Christ must go with him to the cross. Because of their truth and freedom they will be hated by the world. Nor can a people find truth and freedom if they do not place themselves in the judgment of God's truth. Likewise, a people will remain in untruth and slavery until such time as they receive and continue to receive their truth and their freedom from God alone, until they know that truth and freedom lead to love; indeed, until they know that the way of love leads to the cross. If a people are really able to acknowledge this today, then they will be the only people who have the right to call themselves a free people, the only people that are not slaves to themselves, but who are the free servants of God's truth. [GS, IV, pp. 79, 86–87]

SERMONS, 1933–1934
BERLIN, LONDON, FANØ

During 1933, the year that Adolf Hitler came to power in Germany, Bonhoeffer preached on several occasions, including a sermon in the prestigious Kaiser Wilhelm Memorial Church in Berlin. Bonhoeffer was only twenty-seven years old at this time, and his sermons were remarkable for their clarity, order, and depth. Many of them contained less than subtle reminders of the dangers posed to Christian faith by the rise of Adolf Hitler and the church struggle.

In his sermon, "A Church of the World or a Church of the Word?" he sees, for example, the biblical characters Moses and Aaron as representing a perennial struggle in the church of Christ. The "worldly church" is impatient to see results; hence it fashions false gods in its own image. The church of the Word, on the contrary, hears the lofty challenge of Moses and rejects the glittering temptation of idolatry. For Bonhoeffer, at the time, the people of Germany seemed to be approaching the moment of decision between Germanism or genuine Christianity. The crisis was both a threat and an opportunity for faith.

The timeliness of his Church Election sermon on July 23, 1933 in Berlin is, therefore, all the more striking for its urging the people to make a courageous choice on behalf of their faith threatened by cleverly crafted, political idols. In the selection included here, Bonhoeffer sounds like a bellringer as he calls Christians' attention to the ominous character of the times. Along with a pointed reminder of how critical this hour was in the nation's history, Bonhoeffer entreats the church to be the true church of Christ and to confess Christ alone as Lord.

In October 1933, Bonhoeffer arrived in London to assume the pastoral responsibiliities of two of the six German congregations in the sprawling city Sydenham, in the Forest Hills section of South London and St. Paul's in Petticoat Lane in the East End. Week by week he prepared sermons for the worshippers of the two congregations, which consisted of about thirty to forty people in Sydenham and about fifty people in St. Paul. Many of these sermons have survived and remain models of exceptional preaching for the time. It was clear that Bonhoeffer conceived of the sermon as a grappling with the text for the day, certainly not in a sealed vacuum, but in relationship to the context of time and place. For Bonhoeffer, it was a privileged way for Christ to live on as community, in this case a community separated from native country and anxious about the impact of the changes on their faith and their future.

In his preaching on judgment and repentance, for instance, Bonhoeffer stands like a sentinel, pointing the church to Jesus Christ as the compassionate judge of the way Christians should follow the truth of Christ's gospel. He offers the assurance and encouragement of the gospel, especially as it confronts the specter of death, reminding his hearers that they have been called "children of the resurrection." Advent, he says, comes in the church year like a rescuer who grants freedom to those in captivity, like a doctor who delivers from pain, like a father who hears the cries of his children. These are sermons which offer hope in the midst of the ever growing chaos of a world become more and more immersed in national distrust and enmity.

During the period of his London pastorate, Bonhoeffer participated in the ecumenical conference at Fanø, Denmark, in August 1934. While there, he preached to a very formidable congregation: Christian leaders drawn from over fifteen nations and representing an extremely diverse variety of individual churches. As one can see in the text included here, his sermon, "The Church and the People of the World," forcefully challenges all churches to the pursuit of peace in a world seemingly preparing for another round of violence. With a profound capacity for the provocative, even prophetic, word and the personal courage that refuses to be deterred from his objective, Bonhoeffer pleads his case. "Peace must be dared. It is the great venture. . . . The hour is late. The world is choked with weapons, and dreadful is the distrust which looks out of every human being's eyes. . . ."

Back again in his London pulpits, Bonhoeffer preached, among other sermons, a series on *agape* love, primarily related to 1 Corinthians 13. As can be seen in the selections included here, these are not sentimental homilies that have no concrete application. Rather, they are sobering descriptions of what genuine *agape* can mean, not only for the individual person and for the church, but also for all of humanity, the world beyond Christianity. These sermons, along with the other selections of this section, bring out the alertness of Bonhoeffer both to the needs of his parishioners and to the manner in which God's word must be heard in its proper historical context.

27

A Church of the World or a Church of the Word?

(Kaiser Wilhelm Memorial Church, Berlin)

May 28, 1933

TEXT: Exod. 32:1–7, 32:15, 32:19ff., 32:30–34

Priest against prophet, worldly church against the church of faith, the church of Aaron against the church of Moses—this is the eternal conflict in the church of Christ. And it is this conflict and its resolution that we are to consider today.

Moses and Aaron, the two brothers, of the same tribe, of the same blood, sharing the same history, going for part of the way side by side—then wrenched apart. Moses, the first prophet, Aaron, the first priest; Moses, called of God, chosen without regard of his person, the man who was slow of tongue, the servant of God, living solely to hear the Word of his Lord; Aaron, the man with the purple robe and the holy diadem, the consecrated and sanctified priest, who must maintain his service of God for the people. And now, in our story: Moses, called alone into the presence of the living God, high above on the mount of fear, between life and death in the thunder and lightning, to receive the law of the covenant of God with his people—and there down below in the valley, the people of Israel with their priest in his purple robe, sacrificing, far from God.

Why must Moses and Aaron be in conflict? Why cannot they stand side by side in the same service? Why must the church of Moses and the church of Aaron, the church of the Word and the worldly church break apart time and again? The answer to this question is given in our text.

Moses is called up the mountain by God for his people. It is God's will to speak with him up there. The children of Israel know that. They know that up there Moses is standing, fighting, praying, suffering for them. He wears no purple robe, he is no priest; he is nothing at all, nothing but the servant who waits on the Word of his Lord, gets sick, tormented when he is not allowed to hear this word. He is nothing— nothing but the prophet of his God. But the church of Aaron, the church of the world cannot wait. It is impatient. Where has Moses gone? Why does he not come back? Perhaps we will not see him again. Where is he, with his God? "As for this Moses . . . we do not know what has become of him." It may be that he no longer exists, that he is dead.

These are the questions which the church of Aaron, at all times puts to the church of the Word. "We cannot see it. Where are its works? What is its contribution? No doubt at all, it is dead." Do we not then understand that perhaps God himself is keeping Moses up on the mountain, that he is not yet letting him go because he still has some- thing to say to him? Do we not understand that perhaps even today he is not yet letting the church of Moses go, the church whose wish is to hear only the Word of God, because he has still something to say in the quietness? Even God needs time with his prophet and with his church. Is it for us to be impatient? Certainly, the church of the Word is once again on Sinai, and in fear and trembling, amidst the thunder and light- ning, withstands the Word of God, waits, believes, prays, fights. . . . For whom? For the church of Aaron, for the church down there in the valley, for the worldly church. The unwillingness of the worldly church to wait, its impatience, is the first stage of its clash with the church of the Word. So it has always been, and so it will continue to be.

"As for this Moses . . . we do not know what has become of him. Arise, Aaron, make us gods, who shall go before us." That is the second stage, which follows immediately upon the first. The worldly church, the church of the priests, wants to see something. Now it wants to wait no longer. It wants to go to work by itself, act by itself, do by itself what God and the prophet are not doing. What is the use of the priest, what is the use of the church, if they are only left to wait? No, our church ought to have something. We want to see something in our church. We do not want to wait. You priests, you are sanctified, you are consecrated. You owe us something. Arise, Aaron the priest, do your duty, attend to the divine service. God has left us, but we need gods. We need religions. If you cannot prevail with the Living God, make us gods yourself!

The concern expressed here is really not as bad as all that. It is even a pious concern. People are not saying, "Away with the gods!" but "We need gods, religions, make us some!" The priest is not driven out, he is told, "Do your duty!" "Preserve religion for the people, give them wor- ship services." They really want to remain a church with gods and priests and religion, but a church of Aaron—without God. And Aaron yields. He looks to his office, to his consecration; he looks to the people. He understands their impatience, their thirst for action, and their pious raging only too well—and he yields. Come, you who have been aban- doned by your God and by your prophet, make yourselves a god who will not leave you again, more splendid, more glorious than the God who has left us. Bring precious jewelry, gold, necklaces, and bracelets, bring it as an offering. And they all come, without exception. They bring their precious offering to their own image of their god. They tear the jewelry from their bodies and throw it into the glowing mass from which Aaron now shapes the glittering, monstrous, golden calf. We hear it said that the people are not so ready for sacrifice. But those who talk like this do not know the world. The human race is ready for any sacrifice in which it may celebrate itself and worship its own work. The worldly church, the church of Aaron, is ready for any sacrifice if it is to be allowed to make its own God. The human race and the worldly church fall on their knees joyfully, and with smiles, before the god whom we make as it pleases us. But *God* finds little readiness for sacrifice. No, the church of Aaron does not stint, it is not mean, it is lavish with its god. Everything that is precious and valuable and holy to it is cast into the glowing fire of the ideal. Everyone must contribute to the glorification of the god, so each one, according to his inclinations and his capabilities, throws his own ideals into the melting pot—and then the orgy begins. The worldly church celebrates its triumph, the priest has shown his power, and now he himself stands in the middle in his purple robe and his holy diadem and worships the creation of his own hand. And round him the people prostrate themselves in ecstasy and look up at the god whom they have made in their own strength, at their own sacrifice. Who would want to stand aside from this pious joy, this unparalleled exuberance, this achievement of human will and ability? The worldly church now has its god, come, sacrifice to enjoy yourselves, play, eat, drink, dance, make money, be thrilled by the spectacle! You have a god again. These are your gods, O Israel, who brought you up out of the land of Egypt! Come, behold, worship!

But there are rumblings on Sinai. For God shows Moses his faithless people. And Moses trembles for his people and comes hastily down from the mountain. He already hears the merrymaking and the shouts of the dance and the tumult and the orgy. He already sees his brother in purple robe and holy diadem, and in the midst the golden god of the worldly church, the worldly god, the god of the priests, the god who is no God. There he stands among them, the unexpected prophet, high in his hands he swings the tables of the law, and they all must see it, the writing engraved by the hand of God, "I am the Lord your God, you shall have no other gods before me!" Dumb terror, dismay, seizes the worldly church at the sight. The party is over. The living God has come amongst them, he rages against them. What will happen? There—a sight unequaled, a fearful moment—and the tables of the law lie shattered on the idol, and the idol itself is broken in pieces and consumed. That is the end of the worldly church. God has appointed it. God has remained Lord. Lord, have mercy . . . !

Church of the priests against church of the Word, church of Aaron against church of Moses—this historical clash at the foot of Sinai, the end of the worldly church and the appearance of the Word of God, repeats itself in our church, day by day, Sunday by Sunday. Time and again we come together for worship as a worldly church, as a church which will not wait, which will not live from the invisible; as a church which makes its own gods; as a church which wants to have the sort of god which pleases it and will not ask how it pleases God; as a church which wants to do by itself what God will not do; as a church which is ready for any sacrifice in the cause of idolatry, in the cause of the divinization of human thoughts and values; as a church which appropriates to itself divine authority in the priesthood. And we should go away again as a church whose idol lies shattered and destroyed on the ground, as a church which must hear afresh, "I am the Lord your God . . . ," as a church which is humbled as it is faced with this Word, as the church of Moses, the church of the Word. The impatient church becomes the quietly waiting church, the church anxious to see sights becomes the church of sober faith, the church which makes its own gods becomes the church which worships the One God. Will this church too find such devotion, such sacrifice?

But the rupture is not the end. Once again Moses climbs the mountain, this time to pray for his people. He offers up himself, "Reject me with my people, for we are still one. Lord, I love my brother." But God's answer remains dark, fearful, threatening. Moses could not make expiation. Who makes expiation here? It is none other than he who is priest and prophet in one, the man with the purple robe and the crown of thorns, the crucified Son of the Father, who stands before God to make intercession for us. Here, in his cross, there is an end of all idolatry. Here, the whole human race, the whole church, is judged and pardoned. Here God is wholly the God who will have no other god before him, but now also wholly God in that he forgives without limit. As the church which is always at the same time the church of Moses and the church of Aaron, we point to this cross and say, "This is your God, O Israel, who brought you out of slavery and will lead you evermore. Come, believe, worship!" Amen. [NRS, pp. 243–48]

28

Peter and the Church Struggle

(Church election sermon, Berlin)

July 23, 1933

TEXT: Matt. 16:13–18

If it were left to us, we would rather avoid the decisions which are now forced upon us; if it were left to us, we would rather not allow ourselves to be caught up in this church struggle; if it were left to us, we would rather not have to insist upon the rightness of our cause and we would so willingly avoid the terrible danger of exalting ourselves over others; if it were left to us, we would retire today rather than tomorrow into private life and leave all the struggle and the pride to others. And yet— thank God—it has not been left to us. Instead, in God's wisdom, everything is going exactly as we would rather not have it go. We are called upon to make a decision from which we cannot escape. We must be content, wherever we are, to face the accusation of being self-righteous, to be suspected of acting and speaking as though we were proud and superior to others. Nothing shall be made easy for us. We are confronted by a decision, and a difference of opinion. For this reason if we are honest with ourselves, we will not try to disguise the true meaning of the church election today. In the midst of the creakings and groanings of a crumbling and tottering church structure, which has been shaken to its very foundations, we hear in this text the promise of the eternal church, against which the gates of hell shall not prevail; of the church founded on a rock, Christ has built and which he continues to build throughout all time. Where is this church? Where do we find it? Where do we hear its voice? Come all you who ask in seriousness, all you who are abandoned and left alone, we will go back to the Holy Scriptures, we will go and look for the church together. Who hath ears to hear, let him hear.

Jesus went out into a deserted place with his disciples, close to the edge of the pagan lands, and there he was alone with them. This is the place where for the first time he promises them the legacy of his church. Not in the midst of the people, not at the visible peak of his popularity; but in a distant and unfrequented spot, far from the orthodox scribes and pharisees, far from the crowds who on Palm Sunday would cry out "Hosanna" and on Good Friday, "Crucify him," he speaks to his disciples of the mystery and the future of his church. He obviously believed that this church could not be built in the first place on the scribes, the priests, or the masses; but that only this tiny group of disciples, who followed him, was called to this work. And clearly he did not think that Jerusalem, the city of the Temple and the center of the life of the people, was the right place for this, but he goes out into the wilderness, where he could not hope that his preaching would achieve any eternal, visible effectiveness. And last of all he did not consider that any of the great feast days would have been suitable time to speak of his church, but rather he promises this church in the face of death, immediately before he tells of his coming passion for the first time. The church of the tiny flock, the church out in the wilderness, the church in the face of death—something like this must be meant.

Jesus himself puts the decisive question, for which the disciples had long been waiting: "Who do people say that the Son of man is?" Answer: "Some say John the Baptist, others say Elijah, and others Jeremiah or one of the prophets." Opinions, nothing but opinions; one could extend this list of opinions as much as one wanted . . . some say you are a great man, some say you are an idealist, some say you are a religious genius, some say you are a great champion and hero, who will lead us to victory and greatness. Opinions, more or less serious opinions—but Jesus does not want to build his church on opinions. And so he addresses himself directly to his disciples: "But who do you say that I am?" In this inevitable confrontation with Christ there can be no "perhaps" or "some say," no opinions but only silence or the answer which Peter gives now: "You are the Christ, the Son of the living God." Here in the midst of human opinions and views, something quite new suddenly becomes visible. Here God's name is named, here the eternal is pronounced, here the mystery is recognized. Here is no longer human opinion, but precisely the opposite, here is divine revelation and confession of faith. "Blessed are you, Simon Bar-Jona! For flesh and blood has not revealed this to you, but my Father who is in heaven. And I tell you, you are Peter, and on this rock I will build my church."

What is the difference between Peter and the others? Is he of such heroic nature that he towers over the others? He is not. Is he endowed with such unheard-of strength of character? He is not. Is he gifted with unshakable loyalty? He is not. Peter is nothing, nothing but a person confessing his faith, a person who has been confronted by Christ and who has recognized Christ, and who now confesses his faith in him, and this confessing Peter is called the rock on which Christ will build his church.

Peter's church—that means the church of rock, the church of the confession of Christ. Peter's church, that does not mean a church of opinions and views, but the church of the revelation; not a church in which what "people say" is talked about but the church in which Peter's confession is made anew and passed on; the church which has no other purpose in song, prayer, preaching, and action than to pass on its confession of faith; the church which is always founded on rock as long as it remains within these limits, but which turns into a house built on sand, which is blown away by the wind, as soon as it is foolhardy enough to think that it may depart from or even for a moment neglect this purpose.

But Peter's church—this is not something which one can say with untroubled pride. Peter, the confessing, believing disciple, Peter denied his Lord on the same night as Judas betrayed him; in that night he stood at the fire and felt ashamed when Jesus stood before the high priest; he is the man of little faith, the timid man who sinks into the sea; Peter is the disciple whom Jesus threatened: "Get thee behind me Satan"; it is he who later was again and again overcome by weakness, who again and again denied and fell, a weak, vacillating man, given over to the whim of the moment. Peter's church, that is the church which shares these weaknesses, the church which itself again and again denies and falls, the unfaithful, fainthearted, timid church which again neglects its charge and looks to the world and its opinions. Peter's church, that is the church of all those who are ashamed of their Lord when they should stand firm confessing him.

But Peter is also the man of whom we read: "He went out and wept bitterly." Of Judas, who also denied the Lord, we read: "He went and hanged himself." That is the difference. Peter went out and wept bitterly. Peter's church is not only the church which confesses its faith, nor only the church which denies its Lord; it is the church which can still weep. "By the waters of Babylon, there we sat down and wept, when we remembered Zion" (Ps. 137:1). This is the church; for what does this weeping mean other than that one has found the way back, than that one is on the way home, than that one has become the prodigal son who falls to his knees weeping before his father? Peter's church is the church with that godly sadness which leads to joy.

It does indeed seem very uncertain ground to build on, doesn't it? And yet it is bedrock, for this Peter, this trembling reed, is called by God, caught by God, held by God. "You are Peter," we all are Peter; not the Pope, as the Roman Catholics would have it; not this person or that, but all of us, who simply live from our confession of faith in Christ, as the timid, faithless, fainthearted, and yet who live as people sustained by God.

But it is not we who build. He builds the church. No human being builds the church but Christ alone. Whoever intends to build the church is surely well on the way to destroying it; for he will build a temple to idols without wishing or knowing it. We must confess—he builds. We must proclaim—he builds. We must pray to him—that he may build. We do not know his plan. We cannot see whether he is building or pulling down. It may be that the times which by human standards are times of collapse are for him the great times of construction. It may be that from a human point of view great times for the church are actually times of demolition. It is a great comfort which Christ gives to his church: you confess, preach, bear witness to me, and I alone will build where it pleases me. Do not meddle in what is my province. Do what is given to you to do well and you have done enough. But do it well. Pay no heed to views and opinions, don't ask for judgments, don't always be calculating what will happen, don't always be on the lookout for another refuge! Let the church remain the church! But church confess, confess, confess! Christ alone is your Lord, from his grace alone can you live as you are. Christ builds.

And the gates of hell shall not prevail against thee. Death, the greatest heir of everything that has existence, here meets its end. Close by the precipice of the valley of death, the church is founded, the church which confesses Christ as its life. The church possesses eternal life just where death seeks to take hold of her; and he seeks to take hold of her precisely because she possesses life. The Confessing Church is the eternal church because Christ protects her. Her eternity is not visible in this world. She is unhindered by the world. The waves pass right over her and sometimes she seems to be completely covered and lost. But the victory is hers, because Christ her Lord is by her side and he has overcome the world of death. Do not ask whether you can see the victory; believe in the victory and it is yours.

In huge capital letters our text is etched into the dome of the great church of St. Peter's, the papal church in Rome. Proudly this church points to its eternity, to its visible victory over the world, across the centuries. Such splendor, which even our Lord did not desire or bear, is denied to us. And yet a splendor which is immeasurably greater than this splendor in the world, is assured to us. Whether the band of believers is great or small, low or high, weak or strong, if it confesses Christ the victory is assured to them in eternity. Fear not, little flock, for it is my Father's pleasure to give you the kingdom. Where two or three are gathered together in my name, there am I in the midst of them. The city of God is built on a sure foundation. Amen. [*NRS*, pp. 212–17]

29

On Repentance

(Repentance Sunday, Forest Hill, London)

November 19, 1933

TEXT: "For we must all appear before the judgment seat of Christ so that each one may receive good or evil, according to what he has done in the body." (2 Cor. 5:10)

The Day of Repentance is the day in which we are reminded through a word of the Bible, truly an inconspicuous instrument of God, that the end will bring a complete uncovering, a complete exposure of our whole life. "We must all appear before the judgment seat of Christ."

This goes against a human being's inner nature. We have something to hide. We have secrets, worries, thoughts, hopes, desires, passions which no one else gets to know. We are sensitive when people get near such domains with their questions. And now, against all rules of tact the Bible speaks of the truth that in the end we will appear before Christ with everything we are and were; and not only before Christ, but also before the people who will stand next to us. And we all know, that we could justify ourselves before any human court, but not before this one. Lord, who can justify himself?

Christ will judge. His Spirit will separate those of different opinion. He who was poor and weak among us, will in the end pass judgment on all the world. There is only one question which is important: What do you think about this spirit, what do you think about this man Jesus Christ? It is possible to take different positions on every other Spirit, on every other person. The ultimate is not subject to such positions. In the face of Christ, there is only a straight "Yes" or a straight "No" because he is the spirit, by which every human spirit must be judged. No one can escape and no one can bypass him—even if he thinks he can, if he frivolously and carelessly thinks he can stand on his own and be his own judge. No one is his own judge. Christ is the judge of humankind. His judgment is eternal. He who passes him by without having clearly said his "Yes" or "No," will have to stand opposite him and look him in the face in the hour of death where his life is weighed in eternity. And his question will be: "Have you lived a life of love toward God and humans, or have you lived for yourself?" Here there is no more subterfuge, no excuses, no beating around the bush, here one's whole life lies open before the light of Christ. "That we may receive either good or evil according to what we have done in the body."

It is a fearful time to think that the book of our life will be opened; that what we have said and done against God's command will be brought before us that we face Christ and cannot defend ourselves. Lord, who will endure?

But the Bible does not really want to frighten us. God does not want people to be afraid. Not even at the last judgment. But he lets the person know so that he may perceive what life is. He lets it be known today so that he may lead a life in openness and in the light of the last judgment. He lets us know—only so that we find the path to Jesus Christ, so that we may turn from our evil way and meet him. God does not want to frighten people; he sends us the word about judgment so that we may all the more passionately, all the more eagerly, seize the promise of grace, so that we recognize that we do not stand before God in our own strength, lest we should perish before him; that in spite of everything he does not desire our death, but rather our life.

Christ judges. It is truly serious. But it also means: the Compassionate One judges, he who lived among tax collectors and sinners, who was tempted even as we are, who carried and endured in his own body our sufferings, our fears, our desires, who knows us and calls us by name. Christ judges; that means, grace is the judge, forgiveness, and love. Whoever clings to these is already acquitted. Of course whoever refers to his own work Christ will judge and condemn according to these works. But we should have joy on that day; we should not tremble and lose heart, but gladly entrust ourselves into his hand. Luther spoke of blessed judgment day. Let us leave this Day of Repentance worship service not with despondent hearts, but with joyous and believing hearts. Come, judgment day—joyfully we wait for you, since we shall see the merciful Lord and take his hand and he will love us.

Finally, what is "good and evil" about which Christ asks us? The good is nothing other than that we ask for his grace and take hold of it. The evil is nothing other than fear and wanting to stand before God on one's own, wanting to be self-righteous. Repentance means a turning from one's own work to the mercy of God. The whole Bible calls to us and cheers us: Turn back, turn back! Return—where to? To the everlasting grace of God, who does not leave us, his creatures, beyond all measure. He will be merciful—so come, judgment day! Lord Jesus, make us ready. We rejoice. Amen. [GS, IV, pp. 154–59]

30

Confident Hope

("Death Sunday," London)

November 26, 1933

TEXT: "But they are in peace." (Wisd. of Sol. 3:3)

Two questions have brought us to church today. They are inexhaustible questions. Now they demand an answer in the church. They are: Where are our dead? Where will we be after our own death? And the church claims it has the answer to this impossible question of humankind. Indeed, the church exists only because it knows the answer to this ultimate question. If it did not know how to speak here quite humbly, but also quite categorically, it would be nothing but an association of the hopeless who attract attention and become a burden on one another with their trials and tribulations. But that is precisely what the church of Christ is not! I am speaking here not of our suffering, but of our salvation; not of skepticism, but of confident hope. Skepticism is uninteresting. What all one does not believe is uninteresting. Rather, what this one and that one believes and hopes is exciting. The church is the place of unshakable hope.

Where are our dead? Today we see before us our loved ones—in that final image impressed on our minds. We feel how terribly vain and empty our own life seemed to us in such times, how our eyes were fixed on this enigmatically mute person who could only fall silent about the secret he had just seen. He is on the path from which no one returns. The solemnity of knowledge no living person receives lies over him. He is a man of earth as never before, one who will soon sleep in the earth— and he is as distant from this earth as never before, marked by another world. The mother calls her child, the child his mother. The husband calls his wife, the friend calls his friend. The brother calls his brother. Love cries for what is lost: Where are you, O dead? You have departed from us in silence, so speak! Why are you so far away?

But they do not speak. If people think they are able to invoke the spirits of the deceased, there may well be all kinds of things between heaven and earth which we cannot know or comprehend—but one thing is certain. It is not our dead who are appearing here; they have been taken from us. They are in God's hands. We cannot torment them with tears, requests, and incantations. They do not speak. They remain silent.

Who then answers this questioning love? Even the church is not able to make the dead talk. Even it is not able to conjure up spirits. But what does it say to the mother who flees to it and asks it about her child? What does it say to the child about its mother? It doesn't point to the dead; it doesn't say this or that about them. It doesn't point to the world of the occult or to the world of the dead; rather it points to God. Occult worlds are still human worlds, worlds accessible through all kinds of conjuring tricks. God's world is beyond all human worlds. No one else can talk about it except God himself and the one whom he has sent, Christ. In *this* world we must seek our dead. Whoever comes to the church with the burning question "Where are my dead?" is first of all pointed to God himself. There is no knowledge about the dead without faith in God. God is Lord of the dead, and he has their destiny in his hands. Whoever knows about him, knows about his dead.

However, that means there must not be any selfish questioning about the dead, for we are not the masters of the dead. The person who asks about the dead and really wants to have an answer, who isn't content with just slight comfort, must venture out on the path that leads to God and ask him—he will answer because that is his will. He shows himself to the person who longs for his answer and his truth and gives him his secret.

And now the God of peace and eternal life gives it to his church today. It is meant for those who believe him: He promises it to his people and gives them his utmost assurance: they are with me, they are in peace. God's world is peace, final peace after the final battle; God's peace means rest for those whom life has made tired; it means security for those who wandered through this life unsheltered and unguarded; a home for the homeless. It means quietness for the battle weary, relief for the tormented, comfort for the distressed and those who weep. God's peace is like a mother tenderly stroking her crying child's forehead. I want to comfort you just as a mother comforts her child. Your dead are comforted with God's comfort. He has wiped away their tears. He has put an end to the ceaseless hustle and bustle of this life. They are in peace.

The saying "But he is in peace" rises over the deathbeds on which a strong, restless life struggles through death with great fear.

Christ appears and speaks "But he is in peace" over the sinner's final hour of need when death holds up the horrors of damnation before his eyes and he despairs of them, becoming disheartened in great remorse.

The angels sing "But he is in peace" over the caskets of children and old people, over the caskets of the pious who in their final hours hoped only for Christ in simple faith.

Where we who are left behind see nothing but distress and fear and agony and self-reproach and remorse, where we see nothing but hopelessness and nothingness, there God says, "But they are in peace."

It is God's "but" that goes against our thinking and seeking. It is God's "but" that does not let the dead die, that raises them and leads them to himself. It is God's "but" that makes death into the sleep which allows us to wake up in a new world. It is God's "but" that takes the dead to paradise. "Truly, I say to you, today you will be with me in paradise." That is what Christ says to the criminal who hangs on the cross next to him and repents. But they are in peace. That means it is not something obvious, but something completely new and final that happens only on God's initiative. It is not our peace, but God's peace.

But once again: There is no room here for selfish questioning. Rather knowledge and hope come when we look to God and put everything in his hands. We believe him because he says, "I am the resurrection and the life; I live and so shall you."

Now we cannot even hear about this world of God which is not our world without an immeasurable longing, an indescribable homesickness for the world creeping over us, just as anticipation creeps over the children before Christmas morning when there will be abundant joy and blessed peace. The person who is himself not homesick and waiting from that time on, joyously waiting for the redemption of the body, has never really believed in God and his kingdom. Such a person has not yet heard anything about the realm of resurrection.

Whether we are young or old makes no difference here. What are twenty or thirty years in God's sight? And who knows how close to the goal he already is? Both young and old should consider that life only begins when it ends here. All the years of this life are only the preliminaries before the curtain is closed. Why are we afraid to think of death? Why are we so frightened? Death is terrible for the person who is afraid. Death is not wild and frightful—if we are quiet and keep God's word. Death is not bitter if we are not embittered. Death is mercy, God's greatest mercy which he gives to those who believe him. Death is gentle, death is sweet, death is peaceful, death lures us with heavenly force if only we know that it is the gateway to home, to the tent of joy, to the eternal realm of peace. Perhaps we say: "I am not afraid of death. I am afraid of dying." But who knows that dying is something terrible? Who knows whether our human anxieties and problems are not just the fear and trembling that comes before the most glorious, the most heavenly, the most blessed event of the world? Is it not like the kicking of a newborn child who sees the light of the world? What are all the curious things we experience at deathbeds but pointers to that final event? What does it mean when a person who struggled, wrestled, and worried for a long time opens his eyes at the last moment, acts as if he has seen something glorious and shouts, "God, is that beautiful!" What does that mean?

Yes, death is frightful; it is the grim reaper with the scythe who demands that one after another dance with him if they do not believe, if they do not belong to the righteous of whom our word is true: "But they are in peace."

Death is hell and night and coldness if our faith does not transform it. That we can transform death is truly miraculous. When our faith in God touches it, the grim reaper who frightens us turns into a friend and messenger of God; then death turns into Christ himself. Yes, those are deeply hidden things. But we are permitted to know them.

Our life hangs on these things. The believers will have peace, and death will not frighten them. It can no longer touch them because they are in God's hands. No pain or anguish can touch them.

Many have tried to make death a friend, yet he became unfaithful to them in the final hour; he became their enemy. There is only one way to have death as a friend, and it is called faith. Then death becomes our best friend. Then one day God's word will be heard over our deathbed. "They are in peace," and our eyes will fill with tears of joy when they see the kingdom and this peace.

Perhaps it seems childish to you that we talk like this. But in the face of such things, do we have any other choice but to talk childishly? In the face of such things are we anything other than children, unsuspecting children? And do we really want to be anything else when we come into his kingdom and are allowed to see that joyous day? Look at children when they are happy. Say to yourself whether you want to be something better. Do we have to feel ashamed of being children? "I want to comfort you as a mother comforts her child."

Christ has called us children of the resurrection. Children who are homesick, that's what we are when things are right with us.

> Thus I do want to carry on my life through this world,
> But I don't intend to stay in this dark tent.
> I journey through streets that lead me home.
> Since my father will comfort me beyond all measure

> [From Paul Gerhardt, "I Am a Guest on Earth"]

Amen. [*GS*, IV, pp. 160–65]

31

Come, O Rescuer

(First Sunday in Advent, London)

December 3, 1933

TEXT: "Now when these things begin to take place, look up and raise your heads, because your redemption is drawing near." (Luke 21:28)

You know what a mine disaster is. In recent weeks we have had to read about one in the newspapers.

The moment even the most courageous miner has dreaded his whole life long is here. It is no use running into the walls, the silence all around him remains. He knows people are crowding together on the surface; but the way out for him is blocked. He knows the people up there are working feverishly to reach the miners who are buried alive. Perhaps someone will be rescued, but here in the last shaft? An agonizing period of waiting and dying is all that remains.

But suddenly a noise that sounds like tapping and breaking in the rock can be heard. Unexpectedly, voices cry out, "Where are you, help is on the way!" Then the disheartened miner picks himself up, his heart leaps, he shouts, "Here I am, come on through and help me! I'll hold out until you come! Just come soon!" A final, desperate hammer blow to his ear, now the rescue is near, just one more step and he is free.

We have spoken of Advent itself. That is how it is with the coming of Christ: "Look up and raise your heads, because your redemption is drawing near."

To whom does one speak in this way? Think of the prisoners. For a long time they have borne the punishment of their captivity. One prisoner tried to escape again and again, but he was dragged back, and then it was even worse. And now all of a sudden a message rings through the prison: in a short while you shall be free, your chains will fall, your oppressors will be bound and you will be redeemed. Then the chorus of prisoners shouts out, "Yes, come, O rescuer!"

Think of the sick person in great pain who longs for the end of the affliction and now the day comes when the doctor tells the ailing one in a reassuring and clear voice, "Today you will be delivered."

Think of the person with the secret we spoke of on the Day of Repentance—the person who lives in unforgiven sin and loses the meaning of life as well as a cheerful nature. Think of those of us who strive to lead a Christian, obedient life and yet fail; think of the son who can no longer look his father straight in the eye or the husband who can no longer look his wife straight in the eye. Think of the disruption of these lives and the hopeless mess they are in. And then let us hear again, "Look up, raise your heads, because your redemption is drawing near." You shall be free! Your souls' anguish and anxiety will end, your redemption is near!

Just as the father says to his child, "Don't look at the ground, look at me, your father," we read here in the gospel: "Look up, raise your heads because your redemption is drawing near."

Who is addressed here? People who know they are enslaved and in chains. People who know that an oppressor has them under control and forces them to do compulsory labor. People like that miner who was buried alive, or like that prisoner; people who would like to be rescued.

This word is not addressed to all those who have become so accustomed to their condition that they no longer notice they are captives; people who have put up with their plight for all kinds of reasons and have become so apathetic that they are not provoked when someone calls out to them, "Your redemption is near." This Advent word is not meant for the well fed and satisfied, but for those who hunger and thirst. There is a knocking at their door, powerful and insistent. And like that miner buried alive in the mine, we hear every blow, every step closer the rescuer takes with extreme alertness. Can one even imagine that the miner ever thought of anything other than the approaching liberation from the moment he heard the first tapping against the rock?

And now the first Sunday in Advent tells us nothing else: "Your redemption is drawing near!" It is already knocking at the door, don't you hear it? It is breaking open its way through the rubble and hard rock of your life and heart. It isn't happening quickly, but it is coming. Christ is breaking open his way to you. He wants to again soften your heart which has become hard. In these weeks of Advent while we are waiting for Christmas, he calls to us that he is coming and that he will rescue us from the prison of our existence, from fear, guilt, and loneliness.

Do you want to be redeemed? That is the one great question Advent puts to us. Does even a vestige of longing burn in us? If not, what do we want from Advent, what do we want from Christmas? A little inner emotion?

However, if there is still something is us that is stirred up by this word, if there is something in us that believes this word, if we sense that a turning to Christ could happen again in our lives—why then aren't we simply obedient? Why then don't we listen to the word "your redemption is near," the word offered to us and shouted in our ears? Don't you hear it? Just wait a short while longer and then the tapping will grow louder and more unmistakable from hour to hour and from day to day! Then Christmas will come and we will be ready! Christ the Savior is here!

Perhaps you will say, "You've always said that in the church and nothing has ever come of it!" Why has nothing ever come of it? Because we didn't want anything to come of it, because we didn't want to hear and believe, because we said, "It may be that one miner or another is rescued, but the Savior will not get through to us—we who are buried so deep, so far away, so unaccustomed to church. We don't have any aptitude for religion. We would like to, but that doesn't speak to us."

But we are only making excuses with that kind of talk. If we really wanted to, if it were not an evasion, we would finally begin to pray that this Advent would make a stop in our hearts. Let us make no mistake about it. Redemption is drawing near. Only the question is: Will we let it come to us as well or will we resist it? Will we let ourselves be pulled into this movement coming down from heaven to earth or will we refuse to have anything to do with it? Either with us or without us, Christmas will come. It is up to each individual to decide what it will be.

That such an Advent event creates something other than a depressed and weak-kneed Christianity becomes clear from the two invitations that introduce our test: "Look up and raise your heads." Advent creates new men and women. Look up, you whose eyes are fixed on this earth, you who are captivated by the events and changes on the surface of this earth. Look up, you who turned away from heaven to this ground because you had become disillusioned. Look up, you whose eyes are laden with tears, you who mourn the loss of all that the earth has snatched away. Look up, you who cannot lift up your eyes because you are so laden with guilt. "Look up, your redemption is drawing near."

Something different than you see daily, something more important, something infinitely greater and more powerful is taking place. Become aware of it, be on guard, wait a short while longer, wait and something new will overtake you! God will come, Jesus will take possession of you and you will be redeemed people!

Lift up your heads, you army of the afflicted, the humbled, the discouraged, you defeated army with bowed heads. The battle is not lost, the victory is yours—take courage, be strong! There is no room here for shaking your heads and doubting, because Christ is coming.

Now we ask again: Do we hear the tapping and driving as the rescuer fights his way forward, do we hear how something in us wants to burst open and become free to move toward Christ? Do we sense that this is not only figurative speech, but that something is really taking place here, that human souls are being raised up, shaken, torn apart and healed; that heaven is bending toward the earth and the earth trembles, and the people lose heart in fear and joy?

Can the miner buried alive pay attention to anything but this hammering and knocking of the rescuers? Can and may something else still be more important to us than paying attention to this hammering and knocking of Jesus Christ in our lives? What else is at issue in all that is taking place but listening and standing up and taking notice? What else is at issue here but trembling and stretching out our arms toward him?

Something is at work that makes it possible for us not to close our hearts but to open up to him who wants to come in. In the middle of the winter Luther once cried out when he preached on our text in the Advent season, "Summer is near, the trees want to burst forth in blossom. It is springtime." They who have ears to hear, listen! Amen. [GS, IV, pp. 166–70]

32

The Church and the People of the World

(Ecumenical Conference, Fanø)

August 28, 1934

TEXT: "I will hear what God the Lord will speak: for he will speak peace unto his people, and to his saints." (Ps. 85:8)

Between the twin crags of nationalism and internationalism ecumenical Christendom calls upon her Lord and asks his guidance. Nationalism and internationalism have to do with political necessities and possibilities. The ecumenical church, however, does not concern itself with these things, but with the commandments of God, and regardless of consequences it transmits these commandments to the world.

Our task as theologians, accordingly, consists only in accepting this commandment as a binding one, not as a question open to discussion. Peace on earth is not a problem, but a commandment given at Christ's coming. There are two ways of reacting to this command of God: the unconditional, blind obedience of action, or the hypocritical question of the serpent: "Yea, hath God said ... ?" This question is the mortal enemy of obedience, and therefore the mortal enemy of all real peace. "Has God not said? Has God not understood human nature well enough to know that wars must occur in this world, like laws of nature? Must God not have meant that we should talk about peace, to be sure, but that it is not to be literally translated into action? Must God not really have said that we should work for peace, of course, but also make ready tanks and poison gas for security?" And then perhaps the most serious question: "Did God say you should not protect your own people? Did God say you should leave your own a prey to the enemy?"

No, God did not say all that. What he has said is that there shall be peace among people—that we shall obey him without further question, that is what he means. He or she who questions the commandment of God before obeying has already denied him.

There shall be peace because of the church of Christ, for the sake of whom the world exists. And this church of Christ lives at one and the same time in all peoples, yet beyond all boundaries, whether national, political, social, or racial. And the brothers who make up this church are bound together, through the commandment of the one Lord Christ, whose Word they hear, more inseparably than people are bound by all the ties of common history, of blood, of class, and of language. All these ties, which are part of our world, are valid ties, not indifferent; but in the presence of Christ they are not ultimate bonds. For the members of the ecumenical church, insofar as they hold to Christ, his word, his commandment of peace is more holy, more inviolable than the most revered words and works of the natural world. For they know that whoso is not able to hate father and mother for his sake is not worthy of him, and lies if he calls himself after Christ's name. These brothers in Christ obey his word; they do not doubt or question, but keep his commandment of peace. They are not ashamed, in defiance of the world, even to speak of eternal peace. They cannot take up arms against Christ himself—yet this is what they do if they take up arms against one another! Even in anguish and distress of conscience there is for them no escape from the commandment of Christ that there shall be peace.

How does peace come about? Through a system of political treaties? Through the investment of international capital in different countries? Through the big banks, through money? Or through universal peaceful rearmament in order to guarantee peace? Through none of these, for the single reason that in all of them peace is confused with safety. There is no way to peace along the way of safety. For peace must be dared. It is the great venture. It can never be safe. Peace is the opposite of security. To demand guarantees is to mistrust, and this mistrust in turn brings forth war. To look for guarantees is to want to protect oneself. Peace means to give oneself altogether to the law of God, wanting no security, but in faith and obedience laying the destiny of the nations in the hand of Almighty God, not trying to direct it for selfish purposes. Battles are won, not with weapons, but with God. They are won where the way leads to the cross. Which of us can say he or she knows what it might mean for the world if one nation should meet the aggressor, not with weapons in hand, but praying, defenseless, and for that very reason protected by "a bulwark never failing"?

Once again, how will peace come? Who will call us to peace so that the world will hear, will have to hear? so that all peoples may rejoice? The individual Christian cannot do it. When all around are silent, he can indeed raise his voice and bear witness, but the powers of this world stride over him without a word. The individual church, too, can witness and suffer—oh, if it only would!—but it also is suffocated by the power of hate. Only the one great Ecumenical Council of the holy church of

Christ over all the world can speak out so that the world, though it gnash its teeth, will have to hear, so that the peoples will rejoice because the church of Christ in the name of Christ has taken the weapons from the hands of their sons, forbidden war, proclaimed the peace of Christ against the raging world.

Why do we fear the fury of the world powers? Why don't we take the power from them and give it back to Christ? We can still do it today. The Ecumenical Council is in session; it can send out to all believers this radical call to peace. The nations are waiting for it in the East and in the West. Must we be put to shame by non-Christian people in the East? Shall we desert the individuals who are risking their lives for this message? The hour is late. The world is choked with weapons, and dreadful is the distrust which looks out of every human being's eyes. The trumpets of war may blow tomorrow. For what are we waiting? Do we want to become involved in this guilt as never before?

> What use to me are crown, land, folk and fame?
> They cannot cheer my breast.
> War's in the land, alas, and on my name
> I pray no guilt may rest.
>
> M. Claudius

We want to give the world a whole word, not a half word—a courageous word, a Christian word. We want to pray that this word may be given us today. Who knows if we shall see each other again another year? [*NRS*, pp. 289–92]

33

The Way that Leads to Renewal

(Sixth Sunday after Trinity Sunday, London)

July 8, 1934

TEXT: Luke 13:1–5

Perhaps you are startled by this text and think it is just too relevant today and thus dangerous for a worship service. We really want to get rid of the world of newpapers and sensational news in the church.* That is quite right. What really matters is getting rid of this world. However that means getting rid of it in such a way that it does not come upon us suddenly and take us captive and tyrannize us again the moment we get out of church. In this way we will have *overcome* the world when we leave the worship service.

Therefore it cannot really be a question of getting rid of these things by closing our eyes to them or by forgetting them as quickly as possible, even if only for a short time. Rather it is a question of knowing that we have to face them as Christians. It is not only important *that* we get rid of these things, but *how* we get rid of them.

There are people who cannot go to any funeral—or better, they do not want to go. Why not? Because they fear the emotional shock they may get by being in the immediate presence of a dead person. They do not want to see this side of human life and think that they can eliminate these things by not looking.

There are even those who think it is especially pious not to see the somber, dark sides of life, to close one's eyes to the catastrophes of this world and to lead one's own contemplative life of piety in a spirit of peaceful optimism.

---

*Sermon preached after the bloody events connected with the so-called Röhm Putsch of June 30, 1934, in Germany.

However it can never be good to cheat oneself out of the truth. Whoever cheats oneself out of truth about one's own life certainly also cheats oneself out of God's truth. It is certainly never pious to close our eyes in situations where they have to see sad, horrible things, especially since God gave us our eyes to see our neighbor in his need. Therefore that is certainly never the right way to get rid of the things that frighten and depress us.

However there is also a more humane and more serious attempt to cope with these things and yet it too will prove to be an unChristian way. Let me give you a simple example. Before our very eyes a serious accident takes place on the street. Someone is run over. We are terribly frightened. For a second we just stand there in a daze. And then our first thought is: "Whose fault is it?" That is a very ordinary example of a very common attitude. Something terrible hits us personally, hits our family or our nation, and when we wake up from our unconscious state, our first question is: "Who is to blame for it?" So now we have no peace of mind. Our thoughts are racing to and fro. All the people who were involved in the accident in any way appear in our mind's eye. Our vision becomes sharper and more penetrating than ever. Growing more and more bitter, we ask the question: "Whose fault is it? Who is right? Who is wrong?" Man is a moralist to the core. He wants to be able to accuse the one and acquit the other. He wants to be the judge of what happens. He wants to cope with a terrible disaster by showing the one to be in the right and the other to be in the wrong. Think of minor events from your life, but think of major disasters as well, like war or revolution. Everywhere it is the same—people want to be the judge themselves.

Now let me pause for a moment. It is of immeasurable value for us that Luke has preserved for us this report which is, by the way, the only one of its kind in the Gospels. It is a report about how Jesus receives such news of a disaster that hit his country, or as we can safely say, how he receives a sensational newspaper report and what he has to say about it.

Eyewitnesses told Jesus how Pilate had several Galileans—Jesus' fellow countrymen—executed, apparently as rebels and enemies of the state. These eyewitnesses told him how these executions took place under circumstances that made the pious Jews' blood boil. The persons involved in the disaster were torn away from their sacrifices in the temple and then killed right there in the temple precincts. It was likely that this news caused a tremendous uproar, provoked an animated exchange of opinions and got political conversations going in a powerful new way. They must have gone back and forth: "Pilate is right—Pilate is wrong; the Galileans are the victims of a tyrant; the Galileans got the punishment they deserved." However, the predominant view seems to have been that such a terrible fate, such horrible deaths would certainly not have hit the Galileans if they had not been guilty. There must have been a very serious offense here. Otherwise God could not have let such a terrible disaster happen. This was the interpretation of the serious-minded and the pious. They were of the opinion that one should not and cannot separate even this event from the fact that there is a God from whom all things come, both good fortune and disaster, and his judgments are just. The only thing one can and must do is turn away from these punished sinners in honor, for God's wrath has struck them down. This is how they coped with the incident. This was the official view of this event, or let's say, the daily press view of it.

And now Jesus walks onto center stage. He evidently picks up on the idea that we must indeed think of God himself as being inextricably connected with these terrible happenings, that in the final analysis it was not Pilate who was acting here, but that in the good as in the bad God himself was acting as the sole effective agent in this world. However, precisely this idea that God had a hand in these events means something quite different to Jesus than to public opinion.

Jesus uttered not one word about Pilate. He did not say whether Pilate was right or wrong. He uttered not one word about the Galileans, not one word of political judgment, not one word of moral judgment. It is quite clear: Jesus does not judge! Jesus agreed with neither of the two opposing groups. He especially did not go along with the pious Jews who interpreted these events in such a serious moral fashion. *Jesus says no to them.*

"Do you think that these Galileans were worse sinners than all the other Galileans, because they suffered this way? I tell you, no!" Jesus says "no" to the pious. He says "no" to their attempt to deal with this horrible incident by setting themselves up as judges over the Galileans. Jesus says "no." First of all, this means that he is telling them to stop all their guessing, their interpreting, their judging, and to put an end to their know-it-all attitude. He is telling them to stop trying to settle these things in such a way. He is saying "stop" because these things are too enormous. God himself is at work here. When Jesus declares, "I tell you, no!" he means that here is *God's mystery.* It would be sheer folly for man to even try to fathom it. Therefore away with all your judging, away with all your attempts to prove the one right and the other wrong. Instead observe restraint and give no answer. . . . Here is God's mystery.

After Jesus commanded silence and reverence, after God himself loomed into view behind his harsh "no," he now takes the offensive and begins to attack those who wanted to be on hand to pass judgment immediately.

"Do you think? . . . No! But unless you repent, you too will all perish." What is going on here? On the basis of this judgment Jesus is doing the very same thing he has done all his whole life—he is calling them to repent. Here is God—therefore repent. So for Jesus this distressing newspaper report about the terrible events in the temple is nothing other than God's renewed, unmistakable call to all those who hear it to repent and change their ways. For him it is nothing less than a plain, living illustration of his preaching. Humanity must humble itself before God's mystery and power; we must repent and admit that God is right.

From now on our situation will become dangerous. We are no longer spectators, observers, judges, of these events. Now we ourselves are the ones addressed, we are the ones affected. This change in our situation has happened for us. God is speaking to us. It is meant for us.

And that means first of all: Do not judge, or you too will be judged! Don't play yourselves up, don't act as if you are better than those Galileans, than Pilate. Faced with such fearful divine behavior, we do not say proudly, "I thank you, God, that I am not like these other people, . . ." but pray for yourselves: "God, be merciful to me a sinner."

Jesus too raises the quesion of guilt here. But he answers it differently. Pilate or the Galileans are not guilty; on the contrary, we ourselves are guilty. In view of such terrible human catastrophes the arrogant spectator attitude of a judge or know-it-all is no longer valid for the Christian. Rather what really counts here is that we realize this one thing: these events took place in my world, the world I live in, the world in which I commit sin, in which I sow hatred and unkindness day by day. These events are the fruit of what I and my brothers have sown. Moreover, those who were involved in the disaster, the Galileans and Pilate, are my family, my brothers in sin, in hatred, in malice, in unkindness, my sisters in guilt. Whatever strikes them should strike me. They are only the warning sign of God's hand that also stands over me. Therefore let us repent and recognize our guilt and not judge.

It is difficult to think this way. It is even more difficult to believe that this attitude alone overcomes the world and that the world can become new through repentance alone. And yet we must believe it even though we ask ourselves: "Isn't that kind of attitude completely unfruitful? Is anything really changed for the better through repentance?" Yes, indeed! Everything is changed for the better in this way. But how? In our act of repentance God's grace can once again find its way to us. When we truly repent, we realize that no human being is ever right in the end. Rather God alone is right in all his ways, in his acts of severity and in his acts of compassion.

A great man of our time, Mahatma Gandhi, is a non-Christian. Yet one is very tempted to say he is a heathen Christian. This man tells in his life story how he once ran a school and gave his support to one young man there to the best of his ability. One day the young men of the school perpetrated an injustice on this boy that deeply shocked him. From this incident he did not hear the call to punish or judge the students, but only the call to repent. He went and did penance for days by fasting and practicing various forms of self-denial. What did that mean? It means first that he recognized in the guilt of his students his own guilt, his own lack of love, patience, and truthfulness. Furthermore, he knew that only in a spirit of humility that recognizes one's own sin could he once again yield to the Spirit of God. Finally he saw here that there is faith and love and hope in repentance alone. We have not yet believed enough, we have not yet loved enough—can we be judges? Jesus says to us: "I tell you, no!"

The way that leads to renewal through repentance is a quiet, a strange, and a slow way. But this way alone is God's way. And if we go home from church with this insight and truly desire to act on it, only then will we have overcome the world of the newspaper, the world of terrors, and the world of judging.

Lord, lead your people to repent and begin with us! Amen. [*GS*, V, pp. 521–27]

34

The One Who Thinks and Lives for Others

(London)

September 1934

TEXT: "Come to me, all you who are weary and burdened, and I will give you rest. Take my yoke upon you and learn from me, for I am gentle and humble in heart, and you will find rest for your souls, for my yoke is easy and my burden is light." (Matt. 11:28–30)

Since Jesus spoke these words, there should be no person on earth who feels so abandoned that he could say of himself: "No one has asked about me. No one has wanted me. No one has ever offered me his help." Whoever has once heard these words in his life and speaks like this is lying. Indeed, such a person despises and mocks Jesus Christ and the seriousness of his words. For he has called all his people who are weary and burdened. He has not made his circle narrow. He has not gathered around himself a spiritual-religious aristocracy. Rather he has made the circle as wide as possible, so wide that actually not a single person could say in good conscience that Jesus' invitation was not meant for him because he was not among the weary and the burdened. On the contrary, what is so astonishing about this invitation is that it actually puts all people in the awkward position of having to admit that Jesus' invitation was meant for them too. In fact, perhaps for them even more than for others.

The weary and burdened—who are they? Jesus intentionally did not speak limiting or qualifying words here. All those who feel weary and burdened qualify. Moreover those who do not feel weary and burdened because they do not want to feel this way are also truly weary and burdened. Surely the men, women, and children who have to bear and work under a hard external fate are weary and burdened. We could almost say that they happened to be born into the darkness of this life, into drudgery as well as external moral distress. I have rarely had such a strong impression of standing among the burdened and weary as in that miner's town in the north of France where I stayed while on vacation this summer. Here one encounters joyless life that has been whipped, humiliated, insulted, and abused. It is passed on and propagated from parents to their children and their children's children. The weary and burdened are found wherever labor is experienced as God's curse on human beings.

However, we are always all too easily in danger of finding such people solely among those who live in outward poverty. Yet Jesus found and sought the most weary of all and the most burdened of all—not among those kinds of people, but among the so-called rich. Think of the rich young ruler whom Jesus loved and who turned away from Jesus full of sorrow because he was too weak to follow Jesus (Matt. 19:16–26). There is hardly anything more depressing for someone than when one realizes that outwardly one has everything one wants, but with all that he has nevertheless remains inwardly hollow and empty and superficial. With all of his possessions he cannot buy the most important things of this earthly life—inner peace, spiritual joy, love in marriage and family. One can see precisely in the homes of apparently successful people just how much unspeakable inward suffering there is and how great a burden of heavy guilt this wealth produces. No, the weary and burdened do not look only the way Rembrandt portrays them in his hunched gulden drawings, the poor, the wretched, the sick, the lepers, the ragged with their furrowed faces. These are weary and burdened under the cover of a pleasant, youthful face or a shining and successful life—people who feel they are totally abandoned in the midst of a large society, people to whom everything seems stale and empty until they feel disgusted by this life because they sense how their soul molds and decays with all these burdens. No one is more lonely than the prosperous person.

However even those who seem to not even feel their loneliness, because they are so intoxicated with life as it rushes along day by day, do not even think of being weary and burdened. Yet in reality they too are a part of this group. It is just the reverse. They plunge into their supposed happiness ever more wildly because they do know or suspect at the bottom of their heart that they too are a part of it and because they are afraid of admitting that to themselves. They are on the run from every word that might tell them the truth. They do not want to be weary and burdened and yet in the eyes of Christ they are doubly so.

All people are. Come to me *all* you who are weary and burdened. This last phrase is not a restriction of the "all," but is *its explanation*. Who would want to say: "It doesn't really concern me" when Jesus makes this appeal. Who would want to say: "I really don't know what it means to be weary and burdened."

Words are no longer of any help, neither are ideals or dreams for the future held out before one's very eyes when a person has once come to the end of his inner resources. When he becomes a burden to himself, when he doesn't want to keep on going, when he is afraid of the mountain lying in front of him, when guilt feelings weigh heavily on his mind, when he feels he has been lied to and victimized by the world, then he needs only one thing—he needs a person whom he can fully trust without reservation, a person who understands everything, hears everything, a person who bears all things, believes all things, hopes all things, forgives all things. He needs a person to whom he can say: "You are rest, you are gentle peace, you are the longing and the one who stills it" (Ruckert). He needs a person under whose eyes our suffering disappears and our heart opens up in silent love, a person who gently takes our burden from us and frees us from our fits of rage and from all our fears. In so doing, he delivers our soul from this world. But who has such a person? Where is there such a person?

Now the greatest of all miracles is that every individual has and can find this person because this person calls each of us to himself on his own initiative, offers himself, invites us. This person who is our rest, our peace, our refreshment, and our deliverance, is Jesus Christ alone. He alone is truly human. And in this true humanity he is God. He is our deliverer and our peace and our rest. "Come to me, all you who are weary and burdened, and I will give you rest." Everything hinges on this "I." Not an idea, not a word, not a preacher, but "I," the man Jesus who knows us all—who suffered and struggled through everything we have to suffer through, the man Jesus, our Redeemer.

There are two possible ways to help a person who is oppressed by a burden. Either you take the whole load off of him so that in the future he has nothing more to carry. Or you help him to carry it by making the carrying easier for him. Jesus does not want to go the first way with us. The load is not taken from us. Jesus who carried his own cross knows that man is destined to be a burden carrier and the bearer of his own cross. Moroever he knows that man is sanctified only under this burden and not without this burden. Jesus does not take from man the burden God has laid upon him. But he makes the burden easier for man by showing him how he must carry it.

"Take my yoke upon you and learn from me." A yoke is a burden itself, a burden in addition to all the other burdens; and yet it has a peculiar way of making the other burdens easier. A burden that would simply weigh a person down and force him on his knees becomes bearable through this yoke. We are familiar with the pictures of water carriers carrying a yoke on their shoulders. We are well acquainted with the yoke of the draft animals. The yoke alone enables them to pull the heavy burden without feeling pain or torment in the process, and without getting sore skin from pulling it. Jesus wants to put us human beings under such a yoke so that our burden does not become too heavy for us. He calls it "my yoke." It is the yoke under which he learned to carry his burden. His burden is a thousand times heavier than all our burdens precisely because he carries all of our burdens. "Take my yoke upon you"—go with me under my yoke, harnessed together with him so that we can no longer break loose; harnessed together with all those who want to carry this yoke; harnessed together until one day the yoke is completely taken from us.

"Learn from me." See how to carry this yoke and carry it in like manner. "Learn from me, for I am gentle and humble in heart." This, then, is the yoke he carries—his gentleness and his humility. That is the yoke we are to take upon ourselves, the yoke Jesus knows will help us to make our burden easy. "Gentle" means not kicking against the pricks, not rebelling against the burden, not objecting to it, and not chafing against it, but keeping quiet and being patient. Being gentle also means carrying what is laid on us because we know that it is God himself who lays this burden on us and continues to help us as well. "Gentle and humble in heart." Being humble surely means giving up one's own will completely, not asserting oneself and getting one's own way but rejoicing more and more when another's will is done than when my will is done. Being humble means knowing that we are the servants and God is the master and that the servants no doubt have to carry the burden. However it also means knowing that we have a good master who will one day take the burden from our shoulders when this burden has sanctified, humbled, and purified us.

The one who will carry this yoke, the one who will learn from Jesus in this manner, has a great promise. "And you will find rest for your souls." That is the end. This rest is the ultimate. Of course, it is already present even here under the yoke of Jesus, harnessed together with him in gentleness and humility. But the complete rest we long for will be present only where all burdens will fall away.

In the light of such blessed hope and such deliverance from the troubles and sin and guilt of this life, it may be said even today: "My yoke is easy and my burden is light." Woe to him who plays with these words and acts as if it meant that Christ's cause is an easy cause. The person who recoils in horror from the seriousness and the frightfulness of this cause of Christ understands much more about these words. The person who really understands it does not dare to approach this cause for fear of what it may mean for our real life. But, of course, then we must say to the one who has once comprehended what Jesus Christ and his will are all about: Now go to Jesus yourself and take his yoke upon yourself and see how everything has suddenly become different and all your fears and all your dismay will vanish. See how all of a sudden it may be said of the one who is with Jesus: "My yoke is easy."

But now one question stands between us here at the conclusion. We have to call it by its name so that it does not confuse us. They say Jesus is dead. How are we supposed to go to him? How is he supposed to comfort us? How is he supposed to help us? What can we answer but this: No, Jesus lives—he lives here in the midst of us. All you have to do is seek him, here or at home. Call on him, ask him, invite him in. And suddenly he will be with you. And you will know that he lives. You do not see him, you feel him. You do not hear him, but you know that he is there. He alone helps and he alone comforts. You take his yoke upon you and rejoice and wait. And you long for final rest with him.

> Only a short while wrought, then it is done.
> Then all the strife will have faded into nothingness.
> Then I can refresh you with living waters.
> And eternally and forever talk to Jesus.

> (Søren Kierkegaard's epitaph)

[*GS*, V, pp. 527–33]

35

Human Greatness under the Judgment of Love

(Twentieth Sunday after Trinity, London)

October 14, 1934

TEXT: "If I speak in the tongues of men and of angels, but have not love, I am a noisy gong or a clanging cymbal. And if I have prophetic powers, and understand all mysteries and all knowledge, and if I have all faith, so as to remove mountains, but have not love, I am nothing. If I give away all I have, and if I deliver my body to be burned, but have not love, I gain nothing." (1 Cor. 13:1–3)

The reasons that have led me to expand this thirteenth chapter of first Corinthians in a series of sermons have been the following. First, it is a chapter that is just as necessary for our congregation as for the one in Corinth. After all, what does it mean to be a Christian congregation when in the midst of many beneficial and nice activities that may take place in it, the one thing needful is not completely clear or obvious— that the members of the congregation are simply to love one another? What kind of picture does a church offer itself and the world when not even this foremost duty is taken seriously? If anything human in the early church was able to convince the pagans it was simply this—they could see, really see with their very eyes, that the two neighbors, the master and his slaves, the brothers on bad terms with each other all at once were no longer against each other, but with each other and for each other. When they became Christians, they simply experienced rad- ical outward changes. Do we think perhaps that because we are already Christians, nothing needs to change anymore? Or hadn't we better say: If we would really become Christians, immediately much would change in our lives too? Do not these words bring judgment even to a Christian community even if everything was happening in a congregation, even if they all came to church, even if they did many good things and yet "if it has not love, it is nothing."

Secondly, I had the special situation of our German churches in mind. Whether you want to see it or not, whether you consider it correct or not, the churches are locked in a struggle for their faith as it has not been for several hundred years. Whether you think it is right or not, what is at stake here is nothing less than its confession of Jesus Christ as the sole Lord and Redeemer of this world. (And yet in spite of all the difficult and depressing events of late we are grateful for this struggle because it has woken up the churches and prepared them to serve their Lord.)

But those who participate both inwardly and outwardly in this struggle for this confession know that such a struggle of faith carries a great temptation within it, the temptation to be self-confident, self-righteous, and dogmatic. However all these things are tantamount to the temptation of being uncharitable and unkind to one's opponent. And yet this opponent can never really be overcome unless by love. No opponent at all is ever overcome except by love. "Father, forgive them, for they know not what they do" (Luke 23:34). How many people have really been overcome by these words of Jesus? Indeed, this sentence could be written over even the most passionate struggle of faith: "But if it has not love, it is nothing."

And with that we come to the third reason. The Protestant church has been able to proclaim the victory and power of faith in the Lord Jesus Christ alone with incomparable confidence and, in so doing, it has allowed the message of the Bible to be heard again in the Word in its pure form. But who still hears these words about the faith in the way they were supposed to be heard? Have they been heard in such a way that nothing else is meant than that God is to be *loved* above everything else. Loving God does not only mean that we say, "God will help us again if things go badly for us one day." That is truly a poor, weak faith. Loving God means rejoicing in him, being eager to think of him and pray to him. It means being glad to be in his presence and to be with him alone. It means waiting for him impatiently, waiting for every word, every request. It means not grieving him, but rejoicing in him simply because it is he, because he is God and because we are permitted to know and have him and to speak with him and live with him. Loving God—and loving the brothers and sisters out of love for him. Do we still understand that in the disillusioned Protestant church? Are we still able to hear that without saying right away: "That is pietism after all?" And what if it were? Don't these words continually stand over the Protestant church too, the one that preaches about faith alone . . . "and if I have not love, I am nothing"?

In what follows we have the firm intention of not looking at the other, but looking only into ourselves and allowing God to question *us* about *our* love. Who knows if perhaps that neighbor who seems so lonesome, strange, eccentric, unfriendly, and egotistical ultimately knows much more about longing for great love. Perhaps it only takes a long, long time before the ice breaks and his heart is freed. And who knows if all our kindness and what we usually care to say about him actually inhibits the real breakthrough of his love for God and his brothers? Therefore we want to look to ourselves alone and allow God to speak to us.

To begin with, what is said here is something very simple. A life has meaning and value only in so far as love is in it. Furthermore, life is nothing, nothing at all, and has not meaning and value if love is not in it. The worth of a life is measured by how much love it has. Everything else is nothing, nothing at all, totally indifferent, totally unimportant. All the bad things and all the good things about life, all the large and small matters of life are unimportant. We are only asked about one thing—whether we have love or not.

We are all familiar with those times when we stood at the grave of people about whom there was absolutely nothing, nothing at all, to say on our part. One terrible feeling depressed us: What unspeakable poverty there was in this life! There was so much meaninglessness, so much lost time and energy in this life! He had not one whom he loved. He had not one who loved him. We watch impassively, without tears, without pain as this life is laid to eternal rest, the rest he himself perhaps longed for. He was a miser. He was a jealous person. He was a tyrant. He knew and sought and wanted only himself. He hated the others. Everybody was in his way as he searched for the happiness he never found. He remained alone and lonely. Will he have to remain alone in eternity as well? These are the graves that probably shake us up most of all because they give us a quite simple but quite vivid sermon on the words, "And have not love, I am nothing."

And we are familiar with the graves at which we look back on the life of a loyal father or a happy child. All those who experienced love from this person are standing around the grave, an immeasurable number. There are many whom no one knows, but who well know why they are there. Our mouth opens and does not want to be silent, it cannot help but extol the love which was glorified in this life.

These are very simple experiences in life in which we think we have grasped from afar why Paul extols love with such single-mindedness. Life is really not worth living at all without love. However, the whole meaning of life is fulfilled where there is love. In comparison to this love everything else pales into insignificance. What do happiness and unhappiness mean, what do wealth and poverty mean, what do honor and disgrace mean, what does living at home or abroad mean, what does life and death mean where people live in love? They do not know. They do not differentiate. They only know that the sole purpose of happiness as well as unhappiness, poverty as well as wealth, honor as well as disgrace, living at home or abroad, living and dying is to love all the more strongly, purely, fully. It is the one thing beyond all distinctions, before all distinctions, in all distinctions. "Love is as strong as death" (Song of Songs 8:6).

It is already becoming clear from what we had to say here last that this praise of God is not exactly a matter of obvious civil morals, but a matter that cuts across our civil orders of life and philosophies of life. It cuts them all up. If the final "condemned" or "saved" that is to be spoken over our life really only depends on whether a person had love or not; if the verdict before God's throne actually needs "love or nothing," then all of a sudden the world looks very different than before, then all of a sudden much of what was previously big in the world abruptly plunges down into this nothingness, this emptiness, this destruction of life. Whoever strived for power and authority and honor, for pleasure and material wealth, whoever elevated oneself up above this world is toppled, judged, destroyed by this simple word of the New Testament. This striving is nothing, nothing at all.

The world order is turned upside down when it takes these words seriously: "and have not love, I am nothing." But what really matters now is that our piety, our Christianity, our religious life, and all its seriousness has also fallen along with the world. The things we have said up to now were so obvious to the majority that they no longer needed to be said. But they would be totally misunderstood if we stopped here and the handful of saved churchgoers and pious believers were pitted against this fallen world. No, these words cut deeply into our own ranks, our church, and our piety. Only here do we recognize the severity the word love contains. This severity protects it from any possible misunderstanding. Only here do we recognize the tremendous aggressive force that is in this word. Consequently, it sets out to take action against the pious believer in order to hurl that person down from the lofty elevation falsely assumed.

In the presence of love, everything else becomes small. Whatever seemed great is shattered and disintegrates; it is a picture of wretchedness and misery. What is a life full of pleasure, honor, fame, and glamor compared to a life lived in love? But of course, the question does not stop here. It has a tremendously aggressive force and pushes on. What even is a life full of piety, morals, discipline, sacrifice, and self-denial if it is not a life lived in love?

Here in our text images of human beings rise up who are among those the whole human race as well as we ourselves are proud of. They are distinguished by their seriousness, their energy, their devotion, and their zeal for piety. In fact we believe the Creator himself would be proud of them. We look up to them with honor; we defer to them without reservation. They are people we would never venture to criticize; people who seem to stand beyond the bounds of all that is human, people in solitary majesty and grandeur. Yet now we observe the enormous spectacle that these people at the summit of a moral earnestness and piety which we could never achieve are attacked and fall by this one little phrase "and have not love, I am nothing." We observe how they become nothing, even though they appeared to be everything to us, nothing in the sight of God who pours out the light of truth over them. It did not remain hidden from him that in spite of all their majesty and strength they carried a cold heart of stone in their chest.

"If I speak in the tongues of men and of angels." What do I speak of? No doubt what is sacred to me, what is important and serious in life. To whom do I speak? No doubt to the one I would like to teach to appreciate these things, whom I would like to gain for the sacred cause. Therefore, supposing we could speak of the greatest and most sacred things in such a way that we forget everything else because we get carried away by our enthusiasm. Suppose we were given the unique gift of being able to say, to put into words what we feel and what others have to carry around silently inside themselves. Suppose we did this with one another in all sincerity and devotion. "If I speak in the tongues of men and of angels, but have not love, I am only a resounding gong or a clanging cymbal." These words strike like a paralyzing and destructive bolt of lightening. We had not bargained for the possibility that even our most sacred words can become unsacred and godless and rotten when they have no heart, when they are without love. Thus it is possible that the *word* that is given to us human beings for the sake of our innermost communion with God is profaned if it is severed from love and ends up serving itself, loving itself. Our words can become a resounding gong, a clanging cymbal—a hollow sound, empty chatter, without heart and without soul. The words we address to one another are often this way. Our most sacred, serious, honest, solemn declarations are like that, even if they are declarations of our love—if they are not made in a spirit of love. The person who uses serious, pious words in such a way is under the judgment of love. He is a resounding gong or a clanging cymbal, a nothing. On the other hand, the person who perhaps has the heavy, stuttering tongue of a Moses, perhaps with a mute, closed mouth, is saved by the same love. The first thing to consider then is the word without love.

Knowledge of the secrets of this world and of that world, the devotion of thinking directed to God, the devotion of meditation on things present and past as well as the illumination of things future, such knowledge lies deeper than the word. Is not this too a form of the pious life that almost makes us shudder? Imagine how much sacrifice and self-denial truth and knowledge require until one achieves it! (The great theologians of all times, the people who possess a knowledge of God.) "And if I have the gift of prophecy and can fathom all mysteries and all knowledge." Yes, indeed. Does not passionate longing seize us when we hear such words? Oh, if only I had them! If only I knew why I have to go this way and why the other person has to go that way, if only I could recognize God's dark, mysterious ways even here, then my thirst would be quenched. Ah, would not that be true bliss? But again we read: "And have not love, I am nothing." Understanding, knowledge, truth without love is nothing. It is not truth, for truth is God and God is love. That is why truth without love is a lie, nothing at all. "Speak the truth in love," says Paul in a different verse (Eph. 4:15). Truth by itself, truth said in enmity, in rancor, is not truth, but a lie because truth places us before God and God is love. Truth is the clarity of love, or else nothing at all.

However we have omitted a little sentence that is sandwiched in-between. In this sentence a terrible mystery is unveiled before us. "And if I have a faith that can move mountains, but have not love, I am nothing." If I have faith. What is meant by this phrase? What cord in our innermost being is struck by it? All faith, all confidence, all certainty that I am with God and God is with me in all the worries and fears of my life; all faith that enables me to no longer fear tomorrow. Is this not what we ask for daily, what we would be satisfied with if only we had it? Is this not what we would cling to until the very end of our life? But now it hits home here too. "And have not love, I am nothing." What kind of puzzling thing is this, a person who has all faith and yet does not love? A person who does not love God and does not love his brother? What kind of dark abyss is this which we have to gaze into here? It is a faith that is overbearing, high-handed, selfish, and egotistical in the innermost recesses of the heart, a faith that only seeks itself. It is a godless faith that believes not for God's sake, but for its own sake. God, keep us away from this abyss, from such superstition that deceives us and makes us think were with you. And yet in fact we are far from you. God, who will help us get out of such a predicament?

And now there is no stopping anymore. Our situation is becoming more and more terrible and more and more desperate. The loving deed which is nevertheless without love is added to faith without God and without love. So too is the deed that looks like love and yet is totally foreign to it. "If I give all I possess to the poor," if I denied myself and made sacrifices as only love can do it, "and have not love," if such sacrifices were to come from the selfishness and vanity of my heart instead, if such sacrifices were intended to cheat God and my neighbor out of the devotion of my heart, "then I gain nothing."

And what can the pious soul give in the end but his love life itself as a sacrifice for God, for Christ so that he may become a martyr? And if I surrendered my body to the flames, if I proved and sealed my seriousness, my piety, even in death, if I became a martyr for the sake of God's cause—God, how merciful you are to allow me to die for you— and have not love, I would truly gain nothing. If I would appear to love God even unto sacrificial death, and yet did not truly love him, but loved only myself and my martyr's fame and my martyr's dream, then judgment would be pronounced on the martyr as well. Love would hurl him down into the nothingness.

Who can even comprehend that? On the other hand, who does not comprehend this: Who does not know that in every respect we are the ones who speak and have knowledge and believe and do good deeds and sacrifice ourselves—for our own sakes, without love, without God? And who does not understand that God's verdict must be pronounced on all such activity because God is love and wants our whole, undivided love and nothing else?

What is this love? This love for God and for humanity? It is not words, not knowledge, not faith, not deeds of love, not living sacrifices in our sense of the word. Do we have it? Has judgment already been pronounced on us too? Now let us call out to it and ask that it may come from God himself and save us and snatch us from the brink of destruction.

You, a God of all love, come into our confused heart and save us out of love, by love. Amen. [GS, V, pp. 534–42]

36

The Unbelieving Way of Love

(Twenty-first Sunday after Trinity, London)

October 21, 1934

TEXT: "Love is patient and kind; love is not jealous or boastful; it is not arrogant or rude. Love does not insist on its own way; it is not irritable or resentful; it does not rejoice at wrong, but rejoices in the right. Love bears all things, believes all things, hopes all things, endures all things. Love never ends." (1 Cor. 13:4–8)

Last Sunday we learned that all our ideals, all our seriousness, our knowledge, our faith, yes, even our deeds of love and our sacrifices are *nothing* if they lack the one thing that Paul calls love. Therefore it is possible for our whole life to be simply nothing even if we live it seriously, fulfill all our duties, and pursue our vocation with total dedication because it does not come from love, but from the pride or the fear or the vanity of our own heart. It is even possible for all our piety to be nothing if we are forced to say of it: "And have no love." It is possible for all human life and endeavor to be nothing unless it comes from love. So we face the questions: What then is this love on which absolutely everything depends? What is this love if indeed we are nothing without it?

It is true that there is not one who lives without love. Each individual has love. He knows about its power and its passion. He even knows that this love makes up the whole meaning of his life. He would be tempted to throw away his whole life if it did not have this love he has experienced because it would not longer be worth living. Everyone knows about the power, passion, and meaning of this love. However, this love is man's love of himself. It is this love that fulfills him and makes him enterprising and resourceful. Without it his life would not longer be worthwhile. This is the way we experience love, but only in its diabolical reflection and caricature as self-love. However this self-love is misguided love that has rebelled against its source, love that does not need the help of others and thus is condemned to be unfruitful, love that is basically enmity toward God and one's neighbor because they could only disturb the immediate circle of myself. Both types of love actually have the same power, the same passion, the same exclusivity. The only thing that sets them apart is the tremendously different goal they each have—in one case, I myself, in the other, God and my neighbor.

However, self-love is clever. It knows that it is merely the caricature of the original image of love. That is why it pretends and hides its true feelings. That is why it veils itself, disguises itself in a thousand different forms, and tries in this way to become like true love. And it is so successful that it is almost no longer even possible for the human eye to distinguish the appearance from the truth. Self-love plays itself up as altruism and charity, as patriotism, as socially concerned love, as love of humanity, and does not want to be identified. But in spite of all its attempts to obscure reality and keep up appearances Paul forces self-love to answer for itself by painting in its presence and in our presence a picture of love that is valid in God's sight. Each of the individual features listed here can also be interpreted somewhat differently if taken by themselves. But where they all appear together it is inevitably true that the spell of self-love is broken and love of God and fellow human has become a reality. But where does that happen? It does not say, *the person* who loves does this or that, but *love* does this and that. Love, who is that? To whom does it apply? How do we know that?

We will give no answer at this point, but first listen to what is said. "Love is patient and kind." That means love can wait, wait a long time, wait to the very end. It never gets impatient. It does not desire to rush or force anything. It expects long periods of time. It counts on one thing—that the other is finally overcome by love. Waiting, being patient, continuing to live and be kind even where it seems to miserably fail, only this kind of love overcomes human beings. This alone loosens the chains that bind everyone, the chains of human anxiety that make people afraid of change and afraid of new life. Patience and long-suffering do not fit at all into our hurried lives. Kindness often seems to be so totally inappropriate. *But love is patient and kind.* It waits as one waits for someone who has lost his way. It waits and is glad if he is actually able to return. . . .

Yet not even the evil and sin of the other can make it bitter because it does not expect any good fortune for itself. It grieves over the other's evil and is saddened by it, yet for that very reason loves him all the more. It does not let itself become exasperated. Where unreturned love could perhaps embitter one's whole life, love says to us: You have not truly loved at all if you allow your love to be crushed by the animosity or thoughtlessness of the other. Otherwise you would be free from any bitterness. You allow yourself to become bitter, but love does not allow itself to become bitter.

Love is not resentful, it keeps no record of wrongs. Where justice seems to command us to keep a record of rights and wrongs, love is blind, knowingly blind. It sees the wrong, but does not keep a record of it. Love forgives the wrong. Only true love can forgive. Love forgets the wrong. It does not hold grudges. If we would only understand this one thing: Love never holds grudges. Every day it faces the other with new love and a fresh start. It forgets what lies behind. By acting this way it makes itself the laughingstock of the people. It makes a fool of itself, but it is not deterred by such ridicule. Instead it continues to love.

Is it then indifferent to right and wrong? No, it does not delight in unrighteousness, but it rejoices with truth. It wants to see things as they are. It would rather see hatred and injustice and falsehood clearly than see all kinds of amiable masks that only cover the enmity and make it even more ugly. Love wants to get things straight and then see them clearly. It rejoices in the truth for it can love again only by being in the truth.

It bears all things. That means it is no longer frightened by evil. It is totally able to accept and look at the terribleness of human sin. It does not look away because it cannot take it or because it cannot look at blood. Love bears all things. No sin, no crime, no vice, no disaster, is so difficult that love would not face it or take it upon itself, for it knows that love is greater than the greatest sin.

It believes all things and becomes a fool because of its faith, yet it is right in the end. It is victimized and duped and lied to as a result, but nevertheless it stands its ground. But isn't it nonsense to believe all things? Doesn't it actually provoke others to consider me stupid? Yes, it is nonsense if I have something in mind I want to get for my love. But if I really want nothing less than to love without conditions, without limit, without prejudice, then it is no nonsense at all; on the contrary, it is then *the* way to overcome people, the very people begin to wonder and then change their ways. Love believes all things because it cannot help but believe that ultimately, when all is said and done, all people are called to be overcome by love. Have you ever come across a situation where you have spoken to a very bad person and no one any longer expected any good or sincere deeds from him? Then you listened to him and believed what he said and he simply broke down when he realized that you had really put your faith in him. And then he told you: "You are the first person who believes me again!" As a result he took new heart from your faith in him. You did so even though he had lied to us just a short while ago. Do you know the despair of a person whom we mistrust and who nonetheless spoke the truth, as it later turned out? And then he began to have his doubts about all faith because of our mistrust. Whoever has experienced this understands that love does not make a distinction between people. Rather it believes all things with open eyes. Or with closed eyes it sees the true future. . . .

That is why it hopes all things, not only for the individual, but also for the nation and for the church. To hope all things without love is idle and foolish optimism. To hope all things with love is the power from which a nation and a church can take courage. It is our task to hope so unconditionally that our hope in the spirit of love may be a source of strength for others.

He who believes all things and hopes all things for the sake of love, for the sake of encouraging and helping, others must suffer and endure. For the world takes him for a fool, perhaps even for a dangerous fool, because his foolishness may even provoke malice into exposing itself. But only when malice comes to light can it ever be fully loved. Therefore loves endures all things and is radiant and happy in this suffering. For this suffering and endurance make love greater and greater and more and more irresistible. Love that endures all things gains the victory.

Who is this love if not the one who bore all things, believed all things, hoped all things, and even had to endure all things all the way to the cross? The one who did not insist on his own way nor seek himself, the one who did not allow himself to become bitter, and who did not keep a record of the evil deeds perpetrated on him and thus was over-whelmed by evil? The one who even prayed on the cross for his enemies and in this act of love utterly overcame evil. Who is this love Paul spoke of in these verses if not Jesus Christ himself? Who is meant here if not Jesus? What is the mark of this whole chapter if not the cross? [*GS*, V, pp. 542–49]

37

Only Love Keeps Us from Being Rigid

(Reformation Sunday, London)

November 4, 1934

TEXT: "So faith, hope, and love abide, these three; but the greatest of these is love." (1 Cor. 13:13)

We have intentionally arranged our sermon series on 1 Corinthians 13 in such a way that this text falls on Reformation Sunday. We mean to say by this arrangement that the church, having spoken as no other about the exclusive power and salvation and victory of faith in Jesus Christ, and having been great in faith, must be even greater in love. Therefore on the one hand we want nothing less than to go back to the original Reformation, but on the other hand we want to confront a dangerous deterioration of the church that has threatened Protestantism from the beginning. The message of saving and redeeming faith alone became rigid, became a dead record because it was not kept alive through love.

However a church of faith—even if it is the most orthodox faith that faithfully adheres to the creeds—is of no use if it is not even more a church of pure and all-embracing love. What does it mean to believe in Christ who was love and still be full of hatred yourself? What does it mean to call Christ one's Lord in faith and not to do his will? Such faith is not faith at all, but hypocrisy. It is of no use to anyone for someone to confess his faith in Christ if he has not gone first and reconciled himself to his brother, to the reality of each of his brothers, even to the godless, racially different, ostracized, and outcast. And a church that calls a nation to faith in Christ must itself be the burning fire of love in this nation, the driving force for reconciliation, the place in which all the fires of hatred are extinguished and prideful, hate-filled people are turned into people who love. Our Reformation churches have accomplished great things, and yet it seems to me that they have not yet succeeded in doing this greatest of all things. Today it is more necessary than ever.

"So faith, hope, and love abide, these three." Now of course that means that no person and no church can live on the greatness of its own deeds. Instead they live solely on the past deed God himself does and has done. This is the decisive point: the great acts of God remain unseen, hidden in the world. What ultimately matters in the world and in the history of nations is being able to point to great feats; it is not this way in the church. The church that tries to achieve such success would have long ago become a slave to the laws and powers of this world. The church of success is truly far from being the church of faith. The deed God has done in this world, the deed the whole world has lived on since then is called the cross of Golgotha. These are God's successes. And the successes of the church and the individual will look like this when they are deeds of faith. That faith remains means it remains true that man must live by what is invisible. He must live not by his visible work but by God's invisible work. He sees error and believes truth. He sees guilt and believes forgiveness. He sees dying and believes eternal life. He sees nothing and believes the deeds and mercy of God. "My grace is sufficient for you, for my power is made perfect in weakness" (2 Cor. 12:9). And that is the way it is in the Reformation church. It never ever lives by its deeds, not even by its deeds of love. Rather it lives by what it cannot see and yet believes. It sees affliction and believes deliverance. It sees false teaching and believes God's truth. It sees betrayal of the gospel and believes God's faithfulness. The Reformation church is never the visible community of saints but the church of sinners that believes in grace and lives by it alone contrary to all appearances. Luther once exclaimed: "Whoever claims to be a saint should get out of the church." A church of sinners, a church of grace, a church of faith, that is what it is. "But now faith remains" because it lives in God's presence and lives by God alone. There is only one sin, and that is living without faith.

However a faith that really keeps to what is invisible and lives by it, acting as if it were already here, hopes at the same time for the time of fulfillment, of seeing and possessing. He hopes for it as confidently as the hungry child to whom his father has promised bread can wait a while because it believes. Yet eventually the child wants to get the bread. Or take the music listener who willingly follows a dark interplay of disharmonies, but only in the certainly that these disharmonies will have to be resolved sooner or later. Or think of the patient who takes a bitter medicine so that the pain is finally taken away. A faith that does not hope is sick. It is like a hungry child who does not want to eat or a tired person who does not want to sleep. Mankind hopes as surely as it believes. And it is not a disgrace to hope even beyond measure. Who would even want to speak of God without hoping to see him one day? Who would want to talk about peace or love among people without wanting to experience them one day in eternity? Who would want to talk about a new world and a new humanity without hoping that we would share in it? And why should we be ashamed of our hope? One day we will have to be ashamed not of our hope but of our pitiful and fearful hopelessness which believes God is capable of very little, and in false humility does not act where God's promises are given. Such hopelessness gives up in this life and is not capable of looking forward to God's eternal power and glory. "We bid you hope!" (Carlyle). "Hope does not disappoint us" (Rom. 5:5). The more a person dares to hope, the greater he becomes with his hope. People grow with their hope, if only it is hope in God and his power alone. Hope remains.

"So faith, hope, love abide, these three; but the greatest of these is love." Once again the first verses of the chapter linger on our minds. "And if I have a faith that can move mountains"—and we add: if I had all the hope in the world—"but have not love, I am nothing," for love is the greatest of these.

What could be greater than to live one's life in faith before God? What could be greater than to live one's life to God in hope? Even greater is the love which lives *in* God. "Walk before me" (Gen. 17:1). "Whoever lives in love lives *in God*" (1 John 4:10). What is greater than the humility of faith which never forgets the infinite distance of the Creator from the creature? What is greater than the confidence of hope which longs for God's coming and longs to see his reality? Even greater is love, for already here it is certain of his nearness and presence everywhere. This love clings to his love and knows that his love wants nothing but our love. What is greater than faith which hopes for its salvation in Christ and holds fast to Christ and is justified in him? What is greater than hope which hour after hour focuses on a blessed experience of dying and a radiant homecoming? Even greater is the love that senses, the love that forgets everything for the other and even sacrifices his own salvation to bring it to his family. For "whoever loses his life for my sake will find it" (Matt. 16:25).

Faith and hope remain. Let us not think that we can have love without faith and without hope! Love without faith is like a river without a source. That would mean we could have love without Christ. *Faith alone justifies us before God.* Hope directs our attention to the end. Love perfects.

Faith alone justifies. Our Protestant church is built on this sentence. Luther found in the Bible the sole answer to man's question: "How can I justify myself in the sight of God?" By believing his grace and mercy in Jesus Christ. The answer to the question of how man is justified in the sight of God is this: by grace alone through faith alone. Therefore we can turn around the final sentence of our chapter here at the end with good reason and say: And if I have all love so that I do all good works but have not faith, I am nothing. Faith alone justifies. But love perfects.

Faith and hope will enter into eternity changed into the form of love. At the end everything must become love. Perfection means love. But the sign of perfection in this world is called "cross." That is the way perfected love must go and always will go in this world. However this truth shows us first that this world is ripe for demolition, overripe. It is only God's indescribable patience that is still waiting to the end. This truth shows us second that the church in this world remains a church under the cross. Woe to the church that already here wants to become a church of visible glory. It has denied its Lord on the cross. Faith, hope, and love all lead to the cross to be perfected.

When we go out of the church now, we go into a world longing for the things we have spoken of here. Of course it longs not only for words, but for the reality. A humanity that has been deceived and disappointed thousands of times needs faith. A wounded and suffering humanity needs hope. A humanity that has fallen into discord and distrust needs love. And if we no longer have any compassion on our own poor soul which truly needs all this too, then at least have compassion on a poor humanity. It wants to learn from us to believe, hope, and love anew. Don't deny it to them. Let's allow God to shout it at us on this Reformation Day: Believe, hope, and, above all, love! And you will overcome the world. Amen. [GS, V, pp. 555–60]

SERMONS, 1935–1939
FINKENWALDE, BERLIN, KIECKOW, AND THE SECRET SEMINARIES

Following his London pastorate, Bonhoeffer returned to Germany to become director of a Confessing Church seminary located first at Zingst, by the Baltic Sea, and later at Finkenwalde, near Stettin. In this role he not only preached but also trained his seminarians in the ministry of preaching. Albrecht Schönherr, one of Bonhoeffer's Finkenwalde students during those years, who eventually became the Bishop of East Berlin, included this description of Bonhoeffer's style of preaching in his recollection of Bonhoeffer's influence over his life: "In his sermons he avoided any rhetorical effect. He never gave us anecdotes in them. He chose the most sober, matter-of-fact form, the homily. In spite of this, or perhaps because of it, they were extraordinarily impressive. There was not a word too many. Only the matter itself came to speech, sometimes in such a compressed way, that what he had to say seemed almost forced out. It may be typical of Bonhoeffer's way of preaching that today, after thirty years, his texts still cling in the memory, whereas the pattern of thought has gone."[8]

The sermons included here are among the most memorable in the recollections of his seminarians, family, and friends. Bonhoeffer speaks of their longing with the psalmist for God amidst the times of trouble and tears. He reminds them that they can never be alone, whether in foreign lands, or in the depths of sorrow, or when seemingly abandoned into the clutches of those who ridicule their faith. He asks for the spirit of forgiveness in the midst of their experience of injustice, a point not lost on his seminarians who had been urged by Bonhoeffer to include their enemies in their prayers. A third sermon in this section addresses the specter of death in the context of John's vision of judgment on Babylon, undoubtedly a cryptic reference to the Babylon of Nazi Germany they were seeking to convert again to the Lord. We find Bonhoeffer here buoying up their spirits in the dangers they were facing. "Blessed are the dead who die in the Lord. To die in Christ" he declares, "that this be granted us, that our last hour not be a weak hour, that we die as confessors of Christ, whether old or young, whether quickly or after long suffering, whether seized and laid hold of by the Lord of Babylon or quietly and gently—that is our prayer today, that our last word might only be: Christ."

We see, too, Bonhoeffer's personal compassion for those whose lives had been victimized by nazism in the sermon for the funeral service of his grandmother, Julie Tafel Bonhoeffer, who had defied the S.S. guards in order to enter a Jewish shop during the Nazi government's first brutal moves against the Jewish people. Bonhoeffer's own solidarity with the Jews comes out in this sermon. At the same time, we can note his optimism in the wedding sermon for his student, Albrecht Schönherr. But these sermons also contain moments of outrage and a sense of guilt at what had transpired in his church and in his country. He confronts the desire for vengeance with Christ's words of forgiveness for the godless, praying that all their enemies be brought under the cross of Christ. Time and again, there are references to the enemies and pleas that his hearers exercise Christian forgiveness, that they rise above the injustices and evils of the structured criminality they were living through.

"Now we must remember quickly: I was met with mercy, not by men, no, but by God himself. And Jesus Christ died for him, our enemy—and all at once everything is different. . . . No Christian is harmed by suffering injustice. But perpetuating injustice does harm. Indeed, the evil one wants to accomplish only one thing with you; namely, that you also become evil. But were that to happen, he would have won. Therefore, repay no one evil for evil."

Finally, in these selections, we read some of the most powerful exhortations to his seminarians to accept the challenge of the cross and suffering as vital to Christian discipleship and their quest for peace on earth. These ministers had been confirmed in the faith that accepts the challenge of the cross. In Christ's resurrection, he assures them, they are granted the comfort of knowing with St. Paul that death and the fear of death have been swallowed up in victory.

In these sermons there are few specific references to Hitler and nazism, or to those events which were molding Germany into a strong, unbending dictatorship. It is clear, however, that the church struggle in which Bonhoeffer was a forceful leader was never far from his mind; this life-and-death context formed the backdrop and background for the sermons. It remained for the hearers to make the precise connections, and thereby to receive inspiration and guidance for their own daily participation in the struggle.

During the Finkenwalde years, a number of Bonhoeffer's sermons were mimeographed and sent to those persons who had been students in the seminary community. One scholar, in assessing the character of Bonhoeffer's ministry, comments that these sermons "are exceptional expositions of Scripture from the heart and mind of a man for whom preaching was an integral part of life."[9] The sermons selected for inclusion here show where Bonhoeffer believed God had led him in his struggle to find meaning and maintain his faith in the Word of God for the people of Nazi Germany.

38

Longing for the Living God

(Exaudi Sermon on Psalm 42,* Zingst)

June 1935

TEXT: "As a hart longs for flowing streams, so longs my soul for thee, O God." (Ps. 44:14)

Have you ever, on a cold autumn night in the forest, heard the piercing cry of a deer? The whole forest shudders with the cry of longing. In the same way here, a human soul longs, not for some earthly good, but for God. Godly persons, whose God has removed himself from them, long for the God of salvation and grace. They know the God they long for; here are no seekers after an unknown God, who will never find anything. At some time they have experienced God's help and nearness. Thus they do not have to cry into a void. They call to their God. We can seek God as we should only when he has already revealed himself to us, when we have already found him once.

Lord God, awake in my soul that great longing for you. You know me and I know you. Help me to seek and to find you. Amen.

> Succor me in fear and need,
> Faithful God, have mercy on me!
> Your beloved child I remain,
> Despite Satan, world, and every stain.

Verse 2. My soul thirsts for God, for the living God. When shall I come and behold the face of God?

Thirst for God. We know the body's thirst when there is no water, and we know passion's thirst for life and happiness. But do we also know the

---

*The form in which it was reproduced and sent out from the seminary as a meditational aid.

thirst of a soul for God? A God that is only an idea or an ideal cannot quench this thirst. Our souls thirst rather for the living God, for the God and source of all true life. When will he quench our thirst? When we are able to behold his face, the face of God. That is the object of all present life and of the eternal life; we see it in Jesus Christ, the crucified. And when we have found it there, then we thirst to behold it in all clarity for eternity. Jesus says, "If any one thirst, let him come to me and drink" (John 7:37).

Lord, we are anxious to see you face to face. Amen.

> Sweet light, sweet light,
> Sun breaking through the clouds all bright:
> Oh when will I have reached that place,
> Where I may look on your sweet face,
> Together with all the meek and right!

Verse 3. My tears have been my food day and night, while people say to me continually, "Where is your God?"

Where is your God?, we are asked, by troubled, doubting, or scornful people. Death, sin, trouble, and war, as well as bravery, power, and honor—these we see. But where is your God? No one need feel ashamed of those tears that fall because we don't see God yet, because we can't show God to our brothers and sisters. They are tears wept for God's sake, and he counts them (Ps. 56:8). Where is your God? How else could we answer than by pointing to the man who in his life, death, and resurrection proved himself to be the true son of God, Jesus Christ? In death he is our life, in sin our forgiveness, in need our helper, in war our peace. "It is to this person that you should point and say: that is God" (Luther).

Lord Jesus, when I am troubled because I can't see God and his power and love in this world, then let me look steadily on you, for you are my Lord and my God. Amen.

> Let him seek, who will, another end
> Than to find salvation.
> Let my heart be alone intent
> To have Christ for its foundation.
> His word is true, and pure His deeds.
> His holy tongue has strength and reason
> To overcome all enemies.

Verse 4. These things I remember, as I pour out my soul: how I went with the throng, and led them in procession to the house of God, with glad shouts and songs of thanksgiving, a multitude keeping festival.

I am alone. No one is there to whom I can pour out my soul; so I do it in solitude and in the presence of the God to whom I cry out. It is good to pour out my soul in loneliness and not to suppress my grief.

But the lonelier I am, the greater becomes my longing for fellowship with other Christians, for collective worship, for collective prayer and song, for praise, thanksgiving, and celebration. I remember them, and my love for them grows great within me. Whoever calls out for God, calls out for Jesus Christ; whoever calls out for Jesus Christ, calls out for the church.

God the Holy Spirit, grant me brothers and sisters with whom I can have fellowship in faith and prayer, with whom I can bear all that is laid upon me. Lead me back to your church, to your Word, and to the Holy Communion. Amen.

> Heart and heart united,
> Seek in God's heart rest.
> Let your love, a spark ignited,
> Burn for the Savior brightest.
> He the head and we his limbs,
> He the shrub and we the flowers,
> He the master and we the brethren,
> We are his and he is ours.

Verse 5. Why are you cast down, O my soul, and why are you disquieted within me? Hope in God; for I shall again praise him, my help, and my God.

Sorrow and unrest last only a short time. They should not imprison my soul. Speak to your soul too; don't let it torment itself or be anxious. Say to it: hope in God! Do not hope in a sudden change of everything for the better, but hope in God! His presence, which is Jesus Christ, will surely help me, and I will surely praise him. When Jesus is with you, all that is left for you to do is to praise.

Triune God, make my heart constant, fix it on you and your help alone. Then I shall be succored and I shall praise you eternally. Amen.

> What cause have I to be cast down?
> While I remain to Jesus bound,
> Who shall take him from me?
> And Heaven—who shall be its thief,
> When the Son of God has already
> Given it to me with my belief?

Verse 6. My soul is cast down within me, therefore I remember thee from the land of Jordan and of Hermon, from Mount Mizar.

Why this relapse? Must solace always be followed by sorrow? That is the human heart, which won't let itself be comforted, which tumbles from one depression into another, and can only be held fast by God. Far from the temple in Jerusalem, far from the church and the community of believers, my longing remains awake and unsatisfied. My thoughts turn toward my spiritual homeland, where there will be peace and joy, where the soul finds refuge with God. When shall I see it again?

Father, when you send me into foreign lands, preserve in me that wholesome longing for my spiritual homeland, and direct my thoughts to the eternal homeland, where you will comfort us. Amen.

> Jerusalem, O noble city that thou art,
> I would to God I were within thee.
> Such great longing hath my ardent heart,
> It bides no more within me.
> Far over mountains and dales,
> Beyond rich pasture and waste,
> Up over all it sails,
> And flies from this world in haste.

Verse 7. Deep calls to deep at the thunder of thy cataracts; all thy waves and thy billows have gone over me.

Cataracts, deeps, billows, and waves—do you hear how the sea of the world falls upon the godly person? It is about to engulf him; he is like a drowning person who no longer reaches bottom and whose strength is failing him. In such a way, the world can gain power over us. But do we also know him whom the wind and sea obey (Matt. 8:23–27), who, in the fullness of time, arises and rebukes the sea, and there is a great calm?

Lord Jesus Christ, do not let me go under. Speak your powerful Word and deliver me. Only you can do it. Amen.

> One day, in my last affliction,
> Let me not go under.
> If bitter death should come,
> Wave on wave like thunder,
> Then reach out, O Lord,
> Your hand of faith to me.
> Lord Christ, come to us,
> Who founder on the sea.

Verse 8. By day the Lord commands his steadfast love; and at night his song is with me, a prayer to the God of my life.

Day and night, how infinitely long and wretched they are, when we are without God. But how joyous can the most evil day be, when I know that in everything, God works for good with those who love him, and how calm and redeeming can the deepest night be, when I sing and pray in it to God, to the God who demands not my death, but my life, to the God of my life. God's promises hold good and fill day and night—week after week, year after year. If only I take hold of them!

God, Holy Spirit, fulfill all your promises in me. I am ready day and night. Fill me completely. Amen.

Should I not raise up my voice in song
To my God, nor praise Him long?
For in everything I see
What good he means for me.
'Tis after all but love alone
That moves his faithful breast,
And supports without end his own,
Who take his service as their quest.
All things have their time to be—
God's love, an eternity.

Verse 9. I say to God, my rock: "Why hast thou forgotten me? why go I mourning because of the oppression of the enemy?

Why hast thou forgotten me? This question passes every Christian's lips sometime, when everything stands against him, when all earthly hope crumbles beneath him, when he feels himself utterly lost in the flow of great world events, when all life's goals are frustrated and everything seems to be senseless. But then it depends of whom he asks this question. I ask not some dark fate, but the God who is and will remain my rock, the eternal foundation on which my life rests. I fall into doubt, God remains steadfast as a rock; I falter, God is imperturbable; I prove unfaithful, God remains faithful, my rock.

Lord my God, be for me a firm foundation on which I can build, in this time and in that time to come. Amen.

Let me be yours and yours continue,
O faithful Lord and God of old,
Let nothing drive me from you,
But to your teachings hold.
Lord, only let me falter not,
And give me tenacity;
Then I shall praise thee, my God,
For all eternity.

Verse 10. As with a deadly wound in my body, my adversaries taunt me, while they say to me continually, "Where is your God?"

It has been a distinction of the godly for millennia that they suffer taunts and are ridiculed for the sake of their belief. Body and soul ache when not a day goes by in which God's name is not doubted and reviled. Where is your God? I profess him to the world and to all God's enemies, when, at times of deepest need, I believe in God's grace, at times of guilt in forgiveness, at times of death in life, at times of defeat in victory, at times of loneliness in God's gracious presence. Whoever have found God at the cross of Jesus Christ knows in what strange manner God has concealed himself in this world, and how he is always nearest just when we believe him to be farthest away. Whoever have found God at the cross also forgives all their enemies, because God has forgiven them.

God, do not forsake me when I must suffer insult; forgive all the godless, because you have forgiven me, and bring us all to you, at last, through the cross of your beloved Son. Amen.

> Lord our God, let them not be undone,
> Who in their need and burden,
> Await your grace, day and night,
> And to you, hopeful, cry.

Verse 11. Why are you cast down, O my soul, and why are you disquieted within me? Hope in God; for I shall again praise him, my help and my God.

Therefore, abandon all sorrow, and wait! God knows when to help you, and he will help, as sure as God is God. You will experience his help, for he knows you, and loved you before he created you. He won't let you fall; you are in his hands. In the end, you will only be able to praise him for all that has befallen you, for you have learned that the all-powerful God is your God. Your salvation is named Jesus Christ.

Triune God, I thank you for choosing and loving me. I thank you for all the paths in which you lead me. I thank you for being my God. Amen.

> Spirit of sorrow take flight,
> For my master of delight,
> Jesus, enters in.
> For those who God adore,
> Life is joyous, evermore,
> Even in affliction.
> Must I now endure derision and disdain,
> Yet even in that sorrow, you remain
> Jesus, my joy.

[*GS*, IV, pp. 391–99]

39

On Forgiveness

(Finkenwalde)

November 17, 1935

TEXT: Matt. 18:21–35

Let us begin this sermon by asking ourselves whether we can think of someone in our neighborhood, in our family, or among our friends whom we have not forgiven a wrong he has done us, of someone whom we have broken with in anger—if not in open anger, then in silent bitterness—with the thought: I can't put up with that anymore, I can no longer have any fellowship with this person.

Or would we really be so absentminded as to say we can't think of any? Are we so indifferent to others that we don't even really know whether we are at peace or at strife with them? Will one after the other stand up and accuse us one day?: "You parted from me in strife—you couldn't stand me—you broke fellowship with me—you disliked me and turned away from me—I hurt you once, and so you left me alone—I offended your honor once, and so you broke with me, and I couldn't find you again—I looked for you many times, but you avoided me— never again was an open word spoken between us, and I didn't want anything more from you, but only your forgiveness, and you were never able to forgive me, I am here now, and accuse you—do you still know me?" Will names that we hardly know anymore come alive before us in that hour—many, many, wounded and cast out, whose sins we did not forgive? And among these people, a good friend, perhaps, a brother, one of our parents?

In that hour a single, terrible, threatening voice will grow against us: "You were a hard person—all your friendliness is of no use. You were hard and proud, and cold as stone; you didn't worry about any of us; we all meant nothing to you, you detested us, you never knew what pardon does; you did not know how much good it does the one who experiences it, nor how free it makes the one who pardons. You were always a hard person."

We make things so easy for ourselves, when it comes to others. We become unfeeling, insensitive, and think that if we harbor no evil thoughts against a person, then that is just the same as if we had forgiven him. And in so doing, we completely fail to see that we don't have any good thoughts about him. Forgiving: that could indeed mean having only good thoughts about him, supporting him whenever we can. Yet it is just that we avoid; we don't support the other, but rather walk beside him and become accustomed to his silence; indeed, we do not take him seriously at all. But it's precisely the supporting that counts; supporting the other at every step, in all his difficult and unpleasant sides, saying nothing about his injustice and sin, even when it is against you; supporting and loving without ceasing—that would come close to forgiveness!

Only one who stands in such a relation to the other, to father, to friend, to spouse—but also to strangers, to all whom he encounters—he alone knows how hard it is. Sometimes, it escapes his lips: I can't do it anymore now; I can bear him no longer; now my strength is at an end. It can't go on forever like this, "Lord, how often shall my brother or sister sin against me, and I forgive?" or how long must I tolerate that he is hard on me, that he offends and injures me, that he lacks all consideration and tenderness, that he causes me pain without measure—Lord, how often . . . ? Surely, it must come to an end sometime; surely, injustice must be called injustice; surely, it cannot be that my rights are being violated continuously—"as many as seven times"? We smile at Peter; seven times, that seems trifling to us. How often have we already forgiven and overlooked! But we shouldn't smile; compared to Peter, we really have no reason to smile. To forgive seven times, really to forgive; that is, to turn the injustice done us completely to best account, to return good completely for evil, to accept the other as if he had always been our dearest brother; that is no small matter. Ah yes, what we call forgive and forget: "Live and let live!" But to forgive, solely from a love that does not want to let go of the other, but carry him farther; that is no small matter.

It is a real torment, this questioning. How am I to cope with this person; how can I bear him? Where do my rights begin with respect to him? Let us always take this question to Jesus alone, as Peter did. For were we to go to someone else, or to ask ourselves, then we would receive no help, or only poor help. But Jesus does help, only he does it in a most peculiar way. Not seven times, Peter, but seventy times seven, says Jesus; and he knows, only in this way does he help him. Do not count, Peter, but forgive without number; do not torment yourself with the question, how long?; without end, Peter, without end. That is what it is to forgive, and that is grace for you; that alone makes you free!

You count, once, twice, three times, and the matter becomes ever more threatening to you, the relationship to your brother even more tormenting. But you have simply not realized then, that as long as you keep counting, as long as you keep on crediting the other's old sins against him, then in reality, you have not yet forgiven—not even once. Free yourself, Peter, from counting; forgiveness and pardon know neither number nor end; you don't have to concern yourself about your own rights, they are surely in safe keeping with God; you may forgive without end! Forgiveness is without beginning and end, it occurs continuously, every day, for it comes from God. That is liberation from everything strained and unnatural in our life together with our fellow human beings. And with real anger, Jesus proceeds to tell that terrible story of the wicked servant, of the man who experienced mercy, and yet remained a hard man: now all mercy is pronounced over him, now the dreadful judgment of God is pronounced over him. And in telling this angry story, he gives us the greatest help he can; he points out the path to real forgiveness. Let us now explore that path.

Does each of us recall a moment in our life when God called us to judgment, when we were lost persons, when our life was at stake, when God demanded an accounting from us, and we had nothing but debts, immeasurably vast debts? Our life was stained and unclean and guilty before him, and we had nothing, nothing at all to show but debts and more debts. Do we recall how we felt then, how we had nothing to hope for, how lost and senseless everything seemed? We couldn't help ourselves anymore, we were utterly alone, and before us there remained only punishment, well-deserved punishment. Before him, we could not stand erect. Before him, in front of God the Lord, we sank to our knees in despair and prayed to him: "Lord, have patience with me"; and all kinds of foolish talk passes our lips, as here in the story of the wicked servant: "I will pay you and make amends for everything." So we said, and yet we knew for certain that we would never be able to pay it. And then, at once, everything changed: God's face was characterized no longer by wrath, but by great sorrow and pain toward us, and he released us from all debt, and we were forgiven. We were free, and the fear had been taken away from us; we were joyful again and could look God in the face and thank him.

So there was a time when we looked like that wicked servant. But how forgetful we are! Now we go and lay hold of him who has done us some small injustice, who has deceived or slandered us, and we say to him: "Make amends for your sin—I can't ever forgive you that!" Don't we see that we should say instead: "What the other has done to us here, that is nothing, nothing at all, compared to what I have done against God and against him as well"? For who called upon us to damn the other, when we have done far worse than he?

Verses 31–34. Now grace has been squandered; now all the old guilt has returned; now we come under wrath; now we are lost people, because we have scorned grace. That is the whole lesson: the sins of others you see, but you own sin you fail to see. In repentance, recognize God's mercy toward you; in this way alone will you be able to forgive.

What path brings us to heartfelt forgiveness of one another for every sin? Dear brothers and sisters, whoever has had the experience of God tearing him out of great sin and forgiving him; whomever God has sent a brother in such an hour to whom he could tell his sin; whoever knows the struggle the sinner wages against this help because he does not want to let himself be helped; and whoever nevertheless has discovered that his brother has absolved him from his sin in the name of God and in prayer—from such a one, all passion for judging and bearing grudges disappears; he wants only one more thing: to share in the plight of his brother, to serve, to help, to forgive, without measure, without conditions, without end. He can hate his sinful brother no longer, but loves him all the more, and forgives him everything, everything. O Lord, our God, let us experience your mercy, that we may practice mercy without end! Amen. Amen. [GS, IV, pp. 399–406]

40

Learning to Die

(Memorial Day, Finkenwalde)

November 24, 1935

TEXT: Rev. 14:6–13

"And I saw"—the curtain tears, and John gets to see that which for us is concealed by a thick veil—the world after death. So much is clear at once: that world is anything but dead; it is alive to the highest degree, full of action, full of visions, full of words, full of torment, and full of bliss—the world after death is life in the highest degree. It is not a nothing, not an extinction that awaits us when we close our eyes for the last time; rather, we go to meet undreamed of events. Let no one take comfort in the false consolation: after all, everything will be over before long; rather, let him be told: before long, everything will begin; before long now, things will become quite grave, quite critical for you.

Our text intends to help us prepare for the step into that other world. *How do Christians, how does Christ's congregation, learn to die?* That is the question, and our text gives the answer. A threefold glad tidings is preached to us from that world today, as a comfort on Memorial Day, as an aid to dying.

"And I saw another angel fly in the midst of heaven, having the everlasting gospel to preach. . . ." When we see such visions, when we see angels of God, then we are no longer in this world; rather we see heaven opened and the new world. The angel flies in the midst of heaven with the *everlasting gospel*. In other words, it belongs in the middle of heaven as it does in the middle of earth—the everlasting gospel. That is great comfort to all the faithful: *the everlasting gospel does remain*—it is an everlasting gospel; our gospel, as we hear it and preach it Sunday after Sunday; the gospel, which we have with us in our Bibles, reading it morning and evening, which gave a new turn to our lives once, when we understood it correctly for the first time; the gospel, here ridiculed and attacked and dragged through the mud—and yet, covertly and secretly believed; the gospel, openly confessed by martyrs of all times—the gospel remains forever. Therefore, we needn't fear or worry at all, even if it looks as if the gospel were foundering today. What are ten years, or even longer, that we pass through and survey at a glance? The gospel is everlasting and remains despite all. It remains the one and only true proclamation of God in all the world.

And if there are thousands of religions and persuasions and beliefs and ideologies in the world; and if they be the most splendid of ideologies and touch and move people's hearts—yet death frustrates them all; they must all break to pieces, because they are not true. Only the gospel remains. And before the end comes, it will be preached to every people, kindred, and tongue, throughout the entire world. Even if it seems here that there would be many ways, yet there is only one way for all people on this earth: the gospel.

And his language is so simple that everyone must understand it: "Fear God, and give glory to him; for the hour of his judgment is come: and worship him that made heaven, and earth, and the sea, and the fountains of waters." That is the first commandment, the entire gospel. "Fear God"—instead of the many things which you fear. Do not fear the coming day, do not fear other people, do not fear power and might, even if they are able to deprive you of property and life; do not fear the great ones of this world; do not even fear yourselves; do not fear sin. All this fear will be the death of you. You are free from all this fear; it isn't there for you. But fear God and him alone; for he has power over the powers of this world; the whole world must fear him—he has power to give us life or to destroy us; everything else is a game—only God is in earnest, entirely in earnest. Fear God's earnestness—and give him the glory. He demands it as the creator of the world, as our creator he demands it as the reconciler, who made peace between God and man in Christ; he demands it as the Savior, who will liberate us in the end from all sin and burden. Give glory to him in his holy gospel—"for the hour of his judgment is come."

What will God ask about on that day of judgment that we are approaching? At the Judgment, God will ask us solely about his everlasting gospel: Did you believe and obey the gospel? He won't ask whether we were Germans or Jews, whether we were Nazis or not, not even whether we belonged to the Confessing Church or not; nor whether we were great and influential and successful, nor whether we have a life's work to show for ourselves, nor whether we were honored by the world or unimportant and insignificant, unsuccessful and unappreciated. All persons shall be asked by God one day whether they could risk submitting to the test of the gospel. The gospel alone shall be our judge.

The road divides for eternity at the gospel. When we know this, and yet see how the gospel is disregarded among us—both in the world *and in the church*—then we may well become fearful.

Therefore, let us make note of that first vision that John saw: an everlasting gospel—the eternal proclamation to all peoples, the eternal judgment on mankind—an everlasting gospel; that is the sole and enduring comfort to the congregation of the faithful; that is glad tidings for all who have yet to die.

"Another angel, a second, followed, saying, 'Fallen, fallen is Babylon the great, she who made all nations drink the wine of her impure passion.'" That is what John saw—but he also saw something else namely, that Babylon was still great, powerful, and full of strength, that Babylon still stood there invincible in the world with all people trembling and throwing themselves down before her—Babylon, the enemy of God— the city which does not cease building her tower up into the heavens— Babylon, which willfully defies Christ the crucified Lord, which intoxicates the world with her glittering and enticing vices, as prostitutes intoxicate their lovers with heavy wine—which transforms and corrupts and woos the world with every kind of pomp and godless splendor— Babylon, whom the world loves, with whom the world is infatuated, running blindly into her nets—Babylon, which demands nothing else from her worshippers than blind love and intoxication—which gives them liberally and prodigally all that their hearts and wild desires crave—who would dare say of this Babylon, she is not eternal, she will have a great fall? With that anxiety does the Christian congregation, which neither can nor desires to be a citizen of this city, which must live and suffer on the margin, outside the city; with what anxiety must it view that city; with how many prayers must it intercede for her; with how many prayers has it longed for her fall to come! Who is Babylon? Was she Rome? Where is she today? Today, we dare not yet say—not because we fear the world! Rather because the Christian community does not know yet—but it sees terrible things and revelations drawing near.

And now—the voice from heaven, the joyful news for the community of the faithful: she is fallen, Babylon the great! Everything is already done; the judgment has already been handed down by God, Babylon is already condemned—Babylon cannot remain standing, because she cannot stand in the sight of God. Therefore, do not fear Babylon; she can do nothing against you—she is already condemned! She is nothing, like dust and gloom and rubble. Don't take her seriously, so deadly seriously; don't be consumed in your hatred or zeal, for it is all so temporary; so temporary—she is no longer the least bit important; but entirely different things are important—remain steadfast in faith, cling to Christ, listen to the voice of God the omnipotent, who says: remain untouched by Babylon; stay sober, and don't let fear overcome you; she is fallen, Babylon the great. That alone is important, that alone leads to life. He who becomes Babylon's slave, however, he becomes slave to death and judgment. Babylon is fallen; let the congregation of the faithful rejoice! That is the second glad tidings to the congregation that must go to death.

"And the third angel followed them, saying with a loud voice, if anyone worship the beast. . . ." The beast is Babylon's lord, the man of blasphemy, presumption, and violence. And this is the terrible thing: it is not enough for the beast that people serve him; rather, he demands that they mark themselves with his sign on foreheads and hands, that they belong to him visibly with will and deed; the beast demands to be professed! As Christians mark themselves with the sign of the Cross, so the beast demands that those who belong to him be marked with an "x" for blasphemy. And they worship the beast, saying: Who is greater or more powerful than this beast? Who would want to resist him? Who is more splendid or godlike? And all those worship him whose names are not written in the Book of Life, whose names are not chosen or pleasing before God and Christ, whose names are a blasphemy of God.

"The same shall drink of the wine of the wrath of God. . . ." The wrath of God is a burning, unmixed wine, which a person feels unto the very core of his being. Unspeakably dreadful things are named now. There is nothing to add. How can such a message give us cause to rejoice? "Tormented with fire and brimstone in the presence of the holy angels, and in the presence of the Lamb." In their torment, they shall have to see Christ, whom they drove away. "The smoke of their torment goes up forever and ever," "no rest day and night." Presented with such words, let us indeed not grow loud; rather, let us reflect silently, saying: God, have mercy upon us sinners and grant your salvation to us all; to you alone belongs the glory. You alone are righteous, you have provided us with peace in the face of our enemies. Yes, you alone are our comfort and our joy!

No, in the face of God's terrible judgment on the world, let us not break out into the howling of a sectarian crusade, but rather ask: God, give your saints patience despite all our impatience: give your congregation obedience to your commandment of love—despite all our disobedience; give faith in Jesus—despite all our unbelief. And then, when you come and approach us, demanding that we stand before you; then say to us too: "Here is the patience of the saints; here are they that keep the commandments of God, and faith in Jesus"—God, it is all your grace.

Will we comprehend now, that in light of this judgment of God, in light of this temptation to fall into hatred and impatience and unbelief—that today it is a blessing to die, to be taken away? For who among us knows whether he will endure to the end? Who knows how he will stand in the hour of the last trial? Therefore: "Blessed are the dead which die in the Lord from henceforth." Blessed are the dead—we must understand this—not from weariness, not from listlessness, but from the fear of not keeping faith, and with the joy of having kept faith—blessed are the dead "from henceforth"—starting from such times when the power of Babylon and the beast grow to be immense. But not all the dead are blessed; rather those "which die in the Lord," those who learned how to die in time, who kept faith, who clung to Jesus up to the last hour, whether amidst the sufferings of the first martyrs, or in the martyrdom of a silent loneliness. The promise of death's blessedness, which is the resurrection, is solely for the congregation of Jesus Christ. It belongs to this congregation, and whoever else lays claim to it stands in God's way. "Blessed are the dead which die *in the Lord.*" To die in Christ—that this be granted us, that our last hour not be a weak hour, that we die as confessors of Christ, whether old or young, whether quickly or after long suffering, whether seized and laid hold of by the lord of Babylon or quietly and gently—that is our prayer today, that our last word might only be: Christ.

"Yes, says the Spirit, that they may rest from their labors; and their works do follow them." And then there shall be rest from our labors, that is, from the strain and the sin and the temptations that we stand under today; there shall be no more fear of growing weak, no fear of sin and of the force of Babylon; then there shall be rest, because we shall see and recognize Christ as the Lord. "And their works do follow them"—they do not pave the way for us to Christ, for faith does that— but they follow, the works that are done in God, in Christ, for which he prepared us from the very beginning of the world; we don't recognize them here; they are hidden; they are the works about which the left hand knows not what the right hand does. But they shall be with us, because they belong to us as the everlasting gift of God.

With your gospel, Lord, teach your congregation to die. Give us strength to endure until you call. We want to behold your eternal gospel! Amen. Amen. [*GS*, V, pp. 569–76]

41

The Legacy of Another Era

(Funeral service for Frau Julie Bonhoeffer,
cemetery chapel, Berlin-Halensee)

January 15, 1936

TEXT: Ps. 90

We stand today with great thankfulness at the grave of our dear departed grandmother. God's hand has favored us by letting her remain among us until today. We cannot imagine our own lives without hers anymore. She belongs to us completely, and she will always belong to us completely. And God's hand favored her to the last as well. He didn't leave her by herself. He allowed her to see children, grandchildren, and great-grandchildren. In the midst of her last grave illness, he let her be happy and well for a few days, so that she could once more celebrate Christmas Eve with the whole big family, as in all the years before. To the last, she was able to share in all the personal and professional concerns of each one of us with great lucidity and love. She cared about all who were close to her, and had good and kind thoughts and wishes for each. God also gave her the ability to see the nature of her condition clearly, and he gave her the strength to be reconciled to it. And if we would be sorrowful today because she is no longer with us, yet we must never forget how thankful we have to be.

"Lord, thou hast been our dwelling place in all generations." In the course of a life as long as hers was, there are hours in which one especially has to learn that one needs a dwelling place, a refuge. She lost her father early in life; she had to give up two sons while they were still children; three grandsons fell in war; in old age it became more silent around her when grandfather died, when her brothers and sisters passed away, and finally, when just a few years before her death, our dear Uncle Otto, her eldest son, departed from us. God intervened visibly in her life many times; at those times, she had to learn again and again that which she had known since childhood: "Lord, thou hast been our dwelling place in all generations. Before the mountains were brought forth, or ever thou hadst formed the earth and world, from everlasting to everlasting thou art God." She held on to that even in her sickness. Resigning oneself to the will of God, bearing that which is imposed upon one; self-possessedly keeping in view what is given, what is real; doing what is necessary and required; coming to terms by oneself, silently and without complaint, when another cannot help; and preserving, in all of that, a great inner joyfulness and vigorous affirmation of life—that was how she conceived of her life and conducted it, that was how she died, and that was how we loved her.

"Thou turnest man back to the dust, and sayest, 'Turn back, O children of men!'" She was allowed to see this in three generations, and it was her greatest joy in life. She was always there for her children, grandchildren, and great-grandchildren; she had time, patience, and counsel, always and for everything. And although she entered wholly into the lives of each, still her judgment and counsel came always out of a broad perspective on whatever was at hand, out of an incomparable knowledge about all human affairs, and out of a great love. And while she saw the generations come and go, she prepared to go herself. One sensed that in all her experience and wisdom she was sustained by a humble recognition of the limits to all human knowledge, judgment, and life. "For a thousand years in thy sight are but as yesterday when it is past, or as a watch in the night."

"The years of our life are threescore and ten, or even by reason of strength fourscore; yet their span is but toil and trouble." She lived to be ninety-three years old, and imparted to us the legacy of another era. For us, a world comes to an end with her, a world which we all somehow bear and want to bear within us. Right that does not compromise, free speech of a free man, the binding character of a word once given, clarity and plainness of speech, integrity and simplicity in private and public life—to this she was devoted with her whole heart. It was her life. In her life, she came to know that it costs toil and trouble to accomplish these ideals in one's own life. She did not avoid this toil and trouble. She couldn't bear to see these ideals disregarded, to see a person's rights violated. That is why her last years were clouded by the great sorrow that she bore on account of the fate of the Jews in our nation. She bore and suffered their fate with them. She came from a different time, from a different spiritual world—and this world does *not* sink with her into the grave. This legacy, which we thank her for, bears with it an obligation.

And it is not only her life that is to become a lesson for us, but precisely her death as well. Lord, "teach us to number our days that we may get a heart of wisdom." Even a life so meaningful and aware is subject to the law of death, which oppresses all that is human. We must also go one day, together with all our ideals, goals, and work. To get a heart of wisdom; that means to be aware of one's boundary, one's end, but even more, to be aware of the other side of this boundary, to be aware of the God who is from all eternity, in whose hands we fall whether we want to or not, in whose hands she is now well cared for through all eternity. What more could we say about such a full and abundant life? We call on the God who is our dwelling place, with whom we can take refuge in all trouble and grief; Jesus Christ, in whom is all truth, all righteousness, all freedom, and all love. We call on the God who conquered all hate, all unkindness, and all anxiety with his invincible love on the cross of Jesus Christ. We ask that she might behold in eternity that which here remains veiled and hidden beneath sin and death, that in peace and clarity she might behold God's eternal face in Jesus Christ.

> Beginning and end, O Lord, they are thine.
> Life, the short space between, that was mine.
> And if I went astray and got lost in the night,
> Yet with you is all clear, Lord,
> And with your dwelling place Light.

And now, let us be sorrowful no more. She would not have wanted that. She never wanted to make anyone sad. We must go back to our work and our daily tasks. She knew it and meant it to be that way. She loved action and the daily task above all. Therefore, let us go forth strengthened from her grave. Strengthened by her image, by her life and death, but even more, by belief in the God who has been her dwelling place and ours in all generations, strengthened by Jesus Christ. "Let the favor of the Lord our God be upon us, and establish thou the work of our hands upon us, yea, the work of our hands establish thou it." Amen. [GS, IV, pp. 456–60]

42

Rejoice Always

(Marriage sermon for H. and A. Schönherr,
Falkensee Church)

April 15, 1936

TEXT: "Rejoice always, pray constantly, give thanks in all circumstances; for this is the will of God in Christ Jesus for you." (1 Thess. 5:16–18)

Let this be our prayer for you and for your desire to obediently say "yes" to this will.

You are about to set out on your own now. You know that these days everything continues to be uncertain, both tomorrow and in the future. However, it should and must be certain that in such a moment we know ourselves to be one with God's will for us. That is enough, and it helps us through all uncertainties.

You are here to make yourselves one with the will of God. You are about to say that you intend to live for and be faithful to one another until death parts you. Two people can lead their lives together only if their two wills become "one." But that isn't done by seeking either our own will or the other's will. The sole assurance that your wills shall become one will depends not on you, but on the will of God. The assurance for the stability of your marriage lies not with you, your love, or your intentions, but with Jesus Christ. Seek it there! There you can and should and will be one. And therefore, we must say on such days as this, when our thoughts revolve around personal matters: seek first the kingdom of God, and all these things shall be added unto you. Through him all the rest will also be given to you. Seek first the kingdom of God!

Thank God, that he does not conceal his will from us, but makes it known. He makes Jesus Christ's will for you known in the Word that you heard at the beginning: "Rejoice always. . . ."

You will rejoice in a joy that you make for and have in one another. There is nothing in life that can make your joy greater than to be together with someone you love, with whom you know yourself to be one. You rejoice, even when there are outward cares, because you have the other. But that doesn't mean: rejoice today, and tomorrow, and here and again rejoice; rather: rejoice *always*. In other words, not only when you are able to take joy in one another, but also when that is denied you, when outward difficulties oppress you and weigh on your mind.

How can that be said without exaggerating? It can only be said and done if one's reason for rejoicing is found in God, in his will. Rejoice always, for you were redeemed by God, freed from all cares and anxiety about the future, and freed from yourselves. You are redeemed, and therefore you rejoice always, for now you are with God always, and God is with you. Know that you are redeemed, and rejoice.

Albrecht, be a joyful minister! He who knows that he is one with Jesus Christ knows that he is redeemed; and he who, for that reason, also appears that way to others will be a great help to his congregation. People will come to him and lay their burdens on him for him to bear. Rejoice always in your duties.

And to you, dear Henriette, I say: always help your husband to rejoice. In this way you serve both your husband and the congregation. Help him to rejoice through your prayers and through your faithfulness. Help by so budgeting your work and your time that you are able to rejoice with him. Then the two of you will understand what Paul says: all is yours, and you are Christ's!

Such joyfulness comes only through prayer without ceasing. There can be no Christian household that does not pray without ceasing. You, Albrecht, have learned with much difficulty in recent years something of what this prayer without ceasing can mean, and you have discovered that it can help a great deal. In your future life you will discover it even more. And you, dear Henriette, remember that your husband is to hold this holy office, and that he can do that as he should only if you help him, and if you have respect for this office and for this prayer without ceasing.

Pray together every day for the stability and endurance of your marriage, and for the forgiveness of your sins. And in this prayer, forgive each other your sins every day. Your married life should always be accompanied by forgiveness; life should always be accompanied by forgiveness; pray together faithfully for that and pray for each other.

Beyond that, I would like to say especially to you, dear H.: there has been many a time in history when the wife, through intercession, has won people back to the gospel. And I would like to urge you very especially to intercede for your husband, for your family, for all who enter your house, and for all with whom you come into contact. And give thanks in all circumstances. You can pray as you should only if you give thanks in all circumstances, if you are able one day, at the hour of death, to say like Chrysostom: "Thank God for everything!" Do not give thanks only for your good fortune, but also for all that is puzzling in your lives, for sickness, suffering, and persecution for the gospel's sake. Give thanks in all circumstances! Give thanks today for all that you have received up to this hour. Give thanks that you have each other. And above all, give thanks that you will have the Word and the will of God until the end. Give thanks that one day, at the end of your lives, you will be able to say joyfully: Yes, thank God for everything!

And now, go forth as one in great joy and assurance, your eyes lifted up to the cross of Jesus Christ, praying joyfully without ceasing. Amen. [GS, IV, pp. 460–63]

43

Christ and the Congregation

(Sermon outline for the Reformation Festival, Finkenwalde)

1936

TEXT: Rev. 2:1–7

1. *Christ himself calls a congregation back to the right path that is Reformation.*
He holds the seven stars in his hand. That means, he rules the whole
church (stars—angels—overseers of the congregations: the number sev-
en means the entirety of the church). He moves among the seven lamp
stands. This means he is always near and present to his church. That is
why he knows the church and is able to call it back.

2. *Christ speaks kindly to his congregation.* I know your deeds, your hard
work and perseverance. He speaks to us as one who knows us. "I
know"—that is, nothing is lost or forgotten that has happened in his
congregation in visible work, in unrest and struggle, in constancy and
perseverance. Our work in our congregations is not esteemed by Christ
for nothing. He who has advanced the congregation a bit in some way
or other by tenacious work, to his Christ says: "I know it." Christ knows
the work of our confessing congregations. He walks among them. When
we do something for someone out of love, then this is our full reward,
when he says: "I know it." It was no empty, fruitless year "I know it."
Jesus speaks kindly to us. An inner danger came over the congregation;
evil broke out in the congregation. But the discipline and the spiritual
power of the congregation was strong enough that it could find no power over it but rather it was separated from it. That cost the congregation
much renunciation and self-denial. Christ says: "I know it;" it is not
forgotten. Worse yet, temptation and seduction did not stay away. Persons, who went by the name of Christ, persons on their own orders
wanted to lead the congregation on the wrong path. Much was broken
up there. There the congregation needed much prudence, prayer, and
understanding drawn from the word of God until they discovered them

as liars and separated themselves from them. All the inner distress, which arose there, all the trouble and struggle of the congregation, in as much as the truth carried the victory, is not forgotten. Christ says: "I know it." To all who had to hear the reproach that they had fought only for their own cause, out of their own obstinacy, and who finally did not know anymore where they stood, Christ says: "I know it." For my name's sake you labor. To all those who in the long nights worried about the need of the congregation and prayed, and who early in the morning again stood at their work, Christ says: "I know it." You did not become tired. "He gathers all my tears into one vessel" (Ps. 56:9). Christ speaks so kindly to us. He does not break or destroy us. He was everywhere himself where it concerned his congregation. He has seen us and speaks kindly to us. He walks in our midst.

3. *Christ accuses his congregation.* Now we have become thankful and trustful concerning our Lord. He is, however, not with us to praise us, but to bring us to the right path. It accords with the truth of Christ that he says to us that in spite of everything he must stand against us. Why? He knows that we were an undaunted, struggling, working, congregation bravely confessing in his name. That is no small thing.

"But I have something against you." Christ stands against his confessing congregation! "That you have abandoned your first love. Remember from what you have fallen." Remember the beginning, the first Christianity. Remember the Reformation. The first love is in danger of disappearing. Much has been done. But much is so harsh, so self-assured, as if defending oneself were the essential thing. So much has been said and done only for one's own cause, for the sake of one's own safety. The first love, the beginning, bound the congregation solely in burning devotion to Jesus and the community. No one wished to have anything for himself; everything belonged to the Lord and to the community. It was a rivalry in a fellowship of service. It was a love for the gospel, for the worship service, for the works of the kingdom of God. Today our love is attached to many other things: the world, security, habit. There was also a willing love for the enemy that could pray, bless, and do good. This first love the Lord had given to his first congregation. Has he also given it to us at one time? Confirmation? Conversion? The beginnings, or rather the beginning, which is Jesus Christ himself. Remember from what you have fallen! That is the ground of all reformation; not the glorification of men and past history, not Lutheran watchwords, but thankfully hearing the call of God to conversion. That is how the beginning was, but how different is the continuation. Do the first works. It is the same Lord, who just spoke to us so kindly and who now threatens us. He threatens to knock down the lampstand of our congregation if we do not repent and return. We should not celebrate Reformation but have a Reformation. On many of our pulpits these words are written: " . . . restored in the year, . . ." if that could only mean our congregation:

Restored in the year 1936 (verse 6 declares to the congregation that they have nevertheless hated the fanatical, lawless love, and in that they did well).

4. *Christ promises his congregation glory.* The goal is that the congregation may hear this promise. In order to achieve this goal, they must repent. Only in repentance can we hope. The path to conversion and hope goes through the ear. The hearing does it. The Word alone works conversion and hope. That was the proclamation of the Reformation. "Who has ears, let him hear. . . ." Therefore it is necessary to overcome that which as an illusion of the world stands against the Word. Each person must achieve this overcoming against himself, so that he is also able to overcome the enemy. In glory, however, the congregation will have what truly makes body, soul, and spirit. It will eat from the tree of life. The promise is paradise, in which we will not only hear, but recognize the glory of God with all our senses. We will be a church triumphant. [*GS*, IV, pp. 193–96]

44

Vengeance and Deliverance

(Finkenwalde)

July 11, 1937

TEXT: Ps. 58

Is this frightful psalm of vengeance our prayer? Are we actually allowed to pray in such a manner? At first the answer to this question is totally clear, "No, we are certainly not permitted to pray like that. Indeed, we have to shoulder much of the blame for the hostility we encounter and which gets us into trouble. We have to confess that it is God's righteous punishment which strikes and humbles us sinful men. Even in these times of the church's distress we are compelled to recognize that God himself in his anger has raised his hand against us to afflict us with our own sin, all our spiritual indolence, our open or inward disobedience, the profound lack of discipline in our everyday lives under his Word. Or would we want to deny that each personal sin even the most hidden, must bring down God's wrath on his church. How then are we supposed to call down God's revenge on our enemies without this revenge hitting us even harder since we are guilty ourselves and deserve God's wrath? We are not able to pray this psalm. Not because we would be too good for it (what a superficial thought, what inconceivable arrogance!), but because we are too sinful, too evil for it.

Only he who is totally without sin can pray like that. This psalm of vengeance is the prayer of the innocent: "For the director of music. To the tune of 'Do Not Destroy.' Of David. A refuge psalm." It is David who prays this psalm. David himself is not innocent. But it pleased God to prepare for himself in David the one who will be called the Son of David, Jesus Christ. The reason David must not lose his life is that the Christ is to come from him. David could never have prayed for himself against his enemies in order to preserve his own life. We know that David humbly endured all personal abuse. But Christ, and therefore the church of God, is in David. Thus his enemies are the enemies of Jesus

Christ and his holy church. For that reason David must not die in the presence of his enemies. For that reason the innocence of Christ himself is praying this psalm in David—and with Christ the universal holy church. No, we sinners are not praying this song of vengeance; innocence itself and no other is praying it. The innocence of Christ steps before the world and accuses it. We do not accuse it, Christ does.

When Christ takes action against sin, aren't we ourselves right in the midst of the accused as well?

"Do you indeed speak righteousness, O you judges, do you judge the children of men fairly?" It is an evil time when the world lets injustice happen silently, when the oppression of the poor and the wretched cries out to heaven in a loud voice and the judges and rulers of the earth keep silent about it, when the persecuted church calls to God for help in the hour of dire distress and exhorts people to do justice, and yet no mouth on earth is opened to bring justice. "Do you indeed speak righteousness, O you judges, do you judge the children of men? It is precisely the humankind on whom injustice is perpetuated. Must that always be forgotten in such times? Do you hear it? Children of humankind who are creatures of God like you, who feel pain and misery like you, you who do violence to them; who have their happiness and hopes like you; who feel their honor and their shame like you; your brothers and sisters! Are you mute?" Oh, no, they are not mute, their voice is heard on earth. But it is an unmerciful, a partisan word they speak. It judges not by what is right, but by a person's standing.

"No, at heart you work iniquity, you deal out the violence of your hands in the land." When the mouths of the world's rulers remain silent about injustice, their hands invariably commit acts of violence. This language of human hands where no justice exists is terrible. It is there that the distress and pain of the body originates. It is there that the persecuted, captive, beaten church longs for deliverance from this body. Let me fall into God's hands, but not into the hands of others! Do we still hear it? Christ is speaking here! He experienced the unrighteous judgment, he fell into the hands of men. Innocence is accusing the unrighteous world. However, only God's righteous wrath befall us sinners. But it can't be any other way.

It is not just a question here of particular transgressions which occur everywhere. No, here the secret of godlessness itself is unveiled. "The godless are perverse from the womb, they go astray from birth, speaking lies." Only perfect innocence looks into this abyss of evil. We would all too gladly like to believe at least something could be changed, improved here, and we try in innumerable ways to achieve something here or there. When serious wrong is done again and again, it makes us very uneasy, repeatedly dismays us, and fills us with indignation. Innocence alone knows that everything has to happen here just as it does happen. It knows of the dark mystery that Satan has already seized his own in their mothers' wombs and is now driving them frantically on. Now they have to do his work. The world continues to be the world; Satan continues to be Satan. At the same time, innocence gains complete peace of mind in this abyss of knowledge. It has to be so, and it does not change.

"Their poison is like a serpent's venom, like a deaf adder that stops its ear so that it does not hear the voice of the charmers charming ever so skillfully." The Orient is full of magicians who subdue snakes with their voices so that they have to obey. A deaf snake, however, doesn't hear this voice and goes after the charmer. The godless are like such deaf snakes. They are not able to hear the voice of the snake charmer even though he is able to charm snakes quite skillfully. God himself is the snake charmer who skillfully charms snakes. He charms and captivates our hearts with his Word of grace. He attracts us with the sweet words of his love. He persuades us and subdues our hearts so that we are compelled to listen to him as if spellbound and be obedient to him. Yet the great mystery remains—there are some who hear and some who have deaf ears and stop up their ears so that they are not able to hear. Indeed, we know of ourselves that there are times when our ears are deaf. Those are the times we harden our hearts against God's will in willful disobedience and heap sin upon sin until we are finally no longer able to hear. At this point Satan has taken possession of us. So Satan hardens the hearts of those who have to serve him in his struggle against God's kingdom and Word. They are no longer able to hear or obey. However, because their ears are deaf to the grace of God, their mouths are also mute to the righteousness of God. They are enemies of God and his church. David, Christ, and the church of God recognize them as such.

This realization leads us into prayer. When this is the enemy, then no human skill or ingenuity can help bring about peace. Then no human strength can help overcome these enemies. God's name must be called. And now those horrible prayer requests we dread begin in our psalm. When we read these words, we can only repeat them with trembling and deep inner resistance. God is called upon to take revenge on enemies. "O God, break the teeth in their mouths. Shatter the fangs of the young lions, O Lord!" Above all let us learn here that faced with the enemies of God and his church all we can do is pray. Our own courage—no matter how great it may be—all our bravery is bound to snap in the presence of this enemy. Here we are dealing with Satan's attack. Here the one who alone has power over Satan, God himself must take the matter into his own hands.

It would mean much if we would learn that we must earnestly pray to God in such distress and that whoever entrusts revenge to God dismisses any thought of ever taking revenge himself, or whoever desires to take revenge on his own does not yet know whom he is up against and still wants to take his cause into his own hands. But whoever leaves revenge in God's hands alone has become willing to suffer and bear it patiently—without vengeance, without a thought of one's own revenge, without hate, and without protest; such a person is meek, peaceable, and loves his enemies. God's cause has become more important to him than his own suffering. He knows God will win the victory in the end. "Vengeance is mine, says the Lord, I will retaliate" (Deut. 32:35)—and he will retaliate. But we are free from vengeance and retribution. Only those who are totally free of their own desire for revenge and free of hate and who are sure not to use their prayers to satisfy their own lust for revenge—only such persons can pray with a pure heart: "Shatter the fangs of the young lions, O Lord, break the teeth in their mouth." That means, "God, it is your cause about to suffer damage here, your honor is being violated. God, step in now and destroy your enemy, exercise your power, let your righteous anger be aroused." God does not let himself be mocked. He will sit in judgment on his enemies. And whether we are taken aback by the dreadful desire of the psalm or not, God's power will be even more dreadful for the person it strikes. And if we are frightened by human fists, how much more must we be frightened by God's fist crushing the godless for the sake of his kingdom, his name, his honor? The Lord of Creation is establishing his kingdom. Vengeance on his enemies is his.

Now David breaks out in immeasurable jubilation. He is fully certain that his prayer will be heard. In images following in rapid succession he already sees the downfall of the godless in the midst of strife, anguish, and suffering. "Let them melt away like water that runs continuously." They will meet their end quickly and suddenly. They will no longer be there just as water quickly runs off. "As he aims his arrows, let those be as split apart"—the deadly arrows are still whizzing by, but they can no longer do any damage, they are powerless. "Let them be like the snail that dissolves into slime." How full of contempt David speaks of his enemies here! God will crush the powerful and great people of this earth just as one crushes a snail underfoot. "Like an untimely birth that never sees the sun." They will be finished so quickly that they will remain in darkness and oblivion and no one will ever ask about them. "Sooner than your pots can feel the heat of thorns, whether green or ablaze, may he sweep them away!" God's wrath will not let his enemies plans mature. The godless are prematurely torn away—by force. They don't finish anything, that is God's revenge. It will come quickly, more quickly than we suspected.

"The righteous will rejoice when he sees such vengeance; he will bathe his feet in the blood of the wicked." Once again we shudder at this psalm. Isn't this ending really quite impossible for us to pray as Christians? Brothers and sisters, if we are still evasive there, we have understood nothing of it at all. Nothing less than God and his righteousness is at stake here. The godless must die so that God's justice may be triumphant. Human friendship and human sympathy are no longer at issue here. The only thing that matters is that God wins the victory in the end. Whoever recoils from this expression of joy at God's revenge and the blood of the godless still doesn't know what happened on the cross of Christ. God's righteous vengeance on the godless one has already come over us. The blood of the godless one has already flowed. God's death sentence on the wicked is pronounced. God's justice is fulfilled. That has taken place in the cross of Jesus Christ.

Jesus Christ died the death of the ungodly, struck down by God's wrath and vengeance. His blood is the blood God's justice demanded for the transgression of his commandments. God's vengeance has been carried out right here on earth, more terribly than the psalmist himself knows. Christ, the innocent one, died the death of a sinner so that we do not have to die. Now we stand as sinners at the foot of his cross and now a puzzle difficult to understand is solved: Jesus Christ, the innocent one, prays as God's vengeance on the godless is fulfilled, he prays as our psalm is fulfilled: "Father, forgive them for they know not what they do" (Luke 23:24). The one who bore the vengeance, he alone was allowed to ask for the forgiveness of the godless. He alone has set us free from God's wrath and revenge; he has brought forgiveness to his enemies and no one before him was allowed to pray like that. He alone is allowed to. If we look at him, the crucified one, we recognize God's true and living anger at us godless and at the same moment, our liberation from this anger, and we hear "Father, forgive them for they know not what they do."

"The righteous will rejoice when he sees such vengeance; he will bathe his feet in the blood of the wicked." Is not the true delight in God? Is not that the joy of the righteous at the triumph of God's justice on the cross, joy at Christ's victory? God's vengeance has died and the blood of the godless one in whom we bathe ourselves gives us a share in God's victory; the blood of the godless one has become our redemption, it cleanses us of all our sin. That is the miracle.

Thus the image of the bloodstained Savior emerges from the midst of this psalm, the Savior who died for the godless, struck down by God's revenge, for our salvation. No one is excluded here. Christ bore all of God's vengeance for everyone. God's wrath and vengeance will no longer strike anyone who comes to him, and stays on his side. They are under the protection of Christ's righteousness, whoever they may be. Yet whoever does not want to come, whoever does not want to prostrate himself at the foot of Christ's cross as a godless sinner, whoever defies the cross of Christ, God's wrathful judgment will come over him—God's vengeance as it came over Christ, however not for life, but for eternal death.

People will say, "Surely there is a reward for the righteous."—Not happiness or power or honor in this world is the fruit of the righteous. It is nothing other than the fellowship of Christ's cross, the redemption from God's wrath. "There is truly a God who judges on earth." Where is God's judgment on the godless of this world? Not invisible misfortune, failure, or disgrace in the eyes of this world, but solely in the cross of

Jesus Christ. Isn't that enough for us? Don't we see all the enemies of God already fallen and condemned in this cross? What is the good of all our anxiety which wants to see even more than this judgment of God? For that reason, when we begin to doubt God's justice on earth, let us look to the cross of Christ—here is judgment, here is free pardon.

Today the crucified One in this love is still concealing from us what we will see one day at the last judgment, the salvation of the just and the damnation of the godless. We couldn't bear it on this earth. But we may be certain that everything will serve to increase the joy of the righteous. On that day, the victory and triumph of Christ will be made known in salvation and judgment. Until that day, however, Satan will continue to incite the enemies of Christ and his church to commit acts of injustice and violence and tell lies. In the middle of this raging battle, Christ vicariously prays this psalm for us. He accuses the godless, he calls down God's vengeance and justice on them and gives himself up for the benefit of all the ungodly with his innocent suffering on the cross.

And now we pray this song with the psalmist, in humble gratitude that we have been granted deliverance from wrath through the cross of Christ. We pray in fervent supplication that God may bring all our enemies under the cross of Christ and grant them mercy. We pray with burning desire that the day may soon come when Christ will visibly triumph over all his enemies and establish his kingdom. We can learn to pray the psalm in this way. Amen. [GS, IV, pp. 413–22]

45

Christ's Love and Our Enemies

(Third Sunday after Epiphany,
at the secret seminary, Gross-Schlonwitz)

January 23, 1938

TEXT: "Repay no one evil for evil, but take thought for what is noble in the sight of all. If possible, so far as it depends upon you, live peaceably with all. Beloved, never avenge yourselves, but leave it to the wrath of God; for it is written, 'Vengeance is mine, I will repay, says the Lord.' No, 'if your enemy is hungry, feed him; if he is thirsty, give him drink; for by so doing you will heap burning coals upon his head.' Do not be overcome by evil, but overcome evil with good." (Rom. 12:17–21)

"I was met with mercy," we have just sung. And so sings the entire Christian community with every new day. "I was met with mercy"—when my heart was hardened against God, when I was following my own path of sin, when I loved my sin more than I loved God, when my sin had led me into sorrow and misery, when I had gone astray and couldn't find the way back—it was then that I was struck by God's Word, and I heard: God loves me. It was then that Jesus found me; he was with me— he, and he alone—he comforted me and forgave me all my sins, imputing none of my evil to me. "I was met with mercy."

At a time when I was God's enemy because of his commandments, He treated me like a friend. When I did him evil, God dealt me good. He did not hold me accountable for my evil, but sought me unceasingly and without bitterness. He suffered with me. He died for me; there was nothing he would not bear for me. It was then that he had overcome me. God had won over his enemy. The Father found his child again. Isn't that what we mean when we sing this song? True, I don't understand why God loves me, why I was dear to him; nor can I comprehend that he was willing to overcome my heart through his life; but now I can say, "I was met with mercy. . . ."

But precisely because I don't comprehend or understand anything, our text says, "Never be conceited." That is, in every other respect you may be very clever in your work, but there is one thing that by nature you can never know enough about, in one matter you are foolish and unwise like an immature child; namely in the divine matters of mercy; or rather, of how an enemy turns into a friend, of how an enemy of God is overcome.

Our text today speaks of the Christians' conduct toward their enemies, or of how Christians "overcome" their enemies. In the life of the individual and of a Christian congregation, this emerges time and again as a question of greatest importance; yet it is just here that we are so utterly foolish and, left to ourselves, have such completely wayward ideas that our text starts out by saying, "Never be conceited."

This serves first of all as a reminder of how incomprehensible God's way with us was to our wisdom. That God sought us, forgave us, sacrificed his son for our sakes, winning over our hearts from us in the process and making them his own; that is to be sure strange and inaccessible to our wisdom. This tells us: when you meet your enemy, remember first your own enmity to God and God's mercy to you.

"Never be conceited"—this serves secondly as a reminder of the beginning of the human race. The devil promised Adam and Eve wisdom. He would make them wise like God; they would know what good and evil were. Thereby, they would be made judges of good and evil. Ever since Adam let the devil give him wisdom, all people have believed that they understand divine matters and have something to say in them. They think that now they know how to get along with God and with people. With the help of their wisdom now, they would indubitably construct a good world. But what happened? The first person born on this earth to mankind murdered his brother. There the seed of evil sprouted. That was the fruit of the first humans' wisdom. Does that give us cause to think? "Never be conceited"—lest you become murderers of your brothers. Don't believe that you know on your own how to get along with people, or how to deal with enemies, or what good and evil are, lest mankind devour itself completely. "Never be conceited"—rather look to God's way with man, with his enemies, that way, which Scripture itself calls foolish, the way of God's love for his enemies, which he demonstrates to them by sending his Son all the way to the cross. The best wisdom is recognizing the cross of Jesus Christ as the insuperable love of God for all people, for us as well as for our enemies. Or are we of the opinion that God loves us more than he loves our enemies: Would we believe that we are God's favorite children? Were we to think that, we would show ourselves to be of like mind with the Pharisees, we would have stopped being Christians. Is God's love any less for our enemies, for whom he just as much came, suffered, and died, as he did for us? The cross is nobody's private property, but belongs to all; it is intended for all mankind. God loves our enemies—the cross tells us that. He suffers on their account, he feels anguish and sorrow because of them, he gave his beloved Son for them. That is the whole point every time we encounter an enemy, we remember at once: God loves him, God gave everything for him. Therefore, never be conceited. With respect to our attitude toward our enemies, this means first, remember that you were God's enemy and that, without having earned it or being worthy of it, you were met with mercy. It means second, remember that God hung on the cross for your enemy too, and love him as he loves you.

Therefore: "Repay no one evil for evil, but be careful to do what is right in the eyes of everybody. If it is possible, as far as it depends on you, live at peace with everyone." There is a neighbor or someone else who continually says evil things about us, who abuses us, who openly wrongs us, who torments and harasses us whenever he can. At the mere sight of him, the blood rushes to our heads, a terrible threatening anger. It is the enemy who provokes such a thing in us. But now we must be on guard. Now we must remember quickly: I was met with mercy, not by people, no, but by God himself, and Jesus Christ died for him, our enemy—and all at once everything is different. Now we hear: repay no one evil for evil. Do not lift up your hand to strike, do not open your mouth in anger, but be still. For what can the one who does you evil do to harm you? It is not you whom it harms, but it does harm him. No Christian is harmed by suffering injustice. But perpetuating injustice does harm. Indeed, the evil one wants to accomplish only one thing with you; namely, that you also become evil. But were that to happen, he would have won. Therefore, repay no one evil for evil. For in so doing, you harm not him, but yourself.

When evil befalls you, it is not you who are in danger, but the other who does you evil; and if you don't help him, he will perish in it. Therefore, for the other's sake, and because of your responsibility to him—repay no one evil for evil. For has God ever repaid you in such a way?

"Be careful to do what is right in the eyes of everybody . . . live at peace with everyone." In the eyes of everybody, with all people there are no exceptions. Do what is right not only to respectable citizens, but especially to the disrespectable ones as well; be at peace not only with those who are peaceable, but especially with those who do not wish to let us live in peace. Even the heathen can live at peace with those who are peaceable to them. But Jesus Christ died not for those who are respectable and peaceable, but for the sinners and enemies, for the disrespectable, for the haters and killers. Our hearts make sure that we only keep the company of friends, of the righteous and the respectable. But Jesus was to be found right in the midst of his enemies. That is precisely where he wanted to be. We should be there too. It is that which distinguishes us from all other teachings and religions. In them, the pious want to be with one another. But Christ wants us to be in the midst of our enemies, as he was; it was in the midst of his enemies that he died the death of God's love and prayed: Father, forgive them for they know not what they do. Christ wants to win his victory among his enemies. Therefore, do not withdraw, do not seclude yourselves, rather seek to do good unto all. Make peace, as far as it depends on you, with all.

"As far as it depends on you"—matters are not in your hand when others do not leave you in peace, when they abuse and persecute you. But "as far as it depends on you"; that is, you should never be the source of strife. Your heart should always be full of peace. Does that mean, that for the sake of beloved peace, even God's Word is to keep silent? Never—but is there a more peaceful word and work, after all, than the preaching of the peace which God has made with his world and his people? "As far as it depends on you"—the one thing you are not do do is to conceal God's Word. But it is up to you, in the midst of a torn, divided mankind, to say it in the cause of peace, in the cause of peace between God and mankind. Christ made peace with us while we were enemies. He made peace with all our enemies too, on the cross. Let us bear witness to this peace to all.

"Do not take revenge, my friend. . . ." Whoever takes vengeance into his own hands makes himself judge over the world and mankind, and the revenge he wanted to take will fall on his own head. Whoever works to take revenge takes his enemy's life in his own hands and forgets that God has already laid his hand on this person by dying for him on the cross. He who seeks vengeance on another person thwarts Christ's death, he sins against the blood of the reconciliation: Christ died for me and for my enemies to save us both. If I seek revenge, then I despise the other's salvation. It may not harm the other, but in that very desire, I renounce Christ's death.

Giving up our desire to take revenge is a hard sacrifice, perhaps the hardest, which Christ requires of us. For our whole human nature cries out for vengeance against our enemies. The desire for revenge is stronger in our human blood than any other desire. But—and we know it— we can no longer take revenge. If my enemy stands there before my eyes, and I am overcome by the obsession to finally be able to take revenge, then Jesus Christ stands at once behind my enemy and entreats me: do not lift up your hand, but leave vengeance to me; I will take it.

" . . . leave room for God's wrath"; for it is written: "It is mine to avenge; I will repay, says the Lord." A terrible word. Can we hear it and know what it means for God to take revenge, without at once imploring: "No, do not take revenge, I cannot and will not wish it even on my enemy, that he fall into the wrathful hands of God"? But God says, "It is mine to avenge, I will repay." God wants to and has to avenge the wicked, but—miracle of miracles—in an incomprehensible way God has already avenged, not us who were his enemies and still sin against him every day, not our enemies, but himself, his beloved Son. He visits all our sins on him and punishes them. It is Jesus whom he cast out into the hell of despair and godforsakenness; and in that same hour, Jesus prays: Father, forgive them. . . . That is God's vengeance, that he inflicts pain and suffering on himself while he spares and accepts us. That is God's vengeance, that he suffers agony himself and forgives his enemies. Does it not echo within me: Never be conceited? God's ways with you are too wonderful and lofty, too merciful and loving!

Are we still astonished to hear now, just after this word of God's wrath: "No, if your enemy is hungry, feed him; if he is thirsty; give him drink; for by so doing you will heap burning coals on his head"? God gave his life, his all, for the enemy; now you, too, give him what you have: bread if he is hungry, water if he is thirsty, aid if he is weak, blessing, compassion, and love for your enemy. Is he worth it? Who indeed could be more worth our love, who could stand in greater need of our love than he who hates? Who is poorer than he, who is more in need of help, who is more in need of love than your enemy? Have you ever looked upon your enemy as the one who, in effect stands destitute before you and, without being able to voice it himself, beseeches you: "Help me, give me the one thing that can still help me out of my hate; give me love, God's love, the love of the crucified Savior"? All the threatening and showing of fist is really the result of this poverty: it is essentially a begging for God's love, for peace, for brotherhood. When you reject your enemy, you turn the poorest of the poor from your door.

Burning coals. Coals burn and hurt when they touch us. Love, too, can burn and hurt. It teaches us to realize how destitute we are. It is the burning pain of repentance that makes itself felt in those who find, despite their hate and intimidation, only love, nothing but love. God taught us to experience this pain. When we felt it, the hour of repentance had arrived.

Now you stand at the goal: "Do not be overcome by evil, but overcome evil with good." That was Christ's way with us. He did not let our evil confuse or overcome him. He overcame our evil with good. Once again, how does this happen? Not by nourishing the other's evil with our own evil, the other's hate with our hate; it happens when evil runs into a void and finds nothing on which it can ignite. How do we overcome evil? By forgiving it without end. How is that done? By seeing our enemy as he really is, as the one for whom Christ died, whom Christ loves. How will the congregation gain victory over its enemies? By letting Christ's love be victorious over them. Amen. [GS, IV, pp. 427–34]

46

The Secret of Suffering

(Finkenwalde)

March 1938

TEXT: "Therefore, since we are justified by faith, we have peace with God through our Lord Jesus Christ. Through him we have attained access to this grace in which we stand, and we rejoice in our hope of sharing the glory of God. More than that, we rejoice in our sufferings, knowing that suffering produces perseverance, and perseverance produces character, and character produces hope, and hope does not disappoint us, because God's love has been poured into our hearts through the Holy Spirit which has been given to us." (Rom. 5:1–5)

"We have peace with God." So, our struggle with God is over now. Our obstinate hearts have yielded to God's will, and our own desires have subsided. It is God's victory, and our flesh and blood, which hate God, have been broken and must keep quiet. "Therefore being justified by faith, we have peace with God." God was right in the end. In the song we have just sung, we say, "You are just, come what may." God is just, whether or not we understand his ways; God is just, whether he corrects and chastises us or pardons us. God is just; we are the transgressors. We don't see it, but our faith must acknowledge: God alone is just. Whoever acknowledges by faith that God is right in judging him has come into the right position before God; he is well prepared to be able to stand in the presence of God; he has been justified by his faith in God's justice, he has found peace with God.

"We have peace with God through our Lord Jesus Christ." Now God's fight against us is also at an end. God hated that will that refused to submit itself to him. He called, admonished, entreated, and threatened, countless times, until his wrath over us knew no more patience. In that moment, he prepared to let loose a blow against us; he let us have it and hit the mark. He struck the only innocent person on earth. It was his beloved Son, our Lord Jesus Christ. Jesus Christ died for us on the cross, struck by God's wrath. God himself sent him for that purpose. When his Son submitted to his will and authority unto death, then God's wrath was satisfied. Wonderful mystery—God had made peace with us through Jesus Christ.

"We have peace with God." Beneath the cross is peace. Here is surrender to God's will; here is the end of our own will; here is rest and tranquility in God; here is peace of conscience in the forgiveness of all our sins. Here beneath the cross is the "access into the grace wherein we stand," the daily access to peace with God. Here is the way that is provided in the world to find peace with God. In Jesus Christ, God's wrath is satisfied, while we are overcome in God's will. That is why, for his congregation, Jesus' cross is an eternal foundation of joy and hope in the coming glory of God. "We rejoice in hope of the glory of God." Here at the cross, God's justice and victory have dawned on earth. Here he will become known to all the world one day. The peace that we receive here will become an eternal, glorious peace in the kingdom of God.

But while we would like most of all to stop here, filled with the greatest joy that human beings can be granted on this earth; filled, that is, filled with the knowledge of God in Jesus Christ, with the peace of God in the cross, Scripture will not yet let us go. "And not only so," it says now. It hasn't all been said yet, after all. But what more could remain to be said after the cross of Jesus Christ and the peace of God in Jesus Christ have been spoken of? Yes, dear friends, there is still a word to be said; namely a word about you, a word about your life beneath the cross, a word about how God is going to test your life in the peace of God, so that the peace of God will not be merely a word, but a reality. There is still a word to be said; that you will live a while longer on this earth, and about how you will preserve the peace of God.

Therefore our text tells us, "And not only so, but we glory in tribulations also." The test of whether we have truly found the peace of God will be in how we face the sufferings which befall us. There are many Christians who bend their knees before the cross of Jesus Christ well enough, but who do nothing but resist and struggle against every affliction in their own lives. They believe that they love Christ's cross, but they hate the cross in their own lives. In reality, therefore, they hate the cross of Jesus Christ as well; in reality, they are despisers of the cross, who for their part, seek to flee the cross by whatever means they can. Whoever knows that he regards suffering and trouble in his own life as something wholly hostile, wholly evil, can know by this that he has not yet found peace with God at all. Actually, he has only sought peace with the world, thinking perhaps that he could cope with himself and all his questions with the cross of Jesus Christ; in other words, that he could find an inner peace of mind. Thus, he needed the cross, but did not love it. He sought peace only for his own sake. When sufferings come, however, this peace quickly disappears. It was no peace with God because he hated the sufferings God sends.

Thus, whoever feels only hate for the sufferings, sacrifice, want, slander, and captivity in his life, however eloquently he may otherwise speak about the cross, he hates Jesus' cross and has no peace with God. But whoever loves the cross of Jesus Christ, whoever has found peace in him, he begins to love even the sufferings in his life, and in the end, he will be able to say with Scripture, "We also rejoice in our sufferings."

Our church has suffered many a tribulation in recent years. As of this hour: destruction of its order, the penetration of a false preaching, much hostility, evil words, and slander, imprisonment, and every kind of affliction, and no one knows what sufferings still await the church. But through all that, we have also realized that God himself intended thereby, and still intends, to put us to the test, that in all that has happened, only one question has been important, namely, do we have peace with God, or have we lived up to now in an entirely worldly peace?

How much grumbling and resisting, how much opposition to, and hatred of, our sufferings, has that revealed within us, and how much betrayal of our own principles, how much standing aside, how much fear, when Jesus' cross so much as begins to cast a tiny shadow on our own lives? How often have we thought that we could well preserve our peace with God, and yet avoid the suffering, the sacrifice, the hatred, the threats to our existence! Yes, worst of all, haven't we had to hear over and over again from Christian brothers and sisters that they despise their suffering?—and for the sole reason that their own consciences give them no peace of mind.

But God will take no one into his kingdom whose faith he has not proved as genuine in tribulation. "We *must* through much tribulation enter into the kingdom of God." Therefore, we should learn to grow fond of our sufferings before it is too late; yes, we should learn to rejoice and boast in them.

How is that to happen? "We know that suffering produces perseverance; perseverance, character; and character, hope. And hope does not disappoint us." In this way, we learn for the first time from God's word how we should look at and understand sufferings. The sufferings, which appear so hard and objectionable to us in our lives, are in reality full of the greatest treasures a Christian can find. They are like the shell in which a pearl rests. They are like a deep shaft, in which, the deeper one climbs down inside, the more things one finds: first ore, then silver, and finally gold. Suffering produces first perseverance, then character, then hope. Whoever avoids suffering rejects with it God's greatest gift for those who belong to him.

"Suffering produces perseverance." Perseverance, translated literally, means: remaining underneath, not throwing off the load, but bearing it. We know much too little in the church today about the peculiar blessing of bearing. Bearing, not shaking off; bearing, but not collapsing either; bearing as Christ bore the cross, remaining underneath, and there beneath it—to find Christ. If God imposes a load; then the one who perseveres bows his head and believes that it is good for him to be humbled—remain *underneath!* But *remaining* underneath. For remaining steadfast, remaining strong is meant here too; not weak acquiescence or surrender, no masochism, but growing stronger under the load, as under God's grace, imperturbably preserving the peace of God. God's peace is found with those who persevere.

"Perseverance produces character." A Christian life proves itself not in words, but character. No one is a Christian without character. Paul is talking here not about the experience of life, but about the experience of God. Nor is he talking about kinds of spiritual experiences, but rather about those experiences which arise in the trial of our faith and our peace with God, about the experience of Jesus' cross. Only those who persevere are experienced and produce character. Those who do not persevere experience nothing that will build character. To whomever God wants to grant such experience—to an individual or to a church— to them he sends much temptation, restlessness, and anxiety; they must cry out daily and hourly for the peace of God. The experience that is talked of here leads us into the depths of hell, to the jaws of death, and into the night of unbelief. But through all of that, God does not want to take his peace from us. Throughout, we experience God's power and victory, and the ultimate peace at Christ's cross more with each passing day.

Therefore, character produces hope. For every temptation overcome is already the prelude to the last conquest; every wave surmounted brings us closer to the longed-for land. This is why hope grows with character; and in the experience of suffering, the reflection of eternal glory can be sensed already.

"And hope does not disappoint us." Where there is still hope, there is no defeat; there may be every kind of weakness, much clamor and complaining, much anxious shouting; nevertheless, because hope is present, the victory has already been won. This is the secret of suffering in the church and in the Christian life; precisely that gate on which it is written: "Abandon all hope," that gate of sorrow, of loss, and of death is to become for us the gate of great hope in God, the gate of splendor and glory. "And hope does not disappoint us." Do we still have this great hope in God himself in our church and for our church? Then everything is won. Do we no longer have it? Then everything is lost. "Suffering produces perseverance; perseverance, character; and character, hope; and hope does not disappoint us"—but all that is only for him who has found and preserves the peace of God in Jesus Christ, and about whom it is written: because God has poured out his love into our hearts by the Holy Spirit, whom he has given us. He who is loved by God, and who therefore loves God alone and above all things, only he is allowed to speak in this way. No, the series of steps from perseverance to hope is no self-evident truth gained by worldly experience. Luther said that it might very well be put in an entirely different manner; namely: suffering produces a lack of perseverance; a lack of perseverance, impenitence; and impenitence despair; And despair utterly disappoints us. Indeed, so it must be, when the peace of God is lost to us, when we prefer an earthly peace with the world to peace with God, when we love the certainties of our life more than we love God. Then suffering must prove to be our ruin.

But the love of God is poured out into our hearts. To whomever God grants, through the Holy Spirit, that the incomprehensible take place within him; that is, that he begins to love God for God's sake, not for the sake of worldly goods and gifts, not even for the sake of peace, but really for God's sake and his sake alone; whoever has encountered the love of God in the cross of Jesus Christ, so that he begins to love God for Jesus Christ's sake, whoever is led by the Holy Spirit to desire nothing more than to share in God's love for eternity, but other than that to desire nothing, nothing at all—such a person speaks out of this love of God's, and with him, the whole congregation of Jesus Christ: We have peace with God. We rejoice in our sufferings. The love of God is poured out into our hearts. Amen. [GS, IV, pp. 434–41]

47

Faith and Daily Bread

(Confirmation sermon, Kieckow)

April 9, 1938

TEXT: "I believe, dear Lord: help my unbelief! (Mark 9:24)

Dear confirmands! That is a very prudent word. But it is good that we accustom ourselves from the start not to boast about our faith. Faith is not indicated by boasting. It is precisely because everything today depends on our *really* having faith that every desire for boasting fades away. Whether we believe or not will become apparent; it will become apparent daily, and declarations will be of no help at all. You all know how, in the passion story, Peter says to Jesus, "Even if I must die with you, I will not deny you!" And Jesus' answer: "Before the cock crows, you will deny me three times." And the story ends: "And Peter went out and wept bitterly." He had denied his Lord. Grand declarations, however sincere, however solemn, are closest to denial. May God keep you and all of us from that.

This confirmation day is an important day for you and for us all. It is no small matter, that you profess the Christian faith today before the all-knowing God and the ears of the Christian community. You should think back to this day with joy your lives long. But for just that reason, I exhort you today to full Christian sobriety. On this day, you should not and must not say or do anything on which you will have to look back later with nothing but bitterness and regret, because you said and vowed more in an hour of inner stirring than a human being ever can or dare say and vow. Your faith is still weak and untried and at its very beginning; therefore, when you make the confession of your faith in just a short while, don't rely on yourselves or on all your good intentions or on the strength of your belief; rather, rely solely on him whom you confess, on God the Father, on Jesus Christ, and on the Holy Spirit, and pray in your heart: I believe, dear Lord; help my unbelief! Who among us adults would not want and need to pray with you?

Confirmation is a solemn day. But you realize, don't you, that it is still easy to profess your faith here within the church, within the fellowship of Christians, of your parents and brothers and sisters and godparents, within the undisturbed celebration of a church service? And let us be thankful that God grants us these hours of collective confession of faith within the church. Yet all of this will not become fully earnest, fully real, until after your confirmation, when everyday life is there again, daily life with all its decisions. It is then that it will be revealed whether this day has been in earnest as well. You do not have your belief once and for all. Your belief, which you profess today with all your hearts, demands to be won anew tomorrow and the day after tomorrow: indeed, it demands to be won anew with every new day. God gives us always just precisely so much faith as we need for the present day. Faith is the daily bread which God gives us. You know the manna story: while the children of Israel were in the wilderness, they received it every day, but as soon as they tried to store it up for the next day, it spoiled. So it is with all God's gifts. So it is with faith too. Either we receive it anew everyday, or it decays. One day is long enough to keep faith. Every morning brings a new struggle to push through all the unbelief, through all the littleness of faith, through all the vagueness and confusion, through all the faintheartedness and uncertainty, to reach faith and wrest it from God. Every morning of your lives will begin with the same prayer: I believe, dear Lord: help my unbelief.

"I believe." When the Christian community recognizes you today as independent members of the church, it expects you to begin to understand that your belief must be your own, your very own decision. The "we believe" must now increasingly become "I believe."

Belief *is* a decision. We can't get away from the fact. "You cannot serve two masters"; from now on you serve God alone or you don't serve God at all. You have only *one* master now—that is the world's master, that is the world's redeemer, that is the world's re-creator. It is your highest honor to serve him. But with this "yes" to God belongs just as clear a "no." Your "yes" to God requires your "no" to all injustice, to all evil, to all lies, to all oppression and violation of the weak and poor, to all ungodliness, and to all mockery of what is holy. Your "yes" to God requires a courageous "no" to everything that tries to interfere with your serving God alone, even if that is your job, your possessions, your home, or your honor in the world. Belief means decision.

But *your* very own decision. No one can relieve you of it. It must arise out of solitude, out of your heart's aloneness with God; it will be born out of fierce struggles against the enemy in your own breast. You are still surrounded by a community, by families which support you, by parents who take care of you, by people who help you whenever they can; thank God for that! But more and more, God will lead you into solitude. He wants to prepare you for the great hours and decisions of your lives, in which no other person will be able to stand by you, in which only one thing will count: I believe, yes, I myself, I cannot do otherwise; dear God, help my unbelief.

Dear confirmands, the church expects of you, therefore, that you mature in handling God's Word and in prayer. Your present faith is a beginning, no conclusion. You must first enter into Scripture and into prayer, you all alone, and you must learn to fight with the weapon of God's Word wherever it is necessary. Christian fellowship is one of God's greatest gifts to us. But God *can* also take this gift away from us if he pleases, as he has already taken it away from many of our brothers today; then we stand and fall on our own belief. But even if we avoid it our whole lives long, each of us will find himself in the solitariness one day, at the hour of death and the last judgment. Then God will ask not, did your parents believe, but: Did *you* believe? God grant, that in that most solitary hour of our lives, we shall still be able to pray: I believe, dear Lord; help my unbelief. Then we will be blessed.

"I believe, *dear Lord.* . . ." In life, it is not always easy to say "dear Lord." But our faith must learn to say it. Who would not like sometimes to say: I believe, hard Lord, stern Lord, dreadful Lord. I submit myself to you, I want to be silent and to obey; but to learn to say "dear Lord," that is a new, hard struggle. And yet, until we have learned to speak this way, we haven't found God, the Father of Jesus Christ.

Your faith will be led into severe temptations. Even Jesus Christ was tempted, more so than any of us. Temptations to no longer obey God's commandments will approach you first. They shall assail you with great force. Beautiful and enticing, innocent and appearing as light, Satan, Lucifer the bearer of light, will come to you. He will obscure God's commandments and raise doubts about them in your mind. He will try to rob you of your joy in God's way. And if the evil one succeeds in so much as making us waver, then he will tear our entire belief from our hearts, crush it, and toss it away. Those will be rough hours in your lives, in which you will be on the verge of wearying of God's Word, in which everything revolts, and no prayer will cross your lips and your heart won't hear anymore. All this must come to pass, as sure as your faith is alive. It must all come to pass, so that your belief is tested and fortified, so that you become equal to ever greater challenges and struggles. God works on us through temptations. God will never play games with you, depend on that; rather, our Father wants to secure his children's hearts. That is why it all happens to you. And when temptation is ever so confusing, when our resistance already threatens to break down completely, yes, and even when defeat is already there, then with the last vestige of our faith, we may and ought to cry: I believe, dear Lord; help my unbelief. Dear Lord—it is our Father who tests and strengthens us in this way. Dear Lord—it is Jesus Christ who suffered all temptations as we do, only without sin, that he may be an example and a help for us. Dear Lord—it is the Holy Spirit who intends to sanctify us in the struggle.

Your faith shall be tried by sorrow. You don't know much about that yet. But God sends his children sorrow just when they need it most, when they have become far too confident on this earth. Then a great hurt comes into our lives, a hard sacrifice, a great loss, sickness, or death. Our unbelief rears up. Why does God demand this of me? Why did God allow it? Why; yes, why? That is unbelief's greatest question; it tries to choke our belief. No one is spared this anguish. It is all so puzzling, so mysterious. In this hour of godforsakenness, we may and ought to say: I believe, *dear* Lord; help my unbelief. Yes, dear Lord, even in darkness, even in doubt, even in godforsakenness. After all, dear Lord, you are my dear Father, who makes all things work together for my good. Dear Lord Jesus Christ, you yourself cried out: My God, why have you forsaken me? You wanted to be where I am. Now you are with me. Now I know that, even in my hour of need, you do not forsake me. I believe, dear Lord; help my unbelief. [*GS*, IV, pp. 441–47]

48

Christus Victor

(Communion Address on Memorial Day at the secret seminary, Wendisch-Tychow—Sigurdshof)

November 26, 1939

TEXT: "Death is swallowed up in victory. O death where is thy sting? O grave, where is thy victory?" (1 Cor. 15:54–55)

"When death and life did battle, that was a singular strife. But death was overcome, and the victory won by life."

You are invited to a victory celebration, to the celebration of the greatest victory that has been won in the world, to the celebration of Jesus' victory over death. Bread and wine, body and blood of our Lord Jesus Christ, are the signs of victory; for in them, Jesus is present and alive today, the same man who was crucified on the cross and laid in the grave almost two thousand years ago. Jesus arose from the dead; he forced open the tombstone; Jesus remained the victor. You, however, are to receive the signs of his victory today. And when you receive the blessed bread and cup in just a short while, then you are to know at the same time, as assuredly as I eat this bread and drink this wine, Jesus Christ has remained victor over death, he is the living Lord who meets us.

In our lives we don't speak readily of victory. It is too big a word for us. We have suffered too many defeats in our lives; victory has been thwarted again and again by too many weak hours, too many gross sins. But isn't it true that the spirit within us yearns for this word, for the final victory over the sin and anxious fear of death in our lives? And now God's Word also says nothing to us about our victory; it doesn't promise us that *we* will be victorious over sin and death from now on; rather, it says with all its might that someone has won this victory, and that this person, if we have him as Lord, will also win the victory over us. It is not we who are victorious, but Jesus.

We proclaim that today and believe it despite all that we see around us, despite the graves of our loved ones, despite the moribund nature outside, despite the death that the war brings upon us again. We see the supremacy of death; yet we proclaim and believe the victory of Jesus Christ over death. Death is swallowed up in victory. Jesus is the victor, the resurrection of the dead, and the everlasting life.

That which Holy Scripture sings here is like an exultant, mocking song about death and sin: O death, where is thy sting? O grave, where is thy victory? We see death and sin puff themselves up and strike fear into the human heart as if they were still lords of the world. But that is mere show. They lost their power long ago. Jesus took it from them. Besides, no one who is with Jesus need fear these sinister lords any longer. The sting of death, which death uses to hurt us—that is sin— has no more power. Hell can do no more against us, who are with Jesus. They are powerless; they still rage, like a mean dog on a chain, but they can do nothing against us, for Jesus holds them fast. He remains the victor.

But if that is the case, we ask ourselves, then why does it seem so entirely different in our lives; why do we see so little of this victory? Why do sin and death rule over us so terribly? Indeed, this question is the very question God addresses to you: All that I have done for you, and you live as if nothing had happened! You submit to sin and the fear of death as if they could still enslave you! Why is there so little victory in your lives? Because you won't believe that Jesus is victor over death and sin, victor over your life. It is your unbelief that leads to your defeats. But now Jesus' victory is proclaimed to you once again today, at the Holy Communion; it is victory over sin and death for you, too, whoever you may be. Take hold of it in belief; today Jesus will once again forgive you all your serious and multiple sins, he will make you wholly pure and innocent, and from now on, you won't have to sin any more; sin won't have to rule over you anymore. Jesus will rule over you, and he is stronger than every temptation. In the hour of your temptation, and in your fear of death, Jesus will conquer you, and you will acknowledge: Jesus has become victor over my sin, over my death. As often as you give up this belief you will flounder and be defeated, sin and die; as often as you lay hold of this belief Jesus will have the victory.

On Memorial Day, we are asked at the graves of our loved ones: How do you intend to die one day? Do we believe in the power of death and sin, or do we believe in the power of Jesus Christ? Of the two there can be only one. In the last century, there was a man of God who had preached often in the course of his life about the victory of Jesus Christ, and who had done wonderful things. As he lay on his deathbed, as he lay in great torment and agony, his son bent down to his ear and cried out to the dying man: Father, victory is won. When dark hours come, and when the darkest hour comes upon us, then let us hear the voice of Jesus Christ, which cries in our ears: victory is won. Death is swallowed up in victory. Be comforted. And God grant that we may be able to say then: I believe in the forgiveness of sins, the resurrection of the body, and the life everlasting. In this belief, let us live and die. To that end, we take the Holy Communion. Amen. [*GS*, IV, pp. 453–55]

Part 5

BONHOEFFER
ON FOLLOWING CHRIST

-Arrival in Stockholm, 1936
From: Eberhard Bethge *Dietrich Bonhoeffer* (New York: Harper & Row, 1970), p. 393.

Introduction: The Costly Grace of Christian Discipleship

As we encounter two of Bonhoeffer's best known writings, *The Cost of Disciple-ship* and *Life Together,* it is clear that much here emanates from his own life story. This is true especially as Bonhoeffer recognized in his university career the self-seeking individual who had until early in the 1930s managed to avoid the sharp challenge of Christ's Sermon on the Mount. He felt compelled to leave the universi-ty and become wholeheartedly dedicated to the church and, through the church, to the concerns of peace and social justice. He was also moved to enter into fierce debate with that church whenever he detected in it the profiteering hucksterism for souls and political opportunism that fed on "the carcass of cheap grace," killing "the life of following Christ."[1]

There is much in these twin books, too, that depicts the spiritual foundations of the seminary community in Finkenwalde. Here we discover Bonhoeffer's primary model for church community over against both the triumphalist church of privilege and the church compromised by its uncritical allegiance to Hitler. Finkenwalde was not to be a monastic community turned in on itself, though Bonhoeffer had to face the carping criticism that such was the case. One answer to that charge appears in a letter to his brother, Karl-Friedrich, in which Bonhoeffer spoke of a church resto-ration that depended "on a new kind of monasticism, having nothing in common with the old, but a life of uncompromising adherence to the Sermon on the Mount in imitation of Christ."[2]

49

The Cost of Discipleship

(Nachfolge)

Advent 1937

In the very opening pages of what has become a genuine classic in Christian spirituality, *The Cost of Discipleship,* we read the answer to Bonhoeffer's personal problem, disturbed as he was by his own self-seeking careerism at the university and the "soft" Christianity he could easily have slipped into within a comfortable church ministry. The question was a troubling intruder into his budding success story: What was he as a Christian to do about the "impossible" demands of Christ's Sermon on the Mount? His answer, like so many of the striking challenges of this book, became a call to a simple, unflinching obedience. "In the last report," he wrote in his foreword, "what we want to know is not, what would this or that man, or this or that church, have of us, but what Jesus Christ himself wants of us."[3]

Though this book was put into its final form in 1935 and 1936, and was published in 1937, the formulations that still excite readers' imaginations were first spoken as early as 1932 in Bonhoeffer's seminars, sermons, and study groups. Bonhoeffer's biographer Eberhard Bethge calls *The Cost of Discipleship* "Finkenwalde's own badge of distinction."[4] Bonhoeffer was finally permitted in that seminary to give more concrete shape to the hold that the Sermon on the Mount had exerted in his own life. For the young seminarians, the thoughts Bonhoeffer shared with them on this theme led to that exhilarating experience of being drawn into a revolutionary movement. At stake were Christianity in Germany and, indeed, Christian faith itself.

The German title of this work (*Nachfolge*) states in one word not only what Bonhoeffer perceived to be the vocation of a Christian minister but also what happened to him at a crucial turning point in his spiritual life. Discipleship! Bonhoeffer had himself become a Christian, a disciple of Christ, not after the model of a knowledgeable academician or a satisfied churchgoer, but as one who had accepted for the first time the stark, unbending command of Christ in the Sermon on the Mount. This freed him to the point that he described the change in his life as "a great liberation."[5]

What that "change" entailed is clear from the text of *The Cost of Discipleship* itself and the uncompromising demands Bonhoeffer formulates in the name of his own experience of the effects of the Sermon on the Mount. In a letter to his agnostic brother, Karl-Friedrich, he remarked that he had "begun to take seriously the Sermon on the Mount. . . . There are things for which an uncompromising stand is worthwhile. And it seems to me that peace and social justice, or Christ himself, are such things."[6]

Those who have detected in Bonhoeffer's exposition of discipleship in this book only a detour away from the worldliness exalted in *Thy Kingdom Come* and earlier lectures, or a deviation from this path toward the euphoric affirmation of secularity in the prison letters, fail to appreciate Bonhoeffer's ever-shifting, dialectical critique of the world. In the mid-1930s, this world was the totalitarian regime of nazism and of a church subverted by the promise of a Nazi millennium and a fallout of ecclesiastical perquisites and privilege when not cowed by Gestapo terrorism and threats against one's economic base. Church leaders were eager to burn their incense at the Nazi altars of blood and battle. While one might have expected Lutheran Bonhoeffer to have brought Luther's insistence on grace and faith alone to bear on the church struggle with this paganism from within and without itself, or to use as weaponry against a new justification by Nazi works alone, Bonhoeffer offered instead the cadences of Christ's own unyielding word against the world. To many, this book seemed to put forth a "Catholic" emphasis on obedience. In reality, the book puts forth what Bonhoeffer himself had come to hear in the Sermon on the Mount: Christ's Word, commanding obedience.

For Bonhoeffer, this word meant abandoning his own careerism and embracing dedicated servanthood—even to the point of becoming a prophetic critic of his church. At a time when Christians needed "more than ever all the fellowship and brotherly help the church can give,"[7] Bonhoeffer encountered only self-serving accommodation to evil and, often, an open endorsement of Hitler's plans for a Nazi millennium. In a time that begged for a spirit of repentance, Bonhoeffer contended that Luther's inspiring theological legacy of reform had been distorted by the churches. As in the day of Christ, there were "bad shepherds" lording "it over the flock by force, forgetting their charges, and pursuing their own interests. Jesus is looking for good shepherds, and there are none to be found."[8]

In the context of such a dismal church, Bonhoeffer's book confronts individual Christian and Christian community alike with the crisis point of their faith: they are called to the same obedience that Christ's first followers heard. This is the "costly grace" of discipleship. "Only he who believes is obedient, and only he who is obedient believes."[9] The situation of Germany under the spell of nazism, Bonhoeffer claims, is identical to that faced by the first disciples asked to choose whether or not to follow Christ. The thorniest aspect of this choice, which is only partially resolved in the book, is how to be fully decisive in one's opposition to the Nazi inculturation of church and society and how, at the same time, to affirm a church presence in and Christ's lordship over the world.

To begin, Bonhoeffer points his readers to Christ's own invitation to follow though they do not know where such discipleship may lead. They can be sure only that following Christ is not the faithless pursuit of "cheap grace," that reduction of

Christianity to abstract doctrine, neatly formulated principles, and nonthreatening systems. Luther's dynamic teaching on justification by faith alone had thus been perverted to an undemanding churchiness resting on "the preaching of forgiveness without requiring repentance, baptism without church discipline, communion without confession, absolution without personal confession . . . grace without discipleship, grace without the cross, grace without Jesus Christ, living and incarnate."[10] The churches had, so it seemed to Bonhoeffer, bartered away "costly grace" for the "cheap grace" of salvation without the cross of Christ. This was the price exacted of them for molding a Christianity without risk in its decision not to oppose the blatant malevolence of state-sanctioned tyranny. The church had become respectably bourgeois, clinging to the assurance that sins were justified beforehand because covered by the "grace of God." In rejecting Christ's cross, Bonhoeffer observed, the Christian religion had become secularized "as never before." Jesus' call in the face of this secularization is specific: obey! The Christian is one who has promised to follow Christ even should this mean an inglorious martyrdom for refusing to worship the god of national socialism. "When Jesus calls a person, he bids him come and die."[11] This was not the time for church leaders to cunningly assess the advantages and disadvantages of resistance. For Bonhoeffer, the call was clear: self-sacrificing faith and wholehearted solidarity with one's neighbor, particularly those of one's community and those cast out by a heartless society.

This solidarity would lead, in turn, to the ultimate demand of faith.

Revival of church life always brings in its train a richer understanding of the Scriptures. Behind all the slogans and catchwords of ecclesiastical controversy, necessary though they are, there arises a more determined quest for him who is the sole object of it all, for Jesus Christ himself. What did Jesus mean to say to us? What is his will for us today? How can he help us to be good Christians in the modern world? In the last resort, what we want to know is not, what would this or that man, or this or that church, have of us, but what Jesus Christ himself wants of us. When we go to church and listen to the sermon, what we want to hear is his Word—and that not merely for selfish reasons, but for the sake of the many for whom the Church and her message are foreign. We have a strange feeling that if Jesus himself—Jesus alone with his Word—could come into our midst at sermon time, we should find quite a different set of people hearing the Word, and quite a different set rejecting it. That is not to deny that the Word of God is to be heard in the preaching which goes on in our church. The real trouble is that the pure word of Jesus has been overlaid with so much human ballast— burdensome rules and regulations, false hopes and consolations—that it has become extremely difficult to make a genuine decision for Christ. Of course it is our aim to preach Christ and Christ alone, but, when all is said and done, it is not the fault of our critics that they find our preaching so hard to understand, so overburdened with ideas and expressions which are hopelessly out of touch with the mental climate in which they live. It is just not true that every word of criticism directed against contemporary preaching is a deliberate rejection of Christ and proceeds from the spirit of antiChrist. So many people come to church with a genuine desire to hear what we have to say, yet they are always going back home with the uncomfortable feeling that we are making it too difficult for them to come to Jesus. Are we determined to have nothing to do with all these people? They are convinced that it is not the Word of Jesus himself that puts them off, but the superstructure of human, institutional, and doctrinal elements in our preaching. Of course we know all the answers to these objections, and those answers certainly make it easy for us to slide out of our responsibilities. But perhaps it would be just as well to ask ourselves whether we do not in fact often act as obstacles to Jesus and his Word. Is it not possible that we cling too closely to our own favorite presentation of the gospel, and to a type of preaching which was all very well in its own time and place and for the social setup for which it was originally intended? Is there not after all an element of truth in the contention that our preaching is too dogmatic, and hopelessly irrelevant to life? Are we not constantly harping on certain ideas at the expense of others which are just as important? Does not our preaching contain too much of our own opinions and convictions, and too little of Jesus Christ? Jesus invites all those that labor and are heavy laden, and nothing could be so contrary to our best intentions, and so fatal to our proclamation, as to drive people away from him by forcing upon them man-made dogmas. If we did so, we should make the love of Jesus Christ a laughingstock to Christians and pagans alike. It is no use taking refuge in abstract discussion, or trying to make excuses, so let us get back to the Scriptures, to the word and call of Jesus Christ himself. Let us try to get away from the poverty and pettiness of our own little convictions and problems, and seek the wealth and splendor which are vouchsafed to us in Jesus Christ. [CD, 37–38]

COSTLY GRACE

Cheap grace is the deadly enemy of our church. We are fighting today for costly grace.

Cheap grace means grace sold on the market like a cheapjack's wares. The sacraments, the forgiveness of sin, and the consolations of religion are thrown away at cut prices. Grace is represented as the church's inexhaustible treasury, from which she showers blessings with generous hands, without asking questions or fixing limits. Grace without price; grace without cost! The essence of grace, we suppose, is that the account has been paid in advance; and, because it has been paid, everything can be had for nothing. Since the cost was infinite, the possibilities of using and spending it are infinite. What would grace be if it were not cheap?

Cheap grace means grace as a doctrine, a principle, a system. It means forgiveness of sins proclaimed as a general truth, the love of God taught as the Christian "conception" of God. An intellectual assent to that idea is held to be of itself sufficient to secure remission of sins. The church which holds the correct doctrine of grace has, it is supposed, *ipso facto* a part in that grace. In such a church the world finds a cheap covering for its sins; no contrition is required, still less any real desire to be delivered from sin. Cheap grace therefore amounts to a denial of the living Word of God, in fact, a denial of the Incarnation of the Word of God.

Cheap grace means the justification of sin without the justification of the sinner. Grace alone does everything, they say, and so everything can remain as it was before. . . . Yet it is imperative for the Christian to achieve renunciation, to practice self-effacement, to distinguish his life from the life of the world. He must let grace be grace indeed, otherwise he will destroy the world's faith in the free gift of grace. Let the Christian rest content with his worldliness and with this renunciation of any higher standard than the world. He is doing it for the sake of the world rather than for the sake of grace. Let him be comforted and rest assured in his possession of this grace—for grace alone does everything. Instead of following Christ, let the Christian enjoy the consolations of his grace! That is what we mean by cheap grace, the grace which amounts to the justification of sin without the justification of the repentant sinner who departs from sin and from whom sin departs. Cheap grace is not the kind of forgiveness of sin which frees us from the toils of sin. Cheap grace is the grace we bestow on ourselves.

Cheap grace is the preaching of forgiveness without requiring repentance, baptism without church discipline, communion without confession, absolution without personal confession. Cheap grace is grace without discipleship, grace without the cross, grace without Jesus Christ, living and incarnate.

Costly grace is the gospel which must be *sought* again and again, the gift which must be *asked* for, the door at which a man must *knock*.

Such grace is *costly* because it calls us to follow, and it is *grace* because it calls us to follow *Jesus Christ*. It is costly because it costs a man his life, and it is grace because it gives a man the only true life. It is costly because it condemns sin, and grace because it justifies the sinner. Above all, it is *costly* because it cost God the life of his Son: "ye were bought at a price," and what has cost God much cannot be cheap for us. Above all, it is *grace* because God did not reckon his Son too dear a price to pay for our life, but delivered him up for us. Costly grace is the Incarnation of God.

Costly grace is the sanctuary of God; it has to be protected from the world, and not thrown to the dogs. It is therefore the living Word, the Word of God, which he speaks as it pleases him. Costly grace confronts us as a gracious call to follow Jesus, it comes as a word of forgiveness to the broken spirit and the contrite heart. Grace is costly because it compels a person to submit to the yoke of Christ and follow him; it is grace because Jesus says: "My yoke is easy and my burden is light. . . ."

It is a fatal misunderstanding of Luther's action to suppose that his rediscovery of the gospel of pure grace offered a general dispensation from obedience to the command of Jesus, or that it was the great discovery of the Reformation that God's forgiving grace automatically confers upon the world both righteousness and holiness. On the contrary, for Luther the Christian's worldly calling is sanctified only in so far as that calling registers the final, radical protest against the world. Only in so far as the Christian's secular calling is exercised in the following of Jesus does it receive from the gospel new sanction and justification. It was not the justification of sin, but the justification of the sinner that drove Luther from the cloister back into the world. The grace he had received was costly grace. It was grace, for it was like water on parched ground, comfort in tribulation, freedom from the bondage of a self-chosen way, and forgiveness of all his sins. And it was costly, for, so far from dispensing him from good works, it meant that he must take the call to discipleship more seriously then ever before. It was grace because it cost so much, and it cost so much because it was grace. That was the secret of the gospel of the Reformation—the justification of the sinner.

Yet the outcome of the Reformation was the victory, not of Luther's perception of grace in all its purity and costliness, but of the vigilant religious instinct of man for the place where grace is to be obtained at the cheapest price. All that was needed was a subtle and almost imperceptible change of emphasis, and the damage was done. Luther had taught that man cannot stand before God, however religious his works and ways may be, because at bottom he is always seeking his own interests. In the depth of his misery, Luther had grasped by faith the free and unconditional forgiveness of all his sins. That experience taught him that this grace had cost him his very life, and must continue to cost him the same price day by day. So far from dispensing him from discipleship, this grace only made him a more earnest disciple. When he spoke of grace, Luther always implied as a corollary that it cost him his own life, the life which was now for the first time subjected to the absolute obedience of Christ. Only so could he speak of grace. Luther had said that grace alone can save; his followers took up his doctrine and repeated it word for word. But they left out its invariable corollary, the obligation of discipleship. There was no need for Luther always to mention that corollary explicitly for he always spoke as one who had been led by grace to the strictest following of Christ. Judged by the standard of Luther's doctrine, that of his follower was unassailable, and yet their orthodoxy spelt the end and destruction of the Reformation as the revelation on earth of the costly grace of God. The justification of the sinner in the world degenerates into the justification of sin and the world. Costly grace was turned into cheap grace without discipleship. . . .

We have gathered like ravens* round the carcass of cheap grace, and there we have drunk of the poison which has killed the life of following Christ. It is true, of course, that we have paid the doctrine of pure grace divine honors unparalleled in Christendom; in fact we have exalted that doctrine to the position of God himself. Everywhere Luther's formula has been repeated, but its truth is perverted into self-deception. So long as our Church holds the correct doctrine of justification, there is no doubt whatever that she is a justified Church! So they said, thinking that we must vindicate our Lutheran heritage by making this grace available on the cheapest and easiest terms. To be "Lutheran" must mean that we leave the following of Christ to legalists, Calvinists, and enthusiasts—and all this for the sake of grace. We justified the world, and condemned as heretics those who tried to follow Christ. The result was that a nation became Christian and Lutheran, but at the cost of true discipleship. The price it was called upon to pay was all too cheap. Cheap grace had won the day.

But do we also realize that this cheap grace has turned back upon us like a boomerang? The price we are having to pay today in the shape of the collapse of the organized church is only the inevitable consequence of our policy of making grace available to all at too low a cost. We gave away the word and sacraments wholesale, we baptized, confirmed, and absolved a whole nation unasked and without condition. Our humanitarian sentiment made us give that which was holy to the scornful and unbelieving. We poured forth unending streams of grace. But the call to follow Jesus in the narrow way was hardly ever heard. Where were those truths which impelled the early church to institute the catechumenate, which enabled a strict watch to be kept over the frontier between the church and the world, and afforded adequate protection for costly grace? What had happened to all those warnings of Luther's against preaching the gospel in such a manner as to make people rest secure in their ungodly living? Was there ever a more terrible or disastrous instance of the Christianizing of the world than this? What are those three thousand Saxons put to death by Charlemagne compared with the millions of spiritual corpses in our country today? With us it has been abundantly proved that the sins of the fathers are visited upon the children unto the third and fourth generations. Cheap grace has turned out to be utterly merciless to our Evangelical Church. ... [CD, pp. 45–58]

THE CALL TO DISCIPLESHIP

The idea of a situation in which faith is possible is only a way of stating the facts of a case in which the following two propositions hold

---

*Translation altered. The original German has *die Raben,* which should be translated as "ravens," not "eagles."

good and are equally true: *only he who believes is obedient, and only he who is obedient believes.*

It is quite unbiblical to hold the first proposition without the second. We think we understand when we hear that obedience is possible only where there is faith. Does not obedience follow faith as good fruit grows on a good tree? First, faith, then obedience. If by that we mean that it is faith which justifies, and not the act of obedience, all well and good, for that is the essential and unexceptionable presupposition of all that follows. If however we make a chronological distinction between faith and obedience, and make obedience subsequent to faith, we are divorcing the one from the other—and then we get the practical question, when must obedience begin? Obedience remains separated from faith. From the point of view of justification it is necessary thus to separate them, but we must never lose sight of their essential unity. For faith is only real when there is obedience, never without it, and faith only becomes faith in the act of obedience.

Since, then, we cannot adequately speak of obedience as the consequence of faith, and since we must never forget the indissoluble unity of the two, we must place the one proposition that only he who believes is obedient alongside the other, that only he who is obedient believes. In the one case faith is the condition of obedience, and in other obedience the condition of faith. In exactly the same way in which obedience is called the consequence of faith, it must also be called the presupposition of faith.

Only the obedient believe. If we are to believe, we must obey a concrete command. Without this preliminary step of obedience, our faith will only be pious humbug, and lead us to the grace which is not costly. Everything depends on the first step. It has a unique quality of its own. The first step of obedience makes Peter leave his nets, and later get out of the ship; it calls upon the young man to leave his riches. Only this new existence, created through obedience, can make faith possible. . . . [*CD*, pp. 69–70]

SINGLE-MINDED OBEDIENCE

The actual call of Jesus and the response of single-minded obedience have an irrevocable significance. By means of them Jesus calls people into an actual situation where faith is possible. For that reason his call is an actual call and he wishes it so to be understood, because he knows that it is only through actual obedience that a man can become liberated to believe.

The elimination of single-minded obedience on principle is but another instance of the perversion of the costly grace of the call of Jesus onto the cheap grace of self-justification. By this means a false law is set up which deafens people to the concrete call of Christ. This false law is the law of the world, of which the law of grace is at once the complement and the antithesis. The "world" here is not the world overcome in Christ, and daily to be overcome anew in fellowship with him, but the world hardened into a rigid, impenetrable, legalistic principle. When that happens grace has ceased to be the gift of the living God, in which we are rescued from the world and put under the obedience of Christ; it is rather a general law, a divine principle, which only needs to be applied to particular cases. Struggling against the legalism of simple obedience, we end by setting up the most dangerous law of all, the law of the world and the law of grace. In our effort to combat legalism we land ourselves in the worst kind of legalism. The only way of overcoming this legalism is by real obedience to Christ when he calls us to follow him; for in Jesus the law is at once fulfilled and cancelled . . . [CD, pp. 91–92]

DISCIPLESHIP AND THE CROSS

. . . Jesus is a rejected Messiah. His rejection robs the passion of its halo of glory. It must be a passion without honor. Suffering and rejection sum up the whole cross of Jesus. To die on the cross means to die despised and rejected of men. Suffering and rejection are laid upon Jesus as a divine necessity, and every attempt to prevent it is the work of the devil, especially when it comes from his own disciples; for it is in fact an attempt to prevent Christ from being Christ. It is Peter, the rock of the church, who commits that sin, immediately after he has confessed Jesus as the Messiah and has been appointed to the primacy. That shows how the very notion of a suffering Messiah was a scandal to the church, even in its earliest days. That is not the kind of Lord it wants, and as the church of Christ it does not like to have the law of suffering imposed upon it by its Lord. Peter's protest displays his own unwillingness to suffer, and that means that Satan has gained entry into the church, and is trying to tear it away from the cross of its Lord.

Jesus must therefore make it clear beyond all doubt that the "must" of suffering applies to his disciples no less than to himself. Just as Christ is Christ only in virtue of his suffering and rejection, so the disciple is a disciple only insofar as he shares his Lord's suffering and rejection and crucifixion. Discipleship means adherence to the person of Jesus, and therefore submission to the law of Christ which is the law of the cross.

Surprisingly enough, when Jesus begins to unfold this inescapable truth to his disciples, he once more sets them free to choose or reject him. "If any man would come after me," he says. For it is not a matter of course, not even among the disciples. Nobody can be forced, nobody can even be expected to come. He says rather "*If* any man" is prepared to spurn all other offers which come his way in order to follow him. Once again, everything is left for the individual to decide. When the disciples are halfway along the road of discipleship, they come to another crossroads. Once more they are left free to choose for themselves, nothing is expected of them, nothing forced upon them. So crucial is the demand of the present hour that the disciples must be left free to make their own choice before they are told of the law of discipleship.

"If any man would come after me, let him deny himself." The disciple must say to himself the same words Peter said of Christ when he denied him: "I know not this man." Self-denial is never just a series of isolated acts of mortification or asceticism. It is not suicide, for there is an element of self-will even in that. To deny oneself is to be aware only of Christ and no more of self, to see only him who goes before and no more the road which is too hard for us. Once more, all that self-denial can say is: "He leads the way, keep close to him."

" . . . and take up his cross." Jesus has graciously prepared the way for this word by speaking first of self-denial. Only when we have become completely oblivious of self are we ready to bear the cross for his sake. If in the end we know only him, if we have ceased to notice the pain of our own cross, we are indeed looking only unto him. If Jesus had not so graciously prepared us for this word, we should have found it unbearable. But by preparing us for it he has enabled us to receive even a word as hard as this as a word of grace. It comes to us in the joy of discipleship and confirms us in it.

To endure the cross is not a tragedy; it is the suffering which is the fruit of an exclusive allegiance to Jesus Christ. When it comes, it is not an accident, but a necessity. It is not the sort of suffering which is inseparable from this mortal life, but the suffering which is an essential part of the specifically Christian life. It is not suffering *per se* but suffering-and-rejection, and not rejection for any cause or conviction of our own, but rejection for the sake of Christ. If our Christianity has ceased to be serious about discipleship, if we have watered down the gospel into emotional uplift which makes no costly demands and which fails to distinguish between natural and Christian existence, then we cannot help regarding the cross as an ordinary everyday calamity, as one of the trials and tribulations of life. We have then forgotten that the cross means rejection and shame as well as suffering. The psalmist was lamenting that he was despised and rejected of men, and that is an essential quality of the suffering of the cross. But this notion has ceased to be intelligible to a Christianity which can no longer see any difference between an ordinary human life and a life committed to Christ. The cross means sharing the suffering of Christ to the last and to the fullest. Only a man thus totally committed in discipleship can experience the meaning of the cross. The cross is there, right from the beginning, he has only got to pick it up; there is no need for him to go out and look for a cross for himself, no need for him deliberately to run after suffering. Jesus says that every Christian has his own cross waiting for him, a cross destined and appointed by God. Each must endure his allotted share of suffering and rejection. But each has a different share: some God deems worthy of the highest form of suffering, and gives them the grace of martyrdom, while others he does not allow to be tempted above that they are able to bear. But it is the one and the same cross in every case.

The cross is laid on every Christian. The first Christ-suffering which every man must experience is the call to abandon the attachments of this world. It is that dying of the old man which is the result of his encounter with Christ. As we embark upon discipleship we surrender ourselves to Christ in union with his death—we give over our lives to death. Thus it begins; the cross is not the terrible end to an otherwise God-fearing and happy life, but it meets us at the beginning of our communion with Christ. When Christ calls a man, he bids him come and die. It may be a death like that of the first disciples who had to leave home and work to follow him, or it may be a death like Luther's, who had to leave the monastery and go out into the world. But it is the same death every time—death in Jesus Christ, the death of the old man at his call. Jesus' summons to the rich young man was calling him to die, because only the man who is dead to his own will can follow Christ. In fact every command of Jesus is a call to die, with all our affections and lusts. But we do not want to die, and therefore Jesus Christ and his call are necessarily our death as well as our life. The call to discipleship, the baptism in the name of Jesus Christ means both death and life. The call of Christ, his baptism, sets the Christian in the middle of the daily arena against sin and the devil. Every day he encounters new temptations, and every day he must suffer anew for Jesus Christ's sake. The wounds and scars he receives in the fray are living tokens of this participation in the cross of his Lord. But there is another kind of suffering and shame which the Christian is not spared. While it is true that only the sufferings of Christ are a means of atonement, yet since he has suffered for and borne the sins of the whole world and shares with his disciples the fruits of his passion, the Christian also has to undergo temptation; he too has to bear the sins of others; he too must bear their shame and be driven like a scapegoat from the gate of the city. But he would certainly break down under this burden, but for the support of him who bore the sins of all. The passion of Christ strengthens him to overcome the sins of others by forgiving them. He becomes the bearer of other men's burdens—"Bear ye one another's burdens, and so fulfill the law of Christ" (Gal. 6:2). As Christ bears our burdens, so ought we to bear the burdens of our fellow men. The law of Christ, which it is our duty to fulfill, is the bearing of the cross. My brother's burden which I must bear is not only his outward lot, his natural characteristics and gifts, but quite literally his sin. And the only way to bear that sin is by forgiving it in the power of the cross of Christ in which I now share. Thus the call to follow Christ always means a call to share the work of forgiving men their sins. Forgiveness is the Christ-like suffering which it is the Christian's duty to bear.

But how is the disciple to know what kind of cross is meant for him? He will find out as soon as he begins to follow his Lord and to share his life.

Suffering, then, is the badge of true discipleship. The disciple is not above his master. Following Christ means *passio passiva*, suffering because we have to suffer. That is why Luther reckoned suffering among the marks of the true church, and one of the memoranda drawn up in preparation for the Augsburg Confession similarly defines the church as the community of those "who are persecuted and martyred for the gospel's sake." If we refuse to take up our cross and submit to suffering and rejection at the hands of men, we forfeit our fellowship with Christ and have ceased to follow him. But if we lose our lives in his service and carry our cross, we shall find our lives again in the fellowship of the cross with Christ. The opposite of discipleship is to be ashamed of Christ and his cross and all the offense which the cross brings in its train.

Discipleship means allegiance to the suffering Christ, and it is therefore not at all surprising that Christians should be called upon to suffer. In fact it is a joy and a token of his grace. The acts of the early Christian martyrs are full of evidence which shows how Christ transfigures for his own the hour of their mortal agony by granting them the unspeakable assurance of his presence. In the hour of the cruelest torture they bear for his sake, they are made partakers in the perfect joy and bliss of fellowship with him. To bear the cross proves to be the only way of triumphing over suffering. This is true for all who follow Christ, because it was true for him. . . .

Suffering means being cut off from God. Therefore those who live in communion with him cannot really suffer. This Old Testament doctrine was expressly reaffirmed by Jesus. That is why he takes upon himself the suffering of the whole world, and in doing so proves victorious over it. He bears the whole burden of man's separation from God, and in the very act of drinking the cup he causes it to pass over him. He sets out to overcome the suffering of the world, and so he must drink it to the dregs. Hence while it is still true that suffering means being cut off from God, yet within the fellowship of Christ's suffering, suffering is overcome by suffering, and becomes the way to communion with God.

Suffering has to be endured in order that it may pass away. Either the world must bear the whole burden and collapse beneath it, or it must fall on Christ to be overcome in him. He therefore suffers vicariously for the world. His is the only suffering which has redemptive efficacy. But the church knows that the world is still seeking for someone to bear its sufferings, and so, as it follows Christ, suffering becomes the church's lot too and bearing it, it is borne up by Christ. As it follows him beneath the cross, the church stands before God as the representative of the world.

For God is a God who *bears*. The Son of God bore our flesh, he bore the cross, he bore our sins, thus making atonement for us. In the same way his followers are also called upon to bear, and that is precisely what it means to be a Christian. Just as Christ maintained his communion with the Father by his endurance, so his followers are to maintain their communion with Christ by their endurance. We can of course shake off the burden which is laid upon us, but only find that we have a still heavier burden to carry—a yoke of our own choosing, the yoke of our self. But Jesus invites all who travail and are heavy laden to throw off their own yoke and take his yoke upon them—and his yoke is easy, and his burden is light. The yoke and the burden of Christ are his cross. To go one's way under the sign of the cross is not misery and desperation, but peace and refreshment for the soul, it is the highest joy. Then we do not walk under our self-made laws and burdens, but under the yoke of him who knows us and who walks under the yoke with us. Under his yoke we are certain of his nearness and communion. It is he whom the disciple finds as he lifts up his cross.

"Discipleship is not limited to what you can comprehend—it must transcend all comprehension. Plunge into the deep waters beyond your own comprehension, and I will help you to comprehend even as I do. Bewilderment is the true comprehension. Not to know where you are going is the true knowledge. My comprehension transcends yours. Thus Abraham went forth from his father and not knowing whither he went. He trusted himself to my knowledge, and cared not for his own, and thus he took the right road and came to his journey's end. Behold, that is the way of the cross. You cannot find it yourself, so you must let me lead you as though you were a blind man. Wherefore it is not you, no man, no living creature, but I myself, who instruct you by my word and Spirit in the way you should go. Not the work which you choose, not the suffering you devise, but the road which is clean contrary to all that you choose or contrive or desire—that is the road you must take. To that I call you and in that you must be my disciple. If you do that, there is the acceptable time and there your master is come" (Luther). [*CD*, pp. 96–103]

REVENGE: "NONRESISTANCE" TO EVIL*

Text: "You have heard that it was said 'An eye for an eye and a tooth for a tooth!' But I say to you, Do not resist one who is evil. But if any one strikes you on the right cheek, turn to him the other also; and if any one would sue you and take your coat, let him have your cloak as well; and if any one forces you to go one mile, go with him two miles. Give to him who begs from you, and do not refuse him who would borrow from you." (Matt. 5:38–42)

---

*In this segment of his book, Bonhoeffer insists that disciples of Jesus Christ must practice a radical pacifism that includes nonresistance to evil. He makes no distinction between nonviolence and nonresistance. He himself was actively engaged in acts of nonviolent resistance as this chapter was being composed. Here he states the ideal of Christian behavior. His joining the political conspiracy cannot be construed as a renunciation of this ideal. The conspiracy was for him a decision of last resort entered into with a sense of responsibility but with regret and with a longing to restore the ideal.

Jesus classes this saying about an eye for an eye and a tooth for a tooth with the commandments which he has already quoted from the Old Testament, for instance, the sixth commandment against murder. He recognizes this saying, like the sixth commandment, as the veritable law of God. This law, like all the others, is not to be abrogated, but fulfilled to the last iota. Jesus will not countenance the modern practice of putting the decalogue on a higher level than the rest of the Old Testament law. For him the law of the Old Testament is a unity, and he insists to his disciples that it must be fulfilled.

The followers of Jesus for his sake renounce every personal right. He calls them blessed because they are meek. If after giving up everything else for his sake they still wanted to cling to their own rights, they would then have ceased to follow him. This passage therefore is simply an elaboration of the beatitudes.

In the Old Testament personal rights are protected by a divinely established system of retribution. Every evil must be requited. The aim of retribution is to establish a proper community, to convict and overcome evil and eradicate it from the body politic of the people of God. That is the purpose of the law which is maintained by retribution.

Jesus takes up this declaration of the divine will and affirms the power of retribution to convict and overcome evil and to ensure the fellowship of the disciples as the true Israel. By exercising the right kind of retribution evil is to be overcome and thus the true disciple will prove himself.

The right way to requite evil, according to Jesus, is not to resist it.

This saying of Christ removes the church from the sphere of politics and law. The church is not to be a national community like the old Israel, but a community of believers without political or national ties. The old Israel had been both—the chosen people of God *and* a national community, and it was therefore his will that they should meet force with force. But with the church it is different: it has abandoned political and national status, and therefore it must patiently endure aggression. Otherwise evil will be heaped upon evil. Only thus can fellowship be established and maintained.

At this point it becomes evident that when a Christian meets with injustice, he no longer clings to his rights and defends them at all costs. He is absolutely free from possessions and bound to Christ alone. Again, his witness to this exclusive adherence to Jesus creates the only workable basis for fellowship, and leaves the aggressor for him to deal with.

The only way to overcome evil is to let it run itself to a standstill because it does not find the resistance it is looking for. Resistance merely creates further evil and adds fuel to the flames. But when evil meets no opposition and encounters no obstacle but only patient endurance, its sting is drawn, and at last it meets an opponent which is more than its match. Of course this can only happen when the last ounce of resistance is abandoned, and the renunciation of revenge is complete. Then evil cannot find its mark, it can breed no further evil, and is left barren.

By willing endurance we cause suffering to pass. Evil becomes a spent force when we put up no resistance. By refusing to pay back the enemy in his own coin, and by preferring to suffer without resistance, the Christian exhibits the sinfulness of contumely and insult. Violence stands condemned by its failure to evoke counterviolence. When a man unjustly demands that I should give him my coat, I offer him my cloak also, and so counter his demand; when he requires me to go the other mile, I go willingly, and show up his exploitation of my service for what it is. To leave everything behind at the call of Christ is to be content with him alone, and to follow only him. By his willingly renouncing self-defense, the Christian affirms his absolute adherence to Jesus, and his freedom from the tyranny of his own ego. The exclusiveness of this adherence is the only power which can overcome evil.

We are concerned not with evil in the abstract, but with the evil *person*. Jesus bluntly calls the evil person evil. If I am assailed, I am not to condone or justify aggression. Patient endurance of evil does not mean a recognition of its rights. That is sheer sentimentality, and Jesus will have nothing to do with it. The shameful assault, the deed of violence and the act of exploitation are still evil. The disciple must realize this, and bear witness to it as Jesus did, just because this is the only way evil can be met and overcome. The very fact that the evil which assaults him is unjustifiable makes it imperative that he should not resist it, but play it out and overcome it by patiently enduring the evil person. Suffering willingly endured is stronger than evil, it spells death to evil.

There is no deed on earth so outrageous as to justify a different attitude. The worse the evil, the readier must the Christian be to suffer; he must let the evil person fall into Jesus' hands.

The Reformers offered a decisively new interpretation of this passage, and contributed a new idea of paramount importance. They distinguished between personal sufferings and those incurred by Christians in the performance of duty as bearers of an office ordained by God, maintaining that the precept of nonviolence applies to the first but not to the second. In the second case we are not only freed from obligation to eschew violence, but if we want to act in a genuine spirit of love we must do the very opposite, and meet force with force in order to check the assault of evil. It was along these lines that the Reformers justified war and other legal sanctions against evil. But this distinction between person and office is wholly alien to the teaching of Jesus. He says nothing about that. He addresses his disciples as people who have left all to follow him, and the precept of nonviolence applies equally to private life and official duty. He is the Lord of all life, and demands undivided allegiance. Furthermore, when it comes to practice, this distinction raises insoluble difficulties. Am I ever acting only as a private person or only in an official capacity? If I am attacked am I not at once the father of my children, the pastor of my flock, and, e.g., a government official? Am I not bound for that very reason to defend myself against every attack, for reason of responsibility to my office? And am I not also always an individual, face to face with Jesus, even in the performance of my official duties? Am I not therefore obliged to resist every attack just because of my responsibility for my office? Is it right to forget that the follower of Jesus is always utterly alone, always the individual, who in the last resort can only decide and act for himself? Don't we act most responsibly on behalf of those entrusted to our care if we act in this aloneness?

How then can the precept of Jesus be justified in the light of experience? It is obvious that weakness and defenselessness only invite aggression. Is then the demand of Jesus nothing but an impracticable ideal? Does he refuse to face up to realities—or shall we say, to the sin of the world? There may of course be a legitimate place for such an ideal in the inner life of the Christian community, but in the outside world such an ideal appears to wear the blinkers of perfectionism, and to take no account of sin. Living as we do in a world of sin and evil, we can have no truck with anything as impracticable as that.

Jesus, however, tells us that it is just *because* we live in the world, and just *because* the world is evil, that the precept of nonresistance must be put into practice. Surely we do not wish to accuse Jesus of ignoring the reality and power of evil! Why, the whole of his life was one long conflict with the devil. He calls evil evil, and that is the very reason why he speaks to his followers in this way. How is that possible?

If we took the precept of nonresistance as an ethical blueprint for general application, we should indeed be indulging in idealistic dreams: we should be dreaming of a utopia with laws which the world would never obey. To make nonresistance a principle for secular life is to deny God, by undermining his gracious ordinance for the preservation of the world. But Jesus is no draftsman of political blueprints; he is the one who vanquished evil through suffering. It looked as though evil had triumphed on the cross, but the real victory belonged to Jesus. And the cross is the only justification for the precept of nonviolence, for it alone can kindle a faith in the victory over evil which will enable men to obey that precept. And only such obedience is blessed with the promise that we shall be partakers of Christ's victory as well as of his sufferings.

The passion of Christ is the victory of divine love over the powers of evil, and therefore it is the only supportable basis for Christian obedience. Once again, Jesus calls those who follow him to share his passion. How can we convince the world by our preaching of the passion when we shrink from that passion in our own lives? On the cross Jesus fulfilled the law he himself established and thus graciously keeps his disciples in the fellowship of his suffering. The cross is the only power in the world which proves that suffering love can avenge and vanquish evil. But it was just this participation in the cross which the disciples were granted when Jesus called them to him. They are called blessed because of their visible participation in his cross. [*CD*, pp. 156–61]

THE ENEMY: THE "EXTRAORDINARY" COMMAND TO LOVE

"Pray for those who hate and persecute you." This is the supreme demand. Through the medium of prayer we go to our enemy, stand by his side, and plead for him to God. Jesus does not promise that when we bless our enemies and do good to them they will not despitefully use and persecute us. They certainly will. But not even that can hurt or overcome us, so long as we pray for them. For if we pray for them, we are taking their distress and poverty, their guilt and perdition, upon ourselves, and pleading to God for them. We are doing vicariously for them what they cannot do for themselves. Every insult they utter only serves to bind us more closely to God and them. Their persecution of us only serves to bring them nearer to reconciliation with God and to further the triumphs of love.

How then does love conquer? By asking not how the enemy treats her but only how Jesus treated her. The love for our enemies takes us along the way of the cross and into fellowship with the crucified. The more we are driven along this road, the more certain is the victory of love over the enemy's hatred. For then it is not the disciple's own love, but the love of Jesus Christ alone, who for the sake of his enemies went to the cross and prayed for them as he hung there. In the face of the cross the disciples realized that they too were his enemies, and that he had overcome them by his love. It is this that opens the disciple's eyes, and enables him to see his enemy as a brother. He knows that he owes his very life to one who, though he was his enemy, treated him as a brother and accepted him, who made him his neighbor, and drew him into fellowship with himself. The disciple can now perceive that even his enemy is the object of God's love, and that he stands like himself beneath the cross of Christ. . . .

This commandment, that we should love our enemies and forgo revenge, will grow even more urgent in the holy struggle which lies before us and in which we partly have already been engaged for years. In it love and hate engage in mortal combat. It is the urgent duty of every Christian soul to prepare itself for it. The time is coming when the confession of the living God will incur not only the hatred and the fury of the world, for on the whole it has come to that already, but complete ostracism from "human society," as they call it. The Christians will be hounded from place to place, subjected to physical assault, maltreatment, and death of every kind. We are approaching an age of widespread persecution. Therein lies the true significance of all the movements and conflicts of our age. Our adversaries seek to root out the Christian Church and the Christian faith because they cannot live side by side with us, because they see in every word we utter and every deed we do, even when they are not specifically directed against them, a condemnation of their own words and deeds. They are not far wrong. They suspect too that we are indifferent to their condemnation. Indeed they must admit that it is utterly futile to condemn us. We do not reciprocate their hatred and contention, although they would like it better if we did, and so sink to their own level. And how is the battle to be fought? Soon the time will come when we shall pray, not as isolated individuals, but as a corporate body, a congregation, a church: we shall pray in multitudes (albeit in relatively small multitudes) and among the thousands and thousands of apostates we shall loudly praise and confess the Lord who was crucified and is risen and shall come again. And what prayer, what confession, what hymn of praise will it be? It will be the prayer of earnest love for these very sons of perdition who stand around and gaze at us with eyes aflame with hatred, and who have perhaps already raised their hands to kill us. It will be prayer for the peace of these erring, devastated, and bewildered souls, a prayer for the same love and peace which we ourselves enjoy, a prayer which will penetrate to the depths of their souls and rend their hearts more grievously than anything they can do to us. Yes, the church which is really waiting for its Lord, and which discerns the signs of the times of decision, must fling itself with its utmost power and with the panoply of its holy life into this prayer of love.

What is undivided love? Love which shows no special favor to those who love us in return. When we love those who love us, our brethren, our nation, our friends, yes, and even our own congregation, we are no better than the heathen and the publicans. Such love is ordinary and natural, and not distinctively Christian. We can love our kith and kin, our fellow countrymen and our friends, whether we are Christians or not, and there is no need for Jesus to teach us that. But he takes that kind of love for granted, and in contrast asserts that we must love our enemies. Thus he shows us what *he* means by love, and the attitude we must display toward it. . . . [*CD*, pp. 166–69]

THE IMAGE OF CHRIST

Now in Jesus Christ this is just what has happened. The image of God has entered our midst, in the form of our fallen life, in the likeness of sinful flesh. In the teaching and acts of Christ, in his life and death, the image of God is revealed. In him the divine image has been re-created on earth. The Incarnation, the words and acts of Jesus, his death on the cross, are all indispensable parts of that image. But it is not the same image as Adam bore in the primal glory of paradise. Rather, it is the image of one who enters a world of sin and death, who takes upon himself all the sorrows of humanity, who meekly bears God's wrath and judgment against sinners, and obeys his will with unswerving devotion in suffering and death, the man born to poverty, the friend of publicans and sinners, the man of sorrows, rejected of man and forsaken of God. Here is God made man, here is man in the new image of God.

We know full well that the marks of the passion, the wounds of the cross, are now become the marks of grace in the body of the risen and glorified Christ. We know that the image of the Crucified lives henceforth in the glory of the eternal High Priest, who ever maketh intercession for us in heaven. That body, in which Christ had lived in the form of a servant, rose on Easter Day as a new body, with heavenly form and radiance. But if we would have a share in that glory and radiance, we must first be conformed to the image of the Suffering Servant who was obedient to the death of the cross. If we would bear the image of his glory, we must first bear the image of his shame. There is no other way to recover the image we lost through the Fall.

To be conformed to the image of Christ is not an ideal to be striven after. It is not as though we had to imitate him as well as we could. We cannot transform ourselves into his image; it is rather the form of Christ which seeks to be formed in us (Gal. 4:19), and to be manifested in us. Christ's work in us is not finished until he has perfected his own form in us. We must be assimilated to the form of Christ in its entirety, the form of Christ incarnate, crucified and glorified.

Christ took upon himself this human form of ours. He became man even as we are men and women. In his humanity and his lowliness we recognize our own form. He has become like a man, so that people should be like him. And in the Incarnation the whole human race recovers the dignity of the image of God. Henceforce, any attack even on the least of people is an attack on Christ, who took the form of man, and in his own person restored the image of God in all that bears a human form. Through fellowship and communion with the incarnate Lord, we recover our humanity, and at the same time we are delivered from that individualism which is the consequence of sin, and retrieve our solidarity with the whole human race. By being partakers of Christ incarnate, we are partakers in the whole humanity which he bore. We now know that we have been taken up and borne in the humanity of Jesus, and therefore that new nature we now enjoy means that we too must bear the sins and sorrows of others. The incarnate Lord makes his followers the brothers and sisters of all humanity. The "philanthropy" of God (Titus 3:4) revealed in the Incarnation is the ground of Christian love toward all on earth that bear the name of human. The form of Christ incarnate makes the church into the body of Christ. All the sorrows of humanity fall upon that form, and only through that form can they be borne.

The earthly form of Christ is the form that died on the cross. The image of God is the image of Christ crucified. It is to this image that the life of the disciples must be conformed: in other words, they must be conformed to his death (Phil. 3:10; Rom. 6:4f.). The Christian life is a life of crucifixion (Gal. 2:19). [CD, pp. 340–42]

50

Life Together

(Gemeinsames Leben)

1939

The editors of the latest German edition of *Life Together* have remarked that we are indebted in a paradoxical way to the Gestapo for this book.[12] It was because the Gestapo had shut down the Preachers' Seminary at Finkenwalde that Dietrich Bonhoeffer was finally moved to compose his thoughts on the nature of Christian community based on the "life together" at the seminary and House of Brethren. Prior to this, except for a brief explanation of the daily meditation, he had been reluctant to publicize his "experiment in community," feeling that the time was not ripe. With the closing of the seminary and the dispersal of the seminarians, however, Bonhoeffer saw the need to record for posterity not only the daily regimen and its rationale, but also to voice his conviction that the church needs to promote a sense of community like this if it is to have new life breathed into it.

With this sense of urgency, Bonhoeffer completed *Life Together* in a single stretch of four weeks. The book was published in 1939 as volume 61 in the series of theological monographs *Theologische Existenz Heute (Theological Existence Today)*. Within one year it had been through a fourth printing. Kaiser Verlag published the fifth edition after World War II, in 1949. Its twenty-first printing in 1986 is a strong testimony to the enduring quality of what has become a genuine classic in contemporary literature.

This book became not only an exposition of the communal life at Bonhoeffer's seminary but also an apologetic for the effectiveness of this approach in achieving strength in Christian solidarity and freedom to become a vortex of service in a land of oppression. Their life together assumed the form of a structured daily prayer, meditation, mutual support, a common theological training, personal confession, and the renunciation of clerical privileges, freeing the "brethren" to accept emergency calls from the church. They were free to leave the community at any time. Criticism of the seminary was never completely silenced in a Protestant church not fully at home with what smacked of a return to monasticism or a withdrawal from the world, with its hints of justification by works and an unevangelical legalism.

But Bonhoeffer wanted to introduce something different, an experiment in brotherhood, called in his proposal to the Council of the Church of the Old Prussian Union an "Evangelical House of Brethren," in which otherwise isolated ministers could find sustenance and enrichment in community. Bonhoeffer likewise contented that the community would become a concrete experience of that discipleship enjoined on his followers in Christ's Sermon on the Mount. Their life together would only enhance their awareness of Christ's word and the church's mission. By renouncing clerical privileges, pastors would become better prepared to meet new demands on them in a country preparing for war and in a church divided by heresy. Bonhoeffer also envisioned that the community could become a refuge and center of renewal for the weary and spiritually drained.

The Gestapo action against the seminary in 1937 ended Bonhoeffer's attempt to form such a community of brethren within the Confessing Church. In retrospect, the community at Finkenwalde was the beginning of an answer to the question about the church's true nature in the crisis years. Bonhoeffer's intense desire was that the community of Finkenwalde not become a monastery secure in its own isolation but a community "at all times ready for the service of the church."[13] The publication of *Life Together* caused a stir in Protestant Germany because of its sensational newness. Though Bonhoeffer argued that the special character of the seminary derived from the difficult situation created by the church struggle, people were surprised by the openings for renewal advocated and described by him in the book. Daily meditation, and even auricular confession of one brother to another, seemed far from typical of the Protestant church in Germany and too much of a premature unveiling of that "discipline of the secret" Bonhoeffer would call for in the prison letters.[14] His seminarians were being asked to pray, study, and serve people both within and without the community. And this community would stand out for its renunciation of typical triumphalist church identity as well as the advantages avidly sought by so many clergy in the Nazi years. It was an alternative church for which most church leaders were unprepared. The selections that follow represent a cross section of what most distinguished that community of brethren and helped provide Bonhoeffer himself with the inner strength he would need in the lonely years of inner exile in the conspiracy and in prison.[15]

COMMUNITY

"Behold, how good and how pleasant it is for brothers and sisters to dwell together in unity!" (Ps. 133:1). In the following we shall consider a number of directions and precepts that the Scriptures provide us for our life together under the Word.

It is not simply to be taken for granted that the Christian has the privilege of living among other Christians. Jesus Christ lived in the midst of his enemies. At the end all his disciples deserted him. On the cross he was utterly alone, surrounded by evildoers and mockers. For this cause he had come, to bring peace to the enemies of God. So the Christian, too, belongs not in the seclusion of a cloistered life but in the thick of foes. There is his commission, his work. "The kingdom is to be in the midst of your enemies. And he who will not suffer this does not want to be of the kingdom of Christ; he wants to be among friends, to sit among roses and lilies, not with the bad people but the devout people. O you blasphemers and betrayers of Christ! If Christ had done what you are doing who would ever have been spared?" (Luther). . . . [LT, pp. 17–18]

So between the death of Christ and the last day it is only by a gracious anticipation of the last things that Christians are privileged to live in visible fellowship with other Christians. It is by the grace of God that a congregation is permitted to gather visibly in this world to share God's Word and sacrament. Not all Christians receive this blessing. The imprisoned, the sick, the scattered lonely, the proclaimers of the gospel in heathen lands stand alone. They know that visible fellowship is a blessing. They remember, as the psalmist did, how they went "with the multitude . . . to the house of God, with the voice of joy and praise, with a multitude that kept holyday" (Ps. 42:4). But they remain alone in far countries, a scattered seed according to God's will. Yet what is denied them as an actual experience they seize upon more fervently in faith. Thus the exiled disciple of the Lord, John the Apocalyptist, celebrates in the loneliness of Patmos the heavenly worship with his congregations "in the Spirit on the Lord's day" (Rev. 1:10). He sees the seven candlesticks, his congregations, the seven stars, the angels of the congregations, and in the midst and above it all the Son of man, Jesus Christ, in all the splendor of the resurrection. He strengthens and fortifies him by his Word. This is the heavenly fellowship, shared by the exile on the day of his Lord's resurrection.

The physical presence of other Christians is a source of incomparable joy and strength to the believer. Longingly, the imprisoned apostle Paul calls his "dearly beloved son in the faith," Timothy, to come to him in prison in the last days of his life; he would see him again and have him near. Paul has not forgotten the tears Timothy shed when last they parted (2 Tim. 1:4). Remembering the congregation in Thessalonica, Paul prays "night and day . . . exceedingly that we might see your face" (1 Thess. 3:10). The aged John knows that his joy will not be full until he can come to his own people and speak face to face instead of writing with ink (2 John 12).

The believer feels no shame, as though he or she were still living too much in the flesh, when he or she yearns for the physical presence of other Christians. The human being was created a body, the Son of God appeared on earth in the body, he was raised in the body, in the sacrament the believer receives the Lord Christ in the body, and the resurrection of the dead will bring about the perfected fellowship of God's spiritual-physical creatures. The believer therefore lauds the Creator, the Redeemer, God, Father, Son, and Holy Spirit, for the bodily presence of a brother and sister. The prisoner, the sick person, the Christian in exile, sees in the companionship of a fellow Christian a physical sign of the gracious presence of the triune God. Visitor and visited in loneliness recognize in each other the Christ who is present in the body; they receive and meet each other as one meets the Lord, in reverence, humility, and joy. They receive each other's benedictions as the benediction of the Lord Jesus Christ. But is there is so much blessing and joy even in a single encounter of brother with brother, how inexhaustible are the riches that open up for those who by God's will are privileged to live in the daily fellowship of life with other Christians!

It is true, of course, that what is an unspeakable gift of God for the lonely individual is easily disregarded and trodden under foot by those who have the gift every day. It is easily forgotten that the fellowship of Christian brothers and sisters is a gift of grace, a gift of the kingdom of God that any day may be taken from us, that the time that still separates us from utter loneliness may be brief indeed. Therefore, let them who until now have had the privilege of living a common Christian life with other Christians praise God's grace from the bottom of their hearts. Let them thank God on their knees and declare: It is grace, nothing but grace, that we are allowed to live in community with Christian brothers and sisters.

The measure with which God bestows the gift of visible community is varied. The Christian in exile is comforted by a brief visit of a Christian brother or sister, a prayer together and a brother's or sister's blessing; indeed, he or she is strengthened by a letter written by the hand of a Christian. The greetings in the letters written with Paul's own hand were doubtless tokens of such community. Others are given the gift of common worship on Sundays. Still others have the privilege of living a Christian life in the fellowship of their families. Seminarians before their ordination receive the gift of common life with their brothers and sisters for a definite period. Among earnest Christians in the church today there is a growing desire to meet together with other Christians in the rest periods of their work for common life under the Word. Communal life is again being recognized by Christians today as the grace that it is, as the extraordinary, the "roses and lilies" of the Christian life.

THROUGH AND IN JESUS CHRIST

Christianity means community through Jesus Christ and in Jesus Christ. No Christian community is more or less than this. Whether it be a brief, single encounter or the daily fellowship of years, Christian community is only this. We belong to one another only through and in Jesus Christ.

What does this mean? It means, first, that a Christian needs others because of Jesus Christ. It means, second, that a Christian comes to others only through Jesus Christ. It means, third, that in Jesus Christ we have been chosen from eternity, accepted in time, and united for eternity. . . . [*LT*, pp. 18–21]

Christ became the Mediator and made peace with God and among us. Without Christ we should not know God, we could not call upon him, nor come to him. But without Christ we also would not know our brothers or sisters, nor could we come to them. The way is blocked by our own ego. Christ opened up the way to God and to our brothers and sisters. Now Christians can live with one another in peace; they can love and serve one another; they can become one. But they can continue to do so only by way of Jesus Christ. Only in Jesus Christ are we one, only through him are we bound together. To eternity he remains the one Mediator. . . . [*LT*, pp. 23–24]

We belong to him because we are in him. That is why the Scriptures call us the body of Christ. But if, before we could know and wish it, we have been chosen and accepted with the whole church in Jesus Christ, then we also belong to him in eternity *with* one another. We who live here in fellowship with him will one day be with him in eternal fellowship. . . . Christian community means community through and in Jesus Christ. On this presupposition rests everything that the Scriptures provide in the way of directions and precepts for the communal life of Christians. . . . [*LT*, p. 24]

 . . . The more genuine and the deeper our community becomes, the more will everything else between us recede, the more clearly and purely will Jesus Christ and his work become the one and only thing that is vital between us. We have one another only through Christ, but through Christ we do have one another, wholly, and for all eternity. . . . [*LT*, p. 26]

NOT AN IDEAL BUT A DIVINE REALITY

Innumerable times a whole Christian community has broken down because it had sprung from wishful dreaming. . . . By sheer grace, God will not permit us to live even for a brief period in a dream world. He does not abandon us to those rapturous experiences and lofty moods that come over us like a dream. God is not a God of the emotions but the God of truth. Only that fellowship which faces such disillusionment, with all its unhappy and ugly aspects, begins to be what it should be in God's sight, begins to grasp in faith the promise that is given to it. The sooner this shock of disillusionment comes to an individual and to a community, the better for both. A community which cannot bear and cannot survive such a crisis, which insists upon keeping its illusion when it should be shattered, permanently loses in that moment the promise of Christian community. Sooner or later it will collapse. Every human wishful dream that is injected into the Christian community is a hindrance to genuine community and must be banished if genuine community is to survive. Those who love their dream of a community more than the Christian community itself become a destroyer of the latter, even though their personal intentions may be ever so honest and earnest and sacrificial. . . . [*LT,* pp. 26–27]

Because God has already laid the only foundation of our fellowship, because God has bound us together in one body with other Christians in Jesus Christ, long before we entered into common life with them, we enter into that common life not as demanders but as thankful recipients. We thank God for what he has done for us. We thank God for giving us those who live by his call, by his forgiveness, and his promise. We do not complain of what God does not give us; we rather thank God for what he does give us daily. And is not what has been given us enough: people who will go on living with us through sin and need under the blessing of his grace? . . . When the morning mists of dreams vanish, then dawns the bright day of Christian fellowship.

In the Christian community thankfulness is just what it is anywhere else in the Christian life. Only the one who gives thanks for little things receives the big things. We prevent God from giving us the great spiritual gifts he has in store for us, because we do not give thanks for daily gifts. We think we dare not be satisfied with the small measure of spiritual knowledge, experience, and love that has been given to us, and that we must constantly be looking forward eagerly for the highest good. Then we deplore the fact that we lack the deep certainty, the strong faith, and the rich experience that God has given to others, and we consider this lament to be pious. We pray for the big things and forget to give thanks for the ordinary, small (and yet really not small) gifts. How can God entrust great things to one who will not thankfully receive from him the little things? If we do not give thanks daily for the Christian fellowship in which we have been placed, even where there is no great experience, no discoverable riches, but much weakness, small faith, and difficulty; if on the contrary, we only keep complaining to God that everything is so paltry and petty, so far from what we expected, then we hinder God from letting our fellowship grow according to the measure and riches which are there for us all in Jesus Christ. . . . [*LT,* pp. 28–29]

Christian community is like the Christian's sanctification. It is a gift of God which we cannot claim. Only God knows the real state of our fellowship, of our sanctification. What may appear weak and trifling to us may be great and glorious to God. Just as Christians should not be constantly feeling their spiritual pulse, so, too, the Christian community has not been given to us by God for us to be constantly taking its temperature. The more thankfully we daily receive what is given to us, the more surely and steadily will fellowship increase and grow from day to day as God pleases.

Christian community is not an ideal which we must realize; it is rather a reality created by God in Christ in which we may participate. The more clearly we learn to recognize that the ground and strength and promise of all our fellowship is in Jesus Christ alone, the more serenely shall we think of our fellowship and pray and hope for it. [*LT*, p. 30]

A SPIRITUAL NOT A HUMAN REALITY

Because Christian community is founded solely on Jesus Christ, it is a spiritual and not a psychic reality. In this it differs absolutely from all other communities. . . . [*LT*, p. 31]

Right here is the point where spiritual love begins. This is why self-centered love becomes personal hatred when it encounters genuine spiritual love, which does not desire but serves. Self-centered love makes itself an end in itself. It creates of itself an end, an idol which it worships, to which it must subject everything. It nurses and cultivates an ideal, it loves itself, and nothing else in the world. Spiritual love, however, comes from Jesus Christ, it serves him alone; it knows that it has no immediate access to other persons.

Jesus Christ stands between the lover and the others he or she loves. I do not know in advance what love of others means on the basis of the general idea of love that grows out of my human desires—all this may rather be hatred and an insidious kind of selfishness in the eyes of Christ. What love is, only Christ tells in his Word. Contrary to all my own opinions and convictions, Jesus Christ will tell me what love toward my brother and sister really is. Therefore, spiritual love is bound solely to the Word of Jesus Christ. Where Christ bids me to maintain fellowship for the sake of love, I will maintain it. Where his truth enjoins me to dissolve a fellowship for my love's sake, there I will dissolve it, despite all the protests of my self-centered love. Because spiritual love does not desire but rather serves, it loves an enemy as a brother or sister. It originates neither in the brother or sister nor in the enemy but in Christ and his Word. Self-centered love can never understand spiritual love, for spiritual love is from above; it is something completely strange, new, and incomprehensible to all earthly love. . . . [*LT*, p. 35]

. . . Spiritual love proves itself in that everything it says and does commends Christ. It will not seek to move others by all too personal, direct influence, by impure interference in the life of another. It will not take pleasure in pious, human fervor and excitement. It will rather meet . . . other people with the clear Word of God and be ready to leave them alone with this Word for a long time, willing to release them again in order that Christ may deal with them. It will respect the line that has

been drawn between them and us by Christ, and it will find full fellowship with them in the Christ who alone binds us together.... [LT,
p. 36]

Life together under the Word will remain sound and healthy only
where it does not form itself into a movement, an order, a society, a
collegium pietatis, but rather where it understands itself as being a part
of the one, holy, catholic, Christian church, where it shares actively and
passively in the sufferings and struggles and promise of the whole
church. Every principle of selection and every separation connected with
it that is not necessitated quite objectively by common work, local conditions, or family connections is of the greatest danger to a Christian
community. When the way of intellectual or spiritual selection is taken
the human element always insinuates itself and robs the fellowship of
its spiritual power and effectiveness for the church, drives it into sectarianism. The exclusion of the weak and insignificant, the seemingly useless people, from a Christian community may actually mean the
exclusion of Christ; in the poor brother or sister, Christ is knocking at
the door. We must, therefore, be very careful at this point.... [LT, pp.
37–38]

There are probably no Christians to whom God has not given the
uplifting *experience* of genuine Christian community at least once in their
lives. But in this world such experiences can be no more than a gracious
extra beyond the daily bread of Christian community life. We have no
claim upon such experiences, and we do not live with other Christians
for the sake of acquiring them. It is not the experience of Christian
brotherhood and sisterhood, but solid and certain faith in community
that holds us together. That God has acted and wants to act upon us
all, this we see in faith as God's greatest gift, this makes us glad and
happy, but it also makes us ready to forgo all such experiences when
God at times does not grant them. We are bound together by faith, not
by experience.

"Behold, how good and how pleasant it is for brethren to dwell together in unity"—this the the Scripture's praise of life together under
the Word. But now we can rightly interpret the words "in unity" and
say, "for brethren to dwell together *through Christ*." For Jesus Christ
alone is our unity. "He is our peace." Through him alone do we have
access to one another, joy in one another, and fellowship in one another.
[LT, p. 39]

THE FELLOWSHIP OF THE TABLE

We have been following the course of Christian community's morning
worship. God's Word, the hymn of the church, and the prayer of the
fellowship stand at the threshold of the day. Not until the fellowship has

been nourished and strengthened with the bread of eternal life does it come together to receive from God earthly bread for this temporal life. Giving thanks and asking God's blessing, the Christian family receives its daily bread from the hand of the Lord. Ever since Jesus Christ sat at table with his disciples, the table fellowship of his community has been blessed by his presence. "And it came to pass, as he sat at meat with them, he took bread, and blessed it, and brake, and gave to them. And their eyes were opened, and they knew him" (Luke 24:30–31).

The Scriptures speak of three kinds of table fellowship that Jesus keeps with his own: daily fellowship at table, the table fellowship of the Lord's Supper, and the final table fellowship in the kingdom of God. But in all three the one thing that counts is that "their eyes were opened, and they knew him."

To know Jesus Christ in the presence of these gifts—what does this mean?

It means, first, to know him as the giver of all gifts, as the Lord and Creator of this our world, with the Father and the Holy Spirit. The table fellowship therefore prays, "And let *thy* gifts to us be blest," and thus acknowledges the eternal divinity of Jesus Christ.

Second, the fellowship acknowledges that all earthly gifts are given to it only for Christ's sake, as this whole world is sustained only for the sake of Jesus Christ, his Word, and his message. He is the true bread of life. He is not only the giver but the gift itself, for whose sake all earthly gifts exist. Only because the message concerning Jesus Christ must still go forth and find believers, and because our task is not yet perfected, does God in his patience continue to sustain us with his good gifts. So the Christian table fellowship prays, in Luther's words: "O Lord God, heavenly Father, bless unto us these thy gifts, which of thy tender kindness thou hast bestowed upon us, through *Jesus Christ our Lord.* Amen," thus confessing that Jesus Christ is the divine Mediator and Savior.

Third, the congregation of Jesus believes that its Lord wills to be present when it prays for his presence. So it prays: "Come, Lord Jesus, be our guest"—and thereby confesses the gracious omnipresence of Jesus Christ. Every mealtime fills Christians with gratitude for the living, present Lord and God, Jesus Christ. Not that they seek any morbid spiritualization of material gifts; on the contrary, Christians, in their wholehearted joy in the good gifts of this physical life, acknowledge their Lord as the true giver of all good gifts; and beyond this, as the true gift; the true bread of life itself; and finally, as the one who is calling them to the banquet of the kingdom of God. So in a singular way, the daily table fellowship binds the Christians to their Lord and one another. At table they know their Lord as the one who breaks bread for them; the eyes of their faith are opened.

The fellowship of the table has a festive quality. It is a constantly recurring reminder in the midst of our everyday work of God's resting after his work, of the Sabbath as the meaning and goal of the week and its toil. Our life is not only travail and labor, it is also refreshment and joy in the goodness of God. We labor, but God nourishes and sustains us. And this is reason for celebrating. People should not eat the bread of sorrows (Ps. 127:2); rather "eat thy bread with joy" (Eccles. 9:7). "I commended mirth, because a human being hath no better thing under the sun, than to eat, and to drink, and to be merry" (Eccles. 8:15); but, of course, "who can eat, or who can have enjoyment apart from him?" (Eccles. 2:25). It is said of the seventy elders of Israel who went up to Mount Sinai with Moses and Aaron that "they beheld God, and did eat and drink" (Ex. 24:11). God cannot endure that unfestive, mirthless attitude of ours in which we eat our bread in sorrow, with pretentious, busy haste, or even with shame. Through our daily meals he is calling us to rejoice, to keep holiday in the midst of our working day.

The table fellowship of Christians implies obligation. It is *our* daily bread that we eat, not my own. We share our bread. Thus we are firmly bound to one another not only in the Spirit but in our whole physical being. The *one* bread that is given to our fellowship links us together in a firm covenant. Now none dares go hungry as long as another has bread, and one who breaks this fellowship of the physical life also breaks the fellowship of the Spirit. "Deal thy bread to the hungry" (Isa. 58:7) . . . for the Lord is meeting us in the hungry (Matt. 25:37). "If a brother or sister be naked and destitute of daily food, and one of you say unto them, Depart in peace, be warmed and filled; notwithstanding you give them not those things which are needful to the body, what doth it profit?" (James 2:15–16). So long as we eat our bread together we shall have sufficient even with the least. Not until one person desires to keep . . . bread for himself or herself does hunger ensue. This is a strange divine law. May not the story of the miraculous feeding of the five thousand with two fishes and five loaves have, along with many others, this meaning also?

The fellowship of the table teaches Christians that here they still eat the perishable bread of the earthly pilgrimage. But if they share this bread with one another, they shall also one day receive the imperishable bread together in the Father's house. "Blessed is the one that shall eat bread in the kingdom of God" (Luke 14:15). . . . [*LT*, pp. 66–69]

EVENING PRAYER

. . . The labor of the day comes to its end. When the day has been hard and toilsome, the Christian will understand what Paul Gerhardt meant when he said.

> My head and hands and feet
> Their rest with gladness greet,
> And know their work is o'er;
> My heart, thou too shalt be

> From sinful works set free,
> Nor pine in weary sorrow more.

A day at a time is long enough to sustain one's faith; the next day will have its own cares.

Again the Christian family gathers together. The fellowship is united at the evening table and the last devotion. With the disciples in Emmaus they pray: "Abide with us: for it is toward evening, and the day is far spent" (Luke 24:29). It is an excellent thing if the evening devotion can be held at the actual end of the day, thus becoming the last word before the night's rest. When the night falls, the true light of God's Word shines brighter for the church. The prayer of the psalms, a hymn, and common prayer close the day, as they opened it.

We have yet to say a few words with regard to evening prayer. This is the appropriate place for common intercessions. After the day's work we pray to God for the blessing, peace, and safety of all Christendom; for our congregation; for the pastor in his ministry; for the poor, the wretched, and lonely; for the sick and dying; for our neighbors, for our own folks at home, and for our fellowship. When can we have any deeper sense of God's power and working than in the hour when our hands lay down their work and we commit ourselves to the hands of God? When are we more ready for the prayer of blessing, peace, and preservation than the time when our own activity ceases? When we grow weary, God does his work. "Behold, he that keepeth Israel shall neither slumber nor sleep" (Ps. 121:4).

Then, too, the evening prayer of the family fellowship should include particularly the petition of forgiveness for every wrong done to God and our brothers and sisters, for God's forgiveness and that of our brothers and sisters, and for readiness gladly to forgive any wrong done to us. It is an ancient monastic custom that by fixed order in the evening devotions the abbot begs the forgiveness of the brothers for all faults and defaults committed against them, and after the brothers assure him of their forgiveness they likewise beg the abbot's forgiveness of their faults and defaults and receive his forgiveness. "Let not the sun go down upon your wrath" (Eph. 4:26). It is a decisive rule of every Christian fellowship that every dissension that the day has brought must be healed in the evening. It is perilous for the Christian to lie down to sleep with an unreconciled heart. Therefore, it is well that there be a special place for the prayer of . . . forgiveness in every evening's devotion, that reconciliation be made and fellowship established anew. . . . [*LT*, pp. 73–74]

SOLITUDE AND SILENCE

Let those who cannot be alone beware of community. They will only do harm to themselves and to the community. Alone you stood before God when he called you; alone you had to answer that call; alone you had to struggle and pray; and alone you will die and give an account to God. You cannot escape from yourself; for God has singled you out. If you refuse to be alone you are rejecting Christ's call to you, and you can have no part in the community of those who are called. "The challenge of death comes to us all, and no one can die for another. All must fight their own battle with death by themselves alone. . . . I will not be with you then, nor you with me" (Luther).

But the reverse is also true: *Let those who are not in community beware of being alone.* Into the community you were called, the call was not meant for you alone; in the community of the called you bear your cross, you struggle, you pray. You are not alone, even in death, and on the last day you will be only one member of the great congregation of Jesus Christ. If you scorn the fellowship of the brothers and sisters, you reject the call of Jesus Christ, and thus your solitude can only be hurtful to you. "If I die, then I am not alone in death; if I suffer they [the fellowship] suffer with me" (Luther).

We recognize, then, that only as we are within the fellowship can we be alone, and only one that is alone can live in the fellowship. Only in the fellowship do we learn to be rightly alone and only in aloneness do we learn to live rightly in the fellowship. It is not as though the one preceded the other; both begin at the same time, namely, with the call of Jesus Christ.

Each by itself has profound pitfalls and perils. One who wants fellowship without solitude plunges into the void of words and feelings, and one who seeks solitude without fellowship perishes in the abyss of vanity, self-infatuation, and despair.

Let those who cannot be alone beware of community. Let those who are not in community beware of being alone.

Along with the day of the Christian family fellowship together there goes the lonely day of the individual. This is as it should be. The day together will be unfruitful without the day alone, both for the fellowship and for the individual.

The mark of solitude is silence, as speech is the mark of community. Silence and speech have the same inner correspondence and difference as do solitude and community. One does not exist without the other. Right speech comes out of silence, and right silence comes out of speech.

Silence does not mean dumbness, as speech does not mean chatter. Dumbness does not create solitude and chatter does not create fellowship. "Silence is the excess, the inebriation, the victim of speech. But dumbness is unholy, like a thing only maimed, not cleanly sacrificed. . . . Zacharias was speechless, instead of being silent. Had he accepted the revelation, he may perhaps have come out of the temple not dumb but silent" (Ernest Hello). The speech, the Word which establishes and binds together the fellowship, is accompanied by silence. "There is a time to keep silence, and a time to speak" (Eccles. 3:7). As there are definite hours in the Christian's day for the Word, particularly the time of common worship and prayer, so the day also needs definite times of silence, silence under the Word and silence that comes out of the Word. These will be especially the times before and after hearing the Word. The Word comes not to chatterers but to those who hold their tongues. The stillness of the temple is the sign of the holy presence of God in his Word. . . . [LT, pp. 77–79]

Silence is nothing else but waiting for God's Word and coming from God's Word with a blessing. But everybody knows that this is something that needs to be practiced and learned, in these days when talkativeness prevails. Real silence, real stillness, really holding one's tongue comes only as the sober consequence of spiritual stillness.

But this stillness before the Word will exert its influence upon the whole day. If we have learned to be silent before the Word, we shall also learn to manage our silence and our speech during the day. There is such a thing as forbidden, self-indulgent silence, a proud, offensive silence. And this means that it can never be merely silence as such. The silence of the Christian is listening silence, humble stillness, that may be interrupted at any time for the sake of humility. It is silence in conjunction with the Word. This is what Thomas à Kempis means when he said: "None speaketh surely but he that would gladly keep silence if he might." There is a wonderful power of clarification, purification, and concentration upon the essential thing in being quiet. This is true as a purely secular fact. But silence before the Word leads to right hearing and thus also to right speaking of the Word of God at the right time. Much that is unnecessary remains unsaid. But the essential and the helpful thing can be said in a few words. . . . [LT, pp. 79–80]

There are three purposes for which Christians need a definite time when they can be alone during the day: Scripture meditation, prayer, and intercession. All three should have their place in the daily period of meditation. The word "meditation" should not frighten us. It is an ancient concept of the church and of the Reformation that we are beginning again to rediscover. [LT, p. 81]

MEDITATION

It might be asked, why is a special time needed for this, since we meditate already during the common devotions? . . .

In our meditation we ponder the chosen text on the strength of the promise that it has something utterly personal to say to us for this day and for our Christian life, that it is not only God's Word for the church, but also God's Word for us individually. We expose ourselves to the specific word until it addresses us personally. And when we do this, we are doing no more than the simplest, untutored Christian does every day; we read God's Word as God's Word for us.

We do not ask what this text has to say to other people. For the preachers this means that they will not ask how they are going to preach or teach on this text, but what it is saying quite directly to them. It is true that to do this we must first have understood the content of the verse, but here we are not expounding it or preparing a sermon or conducting Bible study of any kind; we are rather waiting for God's Word to us. It is not a vacuous waiting, but a waiting on the basis of a clear promise. Often we are so burdened and overwhelmed with other thoughts, images, and concerns that it may take a long time before God's Word has swept all else aside and come through. But it will surely come, just as surely as God himself has come to people and will come again. This is the very reason why we begin our meditation with the prayer that God may send his Holy Spirit to us through his Word and reveal his Word to us and enlighten us.

It is not necessary that we should get through the entire passage in one meditation. Often we shall have to stop with one sentence or even one word, because we have been gripped and arrested and cannot evade it any longer. Is not the word "Father," or "love," "mercy," "cross," "sanctification," "resurrection," often enough to fill far more than the brief period we have at our disposal?

It is not necessary, therefore, that we should be concerned in our meditation to express our thought and prayer in words. Unphrased thought and prayer, which issues only from our hearing, may often be more beneficial.

It is not necessary that we should discover new ideas in our meditation. Often this only diverts us and feeds our vanity. It is sufficient if the Word, as we read and understand it, penetrates and dwells within us. As Mary "pondered in her heart" the things that were told by the shepherds, as what we have casually overheard follows us for a long time, sticks in our mind, occupies, disturbs, or delights us, without our ability to do anything about it, so in meditation God's Word seeks to enter in and remain with us. It strives to stir us, to work and operate in us, so that we shall not get away from it the whole day long. Then it will do its work in us, often without our being conscious of it.

Above all, it is not necessary that we should have any unexpected, extraordinary experiences in meditation. This can happen, but if it does not, it is not a sign that the meditation period has been useless. Not only at the beginning, but repeatedly, there will be times when we feel a great spiritual dryness and apathy, an aversion, even an inability to meditate. We dare not be balked by such experiences. Above all, we must not allow them to keep us from adhering to our meditation period with great patience and fidelity. . . . [LT, pp. 82–84]

PRAYER

The Scripture meditation leads to prayer. We have already said that the most promising method of prayer is to allow oneself to be guided by the word of the Scriptures, to pray on the basis of a word of Scripture. In this way we shall not become the victims of our own emptiness. Prayer means nothing else but the readiness and willingness to receive and appropriate the Word, and, what is more, to accept it in one's personal situation, particular tasks, decisions, sins, and temptations. What can never enter the corporate prayer of the fellowship may here be silently made known to God. According to a word of Scripture we pray for the clarification of our day, for preservation from sin, for growth in sanctification, for faithfulness and strength in our work. And we may be certain that our prayer will be heard, because it is a response to God's Word and promise. Because God's Word has found its fulfillment in Jesus Christ, all prayers that we pray conforming to this Word are certainly heard and answered in Jesus Christ.

It is one of the particular difficulties of meditation that our thoughts are likely to wander and go their own way, toward other persons or to some events in our life. Much as this may distress and shame us again and again, we must not lose heart and become anxious, or even conclude that meditation is really not something for us. When this happens it is often a help not to snatch back our thoughts convulsively, but quite calmly to incorporate into our prayer the people and the events to which our thoughts keep straying and thus in all patience return to the starting point of the meditation.

INTERCESSION

Just as we relate our personal prayer to the Scripture passage so we do the same with our intercessions. It is impossible to mention in the intercessions of corporate worship all the persons who are committed to our care, or at any rate to do so in the way that is required of us. . . .

This brings us to a point at which we hear the pulsing heart of all Christian life in unison. A Christian fellowship lives and exists by the intercession of its members for one another, or it collapses. I can no longer condemn or hate brothers and sisters for whom I pray, no matter how much trouble they cause me. . . . There is no dislike, no personal tension, no estrangement, that cannot be overcome by intercession as far as our side of it is concerned. Intercessory prayer is the purifying bath into which the individual and the fellowship must enter every day. The struggle we undergo with our brothers and sisters in intercession may be a hard one, but that struggle has the promise that it will gain its goal. . . . [LT, 84–86]

This makes it clear that intercession is also a daily service we owe to God and our brothers and sisters. Those who deny their neighbors the service of praying for them deny them the service of a Christian. It is clear, furthermore, that intercession is not general and vague but very concrete: a matter of definite persons and definite difficulties and therefore of definite petitions. The more definite my intercession becomes, the more promising it is.

Finally, we can also no longer escape the realization that the ministry of intercession requires time of every Christian, but most of all of the pastor who has the responsibility of a whole congregation. Intercession alone, if it is thoroughly done, would consume the entire time of daily meditation. So pursued, it will become evident that intercession is a gift of God's grace for every Christian community and for every Christian. Because intercession is such an incalculably great gift of God, we should accept it joyfully. The very time we give to intercession will turn out to be a daily source of new joy in God and in the Christian community.

Since meditation on the Scriptures, prayer, and intercession are a service we owe and because the grace of God is found in this service, we should train ourselves to set apart a regular hour for it, as we do for every other service we perform. This is not "legalism"; it is orderliness and fidelity. For most people the early morning will prove to be the best time. We have a right to this time, even prior to the claims of other people, and we may insist upon having it as a completely undisturbed quiet time despite all external difficulties. . . . [LT, 86–87]

THE MINISTRY OF HOLDING ONE'S TONGUE

. . . Strong and weak, wise and foolish, gifted or ungifted, pious or impious, the diverse individuals in the community, are no longer incentives for talking and judging and condemning, and thus excuses for self-justification. They are rather cause for rejoicing in one another and serving one another. . . .

In a Christian community everything depends upon whether each individual is an indispensable link in a chain. Only when even the smallest link is securely interlocked is the chain unbreakable. A community which allows unemployed members to exist within it will perish because of them. It will be well, therefore, if every member receives a definite task to perform for the community, that they may know in hours of doubt that they, too, are not useless and unusable. Every Christian community must realize that not only do the weak need the strong, but also that the strong cannot exist without the weak. The elimination of the weak is the death of fellowship. . . . [LT, 93–94]

THE MINISTRY OF LISTENING

The first service that one owes to others in the fellowship consists in listening to them. Just as love of God begins with listening to his Word, so the beginning of love for one's brothers and sisters is learning to listen to them. It is God's love for us that he not only gives us his Word but also lends us his ear. So it is his work that we do for our brothers and sisters when we learn to listen to them. Christians, especially ministers, so often think they must always contribute something when they are in the company of others, that this is the one service they have to render. They forget that listening can be a greater service than speaking.

Many people are looking for an ear that will listen. They do not find it among Christians, because these Christians are talking where they should be listening. But the one who can no longer listen to his brother or sister will soon be no longer listening to God either; he or she will be doing nothing but prattle in the presence of God too. This is the beginning of the death of the spiritual life, and in the end there is nothing left but spiritual chatter and clerical condescension arrayed in pious words. One who cannot listen long and patiently will presently be talking beside the point and be never really speaking to others, albeit he or she be not conscious of it. Any who think that their time is too valuable to spend keeping quiet will eventually have no time for God and their brothers and sisters, but only for the self and for their own follies.

. . . Christians have forgotten that the ministry of listening has been committed to them by him who is himself the great listener and whose work they should share. We should listen with the ears of God that we may speak the Word of God. [*LT*, pp. 97–99]

THE MINISTRY OF HELPFULNESS

The second service that one should perform for another in a Christian community is that of active helpfulness. This means, initially, simple assistance in trifling, external matters. There is a multitude of these things wherever people live together. Nobody is too good for the humblest service. Those who worry about the loss of time that such petty, outward acts of helpfulness entail are usually taking the importance of their own careers too solemnly.

We must be ready to allow ourselves to be interrupted by God. God will be constantly crossing our paths and canceling our plans by sending us people with claims and petitions. We may pass them by, preoccupied with our more important tasks, as the priest passed by the man who had fallen among thieves, perhaps—reading the Bible. When we do that we pass by the visible sign of the cross raised athwart our path to show us that, not our way, but God's way must be done. It is a strange fact that Christians and even ministers frequently consider their work so important and urgent that they will allow nothing to disturb them. They think they are doing God a service in this, but actually they are disdaining God's "crooked yet straight path" (Gottfried Arnold). They do not want a life that is crossed and balked. But it is part of the discipline of humility that we must not spare our hand where it can perform a service and that we do not assume that our schedule is our own to manage, but allow it to be arranged by God. [*LT*, p. 99]

THE MINISTRY OF BEARING

We speak . . . of the service that consists in bearing others. "Bear one another's burdens, and so fulfill the law of Christ" (Gal. 6:2). Thus the law of Christ is a law of bearing. Bearing means forbearing and sustaining. The brother or sister, is a burden to Christians, precisely because they are Christians. For the pagans the other person never becomes a burden at all. They simply sidestep every burden that others may impose upon them.

Christians, however, must bear the burden of the brother and sister. They must suffer and endure the other. It is only when he or she is a burden that another person is really a human being and not merely an object to be manipulated. The burden of people was so heavy for God himself that he had to endure the cross. God verily bore the burden of humankind in the body of Jesus Christ. But he bore them as a mother carries her child, as a shepherd enfolds the lost lamb that has been found. God took humankind upon himself and they weighted him to the ground, but God remained with them and they with God. In bearing with people God maintained fellowship with them. . . . [*LT*, p. 100]

The Bible speaks with remarkable frequency of "bearing." It is capable of expressing the whole work of Jesus Christ in this one word. "Surely he has borne our griefs, and carried our sorrows . . . the chastisement of our peace was upon him" (Isa. 53:4–5). Therefore, the Bible can also characterize the whole life of the Christian as bearing the cross. It is the fellowship of the cross to experience the burden of the other. If one does not experience it, the fellowship one belongs to is not Christian. If any members refuse to bear that burden, they deny the law of Christ.

It is first of all the *freedom* of the other person, of which we spoke earlier, that is a burden to the Christian. The other's freedom collides with one's own autonomy, yet one must recognize it. . . . The freedom of the other person includes all that we mean by a person's nature, individuality, endowment. It also includes . . . weakness and oddities, which are such a trial to our patience, everything that produces frictions, conflicts, and collisions among us. To bear the burden of the other person means involvement with the created reality of the other, to accept and affirm it, and, in bearing with it, to break through to the point where we take joy in it.

This will prove especially difficult where varying strength and weakness in faith are bound together in a fellowship. The weak must not judge the strong, the strong must not despise the weak. The weak must guard against pride, the strong against indifference. . . .

Then, besides the other's freedom, there is the abuse of that freedom that becomes a burden for the Christian. The sin of the other person is harder to bear than . . . freedom; for in sin, fellowship with God and with one's brothers and sisters is broken. Here Christians suffer the rupture of their fellowship with the other person that had its basis in Jesus Christ. But here, too, it is only in bearing with them that the great grace of God becomes wholly plain. To cherish no contempt for sinners but rather to prize the privilege of bearing them means not to have to give them up as lost, to be able to accept them, to preserve fellowship with them through forgiveness. "Brethren, if a man be overtaken in a fault, you who are spiritual, restore such a one in the spirit of meekness" (Gal. 6:1). As Christ bore and received us as sinners so we in his fellowship may bear and receive sinners into the fellowship of Jesus Christ through the forgiving of sins. . . .

The service of forgiveness is rendered by one to the others daily. It occurs, without words, in the intercessions for one another. And every member of the fellowship, who does not grow weary in this ministry, can depend upon it that this service is also being rendered him by the brethren. . . .

Then where the ministry of listening, active helpfulness, and bearing with others is faithfully performed, the ultimate and highest service can also be rendered, namely, the ministry of the Word of God. . . . [*LT*, pp. 101–3]

THE JOYFUL SACRAMENT

. . . The day of the Lord's Supper is an occasion of joy for the Christian community. Reconciled in their hearts with God and the brothers and sisters, the congregation receives the gift of the Body and Blood of Jesus Christ, and, receiving that, it receives forgiveness, new life, and salvation. It is given new fellowship with God and humankind. The fellowship of the Lord's Supper is the superlative fulfillment of Christian fellowship. As the members of the congregation are united in body and blood at the table of the Lord so will they be together in eternity. Here the community has reached its goal. Here joy in Christ and his community is complete. The life of Christians together under the Word has reached its perfection in the sacrament. [*LT*, p. 122]

Part 6

BONHOEFFER'S ETHICS

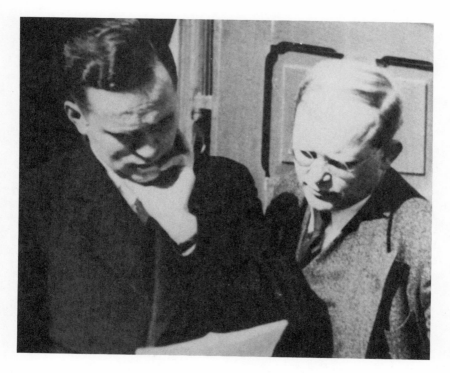

Gross-Schlönwitz, summer 1938. Eberhard Bethge and Dietrich Bonhoeffer, the collective pastorate of Gross-Schlöwitz.
From: Eberhard Bethge, Renate Bethge, Christian Gremmels *Dietrich Bonhoeffer: A Life in Pictures* (Philadelphia: Fortress Press, 1986), p. 168.

Introduction: Freedom and Responsibility

Bonhoeffer often mentioned that his main life's work would be the writing of his *Ethics*. "I sometimes feel as if my life were more or less over, and as if all I had to do now were to finish my *Ethics*."[1] It was a task begun during his pastoral year in Barcelona, with his address "What Is a Christian Ethic?" In one sense, however, the formation of a Christian ethic was something that engaged Bonhoeffer throughout his life. Certainly part of the fallout from his doctoral dissertation was the conviction that there was no Christian ethic if that meant the formulation of an ordered system of principles and values from which moral norms could then be deduced. Christian ethics, for Bonhoeffer at that time, meant simply that one took seriously Christ's command for his community. This was a command set for and in the concrete reality of the Christian community. Christ's vicarious deeds, and particularly his death on our behalf, become in turn the principle and model of the self-sacrifice that makes community possible. In the prison letters this would take on the form of Bonhoeffer's insightful description of the church's vocation: "the church is the church only when it exists for others."[2] According to Bonhoeffer, the movement from life in the Christian community to service of one's neighbor is the only true movement toward God that God's gift of faith makes possible. He argues, moreover, that the demand for spontaneity in one's response to people in need makes it impossible to produce a systematic ethic. Every changing situation of need can become the specific locus of God's command.

In these observations, however sporadic in the earlier literature, we detect Bonhoeffer's suspicion that attempting to formulate Christian principles and laws in the name of establishing a valid-for-all-time Christian ethic was only an attempt to dominate God by religion and to control his law by static legalism. This, he notes, is destructive of the very community such an ethic is designed to protect.

The fragmentary understanding of ethics, evident in the Barcelona lecture, was to be modified by the time Bonhoeffer would begin more formally to study the traditional ethical questions. What still emerges in the more developed segments of his posthumously published *Ethics*, however, is his earlier emphasis on the need to conform to Jesus Christ within the Christian community. It would be inaccurate to say that in the meantime he had mastered a sense of methodology. There is no consistent ethical methodology discernible in his earlier focus on church, though several passages are brimming over with ethical implications. Bonhoeffer rejected religion's churchy way of formulating ethical principles. This negative reaction to what was a constant moral posturing by the churches derives from his aversion for any reduction of Christ and Scripture to ethical commands. It is not the command *per se*, he argued, but God's will, often against ours, and, in Christ, his gift of freedom to act responsibly in every decisive moment that is at the heart of Christian action. Bonhoeffer was aware of the very uniqueness of situations when one is faced with options equally bad or confusing. To resolve conflict situations, he proposed, on the one hand, the observation that one has the support of the community and of one's solidarity with Christ, especially in the person of the needy, and, on the other hand, the strength of faith when one is radically alone before God, called on to trust this God, and to enter into communion with Christ in his own solitary courage.

These qualities were notoriously absent from the compromise morality of too many church leaders advocated in the 1930s. Bonhoeffer's own move from close association with the Confessing Church in the years of the church struggle toward a more expanded activity in resisting nazism signaled at the same time a shift in his ethical perspective. If, in the period prior to 1940, he advanced what can best be described as an ethics of formation, or "conformation to Jesus Christ," in the first section of his published *Ethics,* he speaks pointedly of the wide range of Christ's dominion, the universality of those rights, duties, and relationships included under his rubric of "divine mandates." Even that terminology, with its accent on God's command to people who carry out his will in the important areas governing life, represents a critical departure from an approach to ethical reasoning based on so-called "orders of creation" with its own hints of "natural theology." Drawing ethical conclusions from the "orders of creation" had been a view popularized by Emil Brunner, who asserted that God's will for people was known from the patterns of his creative work. Hence marriage, family, religion, state, and even work and culture demand a specific ordering of one's life as well as certain conditions for proper functioning. Such a perspective was used to link both believers and nonbelievers in a common, fully rational ethic.[3]

Bonhoeffer suspected, however, that this approach neglected the persistent evidence of sin and the inveterate tendency to disobey God's command and thus to corrupt the very order created by him. What is more, Bonhoeffer was disturbed by the potential for Nazi leaders to exploit Brunner's terminology in order to propagate their own version of how best to order the world through structures of Aryanism, nationalism, and salvation through Hitler. In those years of the church crisis, Bonhoeffer spoke by preference of "orders of preservation" to protect people from the consequences of sin of both church and state, of family, and of one's work. As he began his *Ethics,* he likewise wished to endorse a sense of Christian responsibility for the preservation of those orders. This would be a responsibility in conformity with Christ and alert to the needs of an oppressed people, to be sure, but also attuned to God's concrete command amidst the moral dilemmas churned up in Christian consciences by nazism's insidious manipulation of the churches.

The text that consequently became Bonhoeffer's published *Ethics* is, in one respect at least, an attempt to address the great moral dilemmas posed by the war and the need to resist a blatantly evil government. The selections included here trace the main lines of this attempt beginning with his earliest organized thoughts to address the question of what constitutes a Christian ethic.

51

What Is a Christian Ethic?

(Grundfrageneiner christlichen Ethik)

January 25, 1929

In this lecture to his German-speaking parishioners in Barcelona on January 25, 1929, Bonhoeffer attacked religious legalism in the name of freedom. It is one of the main themes, not only of this address, but also of his entire ethical outlook during the years of the church struggle and of the conspiracy. He wrote, therefore, that

> for the Christian there are no ethical principles by means of which he could perhaps civilize himself. Nor can yesterday ever be decisive for my moral action today. Rather must a direct relationship to God's will be ever sought afresh. I do not do something again today because it seemed to me to be good yesterday, but because the will of God points out this way to me today. This is the great moral renewal through Jesus, the renunciation of principles, of rulings, in the words of the Bible, of the law, and this follows as a consequence of the Christian idea of God; for if there was a generally valid moral law, then there would be a way from man to God. . . . And, most important of all, in that case I would once again become a slave to my principles. I would sacrifice man's most precious gift, freedom.[4]

Bonhoeffer wrote these words in the context of his criticism of an explicit Christian morality that, under the aegis of religion, would claim, through law, to govern any and all human contingencies. Against such an authoritarian view, Bonhoeffer retorted that Jesus brought God's Word, not some new ethical revelation. That Word was to become the Christian community, as Bonhoeffer understands that community to be the locus of the command of God.

From this essay and Bonhoeffer's emphasis on Christ's dynamic presence in and command to his community in enunciating anything resembling a Christian ethic, it would appear that Bonhoeffer's earliest views of the ethical were highly contextual and even atomistic. Every situation was unique. Jesus was unique to every situation.

It may seem that this earlier essay reads like an argument on behalf of situation ethics. And, indeed, in this lies one of the essay's main weaknesses. Bonhoeffer seems to meander in too many directions with neither consistent structure nor firmly established ethical principles to guide his audience. He tries to hang ethical decisions on a sense of realism and on being involved. The call to do one's "duty" is, however, interwoven into questionable authoritarian frameworks of mission (which could later create the dilemma of what to do when one is faced with a nationally proclaimed "mission" involving war) and community and God to whom one must ultimately defer. The essay lacks ethical methodology. And there is little continuity in Bonhoeffer's ethics or even order in his insistence on the clarity of God's word and decisiveness of action when one is truly committed. The strength of Bonhoeffer's approach, on the other hand, is his reverence for God's Word, especially that of the Sermon on the Mount, solidarity with the oppressed, concreteness, intelligent assessment of situations, and insistence on freedom, responsibility, and decisiveness, all qualities that will perdure in his subsequent attempts over the ensuing years to develop a consistent Christian ethic.

We will speak today of the basic questions raised by the demand for a Christian ethic, not by making the attempt to lay down generally valid, Christian norms and precepts in contemporary ethical questions—which is in any case completely hopeless—but rather by examining and entering into the characteristic trend of contemporary ethical problems in the light of fundamental Christian ideas. The reason for a limitation of this nature lies in the fact, still to be elaborated in detail, that there are not and cannot be Christian norms and principles of a moral nature; the concepts of "good" and "evil" exist only on the completion of an action, i.e., at any specific present, and hence any attempt to lay down principles is like trying to draw a bird in flight. But more of this later.

Ethics is a matter of history; it is not simply something which has descended from heaven to earth, but is rather a child of the earth. For this reason it changes its appearance with the trends of history and the shift of generations. There is a German ethic and a French ethic, just as there is an American ethic, and none is more ethical or less ethical than the others, but all are firmly fixed in the nexus of history, and all have in our time been decisively influenced by the tremendous experience of the world war, as it has been seen through different eyes. . . .

We said that there was a German, a French, an American ethic, for ethics is a matter of blood and of history. But in that case how does the idea of a so-called *Christian ethic* stand? Are these two words, Christian and ethic, not perhaps completely disparate? Does not the idea "Christian" in this way become secularized, and the so-called Christian ethic become one alongside many, one of many, perhaps rather better or perhaps rather worse, but still in any event completely implicated in the relativity of history? In that case there is a Christian ethic as well as a German ethic, and neither of them is allowed to lay claim to superiority. It is therefore extremely hazardous to speak of a Christian ethic and at the same time to maintain the absolute claim for such an ethic.

In the last address a remark was made which was perhaps not completely comprehensible: that Christianity was basically amoral, i.e., that Christianity and ethics were in fact divergent entities. And why? Because Christianity speaks of the single way of God to man, from the merciful love of God for unrighteous men and sinners, and because ethics speaks of the way of man to God, of the encounter of the holy God with unholy man; because the Christian message speaks of grace and ethics speaks of righteousness. There are countless ways from man to God, and therefore there are also countless ethics, but there is only one way from God to man, and that is the way of love in Christ, the way of the cross. The question of Christianity is not the question of good and evil in man, but the question whether it is God's will to be gracious or not. The Christian message stands beyond good and evil; and that must be the case, for should the grace of God be made dependent upon the extent of man's good or evil, the basis would be laid for a claim of man upon God, and in this way God's sole power and glory would be assailed. It is an extremely profound thing that in the old story of the Fall, the reason for the Fall is eating from the tree of the knowledge of good and evil. The original—shall we say childlike—communion between God and man stands beyond this knowledge of good and evil; it knows only of one thing, of the boundless love of God toward man. Thus the discovery of what is beyond good and evil was not made by Friedrich Nietzsche, who from this standpoint utters polemics against the hypocrisy of Christianity; it belongs to the original material of the Christian message, concealed, of course, as it is.

If the argument up to this point is correct, then the conclusion appears to be quite clear: Christianity and ethics do indeed have nothing to do with one another; there is no Christian ethic and there can be no transition from the idea of Christianity to that of ethics. Yet it is immediately obvious that at this point we are on the wrong track. For we must ask, why then are the Gospels full of evidently ethical directions? What business does the Sermon on the Mount have in the New Testament? The question, obvious as it is important, which confronts us is: What is the significance of the so-called New Testament ethic?

Since the third and fourth centuries there have always been movements which gave out that the preaching of a new ethic was the center of Christianity, and the new commandment was the commandment of love. Such a view, while of course superficial, was possible and tenable right up to the last century. Since, however, investigations into the history of religion and literature have concerned themselves exhaustively with the rabbinic literature of the time of Jesus and earlier, and with the philosophical and ethical tractates of the philosophical schools of that time, it may be held that to make such claims for the New Testament is demonstrably false. The commandment of love is not exclusively Christian, but was already generally recognized and widespread at the time of Jesus. . . .

Had the proclamation of this commandment really stood in the middle of Jesus' preaching, he would always have made a fresh beginning from this point. But that is not the case. This also emerges from a comparison of sayings of Jesus with the sayings of Jewish rabbis and pagan philosophers, which are often similar, right down to their formulation. The Rabbi Hillel is asked what is the greatest commandment and he replies, "Love your neighbour as yourself. That is the greatest commandment." Another says, "Do not do to another what you would not have done to yourself." The Roman philosopher Seneca says, "Let us not become weary of exerting ourselves for the general good, of helping individuals, of bringing aid even to our enemies." To the objection, "But anger affords pleasure. It is even more comfortable to requite pain," he replies, "No, it is honorable in charity to recompense good with good, but not so injustice with injustice. In the one it is disgraceful to let oneself be surpassed, in the other it is disgraceful to prove the victor."

In that case, however, what now remains of a Christian ethic? Has the Sermon on the Mount really nothing new to say to us? Nothing "new" in the sense of a new commandment, but at the same time something quite different. The significance of all Jesus' ethical commandments is rather to say to people: "You stand before the face of God, God's grace rules over you; you are at the disposal of someone else in the world and for him you must act and work. So be mindful in your actions that you are acting under God's eyes, and that his will must needs be done." The nature of this will of God can only be clear in the moment of action; it is only important to be clear that every man's own will must be brought to be God's will, that his own will must be surrendered if God's will is to be realized, and therefore insofar as complete renunciation of personal claims is necessary in acting before the face of God, the Christian's ethical action can be described as love. But this is not a new principle; it derives from the place of man before God. For the Christian there are no ethical principles by means of which he could perhaps civilize himself. Nor can yesterday ever be decisive for my moral action today. Rather must a direct relationship to God's will be ever sought afresh. I do not do something again today because it seemed to me to be good yesterday, but because the will of God points out this way to me today. That is the great moral renewal through Jesus, the renunciation of principles, of rulings, in the words of the Bible, of the law, and this follows as a consequence of the Christian idea of God; for if there was a generally valid moral law, then there would be a way from the human to God—I would have my principles, so I would believe myself assured *sub specie aeternitatis*. So, to some extent, I would have control over my relationship to God, so there would be a moral action without immediate relationship to God. And, most important of all, in that case I would once again become a slave to my principles. I would sacrifice our most precious gift, *freedom*.

When Jesus places people immediately under God, new and afresh at each moment, he restores to mankind the immense gift which it had lost, freedom. Christian ethical action is action from freedom, action from the freedom of a man who has nothing of himself and everything of his God, who ever and again lets his action be confirmed and endorsed by eternity. The New Testament speaks of this freedom in great words. . . .

For the Christian there is no other law than the law of freedom, as the New Testament paradoxically puts it. There is no generally valid law which could be expounded to him by others, or even by himself. The one who surrenders freedom surrenders his very nature as a Christian. The Christian stands free, without any protection, before God and before the world, and he alone is wholly responsible for what he does with the gift of freedom. Now through this freedom the Christian becomes creative in ethical action. Acting in accordance with principles is unproductive, imitating the law, copying. Acting from freedom is creative. The Christian chooses the forms of his ethical action as it were from eternity, he puts them sovereign in the world, as his act, his creation from the freedom of a child of God. The Christian himself creates his standards of good and evil for himself. Only he can justify his own actions, just as only he can bear the responsibility. The Christian creates new tables, a new Decalogue, as Nietzsche said of the Superman. Nietzsche's Superman is not really, as he supposed, the opposite of the Christian; without knowing it, Nietzsche has here introduced many traits of the Christian made free, as Paul and Luther describe him. Time-honored morals—even if they are given out to be the consensus of Christian opinion—can never for the Christian become the standard of his actions. He acts, because the will of God seems to bid him to, without a glance at the others, at what is usually called morals, and no one but himself and God can know whether he has acted well or badly. In ethical decision we are brought into the deepest solitude, the solitude in which a man stands before the living God. No one can stand beside us there, no one can take anything from us, because God lays on us a burden which we alone must bear. Our "I" awakes only in the consciousness of being called, of being claimed by God. Only through the call of God does this "I" become isolated from all others, drawn into responsibility by God, knowing myself to confront eternity alone. And because in the solitude I come face to face with God, I can only know for myself, completely personally, what is good and what is evil. There are no actions which are bad in themselves—even murder can be justified—there is only faithfulness to God's will or deviation from it; there is similarly no law in the sense of a law containing precepts, but only the law of freedom, i.e., of a man's bearing his responsibility alone before God and himself. But because the law remains superseded once for all and because it follows from the Christian idea of God that there can be no more law, the ethical commandments, the apparent laws of the New Testament must also be understood from this standpoint.

It is the greatest of misunderstandings to make the commandments of the Sermon on the Mount into laws once again by referring them literally to the present. This is not only senseless, because it is impracticable, but still more, it is against the spirit of Christ, who brought freedom from the law. The whole life of, say, Count Tolstoy and so many others has been lived under this misunderstanding. There are no ethical directions in the New Testament which we should have, or even could have, taken over literally. The letter kills, the spirit gives life, says Paul; that means, there is only spirit on the completion of the action, in the present; once fixed, the spirit is no longer spirit. Thus, too, there is ethics only on the completion of the act, not in the letter of the law. Now the spirit which is active in us in ethical action is said to be the Holy Spirit. The Holy Spirit is only in the present, in ethical decision, and not in fixed moral precepts, in ethical principles. For this reason, the new commandments of Jesus can never be regarded merely as ethical principles; they are to be understood in their spirit, not literally. And that is no subterfuge, because things would otherwise be too uncomfortable; it is demanded by the idea of freedom and Jesus' concept of God. That the demands of Jesus have got this radical acuteness lies in the fact that the position of man in ethical decision before God demands a radical repudiation of his own person, his own will; but not every single one of Jesus' rules of conduct is valid for us, otherwise the imitation of them would be slavish and unfree. Now it follows from all this that ethical problems of content can never be discussed in a Christian light; there is simply no possibility of erecting generally valid principles, because each moment, lived in God's sight, can bring an unexpected decision. Thus even in our time only one thing can be repeated, over and over again: in ethical decisions a man must put himself under the will of God, he must consider his action *sub specie aeternitatis* and then, however it turns out, it will turn out rightly. Now, day by day, hour by hour, we are confronted with unparalleled situations in which we must make a decision, and in which we make again and again the surprising and terrifying discovery that the will of God does not reveal itself before our eyes as clearly as we had hoped. This comes about because the will of God seems to be self-contradictory, because two ordinances of God seem to conflict with one another, so that we are not in a position to choose between good and evil, but only between one evil and another. And here it is that the real, most difficult problems of ethics lie. And if we set to work to deal with them, it is clear, after what has been said, that we can give no generally valid decisions which we might then hold out to be the only Christian ones, because in so doing we are only setting out new principles and coming into conflict with the law of freedom. Rather can we only seek to be brought into the concrete situation of the decision and to show one of the possibilities of decision which present themselves at that point. The decision which is really required must be made freely by each person in the concrete situation. . . .

We must break off and summarize. Ethics is a matter of earth and of blood, but also of him who made both; the trouble arises from this duality. There can be ethics only in the framework of history, in the concrete situation, at the moment of the divine call, the moment of being addressed, of the claim made by the concrete need and the situation for decision, of the claim which I have to answer and for which I have to make myself responsible. Thus there cannot be ethics in a vacuum, as a principle; there cannot be good and evil as general ideas, but only as qualities of will making a decision. There can be only good and evil as done in freedom; principles are binding under the law. Bound up in the concrete situation, through God and in God the Christian acts in the power of a man who has become free. He is under no judgment but his own and that of God.

But through this freedom from the law, from principle, the Christian must enter into the complexity of the world; he cannot make up his mind *a priori*, but only when he himself has become involved in the emergency and knows himself called by God. He remains earthbound, even when his desire is toward God; he must go through all the anxiety before the laws of the world; he must learn the paradox that the world offers us a choice, not between good and evil, but between one evil and another, and that nevertheless God leads him to himself even through evil. He must feel the gross contradiction between what he would like to do and what he must do; he must grow mature through this distress, grow mature through not leaving hold of God's hand, in the words "Thy will be done." A glimpse of eternity is revealed only through the depths of our earth, only through the storms of a human conscience. The profound old saga tells of the giant Antaeus, who was stronger than any man on earth; no one could overcome him until once in a fight someone lifted him from the ground; then the giant lost all the strength which had flowed into him through his contact with the earth. The man who would leave the earth, who would depart from the present distress, loses the power which still holds him by eternal, mysterious forces. The earth remains our mother, just as God remains our Father, and our mother will only lay in the Father's arms him who remains true to her. That is the Christian's song of earth and her distress.

All the examples which we have hitherto chosen have shown us that it is necessary for a man to be involved in the concrete situation and from there to direct his gaze toward eternity, contending afresh in the ambiguity of the situation always to decide in accordance with the will of God; the decision may then turn out as it will. And then ethics does not become once again a way from man to God, but remains like every-thing that men who know themselves to be freed from the world by Christ can do, a sacrifice, a demonstration of the weak will which springs from thankfulness for what God has done for us; a sacrifice, an offering, a demonstration which God can either accept or refuse; man's action springs from the recognition of the grace of God, toward mankind and toward himself, and man's action hopes for the grace of God which delivers him from the distress of the time. Thus the realm of grace builds itself over the ethical realm. This distress and anxiety of the conscience must find an end, the incomprehensible contradictions of the divine order in the world must become clear, if the kingdom of grace is to take the place of the kingdom of the world, the kingdom of God the place of the kingdom of man. Only the man who has once tasted the utter depth and distress of the kingdom of the world, the ethical realm, longs to be away, and he has one wish, "Let this world pass away, thy kingdom come." [*NRS*, pp. 39–48]

52

Ethics

(Ethik)

1949

The text of *Ethics* was edited by Eberhard Bethge and published posthumously in 1949. As Bethge acknowledges in his preface, the book "is a compilation of the sections which have been preserved, some of them complete and others not, some already partly rewritten and some which have been committed to writing only as preliminary studies for the work which was planned."[5] Bethge restructured this text for the sixth German edition in 1963. The selections here are from the translation by Neville Horton Smith and the arrangement in the Macmillan paperback edition of 1965. *Ethics* is again being revised for the new German and English language editions in the *Dietrich Bonhoeffer Werke* series.[6] This new edition will bring out more clearly the coherence of the original text through a more critical assessment of its "purposeful development, both within the manuscripts themselves and from his writings in the later 1930s to the *Letters and Papers from Prison.*"[7]

The text that consequently became Bonhoeffer's published *Ethics* is, in one respect at least, an attempt to address the great moral dilemmas posed by the war and the need to resist a blatantly evil government. The nature of this work reflects not only different beginnings in search of "foundations" but also the many directions of his own work in the anti-Nazi resistance crowding his writing into smaller chunks of time over a three-year period. The first "beginning" of the text is, from all appearances, an ethical reflection on his mission within the Confessing Church. Here we encounter echoes of *The Cost of Discipleship,* an appeal to the stark command of Jesus' Sermon on the Mount as one way to take one's distance from the evil compromises fostered within churches and readily accepted by a Nazi state. There is, for example, the radical distinction between the values espoused by a follower of Christ and the values of the world. The disciple must not be entrapped by the delusion of grasping for a phariseelike knowledge of good and evil and acquiring, thereby, a self-consciousness of one's own "goodness" guaranteed by the obvious loyalty to law and orthodoxy. Bonhoeffer argues vehemently in that opening section for the simplicity of deeds in response to God's present Word. He advocates a more natural passage between declaring one's commitment to Christ, hearing the word commanding discipleship, and doing the will of God without loitering over problems of self-image or wordly loyalties, such as had divided the German churches in their relationship with the Nazi state. The Christian's gaze must be "fixed" entirely on Jesus Christ but with a zest for "doing" the command of Christ from the attitude of Christ himself so clearly enunciated in the Sermon on the Mount.

There is a disarming simplicity in Bonhoeffer's line of reasoning, reminiscent of what he urged as official attitude and course of action for the churches in the 1930s. More detail was needed, however, to cut through the complexities of the moral decisions created by the increasingly insistent demands for patriotism in a Germany at war. But what appears to be chapter 2 of the text, composed shortly after Bonhoeffer officially joined the *Abwehr* as an unpaid special agent, was not so much a continuation of the reflections of chapter 1 but a section to supplement what would become chapter 3 in Bonhoeffer's original outline 5. In other words, the content of chapter 2, "The Church and the World," was originally to follow Bonhoeffer's analysis "Guilt, Justification, and Renewal." Chapter 3 states that the rich spiritual inheritance of the West, derived from Christ, had fallen into decay. People must now be led back to their origins, even if it be through an antichurch, "promising Godlessness." Such a return calls for a suffering church, willing to heed the "total and exclusive claim of Christ," by becoming itself a credible leader against "the tyrannical despiser of people" who exploits "the baseness of the human heart." The ethical question in this new beginning to the *Ethics* is at once the Christian search for the mode of Christ's taking form in history "in a manner which is neither abstract nor casuistic, neither programmatic nor purely speculative." Such a search takes the Christian to the figure of the crucified Jesus as it also takes one to those prime victims of Nazi hatred, the Jews, who keep "open the question of Christ." Written at the outset of the Jewish deportations, the perspective of this section of the *Ethics* identified the crucified Christ with the suffering Jews. In Bonhoeffer's sober phrase: "An expulsion of the Jews from the West must necessarily bring with it the expulsion of Christ."

Bonhoeffer suggests that counteraction to this and other Nazi evils should spring from Christian confession of Christ as the origin of all good and the center of church in an explicit way and of state in a hidden way. Such a course of resistance implied for Bonhoeffer, not an ecclesially orchestrated "imitation of Christ," but a more robust "Reformation" attitude of accepting Christ's having taken form in human lives, in history, and, more visibly, in the concreteness of church. Faith dictates this acceptance; a Christian ethic would dictate those concrete deeds that directly and indirectly confess such faith. Yet Bonhoeffer also recognized the rot eating away at Western culture through secularized politics and the state's dehumanizing use of technology to support an idolatrous nationalism. He declares this a contempt for people and the laws of reason. Germany, to be sure, but the other Western nations as well, are guilty "of the apostasy from Christ." We find here Bonhoeffer's most enthusiastic statement on the promise of the church in the age of decay that was nazism's "hostility toward Christ."

But with this comes also Bonhoeffer's warning against attempts "to build the world with Christian principles" without a serious confession of one's union with

Christ and without Christ's having taken real form in the church. This leads only to "the total capitulation of the church to the world, as can be seen clearly enough by a glance at the New York church registers. If this does not involve a radical hostility to the church," Bonhoeffer goes on, "that is only because no real distinction has ever been drawn here between the offices of church and state. Godlessness remains more covert. And indeed in this way it deprives the church even of the blessing of suffering and of the possible rebirth which suffering may engender." So went Bonhoeffer's insightful description of one way churches become co-opted to society's "bourgeois" and often perverted values!

Even more unsettling, however, is Bonhoeffer's "confession" that the church not only is guilty in the individuals composing its "collective personality" but also in its corporate failure to uphold the gospel. The church, Bonhoeffer wrote, is guilty of witnessing "the lawless application of brutal force, the physical and spiritual suffering of countless innocent people, oppression, hatred and murder, and . . . has not raised its voice on behalf of the victims and has not found ways to hasten to their aid." And, in a lone word that in a striking way owns up to church complicity in the Nazi Holocaust, he declares the church "guilty of the deaths of the weakest and most defenseless brothers and sisters of Jesus Christ." This was Bonhoeffer's expression for the Jews and the imprisoned pastors. What is astonishing in this "confession of guilt" is that it was written while Germans were still celebrating the greatest victory of their armies, the fall of France, and hailing the enlightened, fearless leadership of Adolf Hitler. While the people rejoiced in the new glory of Germany, Bonhoeffer privately lamented the church's guilt in the suffering inflicted by the Nazi Blitzkrieg and terroristic rule in the occupied countries.

This "confession of guilt" is the highlight of the section entitled "Guilt, Justification, and Renewal." The aim is not merely acknowledgment of sin but forgiveness and healing. That will come about, Bonhoeffer claims, "only when justice, order, and peace are in one way or another restored, when past guilt is thereby 'forgiven,' when it is no longer imagined that what has been done can be undone by means of punitive measures and reprisals, and when the church of Jesus Christ, as the fountainhead of all forgiveness, justification, and renewal, is given room to do its work among the nations." And the guilt, Bonhoeffer adds, is not only that of Germany. All the Western powers have drifted in various degrees into an apostasy from Jesus Christ. And all together must participate in the healing that was the hope of those sharing Bonhoeffer's vision of Christian renewal. There is an implied caution in this downbeat ending to what is presently listed as Chapter III in the original German edition, and in the subsequent English editions. Germany bears the greater guilt, to be sure; but there can be no healing if Germany is to be utterly destroyed or ostracized as a totally immoral reject.

Bonhoeffer also felt the need for a follow-up to describe in more detail the specific mode of the healing a renewed church could spearhead. The section begs for what in part the presently listed Chapter II in the early editions of *Ethics* provides, an elaboration of the relationship between church and world. Though none of this reached a final, developed form, the present Chapter II in *Ethics*, as Clifford Green has so persuasively shown, belongs at the end of what is now Chapter III. Renewal had to be more than restoration of the rule of reason, culture, humanity, tolerance, and self-determination, and similar civil virtues of a new order. All these attributes, rather, had to be affirmed with a "new purpose and a new power in their origin. This origin is Jesus Christ." It is in this setting that Bonhoeffer speaks of "the total and exclusive claim of Christ." The name of Jesus, he notes, has an "unforseen power" as gathering force for those involved in the "struggle for justice, truth, humanity, and freedom." This is not to be mere lip confession of faith in Jesus, however. Bonhoeffer also acknowledges that the exclusive demands made by Jesus led the group of confessing Christians to become more like the small biblical remnant. But this also allowed the church to experience the paradox of Christ's claims both to exclusivity and to totality. Forced now to abandon reliance on the deceptive strength of numbers the remnant of the church could include those who, without any specific church affiliation or without any specific religious justification of their actions, nonetheless were impelled to seek "lawfulness, truth, humanity, and freedom" under the protection that only Jesus could give. It is under the cross of Christ, then, that the few confessing Christians and nonreligious resisters converge in their common cause, that justice incarnated in the humanity of Christ himself.

Bonhoeffer's argument in this section appears to be a deliberate attempt to expand the notion of who should be ranked among the followers of Christ. Certainly not all those who can cry, "Lord, Lord!" in their churches all the while blinded to the injustice around them or even part of that injustice. There is clearly room for the nonreligious humanist. "Jesus," he declares, "gives his support to those who suffer for the sake of a just cause, even if this cause is not precisely the confession of his name; he takes them under his protection, he accepts responsibility for them, and he lays claim to them." In short, Bonhoeffer is asking Christians to enlarge their vision of those with whom Christ identifies and to rethink their categories of "good" and of those thought to be "good people." The "wicked" could very well inhabit the mansions or palaces of bishops; the "good citizen" could paradoxically be the "publicans" and "harlots," provided that these "first become righteous, like those who strive and who suffer for the sake of justice, truth, and humanity."

Bonhoeffer's chapter "The Ultimate and the Penultimate" continues the same kind of reflection. Justification by faith alone is, indeed, something final, encompassing the totality of human life. It is the single event of God's Word breaking into that life and freeing people to be for God and for their brothers and sisters. Faith, Bonhoeffer contends, is being set free to live by the life, death, and resurrection of Jesus Christ. But it is never mere belief devoid of love and hope and, therefore, lost in the religious labyrinth of creed, Bible, and church attendance. The Christian is one who, while living in the grace of God's final Word of justification, participates in the penultimate, "the encounter of Christ with the world." Bonhoeffer mentions that there are two dimensions to the penultimate, namely, being human and being good. Nazism had denied the human and inverted the sense of what was truly "good." If the Christian life is "the dawning of the ultimate," "the life of Jesus Christ in me," it is always life in the penultimate, on that humanity and goodness that herald Christ's advent in the lives of people.

It is here that Bonhoeffer's sense of Christ's compassion and of the problems faced by humans confronted with God's mystery of life and death approaches the edge where the true Christian and the nonreligious humanist meet.

It is not surprising, then, that Bonhoeffer adopts a positive attitude toward what he calls "the natural" and places it after his strong affirmation of the penultimate in *Ethics*. This "natural," though, is, like the penultimate, a preliminary to life with Christ. It is grasped by reason as the "true means of protection of the preserved life." It safeguards life itself against the "unnatural." Bonhoeffer's optimistic assessment of "the natural" stems from his conviction that without such a positive view, the chaos, confusion, and destructiveness so evident in the winter months of 1940–1941, when the text was composed, could go on unchallenged except by a weakened minority. "The unnatural," he insisted, "is the enemy of life." In the background there lurks the specter of the Nazi state reducing individuals and communities to their "utilizable value for some higher institution or organization or idea." When the state becomes an idol, there inevitably results "a certain hostility to life." For this reason Bonhoeffer wanted his ethical reflections to constitute a defense of human rights and, following on that, to speak of duties. If that approach seems out of place to idealistic thinkers, he retorts wryly that "our authority is not Kant; it is the Holy Scripture, and it is precisely for that reason that we must speak first of the rights of natural life, in other words of what is given to life, and only later of what is demanded of life." The detailed ranging of human rights that ensues is far from complete. This is something he admitted in his personal notes, commenting that establishing priorities and resolving conflicts "must be developed later!"

Bonhoeffer's steps toward resolution of these conflicts became the chapters "Christ, Reality and Good" and "History and Good." He aims in these sections to reinvigorate the incarnational perspective that dictated his earlier Christocentric emphasis. In this section of *Ethics*, we can likewise discern an effort on Bonhoeffer's part to interrelate both an ethic of conformation and an ethic of command, each in function of the other, each also in some way expression of the "will of God," which Bonhoeffer asserts to be *the* central question of ethics. The point of departure is, then, "the reality of God as he reveals himself in Jesus Christ." The question of the "good" becomes the question of how one participates in the reality of God. Again, Bonhoeffer makes Jesus Christ the judgment of what is "real" and what is "good"; in him Bonhoeffer sees reconciled "the conflict between what is and what should be."

By further appealing to the incarnational structure of all reality, Bonhoeffer hoped to cut through the main obstacle to a free, responsible decision of resistance to nazism, the tendency of people to divide reality into sacred and profane, Christian and secular spheres. This had permitted Christians to divorce their participation in secular life even from their identity as followers of Christ with consciences relatively intact. Bonhoeffer noticed with frustration how the churches became reduced to purely spiritual adjuncts to the state and were thus led to overlook their responsibility to promote human values and to defend civil rights. The consciences of Christians could, in turn, be dulled by churchy assurances that their routine, periodic sacred performance of listening to a sermon or participating in a harmless, nonthreatening liturgy was sufficient "responsibility." Christian life was split off from one's worldly life. While conceding that the "Christian" was not by that very fact identical with the worldly, nonetheless, Bonhoeffer argued for a unity of the two through one's faith in Christ, the ultimate reality. This would be a polemical unity in Christ through whom a "better secularity" could be achieved. Those who advocated thinking in "two spheres" were accused by Bonhoeffer of denying to people "that fellowship into which God entered with the world in Jesus Christ." The concrete form and the concrete encounter of the world with God's will lie, according to Bonhoeffer, in the "divine mandates" of work, marriage, government, and church. "Human good" has its specific locus, not in the abstraction of religious or universal principles, but in the more definite structure of the mandates governing everyday life.

However, as Bonhoeffer's work for the resistance drew him closer to the actual coup d'état, as the war progressed, and as the deportation and murder of Jews became a fact of life in the terror-filled world of nazism, Bonhoeffer found himself facing a more immediate but related question. Under what ethical rubric could the decent people of the resistance break the law and violate the military oath even to overthrow a criminal regime? Though the question may appear trivial in hindsight, for the conspirators it was especially important to limit any violence to a minimum. They desired neither the repetition of the post–World War I chaos nor a vindictive bloodbath. As a result, their plans lacked the ruthlessness needed for success. That the various attempts on Hitler's life failed is history. The undertaking of the final plot of July 20, 1944, was at best a moral victory costing some six thousand lives in Hitler's retaliatory purge. But one can still note from this section of *Ethics* that part of Bonhoeffer's role in the conspiracy was to stiffen the moral resolve of the resistance and, in particular, to demystify the sacredness of military oaths and the awe surrounding patriotism during a war effort. His argument shrugs the religious considerations to get to the heart of what constitutes true responsibility, at once Christlike and humanistic.

Responsible action in such a clouded-over situation is, Bonhoeffer admits, extraordinary. He can only appeal to the freedom of those who cannot be compelled to be responsible yet who do the deed. They are those who accept their "deputyship" for a nation, acknowledge their guilt in the violence even as they act to stem the violence, trusting in the Lord's forgiveness even as they experience in their deed the paradox of being a lawbreaker for the sake of the law and to restore the original unity of Christ and gospel values to the nation.

In other words, those preparing to deliver their nation and the world from the evil of nazism cannot set their own "innocence" above the needs of the people. They enter into what Bonhoeffer calls a "fellowship of guilt," sustained by the example of Christ, who himself accepted the guilt of his people in opposing the dehumanizing forces within his own religion. He is the model of and inspiration behind every action of responsible deputyship. What we find here in Bonhoeffer's "ethic of responsibility" is what he also recognizes as a special appeal of Christ's Lordship over the world. This is still an ethic of conformation; in this case, however, in the conflict situation where one's conscience is badgered by conflicting considerations of patriotism, abhorrence of violence, respect for oaths of allegiance, and downright guilt feelings over what they must do.

To all this Bonhoeffer answers that Jesus Christ "sets conscience free for the service of God and of our neighbor . . . even . . . when one enters into the fellowship of human guilt." How else could one stop the deportations, the murder, the terror, and the world war? In this, too, we see the sentiments to be echoed by

Bonhoeffer in one of the most memorable passages of "After Ten Years," his essay gift to the conspirators:

> We are not Christ, but if we want to be Christians, we must have some share in Christ's largeheartedness by acting with responsibility and in freedom when the hour of danger comes, and by showing a real sympathy that springs, not from fear, but from the liberating and redeeming love of Christ for all who suffer. Mere waiting and looking on is not Christian behavior. The Christian is called to sympathy and action . . . by the sufferings of his brothers and sisters, for whose sake Christ suffered.[8]

With his arguments neither fully developed nor fully in place, Bonhoeffer, in a last section that could very well have been restructured into new ethical foundations, turned again to the question of God's command. His reading in 1942 of Karl Barth's *Church Dogmatics*, II/2, catalyzed his interest in incorporating his own ethical reflections, smacking as they did in places of as much the rational and pragmatic as they did of the Christic, into the more overarching structure of God's command, freeing and binding and eliciting the human obedient response. This emphasis became chapter VII in the original German edition and in subsequent English editions. God's commandment, he declares, "is the only warrant for ethical discourse."[9] All his previous ethical reasoning would, as a consequence, be subordinated to this ethic of divine command. Yet this is a command heard only in history and nature, and in the existential moments of the "divine mandates."

In short, it is God's command that the concrete structures of human life flourish under a God-given unity. All of the mandated structures with their consequent responsibilities stand in interrelationship with each other; together they stand against the "unnatural" denial of the human. Each structure has its own individual integrity. When violated, as in the case of nazism, one can appeal to God in invoking the support of the other institutions of human life under God. Here we see rejected the claims of state to be legally accountable to no one and, in like manner, the triumphalist claims of church to be the ultimate end of all social life. The command of God in Jesus Christ, on the contrary, leads to an emancipation of all structures to fulfill their functions seen now in the light of Christ's gospel. In Barth's *Church Dogmatics*, II/2, Bonhoeffer seems to have found not only the missing link to his previous arguments on behalf of individual and corporate responsibility in the age of Nazi immorality and chaos but also a better expression of the underlying foundation of ethics. God's command becomes thus the ultimate source of all moral authority and the only ground of meaning for a *Christian* ethic. How this is related to the cross of Jesus Christ is a line of reasoning that will, in turn, become the theological strength of the prison letters. This theme marks the last selection of Bonhoeffer's *Ethics* included here. The selections themselves will show, it is hoped, Bonhoeffer's various attempts to describe why the responsible Christian aroused in conscience, must be free to do the daring deed in the name of human rights, ultimately in the name of Jesus Christ.

GOD'S LOVE AND THE WORLD

It is not said at all that the will of God forces its way into the human heart without further ado, charged with the accent of uniqueness, or that it is simply obvious, and identical with whatever the heart may think. The will of God may lie very deeply concealed beneath a great number of available possibilities. The will of God is not a system of rules which is established from the outset; it is something new and different in each different situation in life, and for this reason a man must ever anew examine what the will of God may be. The heart, the understanding, observation, and experience must all collaborate in this task. It is no longer a matter of a man's knowledge of good and evil, but solely of the living will of God; our knowledge of God's will is not something over which we ourselves dispose, but it depends solely upon the grace of God, and this grace is and requires to be new every morning. That is why this proving or examining of the will of God is so serious a matter. The voice of the heart is not to be confused with the will of God, nor is any kind of inspiration or any general principle, for the will of God discloses itself ever anew only to him who proves it ever anew.

Now how does a man set about this "proving what is the will of God"? ... One cannot, therefore, prove what is the will of God simply from one's own resources, from one's own knowledge of good and evil; on the contrary, only that man can do this who has lost all knowledge of his own of good and evil and who therefore abandons any attempt to know the will of God by his own means, who lives already in the unity of the will of God because the will of God has already been accomplished in him. Proving what is God's will is possible only on the foundation of the knowledge of God's will in Jesus Christ. Only upon the foundation of Jesus Christ, only within the space which is defined by Jesus Christ, only "in" Jesus Christ can man prove what is the will of God. [*E*, pp. 38–39]

It was not metaphysical speculation, it was not a theologumenon of the *logos spermatikos,* but it was the concrete suffering of injustice, of the organized lie, of hostility to mankind and of violence, it was the persecution of lawfulness, truth, humanity and freedom which impelled the men who held these values dear to seek the protection of Jesus Christ and therefore to become subject to his claim, and it was through this that the church of Jesus Christ learnt of the wide extent of her responsibility. The relationship of the church with the world today does not consist, as it did in the Middle Ages, in the calm and steady expansion of the power of the name of Christ, nor yet in an endeavor, such as was undertaken by the apologists of the first centuries of Christianity, to justify and publicize and embellish the name of Jesus Christ before the world by associating it with human names and values, but solely in that recognition of the origin which has been awakened and vouchsafed to people in this suffering, solely in the seeking of refuge from persecution in Christ. It is not Christ who must justify himself before the world by the acknowledgment of the values of justice, truth, and freedom, but it is these values which have come to need justification, and their justification can only be Jesus Christ. It is not that a "Christian culture" must make the name of Jesus Christ acceptable to the world; but the crucified

Christ has become the refuge and the justification, the protection and the claim for the higher values and their defenders that have fallen victim to suffering. It is with the Christ who is persecuted and who suffers in his church that justice, truth, humanity, and freedom now seek refuge; it is with the Christ who found no shelter in the world, the Christ who was cast out from the world, the Christ of the crib and of the cross, under whose protection they now seek sanctuary, and who thereby for the first time displays the full extent of his power. The cross of Christ makes both sayings true: "He that is not with me is against me" and "He that is not against us is for us."

CHRIST AND GOOD PEOPLE

"Blessed are they which are persecuted for righteousness' sake: for theirs is the kingdom of heaven" (Matt. 5:10). This does not refer to the righteousness of God; it does not refer to persecution for Jesus Christ's sake. It is the beatification of those who are persecuted for the sake of a just cause and, as we may now add, for the sake of a true, good, and human cause (cf. 1 Pet. 3:14 and 2:20). This beatitude puts those Christians entirely in the wrong who, in their mistaken anxiety to act rightly, seek to avoid any suffering for the sake of a just, good, and true cause, because, as they maintain, they could with a clear conscience suffer only an explicit profession of faith in Christ; it rebukes them for their ungenerousness and narrowness which looks with suspicion on all suffering for a just cause and keeps its distance from it. Jesus gives his support to those who suffer for the sake of a just cause, even if this cause is not precisely the confession of his name; he takes them under his protection, he accepts responsibility for them, and he lays claim to them. And so the man who is persecuted for the sake of a just cause is led to Christ, so that it happens that in the hour of suffering and of responsibility, perhaps for the first time in his life and in a way which is strange and surprising to him but is nevertheless an inner necessity, such a man appeals to Christ and professes himself a Christian because at this moment, for the first time, he becomes aware that he belongs to Christ. . . .

In times of established order, when the law rules supreme and the transgressor of the law is disgraced and ostracized, it is in relation to the tax gatherer and the prostitute that the gospel of Jesus Christ discloses itself most clearly to people. "The publicans and the harlots go into the kingdom of heaven before you" (Matt. 21:31). In times which are out of joint, in times when lawlessness and wickedness triumph in complete unrestraint it is rather in relation to the few remaining just, truthful and humane people that the gospel will make itself known. It was the experience of other times that the wicked found their way to Christ while the good remained remote from him. The experience of our own time is that it is the good who find their way back to Christ and that the wicked obstinately remain aloof from him. Other times could preach that a man must first become a sinner, like the publican and the harlot, before he could know and find Christ, but we in our time must say rather that before a man can know and find Christ he must first become righteous like those who strive and who suffer for the sake of justice, truth, and humanity. [*E*, pp. 58–61]

ETHICS AS FORMATION

To be conformed with the Incarnate—that is to be a real man. It is man's right and duty that he should be man. The quest for the super-man, the endeavor to outgrow the man within the man, the pursuit of the heroic, the cult of the demigod, all this is not the proper concern of man, for it is untrue. The real man is not an object either for contempt or for deification, but an object of the love of God. The rich and mani-fold variety of God's creation suffers no violence here from false uni-formity or from the forcing of people into the pattern of an ideal or a type or a definite picture of the human character. The real man is at liberty to be his Creator's creature. To be conformed with the Incarnate is to have the right to be the man one really is. Now there is no more pretense, no more hypocrisy or self-violence, no more compulsion to be something other, better, and more ideal than what one is. God loves the real man. God became a real man.

To be formed in the likeness of the Crucified—this means being a man sentenced by God. In his daily existence man carries with him God's sentence of death, the necessity of dying before God for the sake of sin. With his life he testifies that nothing can stand before God save only under God's sentence and grace. . . .

To be conformed with the Risen One—that is to be a new man before God. In the midst of death he is in life. In the midst of sin he is right-eous. In the midst of the old he is new. His secret remains hidden from the world. He lives because Christ lives, and lives in Christ alone. "Christ is my life" (Phil 1:21). . . .

"Formation" consequently means in the first place Jesus' taking form in his church. What takes form here is the form of Jesus Christ himself. The New Testament states the case profoundly and clearly when it calls the church the body of Christ. The body is the form. So the church is not a religious community of worshippers of Christ but is Christ himself who has taken form among people. The church can be called the body of Christ because in Christ's body man is really taken up by him, and so too, therefore, are all humankind. The church, then, bears the form which is in truth the proper form of all humanity. The image in which she is formed is the image of man. What takes place in her takes place as an example and substitute for all people. But it is impossible to state clearly enough that the church, too, is not an independent form by herself, side by side with the form of Christ, and that she, too, can therefore never lay claim to an independent character, title, authority or dignity on her own account and apart from him. The church is nothing but a section of humanity in which Christ has really taken form. What we have here is utterly and completely the form of Jesus Christ and not some other form side by side with him. The church is the man in Christ, incarnate, sentenced, and awakened to new life. . . . [E, pp. 81–83]

Ethics as formation, then, means the bold endeavor to speak about the way in which the form of Jesus Christ takes form in our world, in a manner which is neither abstract nor casuistic, neither programmatic nor purely speculative. Concrete judgments and decisions will have to be ventured here. Decision and action can here no longer be delegated to the personal conscience of the individual. Here there are concrete commandments and instructions for which obedience is demanded.

Ethics as formation is possible only upon the foundation of the form of Jesus Christ which is present in his church. The church is the place where Jesus Christ's taking form is proclaimed and accomplished. It is this proclamation and this event that Christian ethics is designed to serve. . . .

The historical Jesus Christ is the continuity of our history. But Jesus Christ was the promised Messiah of the Israelite-Jewish people, and for that reason the line of our forefathers goes back beyond the appearance of Jesus Christ to the people of Israel. Western history is, by God's will, indissolubly linked with the people of Israel, not only genetically but also in a genuine uninterrupted encounter. The Jew keeps open the question of Christ. He is the sign of the free mercy-choice and of the repudiating wrath of God. "Behold therefore the goodness and severity of God" (Rom. 11:22). An expulsion of the Jews from the West must necessarily bring with it the expulsion of Christ. For Jesus Christ was a Jew. [E, pp. 88–90]

THE CONFESSION OF GUILT

The only way to turn back is through recognition of the guilt toward Christ. What must be recognized as guilt is not the occasional lapse of error, or transgressions against an abstract law, but the defection from Christ, from the form which was ready to take form in us and to lead us to our own true form. True acknowledgment of guilt does not arise from the experience of disruption and decay, but for us, who have encountered the form of Christ, solely from this form. It presupposes, therefore, some measure of communion with this form. . . .

The place where this recognition of guilt becomes real is the church. But this is not to be understood as meaning that the church is the place of genuine recognition of guilt as something additional to the other things which she is and does. The church is precisely that community of human beings which has been led by the grace of Christ to the recognition of guilt toward Christ. To say, therefore, that the church is the place of the recognition of guilt is nothing but a tautology. If it were otherwise, she would no longer be the church. The church today is that community of people which is gripped by the power of the grace of Christ so that, recognizing as guilt toward Jesus Christ both its own personal sin and the apostasy of the Western world from Jesus Christ, it confesses this guilt and accepts the burden of it. It is in her that Jesus realizes his form in the midst of the world. That is why the church alone can be the place of personal and collective rebirth and renewal. . . .

With this confession the entire guilt of the world falls upon the church, upon the Christians, and since this guilt is not denied here, but is confessed, there arises the possibility of forgiveness. . . .

The church confesses that she has witnessed the lawless application of brutal force, the physical and spiritual suffering of countless innocent people, oppression, hatred, and murder, and that she has not raised her voice on behalf of the victims and has not found ways to hasten to their aid. She is guilty of the deaths of the weakest and most defenseless brothers of Jesus Christ. . . . The church confesses that she has witnessed in silence the spoilage and exploitation of the poor and the enrichment and corruption of the strong.

The church confesses herself guilty toward the countless victims of calumny, denunciation, and defamation. She has not convicted the slanderer of his wrongdoing, and she has thereby abandoned the slandered to his fate.

The church confesses that she has desired security, peace and quiet, possessions and honor, to which she had no right, and that in this way she has not bridled the desires of people but has stimulated them still further. . . .

The "justification and renewal" of the West, therefore, will come only when justice, order, and peace are in one way or another restored, when past guilt is thereby "forgiven," when it is no longer imagined that what has been done can be undone by means of punitive measures and reprisals, and when the church of Jesus Christ, as the fountainhead of all forgiveness, justification, and renewal, is given room to do her work among the nations. The guilt of the apostasy from Christ is a guilt which is shared in common by the entire Western world, however greatly the degree of the offense may vary. The justification and the renewal must therefore likewise be shared in common by the whole of the West. No attempt can succeed which aims at saving the West while excluding one of the Western nations. [*E*, pp. 110–19]

LAST AND PENULTIMATE THINGS

THE PENULTIMATE

One must ask the question at this point, without answering it, whether people can live by the ultimate alone, whether faith can, so to speak, be extended in time, or whether faith does not rather always become real in life as the ultimate phase of a span of time or of many spans of time. We are not speaking here of the recollection of past faith, or of the repetition of articles of faith, but of the living faith which justifies a life. We are asking whether this faith is and ought to be realizable every day, at every hour, or whether here too, the length of the penultimate must every time be traversed anew for the sake of the ultimate. We are asking, therefore, about the penultimate in the lives of Christians. We are asking whether to deny it is pious self-deception, or whether to take it seriously in its own way is to incur guilt. This means that we are asking also whether the Word, the gospel, can be extended in time, whether it can be spoken at any time in the same way, or whether here, too, there is a difference between the ultimate and the penultimate. So that this may become quite clear, let us ask why it is that precisely in thoroughly grave situations, for instance when I am with someone who has suffered a bereavement, I often decide to adopt a "penultimate" attitude, particularly when I am dealing with Christians, remaining silent as a sign that I share in the bereaved man's helplessness in the face of such a grievous event, and not speaking the biblical words of comfort which are, in fact, known to me and available to me. Why am I often unable to open my mouth, when I ought to give expression to the ultimate? And why, instead, do I decide on an expression of thoroughly penultimate human solidarity? Is it from mistrust of the power of the ultimate word? Is it from fear of people? Or is there some good positive reason for such an attitude, namely, that my knowledge of the word, my having it at my fingertips, in other words my being, so to speak, spiritually master of the situation, bears only the appearance of the ultimate, but is in reality itself something entirely penultimate? Does one not in some cases, by remaining deliberately in the penultimate, perhaps point all the more genuinely to the ultimate, which God will speak in his own time (though indeed even then through a human mouth)? Does not this mean that, over and over again, the penultimate will be what commends itself precisely for the sake of the ultimate, and that it will have to be done not with a heavy conscience but with a clear one? Of course, this question is not concerned only with a particular case. Fundamentally it embraces the whole domain of Christian social life, and especially the whole range of Christian pastoral activity. What we have said about this particular case applies in countless instances to the daily life of Christians together, and to the whole activity of the Christian preacher with his flock. [E, pp. 125–26]

Preparing the way for the word: this is the purpose of everything that has been said about the things before the last. "Prepare ye the way of the Lord, make his paths straight. Every valley shall be filled, and every mountain and hill shall be brought low; and the crooked shall be made straight, and the rough ways shall be made smooth; and all flesh shall see the salvation of God" (Luke 3:4ff.). Christ indeed makes his own way when he comes; he is the "breaker" of all bonds (Mic. 2:13). "He breaketh the gates of brass, and cutteth the bars of iron in sunder" (Ps. 107:16); "He putteth down the mighty from their seat, and exalteth the humble and meek" (Luke 1:52). His entry is a triumph over his enemies. But lest the might of His coming should overwhelm mankind in anger, and in order that it may find them humble and expectant, the entry is preceded by the summons to the preparation of the way. Yet this making ready of the way is not merely an inward process; it is a formative activity on the very greatest visible scale. "The valleys shall be exalted" (Isa. 40:4). That which has been cast down into the depths of human wretchedness, that which has been abased and humbled, is now to be raised up. There is a depth of human bondage, of human poverty, of human ignorance, which impedes the merciful coming of Christ. "The mountains and hills shall be made low" (Isa. 40:4). If Christ is to come, then all that is proud and haughty must bow down. There is a measure of power, of wealth, of knowledge, which is an impediment to Christ and to his mercy. "The crooked shall be made straight" (Luke 3:5). The way of Christ is a straight way. There is a measure of entanglement in the lie, in guilt, in one's own labor, in one's own work (Ps. 9:16) and in self-love, which makes the coming of grace particularly difficult. That is why the way had to be made straight on which Christ is to come to man. "The rough ways shall be made smooth" (Luke 3:5). Defiance, stubbornness, and unreceptiveness may have hardened a man so much that Christ can now only destroy him in anger as one who resists him, and so that Christ can no longer enter into him in mercy, because the door is bolted against Christ's merciful coming and is not opened to him when he knocks.

Christ comes indeed, and opens up his own way, no matter whether man is ready beforehand or not. No one can hinder his coming, but we can resist his coming in mercy. There are conditions of the heart, of life and of the world which impede the reception of grace in a special way, namely, by rendering faith infinitely difficult. We say that they impede it and render it difficult, but not that they make it impossible. And we are well aware also that even the leveling of the way and the removal of the obstacles cannot compel the imparting of grace. The merciful coming of Christ must still "break the gates of brass and cut the bars of iron" (Ps. 107:16); grace must in the end itself prepare and make level its own way and grace alone must ever anew render possible the impossible. But all this does not release us from our obligation to prepare the way for the coming of grace, and to remove whatever obstructs it and makes it difficult. The state in which grace finds us is not a matter of indifference, even though it is always by grace alone that grace comes to us. We may, among other things, make it difficult for ourselves to attain to faith. For him who is cast into utter shame, desolation, poverty, and helplessness, it is difficult to have faith in the justice and goodness of God. For him whose life has become a prey to disorder and indiscipline, it will be difficult to hear the commandments of God in faith. It is hard for the sated and the mighty to grasp the meaning of God's judgment and God's mercy. And for one who has been disappointed in mistaken belief, and who has become inwardly undisciplined, it is hard to attain to the simplicity of the surrender of the heart to Jesus Christ. That is not said in order either to excuse or to discourage those whom these things have befallen. They must know, on the contrary, that it is precisely to the depths of downfall, of guilt, and of misery, that God stoops down in Jesus Christ; that precisely the dispossessed, the humiliated, and the exploited are especially near to the justice and mercy of God; that it is to the undisciplined that Jesus Christ offers his help and his strength; and that the truth is ready to set upon firm ground those who stray and despair.

But all this does not exclude the task of preparing the way. This task is, on the contrary, a charge of immense responsibility for all those who know of the coming of Christ. The hungry need bread and the homeless need a roof; the dispossessed need justice and the lonely need fellowship; the undisciplined need order and the slave needs freedom. To allow the hungry to remain hungry would be blasphemy against God and one's neighbor, for what is nearest to God is precisely the need of one's neighbor. It is for the love of Christ, which belongs as much to the hungry as to myself, that I share my bread with them and that I share my dwelling with the homeless. If the hungry do not attain to faith, then the guilt falls on those who refused them bread. To provide the hungry with bread is to prepare the way for the coming of grace. [*E*, pp. 135–37]

Christian life is the dawning of the ultimate in me; it is the life of Jesus Christ in me. But it is always also life in the penultimate which waits for the ultimate. The earnestness of Christian life lies solely in the ultimate, but the penultimate, too, has its earnestness, which consists indeed precisely in never confusing the penultimate with the ultimate and in regarding the penultimate as an empty jest in comparison with the ultimate, so that the ultimate and the penultimate may alike retain their seriousness and validity. This demonstrates once again the impossibility of any radical Christianity and of any compromising Christianity in the face of the reality of Jesus Christ and of his coming into the world. [*E*, pp. 141–42]

CHRIST, REALITY AND GOOD

THE CONCEPT OF REALITY

The point of departure for Christian ethics is not the reality of one's own self, or the reality of the world; nor is it the reality of standards and values. It is the reality of God as he reveals himself in Jesus Christ. It is fair to begin by demanding assent to this proposition of anyone who wishes to concern himself with the problem of a Christian ethic. It poses the ultimate and crucial question of the reality which we mean to reckon with in our lives, whether it is to be reality of the revelational word of God or earthly imperfections, whether it is to be resurrection or death. No man can decide this question by himself, by his own choice, without deciding it wrongly, for it presupposes the answer given, namely that, whatever our decision may be, God has already spoken his word of revelation, and even in the false reality we cannot live otherwise than the true reality of the word of God. Thus when we ask about the ultimate reality we are thereby at once inescapably bound by the answers to our question. For the question conveys us into the midst of its origin, the reality of the revelation of God in Jesus Christ. . . . [E, pp. 189–90]

In Christ we are offered the possibility of partaking in the reality of God and in the reality of the world, but not in the one without the other. The reality of God discloses itself only by setting me entirely in the reality of the world, and when I encounter the reality of the world it is always already sustained, accepted, and reconciled in the reality of God. This is the inner meaning of the revelation of God in the man Jesus Christ. Christian ethics inquires about the realization in our world of this divine and cosmic reality which is given in Christ. This does not mean that "our world" is something outside the divine and cosmic reality which is in Christ or that it is not already part of the world which is sustained, accepted, and reconciled in him. It does not mean that one must still begin by applying some kind of "principle" to our situation and our time. The inquiry is directed rather toward the way in which the reality in Christ, which for a long time already has comprised us and our world within itself, is taking effect as something now present, and toward the way in which life may be conducted in this reality. Its purpose is, therefore, participation in the reality of God and of the world in Jesus Christ today, and this participation must be such that I never experience the reality of God without the reality of the world or the reality of the world without the reality of God. [E, p. 195]

THINKING IN TERMS OF TWO SPHERES

One is denying the revelation of God in Jesus Christ if one tries to be "Christian" without seeing and recognizing the world in Christ. There are, therefore, not two spheres, but only the one sphere of the realization of Christ, in which the reality of God and the reality of the world are united. Thus the theme of the two spheres, which has repeatedly become the dominant factor in the history of the church, is foreign to the New Testament. The New Testament is concerned solely with the manner in which the reality of Christ assumes reality in the present world, which it has already encompassed, seized, and possessed. There are not two spheres, standing side by side, competing with each other and attacking each other's frontiers. If that were so, this frontier dispute would always be the decisive problem of history. But the whole reality of the world is already drawn in into Christ and bound together in him, and the movement of history consists solely in divergence and convergence in relation to this center. . . . And yet what is Christian is not identical with what is of the world. The natural is not identical with the supernatural or the revelational with the rational. But between the two there is in each case a unity which derives solely from the reality of Christ, that is to say solely from faith in this ultimate reality. This unity is seen in the way in which the secular and the Christian elements prevent one another from assuming any kind of static independence in their mutual relations. They adopt a polemical attitude toward each other and bear witness precisely in this to their shared reality and to their unity in the reality which is in Christ. . . . [E, pp. 197–199]

And so, too, the church of Jesus Christ is the place, in other words the space in the world, at which the reign of Jesus Christ over the whole world is evidenced and proclaimed. This space of the church, then, is not something which exists on its own account. It is from the outset something which reaches out far beyond itself, for indeed it is not the space of some kind of cultural association such as would have to fight for its own survival in the world but it is the place where testimony is given to the foundation of all reality in Jesus Christ. The church is the place where testimony and serious thought are given to God's reconciliation of the world with himself in Christ, to his having so loved the world that he gave his Son for its sake. The space of the church is not there in order to try to deprive the world of a piece of its territory, but precisely in order to prove to the world that it is still the world, the world which is loved by God and reconciled with him. The church has neither the wish nor the obligation to extend her space to cover the space of the world. She asks for no more space than she needs for the purpose of serving the world by bearing witness to Jesus Christ and to the reconciliation of the world with God through him. The only way in which the church can defend her own territory is by fighting not for it but for the salvation of the world. Otherwise the church becomes a "religious society" which fights in its own interest and thereby ceases at once to be the church of God and of the world. And so the first demand which is made of those who belong to God's church is not that they should be something in themselves, not that they should, for example, set up some religious organization or that they should lead lives of piety, but that they shall be witnesses to Jesus Christ before the world. [E, pp. 202–3]

THE FOUR MANDATES

The world, like all created things, is created through Christ and with Christ as its end, and consists in Christ alone (John 1:10; Col. 1:16). To speak of the world without speaking of Christ is empty and abstract. The world is relative to Christ, no matter whether it knows it or not. This relativeness of the world to Christ assumes concrete form in certain

mandates of God in the world. The Scriptures name four such mandates: labor, marriage, government, and the church. We speak of divine
mandates rather than of divine orders because the word mandate refers
more clearly to a divinely imposed task rather than to a determination
of being. It is God's will that there shall be labor, marriage, government,
and church in the world; and it is his will that all these, each in its own
way, shall be through Christ, directed toward Christ, and in Christ. God
has imposed all these mandates on all people. He has not merely imposed one of these mandates on each individual, but he has imposed all
four on all people. This means that there can be no retreating from a
"secular" into a "spiritual" sphere. There can be only the practice, the
learning of the Christian life under these four mandates of God. And it
will not do to regard the first three mandates as "secular," in contradis-
tinction to the fourth. For even in the midst of the world these are divine
mandates, no matter whether their topic be labor, marriage, government, or the church. These mandates are, indeed, divine only by virtue
of their original and final relation to Christ. [E, p. 207]

HISTORY AND GOOD

If we now return to the question of good, we may say provisionally
that we are, in any case, dealing here with life itself and not with an
abstraction from life, with the realization, for example, of certain definite ideals and values which are independent of life. Good is life as it is
in reality, that is to say, in its origin, essence, and goal; it is life in the
sense of the saying "Christ is my life" (Phil. 1:21). Good is not a quality
of life. It is "life" itself. To be good is to "live."

This life assumes concrete form in the contradictory unity of "yes"
and "no" which life finds outside itself in Jesus Christ. But Jesus Christ
is man and is God in one. In him there takes place the original and
essential encounter with man and with God. Henceforward man cannot
be conceived and known otherwise than in Jesus Christ, and God cannot
be conceived and known otherwise than in the human form of Jesus
Christ. In him we see humanity as that which God has accepted, borne,
and loved, and as that which is reconciled with God. In him we see God
in the form of the poorest of our brothers. There is no man "in himself,"
just as there is no God "in himself"; both of these are empty abstractions. Man is the man who was accepted in the incarnation of Christ,
who was loved, condemned, and reconciled in Christ; and God is God
become man. There is no relation to people without a relation to God,
and no relation to God without a relation to people, and it is only our
relation to Jesus Christ which provides the basis for our relation to people and to God. Jesus Christ is our life, and so now, from the standpoint
of Jesus Christ, we may say that our fellow man is our life and that God
is our life. . . .

We give the name responsibility to this life in its aspect as a response to the life of Jesus Christ as the "yes" and the "no" to our life. This concept of responsibility is intended as referring to the concentrated totality and unity of the response to the reality which is given to us in Jesus Christ, as distinct from the partial responses which might arise, for example, from a consideration of utility or from particular principles. In the face of the life which confronts us in Jesus Christ these partial responses are not enough and nothing less can suffice the entire and single response of our life. Responsibility means, therefore, that the totality of life is pledged and that our action becomes a matter of life and death. . . . [E, pp. 221–22]

Our conclusion from this must be that action which is in accordance with Christ is action which is in accordance with reality. This proposition is not an ideal demanded, but it is an assertion which springs from the knowledge of reality itself. Jesus Christ does not confront reality as one who is alien to it, but it is he who alone has borne and experienced the essence of the real in his own body, who has spoken from the standpoint of reality as no man on earth can do, who alone has fallen victim to no ideology, but who is the truly real one, who has borne within himself and fulfilled the essence of history, and in whom the law of the life of history is embodied. He is the real one, the origin, essence, and goal of all that is real, and for that reason he is himself the Lord and the Law of the real. Consequently the Word of Jesus Christ is the interpretation of his existence, and it is therefore the interpretation of that reality in which history attains to its fulfillment. The words of Jesus are the divine commandment for responsible action in history in so far as this history is the reality of history as it is fulfilled in Christ, the responsibility for man as it is fulfilled in Christ alone. They are not intended to serve the ends of an abstract ethic; for an abstract ethic they are entirely incomprehensible and they lead to conflicts which can never be resolved, but they take effect in the reality of history, for it is from there that they originate. Any attempt to detach them from this origin distorts them into a feeble ideology and robs them of the power, which they possess in their attachment to their origin, of witnessing to reality. Action which is in accordance with Christ is in accordance with reality because it allows the world to be the world; it reckons with the world as the world; and yet it never forgets that in Jesus Christ the world is loved, condemned, and reconciled by God. . . . [E, pp. 229–30]

THE WORLD OF THINGS

In the course of historical life there comes a point where the exact observance of the formal law of a state, of a commercial undertaking, of a family, or for that matter of a scientific discovery, suddenly finds itself in violent conflict with the ineluctable necessities of the lives of humans; at this point responsible and pertinent action leaves behind it the domain of principle and convention, the domain of the normal and regular, and is confronted by the extraordinary situation of ultimate necessities, a situation which no law can control. It was for this situation that Machiavelli in his political theory coined the term *necessità*. In the field of politics this means that the technique of statecraft has now been supplanted by the necessity of state. There can be no doubt that such necessities exist; to deny their existence is to abandon the attempt to act in accordance with reality. But it is equally certain that these necessities are a primary fact of life itself and cannot, therefore, be governed by any law or themselves constitute a law. They appeal directly to the free responsibility of the agent, a responsibility which is bound by no law. They create a situation which is extraordinary; they are by nature peripheral and abnormal events. They no longer leave a multiplicity of courses open to human reason but they confront it with the question of the *ultima ratio*. . . . The extraordinary necessity appeals to the freedom of the person who is responsible. There is now no law behind which the responsible person can seek cover, and there is, therefore, also no law which can compel the responsible person to take any particular decision in the face of such necessities. In this situation there can only be a complete renunciation of every law, together with the knowledge that here one must make one's decision as a free venture, together also with the open admission that here the law is being infringed and violated and that necessity obeys no commandment. Precisely in this breaking of the law, the validity of the law is acknowledged, and in this renunciation of all law, and in this alone, one's own decision and deed are entrusted unreservedly to the divine governance of history. [*E*, pp. 238–40]

THE COMMANDMENT OF GOD

Because the commandment of God is the commandment which is revealed in Jesus Christ, no single authority, among those which are authorized to proclaim the commandment, can claim to be absolute. The authorization to speak is conferred from above on the church, the family, labor, and government, only so long as they do not encroach upon each other's domains and only so long as they give effect to God's commandment in conjunction and collaboration with one another and each in its own way. No single one of these authorities can exclusively identify itself with the commandment of God. The supremacy of the commandment of God is shown precisely by the fact that it juxtaposes and coordinates these authorities in a relation of mutual opposition and complementarity and that it is only in this multiplicity of concrete correlations and limitations that the commandment of God takes effect as the commandment which is manifest in Jesus Christ.

God's commandment, revealed in Jesus Christ, is always concrete speech to somebody. It is never abstract speech about something or about somebody. It is always an address, a claim, and it is so comprehensive and at the same time so definite that it leaves no freedom for interpretation or application, but only the freedom to obey or to disobey.

God's commandment, revealed in Jesus Christ, embraces the whole of life. It does not only, like the ethical, keep watch on the untransgressible frontier of life, but it is at the same time the center and the fullness of life. It is not only obligation but also permission. It does not only forbid, but it also sets free for life; it sets free for unreflected doing. It does not only interrupt the process of life when this process goes astray, but it guides and conducts this process even though there is not always need for consciousness of this fact. God's commandment becomes the daily divine guidance of our lives. . . . [*E*, pp. 279–80]

In the Incarnation God makes himself known as him who wishes to exist not for himself but "for us." Consequently, in view of the Incarnation of God, to live as man before God can mean only to exist not for oneself but for God and for other people.

Jesus Christ, the crucified Reconciler: this means in the first place that the whole world has become godless by its rejection of Jesus Christ and that no effort of its own can rid it of this curse. The reality of the world has been marked once and for all by the cross of Christ, but the cross of Christ is the cross of the reconciliation of the world with God, and for this reason the godless world bears at the same time the mark of reconciliation as the free ordinance of God. The cross of atonement is the setting free for life before God in the midst of the godless world; it is the setting free for life in genuine worldliness. The proclamation of the cross of the atonement is a setting free because it leaves behind it the vain attempts to deify the world and because it has overcome the disunions, tensions, and conflicts between the "Christian" element and the "secular" element and calls for simple life and action in the belief that the reconciliation of the world with God has been accomplished. A life in genuine worldliness is possible only through the proclamation of Christ crucified; true worldly living is not possible or real in contradiction to the proclamation or side by side with it, that is to say, in any kind of autonomy of the secular sphere; it is possible and real only "in, with, and under" the proclamation of Christ. Without or against the proclamation of the cross of Christ there can be no recognition of the godlessness and godforsakenness of the world, but the worldly element will rather seek always to satisfy its insatiable longing for its own deification. If, however, the worldly element establishes its own law side by side with the proclamation of Christ, then it falls victim entirely, to itself and must in the end set itself in the place of God. [*E*, p. 297]

Part 7

BONHOEFFER'S
CORRESPONDENCE

Dietrich Bonhoeffer in the courtyard of the military interrogation prison at Tegel (summer 1944).
From: Eberhard Bethge, Renate Bethge, Christian Gremmels *Dietrich Bonhoeffer: A Life in Pictures* (Philadelphia: Fortress Press, 1986) p. 203.

Introduction:
Who *Is* Jesus Christ for Us Today?

The first acquaintance with the writings and life of Dietrich Bonhoeffer for many people has been through his prison letters. One student of his religious thought has called this final form of his "doing theology," namely, the letters to his friend Eberhard Bethge, "the most interesting and revolutionary relic" Bonhoeffer had left behind. This writer went on to note the "subversive" nature of the prison correspondence. For him, Bonhoeffer's letters signaled "the end of the dominance of care, clarity, and system in theology; the triumph of the communiqué; the notes scribbled for him who must run; disconnected observations on things that matter, written in haste and with passion. . . ."[1] However exaggerated these remarks may be, they nonetheless point to that special fascination for Bonhoeffer's letters and papers from prison among both theologians and the public at large. A Jewish reader wrote to Bethge that upon reading the letters he could understand for the first time why Jesus Christ could be regarded as divine. The famous theologian Karl Barth, himself an influence on Bonhoeffer's theology, called the letters "a particular thorn."

Certainly part of their charm has been the ungoverned spontaneity, even fragmentariness, of Bonhoeffer's reflections. He is a person seemingly in a hurry, and, after the failure of the attempt of July 20, 1944, on Hitler's life, always conscious of the fact that each letter could be his last. Bethge, Bonhoeffer's biographer and editor of the posthumous writings as well as his friend, was astounded at the interest publication of the prison correspondence generated. In fact, initially Bethge was reluctant to share them with others. It was not until 1950 that he sent extracts from the letters to friends and former students of Bonhoeffer and to others who might be interested in Bonhoeffer's final words from prison. From several of these came the encouragement to publish. The noted theologian Gerhard Ebeling, for example, saw in the letters a confirmation of the influence Bonhoeffer continued to exert on him long after he was Bonhoeffer's student at Finkenwalde. Theologian Helmut Thielicke described the letters as exercising "an intensity and living power" he had not experienced for many years. Theologian Ronald Gregor Smith, aware of the inspiring nature of the letters, decided to have them translated into English. With the translation of the letters and the notoriety given to Bonhoeffer by Bishop John A.T. Robinson's *Honest To God*, Bonhoeffer would belong to the world beyond Germany and exert an influence on church and theology beyond anything Bethge had ever imagined.[2]

In a sermon marking the twentieth anniversary of Bonhoeffer's death, on Passion Sunday, April 4, 1965, this same Bishop Robinson spoke of how Bonhoeffer's life and martyrdom proved true Christ's words recorded in the Gospel of John: "Unless a grain of wheat falls into the earth and dies, it remains alone; but if it dies, it bears much fruit [John 12:24.]"

> Had he not died Dietrich Bonhoeffer would have been one among many competing voices for the ear of the Church. Because he died he has been released for all the world, and the seeds of thought which he left have already burst into flower. But they are like passion-flowers—with the markings of the crucifixion on them. And it is fitting that this commemoration of his death should fall on the day which the Church calls Passion Sunday. For he more than any man of our century has extended our insight into its meaning.[3]

At the time Bethge decided to publish excerpts from the letters, however, Bonhoeffer's final thoughts were more like a message one puts inside a bottle to be cast on the seas with only a vague hope the message would reach its destination. In Bonhoeffer's case, the message reached all the continents of the world, prompting one astute observer to entitle the *Festschrift* (celebrative volume) honoring Bethge on his seventieth birthday "Like a Bottled Message on the Seas."[4]

Bethge had already published a version of *Ethics* in 1949. Because of its incomplete nature and comparisons with Bonhoeffer's earlier work *The Cost of Discipleship,* the book did not arouse much consideration either from scholars or from the general public. It was only when the letters from prison appeared that *Ethics* received the attention it deserved. Bethge relates how some of the letters to him had been stored in the attic of his own mother's house back in the country. Some had begun to disintegrate because of the damp mold. Other letters, smuggled out of prison by a friendly guard named Knobloch, had been preserved because Bonhoeffer's niece and Bethge's wife Renate had the foresight to put them in a gas mask canister and bury them in her parents' garden. Some of the correspondence was lost. But, encouraged by Bonhoeffer's friends to make public these dramatic theological probings and sketches and realizing that the ideas were too fragmentary to be published as a theological treatise on the theme "Christ in a World Come of Age," Bethge decided to stick to the letter format.[5] Thus began the process of selecting and abstracting the letters that would be included in the first edition of what Bethge would entitle, *Widerstand und Ergebung* (*Resistance and Submission*), but called in the first English translation *Prisoner for God* and since then entitled *Letters and Papers from Prison.* Bethge made a strong effort to leave untouched the very emotional, personal nature of the letters from one facing a possible death sentence for treason. But it was a treason that in the inverted world of nazism would be looked on as "true patriotism" just as Bonhoeffer's death would be seen as a martyrdom. The book would soon spawn reactions as varied as they were unpredictable. People from all levels of life—except those gnashing their teeth in neo-Nazi rat holes within Germany—began to express openly their admiration for this modern-day martyr of that other, decent Germany, which the victims of nazism had not always known. Theologians found exciting the new directions pointed to in Bonhoeffer's prediction of a nonreligious Christianity and his call for a nonreligious interpretation of biblical concepts. Pastors and people of faith everywhere, puzzled by the sufferings inflicted in a world at war, thrilled to Bonhoeffer's descriptions of how God allows himself to be edged out of the world onto the cross and his portrayal of Jesus as the man for others. People searching for a community would see in the letters an exciting preamble to a church unafraid to speak the controversial word to the world and to do the responsible deed to rescue the nations enslaved by evil. In short, Bonhoeffer, executed at the young age of thirty-nine, began to assume new life, stirring up controversy within the churches and continuing to provoke people even beyond his own church. Through the letters he challenged people to take seriously Christ's Sermon on the Mount and to accept the costly grace of being one of Christ's followers.

The interest provoked by the letters generated more intense questions about Bonhoeffer the man and demands for further clues to the correct understanding of his theology and how best to cope with the ecclesial disturbances created by his radical questions from prison. Theologians and churchpeople wanted to know how to accept this latest shaking of their foundations. "What else had he written?" they asked. What was he like as a teacher? As a pastor? Why had he joined the resistance movement? Were there other letters? What could be remembered about him by his friends? And so Bethge began to make available Bonhoeffer's many other works. Even books like his heavy Berlin dissertations, which Bonhoeffer had quietly disowned, were aroused from a twenty-five-year slumber to new audiences and new life.

The task of collecting, editing, and publishing the extant writings became more imperious, however, as religious writers began to twist the prison letters into their own theological agenda, making them endorse short-lived ideas like the "Death of God" theology, a phenomenon hardly consonant either with Bonhoeffer's theology or his spirituality. Serious scholars, such as those who became the nucleus of the International Bonhoeffer Society in both Europe and North America, assisted Bethge in the work of editing the entire Bonhoeffer literary legacy. Some researchers concentrated on collecting and preserving in "Living History Projects" the recorded memories of those who knew Bonhoeffer most closely. Bethge's work came, therefore, to include Bonhoeffer's personal correspondence with family, friends, fellow theologians, pastors, and churchpeople caught up in the crises provoked by the rise of nazism and the outbreak of war. The letters written before 1943 help to put Bonhoeffer's theological output in better context. At times they are a valuable source of his theology.

But they are more than context. Theologian John Henry Newman once said that "the true life of a man is in his letters." Bonhoeffer's correspondence provides us with invaluable insight into the character of the man as well as an intriguing glance into the troublesome history of this period. We find in the correspondence, too, the special merit of style and substance that enhances the refined quality of Bonhoeffer's more formal writings. The letters likewise reveal a pastor deeply in love with his people and courageous enough to commit himself to a relentless struggle for the truth within his church and country. His letters recount the private turmoil of an individual often in opposition to the mainstream of opinion within his own church. They show a man outraged by his church's public posturing for privilege, security, and power at a time when basic human rights and the freedom to speak dissent were being contravened. Bonhoeffer's letters are, moreover, a testimonial to a person with an extraordinary perception of historical reality and sense of the future.

Bethge's careful collection of Bonhoeffer's letters gives a remarkable portrait of a person who dared to be different at a time when most Germans marched lockstep behind their *Führer*. The letters are, moreover, the correspondence of a man loyal to his friends and willing to sacrifice his time, money, and emotional energies for what he perceived to be the cause of Jesus Christ urging him to compassion and action on behalf of the oppressed of Nazi Germany. Expressed here are the joys of friendship along with anger at the destruction of people and the corruption of both state and church in a twentieth-century reign of terror. The letters give, as few other Bonhoeffer documents do, a penetrating look at Bonhoeffer the man, at the sources of his strength and his attractiveness to those who knew him. And they reveal in their own unique way the love for Jesus Christ that impelled Bonhoeffer in his diversified life as theologian, pastor, ecumenist, and conspirator.

53

Letters from the Year in Barcelona

1928

Before Bonhoeffer could be assigned a pastorate of his own, he was required to spend a year as curate under the supervision of a parish priest. Such a position was offered him under Pastor Fritz Olbricht, chaplain to the German-speaking Lutheran community in Barcelona. Consequently, the year in Barcelona would become Bonhoeffer's first extended stay away from the family and university life to which he had grown accustomed. When Bonhoeffer left Germany in February 1928, he was stepping into a parish where little was demanded of the parishioners. For the most part they were expatriated small-minded businesspeople satisfied with mediocrity in and from their church. He could have been bored—instead he was amused by the situation—or, as he wrote to his grandmother, tempted to become "tremendously lazy." As it was, resisting boredom but trying not to upset the more quietistic pastor, Bonhoeffer quickly entered into the interests of his parishioners, even their business anxieties and failures. He began a special service for the children and became a listener to the fears and expectations of parents. It was a trying time. Soon enough Bonhoeffer had his first experience in one of the most demanding tasks of spiritual care, namely, to console and help those who were beset by poverty, unemployment, and bankruptcy. He assisted his parishioners with gifts and loans. The two letters that follow, one to his father, who had sent him money, medical advice, and prescriptions for the poor, the other to his friend Helmut Rössler, show a characteristic Bonhoeffer, the curate with a deeply rooted concern for people in need. The letter to Rössler tells, too, of his desire that the Word of God be real in the lives of people.

LETTER TO KARL BONHOEFFER

Barcelona, July 7, 1928

. . . One has to deal with the strangest persons, with whom one would otherwise scarcely have exchanged a word, bums, vagabonds, criminals on the run, many foreign legionaries, lion and other animal tamers who have run away from the Krone Circus on its Spanish tour, German dancers from the music halls here, German murderers on the run—all of whom tell one their life story in detail. It is often very difficult in these cases to give or to refuse at one's own discretion. As it is impossible to establish any principles in the matter, the decisive factor has to be one's personal impression; and that can often and easily be mistaken . . . so in the course of time one finds oneself becoming sharper and sharper in defense of the interests of those who are genuinely in distress and cannot be helped adequately. Twice since I have been here I have seen long-established and prosperous families totally ruined, so that they have been unable to go on buying clothes for their children or paying their school fees. . . . Yesterday for the first time I had a man here who behaved so impudently—he claimed that the minister had forged his signature—that I practically shouted at him and threw him out. . . . While taking a hurried departure he cursed and swore, and said something that I have now often heard: "We shall see each other again, just come down to the harbor!" Afterwards I found out at the consulate that he is a well-known swindler who has been hanging about here for a long time, so I was quite pleased that I had dealt with him in the way I had. On the whole, however, I find that kindness and friendliness is the best way of dealing with these people. . . . When Olbricht does not like someone, he gives him a dressing down and throws him out, and he thinks that is more effective. . . . The pleasure of seeing that one has been really helpful is rare, because in most cases the money runs through their fingers as soon as they get it. . . . The real trouble is that we have no employment bureau, and the reason for that is that businesses here are overstaffed already. The Germans are pulling out. . . . We are continually concerned with Germans going home, though we know that things are no better there. [*DB*, pp. 76–77]

LETTER TO HELMUT RÖSSLER

Barcelona, August 7, 1928

. . . You know something about the work that I am doing, from my first letter; it is quite a remarkable experience for one to see work and life really coming together—a synthesis which we all looked for in our student days, but hardly managed to find; really to live *one* life and not two, or rather half a life. It gives the work value and the worker an objectivity, a recognition of his own limitations, such as can only be gained in real life.

I'm getting to know new people every day; here one meets people as they are, away from the masquerade of the "Christian world," people with passions, criminal types, little people with little ambitions, little desires and little sins, all in all people who feel homeless in both senses of the word, who loosen up if one talks to them in a friendly way, real people; I can only say that I have gained the impression that it is just these people who are much more under grace than under wrath, and that it is the Christian world which is more under wrath than under grace. "I was ready to be sought by those who did not ask for me . . . and to a nation that did not call my name I said, 'Here I am'" (Isa. 65:1). Now, during the summer, when I am alone for three months, I have been preaching once every two weeks. And I find the same thing as you. I don't know what to do with the precious half hours which we have; I preach more different things than I would ever have thought possible. . . .

. . . I am thankful that I am allowed to see a result; it is a mixture of personal joy, shall we say self-confidence, and detached thankfulness—but that is the judgment of all religion, this mixture of the personal and the detached, which one can perhaps ennoble, but never completely eliminate, and as a theologian one suffers doubly under it—but on the other hand, who would not rejoice in a full church or over the fact that people are coming who have not been for years, and then again, who is to analyze this joy and see whether it is free from stain? . . .

For a long time I thought that there was a central point in preaching, which, once one touched on it, could move anyone or confront them with a decision. I don't believe that anymore. First, preaching can never apprehend this central point but can only be apprehended by it, by Christ. So Christ becomes flesh as much in the words of the pietists as in those of the churchmen or the Christian Socialists, and these empirical restrictions mean not relative, but in fact absolute difficulties for preaching; people are not the same even at the deepest level, but they are individuals, totally different and only "united" by the Word in the church. I have noticed that the most effective sermons were those in which I spoke enticingly of the gospel, like someone telling children a story of a strange country. The difficulty in principle remains: one should give milk, but one doesn't know what that means and wonders whether one isn't giving sugared water by mistake. It would be a great help if someone would give me an exposition of 1 Corinthians 3:2; both for the "problem of the child in theology"—(on which I hope to work in connection with the problem of consciousness)—and hence for children's services. [NRS, pp. 37–39]

54

Letters to Erwin Sutz
1931–1932

During his year at Union Theological Seminary in New York, Bonhoeffer formed a lasting friendship with a fellow student, the Swiss pastor-theologian Erwin Sutz, who shared with Bonhoeffer a similar continental approach to theology. Eberhard Bethge mentions in his biography that Bonhoeffer and Sutz were also attracted to each other because of a common talent at the piano and a common love for music. In New York they were frequent concertgoers. Sutz understood one of the principal causes of Bonhoeffer's discontent with the theology then in vogue at Union Theological Seminary. He had himself studied under Karl Barth and Emil Brunner. At the time Bonhoeffer was very taken by Barth's approach to theology and had even presented a seminar paper at Union on Barth's theology of crisis ("The Theology of Crisis and Its Attitude Toward Philosophy and Science"). In this paper Bonhoeffer claimed that Barth stood "in the tradition of Paul, Luther, Kierkegaard, in the tradition of genuine Christian thinking."[6] Privately he was able to share with Sutz his misgivings over some of Barth's uncompromising contentions about the way theology and ethics should be structured. His admiration for Barth would, however, continue unabated throughout his life. And all his earlier good impressions would be confirmed once he had met Barth in person. This meeting was made possible through the intervention of Sutz, who had written to Barth about his friend Bonhoeffer. As a result Bonhoeffer made it a point to stop at Bonn and meet Barth before returning to Berlin in 1931. The letter of July 24, 1931, to Sutz, excerpted here, describes this meeting. The other letters are part of correspondence that for Bonhoeffer became a vital contact outside Germany and the church. Two of the letters in this section have become valuable sources for what we know of Bonhoeffer the catechist. In them Bonhoeffer describes his experiences with the fifty young lads from the slum section of Wedding in north Berlin. His care for people in deprived circumstances of life is particularly evident. In Bonhoeffer's hands, as one student remarked, the catechism seemed to come alive.

Bonn, July 24, 1931

. . . They have a sharp scent for thoroughbreds here. No Negro passes "for white"; they even examine his fingernails and the soles of his feet. Up till now they still haven't shown me hospitality as the unknown stranger. Now with Karl Barth himself, of course, everything is completely different. One breathes in an orderly way, one is no longer afraid of dying of suffocation in the thin air. I don't think that I have ever regretted anything that I have failed to do in my theological past as much as the fact that I did not come here earlier. Now there are only three weeks for me to be here, lectures, . . . seminars, meetings, an open evening and now yesterday a couple of hours at lunch with Barth. One hears and sees something there. Of course it's nonsense that I should be writing to you about what you yourself have seen much better. But it is important and surprising in the best way to see how Barth stands over and beyond his books. There is with him an openness, a readiness for any objection which should hit the mark, and along with this such concentration and impetuous insistence on the point, whether it is made arrogantly or modestly, dogmatically or completely uncertainly, and not only when it serves his own theology. I am coming to understand more and more why Barth's writings are so tremendously difficult to understand. I have been impressed even more by discussions with him than by his writings and his lectures. For he is really all there. I have never seen anything like it before and wouldn't have believed it possible.

My visit to him yesterday, which I was really rather hesitant about, especially as I knew how busy he was at the moment, was like other similar occasions which you have told me about. . . .

We very soon came to the problems of ethics and had a long discussion. He would not make concessions to me where I expected that he would have had to. Besides the one great light in the night, he said, there were also many little lamps, so-called "relative ethical criteria"; he could not, however, make their significance and application and nature comprehensible to me—we didn't get beyond his reference to the Bible. Finally, he thought that I was making grace into a principle and killing everything else with it. Of course I disputed his first point and wanted to know why everything else should not be killed. Had you been there, we would have had a third front and perhaps a great deal might have become clearer. But I was glad to be able for once to hear Barth's position in detail. We then went on to speak of a great many other things, and he urged me to develop the small work on the delimitation of Catholicism in contemporary theology about which I have already spoken to you. During our conversation there were many real *bons mots*, but they would be too feeble to repeat. Eventually, after a hard struggle, I went home. [*NRS*, pp. 120–22]

Berlin, October 8, 1931

Now I'm sitting here, preparing for my lecture and also for the post of chaplain to the students, and sometimes wish that I could go somewhere into the country to get out of the way of everything that is wanted and expected of me. It is not that I am afraid of disappointing—at least I hope not that primarily—but that sometimes I simply cannot see how

I am going to get things right. And the cheap consolation that one is doing one's best, and that there are people who would do it still worse, is unfortunately not always sufficient. It is surely not right that one should start such things so early—and with what qualifications? Now and then one could laugh rather furiously at it all.

These things come home to one particularly when one realizes the unprecedented state of our public life in Germany. The outlook is really exceptionally grim. There is in fact no one in Germany who can see ahead even a little way. People generally, however, are under the very definite impression that they are standing at a tremendous turning point in world history. Whether it will lead to bolshevism or to a liberal compromise, who knows? And after all, who knows which is the better? But the coming winter will leave no one in Germany untouched. Seven million unemployed, that is fifteen or twenty million people hungry; I don't know how Germany or the individual will survive it. Economic experts tell me that it looks as though we are being driven at a tremendous rate towards a goal which no one knows and no one can avoid. Will our church survive yet another catastrophe, one wonders, will that not really be the end unless we become something completely different? Speak, live completely differently? But how? Next Wednesday there is a meeting of all the Berlin pastors to discuss the winter problems; and look what problems they are! I have forebodings about this meeting. But nobody knows of anything better to do. And in times like these! Then what's the use of everyone's theology? Work begins in a couple of weeks; the omens are strange— [NRS, pp. 123–24]

Berlin, December 25, 1931

. . . The first half of the semester is over, thank goodness; at least I'm glad it's over. There is perpetually something to do and one is always overwhelmed. But the seminar is really enjoyable. I feel that I do have an elite of interested people, some of whom are remarkably well-read and judicious. My theological extraction is gradually becoming suspect here, and they seem to have the feeling that perhaps they have been nourishing a serpent in their bosom! I see hardly any of the professors, not that this grieves me inconsolably. Since my return from Bonn, things here seem to me to be worse than ever. Recently, on two consecutive days, I had first the lecturers and then my students here at home. I must say that the students were considerably more interested in theology than were the lecturers.

Luckily I still have my practical work. Not so much the Technical University, though of course there's that too, but something which keeps me far busier at the moment. It's the confirmation class which I hold for fifty young people in north Berlin. It is about the most hectic part of Berlin, with the most difficult social and political conditions. At the beginning the young lads behaved crazily, so that for the first time I had real problems of discipline. . . . Now there is absolute quiet, the young men see to that themselves, so I need no longer fear the fate of my predecessor, whom they quite literally worried to death. Recently I was out with some of them for two days; another group is coming tomorrow. We've all enjoyed this being together. As I am keeping them until confirmation, I have to visit the parents of all fifty of them and will be living in the neighborhood for two months in order to get it done. I'm looking forward to this time immensely. That is real work. Their home conditions are generally indescribable: poverty, disorder, immorality. And yet the children are still open; I am often amazed how a young person does not completely come to grief under such conditions; and of course one is always asking oneself how one would react to such surroundings. There must be a great—and I think also a moral—power of resistance in these people. Barth's book about Anselm is a great delight to me; you must read it when you have time. He shows the countless academic cripples, once and for all, that he really does know how to interpret and still remain sovereign. Nothing of course has in fact become any less questionable.

Dibelius recently told us in a lecture that the church has 2,500 theology students too many, and that therefore (!) special demands must be made on the theologians. As a first point for acceptance he put readiness for martyrdom (in a struggle in which religious and political ideals are so intertwined!). By the nature of things, he said, this thought was hard for the younger ones, but the older men had long (!) grown familiar (!) with it and attached to it. The audience stamped their feet like mad. Long live the "violet church."* That's all for today. Many thanks for your letter, and write again soon. Once again, all good wishes for the coming year. [NRS, pp. 139–41, translation slightly altered]

Berlin, February 26, 1932

Tomorrow there's the examination for the confirmation candidates. Confirmation in a fortnight. I have devoted almost all the second half of the semester to the candidates. Since New Year I've been living here in north Berlin so as to be able to have the young men up here every evening. In turns, of course. We eat supper and then we play something—I've introduced them to chess, which they now play with great enthusiasm. In principle anyone can come, even unannounced. And they all love coming. So I don't have to go on prodding them. Then at the end of each evening I read them something from the Bible and after that we have a short spell of catechizing, which often becomes very serious. The instruction went in such a way that I can hardly tear myself

---

*The "violet church" refers to the violet cross on the official church flag. Bonhoeffer was referring sarcastically to Bishop Otto Dibelius's inadequate reply to Barth's address of January 31, 1931, "The Plight of the Protestant Church."

away from it. Of course the young men were often quite dim, but I've sometimes been delighted. It has been really possible to talk to them and they have listened, often with mouths wide open. It is something new to them to be given something other than learning the catechism. I have developed all my instructions on the idea of the community, and these young men who are always listening to party political speeches, know quite well what I'm getting at. But they also see unbelievably clearly what the limitations are, so that again and again when we are talking about the Holy Spirit in the community, the objection comes "But surely, it's not like that at all. In all these things, the church is far behind any political youth organization or sports club. We feel at home in the club, but in the church?"—And again and again we have found our way from faith in the communion of saints to the forgiveness of sins, and I believe that they have now grasped something of it. Nothing sudden has happened, except perhaps that they were paying full attention at this point. But perhaps the foundation has been laid for something which will grow slowly. Perhaps!

I also had some very serious conversations with individual young people. I am reluctant to confess it, but it is true that I never made any detailed preparation for the classes. Of course I had the stuff there, but then I simply went on; first I spoke to the young people for a couple of minutes and then I began. I was not afraid of preaching to the children quite simply, and I believe that in the end anything else is pedagogic doctrinairism. The first thing necessary is to make sure that they understand the sermon. Then one must begin to talk oneself, quite regardless, and then I found in my own case—I don't know why I did—that here the biblical material and references to the great hope which we have, appeared time and time again in sermons like this. And it was just at these points that the young people paid most attention, even if such a sermon lasted more than half an hour. As a contrast to this there are my worst experiences in visiting their homes. I sometimes, indeed often, stand there and think that I would have been as well equipped to do such visits if I had studied chemistry. It sometimes seems to me that all our work comes to grief on the care of souls. To think of those excruciating hours or minutes when I or the other person try to begin a pastoral conversation, and how haltingly and lamely it goes on! And in the background there are always the ghastly home conditions, about which one really cannot say anything. Many people tell one about their most dubious way of life without any misgivings and in a free and easy way, and one feels that if one were to say something then they simply wouldn't understand. [NRS, pp. 150–52]

55

The Rise of Nazism and the Church Struggle: Correspondence with Karl Barth

1932–1933

The letters that Bonhoeffer and Karl Barth exchanged following their initial meeting in 1931 reveal a Bonhoeffer eager to test his ideas and decisions against the critical judgment of the one theologian he had now come to admire the most. Their correspondence reflects the lasting impression Barth had made on him during Bonhoeffer's visit to Bonn in the summer of 1931. These letters likewise provide further insight into the roles these two thinkers played in advancing the cause of the Confessing Church against the Reich Church infiltrated with Nazi ideology.

In his first letter to Barth, Bonhoeffer alludes to their evening together in Berlin and, half apologetic for importuning Barth with "godless" questions but mostly grateful for his straightforward, lucid explanations of things, confides his feelings of gratitude for Barth's guidance. Barth's reply on February 4, 1933, contained an expression of gratitude for the way Bonhoeffer had represented Barth's theological positions at Berlin and also for putting his name forward for Arthur Titius's chair at the University of Berlin (the chair went instead to Georg Wobbemin, a man more sympathetic to the merger of church and culture). Barth mentioned his fears at the political developments and their repercussions on church and theology. They must, he observed, struggle together for the truth—"The world is in a bad way but we mustn't let the light go out at any cost."[13]

Berlin, December 24, 1932

. . . At the end of the year I would like to thank you once again for everything that I have received from you during the course of the year. That evening here in Berlin and then the unforgettably splendid hours with you on the Bergli are among the moments in this year which will always be with me. Please excuse me if I was a burden to you in August with my perhaps too obstinate and—as you once said—"godless" questions. But at the same time I would like you to know that I know no one who can free me from these persistent questions as you can, and that I have to talk to you like that because I feel with you, it is hard to say why, in a strange way quite certain that the way in which you see things is somehow right. When I am talking with you, I am brought right up against the thing itself, whereas before I was only continually circling round it in the distance, and that is for me a quite unmistakable sign that here I've somehow got to the point. And because I never get the feeling in anything like the same intensity anywhere else, I will have to keep on asking you to give me some of your time now and then. Please excuse that too. The brief hours we have been together during the year have succeeded in guiding my thoughts, which are always wanting to sink into "godless" questions, and keeping them to the point. I would like to thank you for that too. [*NRS*, pp. 204–5]

The second exchange of letters makes known Bonhoeffer's disquiet at the rumors about Barth's possible dismissal for his known opposition to nazism and its ideology seeping into university life. Bonhoeffer offers here to circulate a petition against this but needs more information about Barth's "case." Barth's answer reassured Bonhoeffer that he had not as yet appeared on the "proscription lists" and would probably continue on at Bonn. Barth would later be dismissed in the spring of 1935 because of his refusal to take an unconditional oath of loyalty required of all civil servants.

Berlin, April 14, 1933

... There is talk here that you perhaps may not be able to return to Bonn next semester. This rumor is causing no little consternation among many people here. Georg Merz, who was here a day or two ago, gave me further details. Now some theological friends and myself propose in such an event to start a petition to avert a disastrous mistake. To do this, of course, only makes sense if we have some accurate information about the upshot of your case. In other words, may I ask you in the name of those who are most deeply disquieted by the news, to give me some brief details about how things stand? In this case, not a moment should be lost. The attitude of the German Christians toward you does not yet seem to have been clarified.

I only hope that at least this continual unrest has not succeeded in disrupting completely your work and your vacation. We think of you a great deal. Once again many thanks for the evening in Berlin. If something like it happened only once a year, I could bear to stay in Berlin for quite some time still, despite everything. I'm impatient for the beginning of the semester. [*NRS*, p. 206]

The next exchange of letters came at the height of the church crisis. The main issue had become the Aryan Clause adopted at the Old Prussian Synod, nicknamed the Brown Synod because so many of the ministers appeared there wearing the brown uniform and swastikas, emblems of their allegiance to the state. They proceeded to ram through the "Church Law Relating to the Legal Position of Clergy and Church Officers," which effectively limited ordination to those who were prepared to declare unconditional loyalty to the Nazi state and who were of pure Aryan blood. The opposition, led by Präses Koch, was shouted down. Koch then led his supporters out of the hall. As a consequence, none of the Young Reformers to which Bonhoeffer belonged were chosen representatives at the coming Wittenberg National Synod. Bonhoeffer turned to Barth for direction, alluding, as he did so, to Barth's own booklet on the Aryan Clause and to the Bethel Confession composed by Bonhoeffer and Hermann Sasse. The Bethel Confession was to be the only unambiguous defense of the Jewish people during that early phase of nazism. Barth's answer was an enthusiastic endorsement of Bonhoeffer's views. Because of the Aryan Clause, Barth agreed that the church had, indeed, reached a *status confessionis*—a time for confessing one's faith against error. He then went on to declare: "That will first of all mean this, that the church authorities, or the supposed or real majority of church members represented by them, must be told directly, and at the same time publicly, 'Here you are no longer the church of Christ!' And it is clear that this protest cannot be made just once; it must go on and on until the scandal is done away with—or until the church answers by evicting or muzzling those who protest. So the step you had in mind seems to me to be the right one to begin with."[14]

Berlin, September 9, 1933

. . . In your booklet you said that where a church adopted the Aryan Clauses it would cease to be a Christian church. A considerable number of pastors here would agree with you in this view. Now the expected has happened, and I am therefore asking you on behalf of many friends, pastors, and students, to let us know whether you feel that it is possible either to remain in a church which has ceased to be a Christian church or to continue to exercise a ministry which has become a privilege for Aryans. We have in the first place drawn up a declaration in which we wish to inform the church authorities that, with the Aryan Clauses, the Evangelical Church of the Old Prussian Union has cut itself off from the church of Christ. We want to wait for the answer to it, i.e., to see whether the signatories will be dismissed from their posts or whether they will be allowed to say something of this sort unmolested. Several of us are now very drawn to the idea of the Free Church. The difference between our present situation and that of Luther lies in the fact that the Catholic church expelled Luther under its laws against heretics, while our church authorities can do nothing of the sort because they completely lack any concept of heresy. It is therefore by no means simple to argue directly from Luther's attitude. I know that many people now wait on your judgment; I also know that most of them are of the opinion that you will counsel us to wait until we are thrown out. In fact, there are people who have already been thrown out, i.e., the Jewish Christians, and the same thing will very soon happen to others on grounds which have absolutely no connection with the church. What is the consequence for us if the church really is not just an individual congregation in any one place? How do things stand with the solidarity of the pastorate? When is there any possibility of leaving the church? There can be no doubt at all that the *status confessionis* has arrived; what we are by no means clear about is how the *confessio* is most appropriately expressed today.

I permit myself at the same time to send you a copy of the draft of a confession of faith which was made in Bethel and will appear in print very soon. I was expressly asked in Bethel to request your view and your comments. Please excuse these two requests, which will make some inroads on your time. But they are matters which affect thousands of our theologians, and all of us here feel inadequate for them. Your help would be most gratefully received. [*NRS*, pp. 230–31]

Bonhoeffer now requested a leave of absence from the University of Berlin to accept the pastorate of two German-speaking parishes in London. He had already entered into open conflict with the church in Prussia over the Aryan Clause. He was, in effect, removing himself from an unpleasant situation where his conscience dictated stronger resistance to the regime than the church at that time was willing to muster. However, not being completely certain of his decision, he preferred to take his distance from Germany in order to reflect and at the same time to engage in a kind of resistance by keeping the churches outside Germany informed of the extent of the German church crisis. His letter to Barth is thus a *post eventum*. Intimating in advance what Barth's reaction to his leaving at such a crucial moment would have been and unwilling to risk changing his mind through Barth's persuasion, he simply went to England and then exposed himself via letter to a possible scolding from Barth. He admits his doubts to Barth and asks for Barth's "frank opinion," even a "sharp word," if that be called for. The "sharp word" came the following month. Barth's arguments in his reply were a compelling array of reasons for Bonhoeffer's being back in Germany "by the next ship" or at least by "the ship after next" and a devastating criticism of the decision to go to England in the first place. Barth accused him of seemingly having abandoned the struggle and thus wasting his "splendid theological armory" and "upright German figure." He ended with a declaration of the friendship and that special kind of attachment that compelled him to be so harsh with Bonhoeffer.

London, October 24, 1933

. . . I am now writing a letter to you which I wanted to write six weeks ago and which perhaps at that time would have resulted in a completely different turn to my personal life. Why I did not write to you then is now almost incomprehensible to me. I only know that there were two contributory factors. I knew that you were busy with a thousand other things and in those hectic weeks the outward condition of one person seemed to me so utterly insignificant that I simply could not think it important enough to bother you. Second, I believe that there was also a bit of anxiety about it; I knew that I would have to do what you told me and I wanted to remain free; so I simply withdrew myself. I know now that that was wrong, and that I must ask you to forgive me. For I have now made up my mind "freely" without being able to be free in respect of you. I wanted to ask you whether I should go to London as a pastor or not. I simply believed that you would tell me the right thing, you, and only you (except for a man who has such constant concern for my fortunes that he was drawn up into my uncertainty).

I have always very much wanted to become a pastor; I've already told you that a couple of times before. In July the London business came up. I agreed, with reservations, traveled over here for two days, found the congregation quite neglected, and remained uncertain. When the thing had to be decided in September, I said Yes. The formal contract is easy. Six months' notice. I just took leave from the university. How far the link with the congregation is getting stronger is impossible to detect at this stage. I was offered at the same time a pastorate in the east of Berlin; my election was certain. Then came the Aryan Clauses in Prussia and I knew that I could not accept the pastorate I longed for in this particular neighborhood without giving up my attitude of unconditional opposition to the church, without making myself untrustworthy to my people from the start and without betraying my solidarity with the Jewish Christian pastors—my closest friend is one of them and is at the moment on the brink; he is now coming to me in England. So the alternative remained, lecturer or pastor, and if pastor, at any rate not in Prussia. I cannot begin to recount to you the abundance of pros and cons; I haven't got through them by a long way—perhaps I never shall. I hope that I did not come purely out of annoyance at the state of affairs in our church and at the attitude of our particular group. It probably would not have been long before I would have had to part formally from all my friends—but I really believe that all this spoke much more strongly against London than for it. If one is going to discover quite definite reasons for such decisions after the event, one of the strongest,

I believe, was that I simply did not any longer feel up to the questions and demands which came to me. I felt that I was incomprehensibly in radical opposition to all my friends, that my views of matters were taking me more and more into isolation, although I was and remained in the closest personal relationship with these men—and all that made me anxious, made me uncertain. I was afraid I would go wrong out of obstinacy—and I saw no reason why I should see these things more correctly, better than so many able and good pastors, to whom I looked up—and so I thought that it was probably time to go into the wilderness for a while and simply do pastoral work, with as few demands as possible. The danger of making a gesture at the present moment seemed to me greater than that of going off for some quietness. So off I went. Another symptom was that the Bethel Confession, on which I really worked so passionately, met with almost no understanding at all. I think I know for certain that this did not put me personally out of humor; there was really not the slightest occasion for that. I was simply uncertain in my mind.

Then ten days before my departure there came a call from the church chancellery that there were difficulties about my going away because of my hostile attitude toward the German Christians. Luckily I managed to have a conversation with Müller, to whom I said that I could not of course abandon my position and that I would rather remain here than sail under a false flag; I could not represent the German Christians even abroad. This was all put on the record at my request. Müller made an unspeakably poor impression, and said to soothe me, "Besides, I have already taken steps for the existing differences to be smoothed out." But he remained uncertain in my case, and I hoped that the decision would not simply come from outside, and was very glad about it. The next day the news came that I was to go. Worry about the ecumenical movement—tiresome. Now I've been here a week, have to preach every Sunday, and receive news almost daily from Berlin about the state of affairs. That almost tears one apart inside. And now you will soon be in Berlin and I cannot be there. It also occurs to me that I have let you down personally by my going away. Perhaps you will not understand that. But it is a very great reality to me. And despite all this, I am infinitely glad to be among a congregation, even so completely out of things. I also hope that the questions about the ecumenical movement will really clear themselves up for me. I mean to carry on that work over here. Perhaps in this way one can really support the German church once again in something.

I still don't know how long I shall be kept here. If I knew that I was really needed over there—it is so infinitely difficult to know what we should do. "We know not what we should do, but . . ."

So now this letter is written. They are only personal things, but the sort of thing I would very much like you to know about. It would be good if I were to hear a word from you again. I think of you and your work very often, and where we would be but for it. Would you please let me have your frank opinion on all this? I would be ready, and thankful, I think, even for a sharp word—I might write to you again when I have my typewriter. It's too much bother for you this way. [*NRS*, pp. 234–37]

56

Pastorate in London and the Church Struggle: Letter to Bishop Theodor Heckel

October 1933

The "difficulties" in his leaving Germany for London, mentioned in the letter to Barth in chapter 56, became for Bonhoeffer a matter of conscience. Were the German Christians to make his departure dependent on his representing the views of that church abroad, he would prefer to remain at home, loyal to the Confessing Church and still resolute in his opposition to the nazification of the churches. Bonhoeffer's letter to Bishop Theodor Heckel reaffirms his open and honest stand against the Reich Church. He would under no circumstances compromise his integrity in this matter.

Berlin-Grunewald, October 1933

I have just been speaking with the national bishop about my departure for London. He intends to leave the final decision with you. May I therefore once again summarize my standpoint, as I put it forward to him this morning:

I am not a German Christian and cannot honestly advance the cause of the German Christians abroad. I would of course primarily be pastor of the German community, but my relationships with leading circles in the English churches as a result of ecumenical work and my personal interest in the ecumenical task of the church, in my opinion, make it impossible for me not to take up some attitude to questions about the German church and the German Christians because I shall be approached with such questions.

I need not say that I will speak and act in complete political loyalty toward Germany. . . .

I would rather have to give up going to London than give rise to any uncertainties about my position. I regard this as a self-evident act of loyalty towards our church.

May I ask you to put this letter on the record? [*NRS*, pp. 253–54]

57

Letters to Bishop George K. A. Bell of Chichester

1933–1934

Bonhoeffer's desire to continue the church struggle from England and to alert the ecumenical world to the truth of what was happening within the German church led to his meeting with Bishop George Bell, then chairman of the Universal Christian Council for Life and Work and the World Alliance for Promoting International Friendship through the Churches. Soon after his arrival in London, he was invited to visit Bell at Bell's London club. It was the first visit of many that were designed to keep the bishop informed about the situation in Germany. Bell's interest in Bonhoeffer had already been aroused by a letter in October 1933 from Henry L. Henriod, secretary of the Youth Commission of the World Alliance, calling Bonhoeffer "one of the most promising young men in Germany," one who had "made a deep impression on all of us at Sophia."[15]

Later Bell himself would recommend Bonhoeffer both to fellow church leaders and politicians as the best source for "first hand information of the situation in the German Church."[16] Bell soon began to esteem Bonhoeffer's integrity and intellectual gifts and saw in him the decency and faith now under severe threat of extinction within Germany. Their exchange of letters is significant not only as evidence of their close friendship but also for the information it provides on Bonhoeffer's behind-the-scenes agitating on behalf of the Confessing Church. He continually urged Bell to intervene to defend Confessing Church interests at ecumenical gatherings. If the church in Germany had reached a crisis point, it seemed imperative to Bonhoeffer to have the wider assembly of churches declare against the heresy of the Reich Church. In these letters, therefore, Bonhoeffer begged Bell to do all he could to encourage the ecumenical movement to speak out in support of the pastors involved in a seemingly hopeless struggle. This is the gist of Bonhoeffer's first letter to Bell, written after the invitation arrived to have lunch with Bell at his club, the

Athenaeum. The other letters likewise attest that Bonhoeffer found Bell a valuable ally in the struggle against "Nordic heathenism" within the church.

London, November 16, 1933

My Lord:

I thank you very much for your kind invitation to come to Chichester on November 21st. It is indeed a great pleasure for me to come. May I ask you what time would be convenient for you for my arrival?

You certainly know of the recent events within the German church, and I think that there is a great likelihood for a separation of the minority from the *Reichskirche,* and in this case an action of ecumenic[al] support would certainly be of immense value in this tense situation. There is no doubt that any sort of separation would become at once a strong political issue, and for this reason would probably be dealt with by the government in an exclusively political way. It seems to me that the responsibility of the ecumenic[al] work has perhaps never been so far-reaching as in the present moment. If the ecumenic[al] churches would keep silent during those days, I am afraid that all trust put into it by the minority would be destroyed. Undoubtedly—Müller is now in a very precarious situation, and a strong demand from the side of the ecumenic[al] churches could be the last hope for the Christian churches in Germany. We must not leave alone those men who fight—humanly spoken—an almost hopeless struggle. I get news with every mail and also by telephone. If I may, I will forward to you the recent information.

In the enclosed paper you will find some very typical formulations of the German Christians.

I think one ought to try to drive a wedge between Müller and the radicals. On the other hand one cannot rely by any means on Müller's personal theological insight and it is dangerous to put too much trust into such a break. [*NRS,* pp. 254–55]

London, November 25, 1933

My Lord Bishop:

The two days which I spent in your home meant so much to me that I beg to thank you once more for this opportunity which you so kindly gave to me. I have received your letter, and I shall certainly keep all you told me to myself. Things in Germany are getting on—as it seems—more slowly than one could expect, and I am almost afraid that the influence of the radical German Christians becomes once more very strong, and that Müller will yield under this heavy pressure. I shall give you new information as soon as something important will occur.

London, November 27, 1933

My Lord Bishop:

May I draw your attention to the enclosed leaflets. Three pastors have been dismissed only because of their sincere confession to Christ as the only Lord of the church. One of them, Pastor Wilde, is father of seven children. The case is not decided yet definitely, but perhaps the moment has come when the ecumenical movement ought to provide for subsidies and financial support for those who will lose their positions for the only reason of their being confessors of their faith. Things are becoming very acute. Schöffel has resigned, Prof. Fezer has left the German Christian Movement. [*NRS,* p. 256]

London, December 27, 1933

My Lord Bishop,

Thank you very much for your most kind Christmas greetings. It means very much for me indeed to know that you are sharing all the time the sorrows and the troubles which the last year has brought to our church in Germany. So we do not stand alone and whatever may occur to one member of the church universal, we know that all the members suffer with it. This is a great comfort for all of us; and if God will turn back to our church sometime now or later, then we may be certain that if one member be honored, all the members shall rejoice with it.

Things in Germany are going on more slowly than we expected. Müller's position is, of course, very much endangered. But he seems to try to find closer contact with the state to be sure of its protection in case of danger. Only from this point of view can I understand his last agreement with the Hitler Youth. But it seems as if the state is nevertheless very much reserved and does not want to interfere once more. I do not think personally that Müller can keep his position and it will certainly be a great success if he falls. But we must not think that the fight is settled then. On the contrary, it will without any doubt start anew and probably sharper than before with the only advantage that the fronts have been cleared. The trend toward Nordic heathenism is growing tremendously, particularly among very influential circles; and I am afraid, the opposition is not united in their aims. In Berlin they are going to form an Emergency Synod under the leadership of Jacobi next Friday. This is meant to be a legal representation of the oppositional congregations against the illegal synods of last August and September. Jacobi is probably the wisest of the oppositional leaders in the moment and I put much trust into what he is doing. There is a great danger that people who have had a very indefinite attitude toward the German

Christians last summer, jeopardize now the success of the opposition by mingling in and seeking their own personal advantage.

The letter of Müller is as expected very weak and anxious, it really does not mean anything at all. It does not come out of a sound theological but much more of a political argumentation—though one always has to realize his position now is so difficult as never before.

If you allow me I shall be only too glad to come once more to Chichester. I am still having continuous information by telephone and airmail from Berlin. [*NRS*, pp. 265–67]

On January 17, 1934, Bonhoeffer wrote to Bell to thank him for his strong letter in the January 7, 1934, London *Times* protesting Bishop Ludwig Müller's "Muzzling Order" of January 4.[17] This decree forbade pastors to speak or write critically about church government under penalty of suspension and loss of income. It also rescinded Müller's prior annulment of the Aryan Clause. Bell had publicly joined the side of the Confessing Church and for that Bonhoeffer was grateful, mindful of the influence of the entire ecumenical movement Bell could bring to the support of the Confessing pastors. In this letter Bonhoeffer also alludes to the letter of protest he and other German pastors in London had sent to leaders in Nazi Germany expressing their dismay at the latest move against opposition pastors. That letter had noted in very forceful language their dissatisfaction with the national bishop, even stating that "through the 'German Christians' the church and the government of the church have been invaded by a spirit which has shattered the basic principles of the church; despite all protests to the contrary, Holy Scripture and confession have been violated and completely disregarded by the government of the church."[18] Bell's answer on January 18, 1934, asks Bonhoeffer to translate another letter of protest Bell had already sent to Müller in order to forward a copy to President Paul von Hindenburg. Bonhoeffer replied by return post, sending on the translation. His gratitude for this support is tied in with his invocation of Proverbs 31:8, "Open your mouth on behalf of those who have no voice," a scriptural passage Bonhoeffer frequently cited in his attempts to arouse sympathy and help for the German Jews deprived of a voice in their own fate.

London, January 17, 1934

It is my strong desire to thank you most heartily for your letter which I have just read in the *Times*. I am sure it will be of very great importance for the decisive meeting of today. We German pastors in London have sent a telegram to Hindenburg, Hitler, Neurath, Frick, Müller, saying that only the removal of Müller could pacify the highly excited German congregations here in England. You have certainly seen the new order of Rust forbidding all professors of theology to take part in the opposition against Müller and to be members of the Pastors' Emergency League. If this order is the beginning of a state action against the opposition, then, I think, your letter should be enforced by a most drastic disapproval of Müller's policy, and approval and support for the opposition, directed to President von Hindenburg as a *"membrum praecipuum"* of the Protestant church! Any delay of time would then probably be of great danger. A definite disqualification of Müller by the ecumenical movement would perhaps be the last hope—humanly spoken—for a recovery of the German church. It may be, of course, that Rust's order is one of the many attempts from the side of the Prussian government to anticipate the decision of the Reich and to overrule the Reich government. The first print of your book in German has just arrived.

I thank you once more for your help.

London, January 19, 1934

Thank you very much for your wonderful letter to Reichsbischof Müller. One feels that it comes out of such a warm and strong desire to stand for the Christian cause and to "open the mouth of the dumb in the cause of all such as are appointed to destruction" (Prov. 31:8), that it must undoubtedly be convincing for everybody.

I am sending you the translations of the letters and I am absolutely convinced that it would be of immense value if Hindenburg would learn to know this point of view. It has always been the great difficulty to have a free discussion with him about that matter, because there were many people who wanted to prevent it. So it is all the more important that he gets your letter. Once more many thanks. [*GS*, II, pp. 142–44]

Meanwhile Bonhoeffer had twice been recalled to Berlin by the Pastors' Emergency League. Leaders of the Confessing Church were now preparing for the Free National Synod to be held in Barmen in May 1934. The risks were immense. As Bonhoeffer observes in his letter of March 14, 1934, Christianity itself was being undermined by the new idolatry, national racism. Hence he is concerned enough to ask Bell to consider sending a delegation and even an ultimatum to the Reich Church "in the name of Christianity in Europe." A month later Bonhoeffer again wrote to Bell declaring that the crisis had grown to the extent that the pastors had to depend on help from outside the country, here in the form of a direct, forceful intervention by Bell himself and the ecumenical movement. They are, as Bonhoeffer points out, in need of a word from the universal church. The ecumenical movement seems their last hope. In this letter of April 15, 1934, Bonhoeffer singles out the appointment of a Wiesbaden magistrate, August Jäger, to be a member of the *Geistlichen Ministerium* (Ministry for Religious Affairs). This meant a further politicization of the conflict between the Reich Church and the Confessing Church. Clearly Bonhoeffer considered Jäger a ruthless, cunning man, hopeless in his espousal of Nazi ideology and with little appreciation of Christianity. Bonhoeffer's English here is not rigorous. Most probably he intended to say "warning them *not* to take any personal step" rather than "warning them to take" such a step.

Almost as a postscript to the letter of April 15, Bonhoeffer wrote the next day to add a further caution against being deceived by seeming compromises on the part of Müller and the Reich Church, especially by Müller's offer of a partial amnesty to the opposition pastors. The amnesty decree in question exempted the most vocal of these pastors, Martin Niemöller. Bonhoeffer's next letter, undated but probably written on April 25, 1934, mentions the growing opposition to Reich Church tactics as a cause for sedate optimism. Again Bonhoeffer urges Bell to speak that "final word" on the conflict. On May 1, 1934, the mood in Bonhoeffer's letters shifts toward pessimism. The letter of May 1 was written after Bonhoeffer had met with Bell and received further saddening news of the persecution of his fellow pastors. Moves were underway by the Reich Church aimed unmistakably at purifying the German churches of all non-Aryan elements and suppressing the minority opposition.

Bell's answer to this in the beginning of May contained a draft letter to the members of the Ecumenical Council and invited Bonhoeffer's criticism. This was itself a prelude to Bell's famous "Ascensiontide Message," "Regarding the German Evangelical Church to the Representatives of the Churches on the Universal Christian Council for Life and Work from the Bishop of Chichester." One section bears the strong imprint of Bonhoeffer's frequent informative contacts with Bell. Bell writes:

> The exercise of these autocratic powers by the church government appears incompatible with the Christian principle of seeking in brotherly fellowship to receive the guidance of the Holy Spirit. It has had disastrous results on the internal unity of the church; and the disciplinary measures which have been taken by the church government against ministers of the gospel on account of their loyalty to the fundamental principles of Christian truth, have made a painful impression on Christian opinion abroad, already disturbed by the introduction of racial distinctions in the universal fellowship of the Christian church. No wonder that voices should be raised in Germany itself making a solemn pronouncement before the whole Christian world on the dangers to which the spiritual life of the Evangelical Church is exposed.[19]

Bonhoeffer's constructive critique of the original text is contained in the letter of May 3, 1934. His gratitude for and optimistic assessment of the potential impact of the "Ascensiontide Message" can be seen in his letter of May 15, 1934.

London, March 14, 1934

My Lord Bishop:

May I just let you know that I was called last week again to Berlin—this time by the church government. The subject was the ecumenic[al] situation. I also saw Niemöller, Jacobi, and some friends from the Rhineland. The Free Synod in Berlin was a real progress and success. We hope to get ready for a Free National Synod until 18th of April in Barmen. One of the most important things is that the Christian churches of the other countries do not lose their interest in the conflict by the length of time. I know that my friends are looking to you and your further actions with great hope. There is really a moment now as perhaps never before in Germany in which our faith into the ecumenic[al] task of the churches can be shaken and destroyed completely or strengthened and renewed in a surprisingly new way. And it is you, my Lord Bishop, on whom it depends whether this moment shall be used. The question at stake in the German church is no longer an internal issue but is the question of existence of Christianity in Europe; therefore a definite attitude of the ecumenic[al] movement has nothing to do with the "intervention"—but it is just a demonstration to the whole world that church and Christianity as such are at stake. Even if the information of the newspaper is becoming of less interest, the real situation is as tense, as acute, as responsible as ever before. I shall only wish you would see one of the meetings of the Emergency League now—it is always, in spite of all the gravity of the present moments, a real uplift to one's own faith and courage. —Please, do not be silent now! I beg to ask you once more to consider the possibility of an ecumenic[al] delegation and ultimatum. It is not on behalf of any national or denominational interest that this ultimatum should be brought forward but it is in the name of Christianity in Europe. Time passes by very quickly, and it might soon be too late. The 1st of May the "Peace in the Church" shall be declared by Müller. Six weeks only. [*NRS*, pp. 267–68]

London, April 15, 1934

My Lord Bishop:

It is on the urgent request of one of my German friends, whose name I would rather mention to you personally, that I am writing to you again. I have received yesterday this letter which has upset me very much indeed and I think it is necessary that you know how our friends in Germany are feeling about the present situation and about the task of the ecumenic[al] movement now. The letter is really an outcry about the last events in the German church and a last appeal for an "unmisunderstandable" word of the ecumenic[al] movement. This man, who speaks for a few thousand others, states quite frankly: "In the present moment there depends everything, absolutely everything, on the attitude of the bishop of Chichester." If such feeling arises in Germany, it means that the moment has definitely come for the ecumenic[al] movement either to take a definite attitude—perhaps in the way of an ultimatum or in expressing publicly the sympathy with the oppositional pastors—or to lose all confidence among the best elements of the German pastors—an outlook which terrifies me more than anything else. It is for this very reason that I am repeating to you this statement of my friend. Of course, pastors in Germany do not realize all the implications which are connected with such a step taken by the ecumenic[al] movement, but they certainly have a very fine feeling for the right spiritual moment for the churches abroad to speak their word. Please, do not think our friends in Germany are losing all hope, it is only humanly spoken when they look to the ecumenic[al] movement as their "last hope" and it is on the other hand for the ecumenic[al] movement the moment to give test of its reality and vitality. As to the facts there is firstly the appointment of Dr. Jäger, which is considered to be an ostentatious affront to the opposition and which means in fact that all power of the church government has been handed over to political and party authorities. It was much surprising to me that the *Times* gave a rather positive report about this appointment. Jäger is in fact the man with the famous statement about Jesus being only the exponent of a Nordic race, etc. . . . He was the man who caused the retirement of Bodelschwingh and who was considered to be the most ruthless man in the whole church government. Furthermore he is—and remains—the head of the church department in the Prussian Ministry of Education and a leading member of the party. So this appointment must be taken as a significant step toward the complete assimilation of the church to the state and party. Even if Jäger should try to make himself sympathetic to the churches abroad by using mild words now, one must not be deceived by this tactic.

The situation in Westphalia seems even to be much more tense than we know. I could tell you some details personally.

On the other hand it is still the great danger that the attempt of the church government to win the sympathy of the leading men of the churches abroad will succeed as we know of one such case—because many of them do not have enough knowledge to see what is going on behind the scenes. It is therefore that the mentioned letter proposes very strongly if you could not send a letter to all other churches connected with the ecumenic[al] movement warning them [not] to take any personal step toward a recognition of the German church government and giving them the real Christian outlook of the situation which they want. The *Reichsbischof* himself is reported to have said, if we get the churches abroad on our side, we have won. Excuse this long letter, but everything looks so frightfully dark. It is always a great comfort to me that I may tell you frankly and personally our feelings. I hope to have the chance to hear from you soon.

London, April 16, 1934

My Lord Bishop:

May I just add a few words to my letter of yesterday—with regard to the recent decree of Müller. The only reason by which it can be explained is this: the church government has become aware of the fact that the secession of the Westphalian church could no longer be detained, and it was a clever move to delay once more this decision by issuing this new decree. That this offer of peace can not be taken seriously at all, can be proved by the comparison with the Good Friday message. There Müller refuses an "amnesty"; today he has changed once more his mind. The new amnesty is not even complete; Niemöller and other important pastors do not come under the decrees. It is undoubtedly the only intention of this decree to split up the opposition and then to go on freely. The Aryan Clause is still in force, since the law of Nov. 16th is expressly once more canceled. So we can watch this move only with the greatest mistrust.

London, probably April 25, 1934

My Lord Bishop:

Thank you very much for your kind letter and invitation to Chichester. Unfortunately I could not change another arrangement made for Tuesday and so I could not come. In the meantime things are going on rapidly in Germany and the information I get is more optimistic than ever before, at least with regard to the stand of the opposition. The last number of our church paper *Junge Kirche* brings your letter to the *Times* and in addition to that a few voices from Sweden and Switzerland. Today I received the answer of the Emergency League in Berlin to the peace offer of the *Reichsbischof* and I have dared to translate it for you as well as I could, because I thought it very important. I think the moment has come that you should and could speak a final word on this conflict. There are thousands who are anxious to hear that word soon. May I come to the Athenaeum on Friday at 6 o'clock? If I do not hear anything else, I shall be there.

London, May 1, 1934

My Lord Bishop:

Referring to our conversation last Friday, I thought it might be of interest to you and perhaps even for the circular letter that you see the new seal of our German church. It needs no comment.

Second, I have just received the message from my Berlin student friends that they have to prove their Aryan ancestry and descent in order to be admitted to the theological examinations.

Third, two letters of leading oppositionals foretelling a very dark near future. The government seems to be willing to maintain Müller at any cost, even with force. In Saxony the situation seems to be most critical.

There is an idea going about in Berlin concerning the organization of a council of all parties and to bring about the split on such an occasion.

I hope very much that your letter will contain a word of sympathy for the suppressed opposition over there. It would help them much. Sometimes they seem to be rather exhausted. [*NRS*, pp. 269–72]

London, May 3, 1934

My Lord Bishop:

Thank you very much for your most interesting letter. I think it will be a very helpful and important document in the present situation. May I just add a few words with regard to details: you speak "of the loyalty (of the pastors) to what they believe to be Christian truth." Could you not say perhaps: "to what is the Christian truth"—or "to what we believe with them to be the Christian truth"? It sounds as if you want to take distance from their belief. I think even the *Reichsbischof* would be right in taking disciplinary measures against ministers, if they stand for something else but the truth of the gospel (even if they believe it to be the truth)—the real issue is that they are under coercion on account of their loyalty to what is the true gospel—namely their opposition against the racial and political element as constituent for the church of Christ.

Is not perhaps the word "one-sided" (page 2) misleading? It could seem as if one possibly could sympathize with both sides at the same time and as if the difference between both sides were not ultimate, so that one just has to decide for either side. I am afraid Heckel will make use of this "one-sided" in a way you do not want it to be used.—

P.3 "the introduction of racial distinctions" and political principles—could that be added? It is always the same error—the swastika in the church Seal!* Many sources of revelation besides and except Christ. Other constitutive norms for the church than Christ himself.

Finally, I think the stimulating effect of your letter would be still a bit stronger if you would hint at the absolute necessity of [unanimity] with regard to some crucial principles, and that any further cooperation would be useless and unchristian, if such unity would prove unreal.

If there would be no word of that sort, Müller and his men will not be afraid of any definite action from your side in the near future anymore. The policy of the more intelligent people in the church government has always been: "discuss problems as much as you want, but let us act"—the thing they are afraid of is not discussion but action. If they could gather from this letter that the ecumenic[al] movement would leave them alone for a certain while, they would consider it a success for themselves. So I think it necessary not to give them the possibility of such an illusion (of which they would make any political use they can!).

---

* A few days before this letter, Bonhoeffer had sent the bishop a new church seal from Berlin containing a swastika in the emblem.

Excuse my frank comments to your letter. You know that I am most thankful to you for giving me the chance of expressing my opinion to you so frankly.

I remain with great gratitude, yours very respectfully,

Dietrich Bonhoeffer

[*GS*, I, pp. 189–91]

London, May 15, 1934

My Lord Bishop:

Your letter has made a very great impression on me and on all my friends here who have read it. In its conciseness it strikes at the chief points and leaves no escape for misinterpretation. I am absolutely sure that this letter of yours will have the greatest effect in Germany and will indebt the opposition very much to you. And what I think is most important, this letter will help the opposition to see that this whole conflict is not only within the church, but strikes at the very roots of national socialism. The issue is the freedom of the church rather then any particular confessional problem. I am very anxious to learn what the effect on the church government will be. Once more I wish to thank you for your letter which is a living document of ecumenic[al] and mutual responsibility. I hope, it will help others to speak out as clearly as you did.

I remain, my Lord Bishop, yours very respectfully,

Dietrich Bonhoffer

[*GS*, I, p. 194]

58

Letters Relating to the Ecumenical Conference at Fanø

1934

Bishop George K.A. Bell's Ascensiontide pastoral letter, though not the ultimatum Bonhoeffer desired, nonetheless, had an impact both on the Barmen Synod at the end of May 1934 and especially on the Ecumenical Conference held in Fanø, Denmark, toward the end of August that same year. Indeed, Bell's message gave the opposition pastors an unexpected show of ecumenical solidarity as the delegates formed their determined stand against the Nazi idolatry. At Fanø, the Universal Christian Council for Life and Work discussed Bell's letter as a matter of ecumenical significance and were moved thereby to approve a strong resolution on behalf of the persecuted brethren of the Confessing Church. The assembly also elected Bonhoeffer and Präses Karl Koch of the Confessing Church "consultative and co-opted members" of the council.

Prior to Fanø, however, Bonhoeffer was involved in the question of who should represent the German Evangelical Church. This led to the allied matter of how the Confessing Church might be designated should delegates from this group be permitted to attend. Would they, for example, be listed as one of the free churches? This became the substance of a friendly letter written by Youth Secretary Henry Henriod to Bonhoeffer. If the Reich Church is represented at Fanø and if the Confessing Church is there too, would this not constitute de facto two churches side by side at the ecumenical conference and could not this arrangement be tolerated by Bonhoeffer for the sake of an uneasy peace? Bonhoeffer's reply is sympathetic to Henriod's seeming dilemma. But it is also uncompromising. For Bonhoeffer, the Confessing Church is "the only theological and legally legitimate church in Germany." Here Bonhoeffer mentions the decree by Wilhelm Frick, Minister of the Interior, issued on July 9, 1934, "for the protection of the national community." In it Frick forbade any discussion of church disputes in the press or any place of public assembly. Although Bonhoeffer declined the invitation to go to Fanø in this letter, he later relented. Pressured to attend by Friedrich Siegmund-Schultze, a German ecumenical leader, and by Bell's friend Bishop Valdemar Ammundsen of Haderslev, by the end of July Bonhoeffer announced his intention to attend after all. His letter to Bishop Ammundsen is a frank avowal of his anxiety for his brethren of the Confessing Church. Here, as in so much of his perception of the church struggle, he declares the real issue to be a choice between national socialism and Christianity. The time for diplomacy and compromise is over. Bonhoeffer again asks for an unambiguous resolution. Though such might imperil the future of the World Alliance in Germany, that would be a better outcome than survival at the price of integrity. Bonhoeffer's letter to Bell, included at the end of this section, thanks the bishop for the unequivocal resolution of support for the Confessing Church. It was, he says, a resolution appreciated by the entire Confessing Church council as "a true expression of a brotherly spirit of justice and truthfulness."

LETTER TO HENRY HENRIOD

London, July 12, 1934

My Dear Henriod:

Thank you very much for your letter. I appreciate your readiness to understand our point of view and your sympathy with our difficulties. Thanks for your friendly words! Now your main point is that the Confessing Church in Germany should notify the Universal Council of its very existence. As I see it, that has been done long ago in Ulm as well as in Barmen where the Confessional Synod made the official claim before the whole Christian world to be the true Evangelical Church in Germany. If this claim is taken at all seriously, then it includes the hope of recognition by the other churches. If I am right, the churches represented on the Universal Christian Council have been invited to send their representatives and have not done so by their own initiative. I have discussed this point with the bishop of Chichester recently and I learn he has written to you already about it. You say: "if the Barmen Synod . . . leads to the constitution of the church distinct from the present recognized official church . . . then, and only then will the question of choice become possible for the ecumenic[al] movement." I think you are misinterpreting the legal construction of the Confessing Church in this point. There is not the claim or even the wish to be a Free Church besides the *Reichskirche*, but there is the claim to be the only theologically and legally legitimate Evangelical Church in Germany, and accordingly you cannot expect this church to set up a new constitution, since it is based on the very constitution which the *Reichskirche* has neglected. It follows that, according to my opinion, a move should be made by the Universal Council in the form of an official invitation to the Confessional Synod to participate in the ecumenic[al] work of the churches. You will realise that it is exceedingly delicate for the Confessing Church to make this move after having already once declared before the whole of Christianity what their claim is. So, I feel strongly that legally and theologically the responsibility for the future relationship between the German church and the ecumenic[al] movement rests with the ecumenic[al] movement itself and its actions.

With regard to the World Alliance I may say, after having attended an important meeting of it two weeks ago, that it is out of the question that the *Reichskirche* should be allowed to take over their business. There is a very strong feeling against Dr. Heckel, so that even the possibility of staying away from Fanø in case Dr. Heckel should be there is being seriously considered.

Finally, you will allow me to correct your statement concerning my recognition of the *Reichskirche* in my personal position. I am in no relation whatever with the *Reichskirche*. I am elected merely by my congregation and this election has neither been confirmed by the *Reichskirche* as it should have been, nor would I accept such a confirmation at all. When I went over to London, there was no Confessing Church, which had made the claim it is making now—this having been one of the reasons why I left Germany. Excuse this lengthy explanation, but I should not like to be misunderstood by my friends.

The Decree of Frick is indeed of the greatest importance. I feel it is once more a great moment for the Ecumene to speak. This decree may mean the definite suppression of Christianity as a place where public Christian opinion can be formed. I am glad you have found so quickly a substitute for me for Fanø and I am sending you the documents under separate cover. You will understand my decision not to go to Fanø better. I frankly admit that I cannot agree with the invitation of Dr. Heckel without inviting the opposition. I have talked all these problems over with Dr. Koch and Niemöller on my trip to Berlin, and we all agreed. [*NRS,* pp. 282–84]

LETTER TO BISHOP VALDEMAR AMMUNDSEN

London, August 8, 1934

Very Reverend, Dear Lord Bishop:

Forgive me for not answering your kind letter before now. I did not want to do so until I had made up my mind. Your letter and then a conversation with Siegmund-Schultze have, however, in fact made it quite clear to me that I must go to Fanø and put aside all personal scruples. Now that an invitation has also gone out to Präses Koch, thus stating more or less officially that we will be given a hearing, the situation is quite clear. Many thanks once again for your remarks; do please write if ever you feel that I am taking a wrong step. For us Germans, these ecumenical matters are something which one learns only with a great deal of attentiveness, experience, and help—and for that I am most grateful.

Now another word about the conference itself. Speaking quite frankly and personally, when I think of Fanø, I am more worried about many of our own people than about the German Christians. On our side, we will have to be terribly careful not to appear unpatriotic; not so much because of anxiety as because of a wrongly understood sense of honor. Many people, even those who have already been involved in ecumenical work for quite some time, cannot understand or believe even now that we are here together really only as Christians. They are fearfully mistrustful, and therefore not completely open. If only you could succeed in breaking this ice, in gaining the trust of these men and opening them up! Precisely because of our attitude to the state, the conversation here must be completely honest, for the sake of Jesus Christ and the ecumenical cause. We must make it clear—fearful as it is—that the time is very near when we shall have to decide between national socialism and Christianity, that we must go a stage further than our last year's position (I know that you already said this then!). It may be fearfully hard and difficult for us all, but we must get right to the root of things, with open Christian speaking and no diplomacy. And in prayer together we will find the way. I would very much like to say that again.

I feel that a resolution ought to be framed—all evasion is useless. And if the World Alliance in Germany is then dissolved—well and good, at least we will have borne witness that we were at fault. Better that than to go on vegetating in this untruthful way. Only complete truth and truthfulness will help us now. I know that many of my German friends think otherwise. But I ask you urgently to appreciate my view.

How splendid that I shall be able to see you again soon. I really look forward to that. After the conference, a small group of German students (about ten) will be having a holiday with me in Denmark—I would be very glad to go on to Copenhagen, where I could then also see your daughter again. That would be a great pleasure. I have a very good friend at the German Embassy in Copenhagen. But whether I shall get there before or after the conference I don't yet know.

I hear that you are in Germany these days. It is so good to know that there are still men willing to help us in all ways, including prayer. [NRS, pp. 286–87]

LETTER TO BISHOP GEORGE K. A. BELL

Bruay en Artois (Calais), September 7, 1934.
(Conférence oecuménique de la jeunesse)

My Lord Bishop:

First of all, I want to thank you very much for the great help you have rendered to the cause of our church at the Fanø conference. The resolution in its final form has become a true expression of a brotherly spirit of justice and truthfulness. And therefore the contents of the resolution will and must strike every one who reads it without prejudice. Immediately after the conference I went to Germany and met Präses Koch with the assembly of the whole Confessing Council. I delivered there a detailed report on the Fanø conference and I felt strongly that the resolution of Fanø had been met with the greatest appreciation. Moreover the Synod Council asked me to express to you in particular their deep gratitude. Präses Koch and the council asked me to express to you at the same time their great desire to have the opportunity of meeting you when you are coming back from Sweden. If any time were convenient to you, Präses Koch would like to meet you at Hamburg. Other representatives of the synod will come with him. Perhaps you would be so very kind as to send a short note to Oeynhausen. [*NRS,* pp. 294–95]

59

Letters to Erwin Sutz

1933–1936

By April 1933, much had changed within Germany as Hitler began in earnest to attain absolute power. The repercussions of Nazi civil legislation and the budding reign of Gestapo terror on church and university were being felt by Bonhoeffer on both of these fronts. As he admitted in the first of this series of letters to Erwin Sutz, he was unable to predict where and how it would all end. We see here some of his thinking, many of his hopes, and much of his determination to resist Nazi policies. We note, too, mention of his longing for a quiet pastorate away from the maddening atmosphere where, as he writes, not even an influential teacher like Karl Barth was secure in his position. There are allusions here to the impact of the "Jewish Question" on church politics and to the idolatry that national socialism was becoming for many. Very early in the church struggle, Bonhoeffer proved himself more perceptive of the longer range effects of the evil than even Martin Niemöller, whom he criticizes as naive for continuing to believe some of the political promises of national socialism. Some of Niemöller's naiveté came out in a telegram expressing his gratitude and allegiance to Hitler on the occasion of Germany's withdrawing from the League of Nations, October 14, 1933. In his diary, Pastor Julius Rieger notes Bonhoeffer's remark at the time: "This has brought the danger of war very much closer."[20] It is, Bonhoeffer argues, an illusion. Bonhoeffer seems ahead of his contemporaries in predicting that the real battle would be an "endurance with faith" demanding the sacrifice of one's life, a battle resolved only through the Sermon on the Mount.

In the letters from London we read of Bonhoeffer's plans to visit India, there to study Gandhi's methods of asceticism and nonviolent resistance. He confesses his complete disaffection with university life in connection with his own hope to revivify the training of seminarians in more monasticlike settings where sound doctrine, the Sermon on the Mount, and worship could be taken seriously. This would be, in his own view of the situation in Germany, a prelude to more direct church action on behalf of the victims of Nazi heartlessness. Citing Proverbs 31:8, "Open your mouth for those who have no voice," Bonhoeffer argues that this is the very least the Bible requires of the German church.

In his letter of October 24, 1936, Bonhoeffer dismisses with mild contempt the flocking of some mainstream people to attractive groups, which were springing up within Germany and elsewhere, attracting people by their appeal for personal conversion, promise of devotional fulfillment, and offer of a nonpolitical, nonthreatening way of being a church. He cautions against surrendering to the lure of such groups because, for him, such a surrender meant being less a mainstream church with critical power in the state and being more a fringe church unable to preach the gospel to the state. The letter is also valuable for its description of the mission work accomplished by the brethren in the seminary at Finkenwalde and for the insight into Bonhoeffer's compassion for the sick. The series closes with his ironic comment that the new golden calf of Germany may bear a distorted resemblance to Luther, undoubtedly an expression of his vexation at so many fellow Lutherans feeling fully justified in terms of their religion in rallying around the swastika.

Berlin, April 14, 1933

. . . Since I last wrote to you much has changed here and, I suppose, we are still in the middle of these changes. Where it's going to end, we cannot yet clearly perceive. We are most directly affected in the church and in the university. That Karl Barth's position is no longer secure is something you will be informed of. For my part I will do everything to avert a fatal and irreparable blunder and I'm already at work on this. A new organization of the church is pending which, as it now appears, will not be detrimental. The German Christians will hopefully seize this opportunity to withdraw voluntarily from both Confessing Churches—the alternative is frightening and so we will, in the confusion of humans and by the providence of God, once again still survive as a church.

The Jewish question troubles the church very much and here even the most intelligent people have entirely lost their heads and their Bibles over it. So one is personally kept busy going in various directions and can hardly find time for quiet vacation work. How I often envy you, or rather, how I don't begrudge the fact that you can pursue in peace and quiet the work which is alone what matters in the church. I often long terribly for a quiet pastorate.

I have always known that you can preach well without having heard you before and Lehmann's letter had confirmed this. It is an awesome responsibility to know this about oneself. . . .

Berlin, July 17, 1933

Now the semester is almost over and you have remained without a reply to your friendly letter. Please forgive me this. However, I believe you know yourself why this had to be. The ecclesial political events have kept me fully occupied. Now a decision is hanging directly over us, a decision, I believe, of the utmost importance for church politics. I have little doubt that the German Christians will emerge victorious and that, because of this, the outlines of the new church will very quickly be revealed. Consequently, it will be rather very questionable whether we can continue as a church. I fear, however, that there will be a gradual but constant breaking up, since one no longer has the strength for a united action. Then it goes back to the assembly.

By the way, I also preached at that time on the golden calf, and on the church of Aaron and the church of Moses, something that today is becoming actual in an uncanny way. On Election Sunday I'll preach on Matthew 16:18.

A few days ago Barth was in Berlin for a short visit. He then told me how highly pleased he was over your visit to Bonn. My personal future may well take a decisive turn rather soon. It has been proposed to me that I go to London as a German pastor with a special commission for ecumenical work. I have been thinking about it very much and I believe, of course, that, given all the possibilities that one must take into consideration for the church, a close touch with the English church can eventually be of the utmost importance. What do you think about it? Or do you have in Switzerland a pleasant professorship open for me that you have to fill? Perhaps I'll come to Geneva at the end of August, but it is not yet certain.

London, April 28, 1934

During recent months I have frequently longed for your quiet pastorate in the mountains. . . . What is going on in the church in Germany you probably know just as well as I. National socialism has brought with it an end to the church in Germany and effectively brought this about. We can be grateful to it for this, just as the Jews were grateful to Sennacherib. That we are faced with this evident fact, I no longer doubt. Imaginative and naive people like Niemöller still believe themselves to be the true national socialists—and it may perhaps be a kindly providence that maintains them in this illusion, and it may well also be in the best interests of the church struggle—if one is at all still interested in this struggle. The issue is no longer in the least what it appears to be there; the front lines of battle lie in a wholly other direction.

And although I am investing all my energies working in the church opposition, it is quite clear to me that this opposition is no more than a provisional stage in transition to an entirely different kind of oppposition, and that the men concerned with this first skirmishing are only to a very minor extent the same ones who will be involved in that second battle. And I believe that the whole of Christendom must pray with us that the resistance becomes a "resistance to the death" ("resistance to the point of blood"), and that people will be found ready to suffer for this purpose. Simply to endure it—that will be what is needed then—not to fight, to strike at, to stand watch—that may be possible for the preliminary skirmish, but the real battle, what it will perhaps later come to, must be simply an endurance with faith and, then, then perhaps God will again acknowledge his Word to his church. But until that time there must be much faith, prayer, and suffering. You know, I believe—perhaps you are surprised by this—that the whole matter will be resolved through the Sermon on the Mount. . . .

How long I shall remain a pastor and how long I shall stay in this church I don't know. Perhaps not much longer. I would like to go to India in the winter.

London, September 11, 1934

Many thanks for your cards. I received both of them. It's a shame we didn't get together in Berlin. Just think, right after the conference in Fanø, I met with Jean [Lasserre] and spent three days with him in Bruay. We enjoyed those days together very much. It meant so much to reflect once again with each other and to reminisce. I admire in an extraordinary way the work Jean is doing. This North French Protestantism has something about it of the fanaticism of a sect. It was the first time that I have really seen a completely proletarian congregation. The surrounding area of the battlegrounds and cemeteries and the terrible poverty of these mining towns form a dark background for the preaching of the gospel.

I am again back in our congregation and struggling over the decision on whether I should go back to Germany as director of the new Preachers' Seminary (still to be established) or whether I should remain here or whether I should go to India. I no longer believe in the university and never really have believed in it—a fact that used to rile you. The entire training of the budding theologians belongs today in church, monasterylike schools in which the pure doctrine, the Sermon on the Mount, and worship can be taken seriously—which is really not the case with all three things at the university and, in present-day circumstances, is impossible. We must also finally do away with the theologically grounded restrictions in regard to action by the state—after all, it is only fear. "Open your mouth for those who have no voice." (Prov. 31:8) Who still knows that in the church today, this is the least requirement of the Bible in such times? And then the questions of arms and war, etc., etc.

At the present time, I believe that any discussion between Hitler and Barth would be quite hopeless and, indeed, no longer to be sanctioned. Hitler has shown himself quite clearly for what he is, and the church ought to know with whom it has to reckon. Likewise, Isaiah did not go to Sennacherib. We have often—too often—attempted to make Hitler aware of what is going on. It may be that we haven't yet gone about it in the right way, but then Barth won't go about it correctly either. Hitler ought to and cannot hear; he is obdurate and, as such, ought to compel us to hear—the question is thus turned completely around. The Oxford Group Movement was naive enough to try to convert Hitler—a laughable failure to understand what is really happpening—it is we who ought to be converted, not Hitler. . . .

Finkenwalde, October 24, 1936

. . . When I returned here in a hurry I found a brother so severely ill that I had to act as nurse for a long time. This has done less good for my work than it did for my soul. Once I had him back on his feet, various other things cropped up, one after the other, that kept me from my work. I had to attend to a few smaller works, among others a less-than-exact study of the catechism by L. Christ in which I believe I have detected a few teaching mistakes which I might perhaps make known to him as the occasion arises in time for a third edition. I have myself completed a lesson plan for confirmation for our seminary brethren which I presented to them during a free time that lasted the entire preceding week. Now the new semester has again begun and the first weeks are filled up with all sorts of new things, besides the rather active outside service that the seminary gradually provides.

You have indeed met in Eberhard Bethge one of the brothers who for a longer period of time are free for the work of the seminary. Besides him there are five others. Each has his particular task, partly within the house and partly outside. We have been especially involved lately in a mission for the people which we are doing together. This means that at least four brothers go out together, speak each evening for ten minutes, visit the entire village in the course of the day, conduct prayer services in the houses and instructions for the children. What is most important is that the Bible is again being read and prayed over. But it is endlessly difficult there, where the people are not "accustomed" to having someone break into their lives like this. There is also a widespread dearth of material that one could give the people. Everything is too difficult. This is especially lacking for young people. There are, indeed, some fairly useful periodicals but guidance for the daily meditation is entirely deficient. Do you have anything along this line? . . .

Right now I'm wholeheartedly involved with the groups movement.* Therefore, things are apparently now getting rather lively even here. The book market has on display whole mountains of literature on groups. The question here, however, now takes on an extremely serious

---

*Bonhoeffer is referring here to the development of parachurch movements such as the Oxford Group and the Berneuchen Movement and others that often became rival to mainstream churches or to a mainstream within a church. It seems clear that he is averse to the focus of these groups on the witness of personal conversion to the detriment of becoming a church unafraid to confront the political powers. Such stress on proclaiming one's personal change toward conversion and on pietistical fulfillment were hardly substitutes for a strong proclamation of the gospel to the state regardless of the dangers. As he wrote in a letter to Dr. Friedrich Schauer, head of the Berneuchen Movement, the Confessing Church could surrender to no power "other than obedience to the truth" for its infusion of new life within the church" (DB, p. 389).

appearance. All the people of the church's mainstream, including church committees, are full of interest and immediately rushing to look at this unpolitical, living phenomenon, and to flirt with it. Here the group doesn't know what is threatening it, that is, it doesn't in the least have enough instinct to recognize that it serves only as instrument of a dark power. Thereupon, it seems to me that its hour has already struck. I believe the group can, humanly speaking, have everything today that it wants here; it can perhaps penetrate the most influential circles, but the price must be that it gives up the Confessing Church. Frankly, this perspective is unsettling. One hungers for a "Christian" movement; for the committees this is merely a matter of existence. We of the Confessing Church could give ourselves over to this and everything would all come together for us [es wäre alles in unseren Händen]. The price we pay is only that we are no longer church, that is, that we are no longer state (polis), that we can no longer preach the gospel to the state (polis). We would have become, in all the publicity we would then enjoy, a fringe church without influence. Unfortunately, after several experiences in regard to the so-called "instinct" of the group, I predict rather dark things. On the other hand, even if this adversary appears, our situation still approaches madness in the eyes of the world. By the way, because of my essay,* which I gave you at that time, I'm being looked on as the most contemptible among those of our persuasion. Recently one Lutheran association even demanded in a petition that I be relieved of my teaching position in the Confessing Church. The Rhinelanders have stood by me splendidly in this. And also some others. It may eventually happen that the beast before which the idolators bend their knees will bear a caricature of Luther's physiognomy. "They adorn the graves of the prophets. . . ." [GS, I, pp. 37–47]

---

*"On the Question of the Church Community" ("Zur Frage nach der Kirchengemeinschaft"), WF, pp. 75–96. It is in this essay that Bonhoeffer declares that anyone who knowingly separates himself from the Confessing Church separates himself from salvation.

60

Letters to Martin Niemöller

1933

Bonhoeffer's letters to Martin Niemöller in the last months of 1933 constitute a further reflection on some of the turning points in the crisis within the German churches as Hitler engineered a plan first to use the German Evangelical Church as an adjunct of the state and an effective propaganda tool and, failing that, to undermine church influence on party politics. The first letter of this exchange, written before the letter to Erwin Sutz, excerpted in the preceding chapter, in which Bonhoeffer calls Niemöller an imaginative, naive type in regard to the full danger of national socialism, is a clear acknowledgment that Niemöller is the leader of the Pastors' Emergency League and that the direction the church opposition must take depends largely on him. Yet there is also detected here a disquietude over what Bonhoeffer had heard of Niemöller's reluctance to join the discussions between regional bishops from the north and south of Germany and the national bishop in order to form a new church government. This situation had been forced by Bishop Ludwig Müller's rescinding the Aryan Clause and Hitler's announcement that he would not intervene in the dispute that had arisen within the church over the Aryan Clause and the confiscation of a proclamation by the Pastors' Emergency League on November 16, 1933. At that time the church struggle seemed more like an internal squabble to the world. The accusations of heresy against the Reich Church and German Christians would only later percolate into the open split signaled by the Barmen and Dahlem synods of 1934 and the Barmen Confession.

The confusion in Berlin seemed to compound the worries of Bonhoeffer and Franz Hildebrandt, who jointly composed the letter that follows. The letter itself contains their proposals for an emergency program to include dissolution of the synods and a machinery to guarantee sound doctrine within the church. Bonhoeffer and Hildebrandt urged Niemöller to see this program through and to stay in control of things in Berlin. It seemed a final opportunity to save the soul of the church. The letter was followed four days later by a telegram from the German pastors in London stating their consternation over rumors that Niemöller and Jacobi had split over how to assess the German church situation and how to devise tactics. In it they state that "Jacobi's exclusion from negotiations would compel us to resign immediately," adding a suggestion that Niemöller "stop shameful fence-sitting and evasion of responsibility."[21] Niemöller assured them in his letter of December 9, 1933, that the Council of Brethren would take a fully united action against the bishops. Bonhoeffer's reply on December 15, however, again urged Niemöller to take a radical stand and not to be timid about the Aryan Clause in dealing with the Nazi government.

These letters show a Bonhoeffer separated from the epicenter of the budding church struggle yet fretfully concerned that the leadership of the Pastors' Emergency League might be fragmented just when it seemed they were successfully eroding Nazi influence on the church. They were still five months away from the Barmen Synod, where the Confessing Church would assume the more united front Bonhoeffer was urging in this correspondence.

London, S.E. 23, November 30, 1933

Dear Brother Niemöller,

We would have preferred to pick up the telephone again in order to embrace you in a brotherly way with the full power of our youth to implore you in this decisive moment not to hand over the guidance of the ship to those who will only steer us again indecisively and give the wheel back only when it is too late. Only admirals can carry on now. The direction you took last summer seems to offer us the only hope that the Council of Brethren would advance by means of a radical attack rather than get bogged down in tactics. Perhaps today is the last chance to save the church and, if we let the opportunity pass by, we'll all stand guilty of this within two years (who can, especially today, even calculate fourteen days ahead?). False modesty and timidity once again brought about our defeat last June. If you or Jacobi do not now take the opportunity, in a short time the old mess will irrevocably come back.

It is indispensable that we attend to the immediate dissolution of the synods and the purging of the whole church of the entire pest—according to the sole viewpoint of strict proceedings for dogmatic discipline (the schools of Sasse as Lutheran, Barth as Reformed)—and the strictest exclusion from membership in our circle of all the old and new halfhearted people. Just because teaching and not positions are at stake, it is really unimportant whether some ignoramuses are speaking about people looking for jobs. Who can believe that! Today only the language of Luther and not of Melanchthon helps—especially for those in authority. Now we are expecting all serious people to know how to assume responsibility and to take over the leadership. What the bumpkins from Bavaria and the old geezers can do, they have proven to us sufficiently in these critical times.

Please listen to these voices from the wilderness and not only to those from the tame West. Accept many heartfelt and caring greetings from

Dietrich Bonhoeffer and Franz Hildebrandt

London, December 15, 1933

Dear Brother Niemöller,

I would like to tell you very briefly that I am thinking about you very much and quietly I continually keep in view the unusual responsibility you have. The clarity with which you set the direction we took last summer keeps both of us full of hope that we are certainly not now at the last moment of a "we don't understand how to win" attitude, and thus allowing ourselves to be pressured away from a sound theological course. We must especially now be radical on every point, and that includes the Aryan Clause, and not shy away from any unpleasant consequences to ourselves. Should we become unfaithful in any way, then we discredit our entire struggle of last summer. Please, please take care to do everything you can that things remain clear, courageous, and accurate. [GS, II, pp. 149–52]

61

Letters to His Grandmother

1933–1934

Bonhoeffer's concerns, expressed in his letters to Martin Niemöller, surface also in a Christmas 1933 letter to his grandmother, Julie Tafel Bonhoeffer. In this letter he mentions that he is ashamed of the unbelievable shortsightedness of his opposition group.[22] Bonhoeffer's letters to his grandmother are noteworthy not only for their openness and for the feelings he was able to share with her but also for what they reveal of his respect for the intelligence, passion for justice, and interest in the church of this remarkable woman, then in her early nineties. Dietrich Bonhoeffer and Julie Tafel Bonhoeffer appreciated each other. Of the many stories told about her, the most compelling describes her courageous, ostentatious walk past the cordon of S.A. troops and Hitler Youth picketing the Jewish shop *Kaufhaus des Wesens* to make her customary purchases. The occasion was the command of April 1, 1933, for Germans to boycott Jewish shops. Bonhoeffer's grandmother was ninety-one at the time. At her funeral service on January 15, 1936, Bonhoeffer gave an address that summarized what he admired most in her and pointed out how these very qualities led to the grief she experienced in nazism's denial of human rights. In part, Bonhoeffer said of her:

> The inflexibility of what is right, the free word of a free person, the obligation to stand by a promise once it is made, clarity and sobriety of speech, uprightness and simplicity in public and private life—on these she set her whole heart. . . . She could not bear to see these aims held in contempt or to see the violation of another's rights. Thus her last years were clouded by the great grief she endured over the fate of the Jews among our people, a fate she bore and suffered in sympathy with them. She was the product of another time, of another spiritual world—and that world does not go down with her to the grave.[23]

The first of Bonhoeffer's letters to his grandmother, excerpted here, gives us information about the atmosphere of work and even the hopes he was experiencing while composing the Bethel Confession for the council of Young Reformers. The text likewise brings out Bonhoeffer's precocious assessment of the real nature of the church struggle: a choice between Christianity and Germanism.

In the second letter Bonhoeffer relates at length his reasons for wanting to go to India. Here we see his growing disaffection for the Western form of Christianity and his longing for some guidance from Gandhi in organizing a resistance to nazism. His fascination with India and the East provide an important clue for interpreting what he meant by his prediction of a nonreligious Christianity in the prison letters. He wished to see a new form of Christianity drawing inspiration from prayer, social justice, a return to the "discipline of the secret" and, at this time, a community life open to all sources of wisdom, among them, the wisdom of Gandhi and India.

Bethel, August 20, 1933

Dear Grandmama,

. . . The time spent here in Bethel has made a very deep impression on me. Here one simply finds a segment of the church which knows what is of importance and what is not of importance to a church. I have just returned from a religious service. It is remarkable to see there crowds of epileptics and other sick people filling the entire church, among them deaconesses and deacons who must help if someone falls; then, too, vagabonds from the streets, theology students, children from the school building for those in good health, doctors, and pastors, with their families. But, nevertheless, the scene is dominated by the sick, who listen with great intensity. Indeed, for these people there must be a unique feeling for life since they certainly cannot have control over themselves and must be prepared at any moment for the illness to seize them. I really caught such a glimpse of this in the church today. This condition of being actually defenseless may perhaps open to these people a much more careful insight into certain realities of human existence, in which we are in fact basically helpless, than is possible to be given to those of us who are healthy. . . .

Our work here gives us much pleasure but also much trouble. We want to try to make the German Christians declare their intentions. Whether we shall succeed I rather doubt. For even now if they officially make concessions in their formulations, the pressure they are placed under is so powerful that sooner or later all promises are bound to be broken. It is becoming increasingly clear to me that we're going to get a big, popular national church whose nature cannot any longer be reconciled with Christianity and that we must be prepared to enter upon entirely new paths which we will have to tread. The question really is: Germanism or Christianity? The sooner the conflict comes out into the open, the better. Nothing is more dangerous than concealing this. . . .
[GS, II, pp. 77–79]

May 22, 1934

Dear Grandmama,

. . . Recently I received a letter from the dean, E. Seeberg, in which he confirmed my present leave and informed me that in case I want to extend my leave of absence, I must obtain the approval of the ministry. And that is indeed very difficult, so I figure that I will then have to finally decide whether or not I will once again return to my academic career. I no longer have any great desire to do so. And I don't believe that the desire will grow any stronger by winter. For me what counts is only to be doing things with students. But perhaps there are still other paths that will be opened.

Before I finally commit myself to anything, however, I am again desirous of going to India. Lately I have been occupied very intensively with questions relating to India and believe that one can perhaps learn a great deal there. In any case, it sometimes seems to me as if in their brand of "paganism" there is placed more Christianity than in our whole Reich Church. Of course, Christianity did indeed come from the East originally, and we have Westernized it in such a way and permeated it with merely civilized considerations that, as we now see it, it is almost lost to us. Unfortunately I have hardly any confidence left in the church opposition. I thoroughly dislike their way of going about things and I really dread the moment when they assume responsibility and we must once again witness a terrible compromising of Christianity. Practically speaking, it is not yet clear to me how the plans for India will develop. It's possible—but please don't say anything about this to students, etc.— I might go to the University of Rabindranath Tagore. I would very much prefer to go instead to Gandhi. I already have good introductions from some close friends of his. I might be able to stay there as his guest for six months or longer. If this can be arranged and I can somehow manage the matter financially, I would go in the winter. . . . [GS, II, pp. 180–82]

62

Bonhoeffer's Inner Liberation: Letters on Becoming a Christian

1935–1939

In his biography of Bonhoeffer, Eberhard Bethge describes three phases in Bonhoeffer's life: when young Dietrich became a theologian, when the theologian became a Christian, and when the theologian-Christian became a "contemporary."[7] This is a rather simplistic structure that is developed with more nuances in the biography itself. The question of turning points or moments of "conversion" has certainly fascinated researchers of Bonhoeffer's life and writings. Some have attempted to pinpoint the American experience as pivotal in the process whereby Bonhoeffer the theologian became a committed Christian, looking back at his pastoral work among blacks in Harlem or at his budding pacifism under the influence of Jean Lasserre. The question of whether Bonhoeffer experienced a momentous conversion, pinpointed in time, or whether what we detect is more precisely the accumulation of subtle changes that constituted a shift in his ways of thinking and acting has never been fully answered. Evidence from his own writings would seem to rule out the possibility of an "instantaneous conversion." He himself says as much in one of his prison letters acknowledging that he didn't think he had

> ever changed very much, except perhaps at the time of my first impressions abroad and under the first conscious influence of my father's personality. It was then that I turned from phraseology to reality. . . . Neither of us has really had a break in our lives. Of course, we have deliberately broken with a good deal, but that again is something quite different. Even our present experiences probably don't represent a break in the passive sense. I sometimes used to long for something of the kind, but today I think differently about it.[8]

This letter would seem to attest to the patterns of continuity so clearly affirmed in serious studies of Bonhoeffer's theology. He speaks of having "deliberately broken with a good deal"; Bethge speaks rather of a momentous change in his outlook even as continuity, integrity, and consistency were among the most impressive features of Bonhoeffer the theologian-pastor. The continual question for Bonhoeffer was centered in the search for concrete forms in which one is addressed by God's Word in Jesus Christ. That Word was to take him to those forms of Christian discipleship that became his life as theologian, pastor, ecumenist, seminary director, agitator for peace, conspirator, prisoner, and martyr. But even with this remarkable consistency, Bethge notes that people close to him did notice changes. Paul Lehmann, his closest American friend from the year at Union Theological Seminary, remarked that when they met again in 1933 he was struck by Bonhoeffer's having become a regular churchgoer.[9] Likewise, he now meditated regularly on the Bible, to the surprise of his students in 1932. The practice provoked their ironic comments. He began to advocate private, oral confession of sins within the church. He also took a quiet, though unpopular, stand on Christian pacifism in the midst of a Germany given to rearming. Most of all, his personal longing for community life began to assert itself in various ways. He often spoke of a community life of prayer, service, and obedience to the Sermon on the Mount that could become a spearhead of renewal both of pastoral ministry and of Christian life within Germany. That desire would be partially satisfied within the House of Brethren at Finkenwalde. Bonhoeffer's piety became more fervent, to be sure, but utterly opposed to any quietist separation from the world. The Sermon on the Mount, he argued, was a Word of Christ commanding a concrete response in decisive action and not a mere idea to be admired for its impossible demands.

Few studies of Bonhoeffer's writings are as perceptive on this question as that of theologian J. Patrick Kelley, who analyzes two changes or shifts in Bonhoeffer's development as a Christian theologian and pastor. "The first," he writes,

> was a movement away from a more exclusive intellectual sort of theology toward an increasing concern to develop the actuality of Christian living within a highly structured and explicitly pious common life, whose norms were regarded as given from the divine source external to it, yet accessible to the empathic student of the Bible. This shift was already under way in 1930–31 in New York, developed significantly at the point of Bonhoeffer's taking up his work in the University and the church in late 1931, and continued to grow until it manifested itself in a mature form in *The Cost of Discipleship* (1937) and *Life Together* (1937) as well as other works from the period 1935–39. The second turn was in some significant respect a disavowal of at least part of that which had predominated in Bonhoeffer's life in the year since that first turn. Any form of piety which publicly separated the Christian from the world at large now came to be avoided at all cost along with the conceptuality which presumes that Christians have access to special sets of ethical principles or special clarity about those available to general ethical reflection.[10]

Eberhard Bethge calls these same shifts a "momentous inner revolution." Bonhoeffer never spoke of these in public. Bethge adds that he greatly disliked stories of conversion told by pietists to edify the congregation.[11]

The three letters excerpted here are Bonhoeffer's most vivid testimony of what the "shifts" in his thinking were that made him much more aware of the demands of and need to respond to the Sermon on the Mount, which became for him a personal liberation. The first letter, to his physicist brother Karl-Friedrich, speaks to the power of the Sermon on the Mount in his life moving him to take uncompromising stands on peace, social justice, and, indeed, Christ himself. The second letter, to a woman to whom he had once been engaged, describes even more personally his change in attitude from being a self-serving theologian to being a committed Christian. It was, again, a liberation through God's Word in the Sermon on the Mount strengthening him for the crisis of 1933. The third letter, to Rüdiger Schleicher, his brother-in-law, father of Renate Bethge, and fellow conspirator, tells of the way he had come to read and appreciate the Bible, one vital source of his growing commitment to be a more genuine Christian, follower of Christ even to the cross.

Finally, we have included another letter to Karl-Friedrich, composed in January 1939, at the height of the crisis provoked by church-state relations in 1938. Many of the younger pastors of the Confessing Church had been thrown into a state of confusion and indecision. The civil authorities had succeeded in driving a wedge into the ranks of the confessing pastors by distinguishing between those who held a legalized pastoral office in the Third Reich and those excluded from such office because their ordination had proceeded according to the Dahlem Declaration rather than through the official church. Although only a few of the young pastors were affected, for Bonhoeffer these were the ones representing the promise of the Barmen and Dahlem Declarations and, therefore, the very heart of the Confessing Church. The pastors found themselves entangled in the network of Nazi regulations, leaving them vulnerable to arrest and prosecution even for exercising the simplest roles in their ministry. At the congregational level such pastors were subject to eviction or the withholding of their salary for any number of real or trumped-up reasons. Their only refuge lay in being ignored by the authorities or in being protected by older official pastors, not under financial squeeze from Berlin. This led to the systematic wooing of these "illegal" pastors by the presidents of the consistories and led many young pastors into an agonizing choice between the way of the Councils of Brethren of the Confessing Church and that of the consistories. The choice was compounded by the many arrests of dissenting pastors in 1937. Now in 1938 and 1939 Bonhoeffer continued to rally the young pastors to stand firm and to resist the national church despite the lure of "legality" and the threat of monetary sanctions. Bonhoeffer encouraged those who were wavering. It was in that context that he wrote to Karl-Friedrich admitting that it was depressing to see so many look for their peace and quiet while he urged them to hold out against the pressures of the national church and the persuasive tactics of Dr. Friedrich Werner, Nazi head of the Church Committee for the German Evangelical Church.[12]

LETTER TO KARL-FRIEDRICH BONHOEFFER

London, January 14, 1935

Dear Karl-Friedrich,

We have seen so terribly little of each other in the last couple of years that our days spent together recently were very beautiful for me. It may be that in many things I seem to you to be somewhat fanatical and crazy. I myself sometimes have anxiety about this. But I know that, if I were more reasonable, for the sake of honor, I should have to, the next day, give up all my theology. When I first began theology, I imagined it to be somewhat different—perhaps more like an academic affair. Now it has become something completely different from that. And I now believe I know at last that I am at least on the right tract—for the first time in my life. And that often makes me very glad. I continue to fear only that I might no longer appreciate the genuine anxiety for meaning of other people, but remain set in my ways. I believe I know that inwardly I shall be really clear and honest only when I have begun to take seriously the Sermon on the Mount. Here is set the only source of power capable of exploding the whole enchantment and specter [Hitler and his rule] so that only a few burnt-out fragments are left remaining from the fireworks. The restoration of the church will surely come from a sort of new monasticism which has in common with the old only the uncompromising attitude of a life lived according to the Sermon on the Mount in the following of Christ. I believe it is now time to call people to this.

Please excuse these somewhat personal expressions but they flowed from my pen as I thought about our recent getting together. But, then too, we are ultimately concerned about each other. I still can't ever believe that you really consider all these thoughts to be so completely insane. At present there are still some things for which an uncompromising stand is worthwhile. And it seems to me that peace and social justice or Christ himself are such.

Recently by chance I happened upon the fairy tale about the emperor's new clothes. That is really very timely today. All we need is the child at the end of the story. One would have to act it through once. . . . [GS, III, pp. 24–25]

LETTER TO A WOMAN TO WHOM BONHOEFFER HAD BEEN ENGAGED

Finkenwalde, January 1, 1936

I plunged into work in a very unChristian way. An . . . ambition that many noticed in me made my life difficult. . . .

Then something happened, something that has changed and transformed my life to the present day. For the first time I discovered the Bible. . . . I had often preached, I had seen a great deal of the church, and talked and preached about it—but I had not yet become a Christian. . . .

I know that at that time I turned the doctrine of Jesus Christ into something of personal advantage for myself. . . . I pray to God that that will never happen again. Also I had never prayed, or prayed only very little. For all my abandonment, I was quite pleased with myself. Then the Bible, and in particular the Sermon on the Mount, freed me from that. Since then everything has changed. I have felt this plainly, and so have other people about me. It was a great liberation. It became clear to me that the life of a servant of Jesus Christ must belong to the church, and step by step it became plainer to me how far that must go.

Then came the crisis of 1933. This strengthened me in it. Also I now found others who shared that aim with me. The revival of the church and of the ministry became my supreme concern. . . .

I suddenly saw as self-evident the Christian pacifism that I had recently passionately opposed—a disputation at which Gerhard [Jacobi] was also present. And so it went on, step by step. I no longer saw or thought anything else. . . .

My calling is quite clear to me. What God will make of it I do not know. . . .

I must follow the path. Perhaps it will not be such a long one. Sometimes we wish that it were so (Phil. 1:23). But it is a fine thing to have realized my calling. . . .

I believe its nobility will become plain to us only in coming times and events. If only we can hold out. [*DB*, pp. 154–55]

LETTER TO RÜDIGER SCHLEICHER

Friedrichsbrunn, April 8, 1936

Dear Rüdiger,

. . . I will first of all quite simply make a confession: I believe that the Bible alone is the answer to all our questions and that we need only to ask insistently and with some humility for us to receive the answer from it. One cannot simply read the Bible like other books. We must be prepared really to question it. Only in this way is it revealed to us. Only if we await the final answer from it does it give that Word to us. The reason for this is that in the Bible God speaks to us. And we cannot simply reflect upon God from ourselves; rather, we must ask him. Only when we seek him does he answer. Naturally one can also read the Bible like any other book, as for example from the viewpoint of textual criticism, etc. There is certainly nothing to be said against this. Only that it is not the way that reveals the essence of the Bible, only its superficial surface. Just as we do not grasp the word of a person whom we love, in order to dissect it, but just as such a word is simply accepted and it then lingers with us all day long, simply as the word of this person whom we love, and just as the one who reveals himself to us as the one who has spoken to us in this word that moves us ever more deeply in our hearts like Mary, so should we treat the Word of God. Only if we dare for once to enter into relationship with the Bible as the place where the God who loves us really speaks to us and will not leave us alone with our questions will we be happy with the Bible. . . .

If I am one who says where God shall be, so I will always find a God there who corresponds in some way to me, is pleasing to me, who belongs to my nature. If it is, however, God who speaks where he chooses to be, then that will probably be a place which does not at all correspond to my nature, which is not at all pleasing to me. But this place is the cross of Christ. And he who will find him there must be with him under this cross, just as the Sermon on the Mount demands. This doesn't suit our nature at all but is completely counter to it. This, however, is the message of the Bible, not only in the New but also in the Old Testament (Isa. 53!). In any event, Jesus and Paul intended this: with the cross of Jesus is the Scripture, that is, the Old Testament, fulfilled. The whole Bible will, therefore, be the Word in which God will allow himself to be discovered by us. This is no place which is pleasing or *a priori* sensible to us, but a place strange to us in every way and which is entirely contrary to us. But this is the very place God has chosen to encounter us.

So I now read the Bible in this way. I ask in every place: What is God saying to us here? I ask God to show us what he wants to say. Thus we are not at all permitted to seek after general, eternal truths which would correspond to our own "everlasting" nature and as such would be made evident. Rather, we seek the will of God who is entirely strange and contrary to us, whose ways are not our ways and whose thoughts are not our thoughts, who hides himself under the sign of the cross at which all our ways and thoughts come to an end. God is wholly other than the so-called eternal truth. That is always still our own thoughts of self and our wished-for life everlasting. God's Word, however, begins where he points us to the cross of Jesus at which all our ways and thoughts, also the so-called "everlasting" converge, namely in death and God's judgment. Is it in any way intelligible to you, if I won't at any point be willing to sacrifice the Bible as this strange Word of God, that, on the contrary, I ask with all my strength what God wants to say to us here? Everything outside the Bible has become too uncertain for me. I am afraid only of running into a heavenly double of myself. Is it also comprehensible to you that I am rather ready for a sacrifice of my intellect (*sacrificium intellectus*) even in these matters and only in these matters, that is, in the sight of the God of truth? And who would not in fact bring his or her own sacrifice of intellect into such a situation, that is, with the acknowledgment one does not yet understand this or that place of the Scripture, in the awareness that even this will one day be revealed as God's own Word? I would rather do this than only to say, following some suitable opinion: "This is divine, that is human."

I also want to say to you quite personally that since I have learned to read the Bible in this way—and that is not so very long ago—it becomes more wonderful to me every day. I read it every morning and evening, often also during the day. And every day I take for myself a text that I will have for the entire week and attempt to immerse myself entirely in it, in order to be able to really listen to it. I know that without this I would no longer be able to live properly. Or, even before that, to believe in the right way. [GS, III, pp. 26–29]

LETTER TO KARL-FRIEDRICH BONHOEFFER

January 28, 1939

Dear Karl-Friedrich,

The reason I didn't write to you punctually can be explained by the fact that much is happening here at present. It has been to some extent quite depressing in recent weeks when one had to see how many with all sorts of pretexts and reasons seek quiet and safety as much as circumstances permit. In such times, which happen again and again, there is always very much to do with visits, lectures, etc. I am quite certain that what matters most of all for the church is that we hold out now even at the cost of great sacrifices. The greatest sacrifices now are small compared with what we would lose by wrongly backing down. I do not know of anything worth our wholehearted commitment today if not this cause. What certainly matters in this regard is not how many there are in it but only that there are at least some involved in it. Naturally it is much more difficult for the married people, but now and again I think that much is also easier for them. I very often admire the courage of the wives of the pastors who would rather take everything on themselves than that they should influence their husbands to give in. Likewise, the members of the congregation are often more ready and resolute than their pastor. In these days it will be our lot to make very important decisions. Things are fine with me now. I would like to visit Sabine in March if it is still possible. [GS, II, pp. 345–46]

63

Letters to Karl Barth

1936, 1942

In the midst of the escalating church struggle, in late August 1936, Bonhoeffer represented the Confessing Church at the ecumenical conference of Chamby. This was the final ecumenical gathering to be held by the Universal Christian Council for Life and Work in preparation for the larger conference scheduled for Oxford in 1937. From the beginning Bonhoeffer made it clear he would not tolerate anything less than full recognition of the Confessing Church. He refused an offer to be present as a mere interpreter, arguing that he was a member of an official delegation. On the other side, the Reich Church, under Bishop Wilhelm Zoellner, insisted that it alone was qualified to represent the German Evangelical church. There seemed no way out of the dilemma. Eventually the conference conveners, notably H.L. Henriod and George K.A. Bell, made it possible for both these groups and a third, the Lutheran Council led by Hans Lilje, to attend. This in effect gave Bonhoeffer the status of representative of the Confessing Church, though the minutes kept the peace by referring to him and the Confessing Church delegates as "co-opted members . . . invited to the meeting (with the right to speak)."[24]

Bonhoeffer openly manifested his resentment of the Reich Church presence at the conference. The atmosphere was otherwise very friendly; the resolutions were sufficiently vague and irenic enough to convince Bonhoeffer he could expect little help from the ecumenical movement in the church struggle.

After the conference Bonhoeffer and Eberhard Bethge journeyed south to Rome. It was a memorable visit; the memories of it would linger on even during the Bonhoeffer's days of imprisonment. Bonhoeffer reminisced about it in his letter of January 23, 1944. On his return home Bonhoeffer stopped at Wiesendangen to meet with Erwin Sutz. Part of his goal on this brief vacation trip was to visit Karl Barth in Basel. However, Bonhoeffer was unable to see Barth at the time Sutz arranged. Later, to his dismay, Bonhoeffer learned that Barth had waited for them an entire Sunday afternoon. This led to their next exchange of letters, after a silence of nearly three years. Bonhoeffer used this letter to explain his silence as a "silent controversy" with Barth brought on by the questions the Bible was posing to him during these years. He then attempted to bounce off Barth a description of seminary life at Finkenwalde. Bonhoeffer was at the time all too aware of criticisms aimed at his way of directing the seminary. For his critics, his style was too "Catholic," or too pietistic, or too legalistic, or simply too monastic, and, therefore, too strict. Here was an opportunity, as in their earlier encounters, to test his ideas and in this case his philosophy of preparing for the ministry against Barth's sharp mind. Barth's answer was not unexpected, given his well-known Reformed perspectives and aversion for aspects of pietism that seemed too close to a salvation by works. For Barth, there was "an almost indefinable odor of a monastic eros and pathos," a judgment qualified by his stated willingness to learn from Bonhoeffer and by his avowal that his knowledge of what Bonhoeffer was attempting at the seminary too scanty for an adequate criticism. This was to be their last exchange until the war years.

By then, Bonhoeffer had become a courier for the *Abwehr* and was thus able to travel to Switzerland. He made three such trips: February 1941, September 1941, and May 1942. He was there to explore possibilities for the delicate communications with the Allies that would have to be set up in an atmosphere of mutual trust. The conspirators felt that Bonhoeffer's reputation as an ecumenist might at least inspire that trust. At the Swiss frontier Bonhoeffer gave Karl Barth's name as his guarantor of security. Barth did, indeed, vouch for him. The fact that he was in Switzerland at a time of nazism's nearly total ban on such travel led, undoubtedly, to some apprehensions and unsettling suspicions about Bonhoeffer—suspicions that Bonhoeffer tried to dispel in the letter quoted here. Had Bonhoeffer gone over to nazism to be permitted such freedom of travel? Bonhoeffer and Barth met, and Bonhoeffer was able to explain his role in the conspiracy and speak of his hopes for toppling the Hitler government and working for the restoration of Christianity after the war. The letter of May 17, 1942, quoted here, is significant because it points to the shadowy existence Bonhoeffer had to endure as a conspirator, what Bethge has called an "inner exile." Barth's reply through his close associate Fraulein Charlotte (Lollo) von Kirschbaum was reassuring to Bonhoeffer, and it set a date for their meeting. "Oh what a mess!" Fraulein von Kirschbaum wrote.

> Believe us, we too laugh about this business, though with tears in our eyes. That such an uproar could arise at all is enough reason to be distressed, and needs to be taken seriously, in its own way, as a "sign of the times." So, Karl Barth has never distrusted you for a moment; or to be precise: whenever he had a question concerning the occasion for your travels, he immediately and directly asked you about it. The question why *you* have this freedom has been put to us again and again. If we talked about it with any of our friends recently—Barth does not recall doing so, and I have not heard anything about it either—the possible foundation for the alleged comment (your presence here is "unsettling to him on account of your assignments") can only be that question they were raising. Since his conversation with you answered that question for him, he affirmed your coming to everybody. The fact that we have to do this again and again shows you how nervous and distrustful people here are even toward "us."[25]

The letter of Bonhoeffer to Barth, quoted in full here, is one of six hitherto unknown letters discovered in June 1981 by the wife of Dr. Hinrich Stoevesandt, curator of the Karl Barth Archives in Basel, Switzerland. Later, in the fall of 1981, two more letters were found in Barth's own files in the Barth Archives. The German text was published by Kaiser Verlag, Munich, as its Christmas greeting in December 1981. The English translation by John D. Godsey appeared in *Newsletter,* no. 22, (June 1982), published by the International Bonhoeffer Society, English Language Section.

Finkenwalde, September 19, 1936

Very Distinguished And Dear Professor:

When I was in Switzerland recently, I very much wanted to visit you, not having seen you for so long. I gather that my friend Sutz had already said that I was coming, unfortunately at a time which I did not suggest to him at all. I have now heard that you waited in vain for Sutz and me one Sunday afternoon. I'm dreadfully sorry. I always find it overwhelming to think that I am taking up a great deal of your time by visiting you when you are already being deprived of it on all sides. And I certainly would not do it if I did not have something of the utmost importance. This time I really would have been glad to do it and then it was too late. It grieved me very much. Now I must at least write to you, as I have really kept silent for long enough. Our last encounter was a telephone conversation in which I was to invite you to Berlin for Jacobi. Since you wrote to me in England that time that I was to return by the next ship or failing that by the ship after next, you have heard nothing from me in person. I must ask you to excuse me for that. But the arrow did strike home! I think it really was the ship after next on which I came home. Now I have been back here eighteen months; in many respects I am glad that I was over there, but I am still more glad that I am back here again. There are all sorts of reasons for my not having written since then. I have always thought that if I write to you I ought to have something reasonable to write, and I never had anything reasonable, at any rate, anything that I thought it worthwhile bothering you with. Nor have I even now.

Then I really wanted first of all to come to some sort of conclusion about the questions which the Bible raised for me and which kept on bothering me, though of course I also recognised time and again that in some respects I was probably departing from your views. The whole period was basically a constant, silent controversy with you, and so I had to keep silence for a while. The chief questions are those of the exposition of the Sermon on the Mount and the Pauline doctrine of justification and sanctification. I am engaged in a work [*The Cost of Discipleship*] on the subject and would have asked and learnt a very, very great deal from you. Most of us who feel that they had to keep away from you for a while for theological reasons of some sort seem to find that afterwards, in a personal conversation with you, they learn that once again they have seen the whole question in terms far too crude. Now I am earnestly hoping for another opportunity of seeing you and talking to you at length. Finally I must say for the sake of clarity—I have said it to no one else—that I felt myself somewhat excluded from your circle by not taking part in your *Festschrift*. I would very much have liked to write a contribution for you; please do not misunderstand that. I simply took it as an objective verdict that I was not counted as one of the theologians associated with you. I was sorry about it, as I know that it is not true. So, those were the reasons why I kept silent for so long.

Work at the seminary gives me great joy. Academic and practical work are combined splendidly. I find that all along the line the young theologians coming into the seminary raise the very questions that have been troubling me recently, and of course our life together is strongly influenced by this. I am firmly convinced that in view of what the young theologians bring with them from the university and in view of the independent work which will be demanded of them in the parishes— particularly here in the East—they need a completely different kind of training which life together in a seminary like this unquestionably gives. You can hardly imagine how empty, how completely burnt out, most of the brothers are when they come to the seminary. Empty not only as regards theological insights and still more as regards knowledge of the Bible, but also as regards their personal life. On an open evening—the only one in which I shared—you once said very seriously to the students that you sometimes felt as though you would rather give up all lectures and instead pay a surprise visit on someone and ask him, like old Tholuck, "How goes it with your soul?" The need has not been met since then, not even by the Confessing Church. But there are very few who recognize this sort of work with young theologians as a task of the church and do something about it. And it is really what everyone is waiting for. Unfortunately I am not up to it, but I remind the brothers of each other, and that seems to me to be the most important thing. It is, though, certain that both theological work and real pastoral fellowship can only grow in a life which is governed by gathering round the Word morning and evening and by fixed times of prayer. And it is in fact only the consequence of what you have made very clear in "Anselm." The charge of legalism does not seem to me to fit at all. What is there legalistic in a Christian setting to work to learn what prayer is and in his spending a good deal of his time in this learning? A leading man in the Confessing Church recently said to me: "We have no time for meditation now, the ordinands should learn how to preach and to catechize." That seems to me either a complete misunderstanding of what young theologians are like today or a culpable ignorance of how preaching and catechism come to life. The questions that are seriously put to us today by young theologians are: How do I learn to pray? How do I learn to read the Bible? If we cannot help them there we cannot help them at all. And there is really nothing obvious about it. To say, "If someone does not know that, then he should not be a minister" would be to exclude most of us from our profession. It is quite clear to me that all these things are only justified when alongside them and with them—at just the same time!—there is really serious and sober theological, exegetical, and dogmatic work going on. Otherwise all these questions are given the wrong emphasis. But I do not mean to ignore these questions about everything in the world; they are what I am concerned with! And these are just the things that I would most have liked to discuss with you. [*WF,* pp. 115–18]

Geneva, May 17, 1942

Dear Professor:

Forgive me if what I have to write now turns out foolish and not worth talking about. But I still have to bring it up because the matter bothers me a great deal. Last week in Zurich I learned for the first time that, because of my assignments, my stay here was disquieting [*unheimlich*] for you. When I first heard that I just laughed. Shortly thereafter, again in Zurich, I heard of this alleged utterance of yours a second time; at that point I thought it best not to pursue the matter at all. Now I have already heard the same thing twice here in Geneva; having thought it over for a few days, I simply want to tell you that. I know that in circles as close as this there is often silly talk and quite possibly we are dealing with something blown out of all proportion. However, if this is not so, then I am really quite at a loss for words. In a time when so much must rest simply on personal trust, then *everything* is really over when distrust arises. I can indeed understand that this curse of distrust gradually befalls all of us, but it is difficult to bear when it strikes one personally for the first time. But now it must be terrible for you—perhaps even worse than for me—suddenly to be forced to be suspicious. In that case, our conversations must have been quite unbearable for you. But I did not sense that. Nor can I imagine it now. I was so glad during our last conversation that I could tell you everything in answer to your question. I thought everything was now clear.

Let me just add this: it would be unbearably painful for me if the admittedly difficult effort to continue our solidarity were to end in inner alienation. And why should I conceal my belief that, at least in the eastern part of Germany, there are few who have declared their loyalty to you as often as I have tried in recent years. On the other hand I would like to save us both from the agony of a conversation undermined by distrust. In that case I would rather not come at all, even though in all my trips to Switzerland I have looked forward to nothing so much as my visits with you. I also have a lot of news and greetings for you. But, after all this, Basel has now become somewhat "unsettling" for me, and I do not know what to do. Otherwise I would like to have asked whether the Monday or Tuesday after Pentecost would suit you. On Thursday my visa expires. So please send me some word; the address of Otto

Salomon would be best. What's more, this business throws me into a turmoil vis-a-vis Thurneysen and Vischer.

Let me assure you again that there is no reason at all for you to be suspicious. And, bitter as it is, this whole business can still make me laugh. However, I do need a word from you as to whether I should come.

Forgive this lengthy letter which interrupts you in your work and prevents me from reading your *Dogmatics*.

I greet you with sincere respect.

Your thankful and devoted

Dietrich Bonhoeffer

[Translated by John Godsey]

64

To the Brethren of Finkenwalde and the Pastors of the Confessing Church: Circular Letters in the Church Struggle and War Years

1936–1942

The collection of circular letters to his brethren from the seminary and the pastors of the Confessing Church during the height of the church's struggle and during the war years reveals many things about Bonhoeffer's spirituality. These letters tell us a great deal about the sources of Bonhoeffer's own strength in his life as a double agent, trying to keep alive the communion of Finkenwaldians and Confessing pastors, not with memories of their past peace and idyllic community life but with the freshness of God's Word speaking through the Bible, their prayers, and even their experiences. The letters become a witness to Bonhoeffer's standing by these young ministers in the harsh conditions of being a minority struggling for truth and justice, of military life, and in the repugnant actions forced on them by combat. Here, as at Finkenwalde, we see Bonhoeffer himself struggling to maintain a sense of unity and inner peace amid the deaths and sufferings of his brothers on the front, and in the violence done to their consciences—they as soldiers, he as a double agent engaged in treason—and the horrors he knew the war was perpetrating against civilian populations. In fact, the involvement of his fellow pastors in the inevitable atrocities of war gave a special urgency to his work in the conspiracy.

Little, however, made much sense to these pastors, he points out, except their continued trust that somehow God would bring some good out of their service. "Our only comfort," he writes in his first circular letter of the war years, after announcing the death of the first Confessing pastor killed in action, "is the God of the resurrection. The Father of our Lord Jesus Christ, who also was and is his

God." He openly concedes in that letter that the great gaps torn in one's existence by God could not be filled "with human words," but should rather "remain open." The letters speak of death, separation, troubles of conscience, and meaningless suffering. But they also bring to the forefront eloquent reminders of their Christian heritage and pastoral ministry. "Certainly none of us is ever released from the responsibility of being a Christian and no one may deny that he is a pastor," he wrote. Bonhoeffer's Christmas letter of 1939 speaks of the significance of that feast even in the precariousness of their futures in such a war. Though they could not continue to lead pastors' lives as soldiers, they could take solace in their faith. "God knows your present life," Bonhoeffer wrote in his letter of May 1940, "and finds his way to you even in the most tense, the busiest days, if you can no longer find your way to him." They could praise their God even "in the midst of war."

Finally it is in these letters that we see stated as convincingly as Bonhoeffer could why he was so insistent on the practice of daily meditation. In the circular letter of March 1, 1942, he tells those at the front that this is a precious gift that can become "the focal point of everything which brings inward and outward order into my life." In the midst of the dangers that had made their lives so hellish, meditation, he claimed, gave them a needed constancy, providing a link to that "saving fellowship of the community, the brethren, our spiritual home." These letters give shape to what that community had become in the life of Bonhoeffer and his seminarians. His care for them did not end when the seminary closed. To give a sense of some important aspects of that seminary community, we begin the selections of this section with Bonhoeffer's annual report of 1936, given in the form of a letter addressed to his "brothers and friends." The letter tells of what they had to be grateful for in the seminary's development as the Confessing Church; they were being primed for "great questions, great tasks, and great sufferings." This is followed by the circular letters themselves, beginning with the letter of January 1938 outlining the reasons why they are a "confessing church" and why now, more than ever before, they need faith.

BONHOEFFER'S REPORT FOR 1936

"He has done all things well." (MARK 7:37)

Finkenwalde, December 21, 1936

Dear Brothers and Friends:

. . . . Over the past year God the Lord has deigned to give our Confessing Church great questions, great tasks, and great sufferings. Since the intervention of the state church committees in the life of our church, the Confessing Church has suffered great shocks. There have been hard decisions for you, dear brethren, in the parishes. You have had to lead the struggle and in so doing have gone through much questioning, doubt, and temptation. Our service here in the house was able to consist chiefly in continuing our work quietly and straightforwardly. Our way was shown clearly.

We have been assembling together every day in the old way to pray, to read the Bible, and to praise our God, and as we have done so we have thought of you. Similarly at the end of the day there have been devotions and intercessions for all the concerns of our church for your work and for your struggle. You know that we have joined with you all in our daily time of meditation and have prayed for one another before God. It was a great delight to us that over and above the confines of our brotherhood some members of congregations far and near have also joined our meditations, and we should also keep them in our thoughts. We should also let ourselves be reminded to keep up faithfully the morning half hour each day of considering the Scriptures and interceding. Each of us knows the needs, the inner contradiction, the laziness, which keep on wanting to hold us up, and how to search out what we have recognized as our salvation. We have still been given time and admonition. If one person goes astray, that is a visible or an invisible weakening of every one else in the fellowship of prayer. Let us not despise God's gift.

As well as meditation, however, daily, plentiful reading of Scripture must keep its place. No day of our life in office may go past without our having read the Bible on it. The very controversies of the last months have once again clearly shown to our shame how unversed in Holy Scripture we still are. How ready people were to make the decision for or against the church committees dependent on all sorts of contingencies of this or that kind, instead of asking for and seeking out only the evidence of Scripture. Indeed, how little did people so often listen when the Bible was read out, and how readily did they swallow all the novelties. This must be changed. We must make it a rule to look for the scriptural evidence for every decision that confronts us, and not to rest until we have found it. Our confidence in dealing with the Bible must increase year by year. And there is something else. We know that it was quite a long time before some of the brothers who were arrested were given Bibles. Weeks like that can prove whether we have been faithful in our reading of Scripture and whether in our knowledge of Scripture we have acquired a great treasury.

Lectures and exercises stand now, as ever, under the shadow of biblical work. After dealing with the "Discipleship of Christ" in the first course, the theme "The Visible Church" followed in the second, "The New Life in Paul" in the third, and "Concrete Ethics in Paul" in the present semester. It would take too long to tell you about the Old Testament, homiletic, and catechetical work. A great deal of theological work has been done, from the first course onwards, but I believe that a certain climax has been reached in it with the present course. While I am writing this report, a two and a half day long disputation is going on, from morning to evening, on "The Preaching of the Law." For some weeks a chosen group of brothers has been working in all its free time to prepare this disputation. We can be grateful for the clarification and the furthering of our knowledge and our insights in many important spheres. But at the same time, our community is knit more closely together by this common work on a question which is so significant for our church today.

We have made music, as ever, with great joy. In default of any instruments in Zingst, the first course was predominantly active in singing. The second course at Finkenwalde had two grand pianos and tremendous soloists! The third and fourth sing and make music together. On the third Sunday in Advent we had a musical evening for the parish and the friends of the house, which was repeated in the church at Podejuch. We were able to assemble quite a respectable orchestra for it. It was a great delight to all of us, and I for one cannot imagine our common life here without daily music making together. We have certainly driven out some evil spirits that way.

Although the quietness of domestic life and work must be the real purpose of the short time at the seminary, each course has also had a glimpse of life beyond our walls. In the spring, we accepted an invitation to Sweden. For most people this trip was the first encounter with the Church of Christ beyond the borders of Germany, with the ecumenical world. We were given a most hearty welcome, and ten days were almost overfilled with seeing, hearing, and meetings. The friendship and the love we found there enriched us on our return. Thanks for this time will be equally alive in all of us. For another purpose, the summer course went from the house for almost the same time to a popular mission together in the Belgard district. Four brethren each were housed in six villages; they preached on four evenings of the week and on Sunday. In the evenings these four each expounded a text for ten minutes. This combined proclamation, which derives from shared daily work in the parish and shared prayer, commended itself to all the brethren involved and, we hope, to the parish. After long weeks of silence it is a special delight to be able to preach the gospel again. So this popular mission week has strongly influenced the whole semester. One special benefit from this week has been that since then we have kept close contact with several parishes and a number of people, and that we are continually given indications of Christian love and readiness to help. We have much reason for gratitude. . . . [*WF*, pp. 122–26]

TO THE YOUNG BROTHERS OF THE CHURCH IN POMERANIA

The end of January 1938

Dear Brothers:

During the past few weeks, letters and personal comments have reached me which make it clear that our church, and in Pomerania particularly our group of young theologians, has come to a time of sore trial. It is no longer a question of the troubles of one individual, for a great many people are being threatened by one and the same temptation, so I hope that you won't mind if I try to give a common answer to you all. Of course, the letter is still meant for each of you personally. I shall try to take up all the points that you have severally made, in the course of it.

We have to cover a great deal of ground. We shall all agree that when we embraced the cause of the Confessing Church we took the step with a supreme faith which was, for that very reason, a boldness beyond human understanding. We were glad, certain of victory, ready for sacrifice. Our whole life, both our personal life and our ministry, had taken a new turn. Of course I don't pretend that there weren't all sorts of purely human overtones to our feelings—who knows even his own heart?—but there was one thing that made us so joyful and ready to fight and even ready to suffer. Once again we knew that a life with Jesus Christ and his church is worth staking everything on. We believed that in the Confessing Church we had not only found, but through God's great goodness had also actually experienced, the Church of Jesus Christ. For individuals, for pastors, and for communities, a new life began in the joy of God's Word. As long as God's Word was with us, we no longer wanted to worry and fret about the future. With this Word we were ready to fight, to suffer, to undergo poverty, sin, and death, so as finally to reach God's kingdom. Young people and the fathers of large families stood here side by side. What was it that united us then and gave us such great joy? It was the one, age-old recognition which God himself had granted us again, that Jesus Christ wants to build his church among us, a church which lives only by the preaching of the pure, untainted gospel and the grace of his Sacraments, a church which obeys him alone in everything that it does. Christ himself will stand by a church like this; he will protect and guide it. Only a church like this can be free from all fear. This, and nothing else, was acknowledged by the synods of the Confessing Church at Barmen and at Dahlem. Was it an illusion? Did the synods speak under the pressure of external circumstances, which seemed favorable to a "realization" of this faith? No, it was supreme faith, it was the biblical truth itself that was clearly acknowledged then before the whole world. The witness of Christ conquered our hearts, made us glad, and summoned us to act obediently. Dear brothers, surely we are at least agreed on this much, that this was the case? Or do we now want to abuse the grace of God which he has so richly given to us?

That, then, was the beginning of the fight for the true church of Christ. Or do you perhaps think that the devil took all that trouble to annihilate a band of rabid idealists? No, Christ was in the ship, and so the storm was stilled. The battle demanded sacrifice from the beginning. Perhaps everyone did not always realize how much both individuals and communities would have to give up so that the members of the Councils of Brethren would be able to fulfill their duty to the church. But the sacrifices were joyfully made for the cause of Jesus Christ. Who could hold back as long as Jesus still called, "Be the church. Be the church that serves none but me"? Who could take his leave as long as no one released him from his responsibility to preach the pure gospel and to build up the communities in accordance with Scripture and the confessions of our church?

If we are still in agreement here, too, then let us ask in all openness what has happened between those beginnings and our present situation. Perhaps we might put it another way. What is the difference between the church in those provinces where men still live and work and fight as they did at the beginning, and the church in our province? Why has there been incessant lamentation in Pomerania for several months that our church is paralyzed, that it is under a curse, that an inner narrowness and stubbornness is preventing us from doing fruitful work? How has it happened that brethren who were convinced members of the Confessing Church are now saying that all their joy has gone? That they see no good reason why they could not do their work as well under the consistory of the national church as under the Council of Brethren? And can we deny that the witness of our church in Pomerania has recently been growing weaker and weaker? Can we deny that the word of the Confessing Church has largely lost its power to awaken belief and thus call for a decision? Who can deny that the real theological decisions of the church are continually being obscured by considerations of expediency? And has not all this had its effect on our own preaching, too? We ask why all this happens. I don't think that the answer is as hard as people make out. The so-called paralysis in the Confessing Church, the lack of joy, the weak witness, comes from our own disobedience. We should not be thinking about other people now, but about ourselves and our work. What has become of the first clear decisions of the Confessing Church in our communities? Have our communities taken a really lively part in the church? Have we a parish council or a local Council of Brethren unshakably devoted to the cause of the Confessing Church and to us as its pastors? One which supports us and helps us to try new methods in the community? If we haven't, why not? Are the congregations solely responsible for that? There are those among them who are of a contrary opinion. Are the congregations still too "immature"? As though a congregation could be too immature to hear God's Word and act in obedience to it and yet could be "mature" enough to act outside the church! Who taught us to think so contemptuously of our congregations? Who made the cause of the Confessing Church a concern of "the mature?" As if the maturity of a community did not develop precisely from its days of distress before God! Where are the district Councils of Brethren formed from the parish Councils of Brethren, to help the district pastors with their great responsibility? Where is the Confessing Synod of Pomerania, which could only have been formed properly as we went along, and which should have shown the Pomeranian Church the way? In other words, why have we in Pomerania not taken the decisions of the Synod of Dahlem seriously? And if we did not do that, have we ever taken Barmen seriously at all? Other provinces, with much less of a church, fought the battle of the church of the gospel, with all its promise, on the basis of clear, theological decisions made by the church. And in all their sufferings they were glad of it. Why do we so often miss the mark? Why is theological conversation so meaningless among us? At this moment it is really not a question of one accusing another, but of each acknowledging for himself that through our disobedience we have often all too readily despised the grace of God which we received when the Confessing Church came into being. Our words and our actions have often been very different. And now, when we reap our due reward, we begin to accuse one another, indeed we mutter against the way which has been spoilt through our own disobedience and which consequently no longer gives us any joy.

Let me try to put it in a different way: the church struggle can be law or gospel. At the moment it has largely become law as far as we are concerned. We rebel against it. It has become a threatening, angry law which strikes us down. No man can support and direct the church struggle as law without succumbing to it and failing completely. As law, the church struggle is without joy, without certainty, without authority, and without promise. How is that? It is just the same here as in our personal lives. If through our disobedience we evade the gracious Word of God, it becomes a harsh law for us. What is a gentle and easy yoke when done in obedience becomes an insupportable burden when done in disobedience. The more we have hardened ourselves in disobedience against the gracious Word, the harder it is to change, the more obstinately we rebel against God's claim. But just as in our personal life there is only one way, the way of repentance, of patience under God's Word, in which God restores to us our lost communion, so too it is in the church struggle. Without penitence, i.e., unless the church struggle itself becomes our penitence, we shall never receive back the gift we have lost, the church struggle as gospel. Even if the obedience of penitence is harder now than it was then, because we are hardened in our guilt—it is the only way by which God will help us back to the right road.

My dear brethren, if I may so address those of you who still have no permanent appointment in the church, I know that you are perhaps least of all to blame. Indeed things have happened to you, which the pastor could avoid. But must you not accept them with particular joy, and gratitude that the church expects you to go the way that is quite clear? That today *you* have perhaps a greater responsibility than has ever been laid on a generation of young theologians in our church? First, the Confessing Church in Pomerania must come into being. It will, humanly speaking, also depend on you whether it can come into being or not. In the past week we have shared a meditation text from

Haggai 1; it runs: "This people say, 'The time has not yet come to re-build the house of the Lord.' Then the Word of the Lord came by Haggai the prophet, 'Is it a time for you yourselves to dwell in your paneled houses, while this house lies in ruins?'" (Hag. 1: 2–4). It is none of my business, as they say, to "straighten you out," to convince you. But everything does of course depend on our reawakening in you, with God's Word, the courage, the joy, the faith, in Jesus Christ who is and will remain with the Confessing Church, whether you go along with it or not. You ought to know that the faith which threatens to become extinguished among you still lives as it did in the beginning in many communities and many pastorates, that solitary brethren, in Pomerania and outside, in lonely outposts, bear witness to this faith with the great-est joy. The church of Jesus Christ, which lives only from his Word and which means to be obedient to him alone in all things, still lives and will live, and calls you back from temptation and trial. It calls you to peni-tence and warns you of the unfaithfulness which must ultimately end in despair. It prays for you, that your faith may not fail.

You complain about the Council of Brethren. Do that, if you must, at the council itself. But please also ask yourselves whether you came into the Confessing Church because there was a good Council of Brethren. Ask too whether you would have been prepared to embrace the cause of the Confessing Church even if there had not been a Council of Breth-ren at all. Indeed, ask whether you are ready to bear witness for the Confessing Church and to suffer for it all by yourself, before God and man, cut off from all church government and brotherly fellowship. No, your choice is not a simple one, between two church regimes. You cannot take a positive attitude to what you once rejected on grounds of faith for some completely different reason without also destroying yourselves and your belief. God's Word calls you to more faithful work in the Confessing Church, under the direction of the Council of Brethren, however weak both of them may be.

You no longer hope for the success of the Confessing Church. You cannot see any way out. Indeed, who among us *can* see a way out? Only God can do that, and he will show it to those who humbly wait for it. Perhaps we once hoped that the Confessing Church would gain public recognition in Germany. But was this hope ever promised? Certainly not. Now we have learnt to believe in a church which follows its Lord beneath the cross. That is more like the promise. Finally, you say that you would be ready for all kinds of sacrifice both personally and in your ministry, if only you knew why they were necessary. Why, dear brethren? For no reason that men can see, not for the sake of a flourishing church or of a convincing church government, but simply because the way of the Confessing Church must also be followed through desolate stretches of desert and wilderness and because you do not want to stay in the wilderness. So for the sake of the poor church, which will of course go on under the guidance of its Lord even without you, for the sake of your faith, for your certainty, you should remain with the Confessing Church.

What is to happen now? There are so many reasons, and theologians can prove anything. Everything will depend on whether God gives us his testimony afresh in our hearts. Jesus Christ alone can lead the way. But we should have some tasks clearly in mind. There will never be a renewal of our Confessing Church unless we plead for it before God with vigorous prayer. An hour of prayer for our church and for those who lead it should unite us, and at the same time clean and clarify our thoughts. God will then again lead us by the right way. Then we should go on to what we have neglected. We must struggle for complete theological clarity about the decisions of the Confessing Church. We must not stop until we have firm ground under our feet. We can all too easily neglect questions of truth for questions of daily routine. But how can we have clear guidance for a community or a church without a clear theology? False fronts of the church struggle always develop when the question of truth has been passed over. Let us once again take up our conversation with those who confront us with questions. But let it be a conversation in the ultimate truth! The discipline with which the pastors of other districts do theology, preach, and teach, does great credit to these churches and their pastors. Shouldn't discipline also be possible, not least among the younger brethren of our church, for mutual help and strengthening? All this is simply so that we serve our communities. The real need here is for us to prepare to form a Pomeranian Confessing Synod. For this we need local Councils of Brethren and District Councils of Brethren. And once we get that far, the never-ending work will begin: ordering the church's life for baptisms, arranging godparents, instruction, confirmation, confession and the eucharist, visiting, and so on. There are already groups in the Confessing Church which are beginning to attack these questions seriously. But there is no authority which could do this work under the sole guidance of the Word of God but the organs of the Confessing Church. There is work enough. We must now at last get down to it. [*WF*, pp. 164–72]

Bonhoeffer's Advent Letter of November 20, 1938, is included in these selections because it shows in a remarkable way Bonhoeffer's compassion for and solidarity with the Jewish people in the horrors of *Kristallnacht* (Crystal Night), November 9, 1938. He asks the young pastors to exercise patience in their own sufferings, especially in the face of the repressive measures taken against them in 1937 and 1938. But in a cryptic way he also alludes to the suffering of the Jewish people in this strategic paragraph: "During the past few days I have been thinking a great deal about Psalm 74, Zechariah 2:12, Romans 9:4f. and 11:11–15. That takes us right into prayer." Each of these references is significant for Bonhoeffer's attempt to call his seminarians' attention to the compassion, concern, and solidarity they must have with the Jews who had suffered so much during the terrible events of *Kristall-*

nacht. Psalm 74 contains the line: "They said in their hearts, 'Let us destroy them; let us burn all the shrines of God in the land.'" Eberhard Bethge has pointed out that Bonhoeffer's own Bible has a pencil line at Psalm 74:8 and, in the margin, the date, "9.11.38" (November 9, 1938), with an exclamation point. Further, Zechariah 2:12 reads: "whoever touches you touches the apple of my eye." Romans 9 speaks of Israel having received "the adoption, the glory, the covenants, the law, the worship, and the promises." From the Jews, the Apostle Paul says, came the patriarchs and the Messiah. Then, in chapter 11 to which Bonhoeffer refers, Paul denies that the Jews have been displaced by the Gentile world. In his commentary on this passage of Bonhoeffer's circular letter, Bethge speculates how the "prayer" deriving from the scripture verses just cited might have sounded. "These Bible verses together reveal a new, deeper expression of solidarity with persecuted Israel, with its suffering, and a sense of awe in the contemplation of God's election."[26]

ADVENT LETTER

November 20, 1938

Dear Brothers:

At the end of the old church year and the beginning of the new, my first greeting to you is the saying from last week's meditation text: "May the God of steadfastness and encouragement grant you to live in such harmony with one another, in accord with Christ Jesus" (Rom. 15:5). We have been doing a great deal of work here recently, thinking together about the New Testament concept of patience, during which it has become quite clear to me that all along the line we have got to the point where there is only one fundamental question. Do we want to learn the meaning of patience from the gospel? In my opinion, we do not need to take the numerous questions about which we get impatient so seriously. The only serious thing is that our impatience always wants to play nasty tricks on us, by giving itself out as a special sort of obedience, and leading us into unfaithfulness. Somehow, I'm not quite sure how, we have largely got into a way of thinking which is positively dangerous. We think that we are acting particularly responsibly if every other week we take another look at the question whether the way on which we have set out is the right one. It is particularly noticeable that such a "responsible reappraisal" always begins the moment serious difficulties appear. We then speak as though we no longer had "a proper joy and certainty" about this way, or, still worse, as though God and his Word were no longer as clearly present with us as they used to be. In all this, we are ultimately trying to get round what the New Testament calls "patience" and "testing." Paul, at any rate, did not begin to reflect whether his way was the right one when opposition and suffering threatened, nor did Luther. They were both quite certain and glad that they should remain disciples and followers of their Lord. Dear brethren, our real trouble is not doubt about the way upon which we have set out, but our failure to be patient, to keep quiet. We still cannot imagine that today God really doesn't want anything new from us, but simply to prove us in the old way. That is too petty, too monotonous, too undemanding for us. And we simply cannot be constant with the fact that God's cause is not always the successful one, that we really could be "unsuccessful" and yet be on the right road. But this is where we find out whether we have begun in faith or in a burst of enthusiasm.

The significance of patience in the New Testament is quite striking. Only the patient man receives the promise (Matt. 24:13), only the patient man brings forth good fruit (Luke 8:15). A faith which does not become patience is inauthentic, unusable. Faith must be proved. It can only be proved in suffering. Only suffering and endurance will produce the "perfect work" (James 1:3ff.). If we remember that the word faith (*pistis*) already contains the element of faithfulness, we shall not be surprised at the close connection between faith and patience. There is patience only "in Jesus" (Rev. 1:9) for, Jesus was patient as he bore the cross. Hebrews 12:2 describes Jesus' way of the cross as a way of endurance, of patience. For us, endurance means to stand in the fellowship of Christ's suffering (1 Cor. 1:6ff.), and thereby to gain assurance. If we share in the patience of Jesus, we shall ourselves become patient and we will finally have a share in his kingdom (2 Tim. 2:12). The way to patience leads through discipline (2 Peter 1:6). The freer we are from ease and indolence and personal claims, the more ready we shall be for patience.

Our text tells us that we can remain united only if we remain patient. Impatience makes for division. And unfortunately it cannot be denied that all those who have already gone their own way through impatience have made the struggle and test of patience still more difficult for the other brethren. Impatience disrupts fellowship. In the view of the gospel, it is not just a minor, venial, bad habit; it is a failure in the testing of faith. "Now the God of patience"—the God who himself endured in Jesus Christ and helps us to endure—give you "one mind"—to stand by one another in these hours of testing, to come closer to one another, to strengthen and help one another. It is grim if anyone departs at such a time. But our patience depends, not upon people, but upon Jesus Christ and his patience on the cross. He bore the impatience of all people and so can forgive them. "One mind", i.e., not this way today and another tomorrow: remain firm by what you already know, remain constant, show yourselves faithful. How little importance we attach to constancy, firmness, and faithfulness! In the Scriptures they are right at the top of the list.

God grant them to us by making us patient and promising us his comfort in our endurance. One in patience, one in comfort. We belong together in endurance; we also belong together in comfort and in the final victory. No one fights the battle of proving his faith alone. In the hour in which our patience is tried we are one with those who are of one mind with us. And above all, we know that we are one in the patience and comfort of Jesus. He is our patience and our comfort. And this will also be so in the new church year.

If I may give you some advice, take care and work hard with us at the concepts with which we are so concerned at the moment, temptation, patience, proving, humility, thanksgiving, joy, peace, discipline. We have to learn to hear the gospel all over again in these passages. We are being led through the Scriptures along almost untrodden paths, but the views are indescribably wide and beautiful. The meditation texts in the next few weeks should also help us here.

During the past few days I have been thinking a great deal about Psalm 74, Zechariah 2:12, Romans 9:4 f. and 11:11–15. That takes us right into prayer.

I have been very glad to hear from many of you and also to have been able to read your sermons. May I ask the brethren to whom I return sermons to let me know, at least by a postcard, whether they arrive safely, and whether you agree with my comments or not? Please do not think that I cannot be reached by letter, but keep writing and telling me what happens. I think that I have become better at answering in the last few months, at any rate. I have taken care in this direction, for one should really not let such comradeship dissolve through idleness. Above all, keep up the links between yourselves, write, and visit. That is the most important thing.

I wish you a good Advent with all my heart. God bless your preaching and all your work. May he protect you and your homes. We think of you daily. [*WF,* pp. 199–202]

September 20, 1939

Dear Brothers:

In answer to an official question, I have received the news, which I pass on to you today, that our dear brother Theodor Maass was killed in Poland on September 3rd. You will be as stunned by this news as I was. But I beg you, let us thank God in remembrance of him. He was a good brother, a quiet, faithful pastor of the Confessing Church, a man who lived from Word and Sacrament, whom God has also thought worthy to suffer for the gospel. I am sure that he was prepared to go. Where God tears great gaps we should not try to fill them with human words. They should remain open. Our only comfort is the God of the resurrection, the Father of our Lord Jesus Christ, who also was and is his God. In him we know our brothers and in him is the abiding fellowship of those who have overcome and those who still await their hour. God be praised for our dead brother and be merciful to us all at our end. . . .

Please let me know as soon as anyone is called up, or if there is someone not on the list whom I ought to know about. Let me know all the army post office numbers that you have. And take time to write to the brethren out there as often as possible. And above all, we must not neglect the greatest service that is left to us, our faithful daily intercession. There is so much that we must ask for our brethren with the army, but first and last always this, that at all times they may show themselves to be Christians, that they may do a real service to many of their comrades, and that Jesus Christ may be their sole comfort both in life and death.

Many of us have been inwardly disquieted during the past few weeks. We know that our brethren are out there in all sorts of battles and dangers, we hear of the death of a brother, and we feel an urge, "I too must be where my brethren are, I don't want anything more than they have." This often weighs us down completely, and then everything that we do seems so superfluous. Indeed, even the questions about the life of our church, for which we have fought so far, sometimes seem incidental in the light of events in the outside world. We think that once again everything ought to be completely different, that we should leave the whole past behind us and begin all over again. Who can't understand that? But, dear brethren, those of you who have not yet been called up, it is all-important that we do not throw away the grace that God has so far given to us, that we do not despise our office, but learn to love and honor it highly at this very time. We have been called to be preachers of the gospel and shepherds of the community, and as long as we fulfill this task, God will ask us only one thing, whether faithful service to his community has suffered damage, if only for a moment, through our fault, whether we have despised his community and the brethren whom he has given to us, if only for a single moment.

We may still preach, and so we should do, as before, with good, free consciences. And we should be faithful pastors who do not deny their church even in times of need. We know that God requires this service of us today, and this is the greatest possible service that we can render to people. We do not ask what we may feel like today or tomorrow, but what our task is. So let us not bicker and do each other harm, but be glad, and serve.

The texts for September 1st were surprising and promising enough: "Seek the Lord while he may be found, call upon him while he is near" (Isa. 55:6), "Behold, now is the acceptable time; behold, now is the day of salvation" (2 Cor. 6:2). What does that mean, but that God's hour has struck, it is high time for repentance and prayer, the day of glad tidings has dawned, the harvest of the Word of God will be greater than the harvest of death, victory belongs not to the world but to God? If we really believe that, we and our people will be helped.

We are preachers of justification by grace alone. What must that mean today? It means quite simply that we should no longer equate human ways and aims with divine ways and aims. God is beyond all human plans and actions. Everything must be judged by him. Anyone who evades this judgment of God must die, anyone who subjects himself to it will live; for to be judged by God is grace that leads to life. He judges in order to have mercy, he humbles in order to exalt. Only the humble will succeed. God does not confirm human action, but cuts across it, and thereby draws our gaze above, to his grace. In cutting across our ways, God comes to us and says his gracious "Yes" to us, but only through the cross of Jesus Christ. He has placed this cross upon the earth. Under the cross he returns us to the earth, and its work and toil, but in so doing he binds us anew to the earth and to the people who live, act, fight, and suffer upon it. "You then, my son, be strong in the grace that is in Christ Jesus" (2 Tim. 2:1), "Be strong, and show yourself a man, and keep the charge of the Lord your God" (I Kings 2:2f.).

I don't know whether we shall have as troublesome a time now with the question of the righteousness of God as there was in the last war. It almost seems to me as though there had been a change here. Christians today probably know more about the biblical verdict upon the world and history, so they will perhaps be confirmed in their faith, rather than sorely tried, by present events. The non-Christians have already finished too completely with the question of the righteousness of a personal God to be overcome with it. Nevertheless, under the pressure of events the question cannot be left completely out of account, on either side, and we shall often have to listen, like the writer of the 42nd Psalm, to the complaint, "Where is now thy God?" Is it true that God is silent? It is only true for the one whose God is the God of his own ideals and thoughts.

He will have to be given the biblical message of the power and fearfulness of the Creator and Lord of the whole world. "Who has commanded and it came to pass, unless the Lord has ordained it? Is it not from the mouth of the Most High that good and evil come?" (Lam. 3:37f.). "I am the Lord and there is none other, I form light and create darkness, I make weal and create woe." (Isa. 45:6f.). "Does evil befall a city, unless the Lord has done it?" (Amos 3:6). This God, who makes the nations drink from the cup of his wrath and throws them into confusion (Jer. 25:15ff.) is the father of our Lord Jesus Christ, whose counsel is wonderful and who will carry it out gloriously to the end (Isa. 28:29). Is God silent? No, he speaks the silent language of his fearful power and glory, so that we become small and humble and worship him alone. And in pure grace he speaks the clearly perceptible language of his mercy and loving kindness to the children of men and women through the mouth of Jesus Christ, in whom we have the omnipotent God for our own father. "Holy, holy, holy is the Lord of hosts; the whole earth is full of his glory" (Isa. 6:3).

So our hearts and our eyes cannot be caught and dismayed by daily events, however closely we follow them. Above them, we seek and find

God the Lord, and in reverence look upon his works. We seek and find our Lord Jesus Christ, and firmly believe in his victory and in the glory of his community. We seek and find God the Holy Spirit, who gives his Word power over us, greater power than the world can ever gain over us. And so we pray that the work of the triune God will soon be consummated.

Death has again come among us, and we must think about it, whether we want to or not. Two things have become important to me recently: death is outside us, and it is in us. Death from outside is the fearful foe which comes to us when it will. It is the man with the scythe, under whose stroke the blossoms fall. It guides the bullet that goes home. We can do nothing against it, "it has power from the supreme God." It is the death of the whole human race, God's wrath and the end of all life. But the other is death in us, it is our own death. That too has been in us since the fall of Adam. But it belongs to us. We die daily to it in Jesus Christ or we deny him. This death in us has something to do with love toward Christ and toward people. We die to it when we love Christ and the brethren from the bottom of our hearts, for love is total surrender to what a person loves. This death is grace and the consummation of love. It should be our prayer that we die this death, that it be sent to us, that death only comes to us from outside when we have been made ready for it by this our own death. For our death is really only the way to the perfect love of God.

When fighting and death exercise their wild dominion around us, then we are called to bear witness to God's love and God's peace not only by word and thought, but also by our deeds. Read James 4:1ff.! We should daily ask ourselves where we can bear witness in what we do to the kingdom in which love and peace prevail. The great peace for which we long can only grow again from peace between twos and threes. Let us put an end to all hate, mistrust, envy, disquiet, wherever we can. "Blessed are the peacemakers, for they shall be called the children of God."

I have been back from my travels for some weeks. Fritz got married the day before yesterday. Work in the summer was very enjoyable. I would very much like to send you a report of my travels, but it is a long story, and I don't know how I could tell it to you. It all seems a long time ago now.

I am thinking of you and your work in my prayers. God bless and keep you, your homes and your churches. May he grant us all his peace. [*WF*, pp. 251–55]

Christmas 1939

Dear Brothers

No priest, no theologian stood at the cradle in Bethlehem. And yet all Christian theology has its origin in the wonder of all wonders, that

God became man. "Alongside the brilliance of the holy night there burns the fire of the unfathomable mystery of theology." *Theologia sacra* arises from those on bended knees who do homage to the mystery of the divine child in the stall. Israel had no theology. She did not know God in the flesh. Without the holy night there is no theology. "God revealed in the flesh," the God-man Jesus Christ, is the holy mystery which theology is appointed to guard. What a mistake to think that it is the task of theology to unravel God's mystery, to bring it down to the flat, ordinary human wisdom of experience and reason! It is the task of theology solely to preserve God's wonder as wonder, to understand, to defend, to glorify God's mystery as mystery. This and nothing else was the intention of the ancient church when it fought with unflagging zeal over the mystery of the persons of the Trinity and the natures of Jesus Christ. How superficial and flippant, especially of theologians, to send theology to the slaughterhouse, to make out that one is not a theologian and doesn't want to be, and in so doing to ridicule one's own ministry and ordination and in the end to have, and to advocate, a bad theology instead of a good one! But of course, where in our theological classes were we shown and taught the mystery of God in the flesh, the birth of Jesus Christ, the God-man and Savior, as the unfathomable mystery of God? Where do we hear it preached? Surely Christmas Eve can kindle in us again something like a love of sacred theology, so that, seized and compelled by the wonder of the cradle of the Son of God, we are moved to consider again, reverently, the mysteries of God. But it may well be that the glow of the divine mysteries has already been and has died in our hearts as well.

The ancient church meditated on the question of Christ for several centuries. It imprisoned reason in obedience to Jesus Christ, and in harsh, conflicting sentences gave living witness to the mystery of the person of Jesus Christ. It did not give way to the modern pretense that this mystery could only be felt or experienced, for it knew the corruption and self-deception of all human feeling and experience. Nor, of course, did it think that this mystery could be thought out logically, but by being unafraid to express the ultimate conceptual paradoxes, it bore witness to, and glorified, the mystery as a mystery against all reason. The Christology of the ancient church really arose at the cradle of Bethlehem, and the brightness of Christmas lies on its weather-beaten face. Even today, it wins the hearts of all who come to know it. So at Christmas time we should again go to school with the ancient church and seek to understand in worship what it thought and taught, to glorify and to defend belief in Christ. The hard concepts of that time are like stones from which one strikes fire. . . .

The Fathers were concerned to say that God, the Son, took upon himself *human nature,* not that he took upon himself *a man.* What does that mean? God became man by taking upon himself human nature, not by taking an individual man. This distinction was necessary to preserve the universality of the wonder of Christmas. "Human nature," that is, the nature, essence, flesh of all people, i.e., my nature, my flesh; human nature, that is, the embodiment of all human possibilities. Perhaps we moderns might put it more simply by saying that in the birth of Jesus Christ, God took manhood, and not just an individual man. But this taking happened corporeally, and that is the unique wonder of the incarnation. The body of Jesus Christ is our flesh. He bears our flesh. Therefore, where Jesus Christ is, there we are, whether we know it or not; that is true because of the Incarnation. What happens to Jesus Christ, happens to us. It really is all *our* "poor flesh and blood" which lies there in the crib; it is *our* flesh which dies with him on the cross and is buried with him. He took human nature so that we might be eternally with him. Where the body of Jesus Christ is, there are we; indeed, we are his body. So the Christmas message for all people runs: You are accepted, God has not despised you, but he bears in his body all your flesh and blood. Look at the cradle! In the body of the little child, in the incarnate Son of God, your flesh, all your distress, anxiety, temptation, indeed all your sin, is borne, forgiven, and healed. If you complain, "My nature, my whole being is beyond salvation and I must be eternally lost," the Christmas message replies, "Your nature, your whole being is accepted; Jesus bears it, in this way he has become your saviour." Because Christmas is the physical acceptance of all human flesh by the gracious God, we must affirm that God's Son took human nature upon himself.. . . . [*TP,* pp. 28–30]

May 1940

Dear Brothers:

Today for once I must send you all a combined word of thanks for the greetings and letters which I've had from you recently. I couldn't cope with writing to you otherwise, and I don't want you to have to wait any longer for my thanks. Each greeting and each long letter has given me great delight, and has made it possible for me to adjust my ideas better about individuals. But you mustn't think that I want to make further claims on the little free time which you have and need for your families and yourselves. I can imagine that with all one's experiences one sometimes doesn't want to speak and write about them anymore, particularly when one is already writing home. In that case, I really don't want to extort any letters from you. I often feel ashamed when I get a long letter from the front. I sometimes think then that the person who wrote it could certainly have done with his sleep and his rest. I needn't say that I enjoy every greeting from a really free hour. Thank you for all your sacrifices of time and rest which you have made to write your letters.

Many of you want to hear more of how things are going here, so that we don't lose contact. I can well understand that. But you must remember that it's a consequence of the times in which we live that each person must be content to be able to do his duty in his place. One often loses most of the wider perspective. Sad as that is, it also has its good points; now is a time of testing for the individual, to see whether he can do his work faithfully by himself for a time. We still don't know how it will work out, but as far as I can see, I haven't the impression that the whole thing is suffering damage because of it. Anyone who has learnt so far what is at stake is standing fast, even if he has to stand alone for a while, as long as it is not for too long. The greatest difficulty at the moment, and I think that you will agree, is the question of replacements. All conceivable avenues really have been explored here. In some places it is almost beyond the resources of the brethren. But where we then come up so clearly against the limits of our service, we shouldn't be worried to death by scruples. Prayer, and faith, and thankfulness for what we can still do, fill the gap here. It doesn't seem to me to be right to burden the individual inwardly and outwardly with particular worries. Most people have enough to put up with. Each one must know how he is fighting his way through his tasks with God's Word, and there he can be certain of the intercession of the brethren and the power of Jesus Christ.

It is, I think, time once again to say something about the freedom of our Christian life and of the grace of God. Some of you who are in the field write in a state of depression about the difficulty of combining an ordered Christian life with the daily work which occupies the whole of your time. Many people simply cannot find time and peace for the reading of the Bible, for prayer, and for intercession. In addition, the possibilities of having the sort of conversations that we long for as Christians, and of exercising a degree of influence on the general topics of conversation, seem to vary from place to place. Some write very happily about this, others are equally troubled. I don't know now whether it is quite right to keep writing to you and telling you that even at the front you are and must be "in the ministry." Certainly none of us is ever released from the responsibility of being a Christian and no one may deny that he is a pastor. But isn't that rather different from saying so obviously that even at the front one is "in the ministry"? In my view, you are not, and in that position you really cannot be. I'm afraid here of an illusion which will become a harsh law for the serious ones in particular, against which they will chafe and by which in the end they will be broken. Perhaps you say that your ordination itself laid this law upon you. I won't discuss the theological questions of ordination here, and their significance for the person who for some reason cannot exercise his ministry (for example, in a change of profession). Opinions differ here. But one thing is certain: ordination has been appointed as a comfort and a grace for us, to make us certain in our ministry. It is not meant to trouble us, so that we have our doubts about it, and in any case it will certainly not do that to you now. I think I ought to say that once again. In this matter we must be very careful about enthusiastic thoughts which are perhaps very fine for a while but may one day be very dangerous for us and lead our whole faith astray. One of you writes in some distress that he can only be a soldier among soldiers and that in so doing he is trying to remain a Christian, but that he has no strength for more than this. I would like to reassure him and all who feel the same. I cannot see any unfaithfulness toward one's ministry in this. One simply cannot continue to lead a pastor's life as a soldier, and one should not tear oneself apart inside trying to do so. Of course it's splendid if one's military service leaves one as much time as one needs for God's Word. But whether that is the case or not, most of you are no longer responsible for it. Of course it is cheering to be able to have some influence and to help in conversations. But the limits which are appointed here are certainly not set by our own failings alone. Of course it would be fine if we were able to exercise some influence on certain words that are spoken and on conversations that go on around us. But I don't believe that it is good or advisable to cultivate too great a sensibility in oneself—that perhaps will only make us weak and unable to give any substantial help. Anyone who has learnt in the cross of Jesus Christ to know the power and character of the world and his own wickedness, and who at the same time seriously believes in the infinite love of God for this world, should no longer be too surprised or shaken by certain expressions of this worldliness. Anyway, I hope you understand what I mean. We rejoice with anyone for whom doors have been opened, and with them we give thanks to God, but we also stand alongside anyone with whom things are different, and we would not want them to be misled about their call to the ministry.

The great difference between your existence, my dear brothers in the field, and ours, who still have freedom for our ministry, is that we can put ourselves in a place which in a certain sense we have chosen for ourselves, freely, through our profession, whereas you now share the life of millions of people who have never been free in this sense because of the conditions governing their life and work. The inner change associated with that is probably the most difficult thing of all for us, and sometimes it even makes it no longer easy for us to understand one another.

Apart from all the Christian problems, this deep change in our life certainly also brings with it the need to rearrange our life with the Word of God. Your life hitherto has been determined by a different measure of the consciousness of being a Christian from that which obtains at present. Whereas in our ministry we are reminded hourly of our status as Christians, hours and whole days pass for you without your being left a moment for such reminiscences, just as happens with the majority of working men. If the moment of recollection, which cannot hold off, comes then, in the morning or in the evening, or at an unexpected hour, it is probably so overpowering that we are hardly able to stand up to it.

So we long all the more for that abiding communion with the Word of God which we had in our ministry. And then it can also come about that we make false accusations against ourselves, that we look for a firm routine of Christian life which we cannot have at the time. We do indeed know that order and the consciousness of one's Christian existence is a good and generally helpful thing, but nevertheless it is not everything. The sudden, harsh clash of daily work and the Word of God, which you certainly often experience now, must at times take the place of a regular discipline. We should not let ourselves be made slaves. God knows your present life and finds his way to you even in the most tense, the busiest days, if you can no longer find your way to him.

But now for once let's stop looking at our different situations and tasks and thinking about them, and let's look together at *God's* work, which does not stand still, whether we are this way or that, at his work in us, in his church, and in the whole world. Let's look at his grace, which has preserved us so far through many dark hours, when we were worried about what might happen. Let's look at his faithfulness, which has still always been constant. God has begun with us and our church, and he will also carry things through to the end, so that all will be well for everyone. May the Lord Jesus Christ keep us in his grace to the end. [*TP,* pp. 57–61]

Advent 1940

Dear Brothers:

When war broke out in 1914, it was regarded as an unparalleled turning point. A whole way of thinking and living was overturned, and something completely new took its place. Now this new element which the world war brought did not give way to the old, the "prewar," atmosphere even after the "armistice." The revolution of the age persisted, indeed it grew more acute and clarified itself in continually new phases. It is probably for this reason that we do not again feel the present war, like 1914, to be a radical alteration of our life, but regard it merely as another sharper clarification of our existence in a world whose character we have already sampled in principle for years. Just as a speeded-up film reveals, in a more impressive concentration, movements which otherwise would not be perceptible, so the war makes clear in a particularly vivid and unconcealed form what for years has been becoming more and more uncannily clear as the nature of the world. War isn't the first thing to bring death, to reveal the sorrows and troubles of human bodies and souls, to unleash lies, unlawfulness, and violence. War isn't the first thing to make our existence so utterly insecure, to make man the impotent one, who must see his wishes and plans crossed and destroyed "by higher authority." But war makes all this, which has already existed without it and before it, obvious to us all, however much we would still like to overlook it.

This is the very place where the war gives us in a special way the possibility of a real Christmas. "Farewell world"—that is the only insight from which we can grasp what it means that "Christ is born." But we avoid that knowledge with every possible means. It is indeed an unbearable insight. When faced with it, we want to hide our heads in the sand. It's not as bad as all that! We want to flee to some blessed isle. My life, at least, is still splendid and happy and harmonious! How often is the pastor's house and the pastor's life just such a blessed isle? And to what extent have we Germans made Christmas into just such an island, on which one can save oneself from the true reality of life for a couple of days, or at least hours? How far is all our customary festive celebration, with all the cosiness and loveliness and sweetness and gaiety with which we have adorned it, not tuned in to this "magic," which is meant to transport us to fairyland? Christmas—just a "holiday from myself," "holiday from living." So the real Christmas, as it confronts us in the journey of the shepherds to the cradle, has become days of outward and inward pleasure, for which the message of God's love might make quite a useful background.

This sort of Christmas—and we will readily concede how much it has taken this form even in the homes of pastors—has already been made difficult for us in recent years. The "magic" has completely lost its power today; it no longer has any reality. Escapism is prohibited. It has now become clear to us that the pretty veils which used to be able to deceive us for whole hours and days are cheats and lies. The real nature of the world has been revealed. It is no longer a statement of dogmatic theology to renounce the world; it is clearly the reality in which our actual life is accomplished. So we now hear the old message with new senses and a new desire: "Behold I bring you"—those who are in darkness and in the shadow of death—"tidings of great joy! For to you today is born the Savior, Jesus the Lord!" In the feast of Christmas we are directed in a new way to the very thing that stands in the center of the Bible, to the simple reality of the gracious and merciful action which comes from God into this lost world. We are no longer concerned with elegant and gay pictures and fancies; from the reality which is so plain and from our distress, we thirst for the reality of the great divine help. Our question is whether God really has sent the One who has the right and authority for complete, all-embracing, final redemption. And the Christmas message is the complete, glorious "Yes" of the answer to this question. It is our task, our blessed task, at Christmas to hear the message in all its simplicity and to utter it just as it stands. The world has always been full of thousands of demands, plans, summonses, exhortations with which people seek to overcome the distress of the world, which sooner or later, sadly enough, becomes evident to everyone. We do not have to demand, to plan, and to exhort again, thank God, we simply have to hear and to say what has been given by God as our real, our complete, hope, without any of our doing and our working.

Of course, in this way we simply have the Christmas which the shepherds of Bethlehem had, even if we can take the whole richness of the cross, the resurrection, and the ascension of Christ into our Christmas. Like the shepherds, we remain believers. Like them, we see the child in the cradle, who does not want to be distinguished from other children, and we hear the message "as it had been told them" of this child. The night of the world is as dark to us as it was to the shepherds then. We can no more see now than they could then that the glory of the world is laid on the shoulders of this child, that all power in heaven and earth is given to him, despite all the rich and blessed experiences of all Christendom on earth; today, we can do no more than listen and believe as they did then. Our Christmas, too, does not take us out of the distress, the burdens of our life in the world; it does not take us to paradise. We too must return again, like the shepherds, back into the old conditions, with all the pressure that chafes us. But—only let the shepherds' Christmas be given us if like them we can just hear and believe! The Savior is there! God's hand again rests upon the world and will no longer let it go! The night is far spent, the day is already at hand! The glory of the world has already been taken from the prince of this world and laid on the shoulders of this child! In that case it can also be said of us, as of those shepherds: not only did they "return" into all the old, bitter distress; they also "glorified and praised God for all they had heard and seen, as it had been told them," in the midst of all their personal needs, in the midst of the night of the world, in the midst of war . . . [Letter is incomplete][*TP,* pp. 77–81]

August 15, 1941

Dear Brothers:

. . . They have gone before us on the way that we must all tread one day. God reminds those of you who are at the front in a specially gracious way to be prepared. We will watch over you with unceasing prayer. Of course you, and all of us, will be called by God only at the hour which God has chosen. Until this hour, which lies in God's hands alone, we will all be preserved, even in supreme danger, and our thankfulness for such preservation should lead us to constantly renewed preparedness for the last call.

Who understands the choice of those whom God takes to himself early? Does it not seem to us again and again in the early deaths of Christians as though God were robbing himself of his best instruments at a time when he needed them most? But God makes no mistakes. Does God perhaps need our brothers for some hidden service for us in the heavenly world? We should restrain our human thoughts, which always seek to know more than they can, and keep to what is certain. God has loved anyone whom he has called. "For his soul was pleasing to the Lord, therefore he took him quickly from the midst of wickedness" (Wisd. of Sol. 4:14). We know that God and the devil are locked together in combat over the world and that the devil has a word to say even at death. In the face of death we cannot say in a fatalistic way, "It is God's will"; we must add the opposite: "It is not God's will." Death shows that the world is not what it should be, but that it needs redemption. Christ alone overcomes death. Here, "It is God's will" and "It is not God's will" come to the most acute paradox and balance each other out. God agrees to be involved in something that is not his will, and from now on death must serve God despite itself. From now on, "It is God's will" also embraces "It is not God's will." God's will is the overcoming of death through the death of Jesus Christ. Only in the cross and resurrection of Jesus Christ has death come under God's power, must it serve the purpose of God. Not a fatalistic surrender, but living faith in Jesus Christ, who died and has risen again for us, can seriously make an end of death for us.

In life with Jesus Christ, death as a universal fate which comes to us from outside is contrasted with death from within, one's own death, the free death of dying daily with Jesus Christ. Anyone who lives with Christ dies daily to his own will. Christ in us gives us over to death so that he can live in us. So our inner dying grows up against death from the outside. In this way, the Christian accepts his real death; physical death in the true sense does not become the end, but the consummation of life with Jesus Christ. Here we enter the community of the one who could say at his death, "It is accomplished."

Dear brothers, it may be that you now have little time or inclination for such thoughts. There are times in which all reality is so mysterious and oppresses us so much that any direct word seems to destroy the mystery of God for us, that we speak about and would like to hear about the last things only in hints. Everything that we can say about our belief then seems so flat and empty against the reality which we experience and behind which we believe there is an unspeakable mystery. It is the same with those of you at the front as it is with us at home: whatever is uttered vanishes in a flash; all formulas no longer make contact with reality. There can be something very real in all this, as long as one word does not vanish within us, namely the name of Jesus Christ. This name remains a word, the Word around which we gather all our words. In this Word alone lies clarity and strength. "Within my heart abiding, thy name and cross alone my every thought are guiding, to bring me to thy throne."

Let me end with a request. I know that some of you at the front and here are worried by thoughts about the future of our calling. Let these thoughts rest for a while. So far you have been able to give a good witness for our church, even to suffer for our brothers. Let us not obscure anything now. We need this bit of earthly light and we shall need it still more. Who can ignore the fact that with this war we have been granted an interval which we really cannot bridge with our thoughts? So we should wait patiently.

Any letter, any token of life from you, of course delights me and many others with me. I had greetings from brothers Bojack and Nithack just before their deaths, and I'm particularly glad of those today. Please let me know about changes of address as soon as possible. Often something—a book or a letter—comes back undeliverable. I'm always sorry then because a link has been broken. In that case it's usually very difficult to get the right address again.

I commend you to him who can preserve you by day and night, who can give you power in all your service, who will lead you and all of us to his kingdom. [*TP,* pp. 124–26]

March 1, 1942

Dear Brothers:

Our dear brothers, Bruno Kerlin, Gerhard Vibrans, and Gerhard Lehne, have been killed. Now they sleep with all the brothers who have gone before them, awaiting the great Easter Day of the resurrection. We see the cross, and we believe in the resurrection; we see death, and we believe in eternal life; we trace sorrow and separation, but we believe in an eternal joy and fellowship. Bruno Kerlin was a witness to this Easter faith in the joy of his belief, the transparency of his character, his brotherly readiness to serve, and we thank God for it. Gerhard Vibrans was hit by a flying bomb just as he was about to join companions in singing from the New Hymnal. Anyone who knew this pure, selfless brother, who combined simplicity and maturity so well that he won the confidence of all sorts of people, knows what we lost with him. The text of the day of his death, February, 3rd was particularly moving: Revelation 1:14. The life of this brother stood under the "flaming fire" of the eyes of Christ; he was a reflection of this glaring fire. I shall never forget how he taught me Claudius' hymn, "I thank God and rejoice." His life provided a most convincing exposition of it. Gerhard Lehne was a questioning, seeking, wandering, restless man, with many-sided experiences and interests, and also great boldness and simple honesty. The purpose by which he was grasped shone through everything. He served his church in self-sacrificing faithfulness. Now God has brought him early to rest and peace. We praise and thank God for the life and death of our brothers. Their death reminds us of the blessing which God once gave us through fellowship at his Word and table; we also hear the warning to be true to each other as long as we can.

I have experienced the signs of such faithfulness in an overwhelming way over the past weeks. I can never express my thankfulness for it in words. All through the month letters kept arriving for my birthday from people who are working hard in the homeland and also from the bitterest cold of Russia, some written in brief pauses in the action. How shall I respond to such faithfulness? I thank you from the bottom of my heart. Let us remain firm in prayer for each other. Who knows how much preservation he owes, through God's grace, to the intercession of a brother?

I was surprised to see how it has been recently that there has been an increase in the voices from the front and from home which ask for a new help to meditation. I confess that I would not have ventured to talk about that with you now on my own initiative. I didn't want to add yet one more burden to those you already bear each day. So even today I will do no more than say a few words once again about the precious gift which is given to us in meditation, and in a way which is particularly important for us today. Daily, quiet attention to the Word of God which is meant for me, even if it is only for a few minutes, will become for me the focal point of everything which brings inward and outward order into my life. In the interruption and fragmentation of our previous ordered life which this time brings with it, in the danger of losing inner discipline through the host of events, the incessant claims of work and service, through doubt and temptation, struggle and disquiet of all kinds, meditation gives our life something like constancy, it keeps the link with our previous life, from baptism to confirmation, to ordination. It keeps us in the saving fellowship of the community, the brethren, our spiritual home. It is a spark from that hearth which the communities want to keep at home for you. It is a source of peace, of patience, and of joy; it is like a magnet which attracts all the resources of discipline to its poles; it is like a pure, deep water in which the heaven, with its clouds and its sun, is clearly reflected; but it also serves the Highest in showing him a place of discipline and of quietness, of saving order and peace. Have we not all a desire for such a gift, unacknowledged perhaps, but still profound? Could it not again be a healing power for us, leading to recovery? For several reasons I think it best if we keep to the old Epistles for meditation for the moment. God bless us in these hours.

Today, on the first of March, warm spring sunshine has returned for the first time; the snow is dripping from the roofs, the air is clear, and the earth is appearing again. Our thoughts are with those of you who in the past months have had unimaginable experiences at the front, in winter, with the wish that the sun and warmth and earth may soon delight you again. "He gives snow, he scatters hoar frost, he casts forth ice; who can stand before his cold? He sends forth his Word, and melts them; he makes his wind blow, and the waters flow." One day he will also shatter the winter and the night of the evil one and make a spring of grace and joy appear. "The summer is near at the gate, the winter is past, the pretty flowers appear; he who has begun that will also bring it to a consummation" (Luther).

In the confidence and fellowship of this faith I commend you to God and our Lord Jesus Christ. [TP, pp. 164–67]

November 29, Advent 1, 1942

Dear Brothers:

At the head of a letter which is intended to summon you to joy at a serious hour must stand the names of the brothers who have been killed since last I wrote to you: P. Walde, W. Brandenburg, Hermann Schroder, R. Lynker, Erwin Schutz, K. Rhode, Alfred Viol, Kurt Onnasch, Fritz's second brother, and in addition to them, many of whom are well known to you, Major von Wedemeyer and his oldest son Max, my former pupil for confirmation.

"With everlasting joy upon their heads . . ." (Isa. 35:10). We do not grudge it them; indeed, should we say that sometimes we envy them in the stillness? Since ancient times, *acidia*—sorrowfulness of the heart, "resignation"—has been one of the deadly sins.* "Serve the Lord with gladness" (Ps. 100:2) summons us to the Scriptures. This is what our life has been given to us for, what it has been preserved for up till now. Joy belongs, not only to those who have been called home, but also to the living, and no one shall take it from us. We are one with them in this joy, but never in sorrow. How shall we be able to help those who have become joyless and fearful unless we ourselves are supported by courage and joy? I don't mean by this something fabricated, compelled, but something given, free. Joy dwells with God; it descends from him and seizes spirit, soul, and body, and where this joy has grasped a man it grows greater, carries him away, opens closed doors. There is a joy which knows nothing of sorrow, need, and anxiety of the heart; it has no duration, and it can only drug one for the moment. The joy of God has been through the poverty of the crib and the distress of the cross; therefore it is insuperable, irrefutable. It does not deny the distress where it is, but finds God in the midst of it, indeed precisely there; it does not contest the most grievous sin, but finds forgiveness in just this way; it looks death in the face, yet finds life in death itself. We are concerned with this joy which has overcome. It alone is worth believing; it alone helps and heals. The joy of our friends who have been called home is also the joy of those who have overcome—the risen one bears the marks of the cross upon his body; we are still engaged in conflict daily, they have overcome for all time. God alone knows how near to us or far from us stands the last overcoming, in which our own death can become joy. "With peace and joy I go hence . . ."

Some of us suffer a great deal from having our senses dulled in the face of all the sorrows which these war years have brought with them. Someone said to me recently: "I pray every day for my senses not to become dulled." That is certainly a good prayer. And yet we must be

---

*In monastic spirituality, *acidia* (ακηδια) is also called the noonday demon because it causes the worst trouble when the soul is weakest.

careful not to confuse ourselves with Christ. Christ endured all suffering and all human guilt to the full, indeed he was Christ in that he suffered everything alone. But Christ could suffer alongside people because at the same time he was able to redeem them from suffering. He had his power to suffer with people from his love and his power to redeem people. We are not called to burden ourselves with the sorrows of the whole world; in the end, we cannot suffer with people in our own strength because we are unable to redeem. A suppressed desire to suffer with someone in one's own strength must become resignation. We are simply called to look with utter joy on the one who really suffered with people and became their redeemer. We may joyfully believe that there was, there is, a man to whom no human sorrow and no human sin is strange and who in the profoundest love achieved our redemption. Only in such joy toward Christ, the Redeemer, are we saved from having our senses dulled by the pressure of human sorrow, or from becoming resigned under the experience of suffering. We believe in Christ only as much as ... in Christ ... [Letter incomplete][*TP*, 188–90]

65

Disaffection with the Ecumenical Movement and the Confessing Church

1937–1938

The years 1937 and 1938 were destined to be years of disappointment for Bonhoeffer both on the international ecumenical front and in the church struggle within Germany. On the international scene he had ceased to hope for any significant support from the ecumenical movement in his relentless campaign to deny representation to delegates from the heretical Reich Church. His last years on the Youth Commission were thus filled with rancor over this matter. He had further to contend with the distortions the devious Bishop Theodor Heckel had given to the official report of what took place at the conference of Chamby at which the three groups of the German Evangelical Church were all represented. The report provoked disclaimers from the provisional administration of the Evangelical Church. The already tense situation was compounded with the resignation of the more sympathetic Wilhelm Zoellner, head of the Reich Church Committee, who had made some strides toward rapprochement. This left a clearer field to Bishop Heckel and more zealous members of the Reich Church. Bonhoeffer had already signaled his intention to resign his appointment as youth secretary as early as September 1937, just after the Chamby Conference, but held on to the post until he could be replaced by someone of a noncompromising Confessing Church persuasion. At the meeting in London, February 16 to 24, 1937, preliminary to the Oxford Conference slated for 1938, Bonhoeffer did in fact tender his resignation with the request that he be replaced by Udo Schmidt, a pastor in Wesermunde and secretary of the Schoolchildren's Bible Circles. The minutes of the meeting noted Bonhoeffer's unwillingness to organize a German youth delegation because of the presence of Reich Church delegates.

Again, Bonhoeffer's intransigence over what he considered heresy in the Reich Church, that he could not even *appear* to condone what they had done, created a dilemma for Secretary of the World Alliance for Promoting Friendship through the

Churches, Henry Henriod. Henriod's insistence that there be three groups or none pressured Bonhoeffer to further withdraw from the ecumenical movement. The conference in London would be the last at which delegates from the Confessing Church would be represented. Later the question of representation would become academic as the Church External Affairs Office soon grasped control of all permissions to travel abroad, limiting such permissions to those only who were sympathetic to Nazi policies.[27] Bonhoeffer's letter to Henriod, included here, shows some of the passion Bonhoeffer brought to the question of who had the right to represent the German Evangelical Church. For him, Henriod had missed the point of his opposition; the question was one of the most important battlegrounds for struggling against a church that had falsified the gospel. The letter also brings out why his earlier enthusiasm for the ecumenical movement was growing diminished.

By 1938, morale in the Confessing Church had ebbed to its lowest point. New crises could cause some of the pastors to wonder whether the Confessing Church should disband. While their resolve had been stiffened by the waves of arrests in 1937, by 1938 the mood was more for compromise and survival, something Bonhoeffer would later excoriate in the prison letters. His biographer Eberhard Bethge calls this period, climaxed by "*Kristallnacht* (Crystal Night)," an "evil year" in which "Bonhoeffer began to separate himself from the rearguard actions of the defeated remnants of the Confessing Church."[28]

On the occasion of the Austrian *Anschluss* bishops from Thuringia and Saxony had mustered their pastors to take an oath of loyalty to Hitler. Riding a sycophantic wave of enthusiasm over the *Anschluss,* Dr. Friedrich Werner, state commissar for the Prussian Church, decided that such an oath would be an ideal birthday present from the Evangelical pastors to the *Führer.* Hence he decreed on April 20, 1938, that all pastors on active duty were to take the oath of allegiance. "Anyone who is called to a spiritual office is to affirm his loyal duty with the following oath: 'I swear that I will be faithful and obedient to Adolf Hitler, the *Führer* of the German Reich and people, that I will conscientiously observe the laws and carry out the duties of my office, so help me God.' . . . Anyone who was called before this decree came into force . . . is to take the oath of allegiance retrospectively. . . . Anyone who refuses to take the oath of allegiance is to be dismissed."[29] The announcement plunged the Confessing Church into a crisis. Explanations in the *Law Gazette* attempted to construe the oath as little more than what one ordinarily declares at ordination, namely, making public one's solidarity with the German nation and people. For Bonhoeffer and the "illegal" pastors, the opposite was true; the oath was an implicit denial of the whole basis of ordination since it made the ministry subordinate to one's avowed loyalty to country, interpreted in the narrow-minded Nazi way. The Confessing Church attempted to make the oath palatable to consciences by establishing four conditions, all converging on the one condition that made it clear that the oath was a new civil service law and not an oath introduced by the church or required for the exercise of one's ministry. However, the Confessing Synod of the Old Prussian Union decided to evade the issue by declaring the four conditions already fulfilled and giving general permission to take the oath despite the opposition of a vocal minority led by Bonhoeffer. In short, the synod had shoved responsibility for the oath onto the consciences of individual pastors. The individual dissenters, as Bonhoeffer points out in the letter excerpted here, could be easily identified and punished by the state. The leadership of the Confessing Church had, he argues, shirked its responsibility toward a weak and now endangered minority and taken a safe position. But it was at the cost of betraying God's mandate and denying Christ's care of the weak. The letter is a scathing reproof of such leadership. Barth would write from Basel in July 1938: "I am most deeply shocked by that decision and the arguments used to support it, after I have read and reread them. . . . Was it possible, permissible, or necessary that this defeat should come about? Was there and is there really no one at all among you to take you back to the simplicity of the straight and narrow way? . . . No one to beg you not to hazard the future credibility of the Confessing Church in this dreadful way?"[30] There was one such: Bonhoeffer. His remarks to the synod follow the letter to Henriod in this section.

Berlin-Dahlem, March 24, 1937

To the General Secretary H. L. Henriod, Geneva

Dear Henriod,

Many thanks for your letter. The end of the semester in the seminary caused this reply to be delayed. Please excuse this. Permit me now to present once again the facts of the case as simply as I see them. The matter of our discussion in London was the sending of a German Youth delegation to Oxford. Your purpose was to have a delegation from Dr. Heckel. My aim was to frustrate this. I should mention that I am fully aware that you had taken great pains to be just and to have a comprehensive representation of the German churches at Oxford. My opinion, however, is that such an arrangement could appear to be just only in a formal sense, but in fact is unjust and spiritually indefensible. This is for well-known reasons that need not be argued here. Nevertheless, I will not now go into the question of whether it is at all even formally just; i.e., whether it is based on the statutes of the Youth Commission. To support your wish you pointed out the circumstances of the representation in the Main Conference. You said that the agreement in reference to this was that there would be only *one* German delegation and that this would mean either *all three groups* (Reich Church Committee, Lutheran Council, and Confessing Church) *would be represented or no one would be represented.* You deduced from this the need for an analogous arrangement in the Youth Commission. Otherwise I would not have been able to understand your reference to the Main Conference. I doubted even at that time, as I likewise do now, that this analogy is in accordance with the statutes, and in no way have I been convinced of this up to now. What is more, following my personal knowledge of the discussions in Chamby, I have to question whether these arrangements were to be understood in fact in the way you have reported them. When you thereupon very unwillingly answered: "Please don't raise this question again," I was silent, on the assumption that you must certainly have been more exactly informed than I. With this the discussion took the further direction that we are well aware of. I add here once again that this is the way I understood our debate, and in no other way. Should I be wrong, I would appreciate being corrected on this point since it is doubtless of concern to both of us to agree on this matter. It should come as no wonder to you that it was of the greatest importance to me to learn that indeed one German delegation would be expected and that this did not include your demand that either three groups would be present or no one. This however, was what our whole debate was about. Please let me know plainly now to what extent this assumption ought not be regarded as erroneous. Dear Henriod, it is obvious to me that it can never be a question between us of exchanging personal reproaches with each other, after all that we have gone through together in the last few years.

But is also clear that each of us can err. Since, however, the matter appears to me to be so full of meaning with wide-ranging consequences, we must clarify things here. I am asking you, therefore, before any further decision on my part, to tell me if I might request answers to the following questions:

1. Do you insist, come what may, that there be a delegate from Heckel's group at the Youth Conference in Oxford?

2. How can this decision be justified according to the statutes of the Youth Commission?

3. What leverage do these statutes give us to transfer the ratio of delegations for the Main Conference, which is a conference of official ecclesial representation, over into the Youth Conference that up to now in any case had the character of a free meeting? Shall the official representative character of the Main Conference, which is so strongly burdened with purely organizational points of view now also determine the Youth Conference?

4. How is your decision personally to nominate the youth delegates in conjunction with the church government to be reconciled with the statutes of the Youth Commission and the functions of the Youth Secretary? To what extent is an autocracy being avoided here against which I would be compelled to protest most vehemently in matters affecting the church? I regret that this is in fact where we come into sharp conflict and I have the firm hope that we can be reconciled to each other again through this matter and in this matter. . . . [MW, V, pp. 255–56]

August 11, 1938

To the Old Prussian Council of the Brethren, Berlin,

It means a difficult decision for a Confessing pastor to have to contradict the ruling of an Old Prussian Confessing Synod, especially when he can look back on this synod only with great gratitude and respect, when he is aware of the blessing and promise of God which have come from former synods. However, a synod which has dared to be led by a majority decision and thereby to deviate from the early Christian principle of consensus in synodal decisions (in any case where Christian faith and Christian life are concerned), a synod which believes itself able to answer for the spiritual overpowering of a strong minority (certainly with the intention of providing a crucial brotherly service with a directive in so difficult a matter), must indeed reckon with the fact that dissension on this question reaches far beyond the synod into pastorates and congregations. Therefore, it remains for one, on whom the synodal responsibility has not been incumbent and who in his own judgment on this can only hold to the sufficiently grave results themselves to be moved to set himself against a synod that has stood under the command and direction of the Holy Spirit. He has to be aware of the danger of pride (*superbia*) and ready to let himself be called to better understanding and to obedience. On the basis of the official conclusions of the second session of the Sixth Confessing Synod, however, I can't do anything else but reproach those conclusions for repudiating Christian brotherhood and culpably contributing to the confusion of and the sinning against conscience. . . .

Let us be clear on this entirely disregarded point, that the whole question has been handled and resolved, not under the perspective of what the church of Jesus Christ, for the sake of the holiness of the oath, has to say and to require in any matter of this or any oath, what consequence this can have, but it was asked instead how the individual pastor personally, without too much importunity to conscience, can take the oath. This, however, is another question and, in any case, has not been asked in the Confessing Church until now. This is perhaps the basis for our seeking out reasons why the synod has had such little success and has even allowed this question of the oath to become perceived as confession to the Lord Jesus Christ. . . .

There are only two possibilities. Either it concerns a question of a confession of faith and the majority looks on its decision as the decision of the Holy Spirit. Then after having admonished those erring against this disciplinary teaching, communion with them must be dissolved. Thus, the application of paragraph four (Dismissal from Service), according to the intention of the synod, will with full right become effective for this erring majority. The dissenting brothers are thereby expelled from the community of the Confessing Church.

Or it concerns a difference of judgment of conscience. In that case, however, with the command to forswear ("to eat meat," "to eat offerings set for the gods") one sins against the weak brothers, since in the congregation the rule holds that the strong should rather forsake their freedom than cause the weak to be confused and pressured into sin. Every pressure brought to bear on those whose consciences are weak makes one guilty against Christ, who died for the sake of the weak. The "directive" of the synod means the unbrotherly and culpable abandonment of the weak and the setting up of an intolerable law in the congregation. Just because it is not possible for the majority, on the basis of Scripture and the confession, to convert the dissenters to agreement with the conclusions of the second session, but because it is a question here of a differing interpretation of the facts, the freedom of the individual conscience, which longs for greater truthfulness, must be respected. Frankly, it would be dangerous talk should one persuade these dissenting brothers that their longing is fanatical, that it is our way to be sinners, therefore sin bravely. That would be the greatest misuse of the main articles of our Evangelical Church. It is difficult for me to avoid the impression that in this directive of the synod the judgment of the world has been passed on brotherly love toward the weak and toward the community of the church. The synod shifts the lack of clarity in the matter of the oath onto others and still considers the conscience of those dissenting only as a problem "to be resolved." Where in the New Testament can we actually find this latter idea? (Reference to Matthew 16:19 ought not, I suppose, to be taken seriously here!?)

What is to be done? Swearing the oath will irrevocably take place in the next couple of days and the synod will be responsible for it. Many consciences will have been burdened by this. Humanly speaking, one can never make amends for the disruption that has been caused in the Confessing Church. That is the special seriousness of this matter of the oath. I can view the guilt that the Confessing Church has burdened itself with through the directive on taking the oath only as the consequence of a way of life in which the lack of full power, of joy in confessing, of courage in faith, and of readiness for suffering has already become noticeable among us for quite a long time. The fact cannot be hidden that this means a difficult temptation for many parishioners and pastors. What will we learn from this? Will the Confessing Church be willing openly to confess its guilt and disunity? Will it have room for prayer for forgiveness and for the new beginning that is needed in this hour? Will it pay homage to the truth and be able to again console the consciences of the separated brethren who long only for the truth and be able to unite them in God's Word? Will Confessing Synods learn that it is important to counsel in the peace and patience commanded and to decide in defiance of all dangers and difficulties? Will they ever learn that majority decision in matters of conscience kills the spirit? Does it see the danger it has inflicted on its word through its latest session? These are open questions for today. . . . [GS, II, pp. 308–15]

66

Second Visit to America: Letters and Journal Entries; Report on the American Church

1939

Bonhoeffer's second trip to America in the summer of 1939 was to be a retreat of sorts, not unlike his departure for London in 1933. This time, however, the circumstances of growing Nazi militarization, the annexations of Austria and Czechoslovakia, and the upcoming moves against Poland, coupled with the imminence of Bonhoeffer's being called to military service, converged. Several worlds seemed to be collapsing around him. The churches had become, in his view, dishonorably silent on the major evils structured into official state policies. He was experiencing not only isolation within his own church but also a sense that more effective resistance lay only with those possessing enough influence on the sources of power within the military. Soon he would face the decision of whether to obey the call to arms. In conscience he would have to refuse, thus placing in jeopardy his fellow dissenting pastors and the budding conspiracy to which his brother and two brothers-in-law belonged. A trip abroad looked like the best escape, especially since it offered the prospect of continuing the struggle from afar, ready to return as needed.

Bonhoeffer made the necessary inquiries, therefore, with the intention of coming to America for what he believed would be a year's respite from the dilemmas of conscience. The trip itself was made possible by two of his American friends, Reinhold Niebuhr and Paul Lehmann, both of whom highly regarded Bonhoeffer's talents as a theologian, pastor, and representative of their own hopes for a revitalization of the churches, and feared Nazi moves against him. Niebuhr had succeeded in rescuing theologian Paul Tillich in 1933. Now, in 1939, it seemed that he would have the opportunity to bring Bonhoeffer to the safety of America too. Niebuhr wrote to Lehmann on May 11, 1939, asking Lehmann to join him in a committee of two to set up lecture tours and meetings for Bonhoeffer, explaining that "there will be some difficulty in getting him out and if he fails he will land in prison. He has done a great work for the church."[31]

It was this work for the church and his sense of solidarity with his brothers of the Confessing Church he had left behind that made Bonhoeffer realize, as he would put it to Niebuhr, he had "made a mistake in coming to America." This section includes not only letters from his abbreviated stay in America but also excerpts from his diary. These reveal both his motivation for leaving Germany and the disquiet of his soul at the thought that he had abandoned his people at a turning point in German history. We also note the peace of mind he experienced at finally coming to a decision to return. Students of Bonhoeffer's life and theology are often fascinated that he left behind the security of America to return to the world of Nazi terror and expansionist belligerence. Nevertheless, as Bonhoeffer confides in one of his prison letters, it was a step he would never regret. The excerpts here, from his letter to Bishop George Bell explaining his motivation to his farewell letters to Niebuhr and Bell, help trace the reasons behind Bonhoeffer's decision to leave Germany, his anxiety over his decision, and, finally, his commitment to return to the struggle. This section closes with his "Report" on the American Church.

LETTER TO BISHOP GEORGE BELL

London, March 25, 1939

My Dear Lord Bishop:

Dr. Rieger just tells me that Visser 't Hooft will come to London next week and stay with you at Chichester. I also understand that the next weekend does not suit you well for our visit to Chichester. May I now ask a great favor from you? Would you kindly tell Visser 't Hooft that I am very anxious to see him during his stay in London? Any time except Wednesday when I have to be at Oxford would suit me well. Would you also be so kind as to let me know any time when I could see you once more before I go back to Germany?

In order not to take too much of your time when we meet, I should like to put before you the two questions which I am very anxious to discuss with you before my return to Germany. The first question concerns the Confessing Church; the second one is very personal. Please excuse my troubling you again and again and my placing one burden after another on your shoulders.

With regard to the position of the Confessing Church we feel strongly in Germany that—mainly owing to traveling difficulties—the relationship of our church to the churches abroad is not as it ought to be. The responsibility which is placed upon us makes it more and more necessary to have a permanent exchange of opinion and the advice of other churches. We are fully aware of and gratefully appreciate what is continuously being done for us from individuals to individuals. But I think, we must try to go a step farther and to come to some sort of regular cooperation with and to a better representation of the Confessing Church in the ecumenical movements. If we are not going to take a decisive step forward in this direction I am afraid we shall very soon be cut off entirely from our brethren abroad, and that would at any rate mean a tremendous loss to us. What I therefore think we should try to get is a man who could devote all his time to establishing the necessary contacts, to cooperating in the ecumenical meetings and conferences, learning and contributing. I think we failed in earlier years to give our full assistance in advice and fellowship to the Russian Christians; now a similar situation is clearly developing in Germany. Do you not think, my Lord Bishop, it is urgently necessary to avoid a similar failure? Frankly and with all due respect, the German representatives in Geneva simply cannot represent the cause of the Confessing Church. So there is a real vacancy which must be filled up sooner or later. This is the first question which I should like to raise and to discuss with you before I go home again to see the men of the Brethren Council. I have also an idea in my mind for the eventual financial difficulties.

The second point is of entirely personal character and I am not certain if I may bother you with it. Please, do take it quite apart from the first point. I am thinking of leaving Germany sometime. The main reason is the compulsory military service to which the men of my age (1906) will be called up this year. It seems to me conscientiously impossible to join in a war under the present circumstances. On the other hand, the Confessing Church as such has not taken any definite attitude in this respect and probably cannot take it as things are. So I should cause a tremendous damage to my brethren if I would make a stand on this point which would be regarded by the regime as typical of the hostility of our church toward the state. Perhaps the worst thing of all is the military oath which I should have to swear. So I am rather puzzled in this situation, and perhaps even more because I feel it is really only on Christian grounds that I find it difficult to do military service under the present conditions, and yet there are only very few friends who would approve of my attitude. In spite of much reading and thinking concerning this matter I have not yet made up my mind what I would do under different circumstances. But actually as things are I should have to do violence to my Christian conviction, if I would take up arms "here and now." I have been thinking of going to the Mission Field, not as an escape out of the situation, but because I wish to serve somewhere where service is really wanted. But here also the German foreign exchange situation makes it impossible to send workers abroad. With respect to British Missionary Societies I have no idea of the possibilities there. On the other hand, I still have the great desire to serve the Confessing Church as long as I possibly could. My Lord Bishop, I am very sorry to add trouble to your trouble. But I thought I might speak freely to you and might ask your advice. You know the Confessing Church and you know me a bit. So I thought you could help me best. It was with regard to this matter that I wanted to see Visser 't Hooft too.

Please excuse this long letter. I hope to see you soon. Leibholz asks me to thank you for your letter to Dr. Lindsay. [WF, pp. 204–06]

FROM BONHOEFFER'S DIARY

June 13, 1939

. . . The country house in Lakeville, Connecticut, is in the hills; fresh and luxuriant vegetation. In the evening thousands of fireflies in the garden, flying glowworms. I had never seen them before. Quite a fantastic sight. Very friendly and "informal" reception. All I need is Germany, the brethren. The first lonely hours are hard. I do not understand why I am here, whether it was a sensible thing to do, whether the results will be worthwhile. In the evening, last of all, the readings and thoughts about work at home. I have now been almost two weeks without knowing what is going on there. It is hard to bear. "It is good that one should wait quietly for the salvation of the Lord" (Lam. 3:26).

June 14, 1939

Breakfast on the veranda at eight. It poured in the night. Everything is fresh and clean. Then prayers. I was almost overcome by the short prayer—the whole family knelt down—in which we thought of the German brethren. Then reading, writing, going out to issue invitations for the evening. In the evening about twenty-five people, pastors, teachers, with wives and friends. Very friendly conversations without getting anywhere.

June 15, 1939

Since yesterday evening I haven't been able to stop thinking of Germany. I would not have thought it possible that at my age, after so many years abroad, one could get so dreadfully homesick. What was in itself a wonderful motor expedition this morning to a female acquaintance in the country, i.e., in the hills, became almost unbearable. We sat for an hour and chattered, not in a silly way, true, but about things which left me completely cold—whether it is possible to get a good musical education in New York, about the education of children, etc., etc., and I thought how usefully I could be spending these hours in Germany. I would gladly have taken the next ship home. . . . The whole burden of self-reproach because of a wrong decision comes back again and almost overwhelms one. I was in utter despair. In the afternoon I tried to do some work. Then I was invited for a second trip into the hills of Massachusetts. It was at quite the wrong time. I still hadn't found peace for Bible reading and prayer. The trip was splendid. We went through a whole stretch of laurel wood. The view from above was rather like the

Harz country. But the burden did not leave me all day. Cinema in the evening: Zuarez with P. Muni. A good film. It occupied my thoughts for a while. Another letter to Leiper: I must go back within a year at the latest. How glad I was to begin the readings again in the evening and find "My heart shall rejoice in thy salvation" (Ps. 13:5).

June 16, 1939

A fortnight ago today I left Berlin and already I long so much for work. Return to New York. Evening at last. I needed it badly. One is less lonely when one is alone. The whole afternoon at the World Exhibition . . . The Russians are too ostentatious and quite bourgeois. The majority of the others are too commercial. In general no special impressions. Christians and Jews preach alternately in the "temple of religion." The whole building is dreadful—cinema-like. Other thoughts: How much cleaner New York is than London! No smoking in the subway or on the street. Technically more advanced, too, or more up to date (ventilation in every subway). And how much more international New York is than London. Of the people to whom I talked today at least half spoke a dreadfully broken English. This continual murder of their language must be horrible for the good American. I am waiting for the post! It is almost unbearable. Probably I shall not have to wait long. Today God's Word says, "I am coming soon" (Rev. 3:11). There is no time to lose, and here I am wasting days, perhaps weeks. In any case, it seems like that at the moment. Then I say to myself again, "It is cowardice and weakness to run away here now." Will I ever be able to do any really significant work here?—Disquieting political news from Japan. If it becomes unsettled now I am definitely going back to Germany. I cannot stay outside by myself. That is quite clear. My whole life is still over there.

Spent the whole day in the library, looking through *The Christian Century*. Instructive articles on "How my mind has changed in the last decade." Professors of theology on the change in American theology since 1929. The decisive shift to the Word still does not seem to have been made; instead, the movement seems to be from a belief in progress to nihilism, from ethicism to a philosophy to the "present," the "concrete situation." Account of the last lynching of a Negro. Two white people go into the house and pray with the Negroes that "the day may come when such things will not happen in America." That is a good solution for such happenings. Also a report on the lack of religion among college students—"disinterested." That must happen if one doesn't eventually realize that "religion" is really superfluous.

Sunday, June 18, 1939

Service in Riverside Church. Quite unbearable. Text: a saying from James (!) about "accepting a horizon," how one gets a horizon, namely God as man's necessary horizon.

The whole thing was a respectable, self-indulgent, self-satisfied religious celebration. This sort of idolatrous religion stirs up the flesh which is accustomed to being kept in check by the Word of God. Such sermons make for libertinism, egotism, indifference. Do people not know that one can get on as well, even better, without "religion"—if only there were not God himself and his Word? Perhaps the Anglo-Saxons are really more religious than we are, but they are certainly not more Christian, at least, if they still have sermons like that. I have no doubt at all that one day the storm will blow with full force on this religious handout, if God himself is still anywhere on the scene. Humanly speaking the thing is by no means unattractive, but I prefer the rustic preaching of Br. Schutz. The tasks for a real theologian over here are immeasurable. But only an American himself can shift all this rubbish, and up till now there do not seem to be any about.

How good the readings are today! Psalm 119, 105; Matthew 13:8. Work in the afternoon. Spoke to no one all day. Now I must begin to learn again how fortunate I have been hitherto always to have been in the company of the brethren. And Niemöller has been alone for two years. To imagine it! What a faith, what a discipline, and what a clear act of God!—Now the day has had a good ending. I went to church again. As long as there are lonely Christians there will always be services. It is a great help after a couple of quite lonely days to go into church and there pray together, sing together, listen together. The sermon was astonishing (Broadway Presbyterian Church, Dr. McComb) on "our likeness with Christ." A completely biblical sermon—the sections on "we are *blameless* like Christ," "we are *tempted* like Christ" were particularly good. This will one day be a center of resistance when Riverside Church has long since become a temple of Baal. I was very glad about this sermon. Why does a man who preaches like that not notice what dreadful music he has played? I will ask him. This sermon opened up to me an America of which I was quite ignorant before. Otherwise I would have become quite ungrateful in these days for all the protection which God has given me. With my intention and inner need to think incessantly of the brethren over there and their work I would almost have avoided the task here. It began to seem treacherous not to have all my thoughts over there. I still have to find the right balance. Paul writes that he thinks of his congregation "without ceasing" in his prayers and yet at the same time he devoted himself completely to the task in hand. I must learn to do that. It will probably only come with prayer. God, grant me in the next few weeks clarity about my future and keep me in the communion of prayer with the brethren.

Without news from Germany the whole day, from post to post, waiting in vain. It does not help to get angry and write that sort of letter. The expected news is there long before the letter arrives. I want to know how work is going over there, whether all is well or whether they need me. I want to have some sign from over there before the decisive meeting tomorrow. Perhaps it is a good thing that it has not come. The news about China is disquieting. Will one be able to get home in time if it gets serious?—Spent the whole day in the library. Wrote English lectures. I have great difficulty with the language. They say that I speak English well, and yet I find it so utterly inadequate. How many years, how many decades has it taken to learn German, and even now one does not know it! I will never learn English. That is already one reason for going back home soon. Without language one is lost, hopelessly lonely. In the evening to Times Square, an escape. Newsreel there for an hour. Early to bed. What a day! But: "The name of the Lord Jesus was extolled" (Acts 19:17). It disturbs me that we do not keep the same time as Germany. It hinders and prevents prayer together. It is the same every evening. But: "We thank thee, O God, . . . that thy name is so near" (Ps. 75:1). [*WF*, pp. 230–32]

June 20, 1939

In the morning a letter from my parents from South Germany. Nothing from Stettin. Visit Leiper. The decision has been made. I have refused. They were clearly disappointed, and rather upset. It probably means more for me than I can see at the moment. God alone knows what. It is remarkable how I am never quite clear about the motives for any of my decisions. Is that a sign of confusion, of inner dishonesty, or is it a sign that we are guided without our knowing, or is it both?

Isaiah 45:19; 1 Peter 1:17.

Today the reading speaks dreadfully harshly of God's incorruptible judgment. He certainly sees how much personal feeling, how much anxiety there is in today's decision, however brave it may seem. The reasons one gives for an action to others and to one's self are certainly inadequate. One can give a reason for everything. In the last resort one acts from a level which remains hidden from us. So one can only ask God to judge us and to forgive us.

Visit Dr. Bewer; very friendly reception. In the afternoon David Roberts. Long theological conversation. Criticism of the Fundamentalists, when it comes to the point he does not think that they are any more reliable than the Riverside Church people. Fosdick, the AntiChrist in the eyes of the Broadway Presbyterian. America forty years behind Germany. Twenty years behind Scotland. It seems that Germany is still the land of spiritual discoveries. Evening with Van Dusen. Write letters. Half past nine for an hour with Bewer. How good it is to speak German again. At the end of the day I can only ask God to give a merciful judgement on today and all its decisions. It is now in his hand.

June 21, 1939

. . . Of course I still keep having second thoughts about my decision. One could have also given quite different reasons: first, I am here (and perhaps the very misunderstanding was a guidance); they say that it was like the answer to a prayer when my coming was announced; they would like to have *me;* they cannot understand why I refuse; it upsets all their plans for the future; I have no news from home and perhaps everything is going well without me, etc. Or one could ask: have I simply acted out of a longing for Germany and the work there? And is this almost incomprehensible and hitherto almost completely unknown homesickness an accompanying sign from above to make refusal easier for me? Or, is it not irresponsible toward so many others simply to say *no* to one's own future and that of many others? Will I regret it? I may not. Despite everything there is first of all the promise, then the joy of working at home and finally the other, that I am trying to suppress. The reading is again so harsh: "He will sit as a refiner of gold and silver" (Mal. 3:3). And it is necessary. I don't know where I am. But he knows; and in the end all doings and actions will be pure and clear.

June 22, 1939

No news from over there. Invitation to Boericke's. I am going next week. Worked and wrote in the morning. I am most sorry about my decision for Sabine. Read in the afternoon. Niebuhr, an interpretation of Christian ethics. The questioning is still completely between orthodox and liberal criticism, but there is no really new beginning. "Myth" instead of Word of God. Evening in the newsreel theatre, nothing special. The evening papers bring very excited news about Japan. Bewer calms me down. It is unbearable over here for a German; one is simply torn in two. Whereas a catastrophe here is quite inconceivable, unless it is ordained. But even to be responsible, to have to reproach oneself, for having come out unnecessarily, is certainly crushing. But we cannot part ourselves from our destiny, much less here, outside; here everything lies solely on one's own shoulders, and one has no voice and no rights in a foreign land. Besides, the storm will also soon break here, too. It is already bubbling fiercely under the surface. And woe betide those who are aliens here. It is strange how strongly I have been moved by these particular thoughts in the last few days and how all thoughts about the *Una Sancta* make slow progress. A tremendous amount has already been overwhelmed. I have been writing in bed since yesterday evening. A good ending. All that remains now is the readings and intercessions. In the morning a discussion with Bewer and Van Dusen about the future. I want to go back in August. They urge me to stay longer. But if nothing happens in the meantime I shall stick by August 12th. I shall then stay with Sabine. Lunch with David Roberts and his wife; very nice. We spoke about the Negro question. Nothing seems to have altered, at best the antilynching bill. He thinks that there is considerable danger of revolution in the south. I didn't know before that the Negroes are prevented from exercising their proper voting rights. The great Negro churches are not included in the Methodist Union (May 1939). He could not mention any new literature. Strong increase in anti-Semitism. Mountain resort: "1,000 feet—too high for Jews."—Notice: "Gentiles preferred."

June 24, 1939

I now often wonder whether it is true that America is the country without a Reformation. If Reformation means the God-given knowledge of the failure of all ways of building up a kingdom of God on earth, then it is probably true. But is it not also true of England? The voice of Lutheranism is there in America, but it is one among others: it has never been able to confront the other denominations. There hardly ever seem to be "encounters" in this great country, in which the one can always avoid the other. But where there is no encounter, where liberty is the only unifying factor, one naturally knows nothing of the community which is created through encounter. The whole life together is completely different as a result. Community in our sense, whether cultural or ecclesiastical, cannot develop there. Is that true?—Wrote cards in the evening. Felix Gilbert called.—The newspapers are grim again today. Readings: "The one who believes does not flee" (Isa. 28:16). I'm thinking of work at home. Tomorrow is Sunday. I wonder if I shall hear a *sermon?*

Sunday, June 25, 1939

Service in the Lutheran Church. Church on Central Park, Dr. Scherer. Sermon on Luke 15, on the overcoming of fear. Very forced application of the text. Otherwise lively and original, but too much analysis and too little gospel. It came home when he said of the life of the Christian that it is like the daily joy of the person who is on the way home. Again no real exposition of the text. It is very poor. Lunch with the Bewers. Conversation about the newspapers here, then about the strange silence of the American public over the suffering of Christians in Russia, about their alienation from the Bible, about the bad Sunday schools. Afternoon and evening with Gilbert. Very complimentary to Roosevelt. He explained a great deal to me. Today is the anniversary of the Augsburg Confession. It makes me think of the brethren at home. Romans 1:16.

June 26, 1939

. . . Today, by chance, I read 2 Timothy 4:21, "Do your best to come before winter"—Paul's request to Timothy. Timothy is to share the suffering of the apostle and not to be ashamed. "Do your best to come before winter"—otherwise it might be too late. That has been in my ears all day. We are just like soldiers who come away from the field on leave and despite everything that they expected are forced back there again.

We cannot get away from it. Not as though we were necessary, as though we were needed (by God?!), but simply because our life is there and because we leave our life behind, we destroy it, if we are not back there. There is nothing pious about it, but something almost vital. But God acts not only through pious emotions, but also through these vital ones. "Do your best to come before winter"—It is not a misuse of Scripture if I take that to be said to *me*. If God gives me grace to do it.

June 27, 1939

Letter from my parents. Great joy, quite surprising. Work lunchtime and afternoon in the library. Tillich, Niebuhr. In the evening a visit from Professor Richardson, long conversation. He is an Englishman. One seems to stand nearer to him than to the Americans. I wonder if the Americans do not understand us at all because they are people who left Europe so as to be able to live out their faith for themselves in freedom? i.e., because they did not stand fast by the last decision in the question of belief? I feel that they would understand the fugitive better than the one who stays. Hence the American tolerance, or rather indifference, in dogmatic questions. A warlike encounter is excluded, but so too is the true passionate longing for unity in faith.

June 28, 1939

. . . The newspaper reports get more and more disturbing. They distract one's thoughts. I cannot imagine that it is God's will for me to remain here without anything particular to do in case of war. I must travel at the first possible opportunity.

June 29, 1939

Telegram from Karl Friedrich. Looking for somewhere to stay. Work until noon. Broken engagement in the afternoon. In the evening a good, friendly talk with Roberts, who is going on holiday tomorrow. I gave him two of my books. He promised to send me books if I write to him. The news today is so bad that I am determined to go back with Karl Friedrich. We will discuss it tomorrow. Roberts spoke very critically about the church in America. The need comes from inside. Complete indifference towards its message continually dissolves the church. "Keep away from politics"—says that the church should limit itself to its "religious task," in which no one is interested. I find it more and more difficult to understand how the principle of a separation of church and state fits in with the practice of the social, economic, organizational and political activity of the church. In any case, the separation of church and state does not result in the church continuing to apply itself to its own task; it is no guarantee against secularization. Nowhere is the church more secularised than where it is separated in principle as it is here. This very separation can create an opposition, so that the church engages much more strongly in political and secular things. That is probably important for our decisions over there.

June 30, 1939

Letter from Fritz. Thoughtful and friendly as ever. Unfortunately nothing else. Telegram from Karl Friedrich, who is coming from Chicago. There is much to discuss. He has been offered an excellent professorship there; it means a decision once for all. Then my questions. As in the present situation I would in any case have gone in four weeks at the latest, with things as they are I have decided to go on the eighth with Karl Friedrich. If war breaks out I do not want to be here, and it is impossible to get any objective news about the situation. That was a great decision. In the morning another letter from Paul, who was so optimistic about my staying here. Afternoon and evening the World Exhibition, the technical things. Did not write in the evening for the first time.

July 1, 1939

Went round in the morning. Karl Friedrich at midday. Wrote a bit in the afternoon. Then with K.F. into town, bought presents, Music Hall, cinema, the largest. Dreadful. Gaudy, ostentatious, vulgar colors, music and flesh. One can only find this sort of fantasy in a big city. K. F. disagrees. Home in good time in the evening. I could not get away all day from thinking about the situation in Germany and in the church. The readings are again very good. Job 41:11, "God says, Who has given to me, that I should repay him? Whatever is under the whole heaven is mine." Romans 11:36: "By him and through him and to him are all things. To him be glory forever. Amen." The earth, nations, Germany, and, above all, the church, cannot fall from his hand. It was dreadfully hard for me to think and to pray "Thy will be done"in view of the present situation. But it must be. Tomorrow is Sunday. May God make his Word find a hearing in all the world.

July 2, 1939

. . . The Americans speak so much about freedom in their sermons. Freedom as a possession is a doubtful thing for a church; freedom must be won under the compulsion of a necessity. Freedom for the church comes from the necessity of the Word of God. Otherwise it becomes arbitrariness and ends in a great many new ties. Whether the church in America is really "free," I doubt. They are lonely Sundays over here. Only the Word makes a true community. I need some good communal prayers in my own language. The news is not good. Will we arrive in time? Reading: Isaiah 35:10! Intercessions.

July 5, 1939

The nearer my departure comes the fuller the days become. Morning prayers by Professor Smart. Van Dusen on Descartes . . . Work in the library. Horton, Keller. Continue in the afternoon. Conversation at lunch with two students from the Southern states on the Negro problem. Reception in the common room in the evening. It would be good to stay another four weeks. But the price is too high. Letter from Eberhard, great joy. Good ideas about John 2. Still no answer to my decision. The readings call for thankfulness. [*WF*, pp. 228–42]

July 7, 1939

Last day. Paul tried to keep me back. It's no good. Van Dusen lecture. Pack. With Hans Wedell before lunch. Theological conversation with Paul. Farewell in the seminary. Supper with Van Dusen. Go to the ship with Paul. Farewell half past eleven, sail at half past twelve. Manhattan by night; the moon over the skyscrapers. It is very hot. The visit is at an end. I am glad to have been over and glad that I am on the way home. Perhaps I have learnt more in this month than in a whole year nine years ago; at least I have acquired some important insight for all future decisions. Probably this visit will have a great effect on me. [*WF*, p. 247]

LETTERS TO DR. HENRY LEIPER

"Coombe-Pine," Lakeville, June 15, 1939

Dear Dr. Leiper:

I wish to thank you very much indeed for the reception you gave me on my arrival in New York. I felt quite at home when Mr. Macy gave me your kind letter and when I met you the next morning. It is a great thing to have good friends and fellow-Christians abroad.

These beautiful days at Dr. Coffin's country home are giving me some time to think about my future and I am sure you will understand that I should like to put the situation before you as I see it, and ask your advice. Before I left Germany I had long talks with my brethren from the Brethren Council and pledged myself to return to Germany after about a year's time to take up the training work in the Confessing Church again, unless some unforeseen development would change the whole situation. At first they were very reluctant to let me go at all, since they are in need of teachers. It was only when I expressed my hopes that I could be of some use to them by establishing contacts with American theologians and churchmen through lectures or meetings, that they gave me leave. So from the point of view of the Confessing Church my trip to America was meant to be an ecumenical link between our isolated church in Germany and our friends over here. We all felt that to be very essential from many points of view. My personal question and difficulty with regard to military service, etc., came in only as a second consideration. Of course, my colleagues were glad that I would be able to postpone my decision for at least one year. Now, I am sure, all that could not be made quite clear in correspondence before I left Germany. But before we are going to work out my program for the immediate future, however long it might be, I feel strongly, that everything ought to be quite clear between us. I deeply appreciate, and so did my friends, your readiness to invite me to come to this country and I am most happy indeed to be here again and to meet old friends. There are, however, a few questions which we have to clear up before I start my work over here, and I wish you would help me to do the right thing. The post which you are kindly intending to confer upon me attracts me from every point of view. I feel strongly the necessity of that spiritual help for our refugees. When I was pastor in London I spent most of my time with these people and I felt it was a great privilege to do so. At the same time that post would offer me an unusual opportunity for getting acquainted with the life of the church in this country, which has been one of my greatest hopes for my stay over here. The only thing that makes me hesitate at the present moment of decision is the question of loyalty to my people at home. All of us, of course, were well aware of the fact that it means running a risk for a Confessing pastor to go to America with the intention to go back to Germany, and we all agreed that I should take that risk and pay the price for it, if necessary, if it is of a true value to the church of Christ there and here. But, of course, I must not for the sake of loyalty to the Confessing Church accept a post which on principle would make my return to Germany impossible. Now, my question is whether that would not be the case with any post that is officially concerned with refugee work? As a matter of fact, I am afraid, it would be so. Now, if that is true, what can we do about it? Is there a possibility of giving that post a somewhat larger scope? I have no particular idea, but if, for instance, it were possible to interpret that post as a sort of invitation, as a "guest post" from the Federation of Churches so as to enable me to get acquainted with the church activities in New York and to cooperate in some respect (whereby, of course, some of that pastoral work of which you have been thinking might be conferred upon me on the respective occasions), I think, that would change the matter a good deal. But, of course, I have no idea under what heading such a thing could be done. This is the first point, which I should very much like to have your advice on.

Second, when Reinhold Niebuhr wrote to me first in February he was hoping to provide a few lectureships for me all over the country, so as to give me an opportunity of seeing a good deal of the theological schools and of getting in contact with the professors of theology. That, of course, would be very much in the line of my work in Germany and I should be greatly interested to do that sort of work. Now, do you suppose that the post in New York would leave the necessary time to do some investigation and some visiting of that sort?

Finally, let me add a very personal remark. My best friend in Germany, a young Confessing pastor, who has been working with me for many years, will be in the same conflict with regard to military service, etc., at the latest by next spring, possibly in the fall of this year. I feel it would be an utmost disloyalty to leave him alone in Germany when the conflict comes up for him. I should either have to go back to stand by him and to act with him or to get him out and to share my living with him, whatever it be, though I do not know if he would be willing to leave Germany. That is a last personal, but not only personal reason, why I feel bound to keep my way back open. I am sure, you will appreciate that this is a duty of *Bruderschaft* which in these times one simply has to fulfill.

Now I have put my case before you. I know, I am causing you a lot of trouble with all that. But you know us Germans and that we are sometimes a little complicated, and more than that, you know the Confessing Church and its needs. I need not assure you again how grateful I am for all that you have been doing for our cause and for me personally. It is just therefore that I feel you must know my whole case before you go on with me. If you should think it impossible to find the right post for me, after you have heard all that, please feel entirely free to tell me and then we should try to make the best of the next few months and I should return to Germany, certainly very grateful for all the friendship I have experienced over here again, in the later part of the fall. My friends at home would only be too glad, if I came back a little earlier than they expected. But if you would see a way through all these difficulties, then I shall stay here with great pleasure, interest, and gratefulness.

I am going to Eaglesmere for Saturday. I am looking forward to seeing you next week. The "Prophet's Chamber" at Union is lovely and I am enjoying Union a lot.

With many thanks for everything.

New York, June 19, 1939

Dear Dr. Leiper:

I have just received a letter from Dr. Freudenberg asking me urgently not to take over the refugee post if I wish to go back to Germany. He also calls my attention to the fact that there are many of our Confessing pastors who will never be able to return to Germany and from whom, therefore, I should not take away the chance of this post. I hope you will be able to spare an hour of your time tomorrow for me. We must get clear about it ... I hope you have got my last letter. [*WE*, pp. 245–46]

FROM BONHOEFFER'S LETTER TO REINHOLD NIEBUHR AS RECALLED IN *CHRISTIANITY AND CRISIS*, JUNE 25, 1945

Lakeville, Connecticut, July 1939

... Sitting here in Dr. Coffin's garden I have had the time to think and to pray about my situation and that of my nation and to have God's will for me clarified. I have come to the conclusion that I have made a mistake in coming to America. I must live through this difficult period of our national history with the Christian people of Germany. I will have no right to participate in the reconstruction of Christian life in Germany after the war if I do not share the trials of this time with my people. My brethren in the Confessing Synod wanted me to go. They may have been right in urging me to do so; but I was wrong in going. Such a decision each man must make for himself. Christians in Germany will face the terrible alternative of either willing the defeat of their nation in order that Christian civilization may survive, or willing the victory of their nation and thereby destroying our civilization. I know which of these alternatives I must choose; but I cannot make that choice in security. . . . [*WF*, p. 246]

LETTER TO BISHOP GEORGE K. A. BELL

London, S.E. 23, July 22, 1939

My Dear Lord Bishop:

When you were in London on Thursday I asked Hildebrandt to tell you that I had already come back from U.S.A. and that I am on my way to Germany. Unfortunately, he forgot to tell you. Now I can only write a few words of explanation and to say "goodbye" to you. I shall leave on Tuesday morning. On my arrival in New York Dr. Leiper very kindly offered me the post of a refugee pastor (I mean a pastor for the refugees) in New York. This post was to be connected with lectures in various places. Of course, I was rather surprised about this offer and told Dr. Leiper that I had promised to the Confessing Church to come back at the latest after a year unless the political circumstances would make that impossible. So it was just a question of loyalty whether I could accept a post which by itself would make my return doubtful or even impossible. I discussed the problem with my friends very thoroughly and decided to decline the offer for three reasons: I was bound to my promise to go back next year; there were many non-Aryan brethren who are much more entitled to such a post; I had got my leave of absence for another purpose.

It was a difficult decision, but I am still convinced I was not allowed to decide otherwise. That meant my early return to Germany. Kindly enough, I was invited by Dr. Coffin and Van Dusen to stay at Union Seminary as long as I wanted. But when news about Danzig reached me

I felt compelled to go back as soon as possible and to make my decisions in Germany. I do not regret my trip to U.S.A., though, of course, it had been undertaken under different presuppositions. I have seen and learned much in the few weeks over there and I am looking forward to my work in Germany again. What sort of personal decisions will be asked from me I do not know. But nobody knows that now. . . . [*WF*, pp. 248–49]

REPORT ON THE AMERICAN CHURCH, "PROTESTANTISM WITHOUT REFORMATION," 1939

Toward the end of his brief stay in America Bonhoeffer began to compose an essay reporting on American Christianity as he perceived it. Entitling his thoughts "Protestantism without Reformation," he describes what he, as a critical observer, believes to be the distinctive characteristics of the denominations comprising this phenomenon. In his opinion, the American churches, despite obvious similarities with their European counterparts, lacked both the cutting edge of the Reformation and a "confession of faith" that could challenge their prideful pretentiousness. In his "report" he notes that the American church had begun as a refuge for persecuted Christians, a fact highly significant for Christians who were being forced to choose between resistance and flight in Nazi Germany. But he also chides the American church for its failure to reach out to blacks and to counteract the racism oppressing them. Then, in a dramatic section excerpted here, he criticizes the church's smugness with its institutionalized freedom. This is of a piece with Bonhoeffer's diary entry of July 2, in which he doubts that the American church is really free.

The praise of freedom as the possibility for existence given by the world to the church can stem precisely from an agreement entered upon with this world in which the true freedom of the Word of God is surrendered. Thus it can happen that a church which boasts of its freedom as a possibility offered to it by the world slips back into the world to a special degree, that a church which is free in this way becomes secularized more quickly than a church which does not possess freedom as possibility. The American praise of freedom is more a praise which is directed to the world, the state and society, than a statement about the church. . . . Freedom as an institutional possession is not an essential mark of the church. It can be a gracious gift given to the church by the providence of God; but it can also be the great temptation to which the church succumbs in sacrificing its essential freedom to institutional freedom. Whether the churches of God are really free can only be decided by the actual preaching of the Word of God. Only where this word can be preached concretely, in the midst of historical reality, in judgment, command, forgiveness of sinners and liberation from all human institutions is there freedom of the church. But where thanks for institutional freedom must be rendered by the sacrifice of freedom of preaching, the church is in chains, even if it believes itself to be free. [*NRS*, 104–5]

67

After Ten Years: A Letter to the Family and Conspirators

Christmas 1942

Bonhoeffer's becoming a member of the German Resistance Movement centered in the *Abwehr* was a gradual outgrowth of his political involvement in the 1930s. During this decade, he had pestered both his own church and the ecumenical movement for resolutions with political repercussions. He had a strong sense then of what we call today "public theology." But by 1938, given the mood for compromise, the drive for civil legitimation, and the rise of a national patriotism, then eroding Confessing Church resistance, Bonhoeffer had been edged past mere church agitation toward the murkier actions demanded by a political-military conspiracy. In his biography of Bonhoeffer, Eberhard Bethge traces the stages that brought Bonhoeffer to this point. He notes that Bonhoeffer's having become accessory to damning information from the conspirators forced him into an unusual silence in ecclesiastical circles, much to the disappointment of people like Hellmut Traub, a former student of Karl Barth, who remarked, after one discussion of Romans 13, how disappointed he was in Bonhoeffer. He had expected more dynamism and more of an open opposition to the way the Nazis had co-opted that text from Paul to stifle church opposition. Bonhoeffer had remained silent. Later he had to set Traub straight privately by informing him of the new ways of correcting the situation that were being planned. Bonhoeffer was aware of the potential danger to their hopes should their plotting be revealed prematurely. And so he was plunged into an "inner exile" where he could no longer justify his actions before his church and fellow pastors.[32]

By 1940, however, Bonhoeffer was eager to assume the responsibilities entrusted to him by the *Abwehr* and to be part of the only action that had power adequate to the evil they were conspiring to crush. He ceased, therefore, to propagate what remained still close to his ideals, pacifism and conscientious objection, lest he expose those with whom he had now become associated in the intrigues of the Oster–von Dohnanyi group. In this he no longer had the satisfaction of maintaining his sterling reputation as Christian and pastor. The time of the "less glorious martyrdom" was at hand and he and his coconspirators resolved to risk their lives for the sake of Christianity and their country's honor.

With the poignant awareness of what should be of value and of the fact that their "treason" was the only patriotism which made any sense, Bonhoeffer wrote his essay, "After Ten Years." It was written as a Christmas present to his fellow conspirators, Oster and von Dohnanyi, as well as to members of his immediate family who were directly or indirectly involved in the conspiracy. The essay is a reminder of the ideals for which they were joined in the struggle. They could derive satisfaction only from the example of Christ in his willingness to suffer for others and in that remarkable solidarity with the oppressed that had continued to animate their decisions to deliver their nation from nazism. The selections from this essay, included here as part of Bonhoeffer's correspondence, contain that reference to their sense of "solidarity" which seems to have become a dominant theme in so many of Bonhoeffer's writings and sermons.

SYMPATHY

We must allow for the fact that most people learn wisdom only by personal experience. This explains, first, why so few people are capable of taking precautions in advance—they always fancy that they will somehow or other avoid the danger, till it is too late. Second, it explains their insensibility to the sufferings of others; sympathy grows in proportion to the fear of approaching disaster. There is a good deal of excuse on ethical grounds for this attitude. No one wants to meet fate head-on; inward calling and strength for action are acquired only in the actual emergency. No one is responsible for all the injustice and suffering in the world, and no one wants to set himself up as the judge of the world. Psychologically, our lack of imagination, of sensitivity, and of mental alertness is balanced by a steady composure, an ability to go on working, and a great capacity for suffering. But from a Christian point of view, none of these excuses can obscure the fact that the most important factor, largeheartedness, is lacking. Christ kept himself from suffering till his hour had come, but when it did come he met it as a free man, seized it, and mastered it. Christ, so the Scriptures tell us, bore the sufferings of all humanity in his own body as if they were his own—a thought beyond our comprehension—accepting them of his own free will. We are certainly not Christ; we are not called on to redeem the world by our own deeds and sufferings, and we need not try to assume such an impossible burden. We are not lords, but instruments in the hand of the Lord of history; and we can share in other people's sufferings only to a very limited degree. We are not Christ, but if we want to be Christians, we must have some share in Christ's largeheartedness by acting with responsibility and in freedom when the hour of danger comes, and by showing a real sympathy that springs, not from fear, but from the liberating and redeeming love of Christ for all who suffer.

Mere waiting and looking on is not Christian behavior. The Christian is called to sympathy and action, not in the first place by his own sufferings, but by the sufferings of his brethren, for whose sake Christ suffered.

OF SUFFERING

It is infinitely easier to suffer in obedience to a human command than in the freedom of one's own responsibility. It is infinitely easier to suffer with others than to suffer alone. It is infinitely easier to suffer publicly and honorably than apart and ignominiously. It is infinitely easier to suffer through staking one's life than to suffer spiritually. Christ suffered as a free man alone, apart and in ignominy, in body and spirit; and since then many Christians have suffered with him.

PRESENT AND FUTURE

We used to think that one of the inalienable rights of man was that he should be able to plan both his professional and his private life. That is a thing of the past. The force of circumstances has brought us into a situation where we have to give up being "anxious about tomorrow" (Matt. 6:34). But it makes all the difference whether we accept this willingly and in faith (as the Sermon on the Mount intends), or under continual constraint. For most people, the compulsory abandonment of planning for the future means that they are forced back into living just for the moment, irresponsibly, frivolously, or resignedly; some few dream longingly of better times to come, and try to forget the present. We find both these courses equally impossible, and there remains for us only the very narrow way, often extremely difficult to find, of living every day as if it were our last, and yet living in faith and responsibility as though there were to be a great future: "Houses and fields and vineyards shall again be bought in this land," proclaims Jeremiah (32:15), in paradoxical contrast to his prophecies of woe, just before the destruction of the holy city. It is a sign from God and a pledge of a fresh start and a great future, just when all seems black. Thinking and acting for the sake of the coming generation, but being ready to go any day without fear or anxiety—that, in practice, is the spirit in which we are forced to live. It is not easy to be brave and keep that spirit alive, but it is imperative.

OPTIMISM

It is wiser to be pessimistic; it is a way of avoiding disappointment and ridicule, and so wise people condemn optimism. The essence of optimism is not its view of the present, but the fact that it is the inspiration of life and hope when others give in; it enables a man to hold his head high when everything seems to be going wrong; it gives him strength to sustain reverses and yet to claim the future for himself instead of abandoning it to his opponent. It is true that there is a silly, cowardly kind of optimism, which we must condemn. But the optimism that is will for the future should never be despised, even if it is proved wrong a hundred times; it is health and vitality, and the sick man has no business to impugn it. There are people who regard it as frivolous, and some Christians think it impious for anyone to hope and prepare for a better earthly future. They think that the meaning of present events is chaos, disorder, and catastrophe; and in resignation or pious escapism they surrender all responsibility for reconstruction and for future generations. It may be that the day of judgment will dawn tomorrow; in that case, we shall gladly stop working for a better future. But not before.

INSECURITY AND DEATH

In recent years we have become increasingly familiar with the thought of death. We surprise ourselves by the calmness with which we hear of the death of one of our contemporaries. We cannot hate it as we used to, for we have discovered some good in it, and have almost come to terms with it. Fundamentally we feel that we really belong to death already, and that every new day is a miracle. It would probably not be true to say that we welcome death (although we all know that weariness which we ought to avoid like the plague); we are too inquisitive for that—or, to put it more seriously, we should like to see something more of the meaning of our life's broken fragments. Nor do we try to romanticize death, for life is too great and too precious. Still less do we suppose that danger is the meaning of life—we are not desperate enough for that, and we know too much about the good things that life has to offer, though on the other hand we are only too familiar with life's anxieties and with all the other destructive effects of prolonged personal insecurity. We still love life, but I do not think that death can take us by surprise now. After what we have been through during the war, we hardly dare admit that we should like death to come to us, not accidentally and suddenly through some trivial cause, but in the fullness of life and with everything at stake. It is we ourselves, and not outward circumstances, who make death what it can be, a death freely and voluntarily accepted.

ARE WE STILL OF ANY USE?

We have been silent witnesses of evil deeds; we have been drenched by many storms; we have learnt the arts of equivocation and pretense; experience has made us suspicious of others and kept us from being truthful and open; intolerable conflicts have worn us down and even made us cynical. Are we still of any use? What we shall need is not geniuses, or cynics, or misanthropes, or clever tacticians, but plain, honest, straightforward people. Will our inward power of resistance be strong enough, and our honesty with ourselves remorseless enough, for us to find our way back to simplicity and straightforwardness?

THE VIEW FROM BELOW

There remains an experience of incomparable value. We have for once learnt to see the great events of world history from below, from the perspective of the outcast, the suspects, the maltreated, the powerless, the oppressed, the reviled—in short, from the perspective of those who suffer. The important thing is that neither bitterness nor envy should have gnawed at the heart during this time, that we should have come to look with new eyes at matters great and small, sorrow and joy, strength and weakness, that our perception of generosity, humanity, justice, and mercy should have become clearer, freer, less corruptible. We have to learn that personal suffering is a more effective key, a more rewarding principle for exploring the world in thought and action than personal good fortune. This perspective from below must not become the partisan possession of those who are eternally dissatisfied; rather, we must do justice to life in all its dimensions from a higher satisfaction, whose foundation is beyond any talk of "from below" or "from above." This is the way in which we may affirm it. [*LPP,* pp. 13–17]

68

Letters to His Fiancée

1943–1944

Bonhoeffer's letters from prison to his young fiancée, Maria von Wedemeyer, are now in a special collection at Harvard's Houghton Library and as yet inaccessible to the public. However, in 1967, Maria agreed to write an article on his correspondence to her for a special Bonhoeffer issue of the *Union Seminary Quarterly Review*. She included in that article excerpts from these letters, placing them in the moving context of their relationship both before and during his imprisonment. Several of the letters were smuggled to Maria by a friendly guard; others were part of the letters permitted the prisoners every ten days.[33]

The article is particularly important for the details she adds about her meeting Dietrich and of his "great sensitivity to the changing levels of our friendship and to my willingness to receive his attention." Because of the difference in their ages and the opposition of Maria's mother, they had to refrain from making any public announcement of their engagement. It was Renate Bethge who, before her marriage to Eberhard, arranged for Maria to be presented to Bonhoeffer's family prior to their engagement. Only after Bonhoeffer's arrest and incarceration in Tegel prison was a public announcement made.

Maria's descriptions of her visits to Dietrich in Tegel give us a rare look at the emotional, even passionate, side of Bonhoeffer, breaking past the usual reserve so many admired in him. "Our first meeting thereafter took place in the *Reichskriegsgericht* (military court room) and I found myself being used as a tool by the prosecutor Roeder. I was brought into the room with practically no forewarning, and Dietrich was visibly shaken. He first reacted with silence, but then carried on a normal conversation; his emotions showed only in the pressure with which he held my hand. Thereafter I saw him fairly regularly, at least once a month." These visits became a vital emotional support for his dreams of a future family life. Maria mentions his "reluctance to express his feelings." But she also notes that "when he felt the need to express them in a smuggled letter (or on those few times during my visits when the attending officer would tactfully leave the room), he did so with an intensity that suprised him more than it did me." She mentions that "he enjoyed talking about details of our wedding; he had chosen the 103rd psalm as a text and claimed that he was working on the menu." He was amused that she had found his early book *The Communion of Saints* so opaque, declaring that the only book of concern for him was *Life Together,* but he preferred that she wait for him to be released and to be near her again before reading it. There is a poignancy to these letters, just as there was a poignancy to their visits. At the Easter visit, Bonhoeffer remarked, "Isn't it so that even when we are laughing, we are a bit sad?"

Maria and Dietrich were completely cut off from each other when Dietrich was transferred to the Gestapo prison in Prinz Albrecht-Strasse, Berlin, in October 1944. After he had already been transported to Buchenwald, Maria attempted to locate him, inquiring about her fiancé at various concentration camps amidst the chaos of the last months of the war, but she could not. He perished while she still nurtured faint hopes of their eventual reunion. She had only memories of their love and his letters. The excerpts that follow are from her article "The Other Letters from Prison."

August 12, 1943

You cannot imagine what it means in my present situation to have you. I am certain of God's special guidance here. The way in which we found each other and the time, so shortly before my imprisonment, are a clear sign for this. Again, it was a case of *hominum confusione at dei providencia.* Everyday I am overcome anew at how undeservedly I received this happiness, and each day I am deeply moved at what a hard school God has led you through during the last year. And now it appears to be his will that I have to bring you sorrow and suffering . . . so that our love for each other may achieve the right foundation and the right endurance. When I also think about the situation of the world, the complete darkness over our personal fate and my present imprisonment, then I believe that our union can only be a sign of God's grace and kindness, which calls us to faith. We would be blind if we did not see it. Jeremiah says at the moment of his people's great need "still one shall buy houses and acres in this land" as a sign of trust in the future. This is where faith belongs. May God give it to us daily. And I do not mean the faith which flees the world, but the one that endures the world and which loves and remains true to the world in spite of all the suffering which it contains for us. Our marriage shall be a yes to God's earth; it shall strengthen our courage to act and accomplish something on the earth. I fear that Christians who stand with only one leg upon earth also stand with only one leg in heaven.

August 20, 1943

The sun is a special favorite of mine* and has reminded me often of the fact that man is created from earth and does not consist of air and thoughts. This went so far that once, when I was asked to preach in

---

*Written while Bonhoeffer was permitted to sit in the summer sun.

Cuba at Christmas time, coming from the ice of North America into the blooming vegetation, I almost succumbed to the sun cult and hardly knew what I should have preached. It was a real crisis, and something of this comes over me every summer when I feel the sun. To me the sun is not an astronomical entity, but something like a living power which I love and fear. I find it cowardly to look past these realities rationally. . . . So must patience, joy, gratitude, and calm assert themselves against all sorts of resistance. It says in the psalm "God is sun and shield." To recognize and experience and believe this is a moment of great grace and by no means an everyday wisdom.

It would be better if I succeeded in writing to you only of my gratitude, my joy, and my happiness in having you and in keeping the pressure and the impatience of this long imprisonment out of sight. But that would not be truthful, and it would appear to me as an injustice to you. You must know how I really feel and must not take me for a stone saint [*Saeulenheiligen*]. . . . I can't very well imagine that you would want to marry one in the first place—and I would also advise against it from my knowledge of church history.

September 20, 1943

Slowly it gets to be a waiting whose outward sense I cannot comprehend; the inward reason must be found daily. Both of us have lost infinitely much during the past months; time today is a costly commodity, for who knows how much more time is given to us. And yet I do not dare to think that it was or is lost time either for each of us individually or for both of us together. We have grown together in a different way than we have thought and wished, but these are unusual times and will remain so a while longer, and everything depends on our being one in the essential things and on our remaining with each other. Your life would have been quite different, easier, clearer, simpler had not our path crossed a year ago. But there are only short moments when this thought bothers me. I believe that not only I, but you too, had arrived at the moment in life when we had to meet, neither of us basically has any desire for an easy life, much as we may enjoy beautiful and happy hours in this life, and much as we may have a great longing for these hours today. I believe that happiness lies for both of us at a different and hidden place which is incomprehensible to many. Actually both of us look for challenges [*Aufgaben*], up to now each for oneself, but from now on together. Only in this work will we grow completely together when God gives us the time for it.

November 21, 1943

Stifter once said "pain is a holy angel, who shows treasures to men which otherwise remain forever hidden; through him men have become greater than through all joys of the world." It must be so and I tell this to myself in my present position over and over again—the pain of long-ing which often can be felt even physically, must be there, and we shall not and need not talk it away. But it needs to be overcome every time, and thus there is an even holier angel than the one of pain, that is the one of joy in God. A prison cell, in which one waits, hopes, does various unessential things, and is completely dependent on the fact that the door of freedom has to be opened *from the outside*, is not a bad picture of Advent.

December 1, 1943

You can hardly imagine how I long for everyone: after these long months of solitude. I have a real hunger for people. I am afraid, how-ever, that at first I shall have trouble enduring long gatherings of many people. Even in times past I could endure family festivities, which in fact I love dearly, only if I could escape into my room for half an hour from time to time. From now on I hope you will escape with me. Yet you must not think me unsociable. Unfortunately, I find people ex-tremely exhausting. But of these social vices and virtues you will learn soon enough

FINAL LETTER

December 19, 1944

These will be quiet days in our homes. But I have had the experience over and over again that the quieter it is around me, the clearer do I feel the connection to you. It is as though in solitude the soul develops senses which we hardly know in everyday life. Therefore I have not felt lonely or abandoned for one moment. You, the parents, all of you, the friends and students of mine at the front, all are constantly present to me. Your prayers and good thoughts, words from the Bible, discussions long past, pieces of music, and books—[all these] gain life and reality as never before. It is a great invisible sphere in which one lives and in whose reality there is no doubt. If it says in the old children's song about the angels: "Two, to cover me, two, to wake me," so is this guardianship [*Bewahrung*], by good invisible powers in the morning and at night, something which grownups need today no less than children. Therefore you must not think that I am unhappy. What is happiness and unhap-piness? It depends so little on the circumstances; it depends really only on that which happens inside a person. I am grateful every day that I have you, and that makes me happy. ["The Other Letters from Prison," *Union Seminary Quarterly Review*, vol. 23, no. 1 (Fall 1967), pp. 23–29]

69

Letters to Eberhard Bethge

1940–1944

The collection of Bonhoeffer's letters from prison to Eberhard Bethge have already been recognized as a spiritual classic. What has become more evident in light of more recent Bonhoeffer research is the extraordinary way Bethge himself helped Bonhoeffer to express his most creative thoughts. Bethge has succeeded over the many years of collecting and editing Bonhoeffer's papers and in composing his massive biography—which George Steiner had called "one of the few assured classics of our age"—in hiding his own influence on Bonhoeffer. People who have met the Bethges and read Bonhoeffer extensively sense this. Likewise, in the perceptive questions Bethge puts to Bonhoeffer regarding the prison letters excerpted here, one detects the honest, gently critical reaction Bonhoeffer had come to appreciate in his friend and confidant-confessor. If at times Bonhoeffer had to act against the advice of church leaders to the point that he often seemed to despise their opinions, with Bethge he had reached the point of complete trust. Here was the clear-headed, single-hearted follower of Christ to whom he could entrust not only his ideas and hopes, but also his secrets, his affection, his sins, his life. Their friendship grew in the rich ground of their commitment to Christ and in the rockier ground of their involvement in the church struggle. Bonhoeffer had come to rely on Bethge's judgment during the spiritual hardships brought on both of them by their refusal to compromise the gospel. They had become, as several of the Finkenwaldians had noticed, complementary to each other. Bethge tempered the quick, firelike thrusts of Bonhoeffer's theological mind. He was the steadfast friend whom Bonhoeffer needed when their world began to disintegrate and when the challenges of their frustrations in the church struggle and the dangers to their lives from the conspiracy seemed so overpowering. Out of this friendship and because of this friendship, the prison letters came to be.

The letters included in this final section on Bonhoeffer's correspondence extend into the period before his imprisonment. In 1940 Bonhoeffer was taking a break at the Kleist estate in Klein-Krössin in order to compose parts of *Ethics*. He was already involved with the conspirators and filled with indignation at Hitler's grandiose victories on the western front. These feelings breathed some ire into his "Confession of Guilt" on the part of the churches which had by their silence legitimated the atrocities of the war. His letter of October 9, 1940, contains friendly advice to Bethge as well as allusions to his daily prayer and Bible regimen and the importance of authority structures in church government for the present struggle. In the November letter, Bonhoeffer probes the question of union and cooperation among the churches. "Christ," he writes, "is more important than our thoughts about him and his presence." And decisions of faith, not theological affirmations, will, he argues, determine the reunion of churches. A week later, writing from the Catholic monastery of Ettal, his mind has turned to the Eucharist. He notes the similarity between Ettal and Finkenwalde and wonders why the Protestant churches could not have joined the pope in praying for peace. Then, over a year later, he writes from Munich on Eberhard's birthday, speaking about what their ministry should mean for them. "The ministry," he says, "presupposes an equality of form with Christ." Finally, on the train to Munich the following June, Bonhoeffer expresses himself about his worldliness in a way that seems strikingly close to his utterances on worldliness from prison. He already detects in himself what will be a strong theme of the letters from prison, namely, a growing "rebellion against all things 'religious.'" Still, he "would love to preach just once more."

Bonhoeffer would not preach again, but his prison correspondence with Bethge would become the grist for thousands of sermons by people who have found inspiration in his life and martyrdom. The excerpts from the prison letters included here begin with his assurance that he had no regrets about returning from safe haven in America in 1939. Everything, even his being involved in Germany's fate through his imprisonment, had a unique purpose for him; so he avows in this letter. "All we can do is to live in assurance and faith," he adds. A similar note is struck in the second letter, addressed to Renate and Eberhard, in which Bonhoeffer expresses his confidence that they have all been completely placed "in better and stronger hands." Bonhoeffer's next letter of this section addresses the question of whether he had ever changed. According to his recollections, there had never been a real "break" in his life, though he had broken with a good deal. In this letter he sets in proper context his claim to have turned from the "phraseological to the real," a statement often associated with his dissafection for the merely academic theology in vogue at the university and unconnected with life. This was hardly a "conversion."

At this juncture in the prison letters, Bonhoeffer presents what has caused the most excitement and controversy among his interpreters, his views on religionless Christianity and his call for a nonreligious interpretation of biblical concepts. This is from the famous letter of April 30, 1944. He will stay on this theme until the letters of August. He is, as he says in the April 30th letter, "bothered incessantly" by the question of "what Christianity really is" or "who Christ really is for us today." He immediately attempts to elaborate his own understanding of this puzzle, claiming that for 1,900 years Christian preaching and theology rested on an historically conditioned, transitory, religious a priori. His questions seem to flow from that initial probing into what he felt was the coming religionlessness of Christianity. How, then, was Christ to be recognized as Lord of the world? What role would church preaching, liturgy, or Christian life itself have in a world acknowledged to be nonreligious? What place do worship and prayer have? Does this mean a return to the early church's "discipline of the secret"?

These questions became the heart of his future correspondence and the source of much of the confusion that has beset efforts to either damn the letters as too radical, dismiss them as too cryptic, or use them as part of a program for reshaping Christianity after the war. We have attempted to show in this volume that these letters, though electrifying in their immediate impact, are in continuity with his early writings and reflect his concern to theologize in the concrete and in service to the church and people in need.

This is why so many of the more radical passages from these letters seem to weed out the peripheral from the essential in faith and dare to pose questions often buried in the unsettled intuitions of people of faith. These questions are related to the church's seeming exploitation of God, the description of God in abstract, individualistic, metaphysical language, and the scandalous posturing for privilege, promotion, and survival of the clergy at the expense of a commitment to the truth and to God's Word. All these questions converge, as did Bonhoeffer's own life, on the problem of suffering and the search for meaning in the horrors of war.

Bonhoeffer does battle with a number of significant theological figures and ideas in the letters. Karl Barth, he contends, had not provided any useful guidance for the reinterpretation of theology in the modern world. New Testament Scholar Rudolf Bultmann had not gone far enough with his demythologization. There was still need to prune biblical language of the metaphysical, individualistic interpretations and to honor God not as the beyond of the world, but as the beyond in the midst of life. Christ, too, he insists, is not the object of religion but "really the Lord of the world." In effect, Bonhoeffer is himself exploring the answer to his own question of how one speaks in a "worldly" way about God in a world come of age, that is, a world able to answer the pressing questions of the day without recourse to the God hypothesis or like plays of old, by invoking a *deus ex machina*. This concern comes out most urgently in the letter of May 29, 1944, after Bonhoeffer had read Carl Friedrich von Weizsäcker's book, *The World-View of Physics*. This book had underscored for Bonhoeffer the ludicrousness of using God merely to complement human knowledge or to answer questions only when we are at the limits of our intellectual and spiritual strengths, the problems of death, suffering, and guilt. God, Bonhoeffer contends, must be "recognized at the center of life." The letter of June 8, 1944, affirms the movements toward human autonomy and decries churchly opposition to this autonomy and to the world's adulthood as pointless, ignoble, and unChristian. These rearguard efforts only masked the clerical lust for privilege and survival. By the end of June, Bonhoeffer was insisting that Christianity did not focus on the world beyond death; rather, it sent people to become deeply involved in this life and, like Christ, to drink "the earthly cup to the dregs."

In his letters from July 16 to August 3, 1944, encompassing the intense disappointment of the conspirators at the failure of the July 20 assassination plot, Bonhoeffer touches the heart of his belief that God's sufferings in this world are intimately interlaced into the whole issue of nonreligious Christianity and nonreligious interpretation. It is God, he declares, who would have us live as people "who manage our lives without him." Further, this is the God who wants us to live without him even as "we stand continually in his presence." God "lets himself be pushed out of the world onto the cross." It is in this letter that Bonhoeffer describes the weakness and powerlessness of God in the world that in a paradoxical manner becomes the only mode of his helping. This for Bonhoeffer is the decisive difference between religion that feeds on a sense of power and Christianity that affirms God's strength in weakness as he suffers in the world. The next letter, that of July 18, 1944, calls for a truly "worldly life," one that, far from condoning the ungodliness of the world so evident in the Nazi period, shares in the suffering of God in a godless world. The final letter on these new themes, that of August 3, 1944, is especially memorable for its outline of a book on the church Bonhoeffer never lived to write. The church must, he urged, come out of its stagnation. It must, like Christ, the man for others, live wholly to be of service to others. "The church is the church only when it exists for others," he insisted.

The letters then turn on several personal notes that in themselves seem to be offshoots of these daring reflections. In the letter of August 21, 1944, we have a clear glimpse of the faith that enabled him, as he put it, to take life in stride. His love for Jesus, he confides to Bethge, had made it all, even his possible execution, worthwhile. There is a confidence in this letter that radiates from the source of his strength, his conviction that no power could touch him without God's will and that danger and suffering only brought one closer to God. "It is certain that in all this we are in a fellowship that sustains us. In Jesus God has said Yes and Amen to it all, and that Yes and Amen is the firm ground on which we stand."

What is clear from these letters is that Bonhoeffer's questions about nonreligious Christianity are not in any way a repudiation of liturgy, prayer, devotion, or church. Rather, his remarks were directed against that misuse of religion whereby God was turned into an aloof idol remote from his people and Jesus made into a mere object of religion isolated from responsible action in and for the world. He attacked the immaturity of churches that still desired to keep people in a stunted relationship with God for the sake of conformity with the state and the procuring of clerical privilege that ensued. Bonhoeffer's vision of the challenge of faith to the "world come of age" echoed the call to the costly grace of Christian discipleship in earlier writings. As he tries to pare away the various layers of dishonesty in one's faith, he brings almost hauntingly to mind the figure of Christ crucified. The question of the letters becomes, therefore, the question of Bonhoeffer's whole life: "What do we really believe? I mean, believe in such a way that we stake our lives on it?"

That the faith on which Bonhoeffer staked his life was beset by the complexities of his own life's story is something brought out in several of his poems from prison. Three of these and excerpts from a fourth are included in chapters 72 to 75 by way of conclusion to this collection of readings from the Bonhoeffer legacy. His "The Death of Moses" (chapter 75) was sent to Bethge in September 1944. It seems to be an effort by Bonhoeffer in the more strained circumstances of the Gestapo's tightening grip on the conspirators, to peer into the future and to see some meaning amidst the bleakness. Bonhoeffer likens himself to Moses near the end of his journey to a "promised land," his hope for Germany after the war. His death he now understands and accepts for the sake of his people. He would not live to see their liberation but was content to know he had done all he could to share in the sufferings of Christ at the hands of the godless world of nazism. As he sinks "into eternity," it is enough to see his people marching free.

"Who Am I?" (chapter 72), a poem added to the letter of July 8, 1944, takes us to the inner world of personal struggle to be honest with himself and fully committed to Jesus Christ. It is one of the most autobiographical of Bonhoeffer's writings, acknowledging the contradictions he had to confront within himself, especially in his living out the principles of Sermon on the Mount. In an earlier letter in this collection Bonhoeffer had called his commitment to the Jesus of that Sermon a "great liberation." But it was also a liberation that had the price of a lifelong wrestling with the devils of discouragement and pride. He knew his own weaknesses. Was he that person or the person of strength on whom others leaned for support? "Whoever I am," he concludes, "thou knowest, O God, I am thine."

"Christians and Pagans" (chapter 73), included in the same letter, is, in its own brief, poetic way, a summary of Bonhoeffer's understanding of the essence of one's relationship with God. The first verse describes how religion looks on God as only a supplier of needs and whose usefulness is solely to produce benefits, an attitude hardly different from paganism. The second verse insists that with Christians God is someone wholly other than the "god" of religion. Because of his Word enfleshed in Jesus, God is acknowledged as one who suffers with and in his people. Christians are those who can stand by God, sharing in his pain. The final verse portrays God's presence, caring for those in need, nourishing them with his Eucharist. But for all, whether Christian or pagan, he extends his love in constant forgiveness and in the constant sacrifice of his own life. God lives in solidarity with his people.

Another poem, "Stations on the Road to Freedom" (chapter 74), sent the day after the failure of the July 20th attempt on Hitler's life, recollects the many paths followed in Bonhoeffer's fight for freedom. Here in verse one we see again the issues raised in *The Cost of Discipleship*, the discipline needed in following Christ. Then we also call to mind the daring action demanded in doing the deed necessary to deliver people from their civil and spiritual servitude. The time for thought is past. Now is the time to trust wholly in God and act. Bonhoeffer's imprisonment is relived in verse three. They had come close to victory, tasting the sweetness of freedom. But more sacrifice was required of them. And so verse four, like Bonhoeffer's life, ends in the acceptance of death for the sake of experiencing true freedom. "Dying, now we behold your face in the countenance of God." This final line was echoed in a way in Bonhoeffer's farewell message to Bishop George Bell: "This is the end, but for me the beginning of life."

Klein-Krössin, October 9, 1940

Dear Eberhard:

Tomorrow, when you come home, you ought to have at least a greeting from me. You're now leading a much more active and, on the whole, much richer life than I am; but you mustn't let your energy be sapped by it. Keep your independence as much as possible. I feel that much of the weariness and sterility in our ranks is in the end a result of a lack of "selfless self-love." As this *locus* has no place in official evangelical ethics, people in their pride and their craze for work ignore it, to the loss of the individual and the whole. But it is a part of the human life for which we have been redeemed. So tell yourself that at the right time. I enjoy the daily morning prayers here very much: they make me expound the Bible. I think about you and your work a great deal during them, as I do when reading the Bible. The regular routine of the day makes it easy for me to work and to pray, and to get on with people, and it spares me the discomforts of body, soul, and spirit that come from inactivity. Recently, however, a heavy autumn storm made me quite depressed, and it was not so easy to get my balance again. Work goes on: I'm doing an outline of the whole thing [i.e., his *Ethics*] which is the task I always enjoy most and find most difficult. It will probably take the rest of the week.

We were in Kieckow on Sunday. We also talked about the church situation. Once again it became quite clear to me that the struggle over the government of the church is in fact *the* question, which has inevitably arisen out of the history of the church, the question of the possibility of a "protestant" church for us. It is the question whether, after the split between papal and secular authority in the church, an authority can be appointed in the church which is based solely on the Word and the confessions. If such an authority is not possible, then the last possibility for a "protestant" church has gone; in that case, all that is left is a return to Rome, or to the state church, or a way into isolation, into the "protest" of true Protestantism against false authorities. Our present concern with the authority of the government of the church is not fortuitous, but a divine necessity.

My thoughts are often turning to Sabine. . . . When one has the feeling that others expected something of one and that one has fallen so far short of their expectations, one's memory is filled with a sense of guilt and at the same time a desire for forgiveness and to be able to help again. . . . How's the economic situation? And the air-raid shelters? There was an alert again today in Köslin. All the best. See you next week. [*TP*, pp. 67–68]

November 16, 1940

Dear Eberhard:

I'm sitting in the train to Munich and have just been thoroughly disillusioned. The train doesn't arrive at 8:30, as I thought, but at 10:30. I can't read anymore, so I'm writing an illegible letter to you. . . .

One more word about the Catholic question: How have we Lutherans got along with the Reformed Churches? Really quite untheologically (the theological formulation of Halle is really more a statement of fact than a theological solution). We have managed to work together on the basis of two things: the "guidance" of God (Union, Confessing Church) and the recognition of what is given objectively in the Sacraments: Christ is more important than our thoughts about him and his presence. Both are theologically questionable foundations for unity, and yet the church decided in faith for eucharistic—i.e., interchurch—communion. It decided to recognize the union as the guiding hand of God, and it decided to subordinate its ideas or doctrine about Christ to the objectivity of the presence of Christ (in the Reformed Eucharist, too). But it did not bring about a theological union (except at Halle). . . . One can do anything with it! But have we in the Confessing Church not in fact done just that? Of course, the guidance was much clearer then. I don't think it can happen in a day or two, but I want to keep my eyes open in that direction. The train is jolting too much now. Excuse the shaking. Remember me to all old friends in Jena. Write to me at Ettal, via Oberau (Bavaria), Hotel Ludwig der Bayer. [*TP,* pp. 70–72]

Ettal, Sunday, November 23, 1940

I'm glad, despite everything, that you're now so fully occupied and can really do something which is necessary that takes up all your time. My state of retirement, on the other hand, seems so superfluous; but there's no harm in feeling useless for a while. There's no question about it, at present you are indispensable and that will give you—"penultimate"—satisfaction. . . . I sometimes think that the whole business (if it *is* unavoidable) can be a form of cold storage for the future. But of course, how incomparably easy and pleasant our life has been over the past few years, when one considers the burdens which others have borne for years. And what right would I have to quarrel, even for a moment, with my situation, which for others would be a foretaste of paradise! So please do not think that I am abandoning myself without restraint to resignation; I already know and tell myself every morning and every evening what I have to be thankful for—I've just come from a quite marvelous mass. With *Schott* in one's hand one can still pray a great deal and be utterly affirmative. It's not simply idolatry, even if I find the way from our own sacrifice for God to God's sacrifice for us, with which the mass is concerned a hard and apparently very perverse one. But I must learn to understand it better. I'm still a guest over there. The ordered life suits me very well, and I'm surprised at the similarity to much of what we did of our own accord at the seminary. Moreover, the abbot and a number of the fathers have read *Life Together.* We're going to have a discussion soon. The natural hospitality, which is evidently something specifically Benedictine, the really Christian respect for strangers for Christ's sake, almost makes one ashamed. You should come here some time! It's a real experience. . . . Now goodbye, dear Eberhard. In the peace of my present abode I'm thinking a great deal about the brethren, the Confessing Church, you, and your work.

Today the Pope has ordered prayers for peace throughout the church. Couldn't we have joined them too? I did. [*TP*, pp. 74–75]

Munich, August 28, 1941

The eve of your birthday gives me another quiet opportunity of writing to you once again before I go off. I almost went to the cinema in your honor but, as usual, I prefer a peaceful conversation with you to the doubtful pleasure of the film (though *The Holm Murder* sounds very promising!). If you've had as good weather as we have here, you'll now be celebrating your birthday somewhere on the Havel. I'm very glad. I've been thinking of you a good deal today. In the morning I was delighted with the splendid reading. It turns one's attention to the future of the church, to what Christ has done for us, and finally to our ministry. If we are to be "shepherds" of the community, as Christ was, that means much more than saying that we are to be preachers. All the descriptions of ministry in the NT (*apostolos, prophetes, didaskalos, poimēn*) are indeed original designations of the offices of Christ; they were used by Christ himself. The ministry, too, presupposes an equality of form with Christ. That is the high value of the ministry. How good to be reminded of that again. People need shepherds, Christ was the shepherd, and through him and like him we should be shepherds of people. I myself am thankful to have rediscovered this saying. If only the prohibition which still prevents us from exercising this ministry freely were soon to be lifted—if only our thoughts could again be devoted undividedly to this task. Incidentally, the reading for the 27th was also splendid. So I hope that you will be satisfied in your reading throughout the year.

In the morning I had to make some more preparations for my journey. At noon I had a festive meal in your honor. I've also become conscious, in this lamentable business of eating in restaurants, which have also gone down enormously here, how dreadfully off you are in Berlin. Now you must exploit Reimer systematically. You can promise him coffee, perhaps even take him some. . . . He likes it very much. . . . How tedious good eating will be in Switzerland, all by myself. Perels rang up today from Salzburg, only to say good-bye, and he wanted to let his uncle know some things. . . . I think that you should learn some more English again. Who knows when you might need it? . . . The news about Staude disturbs me considerably. It is really quite dreadful. If you're writing to your mother, remember me to her, tell her that I'm traveling and can't write now. . . . I will try not to worry if I hear of attacks on Berlin. At least be sensible! Now good-bye, dear E., I'll be back on September 25th or 26th at the latest. I'll remember you to everyone. God bless you. Practice, and find something new for the flute! Greetings to your mother! [*TP*, pp. 106–7]

On the train to Munich, June 25, 1942

Once again, a greeting from this train. I'm thinking of your work daily, and would so much like to hear how everything has gone. . . . I'm now flying in the morning and coming back with Hans on the 10th (not the 9th). Where are you then? I've written to Frau von Kleist and invited myself for about July 20th . . . I'm also hoping that Thude's brother-in-law is leaving enough time with his message. So something is certainly on until September. Christel should tell him once again; I don't think it's so good and effective if Thude does it himself.

My recent activity, which has been predominantly in the secular sphere, keeps making me think. I'm amazed that I live, and can live, all day long without the Bible. If I were to force myself to it, I would regard my action, not as obedience, but as autosuggestion. I understand that such autosuggestion could be, and is, a great help, but I would be afraid in this way of falsifying a real experience and ultimately not finding any authentic help. When I open the Bible again, it is new, and more cheering than ever, and I would love to preach just once more. I know that I need only open my own books to hear what can be said against all this. I don't want to justify myself, but I recognize that "spiritually" I have had much richer times. I detect that a rebellion against all things "religious" is growing in me. Often it amounts to an instinctive horror—which is certainly not good. I'm not religious by nature. But I have to think continually of God and Christ; authenticity, life, freedom, and mercy mean a great deal to me. It is just their religious manifestations which are so unattractive. Do you understand? These are no new ideas and insights, but as I believe I'm going to have a knot unraveled here, I'm letting these things have their head and not resisting them. That's the way in which I understand my present activity in the secular sphere. Excuse these confessions; blame the long railway journey. We ought to be able to talk about these things again in peace. . . . [*TP,* pp. 137–38]

Tegel, December 22, 1943

. . . Now I want to assure you that I haven't for a moment regretted coming back in 1939—nor any of the consequences, either. I knew quite well what I was doing, and I acted with a clear conscience. I've no wish to cross out of my life anything that has happened since, either to me personally (would I have got engaged otherwise? would you have married? Sigurdshof, East Prussia, Ettal, my illness and all the help you gave me then, and the time in Berlin), or as regards events in general. And I regard my being kept here (do you remember that I prophesied to you last March about what the year would bring?) as being involved in Germany's fate, as I was resolved to be. I don't look back on the past and accept the present reproachfully, but I don't want the machinations of people to make me waver. All we can do is to live in assurance and faith—you out there with the soldiers, and I in my cell.—I've just come across this in the *Imitation of Christ: Custodi diligenter cellam tuam, et custodiet te* ("Take good care of your cell, and it will take care of you").— May God keep us in faith. [*LPP,* pp. 174–75]

Tegel, January 23, 1944

Dear Renate and Eberhard,

Since the ninth, my thoughts about you have taken a new shape. The fact that shortly before your parting you read the text Isaiah 42:16 together puts these thoughts in a special light; on that day, which I knew had special significance for you, I kept reading the passages with special attention and great gratitude. That Sunday was a wrench for me as well as for you, though in a different way. It's a strange feeling to see a man whose life has in one way or another been so intimately bound up with one's own for years going out to meet an unknown future about which one can do virtually nothing. I think this realization of one's own helplessness has two sides, as you, Renate, also say: it brings both anxiety and relief. As long as we ourselves are trying to help shape someone else's destiny, we are never quite free of the question whether what we're doing is really for the other person's benefit—at least in any matter of great importance. But when all possibility of cooperating in anything is suddenly cut off, then behind any anxiety about him there is the consciousness that his life has now been placed wholly in better and stronger hands. For you, and for us, the greatest task during the coming weeks, and perhaps months, may be to entrust each other to those hands. When I learnt yesterday, Eberhard, that you are now somewhere south of Rome, this task became much clearer to me. I am to suppress all the questions that I may keep wanting to ask myself in this connection. Whatever weaknesses, miscalculations, and guilt there is in what precedes the facts, God is in the facts themselves. If we survive during these coming weeks or months, we shall be able to see quite clearly that all has turned out for the best. The idea that we could have avoided many of life's difficulties if we had taken things more cautiously is too foolish to be entertained for a moment. As I look back on your past I am so convinced that what has happened hitherto has been right, that I feel that what is happening now is right too. To renounce a full life and its real joys in order to avoid pain is neither Christian nor human. . . . [*LPP,* pp. 190–91]

Tegel, April 22, 1944

I've just heard through my parents again about how things are going with you; I would always like to know much more, but it's a great comfort even to know that you are well. Father was very pleased with your letter, and so was Maria with the one of April 5. Many thanks, it was a *very* good, friendly thought on your part.

When you say that my time here will be very important for my practical work, and that you're very much looking forward to what I shall have to tell you later, and to what I've written, you mustn't indulge in any illusions about me. I've certainly learnt a great deal, but I don't think I have changed very much. There are people who change, and others who can hardly change at all. I don't think I've ever changed very much, except perhaps at the time of my first impressions abroad and under the first conscious influence of Father's personality. It was then that I turned from phraseology to reality. I don't think, in fact, that you yourself have changed much. Self-development is, of course, a different matter. Neither of us has really had a break in our lives. Of course, we have deliberately broken with a good deal, but that again is something quite different. Even our present experiences probably don't represent a break in the passive sense. I sometimes used to long for something of the kind, but today I think differently about it. Continuity with one's own past is a great gift, too. Paul wrote 2 Timothy 1:3a as well as 1 Timothy 1:13. I'm often surprised how little (in contrast to nearly all the others here) I grub among my past mistakes and think how different one thing or another would be today if I had acted differently in the past; it doesn't worry me at all. Everything seems to have taken its natural course, and to be determined necessarily and straightforwardly by a higher providence. Do you feel the same? . . . [*LPP,* pp. 275–76]

Tegel, April 30, 1944

. . . How good it would seem to me, for both of us, if we could go through this time together, helping each other. But it's probably "better" for it not to be so, but for each of us to have to go through it alone. I find it hard not to be able to help you in anything—except by thinking of you every morning and evening when I read the Bible, and often during the day as well. You've no need to worry about me at all, as I'm getting on uncommonly well—you would be surprised, if you came to see me. People here keep on telling me (as you can see, I feel very flattered by it) that I'm "radiating so much peace around me," and that I'm "always so cheerful,"—so that the feelings that I sometimes have to the contrary must, I suppose, rest on an illusion (not that I really believe that at all!). You would be surprised, and perhaps even worried, by my theological thoughts and the conclusions that they lead to; and this is where I miss you most of all, because I don't know anyone else with whom I could so well discuss them to have my thinking clarified. What is bothering me incessantly is the question what Christianity really is, or indeed who Christ really is, for us today. The time when people could be told everything by means of words, whether theological or pious, is over, and so is the time of inwardness and conscience—and that means the time of religion in general. We are moving toward a completely religionless time; people as they are now simply cannot be religious any more. Even those who honestly describe themselves as "religious" do not in the least act up to it, and so they presumably mean something quite different by "religious."

Our whole 1,900-year-old Christian preaching and theology rest on the "religious *a priori*" of mankind. "Christianity" has always been a form—perhaps the true form—of "religion." But if one day it becomes clear that this *a priori* does not exist at all, but was a historically conditioned and transient form of human self-expression, and if therefore man becomes radically religionless—and I think that that is already more or less the case (else how is it, for example, that this war, in contrast to all previous ones, is not calling forth any "religious" reaction?)—what does that mean for "Christianity"? It means that the foundation is taken away from the whole of what has up to now been our "Christianity," and that there remain only a few "last survivors of the age of chivalry," or a few intellectually dishonest people, on whom we can descend as "religious." Are they to be the chosen few? Is it on this dubious group of people that we are to pounce in fervor, pique, or indignation, in order to sell them our goods? Are we to fall upon a few unfortunate people in their hour of need and exercise a sort of religious compulsion on them? If we don't want to do all that, if our final judgment must be that the Western form of Christianity, too, was only a preliminary stage to a complete absence of religion, what kind of situation emerges for us, for the church? How can Christ become the Lord of the religionless as well? Are there religionless Christians? If religion is only a garment of Christianity—and even this garment has looked very different at different times—then what is a religionless Christianity?

Barth, who is the only one to have started along this line of thought, did not carry it to completion, but arrived at a positivism of revelation, which in the last analysis is essentially a restoration. For the religionless working man (or any other man) nothing decisive is gained here. The questions to be answered would surely be: What do a church, a community, a sermon, a liturgy, a Christian life mean in a religionless world? How do we speak of God—without religion, i.e., without the temporally conditioned presuppositions of metaphysics, inwardness, and so on? How do we speak (or perhaps we cannot now even "speak" as we used to) in a "secular" way about 'God'? In what way are we "religionless-secular" Christians, in what way are we the εκ-κλησια, those who are called forth, not regarding ourselves from a religious point of view as specially favored, but rather as belonging wholly to the world? In that case Christ is no longer an object of religion, but something quite different, really the Lord of the world. But what does that mean? What is the place of worship and prayer in a religionless situation? Does the secret discipline, or alternatively the difference (which I have suggested to you before) between penultimate and ultimate, take on a new importance here?

I must break off for today, so that the letter can go straight away. I'll write to you again about it in two days' time. I hope you see more or less what I mean, and that it doesn't bore you. Good-bye for the present. It's not easy always to write without an echo, and you must excuse me if that makes it something of a monologue.

I'm thinking of you very much.

I'm not really reproaching you for not writing. You have too much else to do.

I find, after all, that I can write a little more—The Pauline question whether περιτομή [circumcision] is a condition of justification seems to me in present-day terms to be whether religion is a condition of salvation. Freedom from περιτομή is also freedom from religion. I often ask myself why a "Christian instinct" often draws me more to the religionless people than to the religious, by which I don't in the least mean with any evangelizing intention, but, I might almost say, "in brotherhood." While I'm often reluctant to mention God by name to religious people—because that name somehow seems to me here not to ring true, and I feel myself to be slightly dishonest (it's particularly bad when others start to talk in religious jargon; I then dry up almost completely and feel awkward and uncomfortable—to people with no religion I can on occasion mention him by name quite calmly and as a matter of course. Religious people speak of God when human knowledge (perhaps simply because they are too lazy to think) has come to an end, or when human resources fail—in fact it is always the *deus ex machina* that they bring on to the scene, either for the apparent solution of insoluble problems, or as strength in human failure—always, that is to say, exploiting human weakness or human boundaries. Of necessity, that can go on only till people can by their own strength push these boundaries somewhat further out, so that God becomes superfluous as a *deus ex machina*. I've come to be doubtful of talking about any human boundaries (is even death, which people now hardly fear, and is sin, which they now hardly understand, still a genuine boundary today?). It always seems to me that we are trying anxiously in this way to reserve some space for God; I should like to speak of God not on the boundaries but at the center, not in weaknesses but in strength; and therefore not in death and guilt but in man's life and goodness. As to the boundaries, it seems to me better to be silent and leave the insoluble unsolved. Belief in the resurrection is *not* the "solution" of the problem of death. God's "beyond" is not the beyond of our cognitive faculties. The transcendence of epistemological theory has nothing to do with the transcendence of God. God is beyond in the midst of our life. The church stands, not at the boundaries where human powers give out, but in the middle of the village. That is how it is in the Old Testament, and in this sense we still read the New Testament far too little in the light of the Old. How this religionless Christianity looks, what form it takes, is something that I'm thinking about a great deal, and I shall be writing to you again about it soon. It may be that on us in particular, midway between East and West, there will fall a heavy responsibility.

Now I really must stop. It would be fine to have a word from you about all this; it would mean a great deal to me—probably more than you can imagine. Some time, just read Proverbs 22:11–12; there is something that will bar the way to any escapism disguised as piety.

All the very best.

Tegel, May 5, 1944

. . . A few more words about "religionlessness." I expect you remember Bultmann's essay on the "demythologizing" of the New Testament? My view of it today would be, not that he went "too far," as most people thought, but that he didn't go far enough. It's not only the "mythological" concepts, such as miracle, ascension, and so on (which are not in principle separable from the concepts of God, faith, etc.), but "religious" concepts generally, which are problematic. You can't, as Bultmann supposes, separate God and miracle, but you must be able to interpret and proclaim *both* in a "nonreligious" sense. Bultmann's approach is fundamentally still a liberal one (i.e., abridging the gospel), whereas I'm trying to think theologically.

What does it mean to "interpret in a religious sense"? I think it means to speak on the one hand metaphysically, and on the other hand individualistically. Neither of these is relevant to the biblical message or to the man of today. Hasn't the individualistic question about personal salvation almost completely left us all? Aren't we really under the impression that there are more important things than that question (perhaps not more important than the *matter* itself, but more important than the *question!*)? I know it sounds pretty monstrous to say that. But, fundamentally, isn't this in fact biblical? Does the question about saving one's soul appear in the Old Testament at all? Aren't righteousness and the kingdom of God on earth the focus of everything, and isn't it true that Romans 3:24ff. is not an individualistic doctrine of salvation, but the culmination of the view that God alone is righteous? It is not with the beyond that we are concerned, but with this world as created and preserved, subjected to laws, reconciled, and restored. What is above this world is, in the gospel, intended to exist *for* this world; I mean that, not in the anthropocentric sense of liberal, mystic, pietistic, ethical theology, but in the biblical sense of the creation and of the incarnation, crucifixion, and resurrection of Jesus Christ.

Barth was the first theologian to begin the criticism of religion, and that remains his really great merit; but he put in its place a positivist doctrine of revelation which says, in effect, "Like it or lump it": virgin birth, Trinity, or anything else; each is an equally significant and necessary part of the whole, which must simply be swallowed as a whole or not at all. That isn't biblical. There are degrees of knowledge and degrees of significance; that means that a secret discipline must be restored whereby the *mysteries* of the Christian faith are protected against profanation. The positivism of revelation makes it too easy for itself, by setting up, as it does in the last analysis, a law of faith, and so mutilates what is—by Christ's Incarnation!—a gift for us. In the place of religion there now stands the church—that is in itself biblical—but the world is in some degree made to depend on itself and left to its own devices, and that's the mistake.

I'm thinking about how we can reinterpret in a "worldly" sense—in the sense of the Old Testament and of John 1:14—the concepts of repentance, faith, justification, rebirth, and sanctification. I shall be writing to you about it again. . . . [*LPP*, pp. 285–87]

THOUGHTS ON THE DAY OF THE BAPTISM OF DIETRICH WILHELM RÜDIGER BETHGE

Tegel, May 1944

. . . Today you will be baptized a Christian. All those great ancient words of the Christian proclamation will be spoken over you, and the command of Jesus Christ to baptize will be carried out on you, without your knowing anything about it. But we are once again being driven right back to the beginnings of our understanding. Reconciliation and redemption, regeneration and the Holy Spirit, love of our enemies, cross and resurrection, life in Christ and Christian discipleship—all these things are so difficult and so remote that we hardly venture any more to speak of them. In the traditional words and acts we suspect that there may be something quite new and revolutionary, though we cannot as yet grasp or express it. That is our own fault. Our church, which has been fighting in these years only for its self-preservation, as though that were an end in itself, is incapable of taking the word of reconciliation and redemption to mankind and the world. Our earlier words are therefore bound to lose their force and cease, and our being Christians today will be limited to two things: prayer and action by the just person on behalf of people. All Christian thinking, speaking, and organizing must be born anew out of this prayer and action. By the time you have grown up, the church's form will have changed greatly. We are not yet out of the melting period. Any attempt to help the church prematurely to a new expansion of its organization will merely delay its conversion and purification. It is not for us to prophesy the day (though the day will come) when men will once more be called so to utter the word of God that the world will be changed and renewed by it. It will be a new language, perhaps quite nonreligious, but liberating and redeeming— as was Jesus' language; it will shock people and yet overcome them by its power; it will be the language of a new righteousness and truth, proclaiming God's peace with people and the coming of his kingdom. "They shall fear and tremble because of all the good and all the prosperity I provide for it" (Jer. 33:9). Till then the Christian cause will be a silent and hidden affair, but there will be those who pray and do right and wait for God's own time. May you be one of them, and may it be said of you one day. "The path of the righteous is like the light of dawn, which shines brighter and brighter till full day" (Prov. 4:18) [*LPP*, pp. 299-300]

Tegel, May 29, 1944

I hope that, in spite of the alerts, you are enjoying to the full the peace and beauty of these warm, summerlike Whitsuntide days. One gradually learns to acquire an inner detachment from life's menaces—although "acquire detachment" seems too negative, formal, artificial, and stoical; and it's perhaps more accurate to say that we assimilate these menaces into our life as a whole. I notice repeatedly here how few people there are who can harbor conflicting emotions at the same time. When bombers come, they are all fears; when there is something nice to eat, they are all greed; when they are disappointed, they are all despair; when they are successful, they can think of nothing else. They miss the fullness of life and the wholeness of an independent existence; everything objective and subjective is dissolved for them into fragments. By contrast, Christianity puts us into many different dimensions of life at the same time; we make room in ourselves, to some extent, for God and the whole world. We rejoice with those who rejoice, and weep with those who weep; we are anxious (—I was again interrupted just then by the alert, and am now sitting out of doors enjoying the sun—) about our life, but at the same time we must think about things much more important to us than life itself. When the alert goes, for instance: as soon as we turn our minds from worrying about our own safety to the task of helping other people to keep calm, the situation is completely changed; life isn't pushed back into a single dimension, but is kept multidimensional and polyphonous. What a deliverance it is to be able to think, and thereby remain multidimensional. I've almost made it a rule here, simply to tell people who are trembling under an air raid that it would be much worse for a small town. We have to get people out of their one-track minds; that is a kind of "preparation" for faith, or something that makes faith possible, although really it's only faith itself that can make possible a multidimensional life, and so enable us to keep this Whitsuntide, too, in spite of the alarms.

At first I was a bit disconcerted, and perhaps even saddened, not to have a letter from anyone this Whitsuntide. Then I told myself that it was perhaps a good sign, as it meant that no one was worrying about me. It's a strange human characteristic that we like other people to be anxious about us—at least just a trifle anxious.

Weizsäcker's book *The World-View of Physics* is still keeping me very busy. It has again brought home to me quite clearly how wrong it is to use God as a stopgap for the incompleteness of our knowledge. If in fact the frontiers of knowledge are being pushed further and further back (and that is bound to be the case), then God is being pushed back with them, and is therefore continually in retreat. We are to find God in what we know, not in what we don't know; God wants us to realize his presence, not in unsolved problems but in those that are solved. That is true of the relationship between God and scientific knowledge, but it is also true of the wider human problems of death, suffering, and guilt. It is now possible to find, even for these questions, human answers that take no account whatever of God. In point of fact, people deal with these questions without God (it has always been so), and it is simply not true to say that only Christianity has the answers to them. As to the idea of "solving" problems, it may be that the Christian answers are just as unconvincing—or convincing—as any others. Here again, God is no stopgap; he must be recognized at the center of life, not when we are at the end of our resources; it is his will to be recognized in life, and not only when death comes; in health and vigor, and not only in suffering; in our activities, and not only in sin. The ground for this lies in the revelation of God in Jesus Christ. He is the center of life, and he certainly didn't "come" to answer our unsolved problems. From the center of life certain questions, and their answers, are seen to be wholly irrelevant (I'm thinking of the judgment pronounced on Job's friends). In Christ there are no "Christian problems." Enough of this; I've just been disturbed again. [*LPP*, pp. 310–12]

Tegel, June 8, 1944

. . . The movement that began about the thirteenth century (I'm not going to get involved in any argument about the exact date) toward the autonomy of man (in which I should include the discovery of the laws by which the world lives and deals with itself in science, social and political matters, art, ethics, and religion) has in our time reached an undoubted completion. Man has learnt to deal with himself in all questions of importance without recourse to the "working hypothesis" called "God." In questions of science, art, and ethics this has become an understood thing at which one now hardly dares to tilt. But for the last hundred years or so it has also become increasingly true of religious questions; it is becoming evident that everything gets along without "God"—and, in fact, just as well as before. As in the scientific field, so in human affairs generally, "God" is being pushed more and more out of life, losing more and more ground. . . . [*LPP*, p. 325]

The attack by Christian apologetic on the adulthood of the world I consider to be in the first place pointless, in the second place ignoble, and in the third place unChristian. Pointless, because it seems to me like an attempt to put a grown-up man back into adolescence, i.e., to make him dependent on things on which he is, in fact, no longer dependent, and thrusting him into problems that are, in fact, no longer problems to him. Ignoble, because it amounts to an attempt to exploit man's weakness for purposes that are alien to him and to which he has not freely assented. UnChristian, because it confuses Christ with one particular stage in man's religiousness, i.e., with a human law. More about this later.

But first, a little more about the historical position. The question is: Christ and the world that has come of age. The weakness of liberal theology was that it conceded to the world the right to determine Christ's place in the world; in the conflict between the church and the world it accepted the comparatively easy terms of peace that the world dictated. Its strength was that it did not try to put the clock back, and that it genuinely accepted the battle (Troeltsch), even though this ended with its defeat. . . . [*LPP*, p. 327]

Tegel, June 27, 1944

. . . The decisive factor is said to be that in Christianity the hope of resurrection is proclaimed, and that that means the emergence of a genuine religion of redemption, the main emphasis now being on the far side of the boundary drawn by death. But it seems to me that this is just where the mistake and the danger lie. Redemption now means redemption from cares, distress, fears, and longings, from sin and death, in a better world beyond the grave. But is this really the essential character of the proclamation of Christ in the gospels and by Paul? I should say it is not. The difference between the Christian hope of resurrection and the mythological hope is that the former sends a man back to his life on earth in a wholly new way which is even more sharply defined than it is in the Old Testament. The Christian, unlike the devotees of the redemption myths, has no last line of escape available from earthly tasks and difficulties into the eternal, but, like Christ himself ("My God, why hast thou forsaken me?"), he must drink the earthly cup to the dregs, and only in his doing so is the crucified and risen Lord with him, and he crucified and risen with Christ. This world must not be prematurely written off; in this the Old and New Testaments are at one. Redemption myths arise from human boundary experiences, but Christ takes hold of a man at the center of his life. . . . [*LPP*, pp. 336–37]

Tegel, July 16, 1944

. . . And we cannot be honest unless we recognize that we have to live in the world *etsi deus non daretur*. And this is just what we do recognize—before God! God himself compels us to recognize it. So our coming of age leads us to a true recognition of our situation before God. God would have us know that we must live as men who manage our lives without him. The God who is with us is the God who forsakes us (Mark 15:34). The God who lets us live in the world without the working hypothesis of God is the God before whom we stand continually. Before God and with God we live without God. God lets himself be pushed out of the world onto the cross. He is weak and powerless in the world, and that is precisely the way, the only way, in which he is with us and helps us. Matthew 8:17 makes it quite clear that Christ helps us, not by virtue of his omnipotence, but by virtue of his weakness and suffering.

Here is the decisive difference between Christianity and all religions. Man's religiosity makes him look in his distress to the power of God in the world: God is the *deus ex machina*. The Bible directs a person to God's powerlessness and suffering; only the suffering God can help. To that extent we may say that the development toward the world's coming of age outlined above, which has done away with a false conception of God, opens up a way of seeing the God of the Bible, who wins power and space in the world by his weakness. This will probably be the starting point for our "secular interpretation." [*LPP*, pp. 360–61]

Tegel, July 18, 1944

I wonder whether any letters have been lost in the raids on Munich. Did you get the one with the two poems? It was just sent off that evening, and it also contained a few introductory remarks on our theological theme. The poem about Christians and pagans contains an idea that you will recognize: "Christians stand by God in his hour of grieving"; that is what distinguishes Christians from pagans. Jesus asked in Gethsemane, "Could you not watch with me one hour?" That is a reversal of what the religious man expects from God. Man is summoned to share in God's sufferings at the hands of a godless world.

He must therefore really live in the godless world, without attempting to gloss over or explain its ungodliness in some religious way or other. He must live a "secular" life, and thereby share in God's sufferings. He *may* live a "secular" life (as one who has been freed from false religious obligations and inhibitions). To be a Christian does not mean to be religious in a particular way, to make something of oneself (a sinner, a penitent, or a saint) on the basis of some method or other, but to be a man—not a type of man, but the man that Christ creates in us. It is not the religious act that makes the Christian, but participation in the sufferings of God in the secular life. That is *metanoia:* not in the first place thinking about one's own needs, problems, sins, and fears, but allowing oneself to be caught up into the way of Jesus Christ, into the messianic event, thus fulfilling Isaiah 53. . . .

This being caught up into the messianic sufferings of God in Jesus Christ takes a variety of forms in the New Testament. It appears in the call to discipleship, in Jesus' table fellowship with sinners, in "conversions" in the narrower sense of the word (e.g., Zacchaeus), in the act of the woman who was a sinner (Luke 7)—an act that she performed without any confession of sin, in the healing of the sick (Matt. 8:17; see above), in Jesus' acceptance of children. The shepherds, like the wise men from the East, stand at the crib, not as "converted sinners," but simply because they are drawn to the crib by the star just as they are. The centurion of Capernaum (who makes no confession of sin) is held up as a model of faith (cf. Jairus). Jesus "loved" the rich young man. The eunuch (Acts 8) and Cornelius (Acts 10) are not standing at the edge of an abyss. Nathaniel is "an Israelite indeed, in whom there is no guile" (John 1:47). Finally, Joseph of Arimathea and the women at the tomb. The only thing that is common to all these is their sharing in the suffering of God in Christ. That is their "faith." There is nothing of religious method here. The "religious act" is always something partial; "faith" is something whole, involving the whole of one's life. Jesus calls people, not to a new religion, but to life.

But what does this life look like, this participation in the powerlessness of God in the world? I will write about that next time, I hope. Just one more point for today. When we speak of God in a "nonreligious" way, we must speak of him in such a way that the godlessness of the world is not in some way concealed, but rather revealed, and thus exposed to an unexpected light. The world that has come of age is more godless, and perhaps for that very reason nearer to God, than the world before its coming of age. Forgive me for still putting it all so terribly clumsily and badly, as I really feel I am. But perhaps you will help me again to make things clearer and simpler, even if only by my being able to talk about them with you and to hear you, so to speak, keep asking and answering. . . . [LPP, pp. 361–62]

Tegel, July 21, 1944

. . . During the last year or so I've come to know and understand more and more the profound this-worldliness of Christianity. The Christian is not a *homo religiosus*, but simply a man, as Jesus was a man—in contrast, shall we say, to John the Baptist. I don't mean the shallow and banal this-worldliness of the enlightened, the busy, the comfortable, or the lascivious, but the profound this-worldliness, characterized by discipline and the constant knowledge of death and resurrection. I think Luther lived a this-worldly life in this sense.

I remember a conversation that I had in America thirteen years ago with a young French pastor [Jean Lasserre]. We were asking ourselves quite simply what we wanted to do with our lives. He said he would like to become a saint (and I think it's quite likely that he did become one). At the time I was very impressed, but I disagreed with him, and said, in effect, that I should like to learn to have faith. For a long time I didn't realize the depth of the contrast. I thought I could acquire faith by trying to live a holy life, or something like it. I suppose I wrote *The*

Cost of Discipleship as the end of that path. Today I can see the dangers of that book, though I still stand by what I wrote.

I discovered later, and I'm still discovering right up to this moment, that is it only by living completely in this world that one learns to have faith. One must completely abandon any attempt to make something of oneself, whether it be a saint, or a converted sinner, or a churchman (a so-called priestly type!), a righteous man or an unrighteous one, a sick man or a healthy one. By this-worldliness I mean living unreservedly in life's duties, problems, successes and failures, experiences and perplexities. In so doing we throw ourselves completely into the arms of God, taking seriously, not our own sufferings, but those of God in the world—watching with Christ in Gethsemane. That, I think, is faith; that is *metanoia;* and that is how one becomes a man and a Christian (cf. Jer. 45!). How can success make us arrogant, or failure lead us astray, when we share in God's sufferings through a life of this kind? . . . [*LPP*, pp. 369–70]

OUTLINE FOR A BOOK

Tegel, August, 1944

I should like to write a book of not more than 100 pages, divided into three chapters:

1. A Stocktaking of Christianity.
2. The Real Meaning of Christian Faith.
3. Conclusions.

Chapter 1 to deal with:

(*a*) The coming of age of mankind (as already indicated). The safe-guarding of life against "accidents" and "blows of fate"; even if these cannot be eliminated, the danger can be reduced. Insurance (which, although it lives on "accidents," seeks to mitigate their effects) as a Western phenomenon. The aim: to be independent of nature. Nature was formerly conquered by spiritual means, with us by technical organization of all kinds. Our immediate environment is not nature, as formerly, but organization. But with this protection from nature's menace there arises a new one—through organization itself.

But the spiritual force is lacking. The question is: What protects us against the menace of organization? Man is again thrown back on himself. He has managed to deal with everything, only not with himself. He can insure against everything, only not against man. In the last resort it all turns on man.

(*b*) The religionlessness of man who has come of age. "God" as a working hypothesis, as a stopgap for our embarrassments, has become superfluous (as already indicated).

(*c*) The Protestant church: pietism as a last attempt to maintain evangelical Christianity as a religion; Lutheran orthodoxy, the attempt to rescue the church as an institution for salvation; the Confessing Church: the theology of revelation; a δὸς μοὶ ποῦ στῶ ["Give me a place were I may stand"] over against the world, involving a "factual" interest in Christianity; art and science searching for their origin. Generally in the Confessing Church: standing up for the church's "cause," but little personal faith in Christ. "Jesus" is disappearing from sight. Sociologically: no effect on the masses—interest confined to the upper and lower middle classes. A heavy incubus of difficult traditional ideas. The decisive factor: the church on the defensive. No taking risks for others.

(*d*) Public morals—as shown by sexual behavior.

Chapter 2.
(*a*) God and the secular.
(*b*) Who is God? Not in the first place an abstract belief in God, in his omnipotence, etc. That is not a genuine experience of God, but a partial extension of the world. Encounter with Jesus Christ. The experience that a transformation of all human life is given in the fact that "Jesus is there only for others." His "being there for others" is the experience of transcendence. It is only this "being there for others," maintained till death, that is the ground of his omnipotence, omniscience, and omnipresence. Faith is participation in this being of Jesus (Incarnation, cross, and resurrection). Our relation to God is not a "religious" relationship to the highest, most powerful, and best being imaginable—that is not authentic transcendence—but our relation to God is a new life in "existence for others," through participation in the being of Jesus. The transcendental is not infinite and unattainable tasks, but the neighbor who is within reach in any given situation. God in human form—not, as in oriental religions, in animal form, monstrous, chaotic, remote, and terrifying, nor in the conceptual forms of the absolute, metaphysical, infinite, etc., nor yet in the Greek divine-human form of "man in himself," but "the man for others," and therefore the Crucified, the man who lives out of the transcendent. . . .

What do we really believe? I mean, believe in such a way that we stake our lives on it? The problem of the Apostles' Creed? "What *must* I believe?" is the wrong question; antiquated controversies, especially those between the different sects; the Lutheran versus Reformed, and to some extent the Roman Catholic versus Protestant, are now unreal. They may at any time be revived with passion, but they no longer carry conviction. There is no proof of this, and we must simply take it that it is so. All that we can prove is that the faith of the Bible and Christianity does not stand or fall by these issues. Karl Barth and the Confessing Church have encouraged us to entrench ourselves persistently behind the "faith of the church," and evade the honest question as to what we ourselves really believe. That is why the air is not quite fresh, even in the Confessing Church. To say that it is the church's business, not mine, may be a clerical evasion, and outsiders always regard it as such. It is much the same with the dialectical assertion that I do not control my own faith, and that it is therefore not for me to say what my faith is. There may be a place for all these considerations, but they do not absolve us from the duty of being honest with ourselves. We cannot, like the Roman Catholics, simply identify ourselves with the church. . . .

Chapter 3.
Conclusions:
The church is the church only when it exists for others. To make a start, it should give away all its property to those in need. The clergy must live solely on the freewill offerings of their congregations, or possibly engage in some secular calling. The church must share in the secular problems of ordinary human life, not dominating, but helping and serving. It must tell people of every calling what it means to live in Christ, to exist for others. In particular, our own church will have to take the field against the vices of *hubris,* power worship, envy, and humbug, as the roots of all evil. It will have to speak of moderation, purity, trust, loyalty, constancy, patience, discipline, humility, contentment, and modesty. It must not underestimate the importance of human example (which has its origin in the humanity of Jesus and is so important in Paul's teaching); it is not abstract argument, but example, that gives its word emphasis and power. [*LPP,* pp. 380–83]

Tegel, August 21, 1944

It's your birthday in a week's time. Once again I've taken up the readings and meditated on them. The key to everything is the "in him." All that we may rightly expect from God, and ask him for, is to be found in Jesus Christ. The God of Jesus Christ has nothing to do with what God, as we imagine him, could do and ought to do. If we are to learn what God promises, and what he fulfills, we must persevere in quiet meditation on the life, sayings, deeds, sufferings, and death of Jesus. It is certain that we may always live close to God and in the light of his presence, and that such living is an entirely new life for us; that nothing is then impossible for us, because all things are possible with God; that no earthly power can touch us without his will, and that danger and distress can only drive us closer to him. It is certain that we can claim nothing for ourselves, and may yet pray for everything; it is certain that our joy is hidden in suffering, and our life in death; it is certain that in all this we are in a fellowship that sustains us. In Jesus God has said Yes and Amen to it all, and that Yes and Amen is the firm ground on which we stand.

In these turbulent times we repeatedly lose sight of what really makes life worth living. We think that, because this or that person is living, it makes sense for us to live too. But the truth is that if this earth was good enough for the man Jesus Christ, if such a man as Jesus lived, then, and only then, has life a meaning for us. If Jesus had not lived, then our life would be meaningless, in spite of all the other people whom we know and honor and love. Perhaps we now sometimes forget the meaning and purpose of our profession. But isn't this the simplest way of putting it? The unbiblical idea of "meaning" is indeed only a translation of what the Bible calls "promise.". . . [*LPP*, p. 391]

Tegel, August 23, 1944

. . . . Please don't ever get anxious or worried about me, but don't forget to pray for me—I'm sure you don't! I am so sure of God's guiding hand that I hope I shall always be kept in that certainty. You must never doubt that I'm traveling with gratitude and cheerfulness along the road where I'm being led. My past life is brimfull of God's goodness, and my sins are covered by the forgiving love of Christ crucified. I'm most thankful for the people I have met, and I only hope that they never have to grieve about me, but that they, too, will always be certain of, and thankful for, God's mercy and forgiveness. Forgive my writing this. Don't let it grieve or upset you for a moment, but let it make you happy. But I did want to say it for once, and I couldn't think of anyone else who I could be sure would take it aright. . . . [*LPP*, p. 393]

70

Who Am I?

June 1944

Who am I? They often tell me
I would step from my cell's confinement
calmly, cheerfully, firmly,
like a squire from his country house.

Who am I? They often tell me
I would talk to my warders
freely and friendly and clearly,
as though it were mine to command.

Who am I? They also tell me
I would bear the days of misfortune
equably, smilingly, proudly,
like one accustomed to win.

Am I then really all that which other men tell of?
Or am I only what I know of myself,
restless and longing and sick, like a bird in a cage,
struggling for breath, as though hands were compressing my throat,
yearning for colors, for flowers, for the voices of birds,
thirsting for words of kindness, for neighborliness,
trembling with anger at despotisms and petty humiliation,
tossing in expectation of great events,
powerlessly trembling for friends at an infinite distance,
weary and empty at praying, at thinking, at making,
faint, and ready to say farewell to it all?

Who am I? This or the other?
Am I one person today, and tomorrow another?
Am I both at once? A hypocrite before others,

and before myself a contemptibly woebegone weakling?
Or is something within me still like a beaten army,
fleeing in disorder from victory already achieved?

Who am I? They mock me, these lonely questions of mine.
Whoever I am, thou knowest, O God, I am thine.

[*LPP*, pp. 347–48]

Christians and Pagans

July 1944

People turn to God when they're in need,
plead for help, contentment, and for bread,
for rescue from their sickness, guilt, and death.
They all do so, both Christian and pagan.

People turn to God in God's own need,
and find God poor, degraded, without roof or bread,
see God devoured by sin, weakness, and death.
Christians stand with God to share God's pain.

God turns to all people in their need,
nourishes body and soul with God's own bread,
takes up the cross for Christian and pagan, both,
and in forgiving both, is slain.

[Translated from *Widerstand und Ergebung,* p. 382]

Stations on the
Road to Freedom

July 21, 1944

Discipline

If you set out to seek freedom, then learn above all
discipline of soul and senses, so that your passions
and your limbs might not lead you confusedly hither and yon.
Chaste be your spirit and body, subject to your own will,
and obedient to seek out the goal that they have been given.
No one discovers the secret of freedom but through self-control.

Action

Dare to do what is just, not what fancy may call for;
Lose no time with what may be, but boldly grasp what is real.
The world of thought is escape; freedom comes only through action.
Step out beyond anxious waiting and into the storm of events,
carried only by God's command and by your own faith;
then will freedom exultantly cry out to welcome your spirit.

Suffering

Wondrous transformation! Your strong and active hands
are tied now. Powerless, alone, you see the end of your action.
Still, you take a deep breath and lay your struggle for justice,
quietly and in faith, into a mightier hand.
Just for one blissful moment, you tasted the sweetness of freedom,
then you handed it over to God, that he might make it whole.

Death

Come now, highest moment on the road to freedom eternal,
Death, put down the ponderous chains and demolish the walls
of our mortal bodies, the walls of our blinded souls,

that we might finally see what mortals have kept us from seeing.
Freedom, how long we have sought you through discipline, action,
  and suffering.
Dying, now we behold your face in the countenance of God.

Notes by Dietrich Bonhoeffer on "Stations on the Road to Freedom":
Dear Eberhard! I wrote these lines in a few hours this evening. They're
rather crude, but perhaps they'll give you some pleasure, and even serve
me as a sort of birthday present to myself!

  This morning I see that I'll have to reconstruct these lines. Nevertheless, I'll let them go off to you in this unfinished form. After all, I'm no
poet!

[Translated from *Widerstand und Ergebung,* pp. 403−4]

73

The Death of Moses

September 1944

DEUTERONOMY 34:1: "AND THE LORD SHOWED HIM ALL THE LAND . . ."

Up on the mountain peak where few have trod
stands the prophet Moses, man of God.

Absent is his gaze and tired his hand
as he surveys the sacred, promised land.

That he might for Moses' death provide,
the Lord appears now by his servant's side,

wants, in this high place where men are dumb,
to show their leader what is yet to come;

spreads out at the tired wanderer's feet
his homeland, which he still may mutely greet,

offer it his blessing with dying breath,
and so, in peace, to go encounter death.

"You shall glimpse salvation from afar,
but your own feet shall tread that path no more!"

And so the old man's eyes survey—survey
veiled faraway places, as at break of day,

meanwhile mighty hand of God kneads clay
to sacrificial cup—hear Moses pray:

"Thus, o Lord, you keep again your promise,
never has your Word departed from us.

Whether you sent grace or godly wrath—
always they have kept us on our path.

You did ransom us from slavery's chains
and in your gentle arms, did soothe our pains;

through the desert and the threatening tide,
wondrously before us you did stride.

All the peoples' mumbling, whining, wailing
you did hear with patience never failing.

. . . .

Not with kindly hearts were they inclined
to let you lead them forth, faith's way to find.

They fell prey to greed, idolatry,
they saw not that the bread of grace is free,

not until your wrath brought plague and snakes
to tear into your people, for their sakes.

Those who were to be the promised heirs
fell to angry pride, and ruin was theirs.

In the midst of their long pilgrimage,
they were snatched away by you in rage.

One thing of your people you would have:
that they trust in your own power to save.

. . . .

O Lord, your chastising I cannot flee,
and yet upon such heights death comes to me.

You who once were glimpsed on distant wind,
I became your chosen one, your friend,

your mouth, the source of holiness so pure,
your eye to take in sorrows of the poor,

your ear to hear your peoples' sighs and woes,
your arm to break the might of all our foes,

the back on which the weary ones could ride,
which made the fury of friend and foe subside.

Your peoples' mediator, Lord, at prayer,
your instrument and friend and messenger.

For this you let me die here, far above
the plain of human folly, void of love—

the death of one with vision free and far,
of general who has led his men at war;

kind of death at whose dark portals now
the beacon lights of coming ages glow.

As death's dark shroud begins to settle o'er me,
behold, your kingdom is fulfilled before me.

. . . .

So, then, my people, follow now the call,
free earth, free air do beckon to you all.

Go and possess the mountains and the meadows,
Blessed they are by ancient fathers' shadows.

Wipe from your foreheads the hot desert sand
and breathe in freedom in the promised land.

Wake up, take hold, your eyes do not deceive you,
God has saved the weary, he won't leave you.

Behold the splendor of the land you see—
it is God's promise that has set you free!"

Upon the mountain peak where few have trod
stands the prophet Moses, man of God.

Absent is his gaze and tired his hand
as he surveys the sacred, promised land.

"Thus, o Lord, you keep again your promise,
never has your Word departed from us.

Your grace redeems and saves us from our pride,
your wrath is discipline that casts aside.

O faithful Lord, confess to you I must:
your servant knows that you are always just.

Fulfill it, then, your punishment decreed,
and sleep eternal to my soul concede.

Only faith untainted to this hour
can drink the nectar of the new land's flower.

To the doubter, give the bitter potion
and let his faith bring thanks and true devotion.

Wondrous deeds with me you have performed,
bitterness to sweetness here transformed.

You let me glimpse the promise through the veil,
you let my people go, their Lord to hail.

Sinking, o God, into Eternity
I see my people's stride is proud and free.

God, who punishes and then forgives,
this people I have truly loved now lives.

It is enough that I have borne its sorrow
and now have seen the land of its tomorrow.

Hold me fast!—for fallen is my stave,
O faithful God, make ready now my grave."

[Translated from GS, IV, pp. 613–20]

A Bonhoeffer Chronology

1906   February 4. Dietrich Bonhoeffer and twin sister, Sabine, born to Karl Bonhoeffer and Paula von Hase Bonhoeffer in Breslau, Germany.

1912   Spring. Bonhoeffer family moves to Berlin, where Dr. Bonhoeffer assumes teaching responsibilities in neurology and psychiatry at Friedrich Wilhelm University. He also becomes the director of the Charité, the university nerve clinic.

1913   Dietrich Bonhoeffer begins gymnasium studies.

1916   Family moves to Grunewald, Berlin (14 Wangenheimstrasse).

1918   April 28. Oldest brother, Walter, dies in World War I.

1921   Dietrich and Sabine confirmed at Grunewald Church, Berlin.

1923   Dietrich begins theological studies at Tübingen University. Visits ancestral home in Schwäbisch Hall.

1924   Summer. Travels to Rome and North Africa with older brother, Klaus.

1924–27   Studies at Berlin University.

December 17 (1927). Receives licentiate in theology. Successfully defends doctoral thesis, *The Communion of Saints*.

1928   February. Appointed curate in Barcelona, Spain.

1929   Summer. Lectures in systematic theology at Berlin University.

1930   July 18. *Act and Being* accepted as entrance dissertation for professorial post.

July 31. Presents inaugural lecture at Berlin University, "Man in Contemporary Philosophy and Theology."

September 5. Departs for New York to study as a Sloan Fellow at Union Theological Seminary.

Christmas. Travels to Cuba with fellow student Erwin Sutz.

1931   May–June. Travels to Mexico with Jean Lasserre.

July. Meets Karl Barth in Bonn for the first time.

August. Appointed lecturer in theology at Berlin University.

September. Appointed youth secretary for the World Alliance for Promoting International Friendship through the Churches at a conference in Cambridge.

October. Appointed a chaplain at Technical College, Berlin.

November 15. Ordained at St. Matthias Church, Berlin.

Begins teaching confirmation classes at Zion Church, Prenzlauer Berg, Berlin.

1932   Summer. Teaches lecture course at Berlin University, "The Nature of the Church," and seminar, "Is There a Christian Ethic?"

Winter. Teaches lecture course, "Creation and Sin," published as *Creation and Fall*, 1933.

1933   January 30. Adolf Hitler made chancellor of Germany.

February 1. Bonhoeffer's radio broadcast on the leadership principle cut off the air.

February 27. Burning of the Reichstag building in Berlin.

April 1. National one-day boycott of Jewish-owned businesses in Germany.

April 7. Aryan Civil Service legislation bans people with Jewish ancestry from public employment, including holding office in state or church.

April. Bonhoeffer publishes article, "The Church and the Jewish Question."

April 23. Ludwig Müller appointed Hitler's personal representative for the Protestant churches.

June 25. Karl Barth blasts nazism in address, "The Theological Situation of Today." Barth sends manifesto to Hitler.

Summer. Bonhoeffer teaches lecture course on Christology at Berlin University.

August. Paul Tillich expelled from the University of Frankfurt.

September 21. Bonhoeffer cooperates with Pastor Martin Niemöller in organizing the Pastors' Emergency League.

October 17. Bonhoeffer begins pastorate at the German Evangelical Church, Sydenham, and the Reformed Church of St. Paul in London.

Begins friendship with Bishop George K. A. Bell of Chichester, England.

December 20. Protestant youth organizations incorporated into Hitler Youth.

1934   May 10. Bonhoeffer collaborates with Bishop Bell on Bell's Ascensiontide pastoral letter in England.

May 29–31. Confessing Church organized at Barmen, Germany; adopts the Barmen Declaration.

June 30–July 2. Blood Purge in Germany in which Ernst Roehm, head of the SA (*Sturmabteilung*, or "Storm Troopers") is killed, together with scores of others. "Night of the Long Knives."

August 2. German President Paul von Hindenburg dies. Hitler proclaimed both chancellor and president.

August 23–30. Ecumenical Conference at Fanø, Denmark. Bonhoeffer coopted as a member of the Universal Christian Council for Life and Work.

December (and in early 1935). Bonhoeffer visits British Anglican monasteries.

December 15. Karl Barth dismissed from professorial post at Bonn University.

1935   April 26. Preachers' Seminary opens at Zingsthof by the Baltic Sea.

June 24. Seminary relocated in Finkenwalde, near Stettin, in Pomerania.

July. Bonhoeffer publishes article, "The Confessing Church and the Ecumenical Movement."

September 15. Nuremberg Laws passed, cancelling citizenship for German Jews and prohibiting marriage between Jews and Aryans.

October. Bonhoeffer family moves to Charlottenberg, Berlin (43 Marienburger Allee).

December 1. Decree by Heinrich Himmler declares all examinations for the Confessing Church invalid, all Confessing Church training centers invalid, the offenders liable to punishment.

1936   January. Bonhoeffer's grandmother Julie Tafel dies.

February–March. Preachers' Seminary visits Denmark and Sweden.

July 11. Martin Niemöller arrested.

August 5. Bonhoeffer's authorization to teach at Berlin University is withdrawn.

August. Olympic Games in Berlin.

1937   February. Bonhoeffer attends last ecumenical meeting in London, resigns as youth secretary.

March 4. Pope Pius XI issues encyclical, "With Burning Anxiety," charging Hitler's government with infractions of their earlier agreement, the Concordat of 1933.

September. Seminary at Finkenwalde closed by order of Gestapo.

November 27. Twenty-seven pastors, former Finkenwalde students, arrested.

November. Publication of *The Cost of Discipleship*.

December. Collective pastorates begin in Köslin and Gross-Schlönwitz.

1938   January 11. Bonhoeffer excluded from working in Berlin.

February. Bonhoeffer makes initial contacts with leaders of the political resistance to Hitler: Canaris, Oster, Beck, and Sack.

March 12–13. Austria annexed by Germany.

April 20. All pastors in Germany ordered to take the oath of allegiance to Hitler in recognition of his fiftieth birthday.

June. Reunion of Finkenwalde seminary students at Zingst, Germany, from June 20-25. Bonhoeffer lectures and leads Bible study on "Temptation."

September. Writes *Life Together* in Göttingen at home of twin sister, Sabine.

Leibholz family escapes to England by way of Switzerland.

Adolf Hitler and Neville Chamberlain sign Münich agreement for peace in Europe.

November 9. *Kristallnacht* (Crystal Night), initiating the "Week of Broken Glass." Destruction of six hundred synagogues in Germany, looting of 7,500 Jewish-owned shops, arrest of 35,000 Jews.

1939   January 1. All Jewish-owned businesses liquidated by order of Herman Göring.

March. Bonhoeffer travels to London for discussions with Bishop Bell, Reinhold Niebuhr, and Willem Visser 't Hooft. German troops invade Czechoslovakia.

June. Bonhoeffer travels to United States for second time.

July. Returns to Berlin.

August. Bonhoeffer made a civilian agent of the *Abwehr,* German military intelligence agency.

September 1. German troops invade Poland. Great Britain and France declare war on Germany. Hitler's Reichstag speech threatens the extinction of Jewry.

1940   February. Christel Bonhoeffer Dohnanyi types "X Report."

March. Gestapo closes seminary in Köslin and Gross-Schlönwitz.

April 9. German troops invade Denmark and Norway.

May 10. German troops invade Holland, Belgium, Luxembourg, and France.

August 24. Battle of Britain begins; German Luftwaffe bombs London.

September 9. Bonhoeffer prohibited from speaking in public and ordered to report regularly to police.

Begins writing *Ethics* at Klein-Krössin.

November. Assigned to *Abwehr* staff in Münich. Becomes a guest at the Benedictine Abbey in Ettal, near Münich.

1941   February–March. Travels to Switzerland to see Karl Barth and Willem Visser 't Hooft.

April. German troops invade Yugoslavia and Greece.

May 23. Leaders of the Confessing Church arrested.

June 22. German troops invade Soviet Union.

August. Bonhoeffer visits Switzerland for the second time.

September 19. Decree requires all German Jews to wear a yellow star stitched to their clothing.

October. First deportations of Jews from Berlin (Operation 7). First gas chambers installed at Auschwitz, Poland.

December 7. Japan attacks Pearl Harbor.

1942   January 20. Wannsee conference, Berlin. Key Nazi leaders lay plans to implement the "Final Solution."

April 10–18. Bonhoeffer travels to Norway and Sweden with Helmuth Count von Moltke.

May. Visits Switzerland for third time.

May 30–June 2. Bonhoeffer meets with Bishop Bell in Sigtuna, Sweden, on behalf of the resistance.

December 8. Rabbi Stephen Wise presents to President Franklin Roosevelt a twenty-page document, *Blue Print for Extermination,* a country-by-country analysis of the Nazi plans to annihilate the Jews.

1943   January 14. Casablanca talks begin between Franklin Roosevelt, Winston Churchill, and Joseph Stalin.

January 17. Bonhoeffer engaged to Maria von Wedemeyer.

March 31. Celebration of Dr. Karl Bonhoeffer's seventy-fifth birthday in Berlin.

April 5. Bonhoeffer arrested and incarcerated in Tegel Prison, Berlin.

May 15. Wedding of Eberhard Bethge, Bonhoeffer's best friend, and Renate Schleicher, Bonhoeffer's niece.

May 19. Joseph Goebbels, German minister of propaganda, declares that Germany is now *Judenfrei* (free of Jews).

July. Bonhoeffer intensively interrogated in prison.

November. Bonhoeffer writes first letter to Eberhard Bethge.

November 28–December 1. Stalin, Roosevelt, and Churchill meet at Teheran.

December. Bonhoeffer writes Christmas essay, "After Ten Years."

1944   January 22. Allied military forces land at Anzio, Italy.

March 6. First heavy daylight bombing raid over Tegel Prison.

April 30. First of Bonhoeffer's "theological letters."

May 15–July 7. 437,000 Hungarian Jews shipped to Auschwitz.

June 6. Allied military forces land on the Normandy coast, France.

July 20. Count Klaus von Stauffenberg attempts to assassinate Hitler at Rastenburg, East Prussia.

August 23. Bonhoeffer writes last (preserved) letter to Bethge.

September 22. Gestapo discovers incriminating *Abwehr* files at Zossen.

October. Gestapo arrests Klaus Bonhoeffer, and Rüdiger Schleicher, Bonhoeffer's brother-in-law.

October 8. Bonhoeffer moved from Tegel to the Gestapo prison at Prinz-Albrecht-Strasse, Berlin.

December 19. Writes last letter to Maria von Wedemeyer.

1945   February 2. Death sentence pronounced on Klaus Bonhoeffer, Rüdiger Schleicher, F. J. Perels, and Hans John.

February 4–11. Allied conference at Yalta.

Febrary 7. Bonhoeffer moved to the Buchenwald concentration camp.

March 7. American forces cross Rhine River at Remagen.

April 3. Bonhoeffer moved from Buchenwald to Regensburg.

April 5. Heinrich Himmler gives order to annihilate the Canaris resistance group.

April 6. Bonhoeffer moved to Schönberg.

April 8. Bonhoeffer moved to Flossenbürg concentration camp during the night, court-martialed.

April 9. Bonhoeffer executed at Flossenbürg together with other key figures of the resistance: Canaris, Oster, Sack, Gehre, Strünck, and von Rabeneau. Hans von Dohnanyi (brother-in-law) executed at Sachsenhausen concentration camp.

April 12. President Franklin Roosevelt dies; Harry S. Truman sworn in as president.

April 23. Klaus Bonhoeffer, Rüdiger Schleicher, F. J. Perels killed in Berlin.

April 30. Adolf Hitler commits suicide in his Berlin bunker.

May 2. Berlin falls.

May 7. Germany makes unconditional surrender at Rheims, France.

July 6–August 7. Churchill, Stalin, and Truman hold Potsdam conference.

August 6–9. United States drops atomic bombs on Hiroshima and Nagasaki, Japan.

August 15. Hostilities end in the Far East.

October. Stuttgart Declaration of the German church acknowledges the "solidarity of guilt."

November 20. Major war criminal trials begin at Nuremberg.

Notes

Editors' Introduction

1. *LPP*, pp. 347–348.
2. *LPP*, p. 391.
3. *GS*, IV, p. 71.
4. *LPP*, p. 17
5. *DB*, p. 39.
6. *DB*, p. 52.
7. *DB*, p. 53.
8. *GS*, V. pp. 116–17.
9. *GS*, V, p. 117.
10. *AB*, p. 24.
11. *GS*, V, p. 149.
12. *GS*, V, 433.
13. Cited in Edwin H. Robertson, *Christians against Hitler* (London: Student Christian Movement Press), p. 25.
14. *NRS*, p. 91.
15. *NRS*, p. 116.
16. *DB*, p. 119.
17. *GS*, I, pp. 97–98. See also the very helpful article by Ruth Zerner for a well-documented, articulate explanation of this aspect of Bonhoeffer's American experiences. "Dietrich Bonhoeffer's American Experiences: People, Letters, and Papers from Union Seminary," *Union Seminary Quarterly Review*, vol. 31, no. 4 (Summer 1976), pp. 267–69.
18. *NRS*, pp. 113–14 (translation slightly altered).
19. Ruth Zerner, "Dietrich Bonhoeffer's American Experiences," pp. 273–74. Although there has been no direct link established between Bonhoeffer and the social and political concerns of Paul Lehmann, his closest American friend, it has been observed by more than one scholar that Bonhoeffer's admiration for Lehmann's integrity "as a theologian" could not have gone unnoticed. See Ruth Zerner, Ibid p. 274. Zerner mentions that Bonhoeffer must have observed "that Lehmann's social and political concern was energetically practiced as well as preached. There was undoubtedly a reciprocity in terms of ideas and life-styles."
20. See F. Burton Nelson, "The Relationship of Jean Lasserre to Dietrich Bonhoeffer's Peace Concerns in the Struggle of Church and Culture," *Union Seminary Quarterly Review*, vol. 40, nos. 1–2 (1985), p. 74
21. Ibid.
22. *DB*, p. 155.
23. *NRS*, pp. 120–22; *DB*, p. 132.
24. *DB*, p. 132.
25. Ibid.
26. *NRS*, p. 362.
27. *DB*, p. 158.
28. Letter of February 26, 1932, *NRS*, pp. 150–51.
29. Richard Rother, "A Confirmation Class in Wedding," *IKDB*, p. 57.

30. *DB*, pp. 172–73.
31. *DB*, p. 173; *GS*, II, p. 131.
32. *DB*, pp. 193–94.
33. *NRS*, p. 225.
34. *NRS*, p. 226.
35. For further development of the various ways in which Bonhoeffer showed concern for and came to the defense of the Jewish people, see especially Eberhard Bethge, "Dietrich Bonhoeffer and the Jews," in John D. Godsey and Geffrey B. Kelly, *Ethical Responsibility: Bonhoeffer's Legacy to the Churches* (New York and Toronto: Edwin Mellen Press, 1981), pp. 43–96, and Geffrey B. Kelly, "Dietrich Bonhoeffer and the Church Struggle: The Possibility of Jewish-Christian Reconciliation," in F. Burton Nelson, *Holocaust Studies: A Search for Directions* (New York and Toronto: Edwin Mellen Press, 1990).
36. Letter of August 20, 1933, *GS* II, p. 79.
37. *DB*, p. 220.
38. *DB*, p. 220.
39. *DB*, pp. 657–58.
40. *DB*, p. 228.
41. *NRS*, pp. 241–42.
42. *DB*, pp. 240–41.
43. *DB*, pp. 248–50.
44. *IKDB*, p. 71.
45. For this exchange of letters between Barth and Bonhoeffer, see *NRS*, pp. 234–92.
46. *DB*, pp. 289–92.
47. *GS*, I, pp. 192–93.
48. For the text of the Barmen Declaration, see Arthur C. Cochrane, *The Church's Confession Under Hitler* (Pittsburgh, PA: Pickwick Press, 1976), pp. 237–47. The translation here is slightly altered.
49. See Bonhoeffer's essay "Our Way according to the Testimony of Scripture," *WF*, pp. 173–193.
50. Bishop George K. A. Bell, "Significance of the Barmen Declaration for the Ecumenical Church," foreword to *Theology, Occasional Papers*, New Series, no. 5.
51. Eberhard Bethge, "The Holocaust and Christian Anti-Semitism: Perspectives of a Christian Survivor," *Union Seminary Quarterly Review*, vol. 32, nos. 3–4. (1977), p. 114.
52. *GS*, I, p. 204. On the Fanø Conference, see especially *DB*, pp. 298–315.
53. R. Rouse and S. C. Neill, *A History of the Ecumenical Movement, 1517–1948* (London: Society for Promoting Christian Knowledge, 1954), p. 583, cited in *DB*, p. 313.
54. *NRS*, p. 294.
55. *DB*, p. 313; see also *IKDB*, p. 90.
56. *GS*, I, p. 217.
57. *NRS*, p. 291.
58. *NRS*, p. 291.
59. *GS*, I, p. 219. *NRS*, p. 291, uses the more irenic expression "non-Christians" to translate *Heiden*.
60. *DB*, p. 330.
61. The finest treatment of the reasons for Bonhoeffer's interest in learning Gandhi's techniques of nonviolent resistance is to be found in Appendix A of Larry Rasmussen's *Dietrich Bonhoeffer: Reality and Resistance* (Nashville, TN: Abingdon Press, 1972), pp. 213–17.
62. *GS*, I, p. 42
63. *DB*, p. 336.
64. *WF*, p. 35.
65. *DB*, p. 360.
66. *IKDB*, p. 133.
67. *WF*, p. 121.

68. *TP*, p. 166 (translation slightly altered).
69. *DB*, p. 383.
70. *WF*, pp. 30–31.
71. *DB*, p. 385.
72. *DB*, p. 353.
73. *DB*, p. 354. (translation slightly altered).
74. *DB*, pp. 405–6.
75. *DB*, p. 406.
76. *DB*, p. 415.
77. *DB*, p. 421.
78. *WF*, pp. 93–94.
79. *WF*, pp. 92–93.
80. *WF*, p. 80.
81. *WF*, pp. 90–91.
82. *GS*, II, p. 314.
83. *DB*, p. 455.
84. In this case the three groups were to be the Reich Church, the Confessing Church, and the Lutheran Council (*Lutherischer Rat*).
85. *WF*, p. 133.
86. *BEM*, p. 107.
87. *GS*, II, pp. 315–18.
88. Bethge, "Dietrich Bonhoeffer and the Jews," pp. 74–75.
89. *DB*, pp. 528–33.
90. *DB*, p. 541.
91. *DB*, p. 542.
92. *DB*, p. 551.
93. *DB*, p. 552.
94. *DB*, p. 554.
95. *DB*, p. 556.
96. *DB*, p. 557.
97. The original of this letter is lost. Niebuhr published this quotation in *Christianity and Crisis*, June 25, 1945, p. 6. This fragment appears in *NRS*, p. 246, and *DB*, p. 559.
98. *DB*, p. 577.
99. *DB*, p. 579.
100. *DB*, p. 579.
101. See *BEM*, pp. 117–36.
102. *TP*, pp. 63–67.
103. *TP*, p. 60.
104. *LPP*, p. 17.
105. *GS*, I, p. 405.
106. *LPP*, pp. 34–35; see also *DB*, pp. 734–36.
107. *LPP*, p. 162.
108. *LPP*, p. 70.
109. Maria von Wedemeyer-Weller, "The Other Letters from Prison," *USQR*, vol. 23, no. 1 (Fall 1967), p. 26.
110. *LPP*, p. 279.
111. *LPP*, p. 362.
112. *LPP*, p. 282.
113. *E*, p. 114 (translation slightly altered).
114. *LPP*, p. 381.
115. *LPP*, p. 378.
116. Thomas I. Day, *Dietrich Bonhoeffer on Christian Community and Common Sense* (New York and Toronto: Edwin Mellen Press, 1982), p. 203.
117. *LPP*, pp. 382–83.
118. *LPP*, p. 337.

119. *LPP*, p. 361.
120. *DB*, pp. 730–31.
121. *LPP*, p. 399.
122. *DB*, p. 823.
123. *DB*, p. 826.
124. Sigismund Payne Best, *The Venlo Incident* (London: Hutchinson, 1950), p. 200.
125. See *DB*, p. 830, for the explanation of the variations in the "final words" that Bonhoeffer spoke to Payne Best.
126. *DB*, p. 830; *IKDB*, p. 232.

Part 1: Christ as Community

1. *Sanctorum Communio*, edited by Joachim von Soosten in collaboration with Wolfgang Huber, *Dietrich Bonhoeffer Werke* (hereafter *DBW*), Band 1 (Munich: Kaiser Verlag, 1988); *Akt und Sein*, edited by Hans-Richard Reuter, *DBW*, Band 2; *Jugend und Studium: 1918–1927*, edited by Hans Pfeifer in collaboration with Clifford Green and Carl-Jürgen Kaltenborn, *DBW*, Band 9 (Munich: Kaiser Verlag, 1986); *Vikariat und Habilitation: 1928–1931*, edited by Hans Christoph von Hase and Reinhart Staats, *DBW*, Band 10.
2. *DB*, p. 75.
3. Karl Barth, *Church Dogmatics*, IV/2, p. 641.
4. Thomas I. Day, *Dietrich Bonhoeffer on Christian Community and Common Sense* (New York and Toronto: Edwin Mellen Press, 1982), p. 9.
5. Clifford J. Green, *The Sociality of Christ and Humanity: Dietrich Bonhoeffer's Early Theology, 1927–1933* (Missoula, MT: Scholars Press, 1975).
6. See note 1.
7. See Peter Berger, "Sociology and Ecclesiology," in Martin E. Marty, ed., *The Place of Bonhoeffer* (New York: Association Press, 1962), p. 60.
8. Green, *Sociality of Christ and Humanity*, pp. 105–133.

Part 2: Bonhoeffer the Teacher and Lecturer

1. *DB*, pp. 157–58.
2. *IKDB*, p. 57.
3. *IKDB*, pp. 57–58.
4. *IKDB*, pp. 60–61.
5. *IKDB*, p. 61.
6. *IKDB*, p. 68.
7. *IKDB*, p. 62.
8. *IKDB*, p. 126.
9. *IKDB*, p. 128.
10. See W. Visser 't Hooft, "Dietrich Bonhoeffer and the Self-Understanding of the Ecumenical Movement," *The Ecumenical Review*, vol. 17, no. 2 (April 1976), p. 200.
11. *IKDB*, pp. 85, 87.
12. *DB*, pp. 184–85.
13. *IKDB*, p. 90.
14. *DB*, p. 165.
15. *NRS*, pp. 179–82.
16. *DB*, p. 164.

Part 3: Bonhoeffer's Confession of Faith

1. *DB*, p. 220.
2. See *DB*, pp. 206–9; see also Eberhard Bethge, "Dietrich Bonhoeffer and the Jews," in John D. Godsey and Geffrey B. Kelly, eds. *Ethical Responsibility: Bonhoeffer's Legacy to the Churches* (Toronto: Edwin Mellen Press, 1981), pp. 58–61.

3. A case in point is Stanley Rosenbaum's superficially researched and tendentious article "Dietrich Bonhoeffer: A Jewish View," *Journal of Ecumenical Studies,* vol. 18, no. 2 (Spring 1981), pp. 301–7.
4. Cited in Bethge, "Dietrich Bonhoeffer and the Jews," p. 63.
5. Bethge, "Dietrich Bonhoeffer and the Jews," pp. 63–76.
6. *DB,* pp. 231–34.
7. William J. Peck, "From Cain to the Death Camps: An Essay on Bonhoeffer and Judaism" *Union Seminary Quarterly Review,* vol. 28, no. 3 (Winter 1973), p. 174.
8. *NRS,* p. 241; emphasis added.
9. *GS,* 2, pp. 232–33.
10. *DB,* p. 415.
11. *DB,* p. 432.
12. *DB,* pp. 517–18.

Part 4: Bonhoeffer the Pastor

1. *DB,* pp. 174–75.
2. Letter to parents, November 11, 1928, quoted in *DB,* p. 79.
3. *DB,* p. 80.
4. Bonhoeffer's Finkenwalde lectures on homiletics have become available to the English public through the translation by Clyde E. Fant in *Bonhoeffer: Worldly Preaching* (Nashville, TN: Thomas Nelson, 1975).
5. *LT,* p. 99.
6. Cited in Fant, *Bonhoeffer,* p. 23.
7. *DB,* p. 829.
8. Albrecht Schönherr, in *IKDB,* p. 128.
9. John D. Godsey, *The Theology of Dietrich Bonhoeffer* (Philadelphia, PA: Westminster Press, 1960), p. 52.

Part 5: Bonhoeffer on Following Christ

1. *CD,* p. 57.
2. *DB,* p. 380; see also *GS,* III, p. 25.
3. *CD,* p. 37.
4. *DB,* p. 369. On the genesis of this book, see especially *DB,* pp. 369–71.
5. Letter of February 1, 1936, cited in *DB,* pp. 154–55.
6. *DB,* p. 155; see also *GS,* III, pp. 24–5.
7. *CD,* p. 299.
8. *CD,* p. 224.
9. *CD,* p. 69.
10. *CD,* p. 47.
11. *CD,* p. 99.
12. Eds. Gerhard Ludwig Müller and Albrecht Schönherr, *Gemeinsames Leben and Das Gebetbuch der Bibel* (Munich: Kaiser Verlag, 1987), p. 7.
13. *WF,* p. 36.
14. *DB,* pp. 388.
15. See *DB,* p. 390.

Part 6: Bonhoeffer's Ethics

1. *LPP,* p. 163.
2. *LPP,* p. 382.
3. For Brunner's contribution to this debate, see Emil Brunner, *The Divine Imperative,* translated by Oline Wyon (Philadelphia, PA: Westminster Press, 1947). See also Robin Lovin's essay "Biographical Context," in William J. Peck, ed., *New Studies in Bonhoeffer's Ethics* (Lewiston/Queenston: Edwin Mellen Press, 1987), pp. 71–73.
4. "What Is a Christian Ethic?" *NRS,* pp. 43–44.

5. *E*, p. 7.
6. *Ethik*, edited by Ernst Feil, Clifford Green, Heinz Eduard Tödt, and Ilse Tödt, *DBW*, Band 6.
7. Clifford J. Green, "The Text of Bonhoeffer's *Ethics*," in William J. Peck, ed., *New Studies in Bonhoeffer's Ethics* (Lewiston/Queenston: The Edwin Mellen Press, 1987), p. 12.
8. *LPP*, p. 14.
9. *E*, p. 277.

Part 7: Bonhoeffer's Correspondence

1. John A. Phillips, "Dietrich Bonhoeffer: The Letters and the Legacy," *Motive*, vol. 27, no. 5 (February 1969), p. 43.
2. Eberhard Bethge, Foreword, *LPP*, 3rd ed., 1967, pp. 9–15.
3. John A. T. Robinson, "The Saint of the Secular" in Bethge, Foreword, *LPP*, p. 9.
4. Heinz Eduard Tödt, ed., with Hans Pfeifer, Ferdinand Schlingensiepen, and Ilse Tödt, *Wie eine Flaschenpost: Ökumenische Briefe und Beiträge für Eberhard Bethge* (Munich: Kaiser Verlag, 1979).
5. Eberhard Bethge, "The Editing and Publishing of the Bonhoeffer Papers," *The Andover Newton Bulletin*, vol. 52, no. 26 (December 1959), pp. 2–5.
6. *NRS*, p. 362.
7. Hence the subtitle of Bethge's biography: "Theologian, Christian, Contemporary."
8. *LPP*, pp. 275–76.
9. *DB*, P. 154.
10. J. Patrick Kelley, *Revelation and the Secular in the Theology of Dietrich Bonhoeffer*, unpublished doctoral dissertation, Yale University, 1980, p. 141.
11. *DB*, p. 156.
12. *DB*, pp. 512–24.
13. *NRS*, p. 206.
14. *NRS*, pp. 231–32.
15. *DB*, p. 283.
16. *DB*, p. 284.
17. *NRS*, p. 257.
18. *NRS*, pp. 262–63.
19. For the complete text, see *GS*, I, pp. 192–93.
20. *DB*, pp. 252–53.
21. *GS*, II, p. 150.
22. *GS*, II, p. 157.
23. *DB*, p. 420.
24. *DB*, p. 458.
25. "More Bonhoeffer-Barth Correspondence," translated by John D. Godsey, *Newsletter*, International Bonhoeffer Society for Archive and Research, English Language Section, no. 22 (June 1982), p. 7.
26. Eberhard Bethge, "Dietrich Bonhoeffer and the Jews," in John D. Godsey and Geffrey B. Kelly, eds., *Ethical Responsibility: Bonhoeffer's Legacy to the Churches* (New York and Toronto: Edwin Mellen Press, 1981), pp. 74–75.
27. *DB*, p. 468.
28. *DB*, p. 512.
29. *DB*, pp. 504–5.
30. *DB*, p. 506.
31. *WF*, p. 218.
32. *DB*, pp. 524–33.
33. Maria Von Wedemeyer-Weller, "The Other Letters from Prison," *Union Seminary Quarterly Review*, vol. 23, no. 1 (Fall 1967), pp. 23–29.

Glossary of Terms

Abwehr.   The counterintelligence agency of the armed forces in Nazi Germany, the *Abwehr* was a center of the resistance movement against the Nazi government. During the war years, the *Abwehr* provided cover-ups for resistance activities, including assassination attempts against Hitler. The head of this "German Military Intelligence Department" was Admiral Wilhelm Canaris. Major General Hans Oster was his chief of staff and the principal organizer of resistance activities. Oster's assistant was Hans von Dohnanyi, Bonhoeffer's brother-in-law. Bonhoeffer was a civilian member of the *Abwehr* staff from 1939 until his arrest in 1943.

Anschluss.   The forced annexation of Austria by Nazi Germany on March 11, 1938. This annexation, achieved through an invasion of Austrian territory by German military units, was formally ratified by the Austrian people in the plebiscite of April 10, 1938.

Arcani Disciplina (*Arkandisziplin*).   This "Discipline of the Secret," sometimes referred to in English translation as the "arcane discipline," was a practice of the early Christian church to protect the mysteries of the faith. The early Christians were not to mention the Eucharist, or the mysteries of the faith in the presence of the unbaptized. Only those instructed in the faith and willing to make a Christian commitment through baptism were admitted to the Eucharistic communion part of the Lord's Supper. Bonhoeffer referred in several writings to this ancient practice, but it was especially in his prison letters that he developed its meaning in the context of the secular world. Bonhoeffer counsels the church not to force its truths on, or to brandish its dogmas and rituals triumphantly before, an unwilling world. The church, he said, is to preserve the mysteries of the Christian faith, not with defensive fervor, but with prayer, worship, and example.

Aryan Clause (*Arierparagraph*).   Also called the *Aryan paragraph*, this is that section of the "Law for the Reconstruction of the Professional Civil Service," passed by the German Reichstag on April 7, 1933, which banned Jews and any person whose parents or grandparents had been Jewish from government service appointment. This clause became a major factor in the church struggle of the 1930s, when the infamous "Brown Synod" of Prussian church leaders adopted it as a condition for acceptance into church ministry.

Barmen Confession.   The six-point declaration adopted by Protestant church leaders, both clerical and lay, opposed to the German Reich Church at their first synod held in Barmen, Westphalia, from May 29 to 31, 1934. This synod constituted the Confessing Church in Germany. The 139 delegates to the conference, coming from twenty-six land and provincial churches, represented Reformed, Lutheran, and United Church bodies. The initial draft of the confession, written by Karl Barth, was directed against Nazi interference in church affairs and the idolatrous destruction of the gospel through racist policies approved by the "German Christians." The primary motif of the confession was the acknowledgment that Jesus Christ alone is Lord and his

Word alone saves. The confession repudiated "the false teaching that there are areas of ... life in which we belong not to Jesus Christ, but to other lords."

Bethel Confession. A declaration of faith, commissioned by the pastors of the "Pastors' Emergency League," and originally drafted by Dietrich Bonhoeffer and Hermann Sasse at the retreat center in Bethel in August 1933. Bethel was a religious community founded by Friedrich von Bodelschwingh for the treatment of epileptics. This confession included a sharply worded criticism of the racist political philosophy of the Nazi government. After several revisions, rendering it less "offensive," it was finally published by Martin Niemöller in pamphlet form at the end of 1933. The final version was judged to be so watered down from his original that Bonhoeffer himself refused to sign it.

Brown Synod. So-called because many of the ministers showed up wearing their brown uniforms and making the scene look like a paramilitary spectacle, this was the Old Prussian General Synod of Prussian church leaders held at the *Herrenhaus* in Berlin on September 5 and 6, 1933. The synod was dominated by the "German Christians," who incorporated loyalty to the Nazi regime and adoption of the "Aryan Clause" into official church policy. They thus stipulated that only those persons could function as ministers of the church who agreed to give "unconditional support to the National Socialist State and the German Evangelical Church," and who were of Aryan descent. At this synod, too, the "Bishops' Law" was passed, abolishing the systems of general superintendents in Old Prussia and replacing them with ten bishoprics under the domain of the national bishop, Ludwig Müller, a known Nazi sympathizer.

Church Struggle (*Kirchenkampf*). This refers to the conflicts within the German churches and the collective resistance of these churches and of individual churchpeople to the policies of the National Socialist Party under Hitler, as the Nazis attempted to dominate and control the church by integrating it into the Nazi bureaucratic structure. At stake in the struggle were the authenticity and integrity of the churches to be what they were called to be according to biblical and confessional criteria.

Confessing Church (*Bekennende Kirche*). An outgrowth of the "Pastors' Emergency League" (*Pfarrernotbund*), the Confessing Church came into being at the Barmen Synod in May 1934, when a fourth of the German Protestant pastors cast their lot with the opposition to the state-controlled national bishop (*Reichsbischof*), Ludwig Müller, and to adoption of the Aryan Clause within the "German Reich Church." The Confessing Church thus became an active resistance movement within Nazi Germany as its members sought to reestablish church freedom and uncompromised fidelity to God's Word. Its forthright claim was that, because of the idolatrous acquiescence to Nazi church policies within the Reich Church, the Confessing Church alone constituted the Protestant church in Germany. The "Barmen Confession" became its theological charter.

Councils of the Brethren (*Bruderräte*). Regional representative structures for the government of the "Confessing Church" in Germany.

Crystal Night (*Kristallnacht*). Also called "the night of the broken glass," this refers to the wanton destruction of Jewish synagogues and stores and the brutalizing of Jewish citizens on the night of November 9, 1938. The event received its name from the broken glass that littered the streets in German towns and cities after that night of devastation and terror.

Deus ex Machina. Literally the "God from the Machine," this phrase is used by Bonhoeffer in his prison letters to criticize a particular idea of God that tended to make God more remote and more unreal. The phrase comes from the practice in ancient drama of solving the unresolvable dilemmas of the actors by lowering a god figure by mechanical means either onto or floating across the stage in order to intervene and solve the problem. For Bonhoeffer, the God of power who descends at the opportune moment to deliver the world from evil or to cure personal ills is just as unreal as the *deus ex machina*. Such a God was an enemy of autonomy and of the world come of age. Such a God was also a mere hypothesis constructed by religious minds to fill in the gaps of human knowledge and human power, and destined to become largely irrelevant as people came to rely more on their own knowledge and mastery of technology. Against this kind of religiously controlled deity, Bonhoeffer offers the biblical God, father of Jesus, the God who allows himself to be edged out of the world and onto the cross, who relates to people in their strength as well as weakness, who lives to serve his people, and who suffers with them.

Ecumenical Movement. The endeavor to work toward greater visible unity and cooperation among Christian churches that emerged from the missionary activities of the nineteenth century. The Edinburgh World Missionary Conference of 1910 is generally considered to be the landmark event that launched the movement.

Faith and Order. One of the three strands of the ecumenical movement with the specific role of examining points of agreement and difference that centered on doctrine and worship of the various churches represented. Prior to the founding of the World Council of Churches at Amsterdam in 1948, Faith and Order conferences were held in Lausanne in 1927 and Edinburgh in 1937.

Final Solution (*Endlösung*). The plan adopted at the Wannsee Conference of Nazi leaders, on January 20, 1942, making the extermination of the Jews official policy of the Third Reich. Prior to this conference, the genocide had already begun through mass shootings and gassings in the occupied territories and by various cruel means in the concentration camps. Responsibility for the carrying out of this policy was entrusted to Reinhold Heydrich, head of the Reich Security Main Office, and Adolph Eichmann, head of the Office for Jewish Affairs and Evacuation Affairs.

Finkenwalde. One of the five seminaries of the "Confessing Church" in Germany, situated in a rambling schoolhouse near the northern city of Stettin, today incorporated into Poland. Bonhoeffer was selected to serve as spiritual director and teacher in this "Preachers' Seminary," which was opened in 1935 and closed by order of the Gestapo in 1937.

Führer (Leader). *Der Führer* was the title given Hitler by the Nazis to designate his predominant role as the head of the Third Reich and commander in chief of the Armed Forces.

"German Christians" (*Deutsche Christen*). Those Protestants who supported Adolf Hitler and the Nazi ideology gave themselves this designation. They were not a separate church body but constituted a movement within the Protestant church of Germany to endorse and actively participate in the formal structures whereby the church became incorporated into the Nazi state. They were opposed by the Confessing Church in what has been called the "Church Struggle."

German Evangelical Church (*Deutsche Evangelische Kirche*). The largest Protestant church body in Germany, comprised of the twenty-eight regional or territorial churches representing Lutheran, Reformed, and United Church denominations.

Gesammelte Schriften. The collected writings of Dietrich Bonhoeffer, published in six volumes by Christian Kaiser Verlag, Munich, between 1958 and 1974.

Gestapo (*Geheime Staatspolizei*). The secret police of the Nazi state, the Gestapo was an instrument of terror and control throughout Germany and the Nazi occupied territories.

Jewish Question (*Judenfrage*). The phrase "Jewish Question," or, alternately, "Jewish Problem," was used in publications, lectures, and statements of government policy to refer to the issues posed by the presence of a significant Jewish population within many Western nations. These included the question of the place of the Jews within a so-called "Christian" nation, the slanderous anti-Semitism and Jew baiting that aroused hatred of and brutality toward Jews among the non-Jewish citizenry, the issue of the Jews as a Chosen People of God vis-à-vis the imperious claims of some Christian denominations to have replaced the Jews in God's covenant, the Jews as a "nation within a nation," the Jews as refugees, the Jews as scapegoat for a nation's ills, and the alleged international "Jewish conspiracy," deriving from the "Protocols of Zion," a virulent anti-Semitic document claiming the existence of a plot by the "elders of Zion" to take over the world and establish Judaism as the sole religion, in essence a pretext for denying Jews their civil rights within the nations. In Nazi Germany, the "Jewish Question" designated the official policies directed against the Jewish citizens. These included propaganda campaigns against Jews, the denial of the right to civil service employment and to enter the professions including law, medicine, teaching, journalism, etc., the denial of civil rights, the boycott of Jewish shops, the confiscation of Jewish property, forced emigration, and, finally, the genocidal "Final Solution," a carefully planned annihilation of the European Jews. Bonhoeffer's article "The Church and the Jewish Question" was the first public defense of the Jews against the repressive government policies then being enacted.

Justification by Faith. The doctrine that is said to have launched the Protestant Reformation. By this formulation, Luther wished to make clear that it was God alone who justifies the sinner; sinners do not justify themselves through "good works." Of themselves, such good works do not merit God's justification or make salvation something a person could demand by reason of the works performed. Rather, God's gift of faith offered in Jesus Christ was seen as the matrix of living by and in the power of God's gracious giving of himself to be known and loved. Through faith, one was enabled to accept God's Word of love and mercy in Jesus Christ, the ground of the trust in God at the heart of justification and of the process of sanctification. Bonhoeffer's book *The Cost of Discipleship* is, in part, an attempt on his part to nuance this doctrine by emphasizing faith as discipleship in a Christian commitment, not to accept justification on the cheap by mere church affiliation, but to act on the gospel ideals even if this cost a Christian his or her life.

Life and Work. One of the main strands of the ecumenical movement, the Ecumenical Council for Practical Christianity, popularly known as "Life and Work," was organized to explore the possibilities of ecumenical cooperation on peace and social justice issues even though doctrinal differences still presented problems for the reunion of the churches. The first World Conference of Life and Work was held in Stockholm in 1925 and a second conference in Oxford in 1937. The task of this Conference has been carried forward through working groups centered in Geneva. Bonhoeffer's close friend Bishop George K.A. Bell of Chichester was president of the council during the 1930s.

Man for Others (*Mensch für Andere*).   This distinctive title, used by Bonhoeffer to describe Jesus in Bonhoeffer's prison letters, sums up the various aspects that, like a mosaic, form the figure of Christ emerging from Bonhoeffer's theology. For Bonhoeffer, Christ's death on the cross became the supreme expression of his destiny, marking him forever as a person whose whole purpose in life was to serve others. Bonhoeffer describes Christ as the "man for others" because his fundamental idea of God in Christ is of one who exists for people in the most total act of his self-giving: the humiliation of the cross. The whole creaturely existence of Christ is orientated to others. In this, God reveals himself as one willing to sacrifice himself for his people, to become a God who suffers. In the reality behind this title, Bonhoeffer also sets the foundation for his Christocentric ethics and for developing a concept of ethical transcendence based on conformation to Christ.

National Bishop (*Reichsbischof*).   The "German Christians" put forth the idea of having a "national bishop," in April 1933, as part of their plan to form a single German Reich Church based on Nazi doctrine. However, in the church elections of May, Friedrich von Bodelschwingh was elected to the position over the objections of the "German Christians," who claimed that only a person of unquestioned loyalty to the *Führer* could lead a national church. The German Christians enlisted the help of the propaganda office and of party officials to have the election rescinded. As a result, Hitler appointed Ludwig Müller, protector of the German Christians and his confidential adviser. Müller was then elected national bishop at the German National Synod of September 5 and 6, 1933, the infamous "Brown Synod." Later, in July 1935, Hitler established the Ministry of Church Affairs, headed by the pro-Nazi Hanns Kerrl. In September 1935, Kerrl set up the "Law for the Protection of the German Evangelical Church," which was aimed at splitting the ranks of the Confessing Church and promoting the cause of the German Christians.

Nonreligious Christianity (*Religionsloses Christentum*).   One of the theological "catchwords" from Bonhoeffer's prison correspondence, nonreligious Christianity refers to a new "form" of Christianity in which people of a genuine Christian faith would live in a more open, constructive relationship with the world. In this process, religion itself, considered an historically conditioned, transient, dying form of Christianity, would undergo drastic changes as faith is freed from its more Westernized, self-serving constrictions and emphasis on inward piety and empty rituals. Christianity would thus be freed for the integration of new insights from a "this-worldly" faith, from Eastern spirituality (idealized in India and Gandhi), and from the church's bitter war experiences. Bonhoeffer had criticized religion for its having inflicted on people a psychic posture of weakness and immature dependence and for having encouraged individualistic, self-centered attitudes toward God and others. Christians living a "nonreligious" form of Christianity, on the other hand, would draw on the example of Christ, the "man for others," and live in the paradox of being called out of the world while belonging wholly to it. From the prison letters, one can deduce that Bonhoeffer was calling for a complete restructuring of ecclesiastical offices and for a reshaping of the churches so they can become like Christ, divested of their possessiveness and encouraged to live only to serve others. Such a Christianity, with its church, Sacrament, and sermon still needed the "discipline of the secret," in order for Christians to be completely engaged in a more "silent" life of prayer and dedication to social justice. In this way Bonhoeffer hoped that a new form of Christian church would come into being.

Nonreligious Interpretation (*Nicht-religiöse Interpretation*).   The corollary to nonreligious Christianity, the phrase "nonreligious interpretation" is taken from Bonhoeffer's questions in his prison letters about how one can speak coherently of God in a "world come of age," or, alternately, how one can speak of God "without religion." Bonhoeffer criticizes the false images of God conjured up by a religiosity that would make God a *"deus ex machina,"* or a "God of the gaps," a God capitalizing on human weakness and cooperating in clerical blackmail of believers, instead of the God made known in the sufferings of the man Jesus, a God encouraging a faith-inspired responsibility in combating the evils of the Third Reich. Bonhoeffer did not have a fully developed model of nonreligious interpretation. For him, the problem of reinterpreting theological and biblical concepts must be set in the praxis of a genuine faith. The church's form in the world had to be reshaped by prayer and action for social justice. In his prison letters he writes that only when there is a true conversion and purification will a new language emerge out of a new form, a language "quite nonreligious, but liberating and redeeming—as was Jesus' language." *(LPP,* p. 300)

Pastors' Emergency League *(Pfarrernotbund)* An association of pastors organized by Martin Niemöller and Bonhoeffer to muster opposition to the decisions of the "Brown Synod" and to show solidarity with their non-Aryan colleagues in the ministry. The league came about as a direct consequence of the "Aryan Clause" adopted by the "Brown Synod," and the protest to the church government drafted by Bonhoeffer and Niemöller on September 7, 1933. The protest consisted of a denunciation of the illegality of the Aryan Clause in the light of the 16th century confessions of faith, a demand for the reinstatement of those ministers deprived of the right to exercise their profession by the recently enacted Civil Service Law, and the declaration that those who had assented to such a breach of the confessions of faith were themselves separated from the communion of the church. To this was added the promise of help for those affected by the new laws or by other compulsory measures taken against them or their supporters. Together, these constituted the four points of the "Pastors' Emergency League Pledge." In sum, the four points of the pledge called for a new allegiance to the scriptures and to the confession, resistance to any infringement of these in the church, financial help for those victimized by the new civil laws, and the rejection of the Aryan Clause. By the end of the year, some 6,000 pastors had joined the Pastors' Emergency League. At the time of the Barmen Synod in May 1934, this group became the nucleus of the "Confessing Church" of Germany.

Reich Church *(Reichskirche).* The name given to the established Protestant church in Germany dominated by the faction of the "German Christians" during the Nazi years. The idea of a "Reich Church" became a rallying point for the German Christians at their National Conference on April 3 and 4, 1933. In this conference, they stirred up support for the Nazi tenets of undivided loyalty to the *Führer* and racial conformity in what was to become the "Aryan Clause." During that month, the church administrations themselves also addressed the demand for a united "Reich Church" to replace the twenty-eight independent regional churches and announced their plans for a new constitution to effect this. It was in the light of this background agitation that Bonhoeffer composed his paper "The Church and the Jewish Question." He is considered the first to have perceived the crucial nature of the impending church struggle.

S.A. *(Sturmabteilung).* These "storm troopers," also called "Brownshirts" because of their brown uniforms, were originally a squad of volunteers organized by Ernst Roehm to keep order at Nazi rallies and later to break up meetings by opposition parties. The S.A. soon became a vital part of the Nazi movement, engaging in violent street fighting that added to the confused political situation and providing the terror and bullying tactics Hitler needed to muscle his way into power. But because the S.A. had also become a rival to the regular army with thoughts of displacing the old Prussian generals, Hitler, recognizing the need for the army's loyalty and support, ordered the suppression of the S.A. in the murderous purge of its leaders on June 30, 1934, the infamous "Night of the Long Knives."

S.S. (*Schutzstaffel*). Literally, "defense squadron," this elite force, also called "Blackshirts" because of their black uniforms, began as a personal bodyguard of the *Führer*. In 1929, under the leadership of Heinrich Himmler, the S.S. began the process of expansion of their numbers and duties; soon they assumed extraordinary power, becoming the backbone of Hitler's rule by force and terror. Behind the strength of the regular army and the civil police, there lurked in Nazi Germany always the force of the S.S. and their secret police colleagues, the "Gestapo." It was to Himmler and the S.S. that Hitler entrusted the confidential operation of the "Final Solution," the mass extermination of European Jews. The S.S. ruled over the concentration camps and carried out the macabre policy of genocide. The troops of the S.S. became known as a formidable fighting force during World War II, but they are mostly remembered with bitterness for their guilt in the worst atrocities of that war and as a brutal instrument of terror in the occupied nations.

Two Kingdoms Doctrine (*Zwei Reiche-Lehre*). A key teaching of Martin Luther in which Luther attempted to explain the relationship between the law and the gospel, the state and the church, in terms of distinctive spheres and mutual duties. The Nazis capitalized on this distinction in order to elicit unswerving allegiance and an incredibly blind obedience to the German state. The churches, too, invoked this doctrine to encourage good citizenship, patriotism, and compliance with all state laws. In drawing his distinctions, however, Luther insisted that God rules both realms, but his rule is different according to the dynamics of both the Christian and the secular vocations. Hence the judge must see that justice is done in a courtroom, even through the use of the approved coercion. A prince may have to issue a call to arms for the sake of a just cause. But within a family context, wrongs may simply be forgiven according to the dictates of the gospel. Unfortunately, what Luther intended to be a dialectic in which the law and the gospel, the state and the church, would coexist in a dialectical unity became a dualism in which both realms were separated in practice. This led to the churches' policy of non-interference in what was judged to be affairs of the state with the consequence that the churches tended to remain silent and appeared to sanction the abuses of power by the Nazis. Bonhoeffer inveighed against such a misinterpretation of Luther's original intention, arguing that the churches were hiding like cowards behind the doctrine of the two kingdoms. Rather, as Bonhoeffer pointed out in his *Ethics*, Luther intended the two kingdoms to exist in a polemical unity in which Christians may and at times should oppose the secular realm in the name of a better secularity.

World Alliance for Promoting International Friendship through the Churches. This organization of Christians from several nations began its activities at the first post–World War I meeting held at Oud Wassenaar near The Hague from September 30 to October 4, 1919, less than three months after the signing of the Treaty of Versailles. It was attended by some sixty representatives of both belligerent and neutral countries to discuss how the churches could cooperate in an effort to maintain peace among the nations. Though a variety of topics were discussed, such as the evil of blockades, the threat of Bolshevism, the guilt for the recent war, the missions, the most important outcome was the proposal for a world conference of the churches to discuss moral and social questions. Help for victims from World War I, concern for the development of international law, and agitation for disarmament and the settlement of disputes by peaceful and judicial means were all part of the earlier efforts of this alliance to promote international friendship. Although World War II brought the World Alliance to the point of extinction, this ecumenical organization is considered one of the forerunners of the "World Council of Churches," organized in 1948. Bonhoeffer's ecumenical career did, in fact, begin with his participation in the World Alliance Conference in Cambridge, September 1 to 5, 1931, where he was appointed youth secretary, an office he held until his resignation in 1937.

World Come of Age (*mündig gewordene Welt*). This phrase from Bonhoeffer's prison correspondence generated considerable interest and controversy among theologians in the decades following publication of the *Letters and Papers from Prison*. In speaking of the "world come of age," Bonhoeffer was referring to the problem of how one can relate to Christ, speak of God, and act responsibly in a world that in many respects has become more adult in its outlook on religion, more autonomous, and more self-reliant in solving problems previously thought to be strictly in God's domain. In addressing this "world," Bonhoeffer cautions against the misuse of typically irrelevant images of God such as the "*deus ex machina*," the God of the gaps in human knowledge and technology, the problem-solving God, the God unrelated to human life, the blackmailing, vindictive God, and the God impervious to human suffering, etc. Bonhoeffer had likewise contended that the efforts of religion to keep people in childish dependence and insecurity had been self-defeating and were among the reasons for the rise of nazism. Hence he argued that Christ himself had set the example of how to live autonomously and free, keeping laws in their proper perspective without becoming nihilistic. His was a freedom for a mature sense of responsibility, of decisive action in the just cause, and of a robust sense of personal freedom. For Bonhoeffer, the correlative of the world come of age was the need for a "this-worldly" Christianity in which Christians would be actively involved in shaping history according to the gospel of Jesus in a life characterized by courage in social justice, discipline, the willingness to enter into solidarity with oppressed peoples, and the acceptance of the cross in a faith that is so genuine one stakes one's life on it.

World Council of Churches. This central ecumenical organization among the Protestant churches held its first assembly in Amsterdam in August 1948, with representation from 147 churches in forty-four countries which had sent 351 official delegates. Two of the three strands of the ecumenical movement were immediately incorporated into this World Council with headquarters in Geneva, "Faith and Order," and "Life and Work." The third strand, the International Missionary Council, which had held conferences in Edinburgh in 1910, in Jerusalem in 1928, and in Madras in 1938, joined in 1961. The Orthodox Church joined also in 1961. Willem Visser 't Hooft who had served as Executive Director of the World Council in Process of Formation during the war years, was named the first General Secretary of the World Council of Churches in 1948. In a talk commemorating the seventieth anniversary of Bonhoeffer's birth, Visser 't Hooft acknowledged the formative influence of Bonhoeffer in the history of the ecumenical movement.

Bibliography

Works by Dietrich Bonhoeffer in English

Act and Being. Translated by Bernard Noble. New York: Harper & Row, 1962. London: Collins, 1962. Reprint (same pagination), New York: Octagon Books, 1983.

Christ the Center. Revised translation by Edwin H. Robertson. New York: Harper & Row, 1966, 1978. Published as *Christology*, London: Collins, 1966.

The Cost of Discipleship. Translated by R. H. Fuller, revised by Irmgard Booth. New York: Macmillan, 1963. London: SCM, 1963. Hardcover reissue (same pagination), Gloucester, MA: Peter Smith, 1983.

The Communion of Saints. Translated by Ronald Gregor Smith et al. New York: Harper & Row, 1963. Published as *Sanctorum Communio*, London: Collins, 1963.

Creation and Fall: A Theological Interpretation of Genesis 1–3. Translated by John C. Fletcher. Published together with *Temptation*. Translated by Kathleen Downham. Edited by Eberhard Bethge. New York: Macmillan, 1966. London: SCM, 1966.

Ethics. Translated by Neville Horton Smith. Rearranged edition. New York: Macmillan, 1965. Rearranged edition published in hardback with different pagination, London: SCM, 1971.

Fiction from Prison: Gathering up the Past. Edited by Renate Bethge and Eberhard Bethge with Clifford Green (in the English edition), Philadelphia: Fortress Press, 1981.

Letters and Papers from Prison. Enlarged edition. Edited by Eberhard Bethge. Translated by R. H. Fuller et al. New York: Macmillan, 1972. London: SCM, 1971.

Life Together. Translated by John W. Doberstein. New York: Harper & Row, 1954. Paperback edition (same pagination), 1976. London: SCM, 1954.

Meditating on the Word. Edited and translated by David McI. Gracie. Cambridge: Cowley Publications, 1986.

No Rusty Swords: Letters, Lectures and Notes, 1928–1936. Edited by Edwin H. Robertson. New York: Harper & Row, 1965. London: Collins, 1965. Translation revised by John Bowden and Eberhard Bethge, London: Collins, 1970. Cleveland: Collins-World, 1977.

Psalms: The Prayer Book of the Bible. Translated by James H. Burtness. Minneapolis: Augsburg Publishing House, 1970.

Spiritual Care. Translated by Jay C. Rochelle. Philadelphia: Fortress Press, 1985.

True Patriotism: Letters, Lectures and Notes, 1939–1945. Edited by Edwin H. Robertson. Translated by Edwin H. Robertson and John Bowden. New York: Harper & Row, 1973. London: Collins, 1973. Paperback edition (same pagination), Cleveland: Collins-World, 1977.

The Way to Freedom: Letters, Lectures and Notes, 1935–1939. Edited by Edwin H. Robertson. Translated by Edwin H. Robertson and John Bowden. New York: Harper & Row, 1966. London: Collins, 1966. Paperback edition (same pagination), London: Collins, 1972; Cleveland: Collins-World, 1977.

Works About Dietrich Bonhoeffer

Bethge, Eberhard. *Bonhoeffer: Exile and Martyr.* Edited by John W. de Gruchy. New York: Seabury Press, 1975.

————. *Costly Grace: An Illustrated Introduction to Dietrich Bonhoeffer.* Translated by Rosaleen Ockenden. New York: Harper & Row, 1979.

————. *Dietrich Bonhoeffer: A Life in Pictures.* Edited by Eberhard Bethge, Renate Bethge, and Christian Gremmels. Translated by John Bowden. Philadelphia: Fortress Press, 1986.

————. *Dietrich Bonhoeffer: Man of Vision, Man of Courage.* Translated by Eric Mosbacher, Peter Ross, Betty Ross, Frank Clarke, and William Glen-Doepel, under the editorship of Edwin H. Robertson. New York: Harper & Row, 1970.

Bosanquet, Mary. *The Life and Death of Dietrich Bonhoeffer.* Hodder & Stoughton, 1968. New York: Harper & Row, 1969.

Burtness, James. *Shaping the Future: The Ethics of Dietrich Bonhoeffer.* Philadelphia: Fortress Press, 1985.

Clements, Keith W. *A Patriotism for Today: Dialogue with Dietrich Bonhoeffer.* Bristol, England: Bristol Baptist College, 1984. London: Collins, 1986.

Day, Thomas, I. *Dietrich Bonhoeffer on Christian Community and Common Sense.* Lewiston, NY and Toronto: Edwin Mellen Press, 1982.

de Gruchy, John W. *Bonhoeffer and South Africa.* Grand Rapids: Eerdmans. London: Paternoster, 1984.

Dumas, André. *Dietrich Bonhoeffer: Theologian of Reality.* New York: Macmillan, 1971.

Fant, Clyde E. *Bonhoeffer: Worldly Preaching.* Nashville, TN, and New York: Thomas Nelson, 1975.

Feil, Ernst. *The Theology of Dietrich Bonhoeffer.* Translated by Martin Rumscheidt. Philadelphia: Fortress Press, 1985.

Godsey, John D. *Preface to Bonhoeffer: The Man and Two of His Shorter Writings.* Philadelphia: Fortress Press, 1965.

————. *The Theology of Dietrich Bonhoeffer.* Philadelphia: Westminster, 1960. London: SCM, 1960.

Godsey, John D., and Geffrey B. Kelly, eds. *Ethical Responsibility: Bonhoeffer's Legacy to the Churches.* Lewiston, NY and Toronto: Edwin Mellen Press, 1981.

Green, Clifford James. *The Sociality of Christ and Humanity: Dietrich Bonhoeffer's Early Theology, 1927–1933.* Missoula, MT: Scholars Press, 1975.

Hamilton, Kenneth. *Life in One's Stride: A Short Study in Dietrich Bonhoeffer.* Grand Rapids, MI: Eerdmans, 1968.

Hopper, David H. *A Dissent on Bonhoeffer.* Philadelphia: Westminster, 1975.

Kelly, Geffrey B. *Liberating Faith: Bonhoeffer's Message for Today.* Minneapolis: Augsburg Publishing House, 1984.

Klassen, A, J., ed. *A Bonhoeffer Legacy.* Grand Rapids, MI: Eerdmans, 1981.

Kuhns, William. *In Pursuit of Dietrich Bonhoeffer.* London: Burnes and Oates, 1968. Paperback edition, New York: Doubleday, 1969.

Leibholz-Bonhoeffer, Sabine. *The Bonhoeffers: Portrait of a Family.* London: Sidgwick and Jackson, 1971.

Lovin, Robin W. *Christian Faith and Public Choices: The Social Ethics of Barth, Brunner and Bonhoeffer.* Philadelphia: Fortress Press, 1984.

Marty, Martin E., ed. *The Place of Bonhoeffer: Problems and Possibilities in His Thought.* New York: Associated Press, 1962. London: SCM, 1963.

Moltmann, Jürgen, and Jürgen Weissbach. *Two Studies in the Theology of Bonhoeffer.* Introduction by Reginald H. Fuller. Translated by Reginald M. Fuller and Ilse Fuller. New York: Charles Scribner's and Sons, 1967.

Ott, Heinrich. *Reality and Faith.* Translated by Alex A. Morrison. London: Lutterworth Press, 1971.

Peck, William J., ed. *New Studies in Bonhoeffer's Ethics.* New York: Edwin Mellen Press, 1987.

Phillips, John A. *Christ for Us in the Theology of Dietrich Bonhoeffer.* New York: Harper & Row, 1967. British title: *The Form of Christ in the World: A Study of Bonhoeffer's Christology.* London: Collins, 1967.

Rasmussen, Larry. *Dietrich Bonhoeffer: Reality and Resistance.* Nashville: Abingdon, 1972.

————. *Dietrich Bonhoeffer: His Significance for North Americans.* Chapter 1 by Renate Bethge. Translated by Geffrey B. Kelly. Philadelphia: Fortress Press, 1990.

Reist, Benjamin A. *The Promise of Bonhoeffer.* Philadelphia: Lippincott, 1969.

Robertson, Edwin. *The Shame and the Sacrifice: The Life and Martyrdom of Dietrich Bonhoeffer.* London: Hodder and Stoughton, 1987. New York: Macmillan, 1989.

Smith, Ronald Gregor, ed. *World Come of Age.* London: Collins, 1967.

Vorkink, Peter, II, ed. *Bonhoeffer in a World Come of Age.* Philadelphia: Fortress Press, 1968.

Woelfel, James W. *Bonhoeffer's Theology: Classical and Revolutionary.* Nashville: Abingdon, 1970.

Zimmermann, Wolf-Dieter, and Ronald Gregor Smith, eds. *I Knew Dietrich Bonhoeffer: Reminiscences by His Friends.* London: Collins, 1960. New York: Harper & Row, 1966.

Bibliographical Notes

Readers of *A Testament to Freedom: The Essential Writings of Dietrich Bonhoeffer* are apprised of an ambitious publishing venture in German and English. Christian Kaiser Verlag of Munich is in the process of publishing sixteen volumes of a critical edition of Bonhoeffer's works. An English-language edition is also being prepared with the authorization of the German publishers and the sponsorship of the English Language Section of the International Bonhoeffer Society. It is expected that four volumes will be completed by 1992: *Communion of Saints, Act and Being, Life Together,* and *Youth and Studies.* The target date for completing the sixteen English-translation volumes is 1998.

A periodical updating of Bonhoeffer bibliographical items, under the editorship of Clifford J. Green and Wayne Floyd, is available through the newsletter of the International Bonhoeffer Society, English Language Section. Annual updates are included in each February issue of the newsletter. Information regarding the newsletter may be obtained from J. P. Kelley, Managing Editor, Lynchburg College, Lynchburg, VA 24501.

Index of Persons

Index of Subjects